CW00422200

A HISTORY OF PYTHAGOREANISM

This is a comprehensive, authoritative and innovative account of Pythagoras and Pythagoreanism, one of the most enigmatic and influential philosophies in the West. In twenty-one chapters covering a timespan from the sixth century BC to the seventeenth century AD, leading scholars construct a number of different images of Pythagoras and his community, assessing current scholarship and offering new answers to central problems. Chapters are devoted to the early Pythagoreans, and the full breadth of Pythagorean thought is explored including politics, religion, music theory, science, mathematics and magic. Separate chapters consider Pythagoreanism in Plato, Aristotle, the Peripatetics and the later Academic tradition, while others describe Pythagoreanism in the historical tradition, in Rome and in the pseudo-Pythagorean writings. The three great lives of Pythagoras by Diogenes Laertius, Porphyry and Iamblichus are also discussed in detail, as is the significance of Pythagoras for the Middle Ages and Renaissance.

CARL A. HUFFMAN is Research Professor and Emeritus Professor of Classical Studies at DePauw University. He is author of *Archytas of Tarentum: Pythagorean, Philosopher, and Mathematician King* (2005) and *Philolaus of Croton: Pythagorean and Presocratic* (1993).

A HISTORY OF
PYTHAGOREANISM

EDITED BY

CARL A. HUFFMAN

CAMBRIDGE
UNIVERSITY PRESS

CAMBRIDGE
UNIVERSITY PRESS

University Printing House, Cambridge CB2 8BS, United Kingdom

Cambridge University Press is part of the University of Cambridge.

It furthers the University's mission by disseminating knowledge in the pursuit of
education, learning and research at the highest international levels of excellence.

www.cambridge.org
Information on this title: www.cambridge.org/9781107014398

First published 2014

Printed in the United Kingdom by Clays, St Ives plc

A catalogue record for this publication is available from the British Library

Library of Congress Cataloguing in Publication data
A history of Pythagoreanism / edited by Carl A. Huffman.
pages cm
Includes bibliographical references and index.
ISBN 978-1-107-01439-8 (hardback)
1. Pythagoras and Pythagorean school. I. Huffman, Carl A., editor of compilation.
B243.H57 2014
182'.2—dc23 2013050036

ISBN 978-1-107-01439-8 Hardback

Contents

Contributors

MICHAEL J. B. ALLEN
Distinguished Professor Emeritus of English and Italian Renaissance Studies, UCLA

ANDREW BARKER
Emeritus Professor of Classics, University of Birmingham, UK

GÁBOR BETEGH
Professor, Department of Philosophy, Central European University, Budapest

BRUNO CENTRONE
Professor of Ancient Philosophy, Università di Pisa

JOHN DILLON
Regius Professor of Greek (Emeritus), Trinity College, Dublin

JAAP-JAN FLINTERMAN
Lecturer in Ancient History, Vrije Universiteit, Amsterdam

M. LAURA GEMELLI MARCIANO
Titularprofessorin of Classical Philology, Universität Zürich

DANIEL W. GRAHAM
Abraham Owen Smoot Professor of Philosophy, Brigham Young University

ANDREW HICKS
Assistant Professor of Music and Medieval Studies, Cornell University

CARL A. HUFFMAN
Research Professor and Emeritus Professor of Classical Studies, DePauw University

ANDRÉ LAKS
Emeritus Professor of Ancient Philosophy at the Université de
Paris-Sorbonne and Professor at the Universidad Panamericana, Mexico
City

GEOFFREY LLOYD
Emeritus Professor of Ancient Philosophy and Science, University of
Cambridge

CONSTANTINOS MACRIS
Researcher at the CNRS (Centre national de la recherche scientifique),
Paris

REVIEL NETZ
Professor of Classics, Stanford University

DOMINIC J. O'MEARA
Emeritus Professor of Philosophy, Université de Fribourg

JOHN PALMER
Professor of Philosophy, University of Florida

OLIVER PRIMAVESI
Chair of Greek I, Ludwig-Maximilians-Universität, Munich

CATHERINE ROWETT
Professor of Philosophy, University of East Anglia

MALCOLM SCHOFIELD
Emeritus Professor of Ancient Philosophy, University of Cambridge

STEFAN SCHORN
Assistant Professor of Ancient History, KU Leuven

LEONID ZHMUD
Leading Academic Researcher, Institute for the History of Science and
Technology, Russian Academy of the Sciences, St. Petersburg

Abbreviations

ANRW	Temporini, H. and Haase, W. (eds.) 1972–. *Aufstieg und Niedergang der römischen Welt.* Berlin: De Gruyter.
BnF	Bibliothèque nationale de France.
CAG	1882–1909. *Commentaria in Aristotelem Graeca.* Berlin: Reimer.
CCCM	1966–. *Corpus Christianorum, Continuatio Mediaevalis.* Turnhout: Brepols.
DG	Diels, H. 1879. *Doxographi Graeci.* Berlin: De Gruyter.
DK	Diels, H. 1951. *Die Fragmente der Vorsokratiker.* 6th edn. W. Kranz. Berlin: Weidmann.
DNP	Cancik, H., Schneider, H. and Landfester, M. (eds.) 1996–2003. *Der Neue Pauly.* Stuttgart: Metzler. Translated into English in Salazar, C. F. and Gentry, F. G. (eds.) 2002–2010. *Brill's New Pauly.* Leiden: Brill.
FGrHist	Jacoby, F. 1923–. *Die Fragmente der griechischen Historiker.* Berlin: Weidmann; Leiden: Brill.
FHG	Müller, C. and Th. 1841–1870. *Fragmenta historicorum graecorum.* Paris: Didot.
FHS&G	Fortenbaugh, W., Huby, P., Sharples, R. and Gutas, D. (eds.) 1992, repr. with corrections 1993. *Theophrastus of Eresus: Sources for His Life, Writings, Thought and Influence.* Leiden: Brill.
IG	1873–. *Inscriptiones Graecae.*
K-A	Kassel, R. and Austin, C. (eds.) 1983–. *Poetae Comici Graeci.* Berlin: De Gruyter.
KRS	Kirk, G. S., Raven, J. E. and Schofield, M. 1983. *The Presocratic Philosophers.* 2nd edn. Cambridge University Press.

LSAM	Sokolowski, F. (ed.) 1955. *Lois sacrées de l'Asie Mineure.* Paris: De Boccard.
LSCG	Sokolowski, F. (ed.) 1969. *Lois sacrées des cités grecques.* Paris: De Boccard.
LSJ	Liddell, H. G. and Scott, R. 1968. *A Greek-English Lexicon,* revised by H. S. Jones and R. McKenzie. Oxford: Clarendon.
MSG	Jan, C. (ed.) 1895. *Musici Scriptores Graeci.* Leipzig: Teubner.
OCD	Hornblower, S., Spawforth, A. and Eidinow, E. (eds.) 2012. *The Oxford Classical Dictionary.* 4th edn. Oxford University Press.
PEG	Bernabé, A. (ed.) 2004–2005. *Poetae Epici Graeci. Pars II: Orphicorum et Orphicis Similium Testimonia et Fragmenta.* 2 vols. Munich and Leipzig: K. G. Saur.
PGM	Preisendanz, K. and others (eds.) 1973–1974. *Papyri Graecae Magicae: Die griechischen Zauberpapyri.* 2 vols. 2nd edn. Stuttgart: Teubner.
PL	Migne, J.-P. (ed.) 1844–1855. *Patrologiae Cursus Completus, series Latina.* Paris.
RE	Pauly, A., Wissowa, G. and Kroll, W. 1893–. *Real-Encyclopädie der classischen Altertumswissenschaft.* Stuttgart: Metzler.
SEG	1923–. *Supplementum epigraphicum Graecum.*
SSR	Giannantoni, G. 1990. *Socratis et Socraticorum reliquiae.* Naples: Bibliopolis.
SVF	von Arnim, H. 1903–. *Stoicorum Veterum Fragmenta.* Leipzig: Teubner.
Thesleff	Thesleff, H. 1965. *The Pythagorean Texts of the Hellenistic Period.* Åbo: Åbo Akademi.

Introduction

Carl A. Huffman

In recent years, ancient Pythagoreanism has tended to be a field pursued by a narrow group of specialists and ignored by most scholars of ancient philosophy and ancient civilization. The field can look like a morass that is better not entered at all or bridged by time-worn platitudes about Pythagoras. Many discussions of Pythagoras and Pythagoreanism in general works about ancient civilization or Western culture are thus woefully uninformed. For there has been a great deal of important scholarship on Pythagoreanism in the last fifty years, so that the Pythagoras of current scholarship is not your mother's let alone your grandmother's Pythagoras. The crucial moment in modern scholarship on Pythagoreanism was the publication fifty years ago of Walter Burkert's epoch-making study, which appeared ten years later in a revised version translated into English by Edwin Minar with the title *Lore and Science in Ancient Pythagoreanism* (1972). References to Burkert's book in the footnotes of this volume are surely more frequent than those to any other piece of scholarship on Pythagoreanism. Burkert's Pythagoras was a religious leader and founder of a way of life and not the great mathematician to which many general accounts tenaciously cling. Yet even Burkert's view has not won universal acceptance; Pythagoras the mathematician survives among some scholars even in this book, and there has been significant scholarship that both builds on and reacts against Burkert.

The purpose of this book, then, is two-fold. The first goal is to provide a reliable, comprehensive and accessible snapshot of the current state of scholarship on Pythagoras and Pythagoreanism. It is an invitation to the academic community and the educated public to enter the morass and discover that the issues, while complex, are not hopelessly obscure; a considerable amount of clarity, if not consensus, has been achieved. The second goal is to generate interest in Pythagoras and Pythagoreanism by highlighting problems and suggesting new answers to them. The hope is that those who have been tempted to engage some of the complexity of the field would become intrigued enough to contribute to it. So this is not a history whose goal is to suggest that scholarship has arrived at a consensus on a series of issues and to present a static picture; rather it is a history that treats the field as an evolving discussion and presents the current state of that discussion including all its controversies and debates. It attempts to provide the reader with some solid ground in approaching Pythagoreanism, while at the same time showing that there is much that is contested and that many problems need further analysis.

It is crucial to recognize that there are many Pythagorases and many Pythagoreanisms in this book. No one Pythagoras or Pythagoreanism emerges because there is not one Pythagoras in the ancient sources and different modern interpreters derive a different picture even from the same sources. This book can then be seen as a celebration of this diversity of interpretations of Pythagoras and Pythagoreanism and its chapters make engaging reading just because of the sheer variety of uses to which Pythagoreanism has been put. Pythagoras himself is at the same time one of the most intriguing figures in the history of Greek philosophy and also the most enigmatic and frustrating. There can be no doubt that a great legend arose about him and that images of him and his philosophy proliferated. Is there something behind that legend, as most have supposed, or is early Pythagoreanism almost totally the creation of the later tradition with little historical reality to support it? In the first chapter of this volume Geoffrey Lloyd confronts the possibility that the historical Pythagoras is almost totally unrecoverable. He provides important arguments for this analysis. The painting on the cover of this book by Salvator Rosa, *Pythagoras Emerging from the Underworld* (1662), now in the Kimbell Art Museum in Fort Worth, thus nicely encapsulates one of its main lessons. Pythagoras himself is an obscure figure, difficult to make out in the lower right-hand corner of the painting, although a ray of light plays across his crouched figure. What is at the center of the painting and takes up the bulk of the space is the reaction to Pythagoras by the other figures. Thus, the historical Pythagoras may not be as important as the reactions to him.

However, even with the difficulties identified by Lloyd, it is folly to deny our desire as scholars to arrive at a picture of the historical Pythagoras, for we, like the figures in the painting, are drawn to look back to him. If Pythagoreanism has wielded the very considerable influence that this volume documents, it is natural to wonder about the origin of the influence. So, although Lloyd's skepticism is closer to the modern consensus about Pythagoras, even in this volume there are alternatives to it; e.g., Zhmud's account of fifth-century Pythagoreans assumes a picture of Pythagoras who was an important mathematician and scientist after all. Moreover, even if it is difficult to say anything reliable about Pythagoras himself, recent scholarship suggests that we can say something about early Pythagoreanism and particularly about Philolaus and Archytas. One of the important developments in scholarship of the last fifty years has been the emergence of a consensus that a core of the fragments of Philolaus are authentic so that we have some actual early Pythagorean texts, and Chapter 3 below emphasizes Philolaus' importance for Presocratic philosophy. Archytas emerges as a central figure in several of the following chapters (e.g., Chapters 8 and 10), although in the chapter devoted to Archytas himself, Schofield evinces a skepticism about him that is similar to that of Lloyd about Pythagoras. Recent scholarship has also suggested that Aristoxenus' *Pythagorean Precepts* provide accurate information about the Pythagorean way of life in the fourth century, and these *Precepts* figure prominently in several chapters (e.g., Chapters 10 and 13). If it is foolish to suppose that Pythagoras as the origin of Pythagoreanism, or the nature of early Pythagoreanism, will ever lose their allure, it is equal folly to dismiss later images of Pythagoras and Pythagoreanism as unimportant on the grounds that they tell us little about the historical Pythagoras, as sometimes has been done by scholars who reduce later accounts of Pythagoreanism to mines for earlier sources. The Pythagoreanisms of the pseudo-Pythagorean writings, of Cicero, of Iamblichus, of the Middle Ages and the Renaissance are fascinating in their own right.

In attempts to recover the figure of the historical Pythagoras and the nature of early Pythagoreanism, source criticism is, nonetheless, incredibly important. One's view of Pythagoras and the early Pythagoreans is almost totally determined by what one considers reliable testimony, as well as by interpretations of individual words in those testimonia. Because of the weakness of our sources there has been a great deal of reconstruction, some of it brilliant but still based on slender evidence, which, if doubted, leads to a radically different picture. Does Eudemus mention Pythagoras in his overview of the history of Greek geometry, which most scholars think Proclus preserves in the preface to his commentary on Book 1 of Euclid? If he does, then this is a strong reason for thinking that Pythagoras was indeed a mathematician. If he does not, it is an equally strong ground for supposing that he was not (see Chapter 13 below).

In the chapters below the authors will show striking divergences in approach and strong disagreements on specific points. To some extent this reflects my choices in enlisting contributors. My goal was to include not only leading scholars in the study of Pythagoreanism but also leading scholars in the field of ancient philosophy as a whole, who had not done much work on Pythagoreanism and could thus bring fresh ideas to old problems. In addition the contributors are a mix of senior scholars and scholars who are relatively early in their careers. Finally, although this book is in English and is in the first place directed to the English-speaking world, a significant number of the authors are from European universities; these contributors ensure that a wide range of European scholarship is represented in the content of the chapters and in the bibliography. In the rest of this introduction I will highlight some of the points of convergence and divergence from this diverse group of contributors and give a taste of the varieties of Pythagoreanism they depict. My reading is, of course, just one reading of the chapters that follow. It cannot encompass everything important that is discussed in them and represents just one viewpoint on what they do discuss. Each of the chapters has been broken into separate sections so that a relatively clear idea of their contents can be gleaned by skimming those section headings.

In the opening chapter, **Geoffrey Lloyd** concludes that recent scholarship has not produced a clearer picture of Pythagoras but rather clarified the difficulties involved in reaching such a picture. The sharp divergence between two such accomplished scholars as Burkert and Guthrie, in the accounts they gave of Pythagoras some fifty years ago, already heralded the intractable nature of the problem. Lloyd stresses that Pythagoras eludes most modern labels. There is no reliable evidence that he was a mathematician (*pace* Guthrie) but there are also problems with identifying him as a shaman (*pace* Burkert) or charismatic (*pace* Riedweg). Comparisons with other cultural traditions, such as that of China, and advances in the study of the history of science and the ethnography of shamanism can shed some light, but they do not allow us to flesh out the vague image of Pythagoras. He was certainly an historical figure (*c.* 570–490 BC), who had a significant impact on his contemporaries. He spent his early life on the Greek island of Samos but later moved on to the Greek cities of Croton and Metapontum in southern Italy. Lloyd carefully considers the early evidence for Pythagoras' views but finds little firm ground. He was famed for his wisdom, way of life and views about the soul, but, in the end, it remains very unclear in what his wisdom resided and what, in detail, were the nature of his way of life and his views on the soul. The answers that individual scholars give to these questions just seem to reflect the prejudices that they bring to the investigation. It is only with Philolaus (*c.* 470–390 BC) and Archytas (*c.* 430–350 BC), more than fifty years after Pythagoras' death, that we get firm evidence for Pythagorean harmonics, mathematics and cosmology. The next two chapters on Philolaus and Archytas respectively, thus become very important.

Daniel W. Graham embraces the view that Philolaus has emerged from the shadow of Pythagoras to become in many ways the originator of Pythagorean philosophy and one of the most important fifth-century philosophers. Philolaus argues that there are two types of basic realities, limiters and unlimiteds, but a third principle, harmony, is needed to hold them together in a unity. Philolaus drew his unlimiteds from the traditional Presocratic emphasis on elements that were indeterminate stuffs such as air (Anaximenes) and "the unlimited" (Anaximander) as well as indefinite continua of qualities such as the hot and the cold. Philolaus' striking innovation was to insist that limiters (e.g. shapes and structures) were equally important elements. The harmonious combination of limiters and unlimiteds produces concrete physical objects. Philolaus crucially recognized that without limits, i.e., without "structures, patterns and hierarchies," there can be no knowledge, no science. Philolaus' conception of science thus stresses "systematization or classification" of a subject matter. His postulation of limiters and unlimiteds as basic principles as well as this conception of science exercised clear influence on Plato in the *Philebus*, where limit and unlimited appear as principles. With regard to his cosmology, there remains controversy as to what extent Philolaus is attempting to give a rational as opposed to mythical account of the world or if he is giving an account that combines the two. Philolaus is famous as the first thinker to make the earth a planet rather than the immobile center of the universe, but it orbits the central fire rather than the sun. It is Philolaus' postulation of another body, the counter-earth (to bring the bodies arranged around the central fire up to the perfect number ten, according to Aristotle), that has been particularly controversial. Graham provides a revolutionary new analysis of its role in his astronomical scheme. He argues that it, in fact, served to explain certain lunar eclipses. This analysis supports Philolaus' status as one of the most original cosmologists of the fifth century but one who also belongs firmly in the tradition of rational rather than mythic cosmology. In addition Graham underlines Philolaus' development of a new paradigm of scientific investigation and his role in the development of the Greek concepts of cause and starting-point (ἀρχή).

Malcolm Schofield recognizes Archytas as a significant figure in the history of Greek science and the first and only Pythagorean who can confidently be described as a major mathematician. He was also an important political leader. This prominent role for Archytas will be echoed in Netz's chapter on Pythagorean mathematics and Barker's on Pythagorean harmonics. But Schofield asks, was he a philosopher? The quick answer is yes, since he put forth the most famous argument in antiquity for an infinite universe. At this point, however, Schofield adopts a skeptical stance regarding what we can know about Archytas that is similar to that which Lloyd adopts concerning Pythagoras, and for the same reasons, the scarcity and unreliability of our sources. There is information for Archytas' views in a wide range of fields but most of it is fraught with difficulties. For example, Schofield doubts that the evidence allows us to conclude that Archytas made significant contributions to the fields of mechanics or optics as some scholars have supposed. Again he suggests that Aristotle's remarks about Archytas' definitions may not indicate that he had "an explicit theory of definition," as Huffman has suggested, but may rather reflect commentary on poetry and correct usage of words in the fashion of the sophist Prodicus. In addition to encouraging us to be skeptical about some of the evidence for Archytas the philosopher, however, Schofield also makes important advances in the analysis of the fragments of Archytas commonly accepted as authentic (e.g., frs. 1–3). He also provides new arguments against the authenticity of the fragments of *On Law and Justice*, which are the only other fragments whose authenticity a significant number of scholars have defended. In the course of casting further doubt on these fragments, however, he provides further support of the authenticity of fr. 3. He presents a nuanced discussion of the relation between Plato and Archytas, but is skeptical of any significant impact of Archytas on Aristotle; he expresses serious doubts about the authenticity of the works on Archytas that appear in the ancient lists of Aristotle's works.

Leonid Zhmud's chapter on Pythagoreans of the sixth through fourth centuries BC, apart from "the big three" (Pythagoras, Philolaus and Archytas), provides an excellent example of the contested state of the evidence concerning Pythagoreanism. His account of these Pythagoreans is inevitably based on his own view of Pythagoras himself and the nature of early Pythagoreanism as a whole. Zhmud presents a view of Pythagoras as a mathematician who founded the sciences of arithmetic and harmonics, although the dominant view since Burkert's work, a view reflected in Lloyd's chapter on Pythagoras and Netz's chapter on Pythagorean mathematics, is that Pythagoras was not a mathematician. Similarly Zhmud accepts Becker's reconstruction of an early Pythagorean arithmetic, while Netz rejects it. Even more strikingly, Zhmud argues that after Pythagoras we do not find a single religious figure among the Pythagoreans of the sixth through fourth century, whereas Gemelli Marciano argues in her account of the Pythagorean life that religion is central to Pythagoreanism.

Similarly Zhmud maintains that there was no split into *acusmatici*, who followed the oral precepts of Pythagoras known as *acusmata*, and *mathematici*, who focused on more scientific disciplines. He argues that this split is the creation of the later tradition, although Burkert and many others think that it occurred in the fifth century and is already found in the testimony of Aristotle. Thus, Gemelli Marciano finds the *acusmata* central to the Pythagorean way of life. Finally, there is no more hotly debated question than who counts as a Pythagorean. Zhmud treats Alcmaeon as a Pythagorean and makes him crucial to his picture of early Pythagorean natural science, as Theodorus is important to Pythagorean mathematics, while other scholars do not regard Alcmaeon or Theodorus as Pythagoreans at all. Zhmud stresses the great heterogeneity of the Pythagoreans and, borrowing a concept from Wittgenstein, argues that while there was a family resemblance among Pythagoreans, there was no single common characteristic shared by all Pythagoreans (except that apart from Pythagoras none were religious figures). He gives accounts of a number of possible but little known early Pythagoreans such as Hippasus, Hippo, Menestor and Ecphantus.

Focus then turns from individual Pythagoreans to the major areas in which early Pythagoreanism manifested itself: politics, way of life, religion, mathematics and harmonics. **Catherine Rowett** provides a fresh look at the role of Pythagoras and the Pythagorean society in the politics of the Greek city-states of southern Italy. She stresses that Pythagoras' political activity began after leaving Samos for southern Italy (*c.* 530 BC) but suggests that a connection with Apollo and the Delphic oracle had already been established and may have had a role in his choice of Croton as a place to settle and in guiding his actions there. She argues that the groups to which Pythagoras made his addresses upon his first arrival in Croton (the old men, youth, boys and women of the city) were not traditional groupings but represent a radical new approach to teaching. Nonetheless, he speaks to these groups at sites associated with traditional *polis* religion rather than invoking mystery cults. Thus, while he may have taught metempsychosis and rewards and punishments after death to his close followers, his message to the city itself was much more traditional. The emphasis on the role of women in the Pythagorean tradition is striking. Although some sources suggest that he revived traditional values, Rowett argues that he was much more revolutionary. Women were regarded as not just faithful wives but also part of the intellectual life of the community. Pythagoras' division of women into age groupings may have furthered radical goals such as assigning women roles by age and experience rather than status or wealth. She concludes by examining the reports about the attacks on the Pythagoreans in southern Italy and sees in them support for her general view about the Pythagorean political agenda and methods. It is a mistake to understand the attacks in the traditional terms of a conflict between democrats and oligarchs. Pythagoreans did not try to change the constitution but rather offered different policies, which were promoted through the Pythagorean clubs (*hetaireiai*). Thus, the attacks on the Pythagoreans are to be understood as the work of rival clubs of propertied citizens challenging Pythagorean policies and in particular the fundamental Pythagorean idea that "friends have all things in common." They resorted to assassination because the "widespread respect for the Pythagoreans" offered little hope for replacing Pythagorean policies by normal political means.

Surely the way of life that Pythagoras prescribed for his followers must have had a role in the political impact described by Rowett. Moreover, those who follow Burkert's view of Pythagoras recognize that the way of life that Pythagoras left to his followers is crucial in defining Pythagoreanism, yet as Lloyd notes it has been hard to reconstruct confidently what that life was like. **M. Laura Gemelli Marciano** suggests that we can only really understand the way of life in light of a distinction between instrumental and receptive consciousness employed by the psychiatrist A. Deikmann. Pythagoras and the Pythagorean life embody the outlook of receptive consciousness, which tries to act in harmony with and in service to a reality that is seen as a connected whole; moderns, however, often misunderstand them by adopting the view of instrumental consciousness, whose focus is on separation from external reality and domination of it. She argues that the socio-political impact of the movement, which Rowett describes in her chapter, is unintelligible without appreciating it as a manifestation of instrumental consciousness, which acts to help communities on behalf of the divine. She emphasizes that the Pythagorean way of life and Pythagorean ethics cannot be separated from their religious dimension. She argues in particular against Zhmud's view that the ritualistic precepts do not correspond to concrete practice. She says that the precepts not only ritualize the life of the Pythagoreans but also allow them to recognize the divine in this world and understand the cosmos in light of the journey the soul must make to return to its original divine state. These oral maxims of the master (known as *acusmata* = "things heard") are thus not "a hotchpotch of superstitious precepts" full of absurdities, as scholars such as Zhmud suggest, but aim at control over one's acts and purity. Nor would they have been cause for scandal in late-sixth-century Magna Graecia. She argues that the attempts to downplay the *acusmata* both in antiquity and in modern scholarship are part of a tendency to normalize Pythagoras and the Pythagorean way of life.

Gábor Betegh explores the religious dimension of Pythagoreanism highlighted by Gemelli Marciano by comparing it to another controversial Greek religious movement: Orphism. He notes that in late antiquity the relationship between Pythagoreanism and Orphism was largely unproblematic. Pythagoras was initiated into Orphic mysteries and derived his metaphysics and theology from Orphism. Authors of the fifth century BC, on the other hand, while perceiving an affinity between Orphism and Pythagoreanism, were much less clear on which way the influence ran, and many regarded Pythagoras as the central figure. For Betegh the central difficulty in determining the relationship between the two movements is the ultimate impossibility of defining Pythagoreanism or Orphism. For example, the common assumption that Pythagoreanism and Orphism share a belief in metempsychosis and the practice of vegetarianism is problematic. Vegetarianism appears not to have been a core feature of Pythagoreanism, so that Pythagoreans could participate in the sacrificial ritual of polis religion. Hardcore Orphics may have practiced it, but many initiates into Orphic rites did not. Evidence from Plato suggests that Orphics believed in metempsychosis, but the archaeological evidence for Orphic and Bacchic cults provides no unambiguous evidence for it. There is clear evidence for Pythagoras' belief in metempsychosis but none for the most important early Pythagoreans, such as Philolaus and Archytas. Betegh concludes that just as Greek religion as a whole is pluralistic and there is much local variation so also there is a great variety among Orphics and Pythagoreans. In this regard he seems to support Zhmud's pluralistic interpretation of what it means to be a Pythagorean. One common feature that Betegh finds in both Orphic texts, such as the Derveni papyrus, and Pythagorean texts, such as the fragments of Philolaus, is an attempt to take concepts derived from natural philosophy and enrich them with religious meaning. Philolaus' central fire is part of an astronomical system that can explain many of the phenomena, as Graham shows in his chapter, but it at the same time brings with it the religious connotations of the hearth of the household and the state. This methodology reinforces the idea that there need not be any antagonism between Pythagoreanism and traditional religion, as Gemelli Marciano also suggested in her chapter. Pythagorean taboos can be seen as an additional layer on top of traditional practices and not in conflict with them. The Pythagoreans do not criticize religion from a rationalist standpoint as does Xenophanes, nor do they attempt to provide an alternative mythic account as do the Orphics; rather they give new significance to traditional religion. Pythagoras' presentation of himself as the Hyperborean Apollo may be emblematic of this.

One of the most intriguing things about Pythagoreanism has always been that it appears to have both a strong religious and also a strong mathematical and scientific dimension. **Reviel Netz** combines a survey of the most important evidence for early Pythagorean mathematics with an innovative new way of looking at the history of Greek mathematics and the position of Pythagoreanism in that history. He suggests that there were two networks that accounted for most progress in Greek mathematics, one in the fourth century and one in the third. The central figure in the earlier network was Archytas. In contrast to Zhmud's approach in Chapter 4, he emphasizes that the evidence for Pythagorean engagement in mathematics proper prior to Archytas is negligible; on his preferred model Netz suggests that most supposed early Pythagorean work in mathematics, including the "Pythagorean theorem," was projected back onto the earlier period in light of the situation in the fourth century and the prominence of Archytas. He emphasizes, moreover, that fourth-century mathematicians who treated Archytas' approach to mathematics as a paradigm by no means therefore embraced Pythagoreanism as a philosophy. Netz admits that the sources are perilous and that his model is not the only possible one. The central question raised by his investigation is how important and influential Archytas was. His preferred answer applies Bertrand Russell's description of Pythagoras as "one of the most important men who ever lived" to Archytas instead, thus making him an even more prominent figure than is suggested by Schofield in Chapter 3. Netz also provides a new suggestion about one of the most puzzling figures in earlier Pythagoreanism, Eurytus. He argues that Eurytus was not, as has often been supposed, naively creating pebble mosaics of individual things in order to show the number (of pebbles) that constituted them (this traditional view is followed in a slightly modified version by Zhmud, Chapter 4, section 10, pp. 108–9). He was instead manipulating counters ("pebbles") on an abacus to demonstrate the numerical basis of things.

Pythagorean mathematics had its greatest influence on Pythagorean philosophy as a whole through harmonics. In his discussion of Pythagorean harmonics, **Andrew Barker** does not begin with Pythagoras himself, initially because of problems with the sources, but in the end because, so Barker concludes, Pythagoras did not contribute anything to the science of harmonics. The story of his discovery of the ratios that govern the concords in a blacksmith's shop, which is first recounted by Nicomachus in the second century AD, is a myth. Instead, Barker begins by giving us the picture of Pythagorean harmonics seen through the eyes of the only recorded Greek woman harmonic theorist, Ptolemaïs of Cyrene, writing at least 200 years after Pythagoras' death. She identifies the Pythagoreans as one of the two main groups of harmonic theorists in the ancient tradition. Pythagorean harmonics is above all characterized by the use of reason to describe musical scales in terms of ratios of whole numbers in contrast to the Aristoxenians who based their harmonics on sense perception. Ptolemaïs distinguished between two groups of Pythagoreans: some do not conceal the fact that they start from the senses, although arguing that in the end it is reason and not sense perception that judges what is concordant, while others claim that reason is completely self-sufficient, although they are refuted by their forgetting that they had to accept perception at the beginning of their investigation. This latter group seems to be later and influenced by Plato's call in the *Republic* for a harmonics divorced from heard harmonies. Indeed later descriptions of Pythagorean harmonics will be heavily influenced not only by this passage in the *Republic* but by Plato's construction of the World-Soul according to the "Pythagorean" diatonic scale in the *Timaeus*. It is earlier Pythagoreans such as Archytas that are closer to Ptolemaïs' first group, although he is even more empirical. In Barker's account of Pythagorean harmonics just as in Netz's account of Pythagorean mathematics it is Archytas who emerges as the crucial figure. Although other Presocratics had explored the basics of the study of acoustics, the Pythagorean Hippasus first started to develop the field and Archytas made important advances in it, including the most influential theory of pitch in antiquity. Barker suggests that Pythagoreans like Archytas may have developed the science of acoustics in an attempt to find quantitative attributes of sounds to which to attach the numbers in the ratios that defined the concords.

The first nine chapters of this volume thus focus on the major figures of early Pythagoreanism as well as the major areas of Greek life and the Greek intellectual tradition to which they contributed. In keeping with the dominant trend of scholarship on the Pythagoreans over the last fifty years and with the skepticism of Lloyd's initial chapter on Pythagoras, the emphasis has been much less on Pythagoras himself and more on a variety of other early Pythagoreans and particularly Philolaus and Archytas. We now turn to the reception of Pythagoreanism and the emergence of new Pythagorases and new Pythagoreanisms starting with two giants of fourth-century philosophy, Plato and Aristotle.

There is a long tradition according to which Plato was heavily influenced by the Pythagoreans, and this tradition began already among Plato's successors in the Academy and flourished in the Neopythagoreanism of the first centuries AD as Dillon's chapter below demonstrates. Plato's Pythagoreanism has come to be more contested in modern scholarship. There are only two explicit references to Pythagoras and the Pythagoreans in the Platonic corpus, and Aristotle's evidence on the relation between Plato and the Pythagoreans is controversial. **John Palmer** presents a nuanced defense of the view that Pythagorean influence on Plato was substantial. He argues that, despite difficulties in determining the precise nature of the Pythagoreanism that Plato knew and recognizing that Plato's treatment of the Pythagoreans, like his treatment of all the Presocratics, is typically "transformative," we, nonetheless, can see important ways in which the Pythagoreans influenced him. The core of the Pythagorean impact on Plato is found already in "the vision of value, goodness and well-being" that appears in the *Gorgias*, where "wise men" assert that the excellence of both the cosmos and the human soul reside in order and correctness. Palmer argues that there are important parallels between the vision of the wise men in the *Gorgias* and fr. 3 of Archytas and several fragments from Aristoxenus' *Pythagorean Precepts*, so that we are justified in supposing that Plato is primarily drawing on Pythagoreans for this vision. He then traces Plato's development of this central vision and its influence on his conception of the soul and on his ethics through the *Phaedo* and *Republic* to the *Timaeus* and *Philebus*. He is careful throughout to distinguish the Platonic transformation from the Pythagorean core to the extent that this is possible. In many cases Plato provides the rationale that supports the bald assertions of the Pythagoreans, e.g., that the soul is immortal or that suicide is forbidden. Palmer finally argues that two of Plato's latest dialogues, the *Timaeus* and the *Philebus*, show him still articulating the Pythagorean vision originally presented in the *Gorgias*. This can be seen in the importance of mathematics and number in the *Timaeus'* account of the cosmos and in the *Philebus'* assertion that the highest value resides in measure, as part of its analysis of the relation between pleasure and knowledge. As in Netz's chapter on Pythagorean mathematics, Archytas plays a central role in Palmer's account of Pythagorean influence on Plato and he accepts certain key texts as representing genuine Archytan ideas (e.g., Archytas' account of pleasure in A9a) in contrast to Schofield's skepticism. Philolaus' influence on Plato as seen in the *Philebus* is also of central importance.

The relationship between Pythagoreanism and the other giant of Greek philosophy, Plato's pupil Aristotle, has usually been thought to be quite different. Like Plato, Aristotle rarely refers to Pythagoras himself, but unlike Plato Aristotle provides extensive explicit, but often quite critical, discussion of Pythagoreanism. **Oliver Primavesi**'s account of Aristotle's picture of Pythagoreanism is striking both in terms of methodology and conclusions. Rather than giving a grand survey of all Aristotelian references to Pythagoreanism, he focuses on just fourteen lines of text from *Metaphysics* A5 (985b23–986a3), which constitute Aristotle's core characterization of Pythagoreanism. He further elucidates these lines by detailed examination of thirty-one lines (38.10–39.13 and 39.19–22) from Alexander of Aphrodisias' (second to third century AD) commentary on them. Alexander is here relying on Aristotle's lost monograph on the Pythagoreans, so Primavesi is in effect reading the passage in the *Metaphysics* in light of Aristotle's more detailed discussion of Pythagoreanism in his monograph. The results are striking. He argues that scholars have failed to realize that Aristotle is presenting a developmental account of Pythagoreanism. Aristotle has two basic sources for Pythagoreanism: 1. a collection of traditional material that includes not just, as is commonly supposed, elements of the Pythagoras legend (e.g., his role as the Hyperborean Apollo) and the heterogeneous taboos and precepts known as the *acusmata*, but also Pythagorean analysis of the similarities between numbers and things inspired by the advancement of the *mathemata*, which Aristotle attributes to them; and 2. the fragments of the book of Philolaus of Croton. Early Pythagorean analysis of numbers, as reconstructed by Aristotle in his monograph, is not rigorous mathematics, but it is also not simplistic number mysticism and involves sophisticated arguments about the structural features of numbers and the world. In *Metaphysics* A5 Aristotle attempts to build a bridge between this earlier piecemeal Pythagorean analysis of numbers and their relation to things and Philolaus' system of universal principles (limiters and unlimiteds). Aristotle constructs causal connections between isolated Pythagorean beliefs in order to arrive at a coherent account of Pythagoreanism. Primavesi suggests that Aristotle's puzzling description of the Pythagoreanism he presents as the philosophy of the "so-called Pythagoreans" represents his recognition that his account is a reconstruction and that the final phase of that reconstruction, represented by Philolaus, is far removed from anything Pythagoras himself might have taught, even though Philolaus was commonly called a Pythagorean.

In his account of Pythagoreanism in the Academic tradition, **John Dillon** traces the crucial story of the rise of Neopythagoreanism (the branch of Platonism that emphasizes the role of number in the cosmos and regards Pythagoreanism as the source of that emphasis) and argues that it has its origin already in the Old Academy, although some scholars have recently

suggested that it does not arise until the first century BC. According to
Dillon, Speusippus and Xenocrates establish the Pythagorean provenance
of the first principles that will dominate Neopythagoreanism, Plato's One
and Indefinite Dyad. Another member of the Early Academy, Heraclides
of Pontus, on the other hand, inaugurates many of the striking characteristics of the later life-myth of Pythagoras, including his supposed invention
of the word "philosophy." The Neopythagoreanism of Speusippus and
Xenocrates is then revived and developed by Eudorus in Alexandria in the
first century BC evidently partly under the influence of pseudo-Pythagorean
treatises forged in the first century. Dillon shows that the first beneficiary
of this revived Neopythagoreanism was the Jewish philosopher Philo, who
was also from Alexandria. After a quick glance at Plutarch, Dillon then
concludes with an examination of the flowering of Neopythagoreanism in
the second century in the figures of Moderatus, Nicomachus and Numenius. As Dillon notes, these Neopythagoreans were for the most part glad
to celebrate Pythagoras and the Pythagoreans as the forerunners of Plato's
One and Indefinite Dyad and to recognize the continuity of Platonism
and Pythagoreanism. Moderatus alone complains that the Platonists have
stolen the best for themselves and left only the trivial to the Pythagoreans.

Aristotle's school, the Peripatos, is less important for the creation of
the image of Pythagoras in the later tradition but more important in
determining the nature of early Pythagoreanism. Just like Aristotle early
members of his school paid particular attention to Pythagoreans; Aristoxenus devoted five treatises exclusively to them. Here more than anywhere
else in the study of Pythagoreanism it becomes clear that our view of the
Pythagoreans is crucially determined by what we take to be a genuine
fragment by a Peripatetic and what we do not. **Carl A. Huffman** examines
the evidence for what are likely to be genuine fragments of Peripatetic
works. One striking case is a sentence in Proclus' preface to his commentary on Book 1 of Euclid that mentions Pythagoras. If it goes back to the
Peripatetic Eudemus' *History of Geometry*, then it is strong evidence that
Pythagoras was an important mathematician. If it does not and is rather
an insertion by Proclus, then Eudemus' failure to mention Pythagoras is
strong evidence that Pythagoras was not a mathematician. Huffman follows Burkert and most recent scholars in arguing that the sentence does
not go back to Eudemus. The fragments of the Peripatetics indicate that
later Pythagoreans did play an important role in a wide range of mathematical disciplines but were not the decisive figures in any of them. Huffman
thus occupies a middle position between Zhmud (Chapter 4), who would
make even Pythagoras himself an important mathematician, and Netz

(Chapter 8), who is skeptical of most early Pythagorean work in mathematics beyond that of Archytas. Two other Peripatetics, Dicaearchus and Aristoxenus, focus on Pythagoras himself and the Pythagorean way of life. Aristoxenus wrote more about the Pythagoreans than any other Peripatetic; however, Aristoxenus has usually been considered a rabid Pythagorean partisan who ascribed to the Pythagoreans doctrines that were really Platonic and Aristotelian and tried to rationalize Pythagoreanism by removing all religious elements from it. Huffman argues that this view ignores crucial fragments of Aristoxenus and ascribes other texts to him that are not his. He, in fact, gave ample scope to the religious aspect of Pythagoreanism. Although he presents the Pythagoreans in a uniformly positive fashion, he does not engage in hagiography and his *Pythagorean Precepts* are an important guide to the Pythagorean life in the fourth century. A new interpretation of Dicaearchus suggests that his account of Pythagoras was negative and satirical. He reports that one of Pythagoras' rebirths was as the beautiful prostitute Alco! Thus the Peripatos was sharply divided in its presentation of Pythagoras and the Pythagorean way of life.

Interest in Pythagoras and Pythagoreanism was not limited to philosophical schools such as the Academy and Peripatos. The ancient historical tradition paid a surprising amount of attention to Pythagoras, more than to most other philosophers. **Stefan Schorn** provides a fresh examination of the presentation of Pythagoras in the historians, focusing particularly on Herodotus, Timaeus, Neanthes and Diodorus. He concludes that Herodotus thought there was strong Egyptian influence on Pythagoras and supposed that Pythagoreanism influenced Orphic and Bacchic rites. Herodotus is guarded in his presentation of Pythagoras, and it may be that he is hesitant openly to express his criticism of him, because he was writing in the homeland of Pythagoreanism, southern Italy. Schorn accepts that Aristoxenus and Dicaearchus presented a rationalized picture of Pythagoras, at least in contrast to Aristotle's presentation of him as a wonder-worker, and thus is in tension with Huffman's view. Schorn gives special attention to the historian Timaeus of Tauromenium. Timaeus shows particular interest in the rules governing the Pythagorean community and admission to it. His attitude to Pythagoras and Pythagoreanism is complex. He admires the seriousness of Pythagorean education but may have been bothered by its exclusivity. In general he seems to be positive about Pythagoras, without being encomiastic, and shows no particular bias. Schorn shows that Neanthes of Cyzicus, a contemporary of Timaeus, was critical of Timaeus' presentation of Pythagoreanism in a number of ways and in particular argued for the earlier (Aristoxenian) dating of Pythagoras, according to which he died *c.* 490 and thus could not have been the direct teacher of Empedocles as Timaeus supposed. Neanthes appears to have had no particular bias in his reporting about Pythagoras, although he was more interested in his life than his philosophy. He is important as an intermediary. His research into Pythagoras and the Pythagoreans, which may have relied on local traditions (including the story of the Pythagorean husband and wife, Myllias and Timycha), became incorporated into later accounts of Pythagoras. Finally Diodorus includes what initially seems to be a surprising amount on Pythagorean teaching in his universal history. However, the emphasis on Pythagorean ethics, in fact, accords with Diodorus' moralizing tendencies, and he appears to have used the Pythagoreans as models of virtue. It is harder to identify his sources. Some material goes back to Aristoxenus but that material has been reworked and Diodorus' main source is difficult to determine.

Bruno Centrone introduces us to a central phenomenon in Pythagoreanism that is the antithesis of the historical tradition, the tradition of texts forged in the name of Pythagoras and other Pythagoreans. It is this tradition of forgery that makes it so difficult to identify not just the ideas of the historical Pythagoras but also the fragments and ideas of early Pythagoreans such as Philolaus and Archytas. Centrone provides a brief overview of the pseudo-Pythagorean writings that appeared first in the third century BC and became so numerous that many more pseudo-Pythagorean texts and fragments of texts survive than geunuine fragments of works by early Pythagoreans. He distinguishes between treatises forged in Pythagoras' name and those forged in the names of other Pythagoreans and gives an overview of the first type. He recognizes that there is great variety among the pseudo-Pythagorean writings and that they arose in different contexts and different times. However, the bulk of his chapter is devoted to an exposition of the thesis that a very large number of the treatises articulate the same basic system and, therefore, are likely to have arisen at roughly the same time and in roughly the same milieu: Alexandria at the end of the first century BC and the beginning of the first century AD. This group of treatises includes the most famous Pythagorean pseudepigrapha: the works ascribed to Timaeus, Ocellus and Archytas. It also encompasses, however, numerous fragments from treatises forged in the names of more obscure Pythagoreans such as Metopos and Damippus. Centrone provides a remarkably coherent account of a common system found in these treatises, which seeks to unite Platonism with Aristotelianism across the full spectrum of the divisions of philosophy: first principles, logic, theology, cosmology, ethics and politics. He brings out the connections between this system and the work of the Platonist Eudorus and the Jewish philosopher, Philo, both of whom worked in Alexandria and who figure prominently in Dillon's chapter on the Academic tradition. For the first time a significant portion of the pseudo-Pythagorean writings can be seen as a coherent whole.

Jaap-Jan Flinterman examines the various guises of Pythagoreanism in Rome and Asia Minor during the first centuries BC and AD, the time period when the bulk of the pseudo-Pythagorean writings emerged. He emphasizes the problematic nature of our sources for Pythagoreanism around the turn of the Common Era in Rome and Asia Minor. It is particularly difficult to disentangle the posthumous reputations and literary images from the historical reality of figures such as Nigidius Figulus, Apollonius of Tyana and Alexander of Abonouteichos. The evidence for Nigidius, a contemporary of Cicero, does not support claims of a widespread rebirth of Pythagoreanism in Rome, as has sometimes been supposed, nor is such an idea supported by the very questionable suggestion that the intriguing remains of the basilica at Porta Maggiore show that it was a meeting place for Pythagoreans. Nonetheless, there is rich evidence that Pythagorean ideas were of great interest to Roman intellectuals and literary figures, such as Cicero and Ovid, and Pythagoreanism may have received particular attention as a native Italian philosophy. Moreover, individuals like Nigidius, Varro, Sextius and Seneca adopted Pythagorean views and ethical precepts to varying degrees. Flinterman stresses that the label "Pythagorean" had ambiguous connotations throughout the first centuries BC and AD both in Rome and in Asia Minor. While it could refer simply to someone who adopted the supposed beliefs of Pythagoras, it also very commonly referred to individuals who were involved in occult or magical practices. The occult connection could lead "Pythagoreans" to be regarded with suspicion as can be seen in Cicero's attack on Vatinius, Augustus' expulsion of Anaxilaus and Lucian's savage parody of Alexander of Abonouteichos. On the other hand, expertise in the magical properties of plants, for example, which was found in texts by pseudo-Pythagoras and pseudo-Democritus, could be perfectly respectable and this may have been a central part of Nigidius' Pythagoreanism. Moreover, the connection to Pythagoras himself could be used to invest a wonder-working individual such as Apollonius of Tyana with the mantle of "philosopher" and defend him from charges of being just a magician or charlatan. Thus despite the source problems there can be no doubt that the "Pythagoreans and magicians" of Rome around the turn of the Common Era and the itinerant Pythagorean wonder-workers of the early empire are important parts of the intellectual and social history of those periods.

This brings us to the three great lives of Pythagoras dating to the third century AD, which survive largely intact and which have had an enormous impact on depictions of Pythagoras in the Renaissance and the modern world. It is generally agreed that Diogenes Laertius' life is the earliest of the three dating to the first part of the century. **André Laks** concludes that Diogenes Laertius' presentation of Pythagoras is so variegated and its structure so opaque that it is very difficult to determine what attitude he had toward Pythagoreanism. There are few traces of the Neopythagoreanism that was rife at the time of Diogenes in the early third century AD. The only clear emphasis that can be seen in Diogenes' account is on the precepts that governed the Pythagorean way of life, and Laks discusses these in some detail, thus complementing Gemelli Marciano's discussion of them in Chapter 6. The lack of a clear focus in Diogenes' *Life* has been part of the reason that scholars have most typically mined it for evidence of earlier sources, instead of studying it for its own sake. Laks provides a good overview of these sources. His real breakthrough, however, is in the interpretation of the long passage that Diogenes quotes from Alexander Polyhistor. The *Pythagorean Notes* that Alexander is in turn quoting have sometimes been thought to contain evidence for pre-Platonic Pythagoreanism. Laks concludes that it is not implausible that there is early material present but, given the nature of the evidence, any attempt to identify a given portion as early ultimately just reveals the prejudices of the interpreter, the same situation that Lloyd suggests applies to the evidence for Pythagoras himself. Laks shows that the passage is important independently of whether it reveals anything about early Pythagoreanism and that it is thematically unified around the idea of purity. The cosmology and psychology of its first sections reveal a world divided into pure and impure parts and a soul that can be purified because it consists of a spark of aither from the pure regions. This cosmology and psychology then lead naturally to the precepts given at the end of the passage, which provide guidelines for purifying the soul. The whole passage is thus extremely coherent and stands out amidst its rather chaotic surroundings in Diogenes. It provides us with insight into Hellenistic Pythagoreanism, for which there is little other evidence. It might reflect the existence of a Pythagorean community in the period, but it could also be the result of purely scholarly activity. Moreover, this pattern of providing justification for the moral precepts may reflect and be an extension of genuine early Pythagorean practice.

Constantinos Macris emphasizes that Porphyry's *Life of Pythagoras* (*VP*) was originally not an independent work but part of Porphyry's larger *History of Philosophy*, which only survives in fragments of which the *VP* is the only large chunk. The larger work significantly ended with Plato and perhaps his immediate pupils, including Aristotle. Pythagoras and Socrates thus received particularly extensive treatment by Porphyry, since they had traditionally been seen as the major influences on Plato. The extensive section on Pythagoras then evidently became separated from the rest of the *History of Philosophy* because of the enduring interest in Pythagoras in the Byzantine period. Macris shows that Porphyry's *Life* is a scholarly work that carefully collects earlier sources without structuring them according to any overall philosophic purpose such as Iamblichus used in constructing his *On the Pythagorean Life*. This careful scholarship on Porphyry's part gives us important insight into earlier sources. Porphyry's own voice is seldom heard in his *VP* and his influence is mainly to be seen in his choice of sources. Macris shows that Porphyry differs strikingly from Diogenes Laertius, who includes many sources that satirize Pythagoras or portray him in a bad light. Porphyry presents almost exclusively positive reports and does not hesitate to include texts from militant Neopythagoreans, who accuse later philosophers such as Plato and Aristotle of stealing much of what was best in Pythagoreanism. It is striking that Porphyry shows no inclination to be critical about the Pythagorean sources that he reports, even though he displays a well-developed critical sense elsewhere. Porphyry was a committed Platonist with Pythagorean sympathies, who evidently had little inclination to question positive reports about Pythagoras. Macris emphasizes that Porphyry's Pythagoras is the Pythagoras of the Middle-Platonists developed in the first two centuries AD. At the same time he emphasizes that this presentation of Pythagoras, as the quintessential sage who provided a model of an ascetic way of life, was distinct from the picture of Pythagoras later developed by Iamblichus, which depicts Pythagoras as a privileged soul sent to save humanity. Finally Macris shows that Porphyry and some of his compatriots in Plotinus' school followed an ascetic way of life that owed much of its inspiration to Pythagoras and that in the *VP* he appears to regard purification of the soul through asceticism and mathematics as Pythagoras' primary contribution to philosophy. His extensive use of Neopythagorean sources in the *VP* and other writings shows that he had a "Pythagorean" library, although it seems mainly to be composed of works from the first two centuries AD and his knowledge of the work of earlier Pythagoreans, such as Archytas, may have come from later compilations.

As **Dominic J. O'Meara** points out, Iamblichus' *On the Pythagorean Life* is the fullest account of Pythagoras and Pythagoreanism to survive from antiquity and is thus of central importance. O'Meara sharply contrasts Rohde's view of Iamblichus' work as a mere patchwork of earlier sources with more recent work, which has come to appreciate Iamblichus' philosophical purposes in writing and structuring the work. O'Meara demonstrates that *On the Pythagorean Life* can only be understood if we recognize that it is the first part of Iamblichus' ten-part work *On Pythagoreanism*. Moreover, his portrayal of Pythagoras must be interpreted in light of Iamblichus' theory of immaculate souls: Pythagoras' soul was not sent to this world to be punished or purified but rather to purify and perfect the world. O'Meara argues that it is impossible to determine whether Porphyry's or Iamblichus' account of Pythagoras was written first but, whatever the order of priority, they represent two different positions in the attempt to determine Plato's legacy. Porphyry defended the view of Plotinus that Plato was the central figure, who developed into clear ideas what was still obscure in Pythagoras, whereas Iamblichus followed Numenius and Nicomachus in regarding the ancient wisdom that inspired Plato, i.e., Pythagoreanism, as central. O'Meara further argues that Iamblichus' grand project *On Pythagoreanism* is not to be understood as some youthful production that is largely separate from his mature views; Pythagoreanism is just as central in his mature philosophy. O'Meara then turns to the structure of *On the Pythagorean Life* itself. He argues that we will understand it better if we recognize that it differs from a modern biography in having many of the features of an encomium, a work whose goal is to magnify and glorify its subject. Interestingly, *On the Pythagorean Life* shows similarities not just to encomia of individuals but also to encomia of sciences, so that it is perhaps best understood as a work of praise of Pythagorean philosophy as a whole, which is appropriate as an introduction to the curriculum in Pythagoreanism that follows in the other nine parts of Iamblichus' work. Having shown that, if Iamblichus' *On the Pythagorean Life* is a patchwork, it is a patchwork with a very sophisticated structure, O'Meara then turns to the patches, the sources that Iamblichus used. He argues that Rohde's thesis, according to which Iamblichus basically stitched together two sources, is misleading in at least two ways. First, Iamblichus often rewrote the passages to serve his own purposes. Second, he is likely to have used more than just two sources. Iamblichus' work is more a "reweaving" than a "patchwork." Iamblichus' treatment of Pythagoreanism was widely influential among later Neoplatonists, such as Syrianus and Proclus, and in the Renaissance, as becomes clear in Allen's chapter below.

The volume now shifts from the ancient to the medieval and Renaissance world for its final two chapters. **Andrew Hicks** shows that in the medieval period, according to one prominent view, Pythagoras was "the icon of Greek wisdom," who founded the Greek philosophical tradition and was its greatest practitioner. His authority is presented as so great that students received it unquestioningly in a seven-year period of silence that corresponded to the seven liberal arts. The highest truths of his philosophy could only be revealed through analogies and were expressed in veiled language. The medieval view of Pythagoras was not a novel creation but grew directly out of one strand of the late antique presentations of Pythagoras found in such authors as Boethius (drawing on Nicomachus), Calcidius and Macrobius. The medieval image of Pythagoras had little to do with the historical Pythagoras. Its accounts of his life were not based on Iamblichus' or Porphyry's *Lives* of Pythagoras, which were not known in the Middle Ages, but rather on a collection of passages from classical authors and church fathers. Hicks focuses not on the life of Pythagoras, however, but on the legacy of Pythagoreanism in the medieval period in three key areas. First he examines Pythagoras as the central figure in delimiting the famous quadrivium of four sciences, which in turn are the foundation for all philosophy. Boethius is the key figure in the transmission of this image of Pythagoras from late antiquity to the medieval period as he is in the second area, music theory. Here Hicks argues that Boethius presents the Pythagoreans as adopting a position which emphasizes not just the role of reason in musical judgment but that also recognizes more of a role for perception than has usually been recognized. Finally Calcidius and Macrobius are the key figures in determining the medieval picture of Pythagoras as a natural philosopher. The musical nature of the structure of the soul and the harmony of the spheres are contested Pythagorean doctrines in the Middle Ages. The harmony of the spheres became a central feature of medieval cosmologies, but the reintroduction of Aristotle's criticism of that doctrine led to its abandonment in many cases.

Hicks ends with a reference to Marsilio Ficino and **Michael J. B. Allen** in his account of Pythagoras in the early Renaissance focuses on this crucial figure and the impact on Renaissance thought of his translations of Iamblichus' works on Pythagoreanism and in particular *On the Pythagorean Life*. For Ficino and the Renaissance Pythagoras was the most important of the Presocratic philosophers and, although the lack of any monumental body of texts kept him from eclipsing Plato as the preeminent ancient philosopher, Renaissance thinkers saw him as providing a vital link in the transmission to Plato of an ancient wisdom that goes back to Zoroaster and

Moses. Allen emphasizes four areas of Pythagorean impact on the Renaissance: 1. The role of music in the Pythagorean way of life as portrayed in Iamblichus influenced Ficino's own musical practice. 2. The Pythagorean conception of reincarnation provided a profound challenge to Renaissance Christians. Allen shows both that its impact was significant and that various strategies were developed to reconcile it with Christian ideas. 3. Ficino regarded arithmology as inherently Pythagorean, even when there were no specific Pythagorean precedents for his own numerology, such as his emphasis on the number twelve and its role in solving the riddle of Plato's famous nuptial number. 4. The brief Pythagorean precepts known as *symbola* (or *acusmata*) had surprising importance for Renaissance Neoplatonism in light of Ficino's argument that the closer the mind comes to the supreme reality, the One, the fewer words it needs. Thus we end with what some regard as the earliest stratum of Pythagoreanism, the gnomic ritual sayings of the *symbola*, although we also fittingly end with controversy, since, as is documented above, the role played by the *symbola* in early Pythagoreanism is a contested issue (see Chapters 4 and 6).

Even in a volume this large not every topic can be covered and not every topic can be dealt with in the detail it deserves. All of the authors felt the constraints of space. The discipline of word count can, however, help us to produce a more focused and less diffuse picture of Pythagoreanism. Every topic intrinsically deserved much more detailed treatment, but the short chapters on Pythagoreanism in the Middle Ages and Renaissance were particularly constraining. Hicks and Allen provide striking snapshots of Pythagoreanism in these periods, but it is to be hoped that their accounts will be supplemented with new book-length studies in each case. The bibliography given in the notes to the chapters and collected in the general bibliography at the end will allow interested readers to find important scholarship that has already been completed and that cannot be considered in detail here. Most of all, it is my hope that the chapters will inspire other readers to carry out new research.

In a volume such as this, which covers a wide range of disciplines and broad time frame, it is inevitable that many topics will be covered in several different chapters in differing contexts and from different points of view. This repetition is to be welcomed, because it is seldom mere repetition and instead represents important variations on central themes. I have provided a number of cross references in this Introduction and in the notes to the individual chapters, but readers should also use the general index and the index locorum to find the different discussions of texts, topics and individuals. Indeed, this volume will have succeeded if the reader is stimulated not only to trace down and puzzle over the various threads of evidence for the original impact of Pythagoras and the Pythagorean society but also to confront the power of the changing faces of Pythagoras and Pythagoreanism over the centuries.

I would like to thank a number of people at Cambridge University Press for their generous and patient help, especially Hilary Gaskin, Christina Sarigiannidou, Gillian Dadd, Anna Lowe and Rebecca du Plessis. I am also grateful to Stefan Schorn, André Laks, Costas Macris and Martha Rainbolt for the special help that they gave me with the proofs. Any mistakes that remain are, of course, my responsibility.

CHAPTER I

Pythagoras

Geoffrey Lloyd

1. Introduction

More even perhaps than Heraclitus – for whom we have at least a few well-attested original statements – Pythagoras eludes interpretation. How can we distinguish reliable from unreliable testimonies? Are there any fully trustworthy sources in the first place? Some scholars place their faith in the earliest, pre-Platonic, evidence, but how that is to be taken has been interpreted very differently. The evidence for Pythagoras in Aristotle's lost work on the Pythagoreans is problematic, and what he has to say about him in the extant treatises amounts to very little. Twentieth-century scholarship was very dismissive of the far richer accounts of Pythagoras and the Pythagoreans in much later Neopythagorean or Neoplatonic writers who were accused, with some justification, of inventing a picture of Pythagoras who could be cited as authority for their own fantastic doctrines. Yet without a clear basis on which to judge how fantastic Pythagoras' own teachings may have been, it is obviously difficult to decide how far later sources may have distorted them.[1] When every ancient and every modern interpretation suffers from large doses of the speculative, the desperate conclusion seems to loom – that the real Pythagoras is now more or less totally inaccessible.

A recurrent problem relates to the use of modern categories, even when some of these have ancient precursors. Should Pythagoras be considered a mystic, a sage, a religious leader, a charismatic figure, a guru, a magus or magician, a wonder-worker, a shaman, a philosopher, a cosmologist, a mathematician, a scientist? The scholarly literature is full of attempts to shoehorn him into one or other, or more often into a combination of such

---

[1] The mere fact that they are late, separated from Pythagoras by several centuries, has been assumed to discredit them. But if "later" means "worse," how can we avoid that applying also to ourselves in the twenty-first century? The problem is rather with the suspected motives of the interpreters; but of course moderns have not always been innocent of *parti pris* either.

categories. We shall find reason to be cautious about the usefulness of all of these labels.

There are more or less severe problems in all attempts to reconcile the contrasting pictures that such categories offer, either with each other, or with such evidence as is available to us. How is the mathematician to be squared with the mystic? How is the philosopher, even, compatible with the scientist? The Greek term *philosophia* is attested in some late testimonies for Pythagoras[2] and the question has been debated whether he had a special way of construing the role of a philosopher and even whether he may have coined that term. But even if we knew that he or his immediate followers used that label, it is far from clear what they would have meant by it. What kind of "love" for what type of "wisdom" would they have had in mind? The modern answers have varied widely between on the one hand taking some type of physical or mathematical research as the main component, and on the other putting the emphasis on religious practices and the cultivation of the self.

We can begin our attempts to discuss the issues by going back some fifty years, to 1962, which happens to be the date of two highly influential books by supremely distinguished scholars. The first is W. K. C. Guthrie, the first volume of whose magisterial *History of Greek Philosophy* appeared in that year. The second is Walter Burkert, whose *Weisheit und Wissenschaft* was also published that year; the revised English edition, *Lore and Science in Ancient Pythagoreanism*, did not appear until 1972.[3]

In an effort to get to the real Pythagoras, Guthrie proceeded with meticulous care through the earliest, pre-Platonic, sources, the most reliable ones, since they were not contaminated by later Neopythagorean influences. All of that looks and is very scrupulous. Yet he allowed himself to suspend the principle of relying just on those sources on one crucial matter in particular, namely Pythagoras' role as a mathematician. "As for the silence of our early sources on Pythagoras as a philosopher and mathematician," he wrote (1962: 168) "it is enough to say that all the later biographical writers show him as such, and they obviously preserve much early material. It would be absurd to suggest that the authors down to Plato's time constitute our only hope of learning anything about him."

---

[2] Aët. 1.3.8, DK 58B15, Diog. Laert. 1.12 (purporting to draw on Heraclides Ponticus) and 8.8, and Cic. *Tusc.* 5.3.8.

[3] In the English edition of his book, published in 1972, Burkert undertook a masterly review of the modern literature to that date, which I shall not repeat here, though all the main commentators will be found in the bibliography, along with the most prominent later interpreters: Kahn (1993, 2001), Kingsley (1995), Zhmud (1997, 2012b), Riedweg (2005) and Huffman (2008c, 2011b).

Additionally Guthrie allowed himself what he calls an "*a priori* method" (1962: 171ff.), though it is one to be used only "with the greatest possible caution." It is possible to make judgments on the basis of our general knowledge of the evolution of Greek philosophy. That of course runs the risk of circularity, but worse, some of the categories that Guthrie used in his reconstruction are much more problematic than he appeared to acknowledge. True, he did not fall into the trap of taking "science" and "religion" as exclusive alternatives. But first, his "science" is a very loose category, which allows in much fanciful speculation without much regard for how it was arrived at. Second, where religion was concerned, he drew a pretty sharp contrast between it and what he labeled superstition. The latter did not rate as proper religion, though again there were unexamined assumptions at work as to why that was so, and on whether or how far the contrast was valid.

To turn from Guthrie to Burkert is to enter a very different world. A contrast is attested in late sources[4] between two groups of Pythagoreans, the *acusmatici* and the *mathematici*, with two corresponding sets of interests, the first including many pithy sayings with ritual or symbolic significance, the second centering around "mathematics," especially number theory. Burkert rejected the view that Pythagoras himself engaged in sophisticated mathematical research with a two-pronged argument. On the one hand he insisted that there was no good early evidence that such researches were undertaken by Pythagoras himself. On the other, he offered a new account of the sources of the mathematical philosophy ascribed to unnamed Pythagoreans in Aristotle's *Metaphysics*. The fragments of Philolaus (fifth century BC) and of Archytas (in the next century) had generally been treated as late fabrications. Burkert's re-examination of the question suggested, on the contrary, that some of the key testimonies are authentic, and provided indeed Aristotle's main sources in the relevant chapters of the *Metaphysics*. So the Aristotelian account there should be taken as evidence not for Pythagoras himself, but for later Pythagoreans of the fifth and fourth centuries. As for Pythagoras himself, that left us with a picture of a sage almost exclusively concerned with religion, with ritual and with practical injunctions for everyday life, many based on ideas about the symbolic associations between things.

The fact that two highly conscientious and eminently well qualified scholars could come to such divergent conclusions should give us pause.

---

[4] Iambl. *De Communi Mathematica Scientia* 25, 76.16–78.8 which is preferable to the version in *VP* 81–6 = DK 18.2 and 58C4 (Burkert 1972a: 193), and Porphyry *VP* 37, DK 18.2.

We should be reminded of the fact that there is no such thing as a neutral, value-free reconstruction in history, any more than there is in science itself. What was felt to be needed was some model that can answer the question of the type of figure that Pythagoras was. Yet obviously to select a model is almost inevitably to beg the important questions. If we knew what sort of a persona Pythagoras had, we would be half way to giving a decent account of his work. But to get to such a model, we need first to have that decent account.

The impasse is clear. Nor of course can I claim some Olympian vantage point enabling me to resolve the issues: in fact some of them seem to me to be irresolvable. Yet we can avoid some earlier mistakes, and in certain respects we can now bring to bear new understanding not available previously to clarify some problems. We can tap into more detailed knowledge of ancient near eastern, Indian and even Chinese work to throw some light on the possible connections, and the similarities and differences, between Greek ideas and those found in other traditions. We can use recent developments in the history of mathematics and science to clarify, in particular, how we should or should not use those two terms in relation to very early systems of ideas. We can bring recent ethnography to bear on the thorny question of "shamanism." Yet if certain advances can be made, they are modest and we have to acknowledge that fundamental obscurities remain, representing a major trap for the unwary.

2. Pythagoras' life

First, however, we must rehearse what we can be said to know concerning Pythagoras' life, even though this will not take us very far. His birthplace is usually given as Samos, which he is said to have left during the tyranny of Polycrates (according to some because of it).[5] There are many stories about his travels, from which no entirely consistent picture emerges. He is reported as visiting Egypt and Babylonia,[6] in addition to many countries much further afield, but in all such cases we have to be careful, since many such stories about Greek thinkers were concocted in part to fit a picture of them as the inheritors of "Eastern" wisdom. But conversely the denial that any prominent Greek thinker owed anything to non-Greek sources was a view promulgated already in antiquity and much bandied about in

---

[5] Cf. Diog. Laert. 8.1–3, Porphyry *VP* 9.

[6] Isocrates (*Bus.* 28) claims that Pythagoras studied with the Egyptians and was the first to bring philosophy and ritual lore to the Greeks, cf. Diog. Laert. 8.3.

the nineteenth and early twentieth century, often in a bid to defend the image of a pure Greek rationality, if not one of a Greek "miracle."

However, there is converging evidence to suggest that he lived the latter part of his life in Magna Graecia, specifically first at Croton, then in Metapontum. There and elsewhere communities that were labeled Pythagoreans came to be established. They appear to have been actively involved, on occasion, in politics.[7] Certainly they are reported as being the subject of some violent anti-Pythagorean reactions in Croton in particular, though quite what the issues were is unclear. Nor can we be certain of Pythagoras' own personal involvement in these political upheavals, nor even where his own political inclinations lay, though it is generally assumed that (unlike his follower Empedocles, let alone the remarkable statesman-leader Archytas) he was no democrat.

3. Pythagoras in the early sources

So we must turn (as others have done) to the more concrete evidence we have in our main earliest sources to see what impression Pythagoras himself made on his near contemporaries. There are five of these, namely Xenophanes, Heraclitus, Empedocles, Herodotus and Ion of Chios and already certain interesting divergences and convergences emerge in the pictures they presented.

In one fragment (7) Xenophanes pokes fun at someone who apparently believed in metempsychosis. He saw a man beating a dog and told him to stop: "Do not beat him: it is the soul of a friend, I recognize his voice." The person who was supposed to make this statement is not named, but our sources identify him as Pythagoras, who is indeed a likely candidate. If so, this would count as the earliest extant Greek evidence for his belief in the transmigration of souls, also ascribed, though on the testimony of much later writers, to the legendary figure of Orpheus. Yet we should also register that that belief cut no ice with Xenophanes himself, who is well known for his attacks on other, more traditional, Greek religious beliefs, such as the conception of the gods as anthropomorphic. So it is difficult to say how far Xenophanes may have exaggerated, in his dog story, for polemical effect.

Heraclitus, our next witness, associates Pythagoras with πολυμαθίη, "much learning" (fr. 40). Evidently Pythagoras did not adopt Heraclitus' own policy of "searching himself." Rather he practiced *historiē*, inquiry, as

---

[7] Widely differing interpretations of Pythagorean involvement in politics have been proposed by, among others, Delatte 1922a, Frank 1923, Fritz 1940, Minar 1942, Dunbabin 1948, Giangiulio 1989. See Chapter 5 below.

another fragment (129) of Heraclitus also suggests.[8] Yet both sayings leave entirely open what kind of "inquiry" Pythagoras engaged in, or what type of "much learning" he was criticized for. We should remember that the term *historiē* can be used of any type of investigation or its end result, ranging from the study of animals (as in Aristotle's treatise that is called *peri zōōn historiē*) to historiography in our sense.

The potential scope of "much learning" is, if anything, even wider. Heraclitus targets three others, besides Pythagoras himself, in that category. "Much learning does not teach sense: otherwise it would have taught Hesiod and Pythagoras, and again Xenophanes and Hecataeus." The grouping of these four into two pairs has often been thought to be significant. If that is the case Pythagoras may be associated particularly with Hesiod who wrote a *Theogony* telling the story of the generations of the gods and the creation of the world, and the *Works and Days* that is full of advice about ritual avoidances and how to behave more generally.[9] Some scholars accordingly use this as an indication of the importance of Pythagoras' religious and moral teaching, though no one goes so far as to suggest that he composed poetry that followed those Hesiodic models. Nor should we forget the other two characters whom Heraclitus also considers "polymaths," namely Xenophanes and Hecataeus. To judge from the latter case, πολυμαθίη does not necessarily involve religious teaching, but conversely nor can it be said to be tied to the kinds of historical, geographical and genealogical investigations we associate with Hecataeus. Given the heterogeneity of the other three characters who are criticized, that might be thought to weaken any case for associating Pythagoras with Hesiodic lore in particular, leaving us with a major question mark over what kind of πολυμαθίη was his.

Heraclitus, like Xenophanes, shows that Pythagoras attracted criticism and satire. Our next witness is Empedocles, often represented, in our sources, as a "Pythagorean," and indeed an explicit proponent of the doctrine of transmigration involving humans, other animals and plants. A tantalizing statement (fr. 129) speaks of someone (unnamed) who was

---

[8] Heraclitus fr. 129 also speaks of Pythagoras' contriving a "wisdom" and "polymathy," saying that he made a selection from (or collected) the writings of others to that end. Is this a charge of plagiarism? Does it suggest that Pythagoras composed prose works himself? The latter goes against the tradition that he left no writings, though that in turn may have been concocted to justify the idea of the secretiveness of his teaching. In the absence of a clear idea of what Pythagoras was reputed to have copied, the charge of plagiarism is impossible to evaluate. The most recent studies are Mansfeld (1989a), Huffman (2008c) and Schofield (unpublished).

[9] At least one of the injunctions at the end of Hesiod's *Works and Days* is similar to a reported Pythagorean *acusma*, namely the prohibition not to urinate while standing facing the sun, Hes. *Op.* 727, Diog. Laert. 8.17 and Iambl. *Protrepticus* 21.15.

exceptionally knowledgeable (εἰδώς), who had the widest wealth of under-standing, in command of all kinds of "wise" (σοφῶν) deeds. If he exerted himself, he could easily see everything in ten or even twenty human lifetimes – which is obviously compatible with and may even suggest reincarnation. This would make Pythagoras (if indeed it was he)[10] some type of seer, gifted with knowledge far beyond the limits of ordinary human cognition. We have, of course, to bear in mind that Empedocles himself not only developed a complex physical system and cosmology, and a doctrine of a transmigrating soul that could be reborn in animals and plants, but also claimed to be a healer, and indeed to be able to bring the dead back to life.

Our next source, Herodotus, is more complimentary than Xenophanes or Heraclitus, but at the same time very guarded, and possibly inconsistent. Book 2.81, in the account of Egypt, refers to a certain proscription against wearing wool in temples. The text is corrupt, but it seems to say that Orphics and Pythagoreans agreed with this Egyptian rule. In 2.123, still in the Egyptian *logos*, Herodotus says that the Egyptians believed that the soul is immortal and reborn in other animals. He goes on to remark that there were Greeks too ("some earlier, some later") who held that doctrine. He says he knows their names but will not record them. However, in 4.94–6, when dealing with the Thracian Getae, he tells us they believe they are immortal and on death are transported to their God Salmoxis. But certain Greeks in the Black Sea contradict this and say that Salmoxis was actually a human being and had been Pythagoras' slave on Samos. He had gained his freedom, amassed a fortune, and having learnt many things from the Greeks – including from Pythagoras, described as "not the weakest wise man (σοφιστής)" – he set about teaching his fellow-countrymen that they would live in bliss forever. He built himself an underground chamber where he hid for three years, emerging on the fourth to persuade the Thracians that his stories and account of the afterlife were true. Herodotus does not credit this story, saying that Salmoxis must have lived long before Pythagoras; but nowhere in this account is there any mention of transmigration.

Leaving aside the inaccuracies in what Herodotus has to say about the Egyptians (where there is otherwise no other evidence for their holding metempsychosis) and discounting the fact that he may well have garbled both the Thracian beliefs he reports and the deflationary account the Black Sea Greeks gave of them, we may at least remark that he endorses

---

[10] But according to one view (Diog. Laert. 8.54) Empedocles was referring to Parmenides, not to Pythagoras himself. That suggests that the matter was left obscure in that part of Empedocles' work that was available to the source quoting him.

Pythagoras' fame as some kind of wise man. As for Pythagoras' views about the soul, we should note that the notions of immortality in play in the Herodotean texts we have considered differ, though there is a recurrent suggestion of a possible connection between certain Greek and certain non-Greek beliefs.

Our final witness is Ion of Chios who is twice quoted in Diogenes Laertius. At 8.8 Pythagoras is said to have ascribed some of his own poems to Orpheus. This is in a context where Diogenes cites a number of authors to support the claim that Pythagoras was quite a prolific writer, though it is generally thought this was in a bid to provide a core of canonical texts much later Pythagoreans could claim originated with the founder, and I have already noted the contrary tradition that Pythagoras left nothing in writing.[11] The other citation is in the life of Pherecydes (1.120) who is there said to have been Pythagoras' teacher (1.119). Ion is quoted as saying that "if indeed Pythagoras, wise in all things, truly knew and understood the minds of all men," then even in death a good and modest man (that is Pherecydes) lives a delightful life. As in the Salmoxis story, as reported by Herodotus, this brand of immortality makes no mention of reincarnation.

There is clearly some convergence in some of this evidence. An interest in the fate of the soul occurs in four of the five (Heraclitus being the exception), though there is no exact agreement on what that fate was. Transmigration is only reconcilable with a blissful afterlife if there is some notion of an eventual escape from the cycle of rebirth, and that escape does not figure explicitly in connection with Pythagoras in any of our five earliest sources. If Empedocles' version of transmigration stays close to Pythagoras' own teaching (a big if), it is likely that the creature into which you were reborn reflected the life you had led as a human, and that may correspond to what we have in Xenophanes and in Herodotus 2.123. But if Ion is to be trusted, good persons live a blissful life after death, which would only be possible if there is (eventual) immunity to reincarnation. Access to special knowledge is a recurrent theme, though again Heraclitus stands out with his criticism that wide learning does not teach good sense. Yet with the exception of the proscription against wearing wool, our earliest sources supply no content to his rules for behavior, though if we allow ourselves to treat Empedocles as mirroring Pythagoras' own views, the situation changes dramatically.[12]

---

[11] This is the view found in Plutarch and Josephus (DK 14A18) and mentioned in Diog. Laert. 1.16, though contradicted in 8.6 where Diogenes cites Heraclitus fr. 129.

[12] In addition to the proscription against wearing wool, there is evidence that Empedocles laid down certain rules about diet, first an abstention from eating beans (fr. 141) and then more importantly the prohibition against taking the life of any living thing. The question of whether the Pythagoreans in

That Pythagoras had a reputation, early on, for wisdom is clear; but we are still left with systemic puzzles concerning what that wisdom consisted in, a theme to which we shall have to return again and again.[13] None of the five earliest sources mentions mathematics or harmonics, none refers to any astronomical or cosmological theories, and the evidence for a moral philosophy as such is slender.

4. Pythagoras in fourth-century evidence

Our next task is to see whether we can build up a more determinate picture by using some of our later evidence. Plato has one important reference to Pythagoras, namely to the point that he taught his followers a way of life which later Pythagoreans continued to pursue (*Resp.* 600b). We find a similar theme also in Isocrates (*Bus.* 28), although his views on education are very different from Plato's, and in that particular passage he puts the emphasis on Pythagoras' interest in sacrifices and ritual purity. In any case the remark in the *Republic* leaves entirely open what kind of life that was, but it does at least suggest that he was a teacher and had pupils who revered him. We should note that in that dialogue Plato contrasts Pythagoras not just with Homer, who failed to be a teacher, but also with Hesiod, mentioned at 600d, as someone who if he had anything of genuine educational value to transmit would not have been confined to life as a rhapsode. Clearly the kind of advice we find on behavior in the *Works and Days* is not allowed to count for much, and that would suggest that the Pythagorean *acusmata* that resemble them would not either. However, Plato also says that the Pythagoreans held that astronomy and harmonics are sister sciences (*Resp.* 530d), and this takes us to the crucial question of Pythagoras' own involvement in mathematics.

A couple of cautionary remarks are needed at the outset. The first concerns what "mathematics" may cover. In Greece, as in many other ancient cultures,[14] an interest in numbers and shapes may take many different

general abstained from meat-eating is controversial, since our sources provide conflicting evidence on the point. On the one side, Diog. Laert. 8.33, for example, speaks of abstaining from meat in general as well as from certain fish, but on the other, Aristoxenus, quoted by Aul. Gell. 4.11, refers to a ban only on certain meats, and that is also the view expressed in various passages from Aristotle's lost treatise *On the Pythagoreans*, which I shall be considering later.

[13] The fact that both Herodotus and Empedocles report what may be Pythagoras' views without naming him provides early evidence of a certain concern for discretion. The idea that much of his teaching was kept secret eventually came to be a recurrent *topos* used, in part, to justify the attribution to Pythagoras himself of views for which no direct evidence existed, cf. e.g., Guthrie 1962: 150–1, who cites Aristotle and Aristoxenus as well as Isoc. *Bus.* 29.

[14] There is an excellent survey of the divergent construals of "mathematics" in different cultures, ancient and modern, in Robson and Stedall 2009.

forms. At one end of the spectrum are what we would recognize as investigations in geometry, arithmetic, number-theory, astronomy, harmonics
and so on. But at the other, the symbolic associations of numbers and other
aspects of what is often labeled number-mysticism would also be included
under the term *mathēmatikē* in Greece and under other analogous terms
in other ancient languages. The Chinese terms for the "art of numbers"
or of calculation, *suan shu* or *shu shu*, had a similarly wide range as Greek
mathēmatikē.

The second cautionary point is that much of what we know about
early Greek mathematics has nothing to do with Pythagoras or with those
who passed as Pythagoreans. True, Aristotle (as we shall be noting) says that
certain Pythagoreans were the first to apply mathematics to the problems of
the principles that he is discussing in the *Metaphysics*. But several of the key
figures in pre-Euclidean geometry have no clear Pythagorean connections.
This is true particularly of Hippocrates of Chios, whom I shall be discussing
shortly. But this observation about non-Pythagorean involvement applies
also to the number symbolism that I said could be included in *mathēmatikē*.
Aristotle reporting what are evidently Pythagorean views tells us that they
found significant connections between items that all numbered seven:
vowels, strings in the scale, the Pleiades and even the number of heroes
who attacked Thebes (*Metaph.* 1093a11ff.) – an idea that Aristotle finds
contemptible. But already Solon (fr. 27) had focused on the importance of
the number seven, as determining the main periods of human life. Insofar
as the Pythagoreans or even Pythagoras himself were just interested in such
symbolic associations, there was nothing distinctive about this.

After these preliminaries we may turn to the information contained
in Aristotle's chapters on the Pythagoreans in *Metaphysics* A especially,
where, as has long been appreciated, there is, with the exception of one
quite possibly interpolated phrase, no reference to Pythagoras himself. In
Chapter 5 Aristotle distinguishes two groups of theorists. At 985b23 he has
just been dealing with Leucippus and Democritus and he goes on to say that
contemporary with them and before them those called Pythagoreans came
to believe that the principles of numbers are the principles of all things.
There follow some severe criticisms of the arbitrariness of the associations
they suggested and in particular the way in which, finding only nine visible
heavenly bodies (the stars counting as one sphere) they invented a tenth to
bring the total up to the perfect number ten, a view that the commentators
ascribe to Philolaus in the fifth century, not to Pythagoras himself in the
sixth.[15]

---

[15] Aët. 3.11.3 DK 44A17.

But what of the second group to whom Aristotle next turns, when he reports the famous Table of Opposites and contrasts the determinate Pythagorean view that there are ten such pairs, with the vaguer and more general opinion of Alcmaeon according to which many human affairs go in opposites? It is here that our texts include a phrase to the effect that Alcmaeon was born, or at least lived, "in the old age of Pythagoras." Yet the negative implications of that remark have sometimes not been noticed. If it is genuine, it would indicate that Aristotle had no compunction, here, in naming Pythagoras in person, and yet he does not mention him as or even as among the authors of the Table. If, as is generally thought more likely, the phrase is in any case an interpolation, we are still left without an attribution of this Table of Opposites to Pythagoras. Moreover the reference to Alcmaeon does provide a chronological anchor, of a sort, for the views on opposites that Aristotle is concerned with. Aristotle says he does not know whether Alcmaeon got his – general – ideas from those Pythagoreans or vice versa. But on what I hold to be the most likely date for Alcmaeon, that would suggest that the Pythagorean systematization of the ten-pair Table of Opposites (starting with Limit and the Unlimited, and Odd and Even) is a fifth-century development, not one that Aristotle thinks goes back to the time of Pythagoras himself.[16] When later commentators go on to speculate that Pythagoras advanced a doctrine based on the principles of the One and the Indefinite Dyad (the Great and the Small) they are reading Plato's ideas back into the founder of the sect, for Aristotle clearly states that those principles originated with Plato himself (*Metaph.* 987b19ff., 26ff.).

5. Pythagoras and the "Pythagorean theorem"

But what about other evidence that Pythagoras himself engaged in geometrical inquiry? Let us take as our prime example the theorem we still name after him. One admittedly rather opaque and possibly corrupt passage in Proclus suggests that Pythagoras sacrificed an ox on his discovery of that theorem.[17] That involves a ritual that Empedocles would have condemned, but we may let that pass. The question is: did Pythagoras himself discover the theorem or did he rather discover its (or a) proof. The first option

[16] An interest in several of the pairs of opposites in the Table was certainly not confined to the Pythagoreans. That applies particularly to Right and Left, which already figure in divination practices and certain social customs in Homer, as well as to Light and Night.

[17] Proclus *in Euc.* 1.47, 426.6–9 (DK 58B19). But Proclus does not himself endorse this report. The story of sacrificing an ox on the occasion of a mathematical discovery appears also in the traditions for Thales, in connection with the theorem that the angle in a semi-circle is right (Diog. Laert. 1.24).

certainly has to be rejected, since there is clear evidence that the Babylonians were well aware of the relationship between sets of what are called Pythagorean triplets, that is numbers such that the squares of the first and the second equal the square on the third ($a^2 + b^2 = c^2$). A Babylonian clay tablet in the Plimpton collection at Columbia University (Plimpton 322) contains a list of such triplets and dates from the second millennium BC. At most Pythagoras might be the first Greek to have discovered this relationship or to have introduced it to the Greeks, but this too seems unlikely. At least in the particular case of a triangle with sides 3, 4, 5, the knowledge that the angle opposite the side of 5 is right is a piece of craft expertise that is widely distributed across many cultures.

But what about the possibility that Pythagoras discovered the or a demonstration? There are plenty of other instances where the knowledge of a geometrical theorem antedated its rigorous proof. A well-attested later example (for which Archimedes, no less, is our authority) are the theorems enunciating the formulae that give the volumes of a cone and a pyramid. Archimedes tells us, in the *Method*,[18] that Democritus discovered these, but it was Eudoxus who proved them. Analogously Proclus cites Eudemus for the point that the theorem later set out by Euclid, *Elements*, 1.15, was known to Thales even though he had not given it a rigorous proof.[19]

Should we credit Pythagoras with some demonstration of the theorem named after him? That cannot be answered until we have some idea of what demonstration that would have been and more generally of what kind of demonstration might have been attempted in Pythagoras' day. Once again there is room for considerable disagreement on both questions. The demonstration we are eventually given in Euclid 1.47 is itself very carefully prepared for by the previous material in that book. That starts with definitions, postulates and common opinions or axioms, and it proceeds by rigorous axiomatic-deductive argument to build up a sequence of theorems leading to 1.47, which has indeed been thought to have been the main goal of the presentation of the materials in that first book.

But how far back does that axiomatic-deductive method go? Our earliest extant piece of deductive geometrical reasoning relates to the investigation of the quadratures of lunules in Hippocrates of Chios, some time in the mid fifth century BC, and he was no Pythagorean, to judge from the way his views on comets are dealt with separately from theirs in Aristotle's *Meteorologica* 342b29ff. According to our source for the lunules quadratures, Simplicius (*in Ph.* 55.25–57.29, 61.5ff.), Hippocrates took as the ἀρχή or

---

[18] Archim. *Method* 2.430.1ff. HS.   [19] Proclus *in Euc.* 299.1 (DK 11A20).

starting-point for his proof, a certain proposition that was clearly not treated as a primary self-evident axiom, since Hippocrates endeavored to establish it. The proposition stated that similar circles have the same ratios as the squares on their bases; and this Hippocrates "proved" by showing that the squares on the diameters have the same ratios as the circles (though Simplicius does not elaborate on the nature of that proof). That would not necessarily suggest that Hippocrates had no clear notion of an axiom in the sense of a primary self-evident premise, but that suspicion gains some support from what we find in Plato. When Plato himself discusses the notion of "hypotheses" in the *Republic* (510c ff.), he states that the geometers take certain starting-points for granted and give no account of them. If the notion of an indemonstrable axiom was already clearly established in Greek geometry, the very idea that an account should or could be given of them would be recognized to be absurd.

Yet on the other side, Proclus, who is thought to be drawing on Eudemus (*Commentary on Euclid Book 1* (*In Primum Euclidis Librum Commentarius*; henceforward *in Euc.*) Prologue 2.66.4), reports that Hippocrates was said to have been the first to have composed a book of *Elements*. Once again there are problems. We do not know whether that was the title that Hippocrates gave his work, nor whether it had the structure of Euclid's later book of that name. As usual we are in the realms of conjecture. Some would say that despite the arguments I have just rehearsed, Hippocrates had some notion of axiomatic premises. Yet even if we accept that conclusion, the fact that in Proclus he was the first to write an "elements" tells strongly against the conclusion that that notion was available already several decades before to Pythagoras himself.[20]

However, a strict axiomatic-deductive proof of Pythagoras' theorem is not the only way it might have been established. Knowledge of the relationship between the sides of right-angled triangles crops up in a number of civilizations, and when they were the subject of some explicit discussion, that discussion proceeds in a variety of ways. In both China and India, as Heath pointed out long ago (1926: 1.350ff.), we have techniques that use the cutting and pasting of squares or triangles to establish the proposition concerning the square of the side subtending the right angle.[21] Such methods would certainly not have passed muster with Euclid himself, for they

---

[20] The strongest statement of the more optimistic view of Pythagoras' involvement in mathematics is to be found in Zhmud 2012b, modifying his earlier discussion, 1997.

[21] The actual diagrams used in the Indian and Chinese demonstrations are, however, disputed, since those in our editions do not tally with one another and with the contents of the text. On the Chinese ones, in the *Zhoubi suanjing*, see Cullen 1996, and in the *Jiuzhang suanshu*, Chemla and Guo 2004.

assume, what he would say had to be proved, namely that the figures when joined up constitute true squares.

We come back to the point that it is only after Euclid that Pythagoras comes to be associated with his famous theorem, and the writers who do so are of course inevitably influenced by Euclidean standards of rigor. The history of the gradual development and clarification of the notion of an axiom, and indeed of deductive argument, or indirect proof as a whole, should make us cautious about reading too much back to the earliest geometrical investigations, a warning that is all the more necessary given the well-known proclivity of Greeks to seek a "first inventor," a πρῶτος εὑρετής, for all sorts and types of cultural items.[22]

6. Pythagoras and harmonic theory

But if there are those strong considerations that tell against Pythagoras himself carrying out Euclidean style demonstrations of geometrical theorems, we may now turn to the particular mathematical discovery that has been thought to have a strong influence on, if it is not the origin of, the Pythagorean view that (as Aristotle reported it) things either are numbers or are like them.[23] I refer of course to the discovery that the main concords of octave, fifth and fourth are expressible as the numerical ratios 2:1, 3:2 and 4:3. Here too we must distinguish between recognition of the fact and the methods that might be used to demonstrate it. Our late sources are full of accounts of how Pythagoras discovered the relationship experimentally. One story has it that he did so when he passed a smithy, heard the different notes that different hammers made, weighed the hammers, and so discovered the relationship. A second was that he found the relationship by attaching weights to strings and noticing that the weights yield the numerical relations of the concords. A third that he filled jars with water and discovered the concords by noting the relation between the amounts of water in the jars when they were struck. But as is by now well known, none of those stories can be true, for the simple reason that they do not in fact produce the results claimed. The fact that no fewer than eight ancient authors repeat one or other version of these fictions is a shocking indication of the way one writer repeats what he has found in another quite uncritically.[24] It is striking that all capture the idea of the importance of

---

[22] Kleingünther 1933.   [23] Arist. *Metaph.* 985b32ff., 987b11ff., 27ff.
[24] These are Nicomachus, Theon of Smyrna, Gaudentius, Censorinus, Iamblichus, Macrobius, Boethius and Chalcidius. The two types of tests that could reveal the relations are those with bronze disks (associated with Hippasus) and with lengths of pipe or string. See Lloyd, G. E. R.

undertaking an empirical test, and indeed varying the conditions of the trial; yet none undertook those tests (at least) themselves.

Of course eventually sophisticated analyses of harmonic relations are attributed to Philolaus (B6) and to Archytas (A16, A19, B2), and earlier, Hippasus did some work in this area. Harmonic theory, the development of which has been well studied by Barker (1989, 2007), reached a high level already before Plato, even though in the *Republic* (531aff.) Socrates has some critical remarks to make about the excessively empirical nature of Pythagorean studies in this area. That tallies, to be sure, with Plato's particular interest in using harmonics to train the guardians of the ideal state in totally abstract thought. Philolaus and Archytas themselves had no such aim, but rather sought to understand the harmonies that musicians created and that we can hear, audible ones, in other words, not ones arrived at by abstract reasoning. It is clear that the numerical representation of the relations of the octave, fifth and fourth stands as a prime example of the way in which numbers can *explain* perceptible phenomena. When Aristotle reports the Pythagoreans as holding that things are or are like numbers, that is probably an inference from what he believes they were committed to. Unlike Plato, for whom mathematics studies objects that are ontologically intermediate between the intelligible Forms and perceptible particulars (sharing the intelligibility of the former but the plurality of the latter), Aristotle himself insisted that there are no such special mathematical objects. Rather, what the mathematician studies are the mathematical properties of *physical* objects. It is from that perspective that Aristotle would have seen any Pythagoreans who focused on the numerical expression of perceptible phenomena as *identifying* things with numbers.

With Philolaus and Archytas we are on reasonably firm ground, since the question of the authenticity of the key fragments and reports has, since Burkert and Huffman, generally been resolved in a positive direction. The range of Philolaus' interests is particularly remarkable. They included a cosmological theory in which the earth is no longer imagined as at the center of the universe, but revolves round a central fire, as a planet, and a sophisticated metaphysical theory based on the contrast between limiters and the unlimited, which appears to underlie Aristotle's report concerning the importance of the twin principles of limit and the unlimited in Pythagorean doctrine.[25] There are too embryological theories attributed to Philolaus in *Anonymus Londinensis* (DK 44A27) as well as psychological

1979: 144 n. 95; Barker 1989: 218ff.; and on the history of the monochord in particular, Creese 2010: Chapter 2.
[25] See Huffman 1993.

ones though these are more contested.[26] Archytas' interests are also wide-ranging, and in one striking report he links his notion of harmony to political and moral issues.[27] We can be confident that by the time of Plato thinkers who were labeled (by others) Pythagoreans engaged in empirical and mathematical studies in many fields, and of course much later, in the revival of Pythagoreanism in the likes of Iamblichus and Porphyry, mathematics came to be viewed as the source of all understanding.[28]

But what about Pythagoras himself? If most of the experiments that claim to describe the way he discovered the numerical relations of the concords are fictitious, that does not mean that he had no conception of those relations. Although the point has been doubted, an awareness of the ratios of the distances of the holes in the *aulos* is presupposed in the construction of the instrument (West 1992: 81ff., 97ff.), although how far the instrument-makers had explicitly formulated mathematical rules for the purpose may be doubted. On that basis it seems unlikely that Pythagoras would have been completely unaware of those relations, but it is quite another matter to specify what his positive interests in them may have been, or indeed how far he may have used music as a paradigm for understanding in general. On *those* questions we are, once again, reduced to speculation. It is striking that while Archytas is evidently aware of the work of Philolaus and refers to his predecessors more generally when he discusses the relationships between the mathematical sciences,[29] Philolaus, for his part, did not, so far as we know, mention or even allude to anyone working on harmonics before him, a point that has, however, to be put into perspective by reminding ourselves of the lacunose nature of our evidence.

7. Later evidence on the Pythagorean way of life: Pythagoras as a shaman or charismatic?

Picking up our survey of the earliest sources, we may return to our preliminary observation that the best attested area of Pythagoras' own interests relates to the soul and its fate, and to how we should behave to ensure our

[26] See Huffman 1993 on Philolaus B13 and the very probably spurious B21.
[27] Archytas fr. 3, on which see Huffman 2005: 182ff.
[28] Iamblichus' *De Communi Mathematica Scientia* provides the most comprehensive account of this program. It encompasses harmonic theory at one end of the spectrum, all the way to number symbolism at the other.
[29] Archytas fr. 1. This is reported in different versions in our three main sources, namely Porphyry, Nicomachus and Iamblichus, but all three cite Archytas as referring approvingly to those who concerned themselves with mathematical inquiries that included "arithmetic," "geometry," some form of "astronomy" and harmonics.

well-being. So we should now consider how far we can credit some of the later evidence on these aspects of his interests. We noted the proscription against wearing wool in Herodotus, and the possibility that there were dietary rules for which we can compare Empedocles. We could extend the list of such regulations considerably if we could have confidence in the purported citations of Aristotle's lost treatise on the Pythagoreans in such writers as Iamblichus, Aelian and Diogenes Laertius.[30] Yet the difficulties in doing so are considerable.

First, there is the general problem of the reliability of any of the evidence for the lost works of Aristotle. Sometimes our sources cite a particular text, but sometimes the presence of Aristotelian material is inferred on the basis that his lost works were the source of later, unacknowledged, borrowings. Second, there is the problem of the slippage between what is ascribed to "Pythagoreans" in general and what to Pythagoras himself, where the temptation to move from the former to the latter reflects the common desire to give increased authority to the ideas in question. Third, we are often in the dark as to the context in which Aristotle cited the views he mentions. As already noted, we know from the end of the *Metaphysics* that he was strongly critical of what he considered the random associations of things with numbers.[31] How far he was inclined to approve or applaud the sayings that later writers cite from him is an open question.

That said, however, the material that is quoted from that lost treatise includes first a number of rules for which (as Burkert showed, 1972a: 177ff.) there are parallels in the evidence for certain religious sects. That applies to certain dietary proscriptions, proscriptions against bathing, wearing ornaments and the like. Some of the dietary rules are in any case far from confined to Pythagoreanism, however broadly construed, since they figure also in Greek medical texts. We know in particular from the first chapter of the Hippocratic treatise *On the Sacred Disease* that the quacks or purifiers the author there attacks proscribed certain foodstuffs that the author himself appears to consider harmful.[32] But in addition to such rules we find a series of marvels ascribed to Pythagoras, that he was reported as

---

[30] The main testimonia are collected by Burkert (1972a: 166ff.) who helpfully distinguishes those sources that purport to refer to Pythagoras himself from those that allude rather to Pythagoreans in general. Huffman's chapter in this volume (Chapter 13, "The Peripatetics on the Pythagoreans") carefully sifts the evidence for the Peripatetic reception, pointing out that Dicaearchus and Aristoxenus agree on a focus on the Pythagorean way of life but otherwise diverge sharply in their evaluations.

[31] Some of the examples of such associations recur both in the *Metaphysics* and in fragments of the treatise *On the Pythagoreans*, cited in this case by Alexander. See Chapter 11 in this volume.

[32] *On the Sacred Disease* Ch. 1 writes of certain fish (the *triglē*, *melanouros*, *kestreus* and the eel) as being "most dangerous" and certain meats (goats, deer, pigs and dogs) as disturbing the digestive organs.

being seen in two places at once, that he made extraordinary predictions, that he remembered his own past lives. Pythagoras is not the only figure who is reported as performing miracles of one kind or another, for that is also part of the tradition for Epimenides, Aristeas, Abaris, Phormio and indeed Empedocles himself. The question we must now confront is whether we have good evidence to think of Pythagoras not merely as a religious teacher but as a "shaman."

That term was introduced into the discussion in the wake of anthropological reports from Siberia. The term "shaman" originates with the Tungusi, studied especially by Shirokogoroff (1935). In the same year Meuli wrote an influential article applying the category to the Scythians, though the evidence on which he based his interpretation was meager, and that is before we come to the difficulty that, even if the Scythians had shamans, there is no direct evidence that the Greeks copied that feature of their religion. Despite that difficulty, shamanism was at one time extensively invoked in the hope of achieving a greater understanding of some of the more exotic features of Greek and indeed Mediterranean religious thought and practice.[33] Yet recent work, not just on Siberia, but especially on Amazonia, brings to light some of the dangers of conceiving "shamanism" as a single, well-defined phenomenon. The controversy between Hugh-Jones and Viveiros de Castro over the different modalities of "shamanism" in Amazonia, "vertical" and "horizontal" in Hugh-Jones' terminology, is instructive.[34] Shamans regularly have exceptional powers attributed to them, including divination and healing in particular. They are believed to be able to communicate with the spirit world and they may have their own spirit "familiars." They can bring back information from their spirits that will guide the behavior of the groups to which they belong: they may even be able to control the spirits with whom they are in contact and they are generally feared as much as revered by their own people. However, they are not usually believed to be reborn in other creatures, let alone associated with any teaching that humans in general are subject to such rebirth.

Unlike the proscription of placing foot on foot or hand on hand, which the Hippocratic author reports in *oratio obliqua*, the dietary proscriptions mentioned are in *oratio recta*; the first three fish figure also in our sources for Pythagorean proscriptions.

[33] Dodds (1951: 160 n. 30) acknowledges that his chapter on "The Greek shamans and the origin of Puritanism" owes its chief idea to Meuli. His own definition of the shaman is that of a "psychologically unstable person who has received a call to the religious life" (1951: 140).

[34] Vertical shamanism is associated with comparatively hierarchical societies and is concerned especially with the reproduction of society and the relations between humans and the spirit world. Horizontal shamanism is found in more egalitarian societies and has warfare and hunting as the main foci of interest. See Hugh-Jones 1994 and cf. the cautions of Viveiros de Castro 2009.

While shamanism, wherever it is found, depends on trance-like experiences, there are otherwise important differences in the practices reported. In particular while in some societies shamans are rare (and they may be limited to males), in others they are relatively frequent. Thus among the Sora, studied by Vitebsky (1993), many individuals, both men and women, become shamans.

Yet one crucial point emerges that is relevant to whether the term can be applied to our Greek evidence or whether it is useful to think of such an individual as Pythagoras as a shaman. This is that shamans always perform more or less recognized roles in the societies to which they belong and to that extent may be said to be institutionalized. Even though how a shaman enters a trance may differ from one society to another, each society has a recognized way of doing so. Shamans do not invent their practices, rather those practices conform to certain widespread expectations in the collectivity to which they belong.

While out-of-the-body experiences are described in the lives of several Greek individuals, they are otherwise a heterogeneous group. They may all have had a reputation as "wise men," even as "divine men," but what those terms covered varies a very great deal.[35] Their special powers generally include divination but otherwise cannot be said to fit any determinate, socially recognized, role such as we find in "shamanism." If so, then we have to say that importing the notion of shamanism is something of a red herring, adding a frisson of the exotic, to be sure, but ignoring what is now known about the role or rather roles of shamans in the societies from which they are reported.

Will we do any better if we deploy that other favorite category, of the charismatic figure (Riedweg 2005: 60)? This originated not so much directly from ethnographic reports, as from Weber's theoretical distinctions between different types of leader, those whose position depended on personal charisma being contrasted with those whose authority rested on traditional status or political power (Weber 1948). That category certainly does not suffer from the objection I raised against using the concept of "shamanism" in relation to Pythagoras, for it can certainly do justice to the "one-off" character of his or anyone else's persona. The problem with that label is rather different, namely that it does not help us to fill out the picture

---

[35] The list of the Seven Sages of archaic Greece was notoriously unstable and contains figures with very varied interests and attainments. One feature that links them, and that we find also in the late traditions for Pythagoras, is certain gnomic sayings, about what is best, what should be done or not done, and the like. But that contrasts rather with the claims to out-of-body experiences that were the chief grounds for invoking shamanism.

of his activities. Charismatic leaders share the feature that their position depends on their personalities, but the nature of their authority and how they acquired it remain open, even though many of them are religious innovators. We know a good deal about charismatic healers, for instance (studied by Hsu 1999 for example in China), and Empedocles shares many of their characteristics. As noted, he certainly announced that he could cure the sick and even bring the dead back to life. But there are bound to be doubts about whether Pythagoras did the same. The evidence in Iambl. *VP* 163ff., for instance, such as it is, suggests that in general Pythagorean medicine stayed close to patterns that are familiar from what else we know about Greek practices. There may be something distinctive in the reported disapproval of drug therapies, but in the emphasis on dietetics they joined what we may call the mainstream.

We come full circle. Reaching for labels such as shaman or even charismatic leader to try to characterize Pythagoras does not help, for the justification for their application is always problematic. Indeed even where mathematician, philosopher, scientist, are concerned, those categories too present their problems when applied to a period before there were clear disciplinary boundaries between such fields of investigations.

8. Conclusions

So where does this survey leave us in our search for the real historical Pythagoras? The most important positive point that we can be sure of is that he made a deep impression already on his near contemporaries. He was certainly a historical figure and no mere legend, unlike Orpheus, Musaeus, Abaris and others. The questions then are: what did that reputation consist in, and on what was it based? The problems, as we have seen, are compounded not just by the fact that his approval rating varied, from enormous admiration to accusations of charlatanry, but also because of the discrepancies recorded already in our earliest sources in what there was to approve or criticize. Certainly there is some convergence on the point that his teaching on the soul was exceptional, with most, but not all, our early sources suggesting that he taught a doctrine of metempsychosis. Assuming he did, that doctrine is sufficiently remarkable to have won him a reputation for startling originality. Was he aware of other distant cultures with similar beliefs? All we can say is that there is no good direct evidence that he was. When Herodotus hints at a connection between that doctrine (whose Greek adherents he refuses to name) and Egypt, he is given the lie by what else we know of Egyptian beliefs. If we try a connection with

India, we enter, as so often, the realm of speculation, and gestures towards a connection with "shamanism" ignore that while shamans often have animal familiars, they are rarely supposed to be reborn in other kinds of living creatures.

What sort of life did Pythagoras teach, if we accept Plato's testimony that he did? The evidence for certain ritual and dietary prescriptions and proscriptions is strong, but we may doubt that that cut much ice with Plato; we are on more solid ground when we conjecture that a concern for the future fate of the soul was one important motivation. His followers seem to have been a political force in Magna Graecia and no doubt what bound them together was an admiration for Pythagoras himself. But from that point on we again encounter problems, in particular concerning Pythagoras' own personal involvement in politics. Filling out the further details of what his "polymathy" may have consisted in remains the chief stumbling block in any reconstruction. In particular the exact nature and extent of his interests in "mathematics" and "harmonics" remain obscure.

But once the reputation was in place, it eventually came to be subject to extraordinary inflationary tendencies. It appears that Aristotle already knew of some miracle stories, though how far back these started is quite uncertain, and as I remarked we are in no position confidently to assess how he evaluated them. It is only in the Hellenistic period that Pythagoras' reputation as a mathematician, harmonic theorist and cosmologist takes off.[36] But here at least our evidence for Philolaus and Archytas helps to put this into perspective. Even though they are classified as "Pythagoreans" and may well have admired Pythagoras, their ideas on important metaphysical and mathematical problems were theirs, and there are no good grounds for attributing them to Pythagoras himself. The key to that part of the inflationary story is the evident desire on the part of later writers, and in particular our main Neoplatonic sources, Proclus, Porphyry and Iamblichus, to do just that.

---

[36] It is striking that Eudemus, who was responsible for the first histories of geometry and of astronomy, is so reserved in his ascriptions of work in those fields to Pythagoras himself, as opposed to certain, often anonymous, Pythagoreans, and this despite the fact that he had no compunction in making certain attributions to the even earlier Thales. The discovery of irrationals has been attributed to Pythagoras, on the basis of one probably corrupt reading of a passage in Proclus (*In Euc.* Prologue 2.65), which may or may not derive from Eudemus. But otherwise in the extant fragments of his histories, Eudemus generally assigns mathematical knowledge (e.g. of the application of areas, and of the theorem that the internal angles of a triangle sum to two rights) to "Pythagoreans" rather than to the founder himself. While there is nothing in principle that rules out the idea that he had much more extensive mathematical knowledge, we enter (once again) the field of conjecture, and would be faced with the problem of why Eudemus did not name him in person for other discoveries.

So I come back to the point that I mentioned at the outset, that modern reconstructions often reflect personal preconceptions about the nature of early Greek thought in general, with some stressing its rationality and originality, others focusing on the points of indebtedness or at least possible resemblance to other cultures. The fragmentary evidence at our disposal is unable to settle the main issues definitively. Such additional considerations as can be adduced in the fifty years since Guthrie and Burkert tell, not for a resolution of the problems, but rather for greater caution than either of those two great scholars displayed. When it comes to the choice that we face between asserting what is not ruled out, or sticking to what is positively attributable on well-tested evidence, modern historians will no doubt continue to follow their own inclinations, but one thing we should surely avoid is the muddle that arises from failing to distinguish those two categories.

CHAPTER 2

Philolaus

Daniel W. Graham

1. Introduction

Philolaus of Croton was the first Pythagorean to write a book and so he should be of central importance for an understanding of the movement. Yet there have been persistent questions about the genuineness of his fragments, and so he has occupied an anomalous position in many accounts. In the later twentieth century, studies have sorted out the genuine from the spurious in Philolaus, and with those studies has come a new understanding of the philosopher. He has emerged as a major thinker in his own right. Increasingly he has come to be appreciated, not just as a Pythagorean, but also as an independent philosopher who interacts with the ontology, epistemology, cosmology and astronomy of his time. In this chapter we will examine Philolaus the philosopher in an attempt to understand his contributions to fifth-century thought.

2. Scholarly judgments

The dominant view of Philolaus in connection with Pythagoras in the mid-twentieth century can be found in J. E. Raven's treatment of the two thinkers in G. S. Kirk and J. E. Raven's influential textbook *The Presocratic Philosophers* (1957). On Raven's view, Pythagoras or his early followers developed two major "scientific doctrines," "first, the ultimate dualism between Limit and Unlimited, and second, the equation of things with numbers" (229). Pythagoras himself is likely to have discovered the simple numerical ratios of musical intervals, using the length of strings on a monochord (a simple stringed instrument). He may have invented the Pythagorean theorem, recognized the incommensurability of the diagonal with the sides of a square, and enunciated the harmony of the spheres doctrine. Meanwhile, the surviving fragments of Philolaus, who allegedly philosophized in the late fifth century, were highly suspect. There were,

46

to be sure, close parallels between Aristotle's reports of "the so-called Pythagoreans" and the Philolaus fragments, but these latter looked suspiciously like *ex post facto* imitations of Aristotle, and they contained epistemological speculations that seemed anachronistic; besides, Aristotle only mentioned Philolaus once, and then on a topic of moral psychology (309–11). Accordingly, "the fragments attributed to Philolaus can be dismissed, with regret but little hesitation, as part of a post-Aristotelian forgery" (311).

In his *History of Greek Philosophy*, Vol. 1 (1962), W. K. C. Guthrie was more positive about Philolaus (329–33 *et passim*). Guthrie saw him as the originator of a number of Pythagorean doctrines, including the unique cosmology that puts a fiery "hearth" at the center of the cosmos and makes the earth a planet traveling around the hearth (282–301, esp. 286–7). Yet Philolaus was for the most part just an appendage to Guthrie's reconstruction of Pythagorean theories.

In the same year as Guthrie's first volume appeared, Walter Burkert published *Weisheit und Wissenschaft: Studien zu Pythagoras, Philolaos und Platon* (1962b English translation: *Lore and Science in Ancient Pythagoreanism*, 1972a), a remarkably detailed analysis of the historical development of Pythagoreanism. The study distinguished early accounts of Pythagoras from later ones, noting that the only distinctive doctrine credited to him in early sources was transmigration of souls. It identified Platonic elements in number theory that were later attributed to early Pythagoreans. And it used the criteria derived from studying Platonizing imitators to distinguish between genuine and spurious fragments of Philolaus. On the basis of his analysis, Burkert established as genuine (of twenty-three fragments found in DK) frs. 1–7, 13 and 17. He went on to discuss early astronomy, music theory and mathematical theory in light of an improved understanding of Philolaus' contributions.

The upshot of Burkert's study was a picture of Pythagoras as a religious guru. The "scientific" development of Pythagoreanism arose later, and at least largely because of the efforts of Philolaus and some other second- or third-generation Pythagoreans. Burkert's reconstruction has formed the basis of much subsequent scholarship, for instance by Jonathan Barnes' *The Presocratic Philosophers* (1979, rev. edn. 1982) and Malcolm Schofield in Kirk, Raven and Schofield, *The Presocratic Philosophers* (1983; the second edition of Kirk and Raven 1957). In particular, the edition of Carl Huffman, *Philolaus of Croton: Pythagorean and Presocratic* (1993), builds on the foundations laid by Burkert (making some minor modifications to his list of genuine texts and significant improvements to his interpretation) to put

Philolaus in his philosophical and historical context as a philosopher of the later fifth century, with a coherent philosophical position.

Works continue to be written which attribute more than a religious content to Pythagoras and assume a robust philosophical tradition prior to Philolaus, including Zhmud 1997, Kahn 2001 and Riedweg 2005. But attitudes have shifted significantly since Burkert's book: those who would establish a strong philosophical tradition before Philolaus must now assume the burden of proof. Increasingly, Philolaus is seen as the starting-point of research on Pythagorean philosophy, not as a mere transmitter or a historical cipher.

Burkert and Huffman have shown that the Pythagorean theory that Aristotle seems to describe and criticize in most cases in his *Metaphysics* A5 and the *De caelo* is that of Philolaus. Yet the theory of the fragments is not just what Aristotle reports; we find in them subtle arguments and claims that Aristotle seems to misunderstand. Thus we can learn things about Philolaus' theory from the horse's mouth. As with other Presocratics, the present state of historiography and philosophical analysis allows us to go beyond Aristotle and other ancient witnesses to gain an improved understanding of Philolaus himself. As always, we are deeply indebted to Plato, Aristotle, Theophrastus and other ancient students of Presocratic philosophy for their reports, but we are no longer wholly dependent on them for our understanding.

Whatever Pythagorean practices and beliefs Philolaus may have inherited with the Pythagorean life, when he published a book in a genre already widely used by philosophers, namely the cosmological treatise, he entered into a larger conversation. He had to speak the language of other philosophers and respond to their intellectual constructs as he presented his own. Whether his predecessors had been silent for religious reasons, or because they operated within a closed oral tradition, when Philolaus made a public statement he subjected Pythagorean views to scrutiny in the agora of ideas. The shadowy world of Pythagorean lore emerged into daylight and henceforth became part of the Greek philosophical conversation. In this transformation it is likely that Philolaus played the role of inventor of "Pythagorean" philosophy more than of transmitter.[1] And it is perhaps partly in recognition of this possibility that Aristotle hedged his exposition of Pythagorean philosophy with disclaimers.

---

[1] As Huffman 2013b shows, Pythagoras' own cosmic views, as reflected in the *acusmata*, are religious rather than scientific in character. We know of no philosophical/scientific cosmological views of Pythagoreans before those of Philolaus.

3. Principles and ontology

Philolaus lived about the same time as Socrates (KRS 323). Born in Croton in southern Italy (the adopted home of Pythagoras, who died before Philolaus was born), he migrated to Greece and taught in Thebes at the end of the fifth century.[2] He wrote a single book, as did most Presocratics.[3] His began as follows:

> Nature in the world-order was fitted together both out of things which are unlimited and out of things which are limiting, both the world-order as a whole and the things in it. (fr. 1, tr. Huffman)[4]

What is remarkable here is the fact that Philolaus immediately addresses nature (*phusis*) and the world-order (*kosmos*), two of the major preoccupations of the "philosophers of nature" (*phusiologoi* or *phusikoi*, Aristotle). In some important sense his subject is cosmology, as in the Ionian tradition that goes back to Anaximander and perhaps to Thales. The world we live in is orderly and operates on the basis of the natural actions and reactions of natural objects. The world, in other words, consists of natural phenomena that are to be understood on the basis of natural events and processes, rather than of actions caused by the will of divine beings.

This natural order "was fitted together" (*harmochthē*) out of unlimited things (*apeira*) and limiting things (*perainonta*). So there are two kinds of building blocks, for both the universe as a whole and the particular things in it, namely limiters and unlimiteds, which combine by a kind of fitting process. Right at the outset, Philolaus presents his interpretation of the fundamental components of the world and their connection. Philolaus seems to give us something like basic categories of reality. But as Huffman points out (1993: 39–40), he always talks in terms of plural instances rather than a singular sort or type. Thus he seems to think of classes of things rather than abstract categories or types. And he argues for them:

> It is necessary that the things that are be all either (a) limiting, or (b) unlimited, or (c) both limiting and unlimited but not in every case unlimited alone. Well then, since it is manifest that they are neither from limiting things alone, nor from unlimited things alone, it is clear then that the world-order and the things in it were fitted together from both limiting and unlimited things. Things in their actions also make this clear. For some of them from limiting (constituents) limit, others from both limiting and

---

[2] Pl. *Phd.* 61d–e, DK 44B15.   [3] Diog. Laert. 8.85, DK A4.
[4] I will use Huffman's translations of Philolaus' fragments throughout.

unlimited (constituents) both limit and do not limit, others from unlimited (constituents) will be manifestly unlimited. (fr. 2)

Here we get a simple argument for the thesis in fr. 1:
1. Necessarily, (a) the basic realities (things that are) are all limiters, or (b) they are all unlimiteds, or (c) they include both limiters and unlimiteds.
2. Not-(1a).
3. Not-(1b).
Therefore
4. (1c).

Philolaus gives us three options that must exhaust the ontology. He eliminates two of these to arrive at the conclusion. The necessity in question may just be the logical necessity of an exhaustive classification; if so, the argument does not (or should not) entail that (4) is necessarily true. The argument is valid. But to know whether it is sound (whether the premises are true) we need to find out what Philolaus means by limiters and unlimiteds. I shall turn to that question in a minute.

For now consider fr. 3:

> There will not be anything that is going to know at all, if everything is unlimited. (fr. 3)

There seems to be a tacit argument in this statement that supports the previous argument:
5. If everything is unlimited, there will be no knowledge.
[6.] There is knowledge.
Therefore,
[7.] Not everything is unlimited.

The bracketed numbers indicate tacit statements. On the assumption that there is knowledge, we conclude that not everything is unlimited, or not-(1b). Thus we do not need to fall back on the "it is manifest" of fr. 1 to get one of the premises.[5] There may be a corresponding argument for not-(1a), but we do not have it. This argument looks surprisingly like a transcendental argument such as Immanuel Kant developed: given that there is a certain kind of knowledge of the world (for Kant scientific knowledge), what can we infer about the necessary conditions of such knowledge?[6] For Philolaus, knowledge presupposes some sort of limiting conditions on a background of unlimited objects of cognition.

One fragment will help to understand the relation between limiters and unlimiteds:

---

[5] See Nussbaum 1979: 98 and Barnes 1982: 386–7.   [6] Cf. Nussbaum 1979: 65–6, 102.

Concerning nature and harmony the situation is this: the being of things, which is eternal, and nature itself admit of divine and not human knowledge, except that it was impossible for any of the things that are and are known by us to have come to be, if the being of the things from which the world-order came together, both the limiting things and the unlimited things, did not preexist. But since these beginnings preexisted and were neither alike nor even related, it would have been impossible for them to be ordered, if a harmony had not come upon them, in whatever way it came to be. Like things and related things did not in addition require any harmony, but things that are unlike and not even related,[7] it is necessary that such things be bonded together by harmony, if they are going to be held in an order. (fr. 6)

Philolaus makes it clear that his subject is not divine, but human knowledge. Whereas the gods may grasp the ultimate being of things, presumably it remains inaccessible to us. And in this Philolaus seems to take a stand with the natural philosophers as against the Pythagoreans,[8] at least insofar as they are a religious society laying claim to an esoteric knowledge of divine things. The only condition under which "the things that are and are known by us" could "have come to be" (*gegenēsthai*) is that their components preexisted (*huparchein*). This suggests an Eleatic background according to which the things that really exist are eternal or atemporal.[9] After Parmenides of Elea "pluralist" philosophers posited the existence of eternal elements that could combine to generate ephemeral beings and later separate to destroy them. But the only real beings would be the elements that exist prior to and independently of the perishable compounds.

Philolaus offers a dualism of elemental realities, limiters and unlimiteds, which he asserts are necessary to enable the production of compounds. They are not alike or even related. Parmenides had presented a "deceptive" cosmology based on a dualism of opposite beings, light and night, which had completely contrary features.[10] Philolaus seems to stick close to Parmenides' formula, even though Parmenides may diagnose the formula as being flawed from the outset.[11] In any case Parmenides' cosmology seems to offer a kind of paradigm that later cosmologies followed for better or worse.[12]

In addition to limiters and unlimiteds, there must be a harmony (*harmonia*) that binds them into a unity. Thus besides the primary entities,

---

[7] Omitting μηδὲ ἰσοταχῆ, "nor of the same speed," which is corrupt and is not found in the parallel text that precedes.
[8] Cf. Xenophanes DK B34, B18; Alcmaeon DK B1.   [9] Cf. Barnes 1982: 385–6.
[10] Parmenides DK 28B8.50–61.   [11] Parmenides DK B8.53–4; cf. Nussbaum 1979: 73–7.
[12] See Graham 1999, Ch. 7.

limiters and unlimiteds, we must have some sort of "glue" to hold them together in those things in which they are joined.[13] The term *harmonia* is a cognate of the verb *harmochthē* ("was fitted together"), which we met in B1.

So now we have all the *dramatis personae*, but we are not yet sure of their identity. Going back to fr. 2, we find that Philolaus formally distinguishes between the things that are, the ultimate realities, and the things in the world, the derivative realities, which correspond to the things that come to be in fr. 6. Having argued in fr. 2 that the ultimate realities must include both limiters and unlimiteds, he goes on in the last sentence to identify derivative realities that are composed variously (1) of only limiters, (2) of both limiters and unlimiteds or (3) of only unlimiteds. Thus the two classes of primary realities L and U evidently give rise to three classes of derivative realities LL, LU and UU.

Scholars do not agree on what exactly Philolaus has in mind with his limiters and unlimiteds. Burkert takes limiters to be atoms, unlimiteds to be void, in a parallel to atomic theory (1972a: 258–9). Barnes understands them as like Aristotelian form and matter, respectively; for instance a bronze sphere is made up of bronze, an unlimited matter, in the shape of a sphere, a determinate form (1982: 388–9). Schofield takes limiters to be odd numbers, unlimiteds to be even numbers (KRS 326). Huffman (1993: 37–53) cautiously points out that Philolaus leaves open-ended the question of what limiters and unlimiteds are. Yet Philolaus claims that their existence is "manifest" or "clear," so that, while the examples of each kind may be diverse, they are present to our experience. Huffman understands an unlimited as a continuum, and a limiter as a boundary (1993: 43–4). He seems to be right to allow the terms their broadest possible scope.

We may see much of Presocratic theory as focusing on the unlimiteds of the world. Anaximander said the world arose from the boundless (*apeiron*, unlimited, DK A9, A11); Xenophanes stressed earth and water as components of reality and also makes earth and air *apeira* (DK B29, B28); Anaxagoras spoke of things "boundless [*apeira*] both in quantity and in smallness" (DK B1) and continua of wet and dry, hot and cold, bright and dark (DK B4, B8); Empedocles recognized four "roots" (*rhizōmata*) or elements: earth, water, air, fire, each of which is in itself unlimited (DK B6); Diogenes of Apollonia said that the ultimate reality was air, which is of itself indeterminate and admits of continuous variation in several features (DK B5); Melissus argued that what-is is unlimited

---

[13] Thus Huffman 1993: 41.

(DK B2, B3, B6). Historically, then, the claim that there are unlimiteds in the world was uncontroversial; Philolaus' predecessors had recognized indeterminate stuffs and continua of qualities and quantities as basic realities. That they could mix together (class UU) was common belief, for clearly elements such as earth, water, air and fire make mixtures or compounds.

What was innovative in Philolaus was the claim that limiters too were essential to the constitution of the world. Parmenides had insisted on the limitedness of what-is (DK B8.30–8, 42–9). Diogenes saw order in the world as arising from measures (*metra*) (DK B3). Earlier, Heraclitus had described the world as a balanced transformation of measured changes (*metra, metreetai,* DK B30, B31). The atomists made shape or "contour" (*rhusmos*) an important feature of atoms (DK 67A6). Yet none of these philosophers made limit or the class of limiting things a *principle* or *element* of reality. Philolaus, by contrast, makes limiters essential ingredients in the world, without which the world could not be an ordered whole (*kosmos*) or its furnishings determinate objects. He puts limiters on the same theoretical footing as unlimiteds, recognizing their indispensable contributions to ontology and epistemology. Philolaus allows limiters to be mixed together (class LL), presumably to include combinations of numbers (to yield sums, products, ratios), shapes, figures and relations.

This leaves the class in which limiters and unlimiteds are combined (LU). Here, presumably, we get concrete physical objects, such as a bronze sphere and, more important, the individual biological specimen. (Philolaus may allow for many other types of combinations of limiters and unlimiteds, but this type is the most philosophically compelling.) What seems to be missing from many of Philolaus' philosophical contemporaries is just a theory of how earth, water, air and fire (or whatever the list of stuffs is) can come together in one place as a horse, in another place as a cow, in another place as a human being. The unlimiteds by themselves cannot explain the structural and functional differences arising in combinations of elements (or in derivative stuffs such as flesh, blood and bone). There has to be something else organizing the elements and metabolizing them into some determinate kind of thing (more on this later). Philolaus posits the existence of a class of entities that provide order to the unlimiteds. But limiters cannot do their job of limiting unless they can connect with unlimiteds. Hence Philolaus recognizes also the need for harmony, some sort of principle of combination that allows unlikes to combine in a unity. We need some sort of "supervenience" (*epigignesthai*, B6) to allow an unlimited to take on a limiting character. Philolaus' harmony prefigures Plato's participation and

Aristotle's predication (where the latter is an ontological, not a grammatical connection).

We have seen that Philolaus' stress on limit is in part driven by epistemological considerations. Without limit, there could be no knowledge (fr. 3). We could, presumably, have primitive perceptual knowledge of things, or rather sense data: hot here, cold there. But without limiters there would not even be particular things delimited from other things, nor types and classes of things. There could be no scientific knowledge, no understanding of complex objects and their connections to one another. For science to be possible there must be structures, patterns and hierarchies. And that brings us to another crux in Philolaus' theory.

4. Number and knowledge

> And indeed all things that are known have number. For it is not possible that anything whatsoever be understood or known without this.   (fr. 4)

Much ink has been spilled on how "all is number" for the Pythagoreans. But Philolaus never makes this strong identity claim, and Aristotle's statements to this effect seem to arise from a misreading of the weaker claim embodied in fr. 4.[14] Philolaus' *principles* are limiters and unlimiteds. Numbers probably belong to the class of limiters but they are not themselves principles of all things. We have seen that limiters are necessary to knowledge. But why number?

The phrase "having number" seems to have a set meaning in the Pythagorean tradition. A survey of examples shows that "things 'have number' in so far as they are constituted [as wholes] in some fashion by ordered pluralities or relations between ordered pluralities" (Huffman 1993: 175). Philolaus gives one extended example of something having number in the form of an account of the octave in music (fr. 6a). Here the various musical intervals are explained as whole-number ratios, and larger intervals are equated to a number of smaller intervals. There has been much debate about whether the analysis of music intervals goes back to Pythagoras or to some earlier figure. What I am interested in is not the origins of the theory but the place of the theory in Philolaus' understanding. Here, it seems, we have a scientific theory in which an octave, or more generally audible sound, "has number."

We find a similar example in Plato. In the *Philebus*, where Plato seems to be drawing on inspiration from Philolaus, he speaks of a gift from

---

[14] See Huffman 1993: 57–64.

some Prometheus according to which "whatever is said to be consists of one and many, having in its nature limit and unlimitedness" (16c, trans. D. Frede).[15] Plato mentions music theory as an example (17b–d), and then goes on to speak in more detail about the art of letters or reading (*grammatikē technē*, 18b–d). Here we distinguish something like vowels, semivowels and consonants.[16] We can further subdivide, for instance consonants into unvoiced, voiced and aspirated, until we reach a level of single sounds, which Plato identifies with letters of the alphabet. If we follow the picture out, we would arrive at a kind of matrix of letters giving perhaps the twenty-four letters of the Ionic alphabet. Now in fact a good list of phonemes would not quite correspond to the letters of the alphabet, since some of these are double letters (ζ, ξ, ψ) representing two sounds, while some sounds might not have their own letter.[17] But in principle the approach will work to distinguish phonemes on the one hand and letters on the other. The result of the art of letters is a great power, literacy, that will enable us to communicate with each other through symbols written on a page. We have here another science (beside music theory) in which by "having number," that is, consisting of an ordered set of elements (*stoicheia*, originally meaning "members of a series"), a subject matter can be learned and its elements applied to explain or manipulate the world.

What emerges is an epistemology in which a science is understood as a classification or systematization of a subject matter. A science that "has number" is not unlike a science arrived at by a process of collection and division as in Plato. The subject matter ("spoken sound") is divided into subordinate types (vowel, semivowel, consonant), and each of them subdivided by distinguishing features. This type of enterprise seems to offer a paradigm of scientific investigation, which potentially can be applied to new fields of study to yield new results.[18]

5. Cosmology and astronomy

From Anaximander on, philosophy was often understood as the study of nature, and the study of nature began with cosmogony and cosmology.

---

[15] Plato then envisages a transition from a one to an infinite number of things, which is mediated by a finite number of entities that are the terms of the theory. This part seems to be original with Plato. On Plato's use of Philolaus see Huffman 2001 and Meinwald 2002.

[16] Cf. Arist. *Poet.* 1456b 24–5. I am not concerned here with the details of the theory, but rather its overall structure.

[17] E.g. the *h* sound is represented by a rough breathing, the *w* sound in some dialects was once represented by a digamma that disappeared from standard alphabets.

[18] See Archytas B1 with Huffman 2005: 57–64 for a continuation of the tradition.

Perhaps the standard of success for a philosophical theory in the Presocratic era was its ability to illuminate cosmology. Burkert recognizes Philolaus' efforts in cosmology and astronomy, but he views them as "mythology in scientific clothing, rather than an effort, in accord with scientific method, to 'save the phenomena'" and concludes that "The system of Philolaus is not a scientific astronomy" (1972a: 342). David Furley views Philolaus' astronomy as consisting of "Pythagorean fantasies."[19] Huffman, on the other hand (1993: 231ff.), has done much to rehabilitate Philolaus' astronomy as a viable theory in the context of fifth-century knowledge, and I shall attempt to add some support for Huffman's assessment.[20]

As we have seen, Philolaus' book began with a statement of the ultimate components of the cosmos. He began his cosmogony as follows:

> The first thing fitted together, the one in the center of the sphere, is called the hearth. (fr. 7)

The original heavenly body that was fitted together (*harmosthen*, "harmonized") is the hearth (*hestia*). The starting-point then is a body composed of an unlimited, fire, limited by its placement in the center of the universe. What is immediately remarkable about Philolaus' cosmology is the fact that the earth is not in the center, as it had been for every other philosopher except Leucippus and Democritus.[21] Aristotle reports that for the Pythagoreans "the world is one, and from the unlimited time and breath were brought in, as well as the void which distinguishes the place of each thing in each case."[22] The birth of the world seems to have been comparable to the birth of a child, as it takes in breath from the environs. Time and void are also breathed in. This sounds strange and exotic, but we may compare the Big Bang theory of modern cosmology, that postulates cosmic inflation in which space rapidly expands.

Philolaus presents a spherical world in which the lower and upper parts are mirror images of each other, or more precisely, in which rotational symmetry is found (fr. 17). Besides the central fire Philolaus makes the earth as a planet revolving around it along with a counter-earth (*antichthōn*).

---

[19] Furley 1987: 57. "[T]he system as a whole makes very little astronomical sense, and it is hard to believe it was intended to do so" (58).

[20] The contrast Burkert makes with "scientific" astronomy seems dubious, because astronomy was not yet fully scientific in any philosopher; further, the notion of a unified scientific method has been called into question in recent history and philosophy of science. Nevertheless, I do believe that scientific progress was made by philosophers of the fifth century, specifically in the realm of astronomy, and that Philolaus accepted important advances and incorporated them into his theory.

[21] The atomists recognized plural worlds or *kosmoi* in the universe. They did, however, see the earth as the center of its world. Hippol. *Haer.* 1.13.2, DK 68A40.

[22] Fr. 201, tr. Huffman.

Outside the orbit of the earth in order are the moon, the sun, the five visible planets, and the sphere of the fixed stars. The one anomaly in this picture (besides the central fire) is the counter-earth. It is, by hypothesis, not visible from earth, and so not amenable to direct empirical confirmation.

Philolaus' astronomical scheme is praised on the one hand for anticipating the heliocentric theory, and damned on the other for being based on *a priori* assumptions. Since it puts the central fire, or hearth at the center, we may call it "hestiocentric" rather than heliocentric.[23] There is no direct link between the hestiocentric and the heliocentric theory, but the former does free the earth to move and at least suggest the possibility of seeing the cosmos from a different perspective. The cosmos is "centrifocal" in that it organizes the heavenly bodies around a point that is a center of cosmic motions and presumably also a center of dynamic forces, and thus a forerunner of the cosmologies of Plato and Aristotle, in contrast to the flat-earth models of most Presocratics with vertical and horizontal motions.[24]

To make the hestiocentric theory work, Philolaus supposes that the earth orbits the hearth once per day, traveling from west to east, creating the appearance that the heavenly bodies orbit the earth in that time, traveling east to west. The earth must also rotate once per day on its axis, so that the same side (where Philolaus is located) is always facing away from the hearth. The moon, for its part, revolves around the central fire once per month, traveling west to east, and the sun revolves once per year in the same direction. The planets have their own periods of revolution, while the sphere of fixed stars can be considered to be stationary. We must suppose that the orbit of the earth is relatively small compared to the orbits of the other bodies, so that the effects of parallax (the changing perspective of the bodies' positions against the fixed stars) are not noticeable.

That leaves the counter-earth, which remains unseen and plays no obvious explanatory role in the astronomy. Why is it there and what does it do? Aristotle claims that it is posited only to make up a perfect number of ten bodies surrounding the central fire – for the sake of a satisfying numerology.[25] He does mention that the counter-earth is supposed to account for the greater frequency of lunar than solar eclipses, since not only the earth but also the counter-earth sometimes blocks the sun's rays

---

[23] Maniatis 2009 coins the term "pyrocentric," but fire is not confined to the center of Philolaus' cosmos, so I prefer my term.
[24] See Furley 1987: 59.   [25] Arist. *Metaph.* 986a3–12; *Cael.* 293a23–7.

to the earth.[26] Thus it has an alleged empirical function beyond its *a priori* numerical contribution.

The location and motion of the counter-earth are controversial. Testimonies say that it is located opposite and/or moves opposite the earth.[27] According to one theory, the counter-earth, being earthy and heavy unlike the other heavenly bodies, must be on the earth's orbit and 180° from it to provide a cosmic equilibrium.[28] According to another, it must travel on a lower (interior) orbit and stay between the central fire and the earth to block a possible view of the central fire from travelers to the antipodes.[29] Most interpreters have assumed that the counter-earth cannot fulfill the alleged function of causing some lunar eclipses because it is in the wrong position to do so, on any interpretation of its position.[30]

I believe we can see how the counter-earth can cause eclipses and must do so on the hestiocentric theory. Parmenides seems to have explained correctly the phases of the moon as resulting from the reflection of the sun's light ("heliophotism").[31] Anaxagoras went on to apply that insight to explain a number of astronomical phenomena including solar and lunar eclipses as caused by the blocking of the sun's light (*antiphraxis*) by the moon and the earth, respectively.[32] Philolaus seems to accept both heliophotism and antiphraxis, along with most philosophers of the late fifth century. On Anaxagoras' (scientifically correct) account, lunar eclipses can happen only at the time of the full moon, when the two bodies are in opposition. On Philolaus' hestiocentric theory, this can occur when the sun, the earth and the moon are in line (see fig. 2.1). On this configuration the eclipse happens near midnight for an observer at a position facing away from the central fire, when the earth and sun are in opposition (position A). But what if a lunar eclipse occurs near dawn or dusk (as sometimes happens) – call that a crepuscular eclipse. At this time the earth must be displaced from the diameter on which the sun and moon lie, by about 90° (position B). In this position, it cannot block the sun's light to the moon. If, however, there were an earthlike planet on an inner orbit, it could in principle block the sun's light (position C). Indeed, by being on an inner orbit, it would have a greater probability of being in position to cause an eclipse than the earth,

---

[26] *Cael.* 293b21–5; cf. Aët. 2.29.4 = Stob. 1.26.3, DK 58B36.
[27] Lies opposite the earth: Arist. fr. 204 from Simpl. *In Cael.* 511.27–30; lies and moves opposite, Aët. 3.11.3 = A17.
[28] Burch 1954.
[29] Arist. fr. 204 = Simpl. *In Cael.* 511.27–30; Huffman 1993: 253; Dicks 1970: 66–7, 69.
[30] Dicks 1970: 67; Huffman 1993: 247; Hankinson 1998: 41.
[31] Parmenides B14, B15; Wöhrle 1995; Graham 2002. The term "heliophotism" is from Alexander Mourelatos.
[32] Hippol. *Haer.* 1.8.9 = DK 59A42.

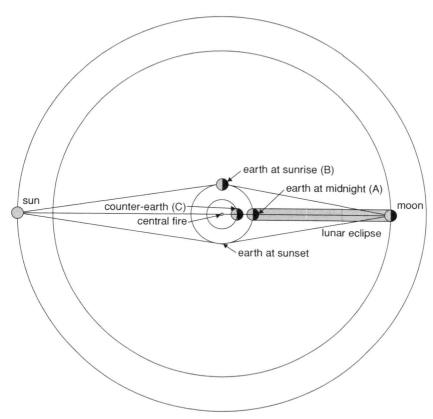

2.1 Lunar eclipes in the astronomical scheme of Philolaus

so that there would be more than twice the probability of a lunar than a solar eclipse; for it would always be close to the diameter joining sun and moon at the time of the full moon. Call that planet the counter-earth. It must be on an inner orbit and traveling independently of the earth to do its work. But with these assumptions, the alleged reason for a tenth heavenly body is vindicated.[33]

If this reconstruction is right, we see Philolaus as accepting the latest developments in astronomy: heliophotism; antiphraxis; the five planets. He

---

[33] The claim that the counter-earth lies or moves opposite the earth seems to be based merely on the name. Yet the prefix *anti-* can signify not only "opposite to" but also "taking the place of" or "like," in which case *antichthōn* would signify "alter-earth" or "earthlike (planet)" – without reference to its position. The moon, we are told is *antichthōn*, for being earthlike without being opposite the earth (Simpl. *In Cael.* 512.17–20). For more on Philolaus' astronomy, see Graham 2013: 192–9.

enters into the world of Ionian natural philosophy, with its cosmological speculations and empirical observations, and constructs a cosmography that is at once original and highly suggestive. He accounts for the daily motions of the heavenly bodies by a daily revolution of the earth, and thereby simplifies the motions. He adapts the latest eclipse theory to his model and makes necessary modifications to ensure that it accounts for all cases of eclipses. He may well have found the resulting numerology a welcome confirmation. But at least the number of the heavenly bodies is not the only motivation for them, and on the present reconstruction all have an empirical justification – except the central fire itself.[34] And here there may be just a hint of preexisting tradition: the central fire "is *called* the hearth" (fr.7) – but by whom? Not by Ionians or Eleatics. By the Pythagorean tradition?

But whatever Philolaus' inheritances, he cannot be following a tradition slavishly. On the contrary, he combines the latest empirical observations and theoretical explanations with (perhaps) traditional beliefs and (certainly) scientific imagination to form an eclectic whole that "has number."

6. Psychology, physiology and biology

There are four principles of the rational animal, just as Philolaus says in *On Nature*: brain, heart, navel, genitals:

> The head [is the seat] of intellect, the heart of life (*psucha*) and sensation, the navel of rooting and first growth, the genitals of sowing of seed and generation. The brain [contains] the origin of man, the heart the origin of animals, the navel the origin of plants, the genitals the origin of all (living things). For all things both flourish and grow from seed. (fr. 13)

In this account Philolaus distinguishes between different life functions, which he associates with key organs or parts of the body. Significantly, he distinguishes between intellect (*noos*) and sensation (*aisthēsis*), recognizing different levels of cognitive activity, as is not often found among Presocratics. We find four kinds of function: (1) intellect, (2) sensation and perhaps emotion, (3) nutrition and (4) reproduction. Connected with each is a ruling organ, respectively (1) the brain, (2) the heart, (3) the navel and (4) the genitals. Philolaus also connects psychic functions with kinds of living things: (1) man, (2) animals, (3) plants and (4) all living things.

We see in this schematic presentation an anticipation of a theory like Aristotle's, in which there are different functions of soul, each associated

---

[34] For the central fire see Huffman 2007 responding to Kingsley 1995: Ch. 13–14.

with a different level of activity. Aristotle's theory is similar to Philolaus' except that the former combines (3) and (4) into a single level. Like Philolaus, Aristotle identifies the levels with different kinds of living things: man, animals and plants; but he does not recognize a further level of a function shared by all animals; in fact he holds that level (3–4) is found in all living things. Both philosophers hold that there is a basis of life shared by all living things. Some living things have in addition the capacity for sensation, and some have that capacity plus the capacity for rational thought.

Plato also recognizes a tripartite division of soul, into mind, spirit (*thumos*) and appetites. Plato similarly assigns the parts of soul to different parts of the body: the head, the chest and the abdomen, respectively.[35] This similarity has led some scholars to think that the fragment is a forgery based on a Platonic theory of soul.[36] But there are significant differences, including the lack of correspondence between the second and third functions of Philolaus and Plato, and Plato's failure to connect thinking with the brain.[37] And again Philolaus thinks in terms of a four-fold rather than a three-fold scheme. Philolaus provides a kind of general psychological analysis like those of Plato and Aristotle, without agreeing with either in detail.

What we do not get in fr. 13 is a statement of what soul is, nor, consequently what its relation is to the psychic functions mentioned. For Plato the discussion is all about soul, and only tangentially about physiology. For Aristotle the functions in question just are manifestations of soul, which is the capacity of naturally organized bodies to act in a self-organized way. Fr. 13 provides a kind of biological basis of life, expounding the seat of each power, and going on to identify an organ that exercises the power. But it does not tell us what the soul is (if anything) in addition to the biological foundation, nor, consequently, how it relates to the biological functioning. There is an ancient debate about the seat of intellect, whether it is the brain or the heart. Philolaus rightly (in retrospect) sides with the brain, following his countryman Alcmaeon and differing from Aristotle's later view.[38] We do not, however, get any argument for this preference, although Philolaus may have supplied one that did not survive.

Philolaus calls the ruling organs the "origin" (*archa*) of the power in question. His use of the term is valuable. Aristotle describes the development of Greek philosophy in terms of different views about the principles (*archai*)

---

[35] Pl. *Ti.* 44d–45b, 69c–70e. [36] Huffman 1993: 307–8.
[37] Plato sees the heart as directing the area of the *thumos* (*Ti.* 70a–b) and the liver the area of the appetites (71a–b). But he fails to connect the brain with thinking, rather associating it with the marrow (76d1).
[38] Aët. 4.17.1 = DK 24A8.

and causes (*aitia*) among the early philosophers, and about how many principles and causes there are and of what sort.[39] Famously, he argues that the
early Ionians hit on the material cause. Belatedly some philosophers saw the
need for a moving or efficient cause. There were hints, especially among the
Pythagoreans, of a formal cause, developed further by the Platonists, but
no one really appreciated the final cause. Until recently, Aristotle's views
on the importance of *archai* have been taken for granted, while his views
on the four causes have been subjected to more scrutiny.

In fact, however, it remains dubious whether the early Presocratics had
a concept of an *archē* in the requisite sense.[40] We find no early fragments
that use the term in a rigorously philosophical way. Certainly the Presocratics seem to be interested with the "starting-point" of cosmogony and
of various component processes in the world, which is one of the senses
of *archē*. But what Aristotle has in mind with his term seems to be the
loaded philosophical sense of a starting-point of being and/or explanation
before which there is no other.[41] This loaded sense may go back only to
Plato's *Phaedrus*, where Plato is doing high-powered metaphysics.[42] Yet
with Philolaus we get an intermediate stage of reflection in which the *archa*
is some kind of starting point of explanation and operation, without the
stronger claim that there is only one unconditioned principle of all reality
and explanation, that is, for all ontology and epistemology.

Indeed, in fr. 6 Philolaus said, "But since these beginnings (*archai*)
preexisted and were neither alike nor even related." The beginnings in
question were limiters and unlimiteds, understood as the primitive entities
of the system. Hence "beginning" here cannot be taken temporally and
must indicate the ontological components of the world. In other words,
Philolaus here uses the term *archa* to mean something like "principle" or
(theoretical) "starting-point." Thus he seems to attain a level of abstraction
that surpasses that of many of his contemporaries and probably all of his
predecessors. He does not yet recognize absolute starting-points of ontology
(e.g. a category) or of explanation (an axiom), but he does recognize
plural relative starting-points for the construction of the world and for
explanations of its workings. He does, as we have seen, distinguish between
formal and material components (limiters and unlimiteds), a step toward
what Aristotle regarded as the inevitable discovery of the four causes.

Scholars have sometimes seen Philolaus as the origin of the doctrine that
the soul is a harmony, which is discussed and refuted in Plato's *Phaedo*.
The basis for the attribution is weak, especially since neither Plato nor

---

[39] *Metaph.* 1.3–10.   [40] See Schofield 1997 and Huffman 1993: 78–92.   [41] *Metaph.* 983b6–13.

[42] *Phdr.* 245c–d. Curiously, Aristotle does not even mention this sense of *archē* in his study of this
term in *Metaph.* 5.1.

Aristotle makes the attribution explicitly, so we have no formal theory of soul that we can connect with Philolaus, other than what is in fr. 13.[43] David Sedley, however, has reconstructed Philolaus' theory of soul, showing soul as a harmony of limiters and unlimited which can survive outside the body.[44] Huffman has built on this account to argue that only the emotional part of the animal or human survives, not the intellect (since the intellectual functions are not associated with the *psucha* in fr. 13). On this basis transmigration can occur between humans and animals, but not plants, which do not have emotions or sensations.[45] This interpretation reconciles Philolaus' psychology with Pythagorean beliefs and provides a kind of missing link for the soul-as-harmony theory criticized by Plato and Aristotle.[46] It does not, however, seem to offer the prospect of a happy future life that inspires the doctrine of transmigration, for the good life seems to require intelligence.[47]

We have an account of Philolaus' physiology and theory of diseases preserved in an anonymous papyrus that seems to follow a medical treatise of Meno, a student of Aristotle (A27).[48] In it we find out that "our bodies are constituted out of the hot." At birth an animal breathes in cold air from the environment, as a cooling mechanism. Philolaus attributes diseases to the action of bile, blood and phlegm, which accordingly are the origin (*archē*) of diseases. Although our knowledge of Philolaus' biology and physiology is sketchy, we can see that he worked out theories in all the areas of natural philosophy, and in the process made use of many current concepts in the field. His account of birth seems to parallel his account of the birth of the cosmos, as the central fire takes in breath and the void from its surroundings.

7. Assessment

In his history of causes in *Metaphysics* 1, Aristotle discusses the contributions of the so-called Pythagoreans (Ch. 5). Because they were steeped in

---

[43] See Huffman 1993: 328–32.

[44] Sedley 1995: 22–6. He bases his reconstruction on fr. 13 and on A27 (see next paragraph). In the latter passage we glimpse the soul as a harmony of hot and cold.

[45] Huffman 2009.   [46] Pl. *Phd.* 91c–95d. Aristotle *De Anima* 407b27–408a30.

[47] Ion of Chios DK 36B4 understands Pythagoras as aiming at a joyful afterlife. Empedocles DK 31B129 (which is about Pythagoras according to Porphyry *Life of Pythagoras* 30, Iamblichus *Life of Pythagoras* 15.67, Diogenes Laertius 8.54) says that Pythagoras can comprehend the works of ten or twenty generations of men, suggesting a memory inhering in a continuing intellect. Thus if the Sedley–Huffman reconstruction is right, Philolaus may offer a more limited kind of psychic survival than Pythagoras did. Could Plato's worries about a life devoid of memory in *Philebus* 21b–d, in a dialogue devoted to doctrines of Philolaus, be a response to this problem?

[48] See Huffman 1993: 289–92.

mathematics and number theory "they supposed the elements of numbers to be the elements of all things" (986a1–2, tr. Ross).[49] In order to make the number of heavenly bodies come out right, they invent a counter-earth (a8–12). "Evidently, then, these thinkers also consider that number is the principle both as matter for things and as forming both their modifications and their permanent states" (a15–17). Aristotle reviews the theories of Presocratic philosophers through the Pythagoreans, and concludes that they had grasped at most only two causes, the material and efficient (987a2–9):

> But the Pythagoreans have said in the same way that there are two principles, but added this much, which is peculiar to them, that they thought that finitude [*to peperasmenon*] and infinity [*to apeiron*] were not attributes of certain other things [but] were the substance [*ousia*] of the things of which they are predicated. This is why number is the substance of all things. (987a13–19)

It seems likely that Aristotle is following Philolaus rather closely in his exposition of Pythagorean philosophy. Two obvious examples are the cosmology with the counter-earth and the ontology based on limiters and unlimiteds. Since Philolaus is the earliest Pythagorean to set his views down in writing, he is the obvious thinker for Aristotle to study. According to Aristotle, the Pythagoreans treat their elements as mere components, and so, presumably as material causes. Yet on the other hand, they treat these elements as forming the "substance" of things, which suggests that they treat them as formal causes. Unfortunately, Aristotle is not very clear about his own analysis of the Pythagoreans. Yet he seems to think we find something like a genuine formal cause only at the next stage in Plato (Ch. 6).

If we see Philolaus as the main representative of the "so-called Pythagoreans," we can at least check Aristotle's comments against one of his main sources. As far as we have seen, Philolaus regards his limiters as structural principles that account for the determinate features of things. These limiters seem to include numbers, ratios, figures and shapes. Unlimiteds, on the other hand, are continua including perhaps space, time and matter. Thus it would appear that at least in some cases limiter is to unlimited as form to matter. On this reading, limiters would be paradigmatic formal causes in Aristotle's sense, and unlimiteds material causes. Hence Philolaus' ontology seems to put him much closer to Aristotle's own theory than Aristotle recognizes.

Aristotle, for his part, seems to think that since odd is limited and even unlimited in a list of opposites recognized by some Pythagoreans (986a23–4), the One is from both limited and unlimited because it is both even and

---

[49] I shall use Ross's translation of Aristotle's *Metaphysics* throughout.

odd (a19–20). And number in turn is derived from the One. In all of this he seems to be thinking of number as some sort of abstract reality derived from some abstract principles of Limited and Unlimited. Yet as far as we have seen, Philolaus does not think of limiters and unlimiteds as abstractions, nor does he construct an abstract One or Number out of these. In his cosmogony Philolaus constructs the first heavenly body out of fire at the center of the cosmos. But this item is not an abstract number, even if it is counted as the first thing in the cosmos.[50] Nor is Philolaus responsible for the list of opposites in which odd–even and limited–unlimited appear; Aristotle notes that this list comes from another Pythagorean source (986a22–3). Philolaus does seem to hold that the number one is both odd and even, but for reasons different from those that can be inferred from the list.

Philolaus seems to be a good candidate for someone who has recognized the importance of structural features as principles of explanation. Despite Aristotle's evaluation, we might say he recognizes both the material and the formal cause. Does he also recognize an efficient cause? Here the evidence is not so clear. What in fact causes limiters and unlimiteds to combine? Philolaus tells us that the two could not connect without harmony. But harmony is not obviously an efficient cause, but rather some sort of categorial link. What determines the cases in which this limiter combines with this unlimited? Here the fragments fail us. We have a cosmogony but no cause that initiates it.[51] We have the many concrete individuals in the cosmos, but no explicit account of what acted to bring them about. Philolaus seems to have a theory of biological generation that may take care of biological individuals. But is there a larger story to tell about cosmic generation?

Plato, who draws on Philolaus' theories in the *Philebus* in his account of the gift of Prometheus, provides an account of how sciences are organized. But Plato goes beyond this to suggest an ontology based on the original insight (23cff.). According to this ontology everything that exists in the universe (*panta ta nun onta en tōi panti*) can be classified into three classes: the unlimited (*to apeiron*), the limit (*to peras*) and the mixture of both. As we have seen, these classes correspond to what we find in Philolaus, even if the first two are stated in more abstract terms than those Philolaus uses. But Plato goes on to add a fourth class, that of the cause (*hē aitia*) that brings about the mixture. Plato recognizes the need for an agent or agency

---

[50] This point remains controversial. In defense of Aristotle's interpretation, see Schibli 1997 and Kahn 2001: 27–9; against these views see Huffman, "Philolaus," in the *Stanford Encyclopedia of Philosophy* § 4.1.

[51] There is one hint of a moving cause: "and the Pythagoreans seemed to say that it [sc. what moves the cosmos] was in the centre" (Simpl. *in Aristotelis de Physica Commentari* 1354.2–3, tr. Huffman). But even this is an inference ("seemed to say") not obviously based on strong textual evidence.

to intervene in the world to bring about the mixing of members of the two opposite classes. In Philolaus we do not find this.

There is, perhaps, one hint we should not overlook. Where Plato talks of the limit (*to peras*) and Aristotle the limited (*to peperasmenon*), using a perfect passive participle, Philolaus uses a present active participle, *perainon* (always in plural, *perainonta*), "limiting (thing)." His structural elements seem to be active in some sense, for they *limit* the unlimiteds. Yet Philolaus was writing in a time when the previous generation of philosophers had distinguished causal agencies from material realities. Anaxagoras had posited *Nous*, Mind, which pervades the world and initiates a cosmic rotation that then separates the primordial mixture (B12). Empedocles had posited *Philotēs* and *Neikos*, Love and Strife, as personified forces of attraction and repulsion, respectively, whose ongoing opposition drives a cosmic cycle (B17, B35). Earlier Parmenides had recognized a goddess "who steers all things" and causes copulation and generation in his cosmology, in other words a goddess of love (B12). Philolaus' contemporary Diogenes of Apollonia speaks of intelligence (*noēsis*) as the organizing power of the universe – though he invests this in one stuff, namely air, in his monistic theory (B3–5). What seems unusual, given the historical context, is Philolaus' reluctance to speak of a principle of change or causation apart from his elements. Plato, who finds Philolaus' ontology a good basis for his own explorations, feels compelled to add a cause, which he later identifies as a crafting power, *dēmiourgoun* (27b).

Aristotle presents the march of philosophy as unfolding a kind of manifest destiny leading to the discovery of the four causes, which are adequately realized only in his own theory (*Metaphysics* 1). While his story is no doubt self-serving, it does bring out successive articulations of different explanatory factors. If we plot Philolaus on Aristotle's grid, he comes off as more advanced in his recognition of formal causality than Aristotle himself allows, but as curiously backward in dealing with efficient causality. And since efficient causation has become explanation par excellence in modern natural philosophy, there seems to be something missing in Philolaus' theory. The hint of efficient causality in limiters remains largely unexplained and unexploited. Aristotle famously complains of Plato's Forms that they do not account for efficient causality, and he raises the same problem for Philolaus and the Pythagoreans:

> They do not tell us at all [. . .] how there can be movement if limit and unlimited and odd and even are the only things assumed, or how without movement and change there can be generation and destruction, or the bodies that move through the heavens can do what they do. (*Metaph.* 990a8–12)

At least we learn from Aristotle that he did not find any ready source of motion in Philolaus' cosmology, or any account of how limiters and unlimiteds join to produce things, or what drives the orbits of the heavenly bodies.

Philolaus allows for a measure of perfection in his cosmos, with fire at the center and ten surrounding bodies. Yet we do not find in him anything quite like a final cause, a purpose or end for which all things happen. This was the one cause Plato found lacking in his predecessors, and Aristotle found lacking even in Plato.[52] Plato felt its absence when he began to think of the world itself as an artifact, a product of divine benevolence.[53] Aristotle saw the world as autonomous or self-caused, but he kept the notion of a cosmic final cause, ultimately the divine activity itself, which somehow inspired the heavenly motions.[54] Modern philosophy and science reject final causes except for human actions, so we cannot fault Philolaus, as did his fourth-century critics.

Overall, Philolaus fits in well with fifth-century natural philosophy. Like most natural philosophers, he rejects divine in favor of human knowledge. Like most of them,[55] he posits a plurality (a minimum plurality of two) of elements from which a multitude of perishable things can be constructed. He recognizes a class of unlimited things like all his contemporaries. Unlike them he recognizes a class of limiters that can account for the formal or structural features of a compound. Thus he approaches the notion of an Aristotelian formal cause more closely than most of his contemporaries. One of his kinds of compound or composite is the union of a limiter with an unlimited. The concrete individual thing seems to be at least one example of such a compound, anticipating the Aristotelian particular substance. In cosmology Philolaus makes the world out of combinations of limiters and unlimiteds. He produces a unique cosmography with ten bodies surrounding a central fire or hearth in a hestiocentric universe. For the first time in Greek cosmology, he recognizes the five visible planets. By making the earth another planet, he allows apparent heavenly motions to be understood as different in principle from real motions. He posits a counter-earth that is justified not solely on a numerical basis, but by providing an explanation for some lunar eclipses that would otherwise not be explained

---

[52] *Metaph.* 988a7–10, b6–16.
[53] *Phd.* 97b–d, 98b–99b; *Ti.* 28b–29a; *Phlb.* 26e–27b; *Legs.* 889b–d, 896b–897c; Sedley 2007: Ch. 4.
[54] *Arist. Ph.* 8; *Metaph.* 12.6–7.
[55] On my view, *pace* Aristotle and most commentators, the Milesians are not material monists, but pluralists; there is only one material monist among the Presocratics, Diogenes of Apollonia. (Melissus surely and Parmenides probably are monists of some type, but not material monists, and Parmenides' cosmology – whatever its epistemological status – is dualistic.) See Graham 2006.

on the hestiocentric theory. He develops a complex psychology based in physiology and makes contributions to medical theory.

In his assessment of the Pythagoreans, Aristotle says they

> treat of principles and elements stranger than those of the physical philoso-phers (the reason is that they got the principles from non-sensible things [. . .]); yet their discussions and investigations are all about nature; for they generate the heavens [. . .] and use up the principles and the causes in explaining these, which implies that they agree with the [. . .] physical philosophers, that the *real* is just all that is perceptible and contained by the so-called "heavens."[56]

He is disappointed that their theory is too physical and not metaphysi-cal enough. Yet to a contemporary audience the loss of the theosophical trappings of pseudo-Pythagorean lore allows us to see him as more, not less, a philosopher. He refuses to speculate about supernatural principles. Instead, he invokes those epistemological principles without which knowl-edge (human knowledge, that is) would not be possible, and posits their existence, while leaving open the question of precisely how those principles are instantiated. He goes on to identify the products of those principles, and then he "generates the heavens" out of those products.

Philolaus has emerged in the twenty-first century as one of the most interesting Presocratic philosophers. Whatever his precise debt to the Pythagorean society, he brought to the philosophical conversation of his time an avid interest in structure, order and "number" (in the sense of an ordered plurality). He seems to have absorbed from the Eleatic tradition a concern for ontology and epistemology and from the Ionian tradition an interest in natural philosophy. If he sometimes seems to be dependent on *a priori* speculations, as with the central fire, he is not obviously more sus-ceptible to conjectures than his contemporaries. And like them, he offers his theories as providing plausible explanations for phenomena. If we look to him for the secrets of the Pythagorean brotherhood we will be disap-pointed. But if we look to him for innovative philosophy that embodies the best of his time, we may be rewarded.

---

[56] *Metaph.* 989b29–990a5; Ross's italics.

CHAPTER 3

Archytas

Malcolm Schofield

1. Introduction

Archytas, a citizen of Tarentum on the Adriatic coast of southern Italy, and a contemporary of Plato, is a significant figure in the history of ancient Greek science. After pioneering work in geometry by Hippocrates of Chios in the later decades of the fifth century BC, Archytas was one of the three or four major contributors to the history of Greek mathematics – in his case geometry and harmonic theory in particular – before Euclid. Detailed discussion of his work in these fields will be found in Chapters 8 and 9. He is in fact the first and only Pythagorean who can be credibly associated with significant technical achievements in mathematics. He was also, as it happens, a considerable figure in politics, who held the office of General probably for seven consecutive years, at a time when there is reason to think that a democratically governed Tarentum was an especially flourishing power in the region.

Was Archytas also a philosopher? He is credited by Aristotle's pupil Eudemus, ordinarily regarded as a reliable witness for this period of Greek thought, with a celebrated argument for the infinite extent of the universe, best known from the version in Lucretius. According to the Aristotelian commentator Simplicius, Eudemus said he used to put the question (A24):[1] "If I arrived at the extremity of the heaven, could I extend my hand or staff into what is outside, or not?" It would be odd to suppose that that would not be possible. But if we suppose it would, and conclude that the boundary must therefore in fact lie further beyond, we then face the same question about what would happen if I tried to extend hand or staff into what is outside *that* boundary. And so on *ad infinitum*. So if I can always reach beyond any putative limit, the conclusion can only be that

---

[1] For convenience I use where possible the reference system in Diels-Kranz, where evidence on Archytas is presented in section 47. Translations of texts quoted are my own, though sometimes based on those in Huffman 2005. Textual choices are likewise my own.

the beyond is in fact unlimited. Therefore, Eudemus' testimony shows that Archytas certainly philosophized.

So much is reasonably secure. To say more is rather difficult. The musical theorist Aristoxenus, another member of Aristotle's school, and originally from Tarentum himself, wrote a life of his compatriot (cf. A9), as well as a work which Diogenes Laertius refers to as *On Pythagoras and his Associates* (Diog. Laert. 1.118). But apart from a few anecdotes from the former[2] and some scraps of narrative from the latter, little about Archytas survives that is identifiable with any certainty as originating with Aristoxenus. Nor is a great deal said about the man in Diogenes Laertius (A1) or the Suda (A2) in their fairly brief biographical entries. One thing they do talk about is the part he was widely believed to have played in extricating Plato from danger when trapped at the court of Dionysius II in Sicily, an incident which caught the imagination of many other writers and is described in some detail in the seventh of the letters attributed to Plato preserved in the Platonic corpus. As for evidence about Archytas' thought, we possess a fairly substantial number of testimonies in quite a range of ancient authors and covering a good deal of intellectual territory. In the end, however, really reliable information of any significance is hard to find beyond that concerning geometry, notably his solution to the "Delian" problem, and harmonic theory. Finally, in some of the later writers – Porphyry, Simplicius, Stobaeus, for example – we encounter a substantial number of extracts from what are claimed to be actual writings of Archytas himself (indeed two entire treatises ascribed to him survive in independent manuscript tradition). Nearly all are nowadays taken to be pseudonymous;[3] the credentials of the few generally regarded as authentic will be briefly reviewed below.

Within the compass of this chapter it is possible to scrutinize only a small portion of the relevant textual material. Readers wanting a fuller treatment are fortunate in having available Carl Huffman's full-scale study of Archytas, published in 2005, which examines all the most important

---

[2] For example, from his father Spintharus Aristoxenus retails the story (A7) that when angered by the extreme negligence of his slaves in their management of his farm during his absence, Archytas said that they were lucky he had lost his temper with them – since otherwise they would never have gone unpunished: evidently implying that he would never act when aware that his capacity for unclouded rational thought was impeded. In A9 he recounts at some length the defense of hedonism he attributes to Polyarchus "the voluptuary," articulated in discussion with Archytas on the occasion of a visit to Tarentum. (Huffman 2005: 323–37 argues that we can reconstruct Archytas' rebuttal from Cic. *Sen.* 39–41; but the ascription to Archytas of the argument against hedonism developed in this passage both attributes to him trains of thought arguably Platonic in cast and also seems to be motivated by a desire to imply Plato's dependence on Archytas – making it hard to know how far one can trust the account, even if it does derive from Aristoxenus.)

[3] See Chapter 15.

evidence in detail.[4] Huffman offers a restrained account of Archytas so far as his work on music and in geometry is concerned, with which the present discussion will be broadly in tune. In other areas, Huffman evinces more optimism about what ideas and activity we can attribute to him than will be found in the pages that follow.

2. Archytas and Plato in the biographical tradition

Diogenes Laertius includes an account of Archytas in the Pythagorean Book 8 of his *Lives*. After substantial sections on Pythagoras himself and on Empedocles (seventy-seven in all), he seems to lose interest, and in just fourteen further sections of text deals with six other thinkers with Pythagorean associations of one sort or another. However Archytas does get more space than anyone else except the important mathematician and astronomer Eudoxus, alleged to have been his student. The relevant section is oddly placed, before those on Alcmaeon, Hippasus and Philolaus, all certainly active one or two generations before him. Fortunately there is plenty of robust evidence that Archytas was indeed Plato's contemporary, such as Proclus' testimony (derived from Eudemus) that he worked at the same time as the mathematicians Leodamas and Theaetetus (A6).

Here is the main substance of Diogenes' biographical account (Diog. Laert. 8.79):

> This is the person who rescued Plato – by means of a letter – from Dionysius, when he was on the point of being killed.[5] But he was also the object of popular admiration for his outstanding qualities all round. And in fact he was his citizens' general seven times, although no one else held the office for more than a year – because the law precluded it. Plato also wrote him two letters, since he had first written to Plato as follows.

The Suda entry amplifies this information on Archytas' military command: "He was the leader of the Italian league, and was chosen general with exceptional powers by the citizens [of Tarentum, doubtless] and the Greeks in the region."

The political history of southern Italy in the fourth century is murky. But several of its Greek cities formed a military alliance in 393 BC against external threats. Then some time after Croton had fallen (in 379/8) like other cities to Dionysius I of Syracuse, the meeting place of the alliance

---

[4] See Huffman 2005.
[5] Translators often make Diogenes say "killed by Dionysius"; but this is not the most natural way of taking the Greek, and it conflicts with the narrative in the Platonic Seventh Letter.

seems to have moved to the Tarentine colony of Heracleia; and it sounds as though Tarentum must have become the major power in the league, with its citizens electing one of their own number as general, and getting that endorsed by the other member cities. According to Strabo, Tarentum was most powerful when it was a democracy (a time he associates with a long period of leadership by Archytas: A4). The best guess for the date of Archytas' political ascendancy is therefore some time in the second quarter of the century.

Like Diogenes, the Suda prefaces its account of Archytas as public figure with a reference to his intervention with Dionysius II on Plato's behalf. But like the Platonic (or "Platonic") Seventh Letter's account of the matter (*Letter* 7.350a–b), the Suda omits any reference to a letter, which is of crucial importance for the way Diogenes constructs the narrative of relations between the two thinkers that is the main focus of his treatment of Archytas the man. "This is the person who rescued Plato" reminds the reader that he has already in Book 3 told the story of Plato's visits to Sicily, and how – on what it represents as the second such occasion – a letter sent by Archytas to the tyrant (a fictive document reproduced by Diogenes) had ensured his safety (Diog. Laert. 3.21–2). Of the two letters he says Plato wrote to Archytas, one must be the ninth in the collection preserved in the Platonic corpus, probably a fictitious rhetorical exercise. The other, the twelfth in the collection, and the only one whose authenticity is questioned in the manuscript tradition itself, is what Diogenes quotes in the sequel to the passage given above, along with the letter of Archytas to which it responds. The exchange concerns the locating and dispatch by Archytas of several works by an early Pythagorean named Ocellus, from the Lucanian region of Italy. It looks as though this pair of letters, with which Diogenes is obviously hoping to impress the reader, were originally forged – as a pair – in an attempt to establish the antiquity, authenticity and authority of writings spuriously ascribed to Ocellus. A fragment of one of those mentioned – *On Law* – survives in Stobaeus, and we have an independent text (with an impressive manuscript tradition) of the whole of another, *On the Nature of the Universe*: samples of the vigorous production of pseudonymous Pythagorean treatises are to be discussed in Chapter 15.

Assuming the historicity at any rate of Archytas' action in supporting Plato in his hour of need, what relationship between himself and Plato will have underpinned it? The sources suggest that the two men had at some point previously established relations at least as "guest-friends," which is to say involving a tacit agreement between persons from different cities to lend each other their good offices in practical matters as circumstances might require. Beyond that the story diverges. According to one strand Plato had learned Pythagoreanism from Archytas. Another reverses the picture and makes Archytas Plato's pupil. The most nuanced account is given in the Platonic Seventh Letter (A5).[6] The writer tells how Plato was reluctantly persuaded, principally at the behest of his old and close friend Dion (the emotional focus of the letter), to accept an invitation to the young Dionysius' court for a second time, and how his mission turned into a disastrous failure. The persuasion to which he yielded included as a significant element assurances, represented as motivated by concern for political relations between Tarentum and Syracuse, from Archytas and others: assurances that the tyrant was making extraordinarily good progress in philosophy. But it transpired that if he had any interest in philosophy, his desire for it was low among his preoccupations (345a–d). The implication, subsequently spelled out explicitly (350c–d), is that Plato was let down by everyone – above all Dion, but including Archytas, even if he and other friends of Plato in Tarentum are later in the letter credited with responding to his pleas for help and with arranging his rescue after he had picked up gossip that some of Dionysius' mercenaries had designs on his life (he has earlier emphasized that he was protected against that by Dionysius, who showed him respect: 340a).

3. Archytas in Plato's *Republic* and *Timaeus*

Whatever we make of Plato's personal relationship with Archytas, is there evidence in the dialogues of impact of Archytas' ideas on his thinking? Both the *Republic* and the *Timaeus* seem (without naming him) to acknowledge it. In the *Republic* the passage in question is the section of Book 7 where Socrates specifies the five mathematical sciences that are to form the educational preparation young philosopher guards will need to master before they are in a position to engage in dialectic, and where he explains how they should be conceived and studied if they are to be appropriate to such a preparation. Having introduced and discussed astronomy as the fourth of them, a fifth is proposed as its counterpart. When asked to identify it, Socrates mentions the Pythagoreans by name for the one and only time in the dialogues (*Resp.* 530d):

---

[6] For discussion see Lloyd 1990. This is not the place to debate the authenticity of the Seventh Letter or its reliability as a historical document.

> "It looks inevitable," I said, "that as the eyes have been compounded with
> a view to astronomy, so the ears were compounded for harmonic motion,
> and that these sciences are siblings of one another, as both the Pythagoreans
> and we agree, Glaucon. Is that the line we take?" "Yes," he said.

The suggestion seems to be that Plato and Pythagoreanism have independently arrived at the same conclusion: they converge. As it happens
we have what Porphyry, commenting on Ptolemy's *Harmonics*, cites as an
actual quotation from Archytas where just such a thesis is propounded.
Here is the beginning of what Porphyry calls his *On Mathematics* (B1):

> Those concerned with the sciences seem to me to make distinctions well, and
> it is not at all surprising that they have correct understanding of their nature
> in each case. For having made good distinctions concerning the nature of
> the wholes, they were set to see the nature of the parts well also. Indeed,
> concerning the speed of the stars and their risings and settings, as well as
> geometry and numbers, and not least concerning music, they handed down
> to us a clear basis for distinguishing them. For these sciences seem to be
> siblings.

The author evidently sees the sciences he discusses as successful because
each of them gives an accurate specification of its subject matter in general
(i.e. of "the whole") before tackling the different elements ("the parts")
of that subject – broadly as in Plato's theory of division. In the sequel to
these introductory remarks he begins his treatment of music by reflection
on how noise in general is produced, before turning to voiced sound more
specifically, thus exemplifying the initial account of the methodology of
the sciences. It is not as clear as in the Plato passage that it is then just
astronomy and music that are "these sciences" identified as siblings. But
the specific focus on the motions of the stars and their speed (there is no
analogue in the references to geometry and arithmetic) is matched by a
similar preoccupation in the account of noise and voiced sound that follows.
So perhaps those are indeed the two sciences that are the intended subject
of the claim, with motion – as in Plato – their common denominator.

If the fragment really is from a treatise by Archytas, then the way the
sibling metaphor is introduced in the two texts makes it sound as though it
might have originated in a conversation between the two thinkers. Happily
there is good reason to accept a genuine Archytan provenance for the text (as
is generally accepted), whether it came from an *On Mathematics* or from a
work with some other title (Iamblichus calls it just "the harmonic work").
Its theoretical vocabulary is free of any of the terminology encountered
in pseudo-Pythagorean writings; the prose sounds more like Presocratic

or early Hippocratic writing. Here is a flavor of the rather repetitious argument in the sequel to our passage:

> Therefore of the sounds that fall upon perception, those that come to be present from blows quickly and forcefully appear high, but those that come slowly and weakly seem to be low. For if someone should pick up a stick and move it sluggishly and weakly, he will make a low sound with the blow, but if both quickly and forcefully, high. Not only by this would we recognize it, but also whenever speaking or singing we wish to voice something loud and high, since we voice it with a violent breath.

The confusion here of pitch with volume (Plato and Aristotle would see that they must be distinct) is another pointer to an early date.

Archytas' most celebrated piece of mathematics was the solution he proposed to the problem of how to construct a cube twice the volume of a given cube: which since Hippocrates of Chios had been recognized to be a matter of finding two mean proportionals in continued proportion, given that no formula expressible in rational numbers was available. It was known in antiquity to Proclus (fifth century AD) and Eutocius (sixth century), and appears also in an Arabic mathematical treatise of the ninth century. Eutocius cites the remarkably rigorous proof in full (A14), in the version he found in the probably reliable Eudemus.[7] References in other authors to Archytas' achievement connect it intriguingly with an incident in which Plato takes center stage. According to the mathematician Theon of Smyrna (second century AD), Eratosthenes, the third century BC Alexandrian polymath, told the following version of the story (*Mathematics Useful for Reading Plato* 2.3–15 Hiller):

> Eratosthenes, in the work entitled *Platonicus*, says that, when the god had ordered the Delians, in an oracle, to construct an altar double the existing one, in order to escape from a plague, great perplexity fell on the builders as to how a solid should become the double of another solid, and they came to ask Plato about this, and he said to them that the god did not give this oracle to the Delians because he wanted an altar twice the size, but in order to bring forward as a reproach against the Greeks that they pay no attention to mathematics and have neglected geometry.

What historical truth might lie behind the legend (in whatever variant: see further A15) we are never likely to know. It is certainly tempting to believe that the Delians' plight did stimulate interest in solving the problem, and that Plato somehow did get involved. It is tempting, too, to try to relate

---

[7] For a full treatment of the mathematics of it see Huffman 2005: 349–61.

to the Delian incident the strange, allusive passage in the mathematical sciences section of Book 7 of the *Republic* on the relatively undeveloped state of the geometry of solids (*Res.* 528a–e). Socrates has initially treated astronomy as the next subject in sequence after geometry (i.e. plane geometry). Then he corrects himself for omitting something else that fits logically between the two: solid geometry (Plato might be meaning us to recall its omission in Archytas' own quartet of mathematical sciences). On one of the perhaps multiple intended readings of the expression "the increase of the cubes" (528b), employed in introducing the topic, Socrates and Glaucon agree that the solution to the puzzle of how the cube is to be duplicated has not yet been discovered.

The first reason given – no city values it – might function as code for reminding the reader that now, however (i.e. at the time of writing, not that of the imagined conversation), Archytas and Eudoxus have come up with solutions, not least because the citizens of Delos decided that they had to take the subject seriously. The second reason Socrates ventures for failure to make progress is the need for researchers to have someone to direct their work. That, he says, is a requirement difficult to satisfy – and as things stand, they are too arrogant to follow the lead of such a director (528b–c). Is this a complaint that Plato's own advice to mathematicians (including Archytas at least) that they needed to develop solid geometry had been ignored, but is now proven timely by the success in tackling the Delian problem now enjoyed by Archytas himself and Eudoxus? None of these possibilities constitutes robust evidence that this stretch of the *Republic* contains further reference to Archytas additional to the sibling sciences passage. But since Plato is here apparently making a necessarily veiled point about the contemporary state of mathematics, it is worth conjuring with such a scenario.

The allusion to Archytas in the *Timaeus* is more oblique and more conjectural. Of Socrates' interlocutors in the dialogue, two – Critias the Athenian and Hermogenes of Syracuse – are historical figures, whereas Timaeus, from the major Italian city of Locri (south of Tarentum), seems to be a Platonic invention. Timaeus has often been taken to be Plato's proxy for Archytas, whose intellectual and political activity postdates the dramatic date of the dialogue. He is described as someone who combines experience of the most important political offices with philosophy (*Ti.* 20a), and as an expert in astronomy who has been particularly energetic in study of the nature of the universe (27a). Introducing an Italian Greek with attributes like these does look like a way of prompting the reader to think of Archytas. As Huffman has argued, however, there is as much contrast as similarity.[8] Thus (for example) Locri had an aristocratic, not a democratic, form of government (Ar. *Pol.* 1307a34–41),[9] as Plato indicates in speaking of the *eunomia* of its constitution (*Ti.* 20a). Of the two sibling sciences, it was in harmonics, not astronomy, that Archytas was expert. And the distinction between the sensible and the intelligible domains, central to Timaeus' cosmological discourse in the dialogue, derives unquestionably from Plato's own metaphysics. It is presumably because he is a consummate Platonist that he is said to have "attained the summit of all philosophy" (20a). Evidence in Ptolemy about Archytas' harmonics (A16), on the other hand, indicates a concern to develop a system that had real empirical application:[10] for Plato quite the wrong agenda (cf. *Resp.* 530c–531c).

Nonetheless, if everything we are told about Timaeus is meant to indicate qualifications superior to Archytas' for the dialogue's intellectual project, there must presumably be something about Archytas' theorizing that made him an appropriate focus of implicit comparison. Here is what purports to be another extract from Archytas, quoted by Porphyry from what he speaks of as *On Music* (B2):

> There are three means in music: one is arithmetic, second is the geometric, third is sub-contrary, which they call harmonic. The mean is arithmetic when three terms are in proportion such that the excess by which the first exceeds the second is that by which the second exceeds the third. In this proportion it turns out that the interval of the greater terms is less, but that of the lesser terms greater. The mean is the geometric when they are such that as the first is to the second, so the second is to the third. Of these terms the greater and the lesser have the interval between them equal. Subcontrary, which we call harmonic, is the mean when they are such that, by whatever part of itself the first term exceeds the second, by that part of the third the middle term exceeds the third. It turns out that in this proportion the interval between the greater terms is greater and that between the lesser terms is less.

The passage's technical content – admittedly not an unimpeachable basis for confidence – has again convinced most scholarly opinion of its probable authenticity.[11]

The most obvious musical application of this system of means is in the construction of concords (octave, fifth, fourth), as is explained in Chapter 9 below. The arithmetic and harmonic means between the numerical values

---

[8] Huffman 2005: 85–8.   [9] On Locri see Redfield 2003.
[10] See further Chapter 9, and more fully Huffman 2005: 402–28, Barker 2007: 287–302.
[11] But as is pointed out by Huffman 2005: 166, 178, the initial use of the term "sub-contrary" for the harmonic mean suggests a pre-Platonic date.

we assign to the two notes of the octave generate the fourth and the fifth (in opposite sequence, depending on which mean is selected); the upper or lower note of the octave itself can be conceived as the geometric mean within a double octave. Some such scheme is evidently what is appropriated by Plato when in the *Timaeus* he gives the World-Soul a complex mathematical ordering, such that the key terms in the formula Timaeus specifies are separated by intervals into each of which are inserted two means: the harmonic and the arithmetic, articulated in the terms we find in the extract above (*Ti.* 35b–36b). The formula itself is a purely theoretical construct, which bears no relationship to the systems of scales that, as we know from Ptolemy, Archytas developed in his effort to capture actual heard harmonies. In any case, what Plato is doing here, of course, is not harmonics but cosmology. In the *Timaeus* scheme of things, the World-Soul and its psychic movements explain above all the motions of the heaven and of the heavenly bodies they carry in their wake. In other words, the mathematical building blocks basic to Pythagorean theory are now put to work in astronomy. It is as though Plato is analyzing with the help of Pythagorean mathematics the sibling relationship between harmonics and astronomy in order to generate his own version of the Pythagorean harmony of the spheres – using in fact the so-called Pythagorean diatonic (the scale employed previously by Philolaus: DK 44B6).

4. Archytas and Aristotle

Does Archytas make himself felt in the work of Aristotle? Later antiquity certainly thought so. In commenting on Aristotle's *Categories* the sixth-century-AD Neoplatonist Simplicius quotes extensively from earlier authorities, included among them Archytas. Here he is in the preface to his commentary, making a work of Archytas the model for Aristotle's *Categories* (13.21–4):

> The Pythagoreans, such as Archytas, with whom Plato also associated, collected the simple expressions into a decad – as he taught in his book *On the Whole System*. It was this teaching of his that Aristotle too followed, even so far as the names [i.e. of the ten sorts of simple expression], though as some think only altering it for the worse, inasmuch as he himself does not take into account also the one (as what includes within it the ten), and he rejects the natural basis of names.

Simplicius' value for the study of early Greek thought is hard to overstate, above all because he deliberately preserved verbatim extracts from books of

Presocratic philosophers, which in his own day were hard to find. Among his many excerpts from *On the Whole System* he allows himself at one point the luxury of reproducing its entire treatment of time (352.24–353.15), "because the Pythagorean treatises are rarities" (352.23). *On the Whole System* in fact survives not just in the snippets Simplicius and other Neoplatonists cite from the original (written in a literary version of a Doric dialectic of Greek), but as a self-standing treatise discovered in the Ambrosian Library in Milan in 1914, where however the Doric has been converted into the *koinē* Greek standard in the early Roman empire.[12]

Not everyone in later antiquity was convinced that this was a work of an Archytas who was Plato's contemporary. Boethius tells us that the fourth-century Aristotelian Themistius did not believe it; Simplicius himself mentions that Iamblichus (later third and early fourth century AD), who evidently championed the importance of *On the Whole System*, felt he had to resist the objection that its definition of time conflated Aristotelian and Stoic doctrine (350.10–16). People asked awkward questions: for example, if the analysis of substance into three (matter, form, the composite) was already there in Archytas, why did Aristotle himself not make use of it in the *Categories* (cf. *Categories* 91.14–33)? Modern scholarship sides with the skeptics. Its verdict is that *On the Whole System* is a forgery, fathered by its author on Archytas. And unlike most of the other forgeries of this kind to which the names of early Pythagoreans were attached, this is a case where the date of its composition can with a fair degree of confidence be conjectured, as the end of the first century BC or not much later. For thanks again to Simplicius, we know that many of its distinctive positions were ones advanced by thinkers such as Eudorus (interestingly a Pythagoreanizing Platonist), Boethus and Andronicus, who were all actively wrestling with the text of the *Categories* in the first century, as the Aristotelian treatises forced themselves once again upon the attention of the philosophical world.

To put into circulation a text designed to use a fashionable philosophical engagement with the *Categories* for promoting interest in the idea of that treatise's fundamental indebtedness to Pythagoreanism was an ingenious stroke at such a historical juncture. Presumably it was designed to capitalize on the Pythagorean resonances of the number ten: if the *Categories* insists that there are just ten basic categories through which we can articulate reality, the treatise surely must have a pedigree in Pythagorean teaching on number as principle of all things, and on ten as the perfection and

---

[12] See the edition of Szlezak 1972 for full discussion of this work and Chapter 15 below.

completion of the number series. Hence the fabrication of an *ur-Categories* attributed to Archytas, to prove that what must be the case was indeed the case. But its author then cleverly crafts his *ur-Categories* so as to encapsulate within it not just some main doctrines of the *Categories*, but reactions or even corrections to them current in the best contemporary work on Aristotle's treatise. That way the forger could show that it was a Pythagorean who had anticipated the sharpest minds recently or currently at work on the theories enshrined in that much pored over text. At the same time, he would feed what appears to have been an inclination to see Pythagoreanism as the original mainspring of all philosophizing that was at that time gathering momentum.[13]

In the surviving authentic treatises of the Aristotelian corpus, there is little to suggest that the work of the real Archytas held much interest for Aristotle. There are in fact only two clear references to points made by Archytas, one in the *Metaphysics*, the other in the *Rhetoric*, together with mention of a children's toy invented by an Archytas. We shall in due course return to Archytas the inventor. The *Metaphysics* passage – concerned with definition – tells us that his definitions included what Aristotle recognized as both formal and material elements. The examples Archytas gave were apparently "windlessness," defined as "stillness in quantity of air," and "calm," taken to be "levelness of sea" (A22). Aristotle implies that these proposals were tendered in illustration of an explicit theory of definition. Perhaps Archytas will have been commenting more immediately on a poetic phrase such as Homer's "and there was windless calm" (*Od.* 5.392) in the style of the sophist Prodicus, notable in his practice of "correctness of names" for his acuteness in distinguishing synonyms. The same kind of context seems likely for a remark of Archytas praised in the *Rhetoric*, to the effect that an arbitrator and an altar are the same – because with both of them someone who has been wronged can take refuge (A12).[14]

To these references we may add a further *Metaphysics* passage (1092b8ff.), where Aristotle mentions the way the Pythagorean Eurytus proposed the view – illustrated with pebbles – that numbers explain things of different species as their differentiated and differentiating boundary markers (DK 45.3).[15] From Theophrastus (DK 45.2) we learn that Archytas must have been the source of this information about a Pythagorean of the previous

---

[13] "Apart from the fourth century BC, the first centuries BC and AD were clearly the period of Archytas' greatest fame in antiquity" (Huffman 2005: 21); and significantly more pseudo-Pythagorean treatises were ascribed to his authorship (B9) than to any other early Pythagorean.

[14] For the scholarly debate about the evidence, see Huffman 2005: 489–507, Barker 2006: 314–18.

[15] See Chapter 8 below.

generation, probably also from Tarentum. We should also register the fact that there was apparently some interest in Archytas' views in the general area of physics among the early Peripatetics. Eudemus' account of his argument for an infinite universe has already been highlighted. Also from Eudemus is the information that Archytas held that motion was caused by inequality or unevenness (A23). No further detail is given by Simplicius. Finally, there is an intriguing entry among the Aristotelian *Problems* (A23a):

> Why is it that the parts of animals and plants (those that are not instrumental) are all rounded (of plants the stem and the shoots, of animals the lower legs, thighs, arms, and trunk), but neither the whole nor the part is triangular or polygonal? Is it, as Archytas used to say, because the proportion of equality is present in natural motion (for all things are moved in proportion), but this proportion alone bends back on itself, so as to make circles and curves, whenever it comes to be present?

There are obvious difficulties of interpretation. How much is the author ascribing to Archytas? The theory of proportion in motion looks designed primarily to explain movements in arcs and circles, such as those of the heavenly bodies, rather than a question in biology. As one would have expected, Archytas looks to mathematics for insight into a physical phenomenon. But as reported the explanation offered is compressed and decidedly obscure, not least because the apparently unparalleled expression "the proportion of equality" admits only of conjectural analysis.

With that glum verdict we might move away from the testimonies of Aristotle and his school. But first we should note two titles relating to Archytas in Diogenes Laertius' catalogue of the writings of Aristotle (Diog. Laert. 5.25): *On the Archytean Philosophy* (three books), and *Extracts from the Timaeus and the Archytean Writings* (one book). Both titles appear in the similar catalogue of Hesychius (A13), and the first of them also in Ptolemy's catalogue. If Aristotle really did write either work, it would be hard to doubt that he thought there was substantial material in Archytas worth serious philosophical attention. In fact it seems doubtful whether there were any such Aristotelian compositions, for which there is very little other evidence.[16] Simplicius knows of an epitome by Aristotle of the *Timaeus*, from which he can quote a sentence, apparently early in the work (*In Cael.* 296.16–18; 379.14–17). But there is no particular reason to think that the book on the *Timaeus* and the Archytas material listed in the catalogues is the same work as the epitome, though perhaps confusion between them might explain the ascription to Aristotle of the *Extracts*.

---

[16] Huffman 2005: 583–94 is more optimistic. But the catalogues are variable in their reliability.

Otherwise Simplicius' contemporary the Neoplatonist Damascius at one point makes the following claim (A13): "Aristotle in the Archytean writings reports that Pythagoras too called matter 'other,' as subject to flux and always becoming other."

The "Archytean writings" sounds like an abbreviated reference to the *Extracts*; and if that work demonstrated similarities between Plato's dialogue and passages from Archytas, the *Timaeus*' account of the receptacle and the movements to which it is subject would be a natural candidate for treatment. However the Pythagoras portrayed in the Damascius quotation is the heavily Platonized figure familiar from the reinvented Pythagoreanism, unrecognizable from Aristotle (who is in any case notoriously chary of ascribing philosophical teaching to Pythagoras himself), which became increasingly dominant from the first century BC onwards. And the attribution to him of a doctrine of matter in flux (cf. Sextus *M* 7.94ff., Aët. 1.9.2, 1.23.1) bears the hallmarks of the attempts characteristic of Neopythagoreanism to make Pythagoras the true author of the philosophical system Plato is then portrayed as inheriting. Indeed the *Extracts* begins to look as though it might be another pseudo-Pythagorean document, whose distinctive purpose was to document that case through a detailed exhibition of relevant textual material.

5. *On Law and Justice* and fr. 3: test cases in authenticity

Nobody in modern times has accepted the Neoplatonist belief that *On the Whole System* is authentic Archytas. Most of the works from which surviving material ascribed to him derives are nowadays taken to be later fictions (B9). But not quite all: a few extracts preserved in late antiquity are thought to be the real thing, a view endorsed above for the fragments from what Porphyry calls *On Mathematics* (B1) and *On Music* (B2); and about a few there is still controversy. In the latter category is a treatise Stobaeus knows as *On Law and Justice*, which I take as a sample case for consideration.[17] Stobaeus preserves five fragments. Here is the first that he quotes, which sounds like the beginning of the work:

> Law relates to human soul and way of life as concord does to both hearing and voice. For law educates the soul and establishes the way of life, while concord causes hearing to understand and voice to be in tune. Now I assert that every community is constituted from ruler and rules and thirdly laws.

---

[17] Huffman 2005: 599–606 thinks the arguments on authenticity equally balanced in this case; Johnson 2008: 194–8 argues for authenticity.

And of laws, that which is living is king, that which is lifeless is letter. So the law is primary – for through the law the king is law-governed, the ruler compliant, the ruled free, and the whole community happy; whereas through contravention of law the king is tyrannical, the ruler non-compliant, the ruled in slavery, and the whole community wretched. For their activities hang together on account of ruling and being ruled and thirdly controlling. Ruling is what is appropriate to the better, being ruled to the worse, and controlling to both of them: for it is what has reason that rules souls, what is non-rational that is ruled, and both control the feelings; for virtue comes into being from the mutual adjustment of each of the two, and that mutual adjustment leads the soul from its pleasures and its pains into quiet and impassivity. (Thesleff 33.3–18)

This is a mish-mash of mostly Platonic, Aristotelian and later philosophical motifs, related at the outset to the kind of harmonic theory there is reason to think the real Archytas did develop, and ingeniously worked up into what sounds like an analysis of communal and psychic harmony – but which makes little sense when examined.

The author's ingenuity begins with his choice of topic and title. While a number of the pseudonymous Pythagorean treatises on political philosophy are concerned with kingship, he is presumably aware that Archytas' Tarentum was not a monarchy, and so makes his focus something else – law and justice (the predominant concern of the third of the extracts Stobaeus quotes, where Archytas' ratio theory is adroitly exploited). The closing sentence of our extract is also cleverly designed to get the reader to conceive that the thesis being propounded about virtue is what Aristotle will have been reacting to at a relevant juncture in the *Nicomachean Ethics*. In his discussion of virtue in Book 2, Aristotle criticizes other thinkers who conclude that, because pleasures and pains are what make people bad, the virtues must be defined as forms of impassivity and quiet (1104b21–6).

So our author is well read, and intellectually supple and well organized. But what he produces is terribly muddled: the kind of muddle that could be perpetrated only by a writer attempting to synthesize other thinkers' ideas, not someone developing a theory more independently. He has a fatal Pythagorizing attraction to triads. This will be no problem when in Stobaeus' third extract he associates aristocracy, democracy and oligarchy with the harmonic, geometric and arithmetic mean respectively, or in the fourth argues rather like Polybius for the superior strength and stability of a constitution such as the Spartans' that combines elements of the simple forms. Here, however, the writer endeavors to superimpose triadicity on a more basic Aristotelian bipartition of constitution and soul alike into a ruling and a ruled element. In the political sphere the third element he introduces is law – which of course is categorially of a different order from ruler and ruled. The problem that creates is then negotiated by attempting to exploit the notion of king as living law found in Philo Judaeus and in the pseudonymous treatise on kingship attributed to the Pythagorean Diotogenes. But of course king and ruler are too close to being the same thing for the triad of king, ruler, ruled to be workable. How the supposedly related triad of ruling, being ruled, and controlling could function in the psychic sphere is left unclear. It transpires that this is really an adaptation of Platonic psychology, where reason and the emotional element that will ideally be responsive to reason cooperate to tame the beast within: the appetites. However once again triadicity comes unstuck, this time because it cannot be coherently mapped on to the bipartite Aristotelian scheme of a rational and a non-rational part of the soul. Within that framework, there remains no logical space for the idea of control after all. Instead mutual adjustment of the rational and irrational parts ends up carrying the entire burden of explanation.[18]

At this point it will be useful by way of contrast to consider another of those few fragments that are often taken to be authentic extracts from Archytas (B3). In the fuller version preserved by Stobaeus, it consists of two passages whose connection with each other is unclear, though both seem to be concerned with intellectual discovery. Text and particularly orthography are problematic (use of Doric forms is fitful). The first and shorter part of the extract, preserved by both Iamblichus and Stobaeus, propounds claims about the constraints on inquiry somewhat reminiscent of the *Meno* paradox. The second part (found only in Stobaeus) might be translated as follows:

> Once calculation was discovered, it caused civic conflict to cease and increased concord. For when calculation gets to be present, there is no grabbing more than one should, and there is fairness – for by calculation we achieve satisfactory exchange regarding our transactions. So it is by this means that the poor get things from those with resources, and the rich give to those in need, both in the confidence that through this they will have what is fair. And it is the standard and preventer of those intent on wrongdoing, making those who know desist from their anger[19] before they commit wrong, persuading them that they will not be able to escape detection when they come to it [i.e. calculation]; and it prevents those who do

---

[18] For further comment on *On Law and Justice* see Chapter 15.

[19] Editors often gratuitously emend the Greek to give "those who know how to calculate desist."

not know from committing wrong, by revealing them in the course of it [i.e. calculation] as they are trying to do wrong.

This piece of writing reads like late fifth or early fourth century BC prose. Its highly rhetorical patterning is full of antitheses reminiscent now of Gorgias, now of the sophist Antiphon. The ideas and vocabulary of the treatment of transfer of resources from rich to poor as the catalyst for civic concord are close to those found in one of Democritus' ethical sayings (DK 68B255). The hope of escaping detection in wrongdoing addressed in the final section echoes such well-known sophistic treatments of justice and the free rider as those of Antiphon (DK 87B44A) and the *Sisyphus* fragment (DK 88B25). The discussion of conflict resolution early in Plato's *Euthyphro* (7a–8a) also talks of "coming to calculation" as remedy for anger and the basis of agreement, but sounds as though it might be arguing against the idea that calculation can achieve as much as is claimed here where justice is concerned.

Was it Archytas who wrote the work from which the fragment was extracted? Its notion of "calculation" is sometimes related by scholars to the idea of "logistic," or the study of numerical proportion, represented as the most perfect of the arts and sciences in what is generally taken to be an authentic fragment, attributed by Stobaeus to what he calls the *Discourses* (B4). But the connection is tenuous; and as Huffman remarks, that extract is "too short to be certain that we can identify the conceptual world in which it is working,"[20] helping to make B4's Archytan credentials relatively weak. Nonetheless there is good reason to think that Stobaeus has managed to find in B3 a genuine piece of early theoretical prose – articulating an utterly different kind of ethical and political theory from that put forward in *On Law and Justice*. It is no less different in style and content from the authentic fragments on music. Yet there is no reason to think that Archytas could not write in a range of registers. And if he participated in the sophistic debate about correctness of names, perhaps he did attempt other writing – such as is represented in B3 – in a sophistic style also.

6. Archytas and the applied sciences

When Diogenes Laertius turns to Archytas' intellectual achievements, he refers to his pioneering duplication of the cube, but he begins by making him "the first to systematize mechanics by using mechanical principles"

---

[20] Huffman 2005: 226.

(editors usually emend the manuscripts' "mechanical" to "mathematical," which is to beg a lot of questions). This idea of Archytas as the founder of the science of mechanics is also found in Plutarch, who writes in his life of Marcellus (14.5):

> This popular and trumpeted science of instruments began to get going in the circle of Eudoxus and Archytas, who with subtlety embellished geometry, and for problems where logical or diagrammatic proof was difficult to come by, they supported their claims by using sensible models as instruments.

He then instances their solutions to the Delian problem as a case in point.

This is the basic evidence, together with a brief comment by Apuleius on Archytas' theory of vision (A25) and a text in Aëtius (4.14.3) on Pythagoras on visual images, underpinning the view of some modern scholarship that Archytas made decisive contributions to the development of the applied sciences as such.[21] However these are shaky foundations for such a hypothesis. For example, Plutarch's story (reproduced above) is hard to reconcile with what Eutocius represents as Eratosthenes' complaint (A15) that Eudoxus and Archytas presented their results in demonstrative format (true, if Eutocius' account of Archytas' proof is correct), and could not put them to use in a physically manipulable form (this seems likely enough). Eratosthenes himself claims in a piece of pentameter verse to be the inventor of an instrumental device that does the job easily. Of course, no smoke without fire: it sounds as though there was current in his day a belief that the credit did indeed belong to Eudoxus and Archytas.

Where the shaping of mechanics and optics as sciences is concerned, we have therefore to be skeptical about Archytas' alleged role. What of his reputation as an inventor? As well as Aristotle's mention of "the clapper of Archytas" (used to keep children occupied: A10), we have a quotation (A10a) from Favorinus (second century AD): "Archytas of Tarentum, an expert in mechanics, made a wooden dove which flew; wherever it alighted, it arose no more." Huffman provides a description of the kind of complicated mechanism (involving tube, valve, compressed air, cord, pulley, counterweight) we must apparently envisage, and a judicious discussion of the chances of such a device being constructed at this early date.[22] One problem with both stories is the identity of the Archytas in question. The clapper is elsewhere represented as the invention of a carpenter of that name; and Diogenes Laertius (8.82) knows a list that includes a master-craftsman called Archytas to whom a book *On Mechanism* is attributed.

---

[21] See for example Burnyeat 2005.   [22] See Huffman 2005: 302–7, 570–9.

Here, as with so much of the relevant evidence, what Archytas of Tarentum did or thought remains hard to pin down. But it would be a pity to end on so downbeat a note. Cicero (*Amic.* 88) gives us one more glimpse of Archytas that speaks volumes. According to him Archytas used to say (A7a Huffman): "If someone had climbed up into the heaven, and gained insight into the nature of the universe and the beauty of the stars, his amazement would turn sour on him. What would have given him the greatest delight would be if he had had someone to tell about it."

CHAPTER 4

Sixth-, fifth- and fourth-century Pythagoreans

Leonid Zhmud

1. What does it mean to be a Pythagorean in the sixth to fourth centuries BC?

Not every Presocratic philosopher had students, but many of them had at least one: Anaximander was reported to be Thales' student; Anaximenes probably was a student of Anaximander. Several thinkers, such as Parmenides of Elea and Leucippus of Abdera, founded philosophical schools, though in each case only one of their immediate students is known: Zeno of Elea and Democritus of Abdera. We hear also about Heracliteans and Anaxagoreans,[1] some of whom are known by name. Cratylus of Athens interpreted Heraclitus' book but was not his personal student. Archelaus and Metrodorus belonged to Anaxagoras' circle in Athens and Lampsacus, respectively. As is often the case, Pythagoras exceeds all the other Presocratics both in the number of his followers and in the continuity of his school. Indeed, Pythagoreanism was the only strain of Presocratic thought to survive, albeit in much-modified form, until the end of antiquity. Even if we limit ourselves to ancient Pythagoreanism, which came to an end around the mid fourth century BC, we still have almost 200 years of its existence and more than 200 names of Pythagoreans.

If we try to uncover the reasons for Pythagoras' extraordinary success, the results are unexpected. The Pythagoreans were not (or at least not originally) organized in a philosophical school, if we understand by this "an identifiable group committed to the teaching and manner of life prescribed by the founder" (Mason 1996: 31). Unlike Plato, Epicurus or Zeno of Citium, Pythagoras founded not an institutionalized philosophical school with a range of well-defined doctrines, varied though these might be at different times, but a political society (ἑταιρεία).[2] Besides, his teachings

[1] Pl. *Tht.* 179e3 ('Ηρακλείτειοι); *Cra.* 409b5; *Two-fold Arguments* (*Dissoi logoi*) 6 ('Αναξαγόρειοι).

[2] Historians of the late fourth century BC – Aristoxenus, Dicaearchus, Neanthes and Timaeus – called the Pythagorean community a ἑταιρεία, and its members "companions" (ἑταῖροι) and "friends"

were not set down in writing and his followers were widely scattered in many cities of Magna Graecia and, after the mid fifth century BC, of mainland Greece as well. Most Pythagoreans were not philosophers, and those who were – Alcmaeon, Hippasus, Hippon, Philolaus, Archytas, Ecphantus and others – did not teach Pythagoras' philosophy but their own theories. Similar in some respects, they were different in many others; no school doctrine shared by all or even most Pythagorean philosophers is known.[3] Some of the Pythagorean philosophers and scientists were united by being teachers and pupils; they worked in related areas and often shared common views, so that in a broad, non-technical sense we can speak of the Pythagorean school as a means of preserving and developing certain intellectual traditions.[4] Of their way of life we know too little reliable to perceive anything they held in common. In his only mention of Pythagoras Plato speaks of him not as a philosopher but as an educator and as the founder of the "Pythagorean way of life" still existent in Plato's days (*Resp.* 600a–b). Regrettably, Plato does not say what it comprised, whereas other classical sources offer conflicting reports. Evidently, different Pythagoreans at different times led different ways of life.[5]

The famous Pythagorean athlete and army commander Milo of Croton, in whose house the Crotonian Pythagoreans met, styled himself Heracles: when leading the Crotoniates in a battle against the Sybarites (*c.* 510), he wore a lion-hide and carried a club.[6] Aristotle called him πολυφάγος ("big eater"); according to later sources, he ate nine kilograms of meat and the same amount of bread every day, and drank ten litres of wine.[7] On the other hand, Iccus of Tarentum, an Olympic victor in 476, a teacher of gymnastics and a doctor, led a life of such moderation that he became proverbial: the Greeks called a frugal meal "an Iccus meal"; while training he adhered to a strict diet and sexual abstinence.[8] Plato's contemporary Archytas, an original thinker and brilliant mathematician, had a feature in

---

(φίλοι). See Aristox. frs. 18, 31; Dicaearchus fr. 34; Neanthes *FGrHist* 84F30–1; Timaeus in Apollonius *FGrHist* 1064 F2; Timaeus in Iustin 20.4.14 (*sodalicium*).

[3] The famous number doctrine of the Pythagoreans was an interpretation of Aristotle (Zhmud 2012b: 433ff.).

[4] On "schools" in Presocratic philosophy, see Laks 2005.

[5] For a more traditional view on the Pythagorean way of life as what made a Pythagorean a Pythagorean, see Huffman 2008e.

[6] Diod. Sic. 12.9.5 (from Timaeus of Tauromenium) = Pythag. DK 14A14.

[7] Arist. fr. 520; Phylarch. *FGrHist* 81F3; Athen. 10 412e–413a.

[8] Pl. *Leg.* 839e–840a = DK 25A2; Ael. *VH* 11.3; *De nat. an.* 6.1. Alongside Iccus, Plato mentions another Pythagorean athlete, the triple Olympic victor (488–480) Astylus of Croton, of whom "similar things are told" (*Leg.* 840a5; cf. Clem. *Strom.* 3.6.50; cf. DK 1.446.20; Paus. 6.13.1).

common with Milo: he was a successful army commander and a leading politician in his native Tarentum. Archytas' moderation, self-control and restraint, praised by his biographer Aristoxenus (frs. 30 and 50, cf. frs. 26–7), place him however closer to Iccus. The more we study figures of individual Pythagoreans the more it appears that all of them were different. It is impossible to find in our sources *any one common* characteristic that applies to all ancient Pythagoreans from the end of the sixth to the middle of the fourth centuries BC. Rather we must speak of a "family resemblance." This means that certain Pythagoreans had characteristics in common with some Pythagoreans, but not with others. Thus, Hippasus, Theodorus of Cyrene, Philolaus and Archytas shared an interest in mathematics; Democedes, Alcmaeon and Iccus were engaged in medicine; Alcmaeon, Hippo, Philolaus and Ecphantus wrote on natural philosophy; Milo, Astylus of Croton, Iccus and Dicon of Kaulonia were Olympic victors, whereas Milo, Democedes, Hippasus and Archytas were involved in politics. What if anything was held in common between Hippasus and Iccus, Milo and Theodorus, we do not know, except that they were Pythagoreans. But what did it mean to be a Pythagorean in the sixth, the fifth and the fourth centuries BC?

The first reference to Pythagoreans (Πυθαγόρειοι) appears in Herodotus. While mentioning the Egyptian custom forbidding the burial of the dead in woolen clothes, he states that the Orphics and the Pythagoreans also forbid it (2.81). This links the Pythagoreans with a cultic society through a common element of burial rite, though we should keep in mind that concern for the burial of their members was a feature of practically all Greek voluntary associations, and not only the religious ones. In the Sophistic treatise *Two-fold Arguments* (*Dissoi logoi* – c. 400 BC) the Anaxagoreans and Pythagoreans figure as acknowledged teachers of wisdom and virtue, typical examples of the philosophical schools (DK 2.414.13). We can only guess which specific Pythagoreans (if any) Herodotus and the author of *Two-fold Arguments* had in mind. Plato (once) and Aristotle (very often) speak of the Pythagoreans in general as a school of thought, but they never call anyone "a Pythagorean." Aristoxenus seems to be the first writer to refer to named persons as Pythagoreans. Born in Tarentum, when it was governed by Archytas, Aristoxenus was closely linked with the Pythagorean circles through his father Spintharus (fr. 30). In Phlius on the Peloponnese he met the last Pythagoreans, the pupils of Philolaus and Eurytus: Echecrates, Phanton, Diocles and Polymnastus of Phlius; in Athens he studied with the Pythagorean musicologist Xenophilus of the Thracian Chalcidice (frs. 18–20). Witnessing the death of ancient Pythagoreanism, Aristoxenus was eager to commemorate in his historical and biographical writings its founder, its history and its most prominent representatives.[9] The remaining fragments of his four "Pythagorean" works are densely populated with individual Pythagoreans; he offers more names than any other ancient writer except for Iamblichus. There are good grounds to believe that the biggest cluster of names, the catalogue of 218 Pythagoreans placed at the very end of Iamblichus' *On the Pythagorean Life*, also comes from Aristoxenus, namely, from his work *On Pythagoras and His Followers*.[10]

The very number of names classified by twenty-seven different city-states and peoples and the fact that only fifty-six of them are known to us from other sources implies that apart from oral tradition, Aristoxenus must have relied on some documentary sources. These sources listed prominent members of the Pythagorean *hetairiai*, in the first place politicians and legislators, who secured the political dominance of the Pythagoreans in Croton, Metapontum, Tarentum, Locri, Rhegium and other cities of Magna Graecia until the mid fifth century. Their deeds are usually unknown to us, if they did not distinguish themselves by something else. Those who did can be placed in four overlapping categories: philosophers, scientists, doctors and athletes; together they constitute about 10–15% of all the names in the catalogue. After the anti-Pythagorean outbreaks of the mid fifth century in Italy, when "the best men in each city" were killed (Polyb. 2.39.1–4, from Timaeus of Tauromenium), while others succeeded in escaping to Greece, the political dimension of Pythagoreanism was drastically diminished. New centers of Pythagoreanism, Thebes and Phlius, were purely intellectual and lacked any perceptible political significance. In Italy, after the seizure of Croton (379) by the Syracusan tyrant Dionysius the Elder, the last important center of Pythagoreanism remains Tarentum, led in 367–361 by Archytas as a democratically elected general (*stratēgos*). Most of the forty-three Tarentine Pythagoreans recorded in Aristoxenus' catalogue must have been politicians rather than Archytas' students in mathematics (of whom we know only Eudoxus of Cnidus: Diog. Laert. 8.86).

2. Were there different classes of Pythagoreans?

After the mid fourth century we have no evidence of any Pythagorean known to us by name. When there were no real Pythagoreans left, two

---

[9] See *On Pythagoras and His Followers* (frs. 11–25), *On Pythagorean Life* (frs. 26–32), *Pythagorean Precepts* (frs. 33–41) and *Life of Archytas* (frs. 47–50). Aristoxenus also mentions the Pythagoreans in other writings: *Rules of Pedagogy* (Παιδευτικοὶ νόμοι; fr. 43), *A Lecture on Music* (Μουσικὴ ἀκρόασις; fr. 90), *Historical Notes* (Ἱστορικὰ ὑπομνήματα; fr. 131); see also fr. 123.

[10] Iambl. *VP* 267 = DK 1.446.8– 448.6; Zhmud 2012b: 109ff.

categories of would-be Pythagoreans appeared: the Pythagorizers and the
so-called Pythagorists of Middle Comedy. The Pythagorizing philosophers,
for example, the Cynic Diodorus of Aspendus (second half of the fourth
century), had nothing to do with the politics, philosophy or science of
the Pythagoreans but merely led an ascetic way of life, which had become
popular by that time. Though they styled and/or called themselves the
Pythagoreans, as Lycon, the critic of Aristotle (last third of the fourth
century), did, their contemporaries regarded them as just pretenders.[11]
Their caricatured reflection in Middle Comedy, the Pythagorists, often
appeared on the Athenian stage as indigent preachers of metempsychosis
and vegetarianism.[12] The Pythagorists of comedy are always dirty; they
constantly go barefoot; they wear only shabby cloaks; they live on grasses
and cereals and drink only water, abstaining from meat and wine. In all
these respects except for vegetarianism they are surprisingly like Socrates
and his pupils in Aristophanes' comedies and other philosophers on the
Athenian stage.[13] One of their actual prototypes, Diodorus of Aspendus,
was an indigent vegetarian, who pretended to be a pupil of the Pythagoreans. If there were in Athens other such figures as Diodorus, comedy could
have taken from them some crucial details, transforming the by-now-dated
character of the poor philosopher, Socrates, into the figure of the indigent
vegetarian-Pythagorist. The readiness of comic authors to adopt the successful devices of their colleagues should caution us against identifying a
particular comic type with some Pythagorean community existing at that
time.

The Pythagorists of comedy and the real Pythagorizers launched the
tradition of the existence (and then the *co*existence) within Pythagoreanism of different groups, as a result of which two fictional categories of
Pythagoreans appeared, the scientific *mathematici* and the religious *acus-*
matici. The latter devoted their lives to the observance of Pythagoras'
"divine commandments" (*acusmata* – literally "things heard"). Admittedly,
this transformation took 500 years. A Hellenistic stage of this tradition is
attested in the scholia on Theocritus:

[11] Timaeus: Diodorus led an eccentric life and pretended to be a pupil of the Pythagoreans (*FGrHist*
      566F16). Sosicrates (*c.* 150 BC): to gratify his vanity, Diodorus began to wear a long beard, long
      hair, and put on a worn cloak, whereas before him the Pythagoreans always went about in white
      clothing, made use of baths and had customary hair-cuts (fr. 15 Giannattasio Andria). On Lycon,
      who wrote all kinds of offensive nonsense about Aristotle, see Aristocl. fr. 2.8 Chiesara.
[12] DK 58E. Not one of the comedies in which Pythagorists figure can be reliably dated before 350;
      some of them were staged in 330–320 (Webster 1970: 53ff.).
[13] In Aristophanes Socrates is poor and dirty, he suffers from cold and hunger and hence is pale, goes
      barefoot and does not drink wine – exactly as the Pythagorists did (*Av.* 1554; *Nub.* 103, 175, 362ff.,
      414ff., 836ff., 1112). See also Amipsias fr. 9 K-A; Antiphanes fr. 120 K-A.

The Pythagoreans differ from the Pythagorists in that the Pythagoreans take great care of their bodies, whereas the Pythagorists lead a very simple and wretched life. Some consider that the Pythagorists accept the rules of Pythagoras, but not his opinions, whereas the Pythagoreans hold to the same way of thinking as Pythagoras. (14.5a)

Up to this point I have avoided mentioning *mathematici* and *acusmatici*, for the simple reason that they figure neither in the classical nor even the Hellenistic sources. In the literature of the first and second centuries AD we find various schemes of dividing up the Pythagoreans, most of which are based on the degree of closeness to Pythagoras: his chosen pupils (Pythagoreans, esoterics, *sebastikoi*) take up worthier things than outside supporters or novices (Pythagorists, exoterics, *akoustikoi*).[14] The first to refer to a division of the school into *mathematici* and *acusmatici* was Clement of Alexandria (*c.* 150–215 AD), to whom belongs also the first use of the term ἀκουσματικοί (*Strom.* 5.9.59). In Neopythagorean biography of the third century AD *mathematici* and *acusmatici* achieved a rapid, but short-lived rise to fame, *viz.*, in Porphyry, where they become the main groupings of Pythagoreans (Porph. *VP* 36–7), and particularly in Iamblichus. After Iamblichus, in fact not a single writer in antiquity mentions them. Iamblichus presents the story in two contradictory versions: in *VP* 81 and 87–8 the *acusmatici* recognize the *mathematici* as Pythagoreans, while the latter do not recognize the former, asserting that the doctrine of the *acusmatici* derives from Hippasus. In *On General Mathematical Science* (*De Communi Mathematica Scientia*; henceforward *Comm. Math.*) 76.16–78.5 all is reversed. Iamblichus copied both versions at different times from the biography of Pythagoras by the Neopythagorean Nicomachus (first half of the second century AD). *Comm. Math.* retained the original text, *VP* changing the *mathematici* and *acusmatici* around and turning Hippasus into an "acusmatic."[15] Since Clement certainly and Porphyry very possibly depend on Nicomachus,[16] whereas there are no traces of the story of the *mathematici* and *acusmatici* before him, much points to Nicomachus as its author.[17] Even if an earlier source

---

[14] Scholia to Theocritus 14.5a; *Greek Anthology* 14.1; Anonymous Photii 438b19–25; Aul. Gell. 1.9.1–8; Hippol. *Haer.* 1.2.4, 1.2.17.

[15] Rohde 1901: 138ff.; Thesleff 1965a: 91; Burkert 1972a: 192ff. Burkert, followed by some other scholars, believes that this account derives from Aristotle, but there is not any evidence for this.

[16] Clement: Burkert 1972a: 459 n. 63; Städele 1980: 204ff., 208 n.12; Porphyry: Zhmud 2012b: 189ff.

[17] The legend of the *mathematici* and *acusmatici* is closely linked with mathematical discoveries and the "disclosure" of Pythagorean geometry (Iambl. *Comm. Math.*, 77.18–78.5 = *VP* 88–9) – both topics must have been of particular interest to Nicomachus as an author of popular introductions to *mathēmata*; cf. next footnote.

for this story did exist, the search for it would be unlikely to take us back further than the first century AD.

3. Hippasus

It is not accidental that Hippasus figured in Nicomachus as Pythagoras' adversary. In the biographical tradition Hippasus is painted in dark colors, which is connected not with his betrayal of the school's mathematical "secrets,"[18] but most probably with his political rivalry with Pythagoras. As distinct from the majority of early Pythagoreans, no pseudo-Pythagorean writings were ascribed to him, apart from a certain *Secret Account* (Μυστικὸς λόγος), which, as Sotion (*c.* 200 BC) reports, he wrote to blacken Pythagoras.[19] In the biography of Pythagoras by another Neopythagorean, Apollonius of Tyana (second half of the first century AD), Hippasus also turns out to be a political adversary of Pythagoras, while belonging to the "thousand," who rule in Croton.[20] It is possible that Hippasus was originally a member of the Pythagorean *hetairia* and turned against his master during the so-called Cylonian revolt and schism in the Pythagorean community, which followed the victory of Croton over Sybaris. He was certainly not the only Pythagorean who did this.[21]

Only two theses are known of the philosophy of Hippasus, who appears not to have left behind a work on natural philosophy: first, Aristotle and Theophrastus report that Hippasus, like Heraclitus, proposed fire as a first principle; second, Aëtius reports that he regarded the soul as fiery by nature.[22] The context of these theses is unknown; their possible connections with the philosophy of Pythagoras are not clear either. Whether Heraclitus knew of his elder contemporary Hippasus,[23] is uncertain. The

---

[18] According to Nicomachus, he gave out the secret of irrational numbers, for which he was expelled from the community and in his lifetime a gravestone was raised for him; in another version, he died the death of the impious at sea for disclosing the secret of the construction of the dodecahedron (Clem. *Strom.* 5.9.57; Iambl. *VP* 246, cf. 88).

[19] Diogenes Laertius 8.7. A similar work was ascribed to Ninon, another political opponent of Pythagoras (Apollonius *FGrHist* 1064 F2).

[20] *FGrHist* 1064 F2 (Apollonius' account of these events depends largely on Theopompus: Zhmud 2012a: 99ff.). How this relates to Hippasus' origin in Metapontum is not clear; other data show his birthplace as Croton (Iambl. *VP* 81; *Comm. Math.* 25); Aristoxenus' catalogue lists him among the Sybarites (DK 1.446.30).

[21] Aristotle names Cylon and Onatas as two of Pythagoras' political opponents (Diogenes Laertius 2.46 = DK 1.103.12 = fr. 21.1 Gigon); Onatas of Croton figures in Aristoxenus' list of the Pythagoreans (DK 1.446.13).

[22] Arist. *Metaph.* 984a7; Theophr. fr. 225 FHS&G = DK 18A7. Aët. 4.3.4 (*Dox.* 388 n.) = DK 18A9. Aëtius' report does not look very reliable.

[23] On Hippasus' chronology see Zhmud 2012b: 124ff.

central fire (*hestia*) that emerged in the center of the cosmos according to Philolaus' cosmogony (B7, A16–17) may have been somehow related to Hippasus' fire.

As distinct from philosophy, everything we know of Hippasus' geometry, arithmetic and harmonics indicates that he continued the researches of Pythagoras. Indeed, before Pythagoras arithmetic and harmonics did not exist and up to the very end of the fifth century they remained a monopoly of the Pythagorean school. In acknowledging Hippasus, we therefore ought to acknowledge Pythagoras, and vice versa: those who deny that Pythagoras was a mathematician usually do the same with Hippasus, or date him much later in the fifth century.[24] It is revealing that Hippasus never figures in our sources as a founder of arithmetic or harmonics, whereas several well-informed authors of the fourth century ascribe such a role to Pythagoras. Thus, Plato's student Xenocrates says: "Pythagoras discovered also that the intervals in music do not come into being apart from number, for they are an interrelation of quantity with quantity."[25] This implies that Pythagoras discovered the numerical ratios of the basic concords, the octave (2:1), the fifth (3:2), and the fourth (4:3), which is confirmed both by the later tradition[26] and by the independent fourth-century evidence for Hippasus. Aristoxenus, an expert in music and in the Pythagorean tradition, reports:

> A certain Hippasus made four bronze discs in such a way that while their diameters were equal, the thickness of the first disc was epitritic in relation to that of the second (4:3), hemiolic in relation to that of the third (3:2), and double that of the fourth (2:1), and when they were struck they produced a concord. (fr. 90 = DK 18A12, tr. A. Barker)

Hippasus' experiment is clearly too complex to be a first attempt, in which the ratios of the octave, fifth and fourth were successfully found (besides, this is not what Aristoxenus says). Rather, it was conducted in order to *confirm* what Pythagoras had already discovered, most likely by observations and/or experiments with a stringed instrument, though hardly with a monochord.[27] The ratios of the first concords are closely bound up with

---

[24] Burkert 1972a: 206ff. and 456 dates him about 460; Knorr 1975: 42ff. and 51 n.7, about 430.

[25] Fr. 87 Isnardi Parente. Xenocrates wrote numerous works on the mathematical sciences (fr. 2); this testimony derives most probably from his work *On Musical Intervals* (Περὶ διαστημάτων).

[26] "It seems that Pythagoras was the first to have identified the concordant notes in their ratios to one another" (Theon of Smyrna 56.10ff., tr. Barker).

[27] The tradition passed down by Diogenes Laertius (8.12), according to which Pythagoras discovered the division of the monochord (i.e. demonstrated the ratios of concords on the monochord) goes back at least as far as the end of the fourth century BC: the historian Duris linked the invention of the monochord with Pythagoras' son Arimnestus (*FGrHist* 76F23). The monochord is not attested before the fourth century.

arithmetic and harmonic means, which Pythagorean harmonics used for dividing the octave into two unequal intervals, the fifth and the fourth $(2:1 = 3:2 + 4:3)$.[28] Further, the fifth (3:2) is the arithmetic mean between the terms of the octave (2:1), and the fourth (4:3) is the harmonic mean between them. According to information that may go back to Aristoxenus' colleague in the Lyceum, Eudemus of Rhodes, the first three means were known to Pythagoras and Hippasus:

> Of old there were but three means in the days of Pythagoras and the mathematicians of his times, the arithmetic, the geometric, and the third in order, which once was called the subcontrary, but had its own name changed forthwith to harmonic by Archytas and Hippasus, because it seemed to embrace the ratios that govern the harmonized and tuneful.[29]

Archytas' fr. 2 confirms this information: in music there are three proportions, arithmetic, geometric and subcontrary, "which we call harmonic."[30] Since Hippasus supposed that consonances were produced by fast and slow movements,[31] it is very possible that Archytas meant him among his predecessors, "those concerned with the sciences" (οἱ περὶ μαθήματα), who contended that there was no sound without movement (DK 47B1). It is clear anyway that Hippasus was interested not only in mathematical harmonics, but also the physics of sound.

A similar relation between Pythagoras and Hippasus is observed in arithmetic. In a fragment of Aristoxenus' work *On Arithmetic* we read:

> Pythagoras more than anybody else seems to have valued the science of numbers and to have advanced it, separating it from the merchants' business and likening all things to numbers. For number contains all things as well, and there is a ratio to each other between all the numbers. (fr. 23)

In the second part of the fragment Aristoxenus quotes definitions of the unit and even and odd numbers, which differ from the definitions in the Euclidean *Elements* (7 def. 1 and 6–7) and derive, to all appearances, from

---

[28] The realization of the fact that an octave could not be divided into two equal parts, because the geometric mean between 2 and 1 is equal to $\sqrt{2}$, should be linked with Hippasus, who discovered irrationality.

[29] Iambl. *On Nicomachus' Introduction to Arithmetic* (*In Nicomachi Arithmeticam Introductionem*), 100.19ff., tr. D'Ooge. On the provenance of this text see Zhmud 2006: 270–2.

[30] Porph. *On Ptolemy's Harmonics* (*In Ptolemaei Harmonica*) 92 = DK 47B2; see Huffman 2005: 162ff.

[31] "Some people thought it proper to derive these concords from weights, some from magnitudes, some from movements and numbers, some from vessels. Lasus of Hermione, so they say, and the followers of Hippasus of Metapontum, a Pythagorean, pursued the speeds and slownesses of the movements [τῶν κινήσεων τὰ τάχη καὶ τὰς βραδυτῆτας], through which the concords arise" (Theon of Smyrna *Mathematics Useful for Reading Plato* (*Expositio Rerum Mathematicarum ad Legendum Platonem Utilium*) 59.4ff. = DK 18A13).

fifth-century Pythagorean work on arithmetic.[32] Philolaus also mentions the division of numbers into even and odd (DK 44B5), and still earlier a fragment of a comedy by Epicharmus (born *c.* 540) plays on Pythagorean operations with even and odd numbers using counting pebbles, *psēphoi* (DK 23B2). However, in the three arithmetical books of the *Elements*, definitions of even and odd are used only once, this being in the theory of even and odd numbers (9.21–34), which, as Becker (1936) demonstrated, belongs to the most ancient stratum of Pythagorean mathematics. Again, the only proposition in the *Elements* in which this theory is used is the ancient proof that the diagonal of a square is incommensurable with its side,[33] whereas the very discovery (or disclosure) of irrationality is ascribed in the ancient tradition to Hippasus.[34] Since the Pythagorean Theodorus of Cyrene demonstrated the irrationality of magnitudes from $\sqrt{3}$ to $\sqrt{17}$, to Hippasus is usually attributed the discovery of the irrationality of $\sqrt{2}$, the classic example of which is the incommensurability of the diagonal of a square with its side. The arithmetical proof of this proposition preserved at the end of Book 10 of the *Elements* (app. 27) makes use of the theory of even and odd numbers, the method of *reductio ad absurdum*, and the least numbers in a given ratio.[35] This all points to its Pythagorean origin. If Hippasus actually did rely on the theory of even and odd numbers, then it must go back to the time of Pythagoras.

4. Alcmaeon

Alcmaeon of Croton, a younger contemporary of Pythagoras (Arist. *Metaph.* 986a29) and older contemporary of Parmenides, was the first Pythagorean to leave behind a written tradition. His book, preserved in several fragments and numerous doxographical testimonies, opens with an address to three Pythagoreans (DK 24B1), one of whom, Brontinus, is known as Pythagoras' coeval and relative.[36] Starting from Aristoxenus'

---

[32] For a detailed analysis of this fragment, see Zhmud 2006: 218ff.

[33] Euc. 10 app. 27. Aristotle referred to it (*An. pr.* 41a24, 50a37). See Heath 1921: 1.90ff.; Becker 1936: 544ff., 547.

[34] See above, n. 18 and von Fritz 1945. The growth of legends on the disclosure of secrets and subsequent punishment was aided by the double meaning of ἄρρητος: "irrational, not able to be expressed in numbers" and "sacred/secret" (Burkert 1972a: 461ff.).

[35] These three things are closely interconnected. Four propositions of the theory of even and odd numbers (Euc. 9.30–1, 33–4) are proved by *reductio ad absurdum*. On the least numbers in a given ratio (πρῶτοι ἀριθμοί or πυθμένες) in the early Pythagorean arithmetic and harmonics, see Archytas DK 47A17, cf. A19; Eudem. fr. 142; Huffman 2005: 428ff.; Zhmud 2012b: 277ff., 295ff.

[36] DK 17; cf. DK 1.446.16, 447.6.

catalogue, Alcmaeon figures in ancient sources as a Pythagorean,[37] but
this nearly unanimous tradition is often outweighed by the fact that Aristotle distinguished Alcmaeon's dualistic theory from the famous table of
ten opposites, which he presented as the teaching of a separate group of
Pythagoreans.[38] However, to be a Pythagorean was not a matter of doctrinal principles: Hippasus and Hippo were monists, Philolaus and Ecphantus dualists, Menestor and Archytas developed no doctrine of principles.
Alcmaeon's teaching on health as a balance of opposing powers (δυνάμεις)
belongs to physiology, not ontology; that it differs from the table of opposites in no way makes him less Pythagorean, the more so as the table itself
has a clear Academic origin (Zhmud 2012b: 434ff., 449ff.). In fact, relying
on Aristotle, we are not in a position to establish who was a Pythagorean
and who was not.

The greater part of Alcmaeon's book was devoted to medicine (τὰ
ἰατρικά) (Diog. Laert. 8.83). Some scholars have asserted that he was a
natural philosopher with an interest in medicine, rather than a doctor, but
from the ancient tradition it seems rather that he combined in himself
the philosopher and the doctor.[39] For the history of Pythagoreanism it
was of great importance that Crotonian medicine and the Pythagorean
school, which arose at almost exactly the same time, were closely linked
with each other. In Pythagoras' lifetime the physicians of Croton enjoyed
the greatest renown (Hdt. 3. 131), and one of them, Democedes of Croton,
was the most famous doctor of his time (3.125). For a substantial fee he
was invited first to Aegina and Athens, and later by Polycrates to Samos.
After the murder of Polycrates he was taken prisoner by the Persians. On
his return to Croton, Democedes married the daughter of Milo the athlete
(3.137) and thus became one of the Pythagorean *hetairoi*.[40] During the
Cylonian revolt, he was one of those who defended the supremacy of the
Pythagoreans (Apollonius of Tyana *FGrHist* 1064 F2).

About Alcmaeon's political activity nothing is known, but his theory of
health and disease – the first rational theory in Greek medicine known to
us – bore the stamp of distinctly anti-tyrannical and aristocratic ideology,

---

[37] DK 1.446.14; Diog. Laert. 8.83; Iambl. *VP* 104, 267; Simpl. *In Libros Aristotelis de Anima Commentaria* 32.3; Philoponus, *In Aristotelis de Anima Libros Commentaria* 88.11; Scholia on Plato's
Alcibiades I 121e.

[38] ἕτεροι δὲ τῶν αὐτῶν τούτων κτλ. (*Metaph.* 986a22ff.). It does not follow from this that Aristotle
had in mind any real group or individual. Rather, we are dealing with a separate theory. Some
scholars relying on this passage deny that Alcmaeon was a Pythagorean, see, e.g., G. E. R. Lloyd
1975: 125ff.

[39] In Photius' *Library* (115b7), Alcmaeon is unambiguously called a doctor (ἰατρός). He appears in the
company of such doctors as Diocles, Euryphon, Erasistratus and others.

[40] According to Hermippus, Democedes' father Calliphon also was a Pythagorean (*FGrHist* 1026 F21).

which was characteristic of the Pythagorean societies (*hetairiai*). "Alcmaeon holds that what preserves health is the equality of the powers [ἰσονομία τῶν δυνάμεων] – moist and dry, cold and hot, bitter and sweet and the rest – and the supremacy [μοναρχία] of any of them causes disease" (DK 24B4). Alcmaeon's "equality" (ἰσονομία) bears no relation to democracy, which it later came to signify (Meier 1970: 40ff.); it refers to equality within the political class, the thousand full citizens, ruling in Croton. *Monarchia*, the power of a tyrant, upsets that equality, just as the supremacy of one of the powers in the organism upsets their balance and leads to illness. This dynamic concept of illness introduced by Alcmaeon into Greek medicine constitutes the basis of humoral pathology, which was developed in several treatises of the Hippocratic Corpus and canonized later by Galen.

Alcmaeon asserted that all the sensory organs were linked with the brain by "passages" (πόροι), carrying sensations, and the brain was also the organ of thought. Only humans think; animals can only feel, and not think.[41] If the brain was disturbed or shifted, the sensory organs were incapacitated, for it obstructed the passages through which the sensations were conveyed (DK 24A5). This explanation, and indeed the whole of Alcmaeon's theory of sensory perception, presupposes that the "passages," of which he wrote, had some definite material substratum. Usually this is taken to mean the optic nerves: first, because they are easy to discover in dissection (the auditory nerves are much smaller in diameter); second, because Chalcidius (fourth century AD) testifies that Alcmaeon was the first to dissect the human eye (DK 24A10). Precisely what anatomical procedure led Alcmaeon to his discovery remains a matter of dispute,[42] as does the question whether he dissected human bodies or only animals, as most scholars suppose. Taking Alcmaeon's statement that goats breathe through their ears (DK 24A7), one may surmise that in dissecting the organs of hearing he found the Eustachian tubes (the ducts between the middle ear and nasopharynx), which he also took to be passages (πόροι) leading to the brain. Having found the "passages" between certain sensory organs and the brain, he postulated their presence for all the others.[43] Alcmaeon's fundamental discoveries were not recognized in full or at once. Philolaus and Plato supported him in what concerned the brain as the organ of thought, while still linking perception with the heart,[44] thus breaking

---

[41] DK 24B1a. Aristotle also stressed this difference (*De an.* 428b6–8).
[42] G. E. R. Lloyd 1975: 118ff., 124, comes to conclusion that Alcmaeon "may have done no more than cut off the eyeball" of an animal; Longrigg 1993: 59ff., on the other hand, believes that what is being discussed is a surgical operation on a human being.
[43] Harris 1973: 6ff.; Longrigg 1993: 58ff. On the Eustachian tubes: G. E. R. Lloyd 1975: 122ff.
[44] Philolaus DK 44B13; Pl. *Ti.* 70a–d, 77c–e; Harris 1973: 116ff.; Huffman 1993: 307ff.

Alcmaeon's causal connection between perception and thought. Even after his theory had been developed and experimentally demonstrated by the Alexandrian doctors Herophilus and Erasistratus (early third century BC), who described the sensory and motor nerves running to the brain, the Stoics, Epicureans and Peripatetics continued to place a reasoning part of the soul in the heart.

Relying on his medical experience and independent research, Alcmaeon was able to lend Presocratic philosophy a new "physiological" direction, focusing its attention on problems of the structure and vital activity of the human organism. Following his lead, other thinkers as diverse as Parmenides, Anaxagoras, and Empedocles turned their attention to these problems, which were absent from the thought of the early Ionians. Soon such problems would become a staple part of works of natural philosophy. Thus, Alcmaeon was first to formulate the basic questions of embryology (including issues of heredity) and try to answer them, though the methods then available very rarely allowed him to achieve definite results. Attributing a central role to the brain, and relying on an outward similarity, he supposed that male semen originated in the brain (DK 24A13). This theory was taken up by Hippo, who took a lively interest in embryology (DK 38A12–18). He linked his vital principle, moisture (ὑγρότης), with the soul, because the soul was born of moist semen, which in turn originated in the brain (DK 38A3). Hippo regarded semen as a product of the spinal marrow. As confirmation of his views, he referred to an original "experiment": "Hippo [...] believed that the seed flows from (spinal) marrow, and thought that his theory was proved by the fact that, if one butchers the males after the animals have mated, no marrow is found, because it has been exhausted, as you might expect" (Aristox. fr. 21 = DK 38A12). Anaxagoras and Democritus opposed the Pythagorean theory that semen originated in the brain and marrow, postulating that it was a product of the whole body.[45] They maintained that after copulation males lost not only part of their marrow, but also a substantial proportion of their fat and flesh (DK 59A107, B10; 68A141).

The notion of semen originating in the brain and spinal marrow survived in European science until the beginning of the eighteenth century. Alcmaeon's idea that there existed both male and female semen had an even longer life; from their union an embryo was formed, and the semen that prevailed determined the sex of the child.[46] This theory, which ran

---

[45] The last theory was widely accepted among the Hippocratics (Lesky 1950: 70ff.; Lonie 1981: 66ff., 115ff.).

[46] DK 38A13–14. Lesky 1950: 24ff., 162ff.; Lonie 1981: 125ff.

counter to traditional views,[47] took hold because it provided a more rational explanation of sex determination and the way a child inherited paternal and maternal traits. The theory of two types of semen was shared by Parmenides (DK 28B18), Empedocles (DK 31B63) and Democritus (DK 68A142), all of whom enriched it by adding new features. Hippo took over some embryological theories of Alcmaeon without changes, while modifying others in the monist spirit that was characteristic of him. Thus he thought that although the woman also possesses semen, it plays no part in the formation of the embryo because it does not reach the uterus (DK 38A13). Consequently, the sex of the child depends solely on the quality of the male semen: thick and potent semen produces boys, thin and weak semen girls (DK 38A14).

The more links, both apparent and hidden, we find between Alcmaeon, on the one hand, and Iccus, Menestor, Hippo and Philolaus, on the other, the more clear it becomes that he was the central figure in early Pythagorean natural philosophy. It is possible to discern in his book the common source of such divergent fields as Iccus' dietetics,[48] Menestor's botany, Hippo's theory of the soul and Philolaus' epistemology. The mathematical studies (*mathēmata*) of the Pythagoreans are as unthinkable without Hippasus, as their account of the natural world is without Alcmaeon. But whereas Hippasus' dependence on Pythagoras cannot be doubted, the situation with Alcmaeon is quite different. Being an independent thinker and a scientist, he was generally interested in problems not related to the interests of Pythagoras. His theory of the soul is one of the very few points where the influence of Pythagoras seems evident. Alcmaeon was the sole Pythagorean philosopher to teach the immortality of the soul; his theory looks like a transformation of metempsychosis into a purely philosophical doctrine. He understood soul (ψυχή) as the principle of life and movement;[49] its immortality is shown by the fact that, like all divine heavenly bodies, it is in constant motion: "For, indeed, all divine things are always in continuous motion: moon, sun, the planets and the whole heaven" (κινεῖσθαι γὰρ καὶ τὰ θεῖα πάντα συνεχῶς ἀεί, σελήνην, ἥλιον, τοὺς ἀστέρας καὶ τὸν οὐρανὸν ὅλον; DK 24A12). In this context ἀστέρας, which can mean "stars," most probably means "planets," and the emphasis on the continuity of the

---

[47] They are reflected in Aeschylus' *Eumenides* (657ff.), where Apollo asserts that only the father begets the child; the mother merely nourishes the fetus.

[48] The sexual abstinence of Pythagorean athletes (cf. above n. 8) is linked with the theory that semen originated in the brain and the marrow (Fiedler 1985).

[49] Although we have no direct evidence, it is possible that Alcmaeon, like Philolaus (DK 44B13), situated the soul (ψυχή) in the heart.

motion of all celestial bodies suggests that it was circular.[50] If this is so, there are good grounds to believe that Alcmaeon gained this idea from Pythagoras or one of his pupils.

5. Menestor

From Aristotle and the Peripatetic Nicolaus of Damascus (first century BC) we know that Alcmaeon in his book wrote also on plants.[51] The interest in plants was shared by Hippo, whose opinions are twice mentioned in Theophrastus' *Enquiry into Plants*,[52] and especially by Menestor, the first known author of a specialized treatise on plants. In the little surviving evidence Menestor appears as a natural philosopher and naturalist competent in matters of agriculture; Theophrastus counted him among the old natural philosophers (οἱ παλαιοὶ τῶν φυσιολόγων; DK 32A7); evidently, he was younger than Alcmaeon and older than Hippo (Zhmud 2012b: 126ff.). Menestor inquired about the causes of all the phenomena he knew of in the vegetable kingdom, and tried to explain the visible phenomena through invisible processes taking place within the plants (Capelle 1961: 65ff.). This method was first formulated by Alcmaeon,[53] who had much in common with Menestor. While Alcmaeon explained health through a balance of opposing "qualities," primarily cold and hot, moist and dry, Menestor transferred this principle to plants, giving primacy to a dynamic equilibrium of internal and external properties, which determined when they sprouted. He viewed moisture, or sap (ὀπός), as the bearer of life in plants (DK 32A2); by its nature this sap was warm, so those plants with most moisture were warm, and those with least, cold (DK 32A5). Excessive cold or heat led to diminished moisture, which meant that a plant either froze or died. Having divided plants into warm and cold, Menestor proceeded to establish their principal properties on the basis of this division: warm plants bear fruit, while cold ones do not; warm plants can survive only in cold places, and cold plants in warm places; evergreen plants retained their leaves because of their warmth, while those with insufficient

---

[50] According to Alcmaeon, people die because "they cannot join the beginning to the end" (DK 24B2), when the cycle through which life moves is broken. The planets were often called οἱ ἀστέρες, e.g., in Aristotle. Only a circular motion is continuous (συνεχής). In it the beginning and the end are joined (Arist. *Ph.* 264b9–28).

[51] Arist. *Hist. An.* 581a12 = DK 24A15; Nic. Dam. *De plantis* 1.2.44: "a man called Alcmaeon says that the earth is the mother of plants and the sun their father."

[52] See *Historia Plantarum* 1.3.5, 3.2.2, on the distinction between wild and cultivated plants.

[53] DK 24B1: "Only the gods have clear knowledge [σαφήνεια] of invisible things [περὶ τῶν ἀφανέων]; humans can judge only on the basis of evidence [τεκμαίρεσθαι]."

warmth shed their leaves, and so on (DK 32A3, 5). The maintenance of equilibrium between internal and external warmth and cold was evidently central to Menestor's theory, but it was not the only point. Location apart, he included the soil in the list of external factors (DK 32A6). It seems that Menestor, like Alcmaeon, did not place any limit on the number of opposing properties by which he explained the phenomena of the vegetable kingdom. At any rate, he wrote of an infinite number of savors (χυμοί), found in plants and distributed in pairs: bitter and sweet, tart and rich, and so on; whatever the mixture of internal moisture in a plant, such was its taste (DK 32A7).[54] Theophrastus took issue with Menestor, claiming, like Aristotle, that there are seven basic savors, because the number seven is "most appropriate and natural" (καιριώτατος καὶ φυσικώτατος).[55] On this question, paradoxically, Aristotle and Theophrastus occupy the position that Aristotle ascribed to the Pythagoreans and for which he criticized them, while Menestor – a real, not an imaginary, Pythagorean! – is untouched by the magic of numbers.

6. Hippo

Hippo, who has already figured in this chapter, was born *c.* 480–470. The author of at least two works of natural philosophy (DK 38A11), he was popular enough to be mocked by the comic poet Cratinus in his *All-Seeing Ones* (*Panoptai*) (DK 38A2), staged *c.* 435–431. Hippo's reputation (perhaps undeserved) of a staunch atheist goes back to Cratinus.[56] Since Aristoxenus named Hippo's birthplace as Samos (fr. 21), and Aristotle (*Metaph.* 984a4) and Theophrastus (fr. 225 FHS&G) attributed to him the same first principle as Thales, he was sometimes regarded as an epigon of the Milesian school. This is, of course, a misunderstanding, if only because Aristoxenus himself considered him to be a Pythagorean (DK 1.447.13). All other sources associate Hippo with the Pythagorean city-states of southern Italy.[57] Continuing the "physiological" trend of Pythagorean natural philosophy, Hippo mostly studied problems of physiology, embryology, botany and medicine. Even more than Alcmaeon he focused his attention on living nature, rather than nature as a whole; in the evidence available to

---

[54] Cf. χυμοί in Alcmaeon (DK 24A5) and Empedocles (DK 31A70).
[55] *De Causis Plantarum* 6.4.1–2. Cf. Arist. *Sens.* 442a12–28: the number of savors corresponds to the number of flowers, i.e. to seven.
[56] See DK 38A2, 4, 6, 8, 9. In Cratinus' *All-Seeing Ones* (*Panoptai*) Hippon asserted that the sun is a brazier and people are coals (DK 38A2).
[57] Croton (DK 38A11); Metapontum (DK 38A1); Rhegium (DK 38A3, 5; *DG* 610.14).

us there are no traces of cosmogony and hardly any of cosmology (cf. DK 38B1). His principle, moisture (ὑγρότης, τὸ ὑγρόν), is only superficially similar to Thales' water; strictly speaking, it is not the origin of all that exists, like air in Anaximenes or fire in Heraclitus, but only the origin of all *life*. In Hippo, soul (ψυχή) derives from moist semen, the source of which is the brain (DK 38A3). The soul is the principle of life and the senses and to all appearances is located in the head (DK 38A3). The soul is mortal, since, according to Hippo, the drying up of moisture is the cause of death (DK 38A11).

As Aristotle's student Meno reports, Hippo supposed that the bodies of all living things contain moisture that is characteristic of them (οἰκεία ὑγρότης),[58] and thanks to which they live and feel: "When such moisture is in its normal condition, the living creature is healthy, but when it dries up, the animal loses consciousness and dies [...] In another book the same author says that the aforementioned moisture changes through excess of heat and excess of cold, and thus brings on diseases" (DK 38A11, tr. J. Longrigg). Hippo and Philolaus are the only Presocratics mentioned in Meno's *Medical Collection*, a doxographical compendium containing theories of the origins of disease; all the other individuals mentioned here, except for Plato, were doctors. Hippo's material monism seemed primitive and vulgar to Aristotle,[59] but Theophrastus,[60] Aristoxenus (fr. 21) and Meno considered him as an expert at least on particular questions of what we call the natural and life sciences.

7. Theodorus

A mathematician, Theodorus of Cyrene (*c.* 475/470 – *c.* 400), was a very different figure. Theodorus figures in three of Plato's dialogues, but very little is reliably known about him. Apart from him, there are three other Pythagoreans from Cyrene in Aristoxenus' catalogue; one of them, Prorus, is featured in Aristoxenus' stories about Pythagorean friendship.[61] Most probably Theodorus came to Athens and lived there for a long period. Plato says that Theodorus' companion was Protagoras and his pupil Theaetetus

[58] By ὑγρότης in this context Hippon evidently meant the element common to all physiological fluids in the body, the element that in its turn depended on liquid food.

[59] *Metaph.* 984a3; *De an.* 405b1. Note that Aristotle (*Metaph.* 983b22–6) and after him Theophrastus (fr. 225 FHS&G) wrongly transferred to Thales Hippo's argument that the semen of all living creatures is moist (DK 38A3).

[60] See above, n. 52.

[61] DK 54A1, 3. How the Pythagorean community appeared in Cyrene remains beyond the reach of our knowledge.

(DK 43A4); his own teachers are unknown. The philosophy of Theodorus, if it existed, has not come down to us; indeed, Plato's words suggest that he did not engage in philosophy (*Tht.* 165a1–2). Xenophon referred to Theodorus as a "good geometer" (DK 43A5). In the later biographical tradition he appears as a teacher of Plato (DK 43A3), which is confirmed by the fact that Plato is the only source to mention his specific contribution to geometry.

Theodorus was the first mathematician known to us who taught professionally all four sciences of the Pythagorean quadrivium – geometry, arithmetic, astronomy and harmonics (DK 43A4). The formation of the quadrivium must go back to the Pythagoreans of the early fifth century, since Hippasus was familiar with all these sciences except astronomy. In the so-called catalogue of geometers in Proclus that goes back to Eudemus' *History of Geometry* we read that, after Oenopides of Chios, Theodorus and Hippocrates of Chios won fame in geometry (Eudem. fr. 133). This implies that Eudemus described at least some of Theodorus' discoveries (he dealt with Hippocrates in great detail), though this information has not come to us. Plato ascribes to Theodorus a proof of irrationality of the magnitudes between $\sqrt{3}$ to $\sqrt{17}$ (*Tht.* 147d = DK 43A4), which means that Theodorus relied on the proof of the irrationality of $\sqrt{2}$ that was found by Hippasus.[62] Theodorus' discoveries were further incorporated in the general theory of irrational magnitudes, developed by his student Theaetetus and set forth in Book 10 of Euclid's *Elements*. One more line connecting Theaetetus with the Pythagoreans, probably via Theodorus, is the construction of the five regular solids. Adding the icosahedron and the octahedron to the three regular solids known to the Pythagoreans – cube, pyramid and dodecahedron,[63] Theaetetus developed a general theory of regular solids.[64]

8. Echecrates, Simmias and Cebes

Theodorus was probably the eldest among the Pythagoreans who communicated with Plato. Philolaus' pupils Echecrates of Phlius and Simmias and Cebes of Thebes, who feature in the *Phaedo* as acquaintances and

---

[62] For reconstructions of Theodorus' proof, see, e.g., Heath 1921: 1.202ff.; Knorr 1975: 109ff.

[63] Scholia on Euclid 654.3. It is very likely that this information goes back to Eudemus.

[64] Theaetetus classified the irrational lines in accordance with the geometric, the arithmetic and the harmonic means, which also reveals his Pythagorean connections; on these three means, see above p. 96.

interlocutors of Socrates, belong to the next generation.[65] Interestingly, it is Socrates who, on the day of his death, teaches the immortality of the soul to skeptically minded Pythagoreans, whereas Simmias and Echecrates share a materialistic view of the soul. Contesting Socrates' arguments, Simmias says: our body is held together and tensioned by warmth, cold, dryness, and moisture, and other similar things, and the soul is their "blending and attunement" (κρᾶσιν καὶ ἁρμονίαν). Once the body is mortal, then the soul, as a combination of bodily properties, is also mortal (86b–d, cf. 88d3–4). The theory of the soul as an attunement (*harmonia*) was shared by Aristoxenus (fr. 118–21), who in his youth had heard Echecrates, and by his colleague and friend Dicaearchus (fr. 5–12). This theory is frequently connected with one of the metaphysical principles of Philolaus, harmony (ἁρμονία), which unites the unlimiteds (τὰ ἄπειρα) and limiters (τὰ περαίνοντα; DK 44B6–7),[66] though this leaves out of consideration that the cosmic harmony, unlike the mortal soul as harmony, is eternal.[67] That the theory of the soul as an attunement of bodily constituents could derive from medicine seems more convincing. In particular this is indicated by its similarity with Alcmaeon's teaching of health as a balance of moisture, dryness, cold, heat and other qualities, and of illness as a disruption of this balance (Burkert 1972a: 272). Revealingly, Simmias asserts that illness immediately destroys the soul as harmony (*Phd.* 86c), while Aristotle, criticizing this theory, insisted that it was not the soul that was harmony, but rather that harmony was health (fr. 45; *De an.* 408a1).

9.   Ecphantus and Hicetas

Simmias and Echecrates were the only Pythagoreans to share identical views on the soul; all the others known to us, from Alcmaeon to Ecphantus, one of the last Pythagoreans, held different theories of the soul. Ecphantus (first half of the fourth century) belongs to a group of Syracusan Pythagoreans, though in the catalogue he appears among the Crotoniates (DK 1.446.11), whereas his fellow-countryman and contemporary Hicetas, mentioned by Theophrastus (DK 50A1), does not appear at all. Ecphantus and Hicetas were first and foremost known for their theory of the earth's diurnal

---

[65] For some reason Thebes, one of the centers of Pythagoreanism in the fifth century, fell out of Aristoxenus' catalogue, so that Simmias and Cebes are absent from it. Besides Philolaus, Lysis of Tarentum also settled at Thebes and became the teacher of Epaminondas (Aristox. fr. 18).

[66] See, e.g., Huffman 2009.

[67] The first to attribute to Philolaus the theory of the soul as *harmonia* was Macrobius (fourth to fifth century AD), but his report (DK 44A23) could be based solely on an interpretation of the *Phaedo*.

rotation about its own axis (DK 50A1; DK 51 A1, 5), which was a modification of Philolaus' teaching that the earth rotates in twenty-four hours around the central fire. Ecphantus was the author of a philosophical treatise available to Theophrastus, who set out his views in some detail (DK 51A1–5), whereas Hicetas figures in the doxography only in connection with the theory of the rotation of the earth. Plato's student Heraclides of Pontus subscribed to Ecphantus' teaching that the earth revolves on its own axis;[68] through the late doxography this idea became available to Copernicus, who considered Ecphantus, Hicetas and Heraclides as predecessors of his heliocentric theory.[69]

In physics Ecphantus was an eclectic who combined the traditions of various schools. Following the atomists, he taught that the world consists of "indivisible bodies," differing in size, form and power, and the void (DK 51A1–2), but these bodies are moved "not by weight nor impact but by a divine power which he calls mind and soul" (DK 51A1). The latter idea recalls the theory of Anaxagoras, with, however, the difference that his Mind (Νοῦς) provided only the primal impulse to the cosmos, while ψυχή had the meaning simply of "life" and played no independent role (DK 59B12, A99–100). Combining the mind and the soul, like Democritus,[70] Ecphantus makes them the force that constantly moves both the atoms and the whole cosmos. As distinct from the theories of Alcmaeon and Philolaus, in which soul (ψυχή), separated from mind (νοῦς), was the principle of human life and movement, Ecphantus gives soul and mind a cosmological dimension. Though Ecphantus' philosophy differed from philosophies of the other Pythagoreans no more than was usual for this school, he seems to be an exception in being so heavily influenced by the theories of the other schools. In any event, he confirms once more that no "all-Pythagorean" philosophical doctrine was formulated up to the very end of ancient Pythagoreanism. Orthodoxy appears only in the late Hellenistic pseudo-Pythagorean literature, but this is founded not on the authentic Pythagorean tradition, but on Platonism and/or Aristotelianism.

Ecphantus' first principles are presented in the late doxography in two versions, according to Hippolytus (DK 51A1) and Aëtius (DK 51A2, 4), Hippolytus' account being more complete and reliable. The short lemma in Aëtius on the principles of Ecphantus, indivisible bodies and the void

---

[68] Fr. 104 Wehrli = 65A Schütrumpf. The idea of Voss and Tannery that Ecphantus and Hicetas were fictitious figures in Heraclides' dialogues was discarded long ago.

[69] *De revolutionibus*, Book 1.5.

[70] According to Aristotle, Democritus made no distinction between mind (νοῦς) and soul (ψυχή). See *De an.* 404a27 = DK 68A101, *De resp.* 471b30ff. = DK 68A106.

(DK 51A2), has this note attached to it: "for he was the first to declare the Pythagorean monads corporeal" (τὰς γὰρ Πυθαγορικὰς μονάδας οὗτος πρῶτος ἀπεφήνατο σωματικάς). Obviously, this has to mean that Ecphantus radically changed Pythagorean teaching, transforming originally incorporeal mathematical units, monads, into sensible bodies. Were it possible to trace this note back to Theophrastus' *Opinions of the Physicists*, an old theory of Tannery and Cornford on Pythagorean number atomism would gain support from a very reliable source.[71] But Pythagorean monads, which are absent in Hippolytus and the other testimonies of Aëtius, hardly have any chance of going back to Theophrastus' doxographical compendium. In Theophrastus we find only the teachings of individual Pythagoreans from Alcmaeon to Hicetas and Ecphantus, but not a trace of the collective Pythagorean theories, such as the number doctrine that Aristotle attributed to the Pythagoreans in general but to no single individual. The note in Aëtius, however, contradicts the logic and chronology of Aristotle, according to whom Pythagoreans constructed the world out of corporeal units, whereas Plato and the Platonists accepted numbers composed of abstract units, μοναδικοὶ ἀριθμοί (*Metaph.* 1080b16ff., b30ff.). In Aëtius, Ecphantus, a contemporary of Plato, appears as the first to declare "Pythagorean units" corporeal, as if hitherto they had been incorporeal! It is much more likely that the first to declare Ecphantus' indivisible bodies the "Pythagorean monads" was a Hellenistic doxographer interpreting his atomism in the spirit of number doctrine, known from Aristotle.

10.   Eurytus

The only individual Pythagorean to be connected with number philosophy by Aristotle and Theophrastus was Eurytus of Tarentum, Philolaus' pupil and teacher of the last Pythagoreans (Aristox. fr. 18). He left no written works, but one of his ideas is known from an account by Archytas, which was preserved in Aristotle and Theophrastus through the Academy.[72] Aristotle refers to Eurytus in the *Metaphysics* 13–14, in the context of criticism of the number theories of Plato and the Platonists. Discussing whether numbers can be the causes of things, he notes:

---

[71] For criticism of number atomism see, e.g., Vlastos 1996; Burkert 1972a: 41ff., 285ff. Knorr (1975: 43ff.) believed Ecphantus' ideas to be "the single potential confirmation of the thesis of Pythagorean 'number-atomism.'"

[72] Theophr. *Metaph.* 6a19ff. Theophrastus makes it clear that Archytas' account was oral: "the very thing that Archytas once said" (ὅ περ Ἀρχύτας ποτ᾽ ἔφη). See Burkert 1972a: 47; Huffman 2005: 593. For a different view of Eurytus see Ch. 8 below.

Once more, it has not been determined at all in which way numbers are the causes of substances and of being – whether as boundaries (as points are of spatial magnitudes). This is how Eurytus decided what was the number of what (e.g. one of man and another of horse), viz. by imitating the figures of plants with pebbles, as some people bring numbers into the forms of triangle and square. (1092b8–13, tr. after W. D. Ross)

Evidently Eurytus drew a silhouette, placed pebbles along the outline and by this means determined the number of a man or a horse.[73] However, to make use of man and horse in explanatory examples is a favorite device of Aristotle, one that he evidently took from Plato; it does not occur in the Presocratics. This makes it possible to explain why Aristotle says "by imitating the figures of plants with pebbles," although man and horse are mentioned earlier: Eurytus outlined plants with pebbles, and "e.g. one of man and one of horse" should be read as Aristotle's parenthetic remark. The expression "as points are boundaries [ὅροι] of spatial magnitudes" implies a line, a one-dimensional magnitude, the ends (limits) of which are points marked by pebbles.[74] The outline of a plant was composed of these lines. It is not clear what Eurytus meant by this; possibly it was a not altogether successful interpretation of Philolaus' thesis "all that is knowable has number" (DK 44B4).

11. Pythagorean friends

Most Pythagoreans of Plato's age listed by Aristoxenus remain just names, though sometimes he furnishes additional evidence about them. Thus, he tells an anecdote according to which Plato wanted to collect all Democritus' books and burn them, but the Pythagoreans Amyclas and Cleinias persuaded him not to do this, explaining that too many people already had copies of them (fr. 131 = DK 54A2). We encounter Cleinias of Tarentum in Aristoxenus' list and in one of his numerous stories about Pythagorean friends,[75] whereas Amyclas of Heraclea figures only in Proclus' catalogue of geometers as a mathematician and one of Plato's followers.[76] Aristoxenus' praise of his mentor Xenophilus, who died in Athens at the age of 105 "in

---

[73] Aristotle and Theophrastus cite no numbers, and those given by pseudo-Alexander (*In Metaph.*, 826.35ff. = DK 45A3), 250 and 360, are taken *exempli gratia*.

[74] By Euclid's definition, "points are the limits of a line" (γραμμῆς δὲ πέρατα σημεῖα; Book 1, def. 3). Aristotle treated πέρατα and ὅροι as synonyms.

[75] DK 1.446.28; Diod. Sic. 10.4.1 = DK 54A3; Iambl. *VP* 127, 239 = DK 58D7, on Cleinias of Tarentum and Prorus of Cyrene.

[76] *Commentary on Euclid Book I* (*In Primum Euclidis Librum Commentarius*), 67.8. On the Platonizing tendency of this catalogue see Zhmud 2006: 89ff., 179ff.

the full brilliance of the most consummate learning" ("in summo perfec-
tissimae doctrinae splendore" – fr. 20b, tr. Shackleton Bailey), presupposes
some philosophical activity of the latter. Among the non-philosophical
Pythagoreans of this time Damon and Phintias are worthy of mentioning. They feature in probably the most famous of Aristoxenus' stories
about Pythagorean friendship (φιλία).[77] Generally, φιλία is broader than
the relations between two close friends; it links even Pythagoreans who
are unacquainted one with another, obliging each of them to employ all
means to aid their "friends" where their lives or welfare are threatened.[78]
As distinct from the other heroes of such stories, Damon and Phintias
were close friends living together in Syracuse, when it was ruled by the
tyrant Dionysius the Younger. It was Dionysius himself who told Aristoxenus the story, after he had lost his power and was living in Corinth as
a schoolteacher. Some of his associates could not stand the Pythagoreans,
"claiming that their dignity, pretended trustworthiness, and freedom from
emotion would collapse if one inflicted on them with any considerable
degree of terror."[79] In a cruel test, Phintias was accused of being involved
in a plot against Dionysius and sentenced to death. He asked for a tempo-
rary release to settle the affairs that he and Damon had in common, left his
friend as security for his appearance and was allowed to go. When Phintias
against all expectations came back to die, all were astonished; Dionysius
asked Damon and Phintias to be their friend, but was refused.

12. Conclusion

In the variety of the figures of the sixth-, fifth- and fourth-century
Pythagoreans it is possible to perceive partly overlapping categories, but
hardly any feature common to all of them. It is only in the negative sense,
viz., in what is *not* to be found in the individual Pythagoreans, that they
constitute a remarkably homogeneous group. Indeed, we do not encounter
among them a single religious figure with even a distant resemblance to
Pythagoras the mystagogue and wonder-worker. No Pythagorean known
to us by name claimed to possess supernatural powers or was a proponent
of metempsychosis; no one looks like a member of a secret sect. They all

---

[77] Fr. 31 = DK 58D7; Diod. Sic. 10.4.3 = DK 55.

[78] Such are the stories about Thestor of Posidonia and Thymaridas of Paros, Miltiades of Carthage
and Posides of Argos, and other pairs of friends (Iambl. *VP* 127–8, 238–9 = DK 58D7).

[79] Aristox. fr. 31, tr. J. Dillon and J. Hershbell.

appear as rational as they can be, given the historical context.[80] Superstitious ritualists who avoided walking along main roads, bathing in public baths, talking in the dark, stepping over yokes and using knives to stoke fires, always turn out to be anonymous figures from the legendary, not the historical tradition – unlike the Pythagorean politicians, athletes, doctors, natural philosophers and mathematicians. If we do not want to isolate Pythagoras, separating him from the ancient Pythagoreans, his followers and the followers of his followers, we have to find a kind of common ground for them. Religion, however great a role it played in Pythagoras' life, does not seem to be such a common ground.

---

[80] The only religious figures among Aristoxenus' Pythagoreans were Aristeas, a famous wonder-worker of the seventh century, and Abaris, a mythical priest of Apollo (DK 1.446.16, 447.10). Both were associated with Pythagoras in the legendary tradition of the fifth century.

CHAPTER 5

The Pythagorean society and politics

Catherine Rowett

1. Introduction

It is not easy to discover the truth about Pythagoras or the early Pythagoreans. In this chapter, I draw on a variety of evidence about the political life of the period, and the Pythagoreans' involvement in it, some from authors concerned with the Pythagorean heritage, and some from historians interested more generally in the cities of southern Italy. I then add my own speculative reasoning, and a critique of the speculations of others. My aim is to give the reader some sense of the historical context, the problems involved in reconstructing the story, and plentiful references to the primary texts where what counts as evidence can be found.

2. Pythagoras in Samos, Delos and Delphi

All our sources attribute Pythagoras' political activity to his period in Croton. For the period before his emigration from Samos, the ancient biographers (citing various earlier sources, mostly of dubious quality) mention his birth, parentage, upbringing, higher education and research travels (to Egypt and Babylon, among other places).[1] We hear that he left Samos, aged about forty,[2] because Polycrates' dictatorship had rendered Samos inhospitable for a free and philosophically inclined person.[3]

Porphyry reports that Pythagoras established some institutions on Samos (including a school called Pythagoras' Semicircle, "where the Samians gather to discuss community matters").[4] So let us imagine that Pythagoras,

---

[1] Iambl. *VP* 19; Diog. Laert. 8.2–3; Porph. *VP* 11–12.
[2] On this chronology see Philip 1966: 195–6.
[3] Porph. *VP* 9 (citing Aristoxenus); 16; Strabo 14 638 (probably using Timaeus of Tauromenium, a fourth-century BC historian). Iamblichus places the departure from Samos later. See von Fritz 1940: 47–57.
[4] Porph. *VP* 9. The testimony sounds like speculation from contemporary geography.

after spending the first forty years studying and traveling in the East, leaves Samos, around 529 or 530 BC.[5] Then the second half of his life is spent establishing his own influence in the West. He was not absurdly young when he left Samos. Maybe he had already acquired a pious devotion to Apollo, after nursing his teacher Pherecydes through his final illness on Delos.[6] Such a formative event would explain why, according to the tradition, he first called at Apollo's oracle at Delphi, after leaving Samos. Perhaps it was Delphi that sent him to a part of Italy already linked to the name of Apollo.[7] Aristoxenus apparently claimed that all Pythagoras' ethical doctrines came from the Delphic priestess Themistocleia.[8] There is surely some truth in this idea. We know that Delphi took a cosmopolitan interest in the cities of Italy and Greece and was certainly capable of deciding that Croton needed a visitation.

The idea that Pythagoras arrived in Croton around 530 BC is based on the standard dating for Croton's conquest of Sybaris (510 BC),[9] and the assumption that Pythagoras was politically involved by then. We shall reconsider these constraints below.

3. Pythagoras in Croton

What happened when Pythagoras arrived in Croton? It is hard to say exactly, but all sources agree that his impact was dramatic and pervasive. Diogenes Laertius gives no detail:

> He set sail for Croton. And there he legislated for the Italians, and was greatly honored together with his disciples. They numbered something approaching 300 and they ran the city in the best possible way, so that the constitution was more or less literally "an aristocracy."[10]

---

[5] See von Fritz 1940: 91–2, favoring the testimony of Timaeus. On this date see further below.

[6] Porph. *VP* 15; Diod. Sic. 10.3.4, probably derived from Aristoxenus. Although some sources place these events later, they seem to me to belong here, though this is incompatible with the supposition that Pherecydes lived to eighty-five (as ps.-Lucian *Macrobioi* 22 claims; for Pherecydes' dates see Schibli 1990: 1–13). The claim that he died on Delos (not far from his native Syros) seems authentic.

[7] For Croton itself, Giannelli 1924 has only late evidence, from the lives of Pythagoras (e.g. Iambl. *VP* 50 presupposes an existing temple of Pythian Apollo in which Pythagoras addressed the children). But see Giangiulio 1989: 134–60 on connections between Croton and Delphi. If Croton's coins (with their tripod motif) antedate Pythagoras' arrival, they too testify to an existing Apollo cult (Burkert 1972a: 113). See the discussion of coinage below, and on the cult of Apollo Lykeios, note 23.

[8] Diog. Laert. 8.8. See Chapter 13 below. The very name "Pythagoras" may allude to Pythian Apollo, as Aristippus of Cyrene (fifth to fourth centuries BC), not entirely fancifully, suggests (Diog. Laert. 8.21).

[9] For alternatives, see below, section 4.   [10] Diog. Laert. 8.3.

Porphyry has a more elaborate legend:

> When he disembarked in Italy and arrived in Croton, so Dicaearchus says,[11] they were struck by his appearance: he had the look of a gentleman of liberal birth, with a gracious and orderly manner, voice and everything, and he seemed like someone well-travelled, naturally blessed by fortune and remarkably gifted in every way. Such an effect did he have on the city of Crotonians that when he had inspired the council of elder statesmen that was in charge of the city, by presenting a range of admirable ideas to them, the rulers then appointed him to deliver a youth mission program to the adolescents. And after that he was asked to address the children from the schools all congregated together, and then the women. Even a meeting of women was fixed up for him. (*VP* 18)

In Dicaearchus' imagination, Pythagoras' influence flowed from a charismatic personality. Perhaps this is the best available explanation, but if he arrived with a Delphic testimonial that will also have helped.

But what did Pythagoras say to these groups of citizens, and why these ones? Notice that Porphyry mentions no assembly of adult male citizens: Pythagoras first inspires the old men (γέροντες) – presumably the governing council; he then addresses young adults (perhaps males only), school-age children (perhaps boys only), and women (of unspecified age range). That the young people are late teenagers seems confirmed by the Council's instruction to deliver a youth mission (ἡβητικὰς παραινέσεις) – something for adolescents.

It has been suggested that these age-group assemblies indicate that Croton was a traditional society organized into age-related clubs (*hetaireiai*).[12] But no such context is implied: the assemblies seem to be newly arranged for Pythagoras, to enable him to instruct each group separately. The children are collected "from the schools," which probably implies that citizen children went to various private schools, not to a communal age-related training.[13] Some institutional structure – for military training and athletics – probably existed for the ephebic age-group, so that an assembly of young men would be easily arranged,[14] but Dicaearchus implies that a

---

[11] Dicaearchus was a pupil of Aristotle, late fourth century, and a contemporary of Aristoxenus. Fragments collected in Fortenbaugh and Schütrumpf 2001. His attitude to Pythagoras is skeptical, emphasizing the charismatic personality. See Chapter 13 below.

[12] Burkert 1972a: 115 (followed by Kahn 2001: 8). But Morrison 1956: 144–5 (to whom Burkert refers) is clearer that Pythagoras does not find this organization already in place, but rather "either reformed or reintroduced" institutions of the older Greek civilization.

[13] "Schools" could mean a series of age-group schools (junior to senior). But it makes better sense if boys were traditionally dispersed to random teachers, learning in small groups to no common agenda.

[14] See below on the connection with Apollo Lykeios.

gathering of women is unconventional, created especially for the occasion.[15] We should not anticipate the women's groupings that figure later in the story, nor assume that they were typical.[16] If Pythagoras later developed a program of social education through such groupings, he was probably doing something radical, not reviving the failed structures of archaic cities. It is more helpful to compare his project to Plato's famous suggestion, 150 years later, for founding a new society:

> They must send all the people older than ten years old into the fields, and remove their children from their current habits, which their parents also have, and raise them instead in their own ways and customs, which are the ones we described then. Would this not be the way they will most quickly and easily establish the city and constitution of which we have spoken. (*Resp.* 541a)

Indeed I would argue that there is more of Pythagoras in Plato's imaginary city than is traditionally supposed – much besides the saying that friends hold things in common, which is widely attested as Pythagorean.[17] Other aspects of the *Republic* – its philosopher rulers, their ascetic and coenobitic life, philosophy for women, the training in geometry, harmonics, rotational geometry and so on – mimic what Plato knew of earlier Pythagorean political establishments. Arguably, Plato's *Republic* is among our earliest evidence for Pythagorean politics, since it antedates virtually all our other sources.[18]

In our story, Pythagoras arrives with a mission from the Delphic priestess to instill excellence in Apollo's other city. His mission begins not with adult males, but with those still open to adjusting their expectations and aspirations: the children, the adolescents, the women.[19] Having won the

---

[15] Porph. *VP* 18. With *kai* in emphatic position, and no definite article, this means "*even* of women" (not "of the women too"). On women see below.

[16] As Burkert 1972a: 115 implies.

[17] κοινὰ τὰ τῶν φίλων. Pl. *Resp.* 424a, 449c5. Cf. *Phdr.* 279c; *Lysis* 207c10; *Criti.* 112e10; *Leg.* 739c2–d5. See Timaeus in Diog. Laert. 8.10, Schol. in Platonis Phaedrum 279, and Iambl. *VP* 81; von Fritz 1940: 35, 39. Porph. *VP* 33 attributes to Pythagoras both κοινὰ τὰ τῶν φίλων and ὁ φίλος ἄλλος ἑαυτός ("the friend is another self"). Iambl. *VP* 167 traces the notion of "calling the same things 'mine' and 'not mine'" (*Resp.* 462c) to the Pythagorean model. For resistance to these themes see Philip 1966: 140–1 and Garnsey 2005 (who ignores Plato's emphasis on shared property).

[18] I have not found this view in the literature. But cf. Pl. *Leg.* 711e; Morrison 1958; Minar 1942: 96–8. Aristophanes may also provide hints, including his portrait of Socrates in the *Clouds* (see Demand 1982).

[19] Interestingly Justin, *Epitome of the Philippic History of Pompeius Trogus* 20.4.13, reporting Pythagoras' missionary meetings, remarks that women are notoriously negatively disposed. He takes Pythagoras' success with them as evidence of his effective communication with the young (implying that the women were juveniles).

trust of the council, Pythagoras summons these assemblies. Where does he hold them? What does he say?

The earliest sources, relayed in Diogenes and Porphyry, record none of the content of these speeches. Yet Iamblichus, somewhat implausibly, recounts each one in detail, but without naming any authority. Perhaps he is using the opportunity to elaborate his own Pythagorean moral teaching,[20] or that of his source (conceivably Apollonius). Nevertheless it is possible that some details are authentic. For instance, Pythagoras does not speak to the different groups successively in one theater, but takes them severally to different sanctuaries: the boys to that of Pythian Apollo, the women to that of Hera.[21] What about the youths? One account reports that they were in "the gymnasium,"[22] most likely the military gymnasium under the protection of Apollo Lykeios.[23] As elsewhere, most famously the Lyceum in Athens, the ephebic gymnasium would be sacred to the wolf-god.[24]

There is surely something authentic in the way that Iamblichus distributes these meetings to chosen cult centers. Pythagoras was clearly involving the community groups in ritual activities, focused on Pythian Apollo for the children, Wolf-Apollo for the youths, and Hera for at least some of the women. In Pythagoras' speech to the schoolboys (imagined by Iamblichus), the association of Pythian Apollo with pre-pubescent boyhood is a running theme.[25]

One thing worth noting here is that the tradition clearly insists that Pythagoras spoke to the assemblies *within the context of polis religion*, invoking the cults of Hera, Apollo, the Muses and so on.[26] No "South Italian" religions or mystery cults are mentioned: there is nothing about life after death, reincarnation, abstinence or magic words. Iamblichus describes a Pythagoras who speaks of virtue, education, care of oneself, purity, sexual mores and honoring the gods. He does not think that Pythagoras gave Croton new doctrines or a strange way of life; his persuasion does not

---

[20] Dillon and Hershbell 1991: 63 n. 4 compare the speeches to those in St. John's Gospel.
[21] Justin 20.4.11. (Supposedly derived from Timaeus. See von Fritz 1940: 34; Morrison 1956: 143–4.) Iambl. *VP* 50.
[22] Iambl. *VP* 37.
[23] On Apollo Lykeios and the initiation of ephebes, see Graf 2009: Ch. 5.
[24] There is epigraphic evidence for a sixth-century cult of Apollo Lykeios in Metapontum and areas in the immediate vicinity of Croton. See *IG* XIV 647 (revised reading in *SEG* XLVI.1322), and *SEG* XXIX 956–62 (mid sixth century). Discussion in Graf 1987. See Hdt. 4.15; and for Crimissa, Macalla, Chone and Petelia in the hinterland of Croton, see Giannelli 1924: 188–95. Literary sources for an ancient cult of Apollo Lykeios in Metapontum are assembled in Giannelli 1924: 61–8.
[25] Iambl. *VP* 51–3.   [26] On the Muses see further below.

rely on rewards or punishments after death. Iamblichus maintains a clear distinction between the moral discourse to the city, couched in exoteric terms, and the secret teachings of the Pythagorean brotherhood.

4. Social and historical considerations

If the traditional dating is right Pythagoreans were the leading political influence in Croton and its regional cities for about eighty years after Pythagoras' arrival. But what exactly was their role? We are faced with a persistent difficulty, of disentangling stories about the Pythagorean "brotherhood" – an inner circle who studied arcane matters, shared some kind of secret passwords, perhaps a coenobitic life – from information concerning the influence that Pythagorean political leaders had on a larger community, the whole city of Croton, and the subsequent alliance of cities in southern Italy. It is implausible to imagine the whole population joining the Pythagorean philosophical circle.[27] What, then, was the wider political role of Pythagoras and the Pythagoreans?[28]

First let us sketch the political situation when Pythagoras arrived. It is widely thought that he came to Croton shortly after Croton was defeated by Locri at the Battle of the Sagra River, conventionally dated *c.* 530 BC.[29] Justin (epitomizing Trogus) suggests that Pythagoras revives the Crotonians' morale in the aftermath of that defeat:

> After this the Crotonians lost their interest in the exercise of military prowess or arms. For they hated the arms that they had taken up with such bad luck; and had Pythagoras the philosopher not been there, they would have given their life over to luxury [. . .] Having studied under all these [sc. the Egyptians, Babylonians etc.], Pythagoras came to Croton and by his authority recalled the citizens from the luxury they had fallen into, bringing them back to frugal ways. Every day he praised excellence. (Justin 20.4.1–2, 5–6)

Justin sees the city's post-traumatic disillusionment as the context for Pythagoras' mission, and thinks that the aim was to inspire the young men and boys to military enterprise.

---

[27] On the Pythagorean way of life, see Chapter 6 in this volume.

[28] For more detail on the historical evidence for this period see Minar 1942: Ch. 3. I dispute Minar's interpretation, particularly his insistence that the Pythagoreans were aristocratic and reactionary in their political leanings.

[29] Strabo 261, 263; Justin 20.2.10–3.9. Bicknell 1966 argues for a much earlier dating (570s) using material from Theopompus found in *Suda: Phormio*.

If Justin is right, Croton would evidently have lost a generation of young men in the disastrous battle, less than a decade before Pythagoras arrived. The citizens are now reluctant to risk provoking war; a whole generation of youth has been raised with a desire to enjoy life while they can, and not to follow their lost brothers into battle. Matching the lost generation of boys would be a generation of young women without husbands or potential husbands. It makes sense that Pythagoras needed to engage the women, and the younger children of both sexes, in raising aspirations.[30]

Besides this attention to women and children, we hear of young men flocking to join up with Pythagoras. Joining the clique apparently committed the member to a special kind of friendship, sharing of personal property, secrecy and a variety of special rituals or passwords whereby the members could identify who did or did not belong.[31] These details tell us little about what the recruits would have learned, or how it might bear on politics in Croton or in other cities where, eventually, they obtained positions of power and influence. As I shall go on to suggest, it is not helpful to think of the emergence (or decline) of Pythagorean influence in the traditional terms used for describing political conflict. The emergence of Pythagorean politics is not a coup or a revolution. It is a creeping enthusiasm for certain ideas and ideals. How would Pythagorean thinking have come to replace the earlier approach to government? If, as seems likely, the 2000 followers who joined, with wives and children, after Pythagoras' first speech,[32] were mainly younger citizens, rather than serving council members, then we can imagine that Pythagorean ideas would have spread upwards, partly as younger men became elders in their family, and partly as their attitudes and values spread to others, not just the wealthy but also ordinary citizens, thereby changing the rulers' options for internal policy. Similarly, as Pythagorean groups emerged elsewhere in the region, their greater loyalty to the Pythagorean way of life than to their separate *poleis*, and their pact of *philia* towards fellow members, would facilitate the growth of an alliance among the cities of Magna Graecia.[33] Not that this happened entirely without violence, however.

---

[30] On women see further below.   [31] See Chapter 6 in this volume.

[32] Porph. *VP* 20, citing Nicomachus (1st-century-AD Pythagorean mathematician, whose biography of Pythagoras is used by Porphyry and Iamblichus). See Burkert 1972a: 98–9.

[33] Porph. *VP* 20 seems to use the term "Magna Graecia," normally used to refer generally to the Greek colonies in southern Italy, to mean the voluntary adherence of members to the Pythagorean discipleship and community living, as though it named the Pythagorean political alliance. On the league of cities see below.

Many recent and not-so-recent accounts have suggested that Pythagorean ideology was reactionary, oligarchic, aristocratic and anti-democratic.[34] But thinking in terms of oligarchy versus democracy seems quite unhelpful here. The existing regime, when Pythagoras arrived, was evidently a council of elders (resembling the Areopagus).[35] No revolution or constitutional disruption is mentioned as Pythagoreans gain influence.[36] It seems more likely that the governing elders were themselves impressed by Pythagoras, and impressed by the ideas that their young men and boys were acquiring. There was a change in morale, and values, not in regime or constitution. There is no revolution but instead a creeping enthusiasm for Pythagorean ideas.[37]

Probably Croton remained an oligarchy under Pythagorean influence and beyond. But this need not mean that the Pythagoreans favored aristocratic oligarchy over other systems.[38] For the most part, the ancient sources do not speak, as modern histories do, of competing parties seeking power, or angling for popular support.[39] The Pythagoreans can hardly favor "aristocracy," if "aristocracy" makes property a criterion for influence. For, by all accounts, Pythagoreans owned no private property, lived a life of simple frugality, and promoted non-materialist values among both themselves and those they governed. Joining meant handing over one's entire wealth, for five years' probation. Only if not admitted could one reclaim the property.[40] A Pythagorean considers nothing *idion* (private): for friends everything is *koinon* (common).[41] So private property would be no mark of esteem or qualification for government, but rather the reverse. When Diogenes remarks that the 300 disciples who ran the city "in the best possible way" constituted literally an "aristocracy," he means neither that they were, nor that they were not, promoting aristocracy: he means that they ruled well.[42] Surely Pythagoras' age-related *hetaireiai*, his distribution of cult duties by age rather than inherited priesthoods, and his confiscation of members' property, precisely preclude inherited

---

[34] See Minar 1942: v–vii and Ch. 2, citing Krische 1830 and Oldfather 1938, against a minority represented by Burnet 1930, Thomson 1938: 349 and Thomson 1941: 210–19 (who had suggested that Pythagorean politics was mildly democratic).
[35] See Giangiulio 1989: 29.   [36] Cf. Delatte 1922a: 18; Minar 1942: 17.
[37] On the absence of any coup d'état, see Minar 1942: 8, 17.   [38] *Pace* Minar 1942.
[39] For caveats see n. 51 below. Also Timaeus supposes that the factions seeking to bring down the Pythagoreans opposed inherited privilege (see section 6 below), which has led to the idea that the Pythagoreans favored it, but there seems little evidence for either idea.
[40] Diog. Laert. 8.10; on issues of the monetary value of property see below.
[41] Diog. Laert. 8.23. See above, n. 17.   [42] Diog. Laert. 8.3.

status. Again the egalitarian aims of Plato's myth of the metals come to mind.[43]

These egalitarian ideals – against privilege, private property, depravity, hostility; for equality of opportunity, communism, the life of the mind and virtuous friendship – can we square these ideals with the history of southern Italy after Pythagoras' arrival? Two key events are, first, Croton's defeat of Sybaris,[44] and, second, Croton's dominance in an unusual political and monetary league of cities. The latter (to which we shall return, under *Coinage*) fits well with the idea canvassed here, of a spreading undercurrent of allegiance, as Pythagoreans with an overriding loyalty to each other increasingly dominated neighboring cities. Of this period, Iamblichus writes:

> It is said, then, that on moving to Italy and Sicily, he found those cities enslaved to one another – some for many years, and others just recently. By filling these cities with thoughts of freedom by way of his "hearers" in each city, he pulled them back and made them free: Croton and Sybaris and Catania and Rhegium and Himera and Acragas and Tauromenium and some others, for which he established laws through Charondas of Catania and Zaleucus of Locri. As a result of these laws these cities were the most well-provisioned legally and the most worthy of admiration for those dwelling in the vicinity, for a long time. He completely removed civil strife and rival views and difference of opinion, not just among his own associates and their offspring during several generations (as is recorded) but also generally from all the cities in Italy and Sicily, both in terms of their internal affairs and in their relations with the other cities. (*VP* 33–4)[45]

This supports my suggestion that the Pythagorean "revolution" was more philosophical than political. People came from afar to enroll, and to invite Pythagorean communities into their city. Such non-violent change side-steps conventional categories like tyranny, oligarchy, aristocracy and democracy; likewise it eludes standard models of revolution and regime-change. Immaterial ideas, values and allegiance spread by contagion, not by power, force or military success.

Croton's conquest of the notoriously wealthy city of Sybaris is harder to square with this picture. Roughly ten years after Pythagoras arrived,

---

[43] Plato's system for eliminating inherited privilege has been similarly misunderstood by those who use a simple-minded dichotomy between "elitist" and "egalitarian" political systems. An egalitarian system to facilitate equality of opportunity will reject existing criteria of privilege, but have its own criteria to select an elite by merit.

[44] Probably 510 BC, but see further below.

[45] Iamblichus' source is probably Nicomachus. Cf. Porph. *VP* 21–2. Porphyry inserts the comment "When Simichus the dictator of Centuripa heard him, he laid aside his dictatorship and he gave some of his property to his sister and some to the citizens" (*VP* 21).

according to the standard chronology, Croton defeated Sybaris at the river Traeis. Not content with victory, they then massacred the survivors, flooded the city and killed the civilians.[46] This genocide became a byword in the history of hostility of Greek against Greek.

Was this what Pythagoras had taught them to do? Diodorus, placing the battle in 510 BC,[47] explains it thus: the new despot in Sybaris demands the return and execution of some refugees, presumably his political opponents, who are seeking asylum in the agora at Croton – probably at the shrine of Hera.[48] Croton must choose: betray the suppliants, or protect them and expect retaliation. At first they favor betrayal, but they are then converted to the nobler choice by Pythagoras. This leads to hostilities. After a surprising victory, given their small army, the Crotoniates, angry and triumphant, kill everyone, instead of taking prisoners of war.[49]

There is nothing here about ideological conflicts between democrats and aristocrats, or commerce and gentry.[50] Diodorus mentions no such ideologies,[51] but speaks of moral motivation: whether to betray suppliants at Hera's altar, zealous hatred of a demonized enemy and so on. Such explanations, in terms of human psychology, are compatible with seeing Pythagoras as Croton's moral conscience rather than its political leader.[52]

If this still seems too violent for Pythagoras to have been responsible, we could experiment with an alternative chronology. Suppose that Pythagoras was prompted to begin his teaching by the moral decline associated with Croton's victory over Sybaris, not by falling morale after the defeat at Sagra River, as Justin had suggested.[53] His teaching on friendship and not punishing in anger might be measures to prevent a repeat of such atrocities, to replace rivalry with collaboration, substitute common frugality for competitive consumption, and devise a politics of friendship and humane justice: all corrections to the arrogance resulting from a magnificent defeat of the

---

[46] Sources for these events include Diod. Sic. 12.9.3; Strabo 6.1.13; Hdt. 5.44; Ath. *Deipn.* 12 521e–f. Some cite the lack of archaeological traces of Sybaris to support the genocide story (but see below on later references to "Sybaris").

[47] Diod. Sic. 12.9–10.   [48] See Ath. 12 522a for implied offence to Hera.

[49] Diod. Sic. 12.10.1.

[50] For explanations deploying these concepts see Minar 1942: 12–14.

[51] Minar finds support where Diodorus describes the dictator (Telys) as a demagogue and the exiles as *megistoi andres* and *euporotatoi*. Diod. Sic. 12.9.2. But surely Diodorus simply means that Telys bought the people's support by confiscating wealth from some fat cats and distributing it to the rest. It says nothing about what existing support he had: arguably it implies that he did not already have popular support; nor whether the fat cats were traditional gentry or commercial types.

[52] In Athenaeus the Sybarites not only killed Telys' opponents, but also some Crotoniate ambassadors, and had established some extravagant games to undermine the Olympics. These crimes cause Hera to vomit bile in the agora, and a fountain of blood appears in her temple (12 521d–e).

[53] See above, n. 29.

world's most gluttonous city. This otherwise speculative hypothesis finds support in Athenaeus (following Timaeus), who says that Croton became decadent *after* defeating Sybaris,[54] not after losing at Sagra River, and that Pythagoras' mission to Croton came *after*, not *before*, the destruction of Sybaris. Either chronology makes sense. Perhaps we could even combine them, if Pythagoras has to add new measures to curb the zeal resulting from his first revival of piety.

5. Pythagoras and the women

We have mentioned that Pythagoras chose to speak not just to men and boys, but also to women. They too would have a role in moral support,[55] and also in the renewal of cult. Pythagoras apparently introduced a combined sanctuary for the Muses, to regularize an earlier plurality of separate cults.[56] It is not clear why, though a connection with Pythagorean interests in music is tempting. There is no historical evidence to support Morrison's suggestion that the earlier cults involved ritual prostitution,[57] although Iamblichus' remark that having prostitutes was a regional custom (*epichorion*) is certainly strange.[58]

In Iamblichus' account, Pythagoras urges women to avoid animal sacrifice, to offer frugal home-baked goods, and to take their offerings to the sanctuary in person, not by sending a slave. He pictures Pythagoras reviving old-fashioned values, with time-honored domestic and religious roles for men and women. But should we not prefer a different picture, in which Pythagoras has a quite revolutionary and unconventional effect? Notice a widespread tradition whereby Pythagoras did not just teach women to be faithful wives, but made them part of an intellectual project.[59] As ever, it is hard to separate evidence about polis structures from accounts of the inner Pythagorean circle, but Iamblichus (*VP* 56, following Timaeus, it seems)[60] says that Pythagoras created an age-related *cursus* for women, identifying them with different deities at different stages of their lives (based on some arcane interest in the meaning of names). A woman starts as a *korē* when

---

[54] Ath. 12 522a.
[55] In Iambl. *VP* 54 wives are to take pride in letting the husband win an argument.
[56] Iambl. *VP* 45. Cf. *VP* 264 (from Apollonius) where a Pythagorean revival is marked by public sacrifice at "the shrine to the Muses established by Pythagoras"; and Diog. Laert. 8.40. See Boyancé 1937.
[57] Morrison 1956: 145–6.
[58] Iambl. *VP* 50. Morrison suggests that Iamblichus does not understand his source. But Iambl. *VP* 210, mentioning a preexisting taboo on sex in sanctuaries and public places is counter-evidence.
[59] Porph. *VP* 19.   [60] See also Diog. Laert. 8.11.

unmarried, becomes a *nymphē* when betrothed, a *mētēr* when producing children, and *maia* (a Doric dialect term) when her child has children.[61] What might such life-stage-groupings be for? Were they to privilege those with children and grandchildren over the childless? To encourage competitive virtue within each category? To distribute cult and ritual duties to different age groups? To provide support and opportunities for unmarried girls and childless widows in the aftermath of war? To assign identities and roles by age or experience, not social status or wealth? While some of these (particularly the first) could be ways to reinforce traditional aristocratic values, others (especially the last two) would be radical egalitarian projects. So which is the better reconstruction?

Another tradition names some women who held important positions in this sequence of sacralized life-stages: Porphyry (*VP* 4, based on Timaeus) says that Pythagoras' daughter "led the girls in Croton" and his wife led the wives. Since these were educated women, "leading the girls" might not just mean leading cult or maidenly duties, but might identify the girl's rank among students; or her role as an instructor for the women's class. Some sayings are attributed to Theano, his wife,[62] concerning modesty and ritual purity around sexual intercourse.[63] She is also said to have written "some things" (unlike her son, Telauges).[64] Diogenes and Iamblichus give the name Damo for their daughter,[65] and Bitale for a granddaughter (Damo's daughter, later Telauges' wife – Telauges being much younger than Damo, and raised by Theano after Pythagoras' death).[66] Much of this must be legend, but the names seem to be authentic, and the tradition that Telauges taught Empedocles fits the chronology, if nothing else.[67]

6. Coinage, money and measures

Many have been tempted by the thought that there could be some link between, on the one hand, the arrival of a monetized economy first in Ionia

---

[61] Diog. Laert. 8.10 describes a similar fourfold division of life for males in terms of seasons of the year.

[62] Diogenes Laertius attributes both to Theano. Iamblichus attributes one to Pythagoras (*VP* 55), the other to "Deino, wife of Brontinos" though he knows another tradition ascribing it to Theano (*VP* 132). Some traditions evidently made Pythagoras celibate, and Theano or Deino the wife or daughter of Brontinus.

[63] Diog. Laert. 8.43. The point of the remark that "when she puts on her shame again, after removing it for intercourse, she puts on what makes her a woman" is probably that apart from womanly modesty, which is a superficial mark of gender, there is no real distinction between a man and a woman.

[64] Diog. Laert. 8.43.   [65] Diog. Laert. 8.42.   [66] Iambl. *VP* 146.

[67] See the allegedly spurious verse of Empedocles, DK 31B155, quoted by Diog. Laert. 8.43.

and then in western Greece, and on the other hand, Pythagorean number
theory and Pythagorean politics. Pythagoras, growing up in Samos, would
have encountered coinage, newly invented in Lydia, as its applications
were first becoming apparent and as small denomination coins were being
invented to service a wide variety of transactions. This happened first in
his native Ionia. Coins start to appear in the western colonies marginally
later in the sixth century.

Could Pythagoras himself have brought the practice of making and using
coins, to places that had not previously had them? This idea is not entirely
plausible. In defending it, C. J. Seltman[68] appealed to the distinctive
incuse coinage[69] in Magna Graecia, and to the fact that in the late sixth
century (the period of rising Pythagorean influence and Croton's regional
dominance) there was some kind of "monetary union," characterized by
coins bearing Croton's tripod and initials (qoppa, rho, omicron), on one
side, and the motif and initials of another city on the other,[70] suggesting a
system of mutually recognized currency across the region. Seltman argued
that the chronology suggested a causal connection with Pythagoras.

The fact that these "monetary union" coins occur during the
Pythagorean period need not mean that the coinage was designed to secure
Croton's dominance, nor that it was inspired by Pythagorean policy, though
it may be symptomatic of these things. Seltman suggested that Pythagoras
himself invented the incuse coins, to illustrate his "Table of Opposites."
This seems unlikely.[71] Nevertheless the idea that Pythagoras might have
brought coinage with him from Ionia is partially credible, and was taken up
recently in Richard Seaford's ambitious attempt to connect the invention
of money with the invention of philosophy, in *Money and the Early Greek
Mind*.[72] Pythagoras is a prime example for Seaford, who suggests that by
introducing coinage, with the associated notions of value abstracted from
physical substance, and of measuring in discrete multiples of a common
(though arbitrary) unit, Pythagoras caused significant and related changes
in economic organization and metaphysical thought.

No ancient texts support this idea, unless the following text (from Aristoxenus, quoted by Stobaeus) is relevant:

---

[68] Seltman 1933: 76–80; Seltman 1949; Seltman 1956.
[69] I.e. coins stamped in relief on one side and the same design in intaglio on the obverse.
[70] Illustrations in Gorini 1975.   [71] Against Seltman see Philip 1966: 197–8.
[72] Seaford (2004: 266–83) considers Pythagoras and Philolaus, but lacks any satisfactory discussion
     of how money reached Italy, or of Xenophanes or Parmenides. On these issues see Philip 1966:
     Appendix I, n. 5.

Pythagoras seems to have revered the business relating to numbers [ἡ περὶ τοὺς ἀριθμοὺς πραγματεία] most of all, and to have advanced [προαγαγεῖν] it for the future by withdrawing [ἀπαγαγὼν] it from the usage of merchants.[73]

Here Pythagoras promotes one kind of "business with numbers," by abstracting them from another kind of "business with numbers." This need not imply that Pythagoras despises commerce; it may simply mean that he starts his inquiries from commercial calculations. Aristoxenus is probably playing with two meanings: does Pythagoras abstract arithmetic from its mercantile use for counting things, or does he take it away from the merchants, in order to move it forward? Aristoxenus might indeed mean that Pythagoras took it away from tradesmen, and into the academy, if the earlier stages of mathematical research had been undertaken by merchants to facilitate complex trading, banking, loans, interest and so on, and then, under Pythagoras, it became the preserve of philosophers and pure mathematicians, and was thereby advanced beyond the limited interests of practitioners.

Clearly Aristoxenus cannot mean that Pythagoras stopped the traders from using sums. Perhaps he even promoted coinage, and other standard units of weight or value in trade. Hints of such intervention have sometimes been detected in Aristoxenus' claim that Pythagoras was the first to introduce weights and measures to the Greeks.[74] This must be false, but could derive from something true. Since early coinage developed from tokens measured by weight, and the names for the older and larger units (antedating small coinage for minor transactions) are the names of old units of weight (e.g. the Stater), introducing those large monetary tokens was, in effect, parasitic upon first introducing standard weights and measures, to which issues of coinage could be pegged, on a local or pan-Hellenic basis. Such measures were surely already in use elsewhere, but in introducing matching coinage, Pythagoras might have standardized Croton's measures to match the ones he had used in the East. Such standardized measures would greatly facilitate shared currencies with other cities, and international trade.

Among recent attempts to discredit Seltman's theories, some are not well founded: Burkert, following De Vogel, argued that Sybaris, not

---

[73] From Aristox. *On Arithmetic*. fr. 23 (Wehrli), Number V 2 05 in Kaiser. Stobaeus *Ecl.* 1. Prooem 6; DK 58B2.

[74] Diog. Laert. 8.14 (DK 14.12).

Croton, had coinage first.[75] But this is apparently largely guesswork,[76] based on Sybaris's mid-sixth-century affluence, prior to its defeat by Croton. Certainly some coins have Sybaris' emblems and initials, so they should antedate its destruction. But the exact dating, relative to the first coins of Croton, is uncertain.[77]

Still, even if coinage arrived before Pythagoras, and the incuse technique was not invented by Pythagoreans but in Sybaris, say, at the very least Pythagoras had come from a culture in which money had been used for longer and for more things; doubtless he could see the potential economic and social advantages for Croton. Even if he did not bring coinage to Croton, he may have made it work as never before. This could indeed have helped with regenerating that city. The ancient sources mention no economic reforms, however.

Another question arises, concerning the fact that you had to deposit your wealth on joining the Pythagorean society. The reports imply that it was not just loaned, but became common property. This raises the following puzzle: in what form did you donate your property? Did owners of land or buildings transfer ownership of their real estate to the community, and then get the same land and buildings back, in sound condition, if expelled? Or did they donate their wealth in the form of money? The latter seems unlikely unless the economy was already fully monetized, with land being bought and sold for cash, not rented out for services or contributions in kind; but it requires a relatively advanced economy to have established a way of determining the uncontroversial monetary value of landed property.

One way to make sense of these traditions is to suppose that most postulants were young men (and women, perhaps) who did not own their family property. Perhaps they were the sons and daughters of propertied families. If some came from trading families, they might not yet own the family's workshop or ships and warehouses. Perhaps many were in their ephebic years. These young adults would not have much wealth to bring. Rarely would they be depositing large sums of money or property. And perhaps if they did own property, buildings or land, it was just ownership of the property that was transferred without measuring its monetary value.

So the idea of a community of friends having all things in common does not require measurable contributions of property, nor any assessment of

[75] Burkert 1972a: 113 n. 125; De Vogel 1966: 52–4.

[76] The idea is still offered as only a hypothesis in Kraay 1976: 163. I have seen no confirmation from datable finds. Detailed discussion on the chronological significance of the region's coinage in von Fritz 1940: 80–6. See also Kahrstedt 1932 and (with caution) Giannelli 1928: Ch. 1.

[77] Further discussion in Gorini 1975: 50–1 (who rejects the connection with Pythagoras, on chronological grounds) and Demand 1976 (who argues the same, on grounds of technique).

monetary value. They could do all this without the notion of monetary value at all.

7. Political opposition to the Pythagoreans

The Pythagoreans' years of political success seem to have extended well into the fifth century and over a large region, although there is only limited evidence for the details.[78] By contrast, the Pythagorean writers have plenty to say about the end of Pythagorean influence in the region, but their reports seem somewhat muddled.

Many authors mention a fire at the house of Milon in Croton, where influential Pythagoreans were meeting at the time. Some accounts say that all the Pythagorean meeting rooms, in all the Pythagorean-dominated cities, were torched.[79] As a result the leading officials in all the cities died, they suggest, and disorder followed. Diogenes Laertius reckons that Pythagoras died in this event (though he knows of variant versions in which he did not);[80] Iamblichus knows a version from Aristoxenus in which the fire happened in Croton, after Pythagoras had moved (in old age) to Metapontum.[81] He also offers a second version, from Nicomachus, and a third, with an alternative chronology, that he found in Apollonius.[82] Plutarch thinks that the arson attack happened in Metapontum, not Croton.[83] Most sources agree that Pythagoras was not killed, though they disagree on whether this was because he had left Croton, was temporarily absent, or was in the house but escaped. Most conclude that he was absent, and that only two people escaped (though there are discrepancies on the names of the two survivors).[84]

Most scholars think that these writers are confusing the circumstances of several periods of political opposition, which they combine into a single story of the end of Pythagorean control in the region.[85] Zhmud and others suggest that the reports of fires in the meeting places across the cities of the region refer to an event in the fifth century that signaled the end of the period of Pythagorean influence. But by then Pythagoras was not just absent but long dead. I do not think that we can be wholly sure about the

---

[78] For details see Minar 1942: Ch. 3.   [79] Polyb. 2.39.

[80] Diog. Laert. 8.39.   [81] Iambl. *VP* 248–9.

[82] Iambl. *VP* 251–3 (citing Nicomachus) and from 254 on (citing Apollonius). Nicomachus thinks Pythagoras was away caring for Pherecydes in Delos (see above, n. 6).

[83] Plut. *De Gen.* 583a–c.

[84] Archippus and Lysis according to Aristoxenus (Iambl. *VP* 250).

[85] See Zhmud 2012b: Ch. 2.4. Also Riedweg 2005: 104; Minar 1942: Ch. 4.

chronology, but investigating the reports will provide further hints about the Pythagorean political agenda and why it was under attack.

We shall start with the period when Pythagoras was still alive. Was there hostility during Pythagoras' own lifetime? Did he have to run for his life? Certainly politics in Croton was not entirely uneventful. Seemingly a dictator named Cleinias seized power briefly around 494,[86] which might conceivably have made Pythagoras emigrate to Metapontum. There are also references to Croton beleaguering "the Sybarites" in *c.* 476, which means either that Sybaris was re-occupied or that some exiles were still called "Sybarites."[87] According to Diodorus Siculus, Sybaris was restored in 453, and destroyed again by Croton not much later.[88] Furthermore the city known as Thurii, founded in either 446 or 444,[89] was apparently first called Sybaris.[90] Its citizens may have called themselves Sybarites.[91] Certainly the old hostilities between Croton and Sybaris extended into the fifth century.

Ancient writers mostly blame a man called Cylon for the fires that killed the Pythagorean leaders, so that the events have become known as the Cylonian conspiracy. Cylon, they claim, was someone who wanted to join the Pythagorean society, but on being refused after some years of probation, he became angry.[92] In distinguishing two distinct periods of hostility, modern scholars generally keep Cylon himself in the late sixth century, but separate him from the fire in the meeting rooms and the end of Pythagorean political dominance. But did Cylon object to Pythagorean political control in Croton? Or was he one of the Pythagoreans? The name "Cylon" appears occasionally among Pythagorean administrators; notably one such is listed as administrator (Exarch) of the subject city Sybaris.[93] So perhaps there was a squabble between Pythagoreans, not challenges from non-Pythagoreans in the sixth century? This is the view recommended by Zhmud.[94]

How might we square Zhmud's idea with the story that Cylon was a Pythagorean reject?[95] Here is one solution, fanciful but not impossible: suppose that Cylon had once applied to join, not because he liked the

---

[86] Dion. Hal. *Ant. Rom.* 20.7 makes Cleinias a contemporary of Anaxilas, 494–76 BC. See von Fritz 1940: 68; Riedweg 2005: 61; Mele 1984: 57; Zhmud 2012b: Ch. 3.1.

[87] Von Fritz 1940: 68–9.   [88] Diod. Sic. 11.90 and 12.10.

[89] Diod. Sic. 12.9–10 gives 446, but pseudo-Plutarch *Lives of the Ten Orators: Lysias* 835d and Dion. Hal. *Lys.* 1 date it 444 BC.

[90] Pseudo-Plutarch *Lives of the Ten Orators: Lysias* 835d. The change of name is confirmed by coinage. The discrepancy on foundation date may reflect the "refounding" under a new name.

[91] Cf. Hdt. 5.45, referring to Sybarites in about 443 BC.   [92] Aristox. fr. 18 in Iambl. *VP* 248.

[93] Iambl. *VP* 74.   [94] Zhmud 2012b: Ch. 2.4.

[95] Iambl. *VP* 252; Diod. Sic. 10.11.1.

Pythagorean ideology, but because he resented its power in Croton. Perhaps Cylon wanted power for himself, and tried to get it under the Pythagorean umbrella, hoping to undermine the Pythagoreans from within. This would explain why his name appears in lists of Pythagoreans; but also his failure in the loyalty tests, his anger, and his violent response. So what looks like a "rift within the Pythagorean society,"[96] could also be a conspiracy against them.

Turning to the fifth century and the end of Pythagorean political success in the region, we should consider what motivated the opposition at that stage. Presumably there was indeed some catastrophic event involving fires in the meeting rooms of the society's political wing; presumably if the attack brought down the administration in all the cities of the region, there must have been coordinated fires in several places, unless several leaders were gathered for some regional council meeting in Croton. But I see no reason to think that opposition to the Pythagoreans was either "democratic" or "oligarchic" in ambition. Apart from the brief period of tyranny under Cleinias, Croton seems throughout to have been run by a council of 1000 citizens. As we saw, Pythagorean political involvement did not alter the number or range of citizens participating in this body. The emergence of Pythagorean *hetaireiai* (clubs) in the cities of southern Italy seems to be the most likely route to influence on the young men from the ruling families. Any opposition to Pythagorean influence would therefore probably come from rival clubs of propertied citizens, offering not a different constitution but *different policies*. Presumably they chose assassination because widespread respect for the Pythagoreans left no prospect of a popular uprising.

As before, the standard political categories seem unhelpful. Perhaps the same is true for most of the political and legislative reforms attributed to intellectuals and philosophers in the archaic period. Not all (if any) of the known cases of this turned out reactionary or aristocratic in spirit. In Athens, the reforms of Solon and Cleisthenes tended toward democracy. And in Tarentum, more than a century after Pythagoras' involvement at Croton, the Pythagorean Archytas served repeatedly as general under a democratic regime.[97]

A complete treatment of Pythagorean political policy would need to investigate the history of Pythagoreanism in Tarentum, and particularly Archytas' influence there during the fourth century.[98] It is striking that the

---

[96] Zhmud 2012b: Ch. 2.4.   [97] See Huffman 2005: 8–18.

[98] For relevant material see Huffman 2005 and Chapter 3 above. Minar 1942: 86–92 suffers from insisting that Pythagoreanism was reactionary.

two survivors of the fifth century fire at the house of Milon, according to Iamblichus, were Archippus and Lysis,[99] apparently from Tarentum (which is whither Archippus then fled, suggesting that Tarentum was already a Pythagorean haven). Given the constraints of space here, we cannot do justice to the later history of that city, but its presence in the Pythagorean circuit already in the fifth century suggests that the Pythagoreans were not anti-democratic in principle. This in turn makes it unlikely that those responsible for overthrowing the Pythagoreans in Croton were motivated by some recognizably ideological considerations, such as promoting democratic or commercial interests over traditional aristocracy. Perhaps the key to the Pythagorean monopoly on power was their notion that friends have all things in common (a belief that eliminates all such ideological divisions). This may also be sufficient to explain why some who were not among their friends and did not have that powerful network of support might feel excluded from the corridors of power.

[99] See n. 84.

CHAPTER 6

The Pythagorean way of life and Pythagorean ethics

M. Laura Gemelli Marciano

1. Problems of method

Discussion of the Pythagorean way of life (*bios pythagorikos*) cannot be undertaken without considering certain methodological presuppositions. The topic has often been treated from a point of view that tends to neglect the fundamental role of the relationship with the divine in ancient Pythagoreanism. In Western civilization, the vision of the world is dominated by what the psychiatrist A. Deikmann calls "instrumental consciousness," a type of consciousness that enables us to act on the environment so that we will survive as biological organisms, but that for this purpose perceives reality as a series of objects that are distinct and separate from each other and from the subject, yet capable of being dominated and manipulated by that subject.[1] Instrumental consciousness employs rational categorization, analysis, control and acting. It emphasizes separation and reinforces egoism, causing people to forget that there is another type of consciousness that Deikmann calls "receptive consciousness," and that perceives reality more as a connected whole, with which one must be in harmony and which one must approach with disinterested attention and a spirit of service. This type of consciousness, in which the boundaries between the subject and environment are blurred, is characterized by intuition, acceptance and surrendering.

The Western scientific approach is on the whole characterized by the first attitude. It puts given items into categories and thereby "appropriates" them, but this practice can lead to distortion if the phenomena to be interpreted belong to the second kind of consciousness. It is far from clear that Pythagoras' actions and his relationship to the divine are rightly interpreted as fabrications, or – to put it more positively – as "devices" to

---

I thank Richard Matthews for translating the first Italian version of this paper and Carl Huffman for helping with the final English version.
[1] Deikmann 2000: 78–90.

impress or beguile the public. Ethnological research shows that shamans, spiritual teachers and other "life guides" are motivated primarily by service, acting mainly to help their communities on behalf of "the divine." What we know of Pythagoras and Pythagoreans calls for a framework of this kind, without which the sociopolitical impact of the movement would remain inexplicable. So such testimonies must be evaluated critically but also remembering that the sources may reveal traces of an original "receptive" attitude, which emphasizes harmony with the divine and one's role of service. A viewpoint dominated by "instrumental consciousness" cannot take adequate account of these features. Assessment of ancient Pythagoreanism has been influenced by the "normalization" of Pythagoras, with the purpose of denigrating him in his own time and of rehabilitating him in later times. Heraclitus tries to strip him of his wonder-worker's halo, calling him "chief of swindlers" (DK 22B81)[2] and a *polymathēs* who has created his own wisdom and "evil trickery" (*kakotechnia)* from books (DK 22B129). Herodotus (4.95) sees him as a *sophistēs*[3] to whom deceptive practices can be attributed (cf. his pupil Salmoxis). Plato transforms him into a *hēgemōn paideias* (*Resp.* 600a): a guide in education, a line taken also by fourth-century BC sources that propagate an image of him and his life that is highly rationalized. But the fact that Pythagoras was thought to be and considered himself as the Hyperborean Apollo[4] implies that the *bios* which he founded was inspired by a different type of "logic."

2.   The Pythagorean way of life: a life in the service of the divine

The *bios* and the ethics of ancient Pythagoreanism cannot be separated from its religious dimension.[5] Such a separation, found in some modern studies,[6] derives from accentuating its educative aspect in Plato and fourth-century-BC sources, but it remains alien not only to ancient Pythagoreanism, but also to the archaic Greek way of thinking whereby all human action is pervaded by religion. The ethical-religious dimension of ancient Pythagoreanism is complex and has a conservative side linked to tradition, but also a certain "otherness" in comparison to contemporary customs. This otherness derives partly from its introduction of elements extraneous to contemporary Greek culture and partly from the manner in which

---

[2] This presupposes the existence of a group of Pythagoreans (Riedweg 2005: 52) who followed their Master's example with regard to "practices."

[3] For the meaning of this term (used also for the purifier Melampus), cf. Burkert 1972a: 211.

[4] Arist. fr. 191 Rose (Ael. *VH* 2.26; 4.17). For Pythagoras' identification with this particular divinity and not with Apollo in general see Kingsley 2010: 39–42 and 100ff.

[5] Burkert 1972a: 185.   [6] E.g. Anton 1992.

it embodies preexisting traditions and precepts. Such an "inherent ambiguity," which characterizes innovative movements within religious and cultural traditions, constitutes the fascination of Pythagoreanism but also sowed the seeds of its own rejection by the very society that it helped to transform.

3. Pythagorean precepts

There is almost universal agreement that the precepts known as *acusmata* ("things heard"), or *symbola* ("tokens," "passwords"), short maxims which were handed down orally[7] and put into practice in everyday life, form the original nucleus of the *bios pythagorikos*.[8] Such precepts not only "ritualize" the life of the Pythagoreans with exacting regulations that frame it within a broad cultic context, but also allow them to recognize the presence of the divine and the *daimonic* in this world and to interpret the *cosmos* and its phenomena against the background of the journey that the soul must undertake to return to its original divinity. These precepts thus enable us to glimpse how the Pythagoreans relate to the mythical and cultic tradition, to the sphere of the divine, to society, to other Pythagoreans and to themselves. Space does not permit a full account of the wealth of these precepts, about which in any case a great deal has already been said.[9] However, three general

---

[7] The first evidence for a written collection and explanation of these sayings goes back to an otherwise unknown author (Anaximander of Miletus) of the end of the fifth century BC, whose book has completely disappeared. Most of them were cited by Aristotle in his work *On the Pythagoreans*. At an uncertain date (before the first century BC) Androcydes wrote a book *On the Pythagorean Symbols*. Both works were used by later sources. For a full treatment of the problems concerning the transmission of the *acusmata*, see Burkert 1972a: 166–92.

[8] Zhmud's (1992a and 2012b: 175–83, 192–205) thesis, whereby the "ritualistic" precepts derive from Anaximander's compilation and do not correspond to any concrete practice, problematically accepts only those *symbola* as original that match with our "rationalistic" point of view and is based on faulty assumptions. For the presupposition that people of wisdom and political judgment would not have been able to actualize such precepts, see below in the text. That the fifth-century-BC sources, the comic poets in particular, do not portray any Pythagorean who practices them is entirely irrelevant. Epicharmus is himself counted among the Pythagoreans; Attic Comedy is a distinctly Athenian affair, which unlike Middle and New Comedy, is not based on types but on the portrayal of real individuals who play, in the broad sense, a "political" role in the city. It is people like Socrates whom the Athenians saw in flesh and blood in the *agora*, who attracted the attention of a large audience, not the Pythagoreans, who were probably almost unknown in Athens at that time. Further, Zhmud forgets that the systematic assemblage of sayings, oracles and traditions of heterogeneous provenance is a specific feature of the *polymathia* not only of the fifth but also and above all of the second half of the sixth century BC (see Gemelli Marciano 2002: 97ff.). This means that the nucleus of the *acusmata* included "ritualistic" *acusmata* going back to Pythagoras himself, who is pictured as a "collector" of wisdom as early as Heraclitus; cf. Huffman 2008c.

[9] Hölk 1894; Böhm 1905; Delatte 1915; Burkert 1972a: 166–92; Thom 1994; Riedweg 2005: 63–77; Hüffmeier 2001.

remarks on their function and significance must be made before suggesting
a new standpoint from which to view them:

1. The *acusmata* are neither a hotchpotch of superstitious precepts, nor
   do they contain "a tremendous amount of absurdities."[10] Instead, they
   reveal full control over and awareness of one's own acts, while aiming
   at uncompromising preservation of purity and "attunement" of the
   individual with the divine and the human worlds. The particular
   attention paid to speech, food, clothing and behavior is crucial.

2. It is anachronistic to assume that the *acusmata* could not have been
   actualized by the aristocratic elite that dominated Croton without its
   being penalized by isolation.[11] At the end of the sixth century BC,
   Magna Graecia is in no way a realm of rationalism[12] and the presence
   of similar traditional and cultic precepts elsewhere shows that they were
   not occasion for scandal.[13] Further, as observed by Burkert (1982/2006:
   207), "much of this would hardly be noticed by people outside."
   Observance of the precepts then did not preclude social life at all, but
   simply dissolved certain unthinking habits and promoted living with
   a greater awareness of the energies that underlie the world and of the
   duties of human beings towards the gods and their own kind.

3. The mainly cognitive approach to these sayings, which characterizes
   many of the ancient sources as well as modern interpretations of them,
   risks obscuring their function and, in part, also their original significance. These precepts above all constituted an orientation towards
   how to live,[14] and had to be assimilated and actualized by individuals
   in order to change their attitudes towards reality. The precepts did
   not require explanation[15] but neither was it excluded *a priori*.[16] Their
   assimilation by individuals could have given rise to the various reworkings and interpretations that may already have been circulating in the

---

[10] Zhmud 1992a: 241.   [11] Centrone 1996: 80; Zhmud 2012b: 176.

[12] Note the flourishing mystery cults of Demeter and Persephone everywhere in the area (Hinz 1998)
and the emergence of the first *defixiones* in Sicily at the end of the sixth century BC (Jordan 1985:
174ff.).

[13] On similar precepts in Hesiod's *Works and Days*, cf. Parker 1983: 291–5. The *Pythagoristai* in fourth-
century-BC Attic Comedy are ridiculed in a very different historical and sociopolitical context.

[14] One may wonder if Philolaus' statement whereby "certain *logoi* are stronger than we are" (fr. 16
Huffman), which has been variously interpreted (Burkert 1972a: 85; Huffman 1993: 333ff.), may not
refer precisely to these "sayings" (this is the usual meaning of *logos* in the fifth century BC) that guide
the action of human beings.

[15] What Iamblichus (*VP* 82) puts in the mouths of the so-called *acusmatici*, viz. that the precepts are
divine maxims to be followed, not to be explained, may in part be true.

[16] Cf. Kingsley 1995: 324 with particular reference to the fifth century BC and to the tendency to
allegorize within Pythagoreanism itself.

second half of the fifth century BC when, after the expulsion and dias-
pora of the Pythagoreans, they needed to accommodate their tradition
and way of life to new geographical and socio-cultural settings.[17]
With these fundamental points in mind two new perspectives on the
acusmata are possible. First, they portray a dedication to and respect for
the divine that calls individuals to attentively, responsibly and correctly
perform the role that has been assigned to them. Second, they presuppose
a constant tension that arises from the individual's striving to be attuned
to the gods and to the cosmos, where bodily entities and phenomena
refer them to stages of the soul's journey or are tangible remains of the
primordial course of divine events.[18] The practice of the *acusmata* is thus
profoundly transformative, not only because it notably increases one's
power of concentration, but above all because it activates the mechanisms
of "receptive consciousness," requiring the subject to abandon egoism and
consciously focus instead on the "signs" of the divine presence and on
how to achieve harmony with its various manifestations in the cosmic and
social context.[19] Pythagoreanism had a great impact at the sociopolitical
level because its devotees were accustomed to making themselves "tools"
in adjusting their words and actions to the divine will. This of course does
not mean that they had to renounce the vigorous exercise of authority or
opposition to the authority of others; rather they did these things from a
standpoint, and with objectives different from those of common politicians.
Qua expression of a kind of open "receptive" consciousness, the practice of
the *acusmata* (*pace* Zhmud 2012b) does not preclude the development of
what we call "science";[20] if anything, it promotes it, since it permits a more
global vision of reality and develops an unusually advanced capacity for

---

[17] It is important to stress here, with Kingsley 1995: 324, that this tradition is "neither rigid nor fixed
but fluid and accommodating."

[18] It is in this sense that one must interpret the physics that emerges from the *acusmata*, since they
define the sea as the tears of Kronos and the Pleiades as the hands of Rhea, etc. (Arist. fr. 196 Rose =
Porph. *VP* 41), with clear allusion to the myth of succession. Here we have to do not with an allegory
that centers on the physical world and explains characters and events in traditional narration as
physical entities, but its exact contrary: a total inversion of perspective in which the physical world
loses its centrality in favor of the manifestation of the divine and the sacred.

[19] This attitude, being inspired by "attunement" and "service" towards the divine, is different from
that described by some scholars (cf., e.g., Bremmer 1999: 76ff.; Macris 2006a: 90) as a rational effort
knowingly calculated so as to attain the "advantageous" objectives desired (better chances in future
reincarnations, or, after death, ascending to the Islands of the Blessed) by "appropriate means."

[20] The dichotomy between religion and science is anachronistic and remote from the full panorama
of Greek wisdom in the period. For a discussion of these "presuppositions" that have their more
immediate roots in the philosophical historiography of the nineteenth century but fundamentally
go back to the *forma mentis* of Aristotle, cf. Gemelli Marciano 2007: 385–9. For further criticism cf.
Kingsley 1995: 292 n. 12.

concentrating and focusing. The development of natural and mathematical science is thus perfectly attuned to the practice of the *acusmata*; even in the later dispute between *mathematici* and *acusmatici*,[21] the *mathematici* do not reject this practice. What distinguishes the Pythagoreans from everybody else is thus primarily their attitude to reality. In what follows I will dwell in particular on precepts and practices concerning their relationship with the gods, the *daimones*, the dead, the family, the group and the outside world.

3.1. *Relationship with the gods and cultic precepts*

The *bios pythagorikos* is characterized by the basic principle that human beings are the property of the gods,[22] and as such must order their whole life towards the honor and overall satisfaction of the divine. All the Pythagorean prescriptions and prohibitions strive for agreement with the divine; their whole life is oriented towards following the gods by correctly interpreting and accepting their will.[23] That the attitude of the Pythagorean is different from that of the ordinary Greek – the latter stressing the egoistic dimension of his relationship with the gods – is exemplified by an anecdote deriving from Androcydes, author of a not-clearly-datable tract, *On Pythagorean Symbols*:[24] someone greets Thymaridas of Tarentum, as he begins a long journey, with the wish (common among Greeks) that he receive from the gods what he desires. He replies "hush!" (*euphēmein*), wishing instead to accept whatever the gods send him.[25] What matters is not the dating of this anecdote, but the attitude it portrays.

This unselfish "acceptance" promotes openness towards all manifestations of the divine, especially what is beyond the capacity of human understanding. One *acusma* says that one should not disbelieve anything about the gods, even if it appears strange;[26] this absolute attention to the divine constrains the natural insolence and varied impulses of man, who always

[21] On this controversial point see Burkert 1972a: 192–208; Riedweg 2005: 106–8; Zhmud 2012b: 183–92.

[22] Pl. *Phd.* 62b (Philolaus).

[23] Iambl. *VP* 86ff.; 137; Aristox. fr. 33 Wehrli (Iambl. *VP* 174). According to Staab (2002: 317ff.) Iamblichus' expression ἀκολουθεῖν τῷ θεῷ is frequent also in Christian writers and reproduces the Delphic maxim ἕπου θεῷ itself variously reused both for Pythagoras/Plato and for Biblical figures, including Christ. Iamblichus would thus ascribe this concept to Pythagoras, transferring it from the Platonic and Judeo-Christian tradition. But Iamblichus' use of contemporary terminology need not imply that the concept cannot also be Pythagorean. Its very closeness to the Delphic maxim, given the Apollonian strain in Pythagoreanism, confirms its authenticity. The Delphic maxims were not the exclusive property of the oracle but were adopted also by "wise men": "know yourself" is also a Socratic principle.

[24] Not later than the first century BC: Burkert 1972a: 167 n. 10.

[25] Iambl. *VP* 145.   [26] Iambl. *Protrepticus* 21 (25); *VP* 148.

needs the gods' threatening supremacy to stay on the straight and narrow.[27] Such attention is reflected in those *acusmata* that regulate attendance at temples, sacrifice, cult and general respect for the gods. These play a central role in the *bios pythagorikos*.

Certain sources suggest that Pythagorean prescriptions on sacrifice and cult must have been more numerous than those that have been handed down. Iamblichus (*VP* 85) states that some *acusmata* went into great detail on how to perform particular sacrifices and on other cultic matters. Iamblichus' assertion is supported by a much earlier source: Isocrates refers ironically to knowledge of and innovations in cult as Pythagoras' special concern.[28] Thus it is highly probable that these prescriptions comprised a significant part of the original *acusmata* and the *bios pythagorikos*, precisely because they regulated the basic relationship with the gods. An almost entirely philosophical interest in Pythagorean teaching and a "normalization" by the later philosophical tradition probably caused many of these prescriptions to sink into oblivion; what remains reveals the tendency to incorporate precepts already in force in normal cult, while making them more restrictive and generalizing their application.

According to the principle that gods have absolute precedence over any other aspect of human life, veneration of them in a temple should exclude all other worldly business; neither speech nor deed should disturb it. Likewise one who passes a temple while engaged in business should not enter it or perform acts of worship, even if he walks right past the door.[29] Various precepts regulate access to the temple and to cult, in order to prevent pollution of the sacredness of the place or the act of veneration by improper behavior. Many sacred laws for specific cults in Greece take on among the Pythagoreans the status of generalized practice. One must honor the god by offering sacrifice barefoot,[30] in awed silence (*euphēmein*), clad in white, and pure.[31] Purification is a must,[32] but as another *acusma* prescribes, not in public baths or with lustral vessels (*perirrhantēria*) in order to avoid contact with impurities transmitted by others.[33]

---

[27] Aristox. fr. 33 Wehrli (Iambl. *VP* 174); cf. also the *acusma* in Iambl. *VP* 82: "What is the truest thing? That men are wicked."

[28] Isoc. *Bus.* 28, cf. Huffman 1999b: 71; Riedweg 2005: 63ff.   [29] Iambl. *Protr.* 21 (1–2).

[30] Iambl. *Protr.* 21 (3); *VP* 85. For the same precept in mystery rites, cf. the sacred laws of Andania (*LSCG* 65.13), Lycosura (*LSCG* 68.6), Ialysus (*LSCG* 136.25ff.) and Delatte 1922b: 231.

[31] Diog. Laert. 8.33 (from Alexander Polyhistor); (for Pythagoras) Iambl. *VP* 100; cf. also Diog. Laert. 8.19. Cf. the sacred law of Andania *LSCG* 65.13 (white garment); 39–41 (awed silence).

[32] Diog. Laert. 8.33 (from Alexander Polyhistor).

[33] Iambl. *VP* 83. In the *perirrhantērion* one was purified by sprinkling oneself with lustral water, in a sacred space (public or private). The Pythagoreans rightly questioned this usage as a source of pollution.

The precepts regarding purity are even more crucial in the case of sacrifice, which plays a central role in Pythagoreanism (one *acusma* defines it as the most just act).[34] Thus, as in Hesiod, it is forbidden to cut one's fingernails at a sacrifice; as bodily discharges, these are impure. Unlike other worshippers, Pythagoreans must pour libations from the handle of the cup, in order that they may not drink – as Iamblichus relates – from the side from which the libation was made.[35]

3.2.   Non-contamination of the divine

The need to avoid contamination of the divine underlies the precepts that forbid using objects normally employed in cult for profane purposes. Thus it is forbidden to purify one's body or clean one's teeth with certain plants such as cedar, laurel and cypress, which are usually dedicated to the gods as sacrificial offerings.[36] Coffins cannot be made of cypress, whose rot-resistant wood was used for statues of the gods and in building temples.[37] The prohibition against plucking a wreath is to be explained in the same way; wreaths are a basic element in Greek cults[38] and as such they belong to the gods.

Various other prohibitions are also directed against contaminating the divine, such as those against wearing rings with a depiction of a god,[39] poking the fire with a knife, cleaning one's seat with a torch,[40] or burning the dead;[41] the latter three seek to avoid contaminating a divine element (fire) with either something offensive (a knife),[42] or something connected with human impurity (a seat), or a corpse. The prohibition against urinating towards the sun, found also in Hesiod, has the same rationale, the sun being divine (and invoked in oaths). Thus the precepts are not "absurd" but consistently directed at respect for the divine.

---

[34] Iambl. *VP* 82.
[35] Porph. *VP* 42 (from Androcydes); Iambl. *VP* 84. The first-century-AD Pythagorean and wonder-worker, Apollonius of Tyana, added some further restrictions to the *acusma* suggesting that one should set aside a cup for libations and never drink from it but reserve it pure for the gods (Philostr. *VA* 4.20). Cf. Chapoutier 1928: 202.
[36] Iambl. *VP* 154.
[37] Hermippus 1026F22 Bollansée 1999a (Diog. Laert. 8.10). For how exceptional cypress-wood was in coffin construction, cf. Böhm 1905: 31ff.; Bollansée 1999b: 250.
[38] Blech 1982: 269–302.   [39] Diog. Laert. 8.17; Porph. *VP* 42; Iambl. *VP* 84; *Protr.* 21 (23).
[40] Diog. Laert. 8.17; Porph. *VP* 42; Iambl. *Protr.* 21 (8).   [41] Iambl. *VP* 154.
[42] It could also be seen as a threat and hence as an impious act.

The prohibition against swearing by the gods may belong here.[43] Syllus, a Pythagorean from Croton (fourth century BC) preferred to pay a fine rather than swear an oath, even though what he was asked to swear was the truth.[44] This anecdote may be authentic since it was possible to avoid taking an oath, although a penalty might be imposed; the sacred law of the mysteries of Andania (92 BC) prescribed that a priest who does not take an oath on investiture will be fined 1000 drachmas and replaced by a fellow-tribesman.[45] The Pythagoreans may have considered the oath superfluous and as contaminating the divine in a courtroom where human questions not involving the gods are treated. Here justice is the only concern, but this had the force of an oath for Pythagoreans.[46]

Avoidance of contaminating what is divine and keeping it separate from what is human explains why novices may attend the Master's teaching only after an apprenticeship in which they are examined, purified and "on trial" for years.[47] Pythagoras' teaching is clearly regarded as a ritual act emanating from a god[48] (the Hyperborean Apollo) and sacralizing the environment. Hence it takes place behind a curtain.[49] Like a temple *adyton* accessible only to priests, the space around the divine Master must be uncontaminated and available only to the completely pure.

3.3.   Purity of life

Even outside the strictly cultic sphere, individual purity is fundamental in avoiding absorption of negative energies that sully not only the divine but also one's own divine component. Thus even everyday Pythagorean life is "ritualized":[50] in their acts, gestures and words they must always consciously aim at preserving purity, respecting the divine and avoiding any action that might damage themselves or others.

The *bios pythagorikos* here exhibits a notable structural affinity with that of the priesthood of ancient Egypt, which was based on purity and

---

[43] Diog. Laert. 8.22 [He is said to have advised them] "Not to swear by the gods, man's duty being rather to render his own words trustworthy." See also Iambl. *VP* 150.

[44] Iambl. *VP* 150.   [45] *LSCG* 65.6–7.

[46] Diog. Laert. 8.33 (from Alexander Polyhistor): ὅρκιόν τ'εῖναι τὸ δίκαιον.

[47] Timaeus *FGrHist* 566F13 (Diog. Laert. 8.10); Iambl. *VP* 72.

[48] A parallel concept of the "lesson" as ritual in sacred space is found in the late work *Corpus Hermeticum*. In particular, this aspect is made clear in §1 of the *Asclepius* ("Hammone etiam adytum ingresso sanctoque illo quattuor virorum religione et divina dei completo praesentia, conpetenti venerabiliter silentio ex ore Hermu animis singulorum mentibusque pendentibus, divinus Cupido sic orsus est dicere").

[49] For this clearly non-Greek custom see Kingsley 2010: 154ff.

[50] On this particular aspect: Burkert 1972a: 190–3; Riedweg 2005: 90–3.

regulated by a series of prescriptions and prohibitions. An oath of Egyptian priests (the Greek text was probably translated from Demotic)[51] of the second century AD but containing precepts found in the *Book of the Dead* and thus preserving ancient Egyptian traditions, displays features akin to certain Pythagorean *acusmata* yet is not influenced by them.[52] We see here again the possible Egyptian influences on ancient Pythagorean rituals and customs.[53] The Egyptian priestly oath forbids going to impure places.[54] The same general principle underlies some Pythagorean prohibitions such as those forbidding travel by the main roads, use of public baths[55] and passing through a place where an ass has crouched down.[56] The meaning of the latter can be explained through the comparison with ancient Egyptian beliefs about the ass as wicked Seth's impure animal. Purity also applies to clothing, which must be of linen. Wool is forbidden, even for burial. As noted by Herodotus (2.81.2), this corresponds to Egyptian customs.

Purity of life entails food prohibitions. In Greece they characterized mystery cults;[57] in Egypt, food prohibitions varied from place to place, in conjunction with the sacred beast venerated in a given temple as a manifestation of a god. In neither case was total vegetarianism practiced. For the Pythagoreans, ancient sources portray much variety in prescriptions regarding meat-eating; these run from absolute vegetarianism[58] (which also forbade certain plants, such as beans and mallow)[59] to limited consumption of meat.[60] There are uncertainties here, but the first Pythagoreans were probably less rigid.[61] The meat prohibition was limited to certain animals or those not destined for sacrifice,[62] and to particular parts of them

---

[51] Quack 1997.   [52] Merkelbach 1968: 14.

[53] For a detailed treatment of the problem see Kingsley 1994: 1–5.

[54] Col. II.10ff. [οὐ μὴ ἐ]πέλθω εἰς τόπον ἀκάθαρτον.

[55] Porph. *VP* 42; Iambl. *VP* 83; Diog. Laert. 8.17. cf. Iambl. *Protr.* 21.

[56] Hermippus 1026F21 Bollansée 1999a (Joseph. *Ap.* 1: 164). The precept is attributed to Pythagoras himself and has been interpreted in the light of mystery cults, where fallen asses were connected with the underworld (Sansone 1997: 53–64), but there is no hint here that ὀκλάζω should mean "to fall" instead of "to crouch down." And besides, this precept focuses on the place where the ass has crouched down, not on the ass itself.

[57] Burkert 1972a: 177ff. pointing (with Delatte 1922b: 232) to the fact that such dietary rules were also typical for purification rites performed by wandering priests such as those portrayed in the Hippocratic treatise *De Morbo Sacro*, whose connection with the Pythagorean tradition is not to be excluded.

[58] Eudoxus fr. 325 Lasserre (Porph. *VP* 7); Diog. Laert. 8.20.

[59] Mallow is the holiest thing (Ael. *VH* 4.17). For its connection with the world of the dead, cf. Burkert 1972a: 185 n. 140. The prohibition of beans is proverbial, with countless ancient and modern explanations (Burkert 1972a: 183–5). For the ritual significance of the beans taboo and its links with dream-divination cf. Kingsley 1995: 283–6.

[60] Aristox. fr. 29a Wehrli (Diog. Laert. 8.20).   [61] Burkert 1972a: 180–3.

[62] Porph. *VP* 42–5; *Abst.* 1.26; Iambl. *VP* 85: the only animals into which the souls of men do not enter are those that can be sacrificed. For abstinence from animals that are not destined for sacrifice

(the *acusmata* list the heart, the womb and the brain, but the metaphorical interpretation foisted on them by the sources is influenced by strict vegetarianism),[63] exactly as happened in certain mystery cults.[64] Later on, as early as the time of Empedocles, vegetarianism may have become stricter. A comparison between the *Book of the Dead* (Ch. 125) and the Egyptian priestly oath of the Roman period referring to animal slaughter attests a similar evolution. The deceased Egyptian swears before Osiris that he has not killed sacred beasts, whereas the Egyptian priest swears that he has not killed any animal.[65]

3.4. Daimones, *heroes, the dead*

Daimones and heroes were an integral part of Pythagorean life, as they were of that of all Greeks.[66] After the gods, they too were recipients of sacrifice. Heroes only from midday onwards.[67] As with the gods, encounters with these numinous figures provoked fear because they could turn out to be destructive, but the Pythagoreans considered them normal, and used to be amazed if anyone claimed never to have seen a *daimōn*.[68] Heroes, commonly defined as *kreittones*,[69] received special cult worship at their tombs (*hērōa*) and were protective, but could be hostile to communities or individuals if disturbed or inadequately honored. In the Battle of Sagra (532 BC, before Pythagoras' arrival), the Crotonians had themselves experienced the power of the hero-protector of Locri, Ajax Oileus.[70] In this, the Pythagoreans are fully integrated into their place and time. They pay close attention to the presence of *daimones* and heroes who "communicate" by means of sounds and ringings, commanding a reverence that cannot be withheld. Some *acusmata* refer to these "voices": the sound of struck bronze is the voice of a *daimōn* entrapped therein;[71] the ringing in one's ears that

---

(*athyta hiera*) cf. the sacred law of Smyrna (cult of Dionysos Bromios, second century AD, *LSAM* 84.11). But already Semonides 7.56, describing a conduct of a careless woman, says that she often eats *athysta hira* (Nock 1944: 155 n. 53).

[63] Porph. *VP* 42ff. For the list of these dietary rules see Burkert 1972a: 180–4.

[64] On this see Burkert 1972a: 181–3.   [65] Merkelbach 1968: 20.

[66] Burkert 2011: 311–18. Although the English word "demon" comes from the Greek *daimōn*, for Greeks *daimones* are not inherently evil, see Burkert 2011: 276–9.

[67] Diog. Laert. 8.33 (from Alexander Polyhistor). The precept fully matches current cultic rules, cf. Rohde 1925: 116 and 140 n. 9.

[68] Arist. fr. 193 Rose (Apul. *De deo Socr.* 20).

[69] Hesychius s.v. κρείττονας· τοὺς ἥρωας οὕτω λέγουσιν, δοκοῦσι δὲ κακωτικοί τινες εἶναι, διὰ τοῦτο καὶ οἱ παριόντες τὰ ἡρῷα σιγὴν ἔχουσιν, μή τι βλαβῶσι. On heroes as protectors and avengers, Ar. fr. 322 K-A, Merkelbach 1967: 97–9.

[70] Burkert 2011: 316 n. 44; Giangiulio 1989: 239ff. n. 88.

[71] Arist. fr. 196 Rose (Porph. *VP* 41).

of the *kreittones*.[72] Sounds and ringings are to be heeded as the actual voices of *daimones* and heroes, whereas the *acusma* that enjoins showing reverence to the echo when it is windy[73] points to the need to appease the *daimones* that make the winds blow.[74] The prohibition against turning to look back on a boundary when leaving on a journey suggests the fear of attacks by *daimones*.[75] Caution in evoking these presences with involuntary acts probably underlies the puzzling prohibition against looking in a mirror beside a lamp. Delatte (1932: 152) explains that in the practice of catoptromancy gazing at a shining mirror causes visions. The reflection of the lamp's light would increase the shine of the mirror, generating worrisome apparitions.

Reverence for heroes explains two further *acusmata*. Since heroes were especially dangerous at nighttime,[76] one *acusma* prescribes silence in the dark,[77] so that heroes may not be disturbed or rendered hostile.[78] Another prohibits picking up food that falls from the table, since it belongs to heroes.[79]

In addition to being unmoved by encounters with *daimones*, the Pythagoreans also regard manifestations of the dead as completely normal, and supply instructions for recognizing them: they do not blink or cast a shadow.[80] One anecdote may go back to Pythagoras himself: he claimed that he was constantly accompanied by the spirit of a deceased follower, Calliphon of Croton.[81] Other anecdotes concern voices or apparitions in dreams of deceased individuals; these were held to be completely normal. When someone, who was grazing animals at the Master's tomb, told Philolaus' pupil Eurytus that he had heard singing, Eurytus expressed no surprise and merely asked what the melody was (Iambl. *VP* 139).

---

[72] Arist. fr. 196 Rose (Ael. *VH* 4.17).   [73] Iambl. *Protr.* 21 (7).

[74] Böhm 1905: 53ff.; cf. Rohde 1925: 204 n. 124.

[75] Porph. *VP* 42; cf. also Diog. Laert. 8.17. In Iambl. *Protr.* 21 (14) (as in Hes. *Op.* 724–59) it is the Erinyes who persecute the one who turns to look back.

[76] Chamaileon fr. 9 Wehrli. This may go back to at least the last third of the fifth century BC, since the Hippocratic treatise *De Morbo Sacro* also mentions nocturnal attacks (*ephodoi*) of heroes (8.13 Jouanna = VI 362 Littré).

[77] Iambl. *VP* 84; *Protr.* 21 (12) ("don't speak of Pythagorean matters in the dark"). Cf. Hesych. s.v. κρείττονας, cf. Böhm 1905: 51.

[78] The same reverence underlies observing silence when walking past a *hērōon* (Epicharm. fr. 163 K-A). See also n. 69 above.

[79] Diog. Laert. 8.34. Cf. Rohde 1925: 202 n. 114.   [80] Plut. *Quaest. Graec.* 300c.

[81] Hermippus 1026F21 Bollansée 1999a (Joseph. *Ap.* 1.164). The precepts that follow this item (not to pass through a place where an ass has crouched down (see above, n. 56), to avoid thirst-causing waters and words of evil omen) are (*pace* Sansone 1997: 59–61) hardly attributed to the deceased Calliphon, but to Pythagoras, to whom the Pythagoreans ascribed all of them. Further arguments in Bollansée 1999b: 235ff.

3.5.   Gestures and behavior

In archaic and classical Greece, gestures were very important as signals of psychological condition, social status and attitude towards others. Pythagorean punctiliousness regarding gestures and their ordering denotes an acute awareness that gestures contribute to the maintenance of cosmic harmony. Thus the prescription of presenting the right foot first, when putting on shoes, and the left, when washing (Iambl. *Protr.* 21 [11]), which is usually explained as "superstition," reflects a concern for order and the appropriate time (*kairos*) typical of other aspects of the Pythagorean life.[82] What one does first presupposes an order of gestures and a right moment for them: the right foot, being nobler, must be protected first, while the left foot, being baser, needs washing first.

In the Greek world as in ours, offering the right hand is a sign of good faith, friendship and alliance; thus for the Pythagoreans it was a sacred gesture not to be made lightly. One *acusma* forbids extending it to all and sundry.[83] In practice this means de-automatizing the display of loyalty and friendship; therefore it is not an expression of "sectarianism," but enjoins a behavioral stance, because it stresses the need for responsible action, no matter what disadvantages ensue (e.g. resentment on the part of those excluded).

For the Pythagoreans, counseling is a sacred duty, not to be undertaken lightly: one should give no other advice than that which is the best for the person advised; for counsel is a sacred thing.[84] This precept sacralizes one's relationship with others, presupposing a conscious assumption of responsibility, and codifying a behavior pattern that may turn out to be an enormous social resource.

Justice is a guiding principle for the Pythagorean community. It had the force of an oath[85] and involves reciprocity (ἀντιπεπονθός) and equivalence (ἴσον),[86] which is to say that it sanctions balance between two parties. The famous *acusma* often cited as an example of nonsense (ζυγὸν μὴ

---

[82] Cf. the training of memory in Iambl. *VP* 164–6 (possibly from Aristoxenus): the Pythagoreans recall in exact order what has happened and what they have said or done the preceding days. Aristotle reports that the Pythagoreans assigned a specific "number" to *kairos* (*Metaph.* 985b30; 990a23; 1078b22).

[83] Iambl. *Protr.* 21 (28); cf. *VP* 257; Diog. Laert. 8.17 (Pythagoreans offer their right hand only to their parents or to other Pythagoreans).

[84] Iambl. *VP* 85. "Advice is sacred" was certainly a widely known maxim (Burkert 1972a: 172 n. 48), but it was not specified that it must always be the best advice.

[85] See above, n. 46.

[86] Iambl. *VP* 179; Arist. *Eth. Nic.* 1132b21; fr. 203 Rose (Alexander of Aphrodisias *In Metaph.* 38.10).

ὑπερβαίνειν)[87] reflects this principle. It does not actually mean "don't step over a yoke" (as it is commonly translated), but "don't overstep the scales" ("scales" is the other meaning of ζυγόν by metonymy), thus don't add to the weight of the balance in one's own favor. Once again, a comparison with ancient Egypt is illuminating: in the *Book of the Dead*, the deceased declares that he has never added anything to the weight of the scales (Ch. 125 A 25–6). The priestly oath of the Roman era (col. II.9ff.) forbids even holding a scale.[88] Thus ancient sources are right in interpreting the *acusma* as forbidding the perversion of justice.[89]

4. Silence

The earliest sources already consider silence to be the hallmark of the movement. Reports that Pythagorean novices had to maintain five years of silence before being admitted to the Master's presence may seem implausible, but silence is not necessarily muteness.[90] In the mysteries, "silence" is mainly reticence about ritual, initiatory experiences, meanings of symbola and sacred tales. Ancient Pythagoreans display similar reticence: while nothing is known about what really happened in their gatherings, their founding myths are mentioned in enigmatic *symbola*, or in comparably obscure allegories; nor is much known about their experiences, other than some hints of Pythagoras' journeys to the underworld (*katabaseis*). In this context silence is likely to mean reticence (*echemythia*): even speech can be silence if it describes something inaccessible to the profane, for whom it remains a closed door. Reticence does not involve the superficial meaning of doctrines but their reception at a deeper level. Commentators are quick to stress that transmigration of souls is a widely known doctrine, but the mere doctrine says nothing specific about how incarnation and the liberation of the soul actually take place. In esoteric teaching, the communication of "doctrines" is actually much less important than the effects arising from practice. Pythagorean silence concerns not doctrine but experience and the profound transformation it brings about.

But silence is also to be interpreted literally: it is deep, attentive listening to the word of the Master[91] and to the divine within and outside individuals (*euphēmein* in mystery cult). The five-year period of silence involves all

---

[87] Diog. Laert. 8.17ff.; Porph. *VP* 42; Iambl. *VP* 186; *Protr.* 21 (13); *Theologumena Arithmeticae* 40.9 De Falco.

[88] Merkelbach 1968: 21.   [89] References in Thom 1994: 97 n. 18.

[90] On Pythagorean silence cf. the stimulating article of Petit 1997.

[91] Empedocles says this expressly (DK 31B5).

these meanings. This silence enables the Pythagorean to live in this world, as mystics working actively in society have always done in all periods, and does not prevent speech or action. The inner space created by this silence has to be protected because it belongs to the divine: hence one precept enjoins mastering the tongue more than anything else,[92] another forbids unrestrained laughter.[93] Too much speech or laughter would divert attention from the inner self, disturbing this silence.

5. Family and conjugal relationships

Pythagoreans thought that after gods and *daimones* one should pay the greatest attention to parents.[94] Family plays a central role in the Pythagorean way of life but, in contrast to the usual Greek picture, it is not seen as the private possession of the individual, but rather as part of one's duties towards the gods. The need to beget children is justified as ensuring continued worship for the gods (Iambl. *VP* 83), moreover procreation must take place in a pure environment and above all with one's legitimate spouse. Thus, if a man wants to beget children, he may not unite with a woman who wears gold jewelry,[95] i.e., with a *hetaira* or concubine.[96] Greeks separated *hetairai,* with whom they consorted for pleasure, from wives, who provided legitimate offspring,[97] but Pythagoras went further by trying to persuade the Crotonians to renounce concubinage.[98] That this was a theme of early Pythagoreanism is indicated by Pythagoras' report that, during a journey to the underworld, he saw adulterers being punished.[99] The same goes for respect for one's legitimate wife, whom one *acusma* equates with a suppliant.[100] As such, she is sacred and enjoys the protection of the gods. A remark by Pythagoras' supposed wife Theano shows that adultery was an ineradicable black mark. Asked when a woman becomes purified after intercourse with a man, she replies "with one's husband, immediately; with

---

[92] Iambl. *Protr.* 21 (6), cf. Riedweg 2005: 101ff.   [93] Iambl. *Protr.* 21 (26).

[94] Aristox. fr. 33 Wehrli (Iambl. *VP* 175). Parents are seen as benefactors (Hermippus 1026F4 Bollansée 1999a; Porph. *VP* 38). Aristoxenus' fragment refers to the conceptions of fourth-century Pythagoreans (see Huffman 2008d: 108), but respect for parents was probably even more important in early Pythagoreanism.

[95] Iambl. *Protr.* 21 (35).   [96] Zoepffel 2001: 178 and 196 n. 34.

[97] Burkert 1982/2006: 210 n. 81.   [98] *VP* 48; 195.

[99] Hieronymus of Rhodes fr. 42 Wehrli (Diog. Laert. 8.21).

[100] Iambl. *VP* 84: "It is not right for a man to pursue his own wife; for she is a suppliant. On this account also we bring her from her hearth, and take her by the right hand." Cf. [Arist.] *Oec.* 1344a10. Offering the right hand is a ritual gesture sealing a pact of fidelity (this character of the matrimonial rite is stressed in the literary sources, especially in Eur. *Med.* 21; *Alc.* 910–14; *Hipp.* 325–35; *IT* 1068–78), but also the acceptance of a supplication and the reception of the suppliant into the group (cf. Eur. *Supp.* 277–85; Naiden 2006: 71).

anyone else, never," thereby agreeing with the sacred laws up to a point but also diverging from them, since they envisage purification following adultery after a certain lapse of time.[101] The wording of the anecdote, although "reconstructed," recalls the atmosphere of the *acusmata*.

6. Friendship: a harmonious equality

Friendship (*philia*) is the cement that holds the group together and is based on "harmonious equality" (ἐναρμόνιον ἰσότητα) as defined by the Pythagoreans.[102] This calls for integration, harmonization and balance between individuals of disparate status within the group. The musical model, in which every sound has its place and cannot be altered without compromising the outcome, shows that the harmony of friendship also entails respect for the hierarchy of authority and awareness of one's position within it. At the top is Pythagoras, undisputed Master; younger pupils must be respectful of the elders assigned to them as mentors,[103] who must in turn provide them with loving service. What "instrumental consciousness" sees as "constriction" is perceived from the standpoint of "receptive consciousness" as the "service" and "obedience" needed to maintain social and cosmic harmony. The case of Damon and Phintias, who model the community of life and goods (according to the famous saying that "friends have all things in common" – κοινὰ τὰ τῶν φίλων)[104] between an old man and a youth, exemplifies the fidelity of the one and the trust and obedience

---

[101] Diog. Laert. 8.43: ἀπὸ μὲν τοῦ ἰδίου παραχρῆμα, ἀπὸ δὲ τοῦ ἀλλοτρίου οὐδέποτε. Cf. also Iambl. *VP* 132 who is uncertain about who said this. On sexual abstinence in the sacred laws, cf. e.g. *LSAM* 12.3–6 (Pergamon): ἀγνευέτωσαν δὲ καὶ εἰσίτωσαν εἰς τὸν τῆς θεο[ῦ ναὸν] οἵ τε πολῖται καὶ οἱ ἄλλοι πάντες ἀπὸ μὲν τῆς ἰδίας γ[υναι]κὸς καὶ τοῦ ἰδίου ἀνδρὸς αὐθημερόν, ἀπὸ δὲ ἀλλοτρίας κ[αὶ] ἀλλοτρίου δευτεραῖοι λουσάμενοι. Cf. also *LSCG* 124.9; 151A42.

[102] Diog. Laert. 8.33 (from Alexander Polyhistor); cf. Timaeus *FGrHist* 566F13 (Diog. Laert. 8.10 φιλίαν ἰσότητα).

[103] Diog. Laert. 8.22–3. Respect for one's elders rests on the principle that what precedes in time is worthy of greater esteem than what follows. In addition to the case of Damon and Phintias, other individual master–pupil relationships in early Pythagoreanism are worth mentioning. According to a source that is trustworthy because it is probably based on an inscription, Parmenides was the disciple of the Pythagorean Ameinias, who had brought him to "stillness" (*hēsychia* – with all the Pythagorean echoes that this entails); after Ameinias' death, Parmenides erected at his own expense a *herōon* in his honor (Diog. Laert. 9.21). This indicates a hero-cult; divinization of the master is in total accord with Pythagorean practices. Parmenides' formal "adoption" of Zeno (Diog. Laert. 9.25), a procedure unattested for any other disciple among the so-called Presocratics, also points to this tradition. This may confirm Strabo's note (6.1.1) that identifies the two Eleatics as *andres pythagoreioi*. Cf. Kingsley 1999: 150–7 and 249; Gemelli Marciano 2009: 120ff. and Gemelli Marciano 2013: 107–9.

[104] Timaeus *FGrHist* 566F13; Burkert 1977/2006: 208–10.

of the other, even in face of death.[105] *Pistis* (the pact of fidelity) may never be violated even in jest, nor should the bonds of friendship be broken with a lie or after misfortune, but only if one's friend is incurably vicious.[106] The image of Pythagorean friendship transmitted by Iamblichus is that of a living organism on which no wounds (ἀμυχαί)[107] may be inflicted. The vividness of this image and its medical terminology suggest that it belongs to the first Pythagoreans.[108]

"Harmonious" friendship applies also to the tutelage of the young by their elders. To define "reproach," the Pythagoreans have recourse to the semantic field of harmony. To reproach means to "re-tune" (πεδαρτᾶν),[109] which must be done gently and cautiously, showing solicitude for the youth and closeness to him.

"Harmonious equality" based on hierarchy includes women who were also possibly admitted to the teaching. Although the earliest sources for this information date back to the end of the fifth century BC,[110] there is no reason to be skeptical about its authenticity. In fact the transmission of esoteric doctrine to women was not unknown in archaic and classical times especially among the families of seers.[111] It is not surprising that Pythagoras, himself a seer, adopted the same practice.

7. Conclusion

This overview of Pythagorean precepts and behavior reveals close attention to all aspects of the visible and invisible worlds, to signs of divine presence and will in the cosmos and to cosmic order. Renunciation of the self and obedience to the gods and to the Master's prescriptions, seen from the viewpoint of "receptive consciousness," do not reveal a group solely

---

[105] Aristox. fr. 31 Wehrli. For this episode, which goes back to the first half of the fourth century see Riedweg 2005: 40–1; cf. also Cohen-Skalli 2010.

[106] Iambl. *VP* 102; 232.   [107] Iambl. *VP* 231.

[108] ἀμυχή ("scratch") is a technical term frequent in Hippocratic medicine (*Internal Affections* 32; *Epidemics* 7.1.32; cf. ἀμύσσω already in Hom. *Il.* 1.243; 19.284). Iamblichus' καὶ ἑλκώσεις reads like a gloss on a rare term.

[109] Diog. Laert. 8.20 (for Pythagoras); cf. Iambl. *VP* 197, 231 (πεδάρτασις = μεθαρμογή). The verb is the Doric form of μεθαρμόζειν (in the language of music "re-tune" [μεθαρμογή "re-tuning"], Ptol. *Harm.* 2.11; Iambl. *VP* 113).

[110] Bollansée 1999b: 275 n. 140. Kingsley 1995: 160–5 has also convincingly demonstrated that the allusion to "men *and women who are wise* about divine matters" in Plato's *Meno*, where Socrates introduces the doctrine of reincarnation (81a), is to Pythagoreans.

[111] Cf. the seers of Telmessos (Arr. *Anab.* 2.3.3), the family of Aeschines' mother (*SEG* XVI 193 and Burkert 1977/2006: 198 n. 29), the statue of the so-called Diotima, holding a liver (a symbol of her craft) in her hand, in Mantinea (420–410 BC; Flower 2008: 212–14 and fig. 18).

concerned with its own salvation and passively following a leader, however charismatic he may be (this is the picture that modern studies tend to give),[112] but rather individuals who have consciously and responsibly decided to subordinate their own individuality not only so as to serve the divine, the community and the world in a particular historical period, but also to leave a heritage for posterity, as in fact happened.

On the basis of the openness fostered by these presuppositions the Pythagoreans were able to lay the foundations for the study of mathematics and of harmony, but within a vision of the world very different from that of modern science, and above all rooted in a particular "receptive" attitude and lifestyle. This approach was also the secret of the success of Pythagorean science.

---

[112] The term "sect" often ascribed to the group is misleading because it suggests a negative image of "dependence." Furthermore unlike sects, the Pythagoreans do not want to proselytize; on the contrary, they limit their numbers and discourage converts (Riedweg 2005: 101).

CHAPTER 7

Pythagoreans, Orphism and Greek religion

Gábor Betegh

1. Pythagoreanism and Orphism: introduction

At the end of antiquity the relationship between Orpheus and Pythagoras seemed unproblematic. These two founding figures of Greek culture were thought to proclaim the same theological and metaphysical doctrines, although formulating them in different genres. Proclus, writing a millennium after Pythagoras founded his association (*hetairia*), declares that

> all that Orpheus transmitted through secret discourses connected to the mysteries, Pythagoras learnt thoroughly when he completed the initiation at Libethra in Thrace, and Aglaophamus, the initiator, revealed to him the wisdom about the gods that Orpheus acquired from his mother Calliope. (*In Ti.* 3.168.8 Diehl)

For Proclus, just as for his teacher Syrianus, Plato expresses the very same teaching in his dialogues. The Muse Calliope, Orpheus, Aglaophamus, Pythagoras, the Pythagorean Timaeus, and Plato are links in the unbroken chain of transmission of divine wisdom that constitutes the backbone of the Greek philosophical tradition and is at the same time the foundation of the right religious attitude towards the gods.

Proclus reproduces here almost verbatim a text that Iamblichus quotes from a work called *Sacred Discourse* (*Hieros Logos*), in which Pythagoras, its purported author, gives a first-person account of the story (Iambl. *VP* 146–7). The quotation enables Iamblichus to demonstrate that the core of Pythagorean theology, which takes numbers to be the divine first principles, as well as the exemplary piety of Pythagoras and his followers manifested in their religious taboos and precepts, issue from Orpheus' teaching. "If someone, then, wishes to learn from whence these men received such a

I am grateful for perceptive comments by Valeria Piano, Máté Veres and Carl Huffman. In preparing this paper, I received support from the MAG ZRT ERC_HU BETEGH09 research grant.

degree of piety, it must be said that a clear model for Pythagorean theology according to number is laid down in (the writings of) Orpheus" (Iambl. *VP* 145, tr. Dillon and Hershbell, slightly modified).

Much closer to the time of Pythagoras, the authors of the classical age show no knowledge of his initiation into the Orphic mysteries by Aglaophamus (the story is never attested before Iamblichus' text)[1] and are often far more skeptical about Orpheus, whom they tend to treat as a mythical character, just as we do. Nonetheless, already the earliest stratum of evidence about Pythagoras and his immediate followers assumes a tight connection with Orphism with regard both to cult and to poems of theological and eschatological content. Herodotus, composing his *Histories* about sixty years after Pythagoras' death, claimed in a much-discussed passage that "the so-called" Orphics and the Pythagoreans shared with the Egyptians a particular ritual prohibition, which is otherwise alien to Greek tradition and which proscribes burying the dead in wool. Because of a discrepancy between two alternative versions of the transmitted text, it is unclear whether Herodotus speaks about Orphics and Pythagoreans, and if so, whether or not he means to equate the two groups or, alternatively, about Orphic and Bacchic rituals, which he identifies as in reality being Egyptian and Pythagorean.[2] On either construal, Herodotus asserts a non-accidental connection between Orphic and Pythagorean funerary ritual, in all probability based on some shared and non-standard eschatological beliefs, which, as Herodotus adds, were explained in sacred discourses (*hieroi logoi*).

Other fifth- and fourth-century BC writers, being doubtful about the historicity of Orpheus, maintained that Pythagoras and his acolytes, far from drawing their wisdom from Orphic writings (as the Neoplatonists would later claim), actually authored those writings. Ion of Chios "says in the *Triagmoi* that he [Pythagoras] composed some poems and attributed them to Orpheus" (Diog. Laert. 8.8 = DK 36B2; cf. Clem. Al. *Strom.* 1.21.131 Stählin). Epigenes, an author plausibly dated to the early fourth century, wrote a treatise with the title *On Works Attributed to Orpheus*. According to the information transmitted by Clement, Epigenes discussed the authorship of four poems, the *Descent to Hades*, the *Sacred Discourse*, the *Robe*, and the *Physica*, and ascribed each of them to authors whom he took

---

[1] Cf. Brisson 2002. Brisson thinks that Iamblichus himself might have invented the story about Aglaophamus (2002: 421).

[2] Hdt. 2.81. The latter version, vindicated somewhat tentatively by Burkert (1972a: 127–8), is favored by most current interpreters. For a detailed, and to my mind still rather persuasive, defense of the former version, see Linforth 1941: 38–50 and now Zhmud 2012b: 224.

to be Pythagoreans – the first two to Cercops, the latter two to Bro(n)tinus.[3] The same tradition is recorded also by Cicero: "Aristotle informs us that the poet Orpheus never existed, and the Pythagoreans maintain that the Orphic poem now current was the work of a certain Cercops" (Cic. *Nat. D.* 1.38.107 = Arist. fr. 7, tr. Walsh). It is tempting to read Herodotus' remark in the same manner. He knew about "sacred discourses" that were attributed to Orpheus, and that provided the justification for the burial taboos, but Herodotus claims these texts to be of Pythagorean origin.[4]

The affinity between Orphism and Pythagoreanism was thus perceived very early on. There is, however, a fundamental difference. Whereas for the Neoplatonists the theology and piety taught and displayed by Orpheus, and following him Pythagoras, were supremely reverent and at the center of the Greek religious tradition, most authors of the classical age consider them as fringe phenomena, proclaiming outlandish myths and prescribing puzzling taboos and alien rituals.[5] While withholding value judgments, modern historians of religion would agree rather with the second view. Traditional forms of religious practice and belief that permeate the life of every Greek, from birth to death, from dawn to evening, during festivals and on regular days, are firmly rooted in the local traditions of the *polis*. As we shall shortly see, neither the phenomena related to Orphism, nor the beliefs and cultic precepts attributable to Pythagoras and his followers were integrated in these local ancestral traditions. What remains debated is how far membership in a Pythagorean *hetairia* or active participation in Orphic cult activities would actually oppose actors to their respective local traditions and exclude them from institutionalized forms of worship in the *polis* religion. Central to this problem is of course the question of vegetarianism, to which we shall return soon.

Modern assessments of the extent, nature and direction, of the connection between Orphism and Pythagoreanism remain widely divergent. Some find the association so close that, following a practice current in the earlier part of the last century, they use the coinage "Orphico-Pythagorean" to describe various cultic practices and eschatological ideas. Others emphasize the "fundamental differences" between Orphism and Pythagoreanism

---

[3] Clem. Al. *Strom.* 5.8.49 and 1.21.131 Stählin. For this dating, see Linforth 1941: 114–18, followed, with some reservations, by Gagné 2007: 7–8. On this dating, Epigenes might be identical with the one mentioned by Plato (*Ap.* 33e; *Phd.* 59b) and Xenophon (*Mem.* 3.12) as an associate of Socrates. For a later, Hellenistic, date, see Zhmud 2012b: 117. See also West 1983: 9.

[4] The text allows two readings. Herodotus might mean that the *hieroi logoi* are Egyptian (so Burkert 1972a: 219 with n. 10) or that they are Orphic/Pythagorean (so Graf and Johnston 2007: 142 and 175). I am inclined to the latter view.

[5] Cf. Edmonds 2008.

(Zhmud 2012b: 228) or argue that they were originally two largely independent and parallel phenomena that got confused on account of some perceived similarities (Kahn 2001: 21). As to the question of historical priority, some think that – even if not quite in the way described by Iamblichus and Proclus – Orphic writings could indeed serve as a major source of inspiration for Pythagorean philosophy and ritual precepts (cf., e.g., Riedweg 2005: 74–6; Guthrie 1993: 219–21). Others suggest that Pythagoreanism came first, so that "Orphism was the product of Pythagorean influence on Bacchic mysteries" (Bremmer 2002: 15) and that early Orphic poems were primarily, or even exclusively, composed by Pythagoreans (West 1983: 7–20; Kahn 2001: 20). Scholars are not less divided on the question whether the doctrine of metempsychosis, often assumed to be among the most important points of contact, originated with Orphism or was rather introduced into Greece by Pythagoras.

There is nothing surprising in this bewildering discord of voices about the nature of the relationship in view of the lack of consensus about the natures of the two terms of the relationship. It seems easy to agree with Guthrie: "Clearly, the best hope of discovering something about the relationship between Orphics and Pythagoreans lies in an examination of the two systems themselves" (Guthrie 1993: 217). But this is exactly where problems erupt; indeed, it is highly doubtful whether one can justifiably speak about "systems" to describe either Orphism or Pythagoreanism.

To be sure, the scholarly landscape has significantly changed since Guthrie first wrote these words in the 1930s. On the side of Pythagoreanism, Walter Burkert's epoch-making *Lore and Science in Ancient Pythagoreanism* (Burkert 1962b; Burkert 1972a) put the study of early Pythagoreanism on a new footing. By accentuating its religious aspects, and formulating strong reservations about its scientific side, Burkert's study inevitably brought Pythagoreanism closer to Orphism. At the same time, a series of fascinating archaeological discoveries has made Orphism considerably more tangible. A collection of tiny inscribed bone plates found in Olbia and dated to the fifth century BC strongly suggests that – at least there and then – Orphic communities existed.[6] The enigmatic inscriptions of the bone plates indicate a connection between Dionysus, Orphic cult, and an interest in the afterlife. The mention of *bacchoi* on the gold tablets found in Hipponion, and the reference to Dionysus Bacchius releasing the souls of the initiates on the gold tablets found in Pelinna, testify further to the Dionysiac nature (of at least some aspects) of Orphism. The same

---

[6] Cf. Rusjaeva 1978; West 1982; Zhmud 1992b.

finds invalidate the attempts of Zuntz to distance the gold tablets from Orphism and to ascribe them to Pythagoreanism.[7] Finally, the Derveni papyrus, the remains of which were found among the ashes of a funerary pyre close to Thessaloniki, and the text of which was probably written around the time of Plato, presents incontrovertible evidence that Orphic poems of theogonic nature were in circulation by the fifth century at the latest.[8] Most scholars would agree that the combined weight of this body of newly found evidence makes the hypercritical position of Wilamowitz and Linforth – according to which Orphism as a religious phenomenon is a figment of ideologically motivated modern scholarship – hardly tenable.

Burkert, already taking into account most of the new evidence and armed with his formidable knowledge of Pythagoreanism, summed up a brief but nuanced analysis of the relationship with a memorable image: "Bacchic, Orphic, and Pythagorean are circles each of which has its own center, and while these circles have areas that coincide, each preserves its own special sphere" (Burkert 1985: 300). This remains the most promising general characterization; it nonetheless requires due caution and possibly some refinements. Above all, it is not obvious what could count as the respective centers of Pythagoreanism and Orphism – or indeed, if they had such identifiable nubs at all. Moreover, we should not, I would insist, take Burkert's circles as referring to systems of beliefs, and practices connected to them, with internal consistency and fixed borders. Rather, I would suggest, there was a group of phenomena that can be by some broad characterization ranged under the heading "Orphism"; yet there is no guarantee that these phenomena have anything clearly specifiable in common, in terms of beliefs and practices, with all the other phenomena that can with equal right be described as "Orphic." The gamut of new and old evidence presses for a non-essentialist conception of Orphism. One common feature in Orphism seems to be an authority granted to poems attributed to Orpheus and their use in rituals, which were assumed to have an effect on the fate of the soul – but even this might be too strict because, for instance, Orpheus is not mentioned on the gold tablets, and we cannot be sure whether, and if so how, they were supposed to be connected to Orphic poems. On the other hand, one shared feature among Pythagoreans seems to be the

---

[7] Zuntz 1971. For recent editions and discussions of the gold tablets, see Graf and Johnston 2007; Bernabé and Jiménez San Cristóbal 2008; Edmonds 2011. For a fascinating account of the history of the scholarship on the gold tablets and Orphism, see Graf in Graf and Johnston 2007: Ch. 2. For a recent, and to my mind somewhat desperate attempt to question that all the gold tablets can be characterized as Orphic, see Edmonds 2011.

[8] Kouremenos, Parássoglou and Tsantsanoglou 2006; Betegh 2004.

observance of a set of religiously motivated precepts sealed by the authority of Pythagoras – but even this might be too strict, because we do not have sufficient evidence to show that all Pythagoreans adhered to these laws of conduct and there is reason to think that different Pythagoreans attributed different precepts to the founder. If so, some elements of the batch of Orphic phenomena can justifiably be linked, more or less closely, with some phenomena, no less multifarious, that we range under the heading "Pythagoreanism."

In the rest of this chapter, I shall substantiate these claims by presenting a number of examples and concentrating on individual actors, phenomena, and specific texts. First I shall focus on those features that are most commonly considered as the principal areas of overlap between Orphism and Pythagoreanism. The outcome, in some respects, will be on the minimalist side. In the second part of the paper I shall, however, suggest a few possible general and specific points of contact that have received relatively little or no attention.

2. Vegetarianism and metempsychosis in Pythagoreanism and Orphism

The most commonly mentioned points of contact between Orphism and Pythagoreanism are a belief in metempsychosis and, closely related to this, vegetarianism. On a common interpretation of Burkert's circles, these two are constitutive, or even essential, features of both Orphism and Pythagoreanism, and can therefore safely be located in the area where the two circles intersect.[9] I would suggest a somewhat different picture.

To begin with, I strongly doubt that all actors who were involved in Orphic religious phenomena were vegetarians or believed in metempsychosis. Take for instance the "Superstitious Man" as sketched by Theophrastus (*Char.* 16). Among the hotchpotch of taboos he observes and rituals he performs, he also visits the local Orphic initiators ('Ορφεοτε-λεσταί) on a monthly basis with his wife and children to repeat a set of rituals (τελεσθησόμενος). Surely, Theophrastus draws a caricature here. Yet the phenomenon he describes finds confirmation in *Republic* 2, where Plato describes itinerant priests, who perform their rituals according to a "hubbub of books of Musaeus and Orpheus," and who make rich individuals

---

[9] Burkert (1972a: 180–3) presents a more nuanced view about the place of vegetarianism among Pythagoreans, but his caveats are often disregarded. For a confident statement that Pythagoreans were vegetarians, see, e.g., Frank 1923: 223.

and whole cities believe that by means of sacrifices, purifications and incantations they can expiate personal and ancestral guilt and cure or cause harm, as the client wishes (*Resp.* 364b–365a). The author of the Derveni papyrus presents a comparable image of gullible people who pay for the services of those "who make craft of the holy rites" (Derveni papyrus, henceforward *PDerv*, col. 20.3–8). Although the clientele of these Orphic initiators was certainly in the sphere of Orphism, there is no compelling reason to suppose that the individuals involved switched to a vegetarian diet, believed in metempsychosis, or had anything to do with Pythagoreanism. The contact with Orphism, Orphic texts and *orpheotelestai* does not seem to bring about any standing alteration in the lifestyle of these people. Indeed, Adeimantus in the *Republic* finds these practices so reprehensible precisely because they make people think that they can secure various advantages for themselves simply by performing some ritual actions, without any deeper and lasting transformation in their ideas or comportment. Similarly, the Derveni author finds it disappointing and pitiable that people who have paid to go through the rites leave without any genuine understanding or real change.

What about the *orpheotelestai* themselves? We simply don't know. There is, however, clear evidence that at least some people connected to Orphism led an alternative lifestyle, that Plato calls "the Orphic life," the most conspicuous features of which were vegetarianism and abstention from bloody sacrifices (Pl. *Leg.* 782c; cf. Eur. *Hipp.* 952; Ar. *Ran.* 1032).

The evidence about vegetarianism among Pythagoreans is notoriously confused and confusing, ranging from a denial of Pythagoras' vegetarianism, emphasizing his predilection for certain types of meat (Aristox. in Aul. Gell. 4.11; cf. Diog. Laert. 8.20), through the attribution of abstention from some animals or parts of animals (e.g., Arist. fr. 195 Rose = Diog. Laert. 8.33–4; Iambl. *VP* 85), to strict vegetarianism (e.g., Eudoxus in Porph. *VP* 7) among some or all members of the group.[10] A unified explanation in which all these pieces of evidence find their places seems impossible. Nonetheless, I find it conceivable that different groups and individuals applied different rules. The very discrepancy among the sources indicates that there was a serious interest in relaxing vegetarianism in such a way that it did not block participation in public rituals involving animal sacrifice and feasting on the ritually slaughtered animals. Although dietary taboos were no doubt important in Pythagoreanism from the beginning and it could be that some Pythagoreans observed a fully meatless diet, it appears that a strict form of

---

[10] For a helpful overview of the different sources, see Guthrie 1962: 187–90. On how the first two might be harmonized, see Huffman 2012a: 167–74.

vegetarianism, allowing no exceptions, was not conceived as a core feature of Pythagoreanism. On the other hand, "hard core" Orphism seems to be characterized precisely by a complete avoidance of bloodshed and the eating of meat and the complementary use of alternative "pure sacrifices" (ἀγνὰ θύματα) based on honey and cakes.[11]

In a great number of sources, starting with Empedocles' staggering image of a father inadvertently slaughtering his son incarnated in a sacrificial animal and children killing their parents and eating their flesh (DK 31B137), adherence to the doctrine of metempsychosis is presented as a preemptory reason for abstention from bloody sacrifices and the eating of meat. The reasoning only works if souls can alternately be incarnated in humans and non-human animals. Yet, apparently even this version of the doctrine does not automatically imply vegetarianism. Plato, to all appearances, was fully committed to metempsychosis, including incarnation in animal bodies, in his late period. Nonetheless, he seems not to have observed or promulgated a meatless diet – indeed, he presents the vegetarian "Orphic life" as something rather distant. Remarkably, his disciple Xenocrates appears to have dissociated the two starting from the opposite direction, observing that the recognition of the fundamental relatedness of all ensouled creatures provides a sufficient reason to become vegetarian, without accepting the doctrine of metempsychosis (Porph. De Abst. 4.22 = fr. 252 Isnardi Parente).[12]

The new pieces of evidence make it more manifest than ever that the soul and its fate after death were of special concern in Orphism. On one of the Olbia bone plates we read "Dio(nysus)," then "truth" and then "body soul," whereas in the gravely damaged first columns of the Derveni papyrus the author discusses eschatological topics, including how to secure a safe passage for the soul by appeasing impeding daimones (PDerv col. 6). The steady growth of gold tablets found in various parts of Greece gives further detail to the picture. However, from this accumulation of data no unified, clearly specifiable doctrine emerges.[13] In particular, the new documents still have not provided incontrovertible evidence for a strong presence of metempsychosis in Orphism. On one of the Olbia bone plates, we read "life death life" below which the word "truth" is inscribed. Prima facie, it is natural to think that the sequence was meant to be repeated, and the

---

[11] See now also PDerv col. 6, where the magoi and following them the initiates perform bloodless sacrifices involving sacrificial cakes, and wineless libations.

[12] See Chapter 12, section 3 below.

[13] In this stronger sense, Wilamowitz's often-quoted dictum "One should still prove that there was an Orphic doctrine of the soul" (Wilamowitz-Moellendorff 1931–1932 Vol. 2: 194) remains valid.

second mention of "life" refers to a new incarnation. This is, however, not necessary. On the Pelinna gold leaves the soul of the deceased is greeted by the words: "Now you have died and now you have been born, O thrice happy, on this very day." Surely, rebirth in this case does not mean reincarnation, but a new, better, life after death; the second mention of life following death might mean the same on the Olbia bone plate (Graf 2011: 56). The most explicit reference to metempsychosis remains line 5 of one of the Thurii tablets (Bernabé no. 488 = Graf–Johnston no. 5): "I have flown out of the heavy difficult circle."

The strongest pieces of evidence come from Plato. In a well-known passage of the *Meno* Socrates evokes "priests and priestesses who have made it their concern to be able to give an account (*logos*) of their practices" and who teach that the immortal soul is periodically reincarnated and punished for previous sins (81a10–d4). Plato also associates the *logoi* of these officiants with a quotation from Pindar in which we hear about "the ancient grief" of Persephone (fr. 133). This, in turn, is often, although by no means unanimously, taken to refer to the myth tracing the origins of mankind to the ashes of the Titans who had torn apart and devoured Persephone's child, the young Dionysus, and were struck by Zeus' thunderbolt in punishment.[14]

Although less often quoted, a passage from the *Laws* is also relevant:

> we must tell the account which is so strongly believed by many when they hear it from those who seriously concern themselves with these matters in the mystic rites [*teletai*]: retribution comes in Hades for such [crimes], and when the person returns to this world again from there, one is necessarily obliged to pay the full penalty according to natural justice and suffer the same thing he had meted out to his victim. (870d5–e2)

Plato leaves the identity of these priests and cults vague in both the *Meno* and the *Laws*. It is nonetheless fair to assume that the reference at least includes Orphic *teletai*.[15] Plato, thus, seems to know about priestly figures connected to Orphism who propagated a retributive eschatology

---

[14] It remains debated whether the "Orphic anthropogony" belongs to the archaic stratum of Orphism or whether it was a later invention. Johnston, in her insightful presentation and analysis of the myth, tentatively dates it to the second half of the sixth century BC (Graf and Johnston 2007: Ch. 3). See also Bernabé 2008 (with bibliography) and Alderink 1981: 55–86. For a staunchly skeptical view, arguing that the anthropogonic narrative is a much later invention, see Edmonds 1999. Holzhausen 2004 questions whether Pindar's verse is a reference to the myth of Dionysus torn apart.

[15] It is often thought (see, e.g., Bernabé 1995) that a further piece in the puzzle is provided by Plato when he quotes in the *Cratylus* (400c1–9) the etymology of "body" (σῶμα) from "tomb" or "sign" (σῆμα), capturing the belief that our souls are locked up in our bodies as a penalty for a sin. The sin in question could then be the crime of the Titans against Dionysus. Yet, I agree with Burkert 1972a: 248, n. 47 and Huffman 2013a that Plato does not attribute this etymology to the Orphics.

involving metempsychosis and might have integrated the Dionysiac myth of the origin of mankind into their *logoi*. This, however, seems meager grounds for the claim that metempsychosis was an inalienable feature of Orphism, so that all the *orpheotelestai* whom we hear about in Adeimantus' harangue, Theophrastus, or the Derveni papyrus, and the initiators who distributed the gold tablets all around Greece, made metempsychosis integral to the practices that they derived from the "books of Orpheus and Musaeus." Notably, the individual constituents of the "maximal picture" reconstructed primarily on the basis of these Platonic passages are not indissociable. The Orphic anthropogony does not imply metempsychosis – later generations can inherit the sin of the Titans without being reincarnations of the first humans stemming from the ashes. The reference to the myth of Dionysus on the Pelinna text can make perfect sense without assuming metempsychosis, just as the Derveni author can expound a retributive eschatology without any indication of such a doctrine. All in all, with respect to metempsychosis, we can observe just the reverse of what I have remarked above about vegetarianism. Metempsychosis is one of the best-documented tenets of Pythagoras[16] – even though it remains unclear whether or not it was standardly accepted by his followers[17] – whereas the evidence for metempsychosis in early Orphism remains relatively scarce and mostly indirect.[18]

To sum up, the evidence invites a decidedly pluralistic picture. There were some actors in the sphere of Orphism, such as some of the *orpheotelestai* and their initiates, who were vegetarians, probably but not necessarily because they believed in metempsychosis, possibly but by no means necessarily in connection with the myth about Dionysus and the Titanic origins of mankind; and there were others who did not avoid meat and had different, more or less clear-cut eschatological conceptions.[19] Greek religion is marked by a high degree of variation at the level of local communities and individual conceptions. I find no reason to believe that phenomena connected with Orphism would constitute an exception to this general

---

[16] See Chapter 1 above. For a balanced recent review of the evidence, see Casadesús 2011, with bibliography of the earlier literature.

[17] Nothing in the fragments of Philolaus and Archytas decides this question. Cebes' report in Plato's *Phaedo* (61d) that Philolaus forbade suicide cannot be taken as conclusive evidence for his belief in metempsychosis. For a fascinating account of Philolaus' concept of *psychē* and its possible connection with Pythagoras' own views, see Huffman 2009.

[18] For a more confident recent statement about the presence of metempsychosis in Orphism, see Bernabé 2011.

[19] Cf. also Johnston in Graf and Johnston 2007: 135.

characteristic. This entails that the relationship of actors, their practices and beliefs, to Pythagoreanism was far from homogeneous.

Let me conclude this part of the chapter with an additional observation. One recurrent element in the different texts connected to Orphism is a focus on *teletai* (mystic rites). Indeed, Orpheus was often supposed to be the one who introduced such rites into Greece (e.g., Ar. *Ran.* 1032; [Eur.] *Rhes.* 943–4; Diod. Sic. 4.25.3). As opposed to the private and communal ritual actions performed at regular intervals according to the laws of the *polis, teletai* were isolated events of special importance, performed once in a lifetime or at times of extreme crisis. (Theophrastus' Superstitious Man becomes ridiculous by performing them on a regular basis.) Contact with Orphism, for most people, focused on these extra-ordinary occasions that were supposed to change the status of the individual into an initiate, remove the malefic effects of personal or ancestral guilt, and hence cure present ills and secure a better afterlife.

The Pythagorean precepts, by contrast, concern primarily actions of everyday life, what to do and what to avoid, from how to leave one's bed in the morning, through what to steer clear of in one's everyday dealings, to observing silence when the lights are out at night. The emphasis is on how to *maintain* purity by a regulated standing praxis, rather than on how to *regain* purity by ritually paying the penalty for personal or inherited sin on the special occasions of the *teletai*. This is fully in line with the sociological aspect of the two phenomena. In Pythagoreanism, membership in a Pythagorean *hetairia* is crucial – and this meant standing social interactions, common meals, and life-long personal ties. Such a set-up is obviously more geared towards a regulation of everyday life than the one-off encounters with an *orpheotelestes*.[20]

3. Reinterpretation of natural philosophy

Up to this point, I have primarily concentrated on the performative side, *teletai* and their participants, as well as broad eschatological conceptions and their possible connections with alternative lifestyle and diet. Let us now turn to the level of literary phenomena, texts written by Pythagoreans and poems attributed to Orpheus, and the more specific doctrinal points expressed in them. After all, our sources from the classical age locate the connections primarily at this level. I will start by bluntly stating three

---

[20] On the sociological differences, see Burkert 1982 (without however accepting Burkert's characterization of Pythagorean *hetairiai* as "sects").

broad structural features, which – I would suggest – are shared by related phenomena within Orphism and Pythagoreanism, once again taken in the highly pluralistic sense for which I have argued above. First, in both cases there is an authority figure, Orpheus and Pythagoras respectively, whose special authority has particular relevance for religious beliefs and practices, although it is not necessarily restricted to such beliefs and practices. It is noteworthy that the early Greek tradition does not know of many such religious authorities apart from these two. Second, the pronouncements of these authority figures, revealed in the Pythagorean *symbola* and the Orphic poems, allow, or indeed require, interpretation. These interpretations can take various forms from literal to strongly allegorical interpretations. Third, both the original pronouncements attributed to the authority figures and the interpretations offered thereof include theoretical considerations and are in constant contact with current philosophical developments. Yet, at the same time, they give these theoretical considerations and concepts a new religious significance. In what follows, I will give examples to unpack these bald statements. I have picked cases that will, I hope, make palpable how these features manifest themselves in Pythagorean and Orphic texts, but which can at the same time point towards more subtle, specific interconnections between Orphic and Pythagorean documents.

Aristotle in the first chapter of *On the Heavens* argues for the claim that the maximal number of dimensions is three, because three is *teleion*, "complete and perfect." He draws his central argument from the Pythagoreans:

> For, just as the Pythagoreans say, the whole and all things are delimited [or "defined," ὥρισται] by the three; for end, middle, and beginning have the number of the whole, which is that of the triad. Wherefore, we use this number also in the worship of the gods, taking it from nature, as a law of it. (268a10–15)[21]

Although Aristotle does not identify the rituals that are supposed to evince the prominence and specific meaning of the number three, we know that several cult actions in Greek religion had to be repeated thrice. Most relevant is that people at *symposia* and other communal meals – which had a central role also in the life of Pythagorean *hetairiai* (associations) – performed the third and final libation to Zeus *Sōtēr* (Deliverer) also called Zeus *Teleios* (Fulfiller).

Attributing a specific significance to the number three appears to be part of typical Pythagorean number speculation. Connecting it with wholeness

---

[21] For a detailed discussion of Aristotle's reference to the Pythagoreans in *Cael.* 1.1, see Betegh, Pedriali and Pfeiffer 2013, esp. Appendix 2.

through the trio of beginning, middle and end is, so to speak, "topic neutral"; Aristotle is just using it for the demonstration of a highly abstract metaphysical point. It is, however, backed up by a reference to standard religious practice, which can also evoke the targeted term *teleios*. The outcome is double. On the one hand, the religious customs regulating the performance of these ritual actions now turn out to be applications of a higher numerological principle: these religious customs (*nomoi*) are derived from the role of the number three in nature, conceived as a law (*nomos*) of it. Yet, the rituals in question do not get thereby "naturalized" in the sense of losing their religious significance; rather, the number three receives religious significance from its application in cult.

Remarkably, some commentators have suggested that the Pythagoreans took their cue from Orphic poetry in elaborating this interpretation of the number three. According to a verse quoted in the Derveni papyrus (col. 17.12), and the pseudo-Aristotelian *De Mundo* (401a29), "Zeus is head, Zeus is middle, all things take their being from Zeus." Plato refers to the same line in the *Laws* (715e7–716a1) when he says "the god, as the ancient *logos* also holds, has the beginning, end, and the middle of all beings."[22] It is important to note that the verse refers to a key episode in the Orphic theogony. At the beginning of his reign, and in order to secure his power, Zeus swallowed the first principle of generation (either the primeval god Phanes or the phallus of Ouranos) and with it all beings that then existed. Zeus then effected a second generation by bringing to light all the constitutive parts of the cosmos and the gods that populate it. It is in this sense that Zeus can be called "beginning, middle and end" and the source of all becoming. The reference to end (τελευτή) seems to mean that Zeus, with his second creation, gives completeness and final form to things. The reference to middle might evoke Zeus' centrality. This staggering myth is a reflection on the "One–Many Problem," that has a central place in Presocratic philosophical speculations: how can all existing things arise from a single *archē* (starting-point, first principle), and how can all things be absorbed into that one entity. At the same time, it is a solution, still in the language of mythology, to a problem inherent in succession myths: how can the most important divinity, who rules the cosmos, be a mere scion and not the *archē*? This problem has, once again, clear resonances in Presocratic philosophy. Yet, crucially, these Orphic poems of theogonic content were not merely expressions of abstract theological and philosophical considerations, but were used in the *teletai*,

---

[22] Cf. Burkert 1972a: 467 n. 6; Moraux 1965: xxx–xxxi.

thus reintegrating theogonic narratives into actual ritual practice. Whether or not they are historically connected, the Pythagorean view about the number three as reported by Aristotle and the central episode of the Orphic theogonic narrative show a comparable interconnectedness of theoretical considerations and religious significance.

My second example comes from Philolaus. This is how he describes the first stage of cosmogony:

> The first thing to be fitted together – the one, in the center of the sphere – is called the Hearth [*hestia*]. (DK 44B7)

The item that has thus come into being is arguably the boldest original constituent of Philolaus' non-geocentric cosmological theory. Modern discussions customarily refer to it periphrastically as "the central fire"; yet, as we can see from this fragment, Philolaus' own preferred term was "hearth" (cf. Arist. fr. 203 Rose = Alex. Aphr. *in Metaph.* 38.20; Aët. 3.11.3, etc.). This appellation is outstandingly rich in signification and we lose a great deal by forgoing it.

First, the Greek proverbial phrase "starting from the hearth" means to begin from a proper starting point (Ar. *Vesp.* 846; Pl. *Euthphr.* 3a7, *Cra.* 401b1, etc.) – already a strong, albeit implicit, argument for starting the cosmogony with the Hearth. Hestia was also the first of the children of Cronus and for this reason the recipient of special honors among humans and gods alike (*Hom. Hymn* 5.31–2; 29.1–4). Second, *hestia* also had strong associations with the middle point: the hearth is at the center of the house (μέσῳ οἴκῳ *Hom. Hymn* 5.30).[23] Priority, location in the middle, and fieriness – Philolaus can draw on the religious tradition in establishing all the key features of his otherwise striking innovation. This novel idea is fully motivated by metaphysical and physical considerations and finds its place in the framework of Presocratic cosmological speculations;[24] yet, at the same time, it incorporates, and thereby reinterprets, elements of the religious tradition. The Hearth can henceforth function not merely as a key element in a cosmological theory, but also as an archetype of the individual hearths of households and communities, and its generation at the start of the cosmogonical process can be conceived as a quasi-aetiological myth for them. Note also, that the priority of Hestia was manifested in cult practice according to which the first (and in some sources also the last) libation had to be offered to it/her at communal meals (*Hom. Hymn* 29.6). One can easily imagine that for members of Philolaus' Pythagorean *hetairia*, and for

---

[23] On the spatial connotations of Hestia, see also Vernant 1983.   [24] See Chapter 2 above.

others familiar with his theory, the libation they performed for Hestia at the start of banquets acquired a new layer of significance.

Similarly, by putting the Hearth at the center of his astronomical system, Philolaus immediately conveys the image that the cosmos is one large household populated by relatives – this might very well be related to the Pythagorean idea of the connectedness and friendship linking the main structural features of the cosmos and all living beings in it (cf. Pl. *Grg.* 507e6–508a4). Then again, one of the most notable rituals connected with Hestia was the *amphidromia*, literally "running-around" the hearth, by which newborns were introduced into the household – this can easily evoke the image of the heavenly bodies orbiting around the Hearth. Moreover, the *polis* also had its own hearth, a permanent fire in the Prytaneum, "the symbolic center of the government of the city," in which Hestia could function as the "unmoving emblem of permanence and legitimacy" (Parker 2005: 404). There is, moreover, reason to think that the Prytaneum was originally the hearth of the monarch (Farnell 1909: 350). If so, it becomes easier to understand why Philolaus also called the Hearth the "tower of Zeus" and "garrison of Zeus" (Huffman 2007: 83). The mythologizing interpretation of major constitutive parts of the physical world and a renewed attribution of religious significance to them, is highly reminiscent of the cosmological Pythagorean *symbola* that call the sea "the tears of Kronos," the Bears "the hands of Rhea," the planets "the hounds of Persephone," the sun and the moon "the Isles of the Blessed," and so forth (Arist. fr. 196 Rose = Porph. *VP* 41; cf. also Arist. *Mete.* 345a14). It is important to emphasize, however, that Philolaus' Hearth is fully incorporated in a developed physical, cosmological theory, whereas the Pythagorean *symbola* are enigmatic snippets.

Philolaus' Hearth might also bring us back to the Derveni papyrus in an unexpected way.[25] In the longer and better preserved second part of the papyrus, the anonymous author offers an allegorical interpretation of a poem he explicitly attributes to Orpheus: the poem relates the peculiar story

---

[25] The Presocratic background of the Derveni author's cosmogony is discussed in detail in Betegh 2004, and in the Introduction and Commentary of Kouremenos, Parássoglou and Tsantsanoglou 2006; Philolaus however receives almost no attention in these treatments. The only sustained effort to show the relevance of the Derveni papyrus for Pythagoreanism is Burkert 1968: esp. 107–9, followed by Riedweg 2005: 89. Burkert, however, focuses not on the Derveni author's interpretation, but rather on the Orphic theogony. He aims to show that there are parallels between Phanes, the primeval double-sexed god of the Orphic theogony, and the One and the central fire of the Pythagorean/Philolaic cosmogony insofar as both embody (1) the ultimate origin of all later beings, (2) the primal co-existence of fundamental pairs of opposites and (3) the first appearance of light and brightness. I agree with Huffman 2008b: 213–15 that the assumed parallels are rather strained.

we have already mentioned above about Zeus' seizing royal power, whereas the Derveni author translates this mythical narrative into a Presocratic type cosmogony. The precosmic – that is pre-Zeus – state of the world was characterized by the disorderly motion of all the elements. The cause of the disarray was that fire intermingled with the other elements, kept them in unceasing motion, and did not let them combine. When the divine Mind wanted to put things into cosmic order, and allow the formation of distinct objects and stable structures, he collected the excess of fire into one large mass, and placed it in the middle (col. 15.3–5). This agglomeration of fire in the Derveni text is not Philolaus' hallmark central fire, but the sun. Nonetheless, no other early cosmogony is triggered by the formation of a ball of fire in the center of the would-be cosmos.[26]

But there is more. In the fragment quoted above, Philolaus states that the Hearth was the first thing "fitted together" (ἁρμοσθέν). In Philolaus' system, this means that the Hearth was the first harmonious combination of the two types of principles, "limiters" and "unlimiteds." Huffman has very plausibly suggested that the "unlimited" in this case is the elemental stuff of fire, unbounded and formless in and of itself. Huffman at the same time maintains that the "limiter" involved is the determinate and fixed location of the geometrical center (Huffman 1993: 227). However, it is just as plausible, it seems to me, that the determinate size and shape – i.e., its actual spatial limits – must also be among the limiters contributing to the formation of the Hearth.[27] If so, not only the position, but also the dimensions of the Hearth are important features that allow a functional, harmonious and stable cosmic order to develop around it. This, in turn, agrees with what the Derveni author says in a key sentence:

> If the god had not wished that the things that are now should exist, he would not have made the sun. But he made it of such a sort and of such a size as is explained in the beginning of the account. (col. 25.10–12)

Both cosmogonical narratives thus start with the formation of a ball of fire at the center, and in both systems the position and dimension of this entity are the preconditions of the ensuing generation of a cosmic order.

---

[26] There is also some similarity between the way Philolaus 44B17 and *PDerv* col. 15.4–5 describe the symmetry relations in terms of the things above and things below the centrally positioned fire.

[27] Note that a combination of "limiters" and "unlimiteds" is harmonious not merely insofar as their product shows internal coherence and stability, but also because the emerging entity fits harmoniously into larger structures of which it forms a part. This is how I read, e.g., the end of DK 44B6.

Moreover, in both systems this primal aggregation of fire remains a motor force and a generative power of life on earth.[28]

Information about the next steps of Philolaus' cosmogony is scarce. Nonetheless, what we do have is noteworthy. A crucial piece of information comes from Aristotle's lost treatise on the Pythagoreans:

> The world is one, and time and breath and the void, which always distinguishes the place of each thing, are drawn in from the unlimited. (Arist. fr. 201 Rose)

As a close parallel with Philolaus' embryological theory proves, breath (πνοή) is necessary for the further development of the cosmos in so far as it can counterbalance the heat of the central fire (Huffman 1993: 213). For his part, the Derveni author identifies the demiurgic divine Mind with elemental air, one aspect of which is breath (πνεῦμα col. 18.2); the primary cosmological function of air is precisely to cool and bridle the excessive heat of fire. Thus, in both theories, the crucial step in the cosmogonic narrative, leading to the formation of individual entities, is the interaction between hot fire and the cooling air.

I have suggested that there are some remarkable points of contact between central elements of the cosmogonical theories of Philolaus and the Derveni author.[29] These and possible further parallels notwithstanding, there is at least one striking difference, which highlights an intriguing feature of early Pythagoreanism. The main character in the Derveni author's cosmogony is the demiurgic divine Mind: it is Mind who forms the sun, thereby organizing the cosmos in a teleological way, and who purposefully bridles the heat of fire and demarcates individual entities. This is fully in line with the fact that the theory is presented as the true meaning of the Orphic poem that relates Zeus' founding of the world. As opposed to this, Philolaus never says what or who brought it about that limiters and unlimiteds suddenly started to fit together, and he never explains why precisely the particular limiters and unlimiteds that constitute the Hearth combined first. This difference might reflect Orphic literature's predilection for mythological narratives about the gods, whereas properly theological considerations are strikingly missing from early Pythagorean documents.[30]

---

[28] For Philolaus, cf., e.g., Simpl. *in Phys.* 1354.2; Arist. fr. 204 Rose.

[29] I develop the parallels between Philolaus and the Derveni author in a separate paper, which is in preparation.

[30] It is a telling fact that authoritative discussions of the theology of the Presocratics such as Jaeger 1947, Vlastos 1952 or Broadie 1999, say next to nothing on the Pythagoreans. The attempt in Drozdek 2007: Chapter 5 to remedy the situation does not yield convincing results.

By juxtaposing these dispersed pieces of evidence, I have tried to suggest that a number of texts coming from Pythagorean and Orphic sources share a general methodology of giving new religious relevance to concepts issuing from and integrated into natural philosophy. Thus, the connection between Orphism and Pythagoreanism might take subtler forms than adherence to metempsychosis and a vegetarian diet. Yet, this is not a unified methodology but can come in many shades and forms. Nor again would it characterize all Orphic or Pythagorean texts or be limited to them. For instance, there is no discernible trace of either in the fragments of Archytas, whose work is otherwise connected in many ways with that of Philolaus. Similarly, it might very well be that the Derveni author is a solitary case within Orphism. On the other hand, this type of reintegration of religious notions into a cosmological framework, once again with different emphases, is characteristic also of Heraclitus and Empedocles. But, crucially, neither of them would accept either Orpheus or Pythagoras as the highest authority in religious or cosmological matters but would want to present themselves as the ultimate source of wisdom. This is where, I think, we have reached the limits of Orphism and Pythagoreanism.

So, in speaking about the relationship between Pythagoreanism and traditional religion, what ultimately matters are the relations between local cults and myths and the Pythagorean precepts and reinterpretations of mythical concepts. There is not any real, deep conflict here. There are additional requirements on a Pythagorean in terms of taboos and rituals but no strong tension or incompatibility. There are re-elaborations and novel layers of significance given to religious ideas but – once again – no antagonism. We find neither overt criticism of traditional beliefs from the side of Pythagorean natural philosophy, in the fashion of Xenophanes, nor an alternative comprehensive mythological account of the gods as in the Orphic theogonies. Pythagoras' privileged relation to Apollo – the exact nature of which has been debated since antiquity – can also be appreciated in this general framework. Pythagoras might well build on already existing local cults of Apollo in Croton, integrate the authority of the pan-Hellenic cult of the Delphic Apollo,[31] and finally introduce the promise of the piety, justice and toil-free existence of the mythical Hyperboreans, by taking up the persona of the Hyperborean Apollo.

---

[31] Cf. Aristoxenus' report (fr. 15) according to which Pythagoras built his ethical doctrines on the teaching of the Delphic priestess Themistoclea. On the relationship between Apollo and Pythagoras, see also the remarks of Rowett in Chapter 5 of this volume.

CHAPTER 8

The problem of Pythagorean mathematics

Reviel Netz

1. The first network of Greek mathematics

Before turning specifically to Pythagorean mathematics we need to consider the development of Greek mathematical culture as a whole. We all know the narratives where impersonal continuities replace individuals, for example, "The History of Greek Mathematics." In fact, Greek mathematics, like most other ancient cultural endeavors, may have been pursued primarily by small networks that did not survive beyond two generations or so. A significant part of the Greek creative achievement in pure mathematics may be assigned to two such networks: the one found in Proclus' summary of early Greek mathematics (*In Eucl.* 65.7–68.4 Friedlein), standardly understood to derive from Eudemus' history of geometry,[1] and the one constituted by Archimedes, his correspondents, and the authors in the following generation. It is the first network that is relevant to Pythagoreanism.

Proclus' list includes three names from the archaic era: Thales, Mamercus[2] and Pythagoras. Hippias of Elis, Anaxagoras and Oenopides are brought in based on their mention in Platonic dialogues; next follow Hippocrates of Chios, Theodorus of Cyrene, (Plato himself) and finally: Leodamas of Thasos, Archytas of Tarentum, Theaetetus of Athens, Neoclides, his pupil Leon, Eudoxus of Cnidus (a little later than Leon), Amyclas of Heracleia, Menaechmus (a student of Eudoxus), Dinostratus, his brother, Theudius of Magnesia, Athenaeus of Cyzicus, Hermotimus of Colophon and Philippus of Mende.

Several are known only from Proclus' summary (Amyclas, Athenaeus, Hermotimus, Leon, Neoclides and Theudius), but the traditions that

---

[1] The best introduction to Eudemus is Zhmud 2002. Eudemus produced his work *c.* 330 BC.

[2] Stesichorus' purported brother; see West 1971b: 303. Apparently, late erudite discussion of Stesichorus, the south Italian poet, used his contemporaneity with Pythagoras to invent a Pythagorean and hence mathematical brother.

Theaetetus, Archytas, Eudoxus and Philippus knew Plato personally are solid, and there is no reason to doubt Proclus' claim that so did the much less well known Leodamas; since we are told that Theaetetus was Theodorus' student, Menaechmus a student of Eudoxus, and Dinostratus Menaechmus' brother, we end up with a tight network whose core is Plato. It is useful to point to contrasts between this network and that centered on Archimedes. There seems to be an entire range of interests central to the first network that is almost entirely absent from the second: *non-configurational classification* (i.e., an interest in the classification of those mathematical terms whose representations in diagrams do not involve complex interacting diagrams).

We may start with a scholion to Euclid's *Elements* V, stating that the results of this book are due to Eudoxus.[3] While not primarily about classification, the theory of proportion in this book is definitely non-configurational. Pappus' commentary to Euclid's *Elements* X states:

> It was [. . .] Theaetetus who distinguished the powers which are commensurable in length from those which are incommensurable, and who divided the more generally known irrational lines according to the different means, assigning the medial lines to geometry, the binomial to arithmetic, and the apotome to harmony, as is stated by Eudemus, the Peripatetic.[4] (Thomson 1930: 63)

This makes Theaetetus the author of a study of irrationals related to that of Euclid's *Elements* X: a classification of non-configurational objects. Furthermore, Archytas developed a system of classification of means between numbers, contributed to the theory of the division of the musical octave, devising a proof equivalent to Euclid's *Sectio Canonis* 3, and was the first to solve the problem of the duplication of the cube, which could have fitted, for Archytas himself, within a program of the study of means and proportionals.[5] Finally, while there is no reliable evidence for the historical origins of the arithmetical books of Euclid's *Elements* (VII–IX),

---

[3] Heiberg 1886: 5.280.

[4] Following Lefkowitz 1981 we may suspect that later biographers derived Theaetetus' achievement from the Platonic dialogue carrying his name. Pappus' reference to Eudemus makes it more likely that Plato, in his fictional vignette, echoes Theaetetus' future biography, than that the biography was fabricated on the basis of a Platonic fiction.

[5] The general theory of means is fr. 2; see Chapter 3 above and Huffman 2005: 162–81; the contribution to music theory is fr. 1 (Huffman 2005: 103–61) and A16 (see Chapter 9 below and Huffman 2005: 402–82). The explicit musical proof is A19 (Huffman 2005: 451–70) from Boethius' *De Institutione Musica* 3.2. It is far from certain that the *Sectio Canonis* is by Euclid himself, though this attribution was favored by Barker (1989: 190). Our evidence for the duplication of the cube comes from a long passage extant via Eutocius (A14–15 Huffman 2005: 342–401; undoubtedly in mediated form), where the problem is, given two line segments A and D, to find two more line segments B and C such that A, B, C and D are in continuous proportion. This problem is equivalent to the extraction of a

it is remarkable how much they engage with the classification of numbers and of their ratios, through categories such as "prime," "square" and "cube" numbers and "continuous" ratios (Books VII–IX.20).

We end up with roughly half of Euclid's *Elements*: Books V, VII–IX and X. There are, of course, exceptions to this pattern: for instance, Hippocrates' quadrature of lunules, an early and isolated result; the elementary results of Euclid's *Elements* I–III, VI, and XI; and one major advanced result, the measurement of the volumes of pyramids, cylinders and cones, in *Elements* XII.[6] It is this result that Archimedes singles out for praise, twice, in both the introduction to *Sphere and Cylinder* I as well as the introduction to the *Method*, and as due to Eudoxus.[7] And for a reason: the great bulk of the work of the second network of Greek mathematics has the same character as this part of Book XII: geometrical exploration, studying complex configurations with an eye not for classification but for brilliant measurement or problem-solving.[8]

The impression therefore is that the first network was typically motivated by questions of classification of non-configurational objects, the most significant exception being Eudoxus' measurement of solid volumes, and that Archimedes made this exceptional result paradigmatic for his own project. Rule and exception, foreground and background, became flipped. Numbers, means, ratios, proportions, irrationals, harmonies: such are the key terms studied – with an eye to classification – around the first half of the fourth century (and almost at no other time), in a network organized around Plato's Athens (and almost in no other context).

These interests could have been informed by Plato's own philosophical agenda. So, was Plato the "architect" of this science? As Zhmud 1998a shows, such an account – familiar from antiquity – derives from the self-propagandizing efforts of the early Academy. It is thus appropriate to ask if the intellectual tendencies of the first network could have reflected the influence of any particular author from *within* the network. Was there

---

cubic root and for this reason naturally became immersed in later Greek mathematics, in geometrical applications ("duplication of the cube") and geometrical techniques (conic sections).

[6] We can generalize further. In Euclid's *Elements*, three geometrical books appear to be less a "toolbox" and more an example of the type of valuable results one achieves with such a toolbox. One is the Eudoxean Book XII; the other two are Books IV (the construction of regular polygons within circles, which a scholion [*Schol. Euc.* 273.3] assigns to "Pythagoreans," in all likelihood mistakenly [*pace* Burkert 1972a: 450], because of the relationship of this task to the Platonic solids) and XIII (the construction of regular solids within spheres). Such tasks are not connected to other geometrical problems and they may be motivated by sheer aesthetic contemplation of geometrical objects as visual patterns.

[7] Heiberg 1910: 4.5, 1913: 430.2 (now revised: Netz, Noel, Tchernetska and Wilson 2011: 297).

[8] Knorr 1986 is the best survey of the achievement of this second network.

any mathematician in this group sufficiently influential so that his works became paradigmatic?

Surely, for Archimedes, Eudoxus served as the paradigmatic mathematician. But we now understand the programmatic meaning of Archimedes' choice of Eudoxus: in a sense, it was a choice *against the grain* of early Greek mathematics. And, in concrete historical terms, it is unlikely that Eudoxus could have been the paradigmatic figure for the first network; he came too late. While contestable, a date of birth somewhere around 395 BC is the most likely.[9] It is hard to see how a thirty-something, however brilliant, could accumulate the cultural capital to be a leading figure among his network of acquaintances and so a central position for Eudoxus cannot be imagined before 360 BC.[10] And yet, Theaetetus was dead by 369.[11] For Archytas, Huffman (2005: 5) suggests a birth between 435 and 410 and a death between 360 and 350. This is likely enough, but I wish to carry a bit further Huffman's reasoning based on Tarentum's political history. The city is assumed to have flourished (as it did under Archytas' tutelage) between 379 and 360. While political authority could have been achieved, in a Greek democracy, at a fairly early age (Pericles was a leading citizen by 450, aged forty to forty-five, at the oldest), the balance of probability remains that a city's leader would not be very young. Thus, a leading position in roughly 379–360 accords best with birth at 420 at the latest or perhaps even closer to Huffman's earliest date of 435.[12] We find that, of the three better-known mathematicians of the first network, Eudoxus was by far the youngest, Archytas almost certainly the oldest and that Archytas and

---

[9] The key, irreconcilable facts are: he is said to have died aged fifty-three (a remarkably precise and young age, so perhaps more reliable than usual?), he seems to have known of Plato's death in 347, and his acme was stated to be 367. Most scholars prefer the first two facts to the third (taken perhaps to synchronize his acme with Aristotle's arrival at the Academy) and so place his birth early in the fourth century (Goulet 2000: Vol. 3, 294–5).

[10] My current research indicates that a substantial fraction of ancient cultural figures died at a very old age and that the only way to account for this is through the inherently plausible assumption that cultural prominence in antiquity was premised on the kind of social prominence one gained at a relatively advanced age (about fifty). Thus our "acme" calculations are off by about a decade.

[11] His death, in a war between Athens and Corinth in 369 BC, is commemorated in Plato's dialogue. The standard view, that Theaetetus was born *c.* 415 BC, is based on a literal reading of the dialogue, as if Socrates actually met the youthful Theaetetus.

[12] This would also fit with Huffman's conjectural reconstruction of the birthdates of lesser-known mathematicians mentioned by Proclus in the immediate context of Archytas (2005: 5 n. 1): Leodamas *c.* 430, Neoclides *c.* 420, Leon *c.* 400. It is plausible that written works in the first network of mathematics began to appear in greater density in the 380s, perhaps first among these being works by Archytas, and that, during the 370s and 360s, several more authors join in, notably Theaetetus and Eudoxus. Under the influence of these three important mathematicians, a larger corpus is formed through the ensuing decades, but, after Theaetetus dies (369) and then Archytas and Eudoxus (the 340s), the group peters out in the 330s.

Theaetetus completed their main achievements by 360 BC. If any single individual was responsible, more than others, for the intellectual character of the first network of mathematics, it surely ought to have been Archytas.[13] He was the older member of the group; more important, perhaps, he had the social capital. He was the leading citizen of a major city. Even among mathematicians this should count for something.

What is meant by "paradigmatic role?" Only that, among the authors of the first network of Greek mathematics, one reason to have been pleased with one's work would be that it was *rather like Archytas'* – rather like the work of the recognized master of one's art. An Archytas interested in the classification of means and the division of the octave; a network where Archytas' work is a supreme model and thus a mathematical culture that puts more emphasis on results of non-configurational classification – I find this a likely enough account. But has this history of Greek mathematics got anything to do with the history of Pythagoreanism?

2. The evidence for Pythagorean mathematics

2.1. *Fairly uncontroversial evidence concerning Aristotle, Archytas and Philolaus*

A.

Aristotle thought that "Pythagoreans" engaged especially with "mathematics," specifically, *numbers*:

> At the same time, and even before them [the Atomists], the so-called "Pythagoreans," having attached themselves to the study of mathematics, both put it first and also, engaged in those studies, thought their [i.e., mathematics'] principles were the principles of all beings. And since, among these, numbers are prior by nature [. . .] they took the elements of numbers to be the elements of all beings. (*Metaph.* 985b23–986a2; cf. 1090a20–5)

This is Aristotle's diagnosis of an error: Pythagoreans were familiar with mathematical studies and noted the role of number in them; for this reason, they concluded that numbers were ontologically fundamental.

B.

Archytas was a major mathematician as well as a "Pythagorean." The range of his mathematical work was likely wider than mentioned above (Roman

---

[13] Whatever the historicity of Diogenes Laertius' assertion that Archytas was Eudoxus' teacher (8.86), it implies a cultural memory where Archytas is the senior partner.

authors referred to Archytas' astronomy; until recently, scholars argued for Archytas' role in the history of mechanics while, more recently, some suggest that he contributed to optics).[14] As for Archytas' Pythagoreanism, this has surprisingly little early support (Huffman 2005: 45. Aristotle never refers to Archytas as a Pythagorean!) and yet, as Huffman puts it (2005: 44), "Archytas . . . fits the popular conception of a Pythagorean better than anyone in the Pythagorean tradition." We should not expect too much fixity of the category, which was hazy already for Aristotle. Archytas was not a card-carrying Pythagorean: there were no cards.

C.

Philolaus, in a sense, *was* early Pythagoreanism: that is, as Huffman points out (1993: 8), Philolaus is likely to have been the first Pythagorean author, the next one being Archytas (Philolaus' book was probably circulating towards the end of the fifth century).[15] Philolaus was not a mathematician; he was an author on nature. He did however pay much more attention than his predecessors to those fields that would emerge, ultimately, as "mathematics." This produces a conundrum: Philolaus' system gave central place to harmony,[16] music,[17] arithmetic,[18] astronomy[19] and even geometry,[20] but just what in Philolaus' doctrines prompted Aristotle's claim that Pythagoreans made numbers the principles of all things? Huffman's measured solution (1993: 57–64), that this was Aristotle's interpretation of what Philolaus'

---

[14] Astronomy: Huffman 2005: 22–4. Huffman refers to a cosmological passage, testimony A24, and bases upon it the image of Archytas the astronomer; it also seems that the Roman authors in question – Horace and Propertius – essentially take Archytas as an expert in mathematics, for which astronomy is perceived, as well it should by their time, as constitutive. Mechanics: Huffman 2005: 77–83. His conclusion is that ancient references to Archytas as an important mechanical author are based on his duplication of the cube, which, in his own context, need not have had the mechanical meaning it would later acquire. Optics: Huffman 2005: 550–69, responding to Burnyeat 2005. Yet, while we do have compelling evidence that Archytas had a theory of the visual ray, would this come naturally in the context of a mathematical optics, rather than that of a physical treatise? I do not wish to deny any of Archytas' contributions but to emphasize that his only certain mathematical interest was in music and means.

[15] Philolaus is, in general terms, "of the generation of Socrates." It is also likely that his single book, summing up his wisdom, would be the outcome, rather than the start, of his reputation as a sage (for both the dating and the single book, see Huffman 1993: 1–16).

[16] Frs. 1–2 use a verbal cognate of "harmony"; fr. 3 discusses harmony explicitly.

[17] Fr. 6a discusses harmony as a musical term, providing our earliest evidence for an account of such harmony in terms of numerical ratios.

[18] Fr. 5 mentions the division of number into odd and even.

[19] Huffman 1993: 202–88. Much of the early reception of Philolaus – indeed, all the way down to Copernicus – focused on his idiosyncratic cosmological system (see Chapter 2 above), which was, among other things, in some sense heliocentric; it could also have included an early formulation of the "harmony of the spheres," although the evidence is weak (Huffman 1993: 279–83).

[20] The "Mother city" of the other (sciences?): Testimony A7a.

system amounted to, is the most likely (if not uncontroversial) and it suggests an important moral. A generalized late-fifth-century interest in such themes as harmony, arithmetic, music, astronomy and geometry could be recalled, almost a century – and much mathematics – later, as an emphasis upon numbers.

2.2. *Problematic evidence*

A.

Eurytus deserves detailed consideration because he has been neglected in scholarship. In *On First Principles,* Theophrastus argues[21] that, when offering an account, one should be explicit about the manner in which the fine details can be deduced from one's principles. Platonism is blamed and Speusippus' followers are mentioned in particular (*Metaph.* 6b6) for positing principles such as "One and the Dyad," whence arise numbers and other general categories, and stopping there. (So how does "One and the Dyad" explain anything, concretely?) Even before blaming Speusippus, however, Theophrastus cites, approvingly,[22] Archytas' apparently firsthand description of Eurytus (a somewhat older Pythagorean than Archytas, from Archytas' own Tarentum):[23]

> For this is the [approach] of an accomplished and sensible man, that very thing which Archytas once said that Eurytus did, in his various *diatheseis* of *psēphoi*;[24] for he said that *this* number turned out to be of *man, that* of *horse, that* of some other thing.

A passage in Aristotle's *Metaphysics* is the only other source to cast light on this practice (we learn of Eurytus' practices from the best possible sources: Archytas, Aristotle, Theophrastus). The context[25] is Aristotle's complaint that those who say that numbers are explanatory/causal (*aitioi*) do not clarify the sense intended (the implication is that numbers, invoked in plausible ways, cannot be explanatory/causal). This is very similar to the context in Theophrastus: the methodological problem of how to use numbers as explanatory principles, for which, we now see, both Aristotle

---

[21] *Metaph.* 6a15–b22.
[22] Is this ironic? So it is usually taken (Zhmud 2012b: 410 offers a compelling reading); but Gutas 2010: 304 notes the "rather sober and decidedly non-playful tone" of Theophrastus' *Metaphysics.* Referring to Eurytus, in this context, as *teleos,* "well-finished," "accomplished," is to the point: he is distinguished by bringing his derivations to a *completion.* See further Chapter 13 in this volume.
[23] *Metaph.* 6a19–22. In the quotations which follow, the emphases are my own.
[24] Literally, "having arranged certain pebbles" (διατιθέντα τινὰς ψήφους). I take the *tinas* to refer not to the pebbles being of some special sort, but to the unspecified plurality of Eurytus' practices.
[25] *Metaph.* 1092b8–25.

and Theophrastus agreed that Eurytus could be taken as a paradigmatic
example:

> Are [numbers explanatory/causal] in the sense of *definitions*,[26] as points are
> of magnitudes?[27] And [so], as Eurytus assigned a certain number to a certain
> thing, e.g., this [number] to *man*, that [number] to *horse* (just as is done,
> making numbers into the figures *triangle* and *square*), making the forms of
> living beings analogous, in this way, to *psēphoi*? (1092b9–13)

The passage gives exactly one example for numbers-explanatory-via-
definitions: Eurytus' practice. To clarify his meaning, Aristotle illustrates
this practice with the aid of two analogies. First, he gives an analogy
for the manner in which anything, in general, can serve as causal/
explanatory through *definition*: Speusippus' derivation of magnitudes from
the point. The relevant sense of "definition" is therefore "serving as the
starting-point in the process of conceptual derivation." Second, he gives an
analogy for how Eurytus' operation could have been considered successful,
i.e., the sense in which one could end up concluding that a number is that
of "man" or that of "horse": the manner in which arithmeticians say that
one number is "triangle," another, "square."

What does Aristotle think of Eurytus' operation? Aristotle goes on to
offer a different account of number as explanatory/causal, in which the
precise numerical ratios that constitute various natural phenomena explain
them. Aristotle insists that, in this case, it is not the numbers that are
explanatory (on the one hand, it is the ratio, as form; on the other
hand, it is the constituents, as matter, but in either case, the numbers
themselves are not explanatory). Thus, Aristotle explicitly refutes the theory of numbers-explanatory-via-numerical-ratios, but he does not provide

---

[26] I am not sure why ὅρος in this passage often gets translated as "boundary." How are boundaries
plausible candidates for examples of causes? Raven (1951: 148) does try to develop an account
wherein "boundary" acts, in a certain doctrine, as an effective "definition"; but why not just have
the meaning "definition" and be done with it? Of course, a *definition* is a likely first candidate to
consider; it is an explanatory category and applies naturally to the notion of *number* as explanatory.
See the following note.

[27] Pseudo-Alexander and Syrianus read γραμμῶν for μεγεθῶν, so that they clearly had in mind ὅρος
as boundary and went on to read the passage in light of Euclid's *Elements* I Def. 3. They missed
Aristotle's intended reference, which must have been to Speusippus' construction of the magnitudes
from the point (this is best preserved in the *Theologumena Arithmeticae*, Speusippus F28.61–2 Tarán:
"For the first principle, towards magnitude, is point; second – line; third – plane; fourth – solid").
Here the point serves as a starting-point in a recursive process of conceptual derivation, so that it is
explanatory/causal of the magnitudes in the manner of a definition. It is not an accident that both
Theophrastus and Aristotle mention Speusippus and Eurytus in the same breath. Their very reason
for pondering Archytas' stories of Eurytus' performances was to account for their philosophical
fruit: Speusippus' metaphysical system. For Theophrastus, Speusippus' system was a watered-down
version of Eurytus' tricks, less flagrantly wrong, but only at the price of losing any definite meaning.

a refutation of the numbers-explanatory-via-definitions. In the case of numbers-explanatory-via-numerical-ratios, Aristotle seems to accept the science (flesh or bone *could* in principle be defined as "three of fire, two of earth" [1092b19]). He thus needs to show that even though this science is valid, its results do not amount to the conclusion that numbers are causal/explanatory. In Eurytus' case, however, no refutation of the use of numbers as explanatory is offered. The implication is that Aristotle would not deny that, had such a derivation held in practice, it should have counted as a case of numbers being causal/explanatory. Aristotle's view is that no such refutation is called for because a derivation such as Eurytus' is patently wrong as a matter of science. *Flesh* might be $Fire_3Earth_2$, but *man* most definitely is not, say, 250. Eurytus' effort is methodologically meaningful (if successful, it would amount to the type of account being sought) but scientifically false; this is exactly the position we see in Theophrastus as well.

While Theophrastus and Aristotle both consider Eurytus' results patently false, nothing suggests they consider his procedure *silly*. Eurytus was not so fortunate in his later reception. Pseudo-Alexander, writing not earlier than late antiquity and probably in Byzantium,[28] tried to imagine Eurytus' procedure; he ended up with Eurytus the *mosaicist*. His Eurytus begins by postulating that the number of man is 250. He then takes small pebbles – should we say tesserae? – of various colors and, "like today's painters," produces a likeness of a man. "There!," pseudo-Alexander has Eurytus conclude by exclamation, just as 250 is the number of small pebbles in the picture, so 250 is the number of monads in man.

Amazingly, scholars of Greek science and philosophy have not dismissed this interpretation. Bélis 1983 is an article entirely based on the assumption that pseudo-Alexander reports what Eurytus actually did. Knorr refers to Aristotle but then adds, simply (1975: 59 n. 81), "The passage is amplified by Theophrastus and Alexander." Annas, too, is led astray:

> All we know about Eurytus comes from the commentator pseudo-Alexander [. . .] There have been many interpretations of what he [Eurytus] could have been getting at in this procedure, and the general assumption is that it cannot have been as simple-minded as it appears. However, in this chapter Aristotle is out to ridicule his opponents, and it can be safely assumed that whatever Eurytus was doing with his pebbles Aristotle took it to be silly. (Annas 1976: 218)

---

[28] Luna 2001 argued, against Tarán 1987 but confirming the consensus of the literature, that the pseudo-Alexander in question was in fact Michael of Ephesus, a twelfth-century Byzantine scholar.

The last claim is importantly wrong. As I note below, Aristotle does quickly dismiss various bits of number symbolism (1093a13–b6) as a kind of reduction to absurdity of the entire enterprise, but the passage in which Eurytus is mentioned is not at this level of dismissiveness and is instead a piece of careful conceptual consideration, based on a view of Eurytus' practice, evidently shared by Theophrastus and Archytas, as wrong but intellectually meaningful. For this reason alone, pseudo-Alexander's picture of Eurytus the mosaicist is a non-starter for it is evidently idiotic. How would Eurytus' numbers *scale*?

The main reason, then, to prefer a more abstract reading of his procedure is to make Eurytus appear somewhat less absurd. Pseudo-Alexander was under no such compulsion. But we are, not just because Theophrastus, Aristotle and apparently Archytas all, arguably, took Eurytus seriously, but more basically, because he was active in the public arena and sufficiently well received to be remembered. The mosaicist-arithmologist would have been laughed down at the first try. How could Eurytus have made sense to anyone? This is the question that scholarship has largely failed to address.[29]

The reason may be scholars' failure to get the right sense of *psēphoi*. There is a reason why I did not translate the *diatheseis* of *psēphoi* in Theophrastus above and the *psēphoi* in Aristotle. Literally, Theophrastus and Aristotle talk about the setting down of pebbles (*psēphoi*) so that it appears to be a reference to some kind of mosaic practice. But this is a misunderstanding of ancient numeracy. Patterned numbers are entirely unremarkable in ancient numeracy. All that we learn from Pythagorean interest in such patterns is that Pythagoreans cared about numbers (Netz 2002: 341). The standard way to calculate was with, well, *calculi* (or *psēphoi*).

> [Counters, for the Greeks] were the medium of numerical manipulation par excellence, in exactly the same way in which, for us, Arabic numerals are the numerical medium par excellence. We imagine numbers as an entity seen

---

[29] I do not say that pseudo-Alexander was an idiot, either. There are two good reasons to read Aristotle's passage as referring to a mosaicist-like procedure. First, since pseudo-Alexander's text read "lines" for "magnitudes" (see note 27), "boundaries" rather than "definitions" becomes a natural sense for ὅροι and this could suggest that Aristotle was talking about shapes. Second, there is the reference to "square" and "triangle" as types of numbers. This could be Aristotle's way of saying that Eurytus had arranged pebbles in the shape of a man or a horse; the main reason to think so is that Aristotle states Eurytus made the forms (μορφαί . . .) of living things analogous to *psēphoi*. But Aristotle does not, in fact, say that Eurytus arranged pebbles into shapes but only that Eurytus' procedure could be understood on analogy with the manner in which numbers can be made into figures. This leaves a much wider conceptual space, ranging between figured representation and a much more abstract operation where numbers are assigned properties that, upon first hearing, one would consider non-arithmetical, such as "square" and "triangle."

on the page; the Greeks imagined them as an entity grasped between the thumb and the finger. (Netz 2002: 341)

Thus, we may spell out our passages as follows. Theophrastus:

> For this is the [approach] of an accomplished and sensible man, that very thing which Archytas once said that Eurytus did, in his arrangements of abacus operations;[30] for he said that *this* number turned out to be of *man*, *that* of *horse*, *that* of some other thing. (*Metaph.* 6a19–22)

Aristotle:

> Are [numbers explanatory/causal] in the sense of *definitions*, as points are of magnitudes? And [so], as Eurytus assigned a certain number to a certain thing, e.g., this [number] to *man*, that [number] to *horse* (just as is done, making numbers into the figures *triangle* and *square*), making the forms of living beings analogous, in this way, to calculations upon the abacus?[31] (*Metaph.* 1092b9–13)

A translation, an interpretation, debatable, for sure. Yet my suggested translation does end up with a version of Eurytus which is much more sensible than that of pseudo-Alexander's mosaicist. What we envisage now is an operation of public calculation, pebbles moved around expertly upon the abacus until the result is obtained: such and such is the number of horse. A further hint is provided by the context in both Theophrastus and Aristotle: this is somehow meant to be a derivation from first principles. We need to imagine Eurytus working from some basic numerical identifications (certain basic properties are identical to certain numerical values; their combination is expressed by certain operations: for potential examples, see n. 40 below). The derivation, then, is a kind of recursive,

---

[30] ψῆφον (-ους) τιθῆναι is the standard way of referring to operations upon counters. If the text read τιθείς τίνας ψήφους, its precise translation would have been "having made certain calculations." Theophrastus, however, uses the participle form διατιθείς, which indicates not merely *laying out counters in the operation of the abacus* but being engaged in *some better-defined arrangement*. This could suggest the interpretation according to which Eurytus prepared mosaics. It could also imply that Theophrastus assumed, based on Archytas, that Eurytus operated not merely with the standard rules of the abacus, but had some special "arrangements," or sets of rules, with which his counters were manipulated (his was a "prepared abacus," in the manner of a "prepared piano").

[31] I take ψῆφοι in Aristotle, as I did in Theophrastus, as synecdoche for the operation of calculating with such pebbles, or for the result of such calculations. See Demosthenes *De Corona* 227.3–4, "the accounts (ψῆφοι) are clean (καθαραί)" where the pebbles are a synecdoche for the result of doing one's accounts. (In general, *psēphos* is a metonym of Greek calculation, in the manner in which the diagram is a metonym of Greek proof: the misunderstanding of *psēphos* in interpreting of Greek mathematics is similar to the misunderstanding of γράφειν: see Knorr 1975: 69–75; Netz 1999: 35–8.)

constructive calculation (akin, then, to Speusippus' recursive construction of the magnitudes from the point).[32]

B.

Diogenes Laertius, in his life of Plato, reported a tradition according to which the comic poet Epicharmus was an influence on Plato; he quotes "philosophical" passages to prove the point.[33] Specifically, in Diog. Laert. 3.11, a comic character points out that if you add one or subtract one from an odd, or even number, they do not remain the same as they were. Even if this is taken to be authentic (should it?) and to refer to an operation upon counters (it should), all that we learn is that: (1) in fifth-century Syracuse the terms "odd" and "even" were already in use and (2) calculations upon counters were well known. Of course: they used the abacus! Attempts to read "Pythagoreanism" into this passage represent a failure to understand ancient numeracy.[34]

The same is true for the use, in the work of a couple of Imperial era Platonist-Pythagorean teachers, of diagrams where notional counters stand for numbers.[35] Further, the understanding of numbers as constituted by counters is evident in the metaphors used for many arithmetical categories beginning with "odd" and "even" themselves (literally "extends beyond" and "exactly fitted": the number is understood to stand in two rows), all the way through "square," and "triangle," to "cubes" and "pyramids." There is nothing remarkable here: the metaphorical domain for the classification of numbers would involve numbers perceived as counters because Greeks perceived numbers as counters.

---

[32] If this was Eurytus' procedure, we have a ready contemporary analogue: Cratylus. Cratylus' proce-dure, too, involved a derivation from first principles – certain basic sound associations were used to derive, through certain rules of etymology, the hidden significance of various words. In Plato, Cratylus is a performer called upon to derive the significance of various words. Substitute num-bers for sounds, abacus manipulation for a verbal performance, and you have Eurytus in action. Sedley 2003 suggested that Plato took Cratylus' procedure seriously. Substitute Archytas for Plato, Eurytus for Cratylus. Why should Archytas not have taken Eurytus' procedure as worthy of serious discussion – even if it, too, might be found ultimately false?

[33] More recently, scholars tend to consider these fragments late fabrications based on Plato's own philosophy; there was, even in antiquity, a widespread understanding that many of the texts ascribed to Epicharmus were pseudepigraphic. See Kerkhof 2001: 65–78.

[34] Knorr 1975: 126–7 says the following to counter Philip 1966 and in defense of Becker 1936 (on which more below): "Philip thus apparently believes that the pebble-arithmetic owed its principal development to the studies in the Platonic period. But this view neglects the fact that these methods are in plain evidence in the Epicharmus-fragment, hence at least date from the mid-fifth century." An entire science, its entire chronology, is conjured out of the misunderstanding of an (apocryphal?) fragment.

[35] Theon of Smyrna 31–40 Hiller; Nicomachus *Introduction to Arithmetic* 2.8–10.

The testimonies for Eurytus, the (pseudo?)-Epicharmus fragment, the later evidence for the use of figured numbers as well as the metaphorical language of figured counters in Greek arithmetic, all change their meaning dramatically once the ancient ubiquity of the abacus, and so the standard use of pebbles as metonyms of "calculation," are taken into consideration. Eurytus, most likely, calculated, somehow, certain symbolically significant numbers; Epicharmus, and other references to numbers-as-constituted-by-counters reflect no distinctive knowledge. And yet, the above evidence provided the basis for a theory, suggested at least since Burnet 1892 [1930]: 99–107, put forward in detail by Becker 1936, and still influential in the historiography of Greek mathematics,[36] according to which there was a distinct form of early Pythagorean arithmetic. In this imagined science, pebble-representations of numbers were invented as tools used to prove theorems (Becker claimed to identify this stratum, more or less intact, in Euclid's treatment of odd and even in *Elements* IX.21–34).[37] We can now see that, however attractive, such a theory has no evidence to support it.

C.

Late in the *Metaphysics* (1093a13–b21), Aristotle does cite several Pythagorean claims more dismissively, for instance, that it is significant that there are seven vowels, strings, Pleiads, heroes against Thebes and an age of seven for animals to lose their teeth or that "(the distance from A to Ω) = (the tone range of an aulos) = (the harmony of the universe)." This is related to Aristotle's account of Pythagoreanism in the first book of the *Metaphysics*. Having explained how, in his view, certain Pythagoreans came to think, under the influence of their close engagement with mathematics, that numbers are in some sense the "principles," he adds (986a22–b8) that others among them arrange the principles in a table of opposites (*sustoichia*): limit/limitless; odd/even; one/multitude; right/left; male/female; stationary/mobile; straight/curved; light/darkness; good/bad; square/rectangle. Thus the Pythagorean target of at least some of the criticism towards the end of the *Metaphysics* is established. The reference to

---

[36] Mueller 1981: 103: "[Becker's] suggestion remains one of the most persuasive historical hypotheses based on the *Elements*." Knorr 1975 is a book-length treatment relying on a version of Becker's hypothesis. More recent work in the historiography of mathematics, mine included, simply tended to avoid the early strata of Greek mathematics, focusing instead on the better-documented Hellenistic period (see Saito 1998 for a historiographical survey).

[37] A further ramification of this theory is that, in a mathematical-metaphysical system where everything is a number understood via discrete representations, the discovery of irrationality creates havoc; this interpretation, once standard in the literature, is transparently a retro-projection of the crisis of foundations of the early twentieth century. The lack of evidence for any "crisis" following the discovery of incommensurability is remarked upon in recent literature; see Fowler 1994.

the harmony of the universe is reminiscent of Aristotle's criticism of the "harmony of the spheres," presented as a Pythagorean theory;[38] clearly this theory is related to a suggested numerical equivalence between the number of notes in the octave and the number of planets, another "seven" observation similar to the other numerical equivalences quoted above.[39]

Finally, Alexander's commentary on Aristotle's account of the role of number in Pythagorean metaphysics (*Metaph.* 985b26) offers an expanded list of "analogies" (*homoiomata*) based on number, some or all of which might come from Aristotle's lost books on the Pythagoreans (this time, the author is Alexander, not pseudo-Alexander). Burkert (1972a: 467), who believes this material does go back to Aristotle and hence may represent historical "Pythagoreans," summarizes it as follows:

> One is *nous* [mind] and *ousia* [being]; two is *doxa* [opinion]; three is the number of the whole [. . .] four is justice – equal times equal – but it is also, in the form of the *tetractys*, the "whole nature of numbers";[40] five is marriage [. . .] seven is opportunity and also Athena; [. . .] ten is the perfect number.

Some people Aristotle identified as "Pythagoreans" engaged in the systematic analogy between mathematical terms (especially numerical and musical) and other, cultural and physical phenomena. The fact that Aristotle refers to this approach as that of "other" Pythagoreans (relative to those who thought that "all is number"), suggests that he associated this approach with Pythagoreans other than Philolaus; if so, he was likely reporting, by hearsay, some unwritten discourses and performances.

D.

There remain a few testimonies ascribing mathematical achievement in the strict sense to Pythagoreans.[41] Some have no authority whatsoever:

[38] The authors of the theory are at first anonymous, and then at *De Caelo* 291a8 Aristotle tries to account for the theory and says that they came to this theory "because *this* [. . .] is what puzzled the Pythagoreans." In truth there is no evidence for the origins of this theory; it might be derived by Aristotle entirely from Plato's myth of Er.

[39] Burkert 1972a: 351.

[40] The discussion of the number 4 shows how number symbolism can be generative in complex ways. Four may be conceived as the result of 2 × 2 and hence as "equal × equal" or justice; or as the last term in a series whose summation is 10, 1+2+3+4, its meaning derived from this position (the finish of the series whose result is the "key" number and therefore the "whole nature of number"). On my interpretation, Eurytus performed by acting out such generative number symbolisms of various more particular concepts including biological species.

[41] My survey concentrates on the more significant examples; for a few others see Chapter 13 in this volume. Was Pythagoras, for instance, a founding author of the *Elements*, as Proclus suggests and, seems to suggest, on the authority of Eudemus? Our ignorance is such that no piece of evidence can be definitively shown to be false. Zhmud (2012b) makes the best case possible for such claims, as against the skepticism made standard since Burkert (1972a).

(1) The tradition according to which Pythagoras was the author of the theorem now known by his name is derived from a (Hellenistic?) joke-epigram which *might* have taken this theorem as a generic representation of mathematical achievement.[42] (2) Late sources routinely ascribe the regular solids to Pythagoreans or indeed to Pythagoras himself; this represents no more than the understanding that Plato's *Timaeus* is "Pythagorean."[43] However, Proclus makes two detailed claims for the "Pythagoreans" based on the authority of Eudemus: that Pythagoreans offered an early version of *Elements* I.32 (dealing with the sum of angles in a triangle; Proclus *in Eucl.* 379.2–18 Friedlein), and that Pythagoreans were the first to use the term, or procedure, of "application" (*in Eucl.* 419.15–420.23). For I.32, Proclus cites a detailed, alternative proof, so that this may be an actual Eudemean fragment. The details offered by Proclus concerning "application" are vague by comparison, the typical fare of a commentator padding his text.

These two points are the most difficult element for our interpretation of Pythagorean mathematics. They are consequential; whether or not we take them to be real determines whether or not we take any Pythagoreans, other than Archytas, to have engaged in mathematics in the modern sense. They are undecidable; one may plausibly deny them entirely, one may plausibly accept them entirely. We end up unable to decide between two starkly contrasting images of Pythagoreanism. What seems clear is that, in Eudemus' time, there were reports ascribing to "Pythagoreans" certain geometrical results.[44] With this, we bring our survey of the evidence for Pythagorean mathematics to an end.

3. Early Pythagorean mathematics: a proposal

Even if we reject "relay-race" historiography, as I have proposed, we should not reduce Greek cultural history to a bad tragedy made of discrete episodes. Continuity is formed by the overlap of networks. Certain ideas, or even members, are shared between groups and so the history of culture becomes a network of networks. The relay is a bad metaphor; gears are more to the point. How did the two gears – that of south Italian "Pythagoreans," and

---

[42] Netz 2009: 196–8.

[43] Aët. *DG* 334.10–335.2; Iambl. *VP* 88; Proclus' assertion (*in Eucl.* 305.3 Friedlein) that the proposition about certain regular polygons filling a plane is Pythagorean is best understood as deriving from such a tradition (a cognate lemma is required to prove that there are only five regular solids). Iamblichus refers to Hippasus, who is sometimes associated with the discovery of irrationality, yet another mathematical result whose ascription to Pythagoreans carries no weight; see n. 37.

[44] Our evidence is shaped by Proclus' project in his commentary on Euclid I. We hear more about geometry, especially that of the *Elements* and especially that of *Elements* I.

that of the first network of Greek mathematics – get engaged? One answer is now obvious. *Archytas belonged to both.* Indeed, Archytas also counts as a presence in yet another network – that of the philosophers whose work was in dialogue with Plato.[45] It was through Archytas, then, that a fairly minor and obscure gear – that of south Italian "Pythagoreans" – became engaged with two other gears – (1) mathematicians and (2) philosophers, networked via Athens of Plato's age. These two gears ended up as the prime motor of Western mathematics and philosophy. When Russell says in his *History of Western Philosophy* (1945: 29) "Pythagoras [. . .] was intellectually one of the most important men that ever lived," he may refer to just this engagement of the gears. Rephrasing Russell, then, Archytas could be one of the most important men that ever lived, not so much because of his contributions (which were remarkable enough) as because of his – literally – pivotal position.

The group of south Italian "Pythagoreans" was interested in pursuing analogies based on mathematical concepts, especially those of music and number. Some members of this group might have found what we would call mathematical results, but it is likely that Archytas was the first "Pythagorean" to pursue and commit to writing such results to any meaningful extent. An entire network of mathematicians was formed during Archytas' lifetime. They knew of each other's work, apparently through Athenian connections (perhaps, above all, Plato), but, as mathematicians, they must have been impressed by Archytas, an older member of the group, in social terms a brilliant figure, and, let us not forget, a great mathematical mind. Archytas' engagement with non-configurational classification was impressive enough that it would become a typical (albeit, not the unique) form of mathematical writing in this network. We should not assume, however, that the mathematical influence of his work implied any Pythagoreanism. Theaetetus could have studied irrationals and Eudoxus general proportions, so as to emulate Archytas' brilliant treatment of means, with or without the implication that they had a metaphysics based upon analogies with numbers. However, it would not have been lost on contemporary observers that the rapidly expanding field of mathematics emphasized matters of value to the "Pythagoreans"; it would become natural for philosophers around Plato – such as Aristotle – to detect an affinity between mathematics, Pythagoreanism and number. This *contemporary* historical contingency could then be projected back onto the "Pythagoreans"

---

[45] A network is formed by personal acknowledgment – in friendship, or in rivalry. Lloyd 1990 points out that Plato might have appeared, to himself or to his followers, as a rival to Archytas; just because, I would add, the two could be assimilated in several ways.

themselves – and so, it became natural for Aristotle to imagine that group as more akin to the first network of Greek mathematics (more engaged in what we would still call mathematics) than it was in fact; natural for Eudemus to look for whatever evidence he could find of the mathematical achievements of that group.

Our evidence is too problematic, however, to support with certainty any single proposal. Having made a proposal, let us now qualify it and admit our ignorance. To start at the minimalist end, the evidence for the specific early Pythagorean contributions to mathematics really is tenuous and could represent no more than a misunderstanding on the part of Eudemus or his readers. We are then left with no more evidence for early Pythagorean mathematics beyond Eurytus' performances and Philolaus' metaphysics. Later authors could refer to "Pythagoreans" as a mere hedge – because they were not sure how far back the tradition actually went – when, in fact, there may have been no tradition at all, just a handful of eccentrics. Similarly, it is quite possible to downplay Archytas' influence: perhaps fourth-century mathematicians were interested in non-configurational classification for a variety of reasons, which had little to do with their admiration for their older (but distant) colleague in Tarentum. "Pythagorean mathematics" as a historical force is then reduced to nearly nothing.

At the maximalist end, it is possible that there were many more figures active in south Italy at the turn of the fifth century sharing broadly the same interests as Philolaus. It is likely that some of them would be inspired to find and proclaim original mathematical results, which might have circulated with enough consistency, even if only orally, so that they became a real historical force in the growth of Greek mathematics. Then again, the maximalist could suggest – more credibly, indeed – that the mathematicians of the fourth century pursued their science in full recognition that it was a Pythagorean tradition, perhaps many of them subscribing to it (or to some Platonist version of it), all the way down to Euclid himself: such, of course, was Proclus' view,[46] and it is not an absurd one.

In my preferred account, the role of Archytas is crucial. In the minimalist account, he is left isolated and less influential; in the maximalist account, he is swamped in a much thicker tradition, where his own personal contribution matters much less. It is hard to tell how to divide the probabilities between the various accounts. Perhaps the real contribution made by this

---

[46] Proclus explicitly claims that Euclid was a Platonist (*in Eucl.* 68.20–3 Friedlein), capping a historical survey, largely of what I refer to as "the first network of Greek mathematics," where the key claim is that of the close relationship between the mathematicians and Plato's Academy.

survey, then, is in focusing our ignorance, our open questions. The historical question – the one whose answer we may never know – turns out to be this: how important was Archytas? How original, how influential?

To conclude on firmer ground, we may once again set the first network of Greek mathematics side by side with the second and notice that the second network is not "Pythagorean."[47] But it did come to represent mathematics. Archimedes, to his future readers, came to *replace* Archytas. This would have consequences for the future history of mathematics. It would be much more difficult to base one's worldview on the metaphysics of number and music, when your mathematics was that of Archimedes. After the third century BC, a mathematically inclined philosopher would have either to invoke an archaizing version of mathematics, or to invent a new kind of mathematical metaphysics going beyond Plato and "Pythagoreanism." The first route would be taken by the Late Ancient Platonists, the second by the authors of the scientific revolution.

[47] Indeed, even its interest in "ratios" appears to be quite un-Pythagorean. I argued this for Archimedes in Netz 2010: 433–43.

CHAPTER 9

Pythagorean harmonics

Andrew Barker

1. Introduction

If we tried to begin this investigation of Pythagorean harmonics with Pythagoras himself (*c.* 500 BC), we would find ourselves floundering through a swamp in darkness, guided by little except Will-o'-the-Wisps, "false deluding lights," as Dryden put it. We shall tiptoe towards this perilous territory in due course, but let us begin in clearer light and on rather more solid ground, with a remark by Ptolemaïs of Cyrene, a scholar writing several hundred years after Pythagoras died:

> A *kanonikos* is a harmonic theorist who constructs the ratios of what is attuned. There is a difference between *mousikoi* and *kanonikoi*: the harmonic theorists who proceed on the basis of sense-perception are called *mousikoi*, and the Pythagorean harmonic theorists are called *kanonikoi*. (Both, however, are *mousikoi* in the generic sense.)[1]

Ptolemaïs is the only Greek woman on record as a musical theorist. Her work is known through quotations by Porphyry, all of which are concerned with the epistemological commitments and methodologies of the various "schools" or traditions of harmonic theory. She divides them into two broad groups, distinguished by the "criteria" on which they principally rely, sense-perception in the case of one group (here called *mousikoi* but in other passages "Aristoxenians"), and reason, *logos*, in the case of the other (*kanonikoi* or "Pythagoreans").

Ptolemaïs' comments are sketchy, but make a useful starting-point. Exponents of Pythagorean harmonics are identified with the *kanonikoi*, people who make use of the *kanōn* or monochord (a single taut string which can be divided at measured points by means of movable bridges); and a *kanonikos*, she says, is a theorist who describes musical scales or systems

---

[1] Ptolemaïs *ap.* Porph. *Harm.* 23.5–9. Porphyry quotes several extracts from her *Pythagorean Musical Elements* at 22.22–26.5 and mentions her briefly at 114.7; we hear nothing of her elsewhere. The fullest modern discussion is Levin 2009, especially 204–40.

of attunement in terms of numerical ratios. This does not imply that everyone who expressed their theories in terms of ratios was a *kanonikos*, a user of the monochord; that would be questionable, if only because theories deploying ratios go back to the mid fifth century BC, whereas our first explicit allusion to the monochord dates from the end of the fourth. But it does imply the converse, that monochord users inevitably express their theories in terms of ratios; and this is true, since the monochord's only purpose was to demonstrate the correlation between each musical interval and the ratio between the lengths of a string that produce its constituent notes.[2] Regardless of the string's absolute length, if we first strike a note from its whole length and then another from its half (separating the two halves by a bridge), the second note will be exactly an octave above the first, giving the ratio 2:1; if the ratio is 3:2 the interval is a perfect fifth; the ratio 4:3 gives a perfect fourth; and so on. Experiments with relevant dimensions of other sound-producing objects – pipes of different lengths, metal disks of different thicknesses (famously used in demonstrations by Hippasus before the mid fifth century)[3] and so on – showed that the ratios remain the same no matter how the notes are generated.[4]

2. Pythagorean acoustics

Early Pythagoreans concluded that since the only constant features of these situations are the pitches themselves, it must be their inter-relations that are consistently reflected in the ratios. Pitches are *quantitative* attributes of sounds, and the relations between them are constituted by the same ratios that are found on the instruments. They interpreted this conclusion through research in the science we call "physical acoustics," the study of the material events involved in the production and transmission of sounds. Their most fundamental hypotheses are not peculiarly Pythagorean; non-Pythagorean Presocratic cosmologists shared with them the thesis that sounds are caused by impacts of objects on the air, that from a physical perspective a sound is the consequent movement in or of the air, and that this movement is perceived *as* a sound when it enters the ear.[5] But no

---

[2] For details of the monochord, its history and its scientific contexts, see Creese 2010.
[3] Hippasus is the earliest Pythagorean connected by reasonably solid evidence with work in mathematics and harmonics. See Burkert 1972a: 193–4, 206–8, and now Horky 2013a: 37–84.
[4] See, e.g., [Arist.] *Pr.* 19.50, 922b–923a; Theon of Smyrna 59.4–61.17, 66.20–4; schol. to Pl. *Phd.* 108d4.
[5] See especially Theophr. *Sens.* 9 (Empedocles), 39–41 (Diogenes of Apollonia), 55–7 (Democritus); cf. Aët. 4.16.1 (Empedocles), 4.16.2 (Alcmaeon), 4.19.5 (Anaxagoras); Hippocrates *Fleshes* 15 and 18.

non-Pythagorean Presocratics are said to have examined the physical difference between high-pitched and low-pitched sounds.

The first Pythagorean to do so was Archytas (fr. 1). He argues, on the basis of a plethora of observable examples, that high-pitched sounds are caused by swifter and more vigorous impacts on the air. Their pitches depend on the speed and vigor of their movement – apparently their movement across the space between the source and the ear. Archytas' theory runs into two main difficulties. First, he apparently conflates the attributes of pitch and volume; an impact that moves the air swiftly also moves it vigorously, and he says explicitly that the resulting sound is both high-pitched and loud, whereas, of course, a high-pitched sound need not be loud. Plato modified the theory, making the movement's speed solely responsible for the sound's pitch and tying its volume to a variable independent of the speed, the movement's "magnitude" (*Ti.* 67b–c). That the pitch of a sound is either caused or constituted by its speed of transmission remained the commonest theory in later centuries.

Second, if either version of the theory is correct, the two notes of a concord transmitted simultaneously from their source cannot reach us at the same moment. Hence the higher will be perceived before the lower. But then they cannot form a concord, since a concord was standardly defined as an undifferentiated blend of two notes neither of which is heard separately. Aristotle ruminated elaborately but inconclusively on the issue in the *De sensu*, and Theophrastus exploited the difficulty in an intricate set of arguments against quantitative theories of pitch in general.[6] Theophrastus found little support among later theorists, but alternatives to the "speed" hypothesis were already being proposed. The most important first appears explicitly around 300 BC in the introduction to a treatise we shall discuss later, the *Sectio canonis*. It argues that each sound is caused not by one impact on the air but by a sequence of impacts; the writer may be thinking of the back-and-forth oscillations of a plucked string, to which several later theorists refer, conceived as beating against the air with each displacement from its position of rest.[7] Notes of higher pitch, he says, occur when the impacts follow in quicker succession, and the airborne impulses impinge on our ears in a more crowded sequence. A similar hypothesis is outlined in a passage quoted by Porphyry (*Harm.* 30.1–31.21) from a certain Heraclides, whom I take to be the fourth-century philosopher Heraclides

---

[6] Arist. *Sens.* 448a–9a, noting that others before him had raised the problem; Theophr. fr. 716 Fortenbaugh, especially lines 64–90.

[7] Cf., e.g., Aelianus *ap.* Porph. *Harm.* 35.1–7.

of Pontus;[8] and other writers of the same period hint at the same idea. I suspect that it may have earlier and specifically Pythagorean origins (cf. n. 26 below).

Theories of these sorts became common currency among philosophers and scientists, but are especially prominent in expositions of Pythagorean harmonics, regularly keeping company with the treatment of musical intervals as ratios. It is easy to see why. Every such hypothesis gives a clear physical interpretation to the thesis that pitch is a quantitative attribute; it is identified either with the speed of a movement[9] or with the number of impulses passing in a given time through the air. Although the Greeks had no technical devices for measuring any sound's speed or the frequency of its impulses, they could readily assign ratios to the relations between the speeds or frequencies of pitches a given interval apart. Other things being equal, a shorter string oscillates more rapidly than a longer one; hence, they concluded, it generates more frequent impulses or causes swifter movements. Since experiments with the monochord or similar devices showed that when the ratio between the lengths of string is 2:1, for instance, the interval between the pitches is an octave, it is a natural inference that the movement generated by the shorter length is twice as swift as the other, or embodies twice as frequent impulses. Hence the ratio between notes an octave apart is also 2:1. It is the mirror-image of the ratio between the lengths; applied to string lengths the larger term belongs to the longer, lower-sounding length; applied to the notes it belongs to the higher note. Through such reasoning Pythagorean harmonics is provided with firm foundations.

3.   Reason and sense-perception in Pythagorean harmonics

Let us return to the evidence of Ptolemaïs. The *mousikoi*, she says, base their work on the evidence of the senses, i.e. the hearing, evidently implying that the *kanonikoi* or Pythagoreans do not. This is confirmed by two other passages quoted from her treatise by Porphyry:

> Pythagoras and his followers wished to treat sense-perception [*aisthēsis*] as a guide for reason [*logos*] at the beginning, to provide it as it were with an initial spark, and after setting off from these starting-points to work with reason by itself, divorced from perception. Hence if the system discovered by reason in the course of their work no longer accords with perception, they

---

[8] His identity has been debated since the nineteenth century; the fullest modern discussion is in Gottschalk 1968: 450–2. He concludes that this Heraclides is a much later writer; most recent scholars follow him, but I do not find his arguments persuasive.

[9] On the definition of a movement's speed cf. Aelianus *ap.* Porph. *Harm.* 36.9–37.5.

do not turn back, but accuse sense-perception of having gone astray, and say that reason by itself has discovered what is correct and refutes perception.[10]

What is the difference between those who are eminent in musical theory? It is that some gave priority to reason by itself, others to sense-perception and others to a combination of both. Reason by itself was given priority by those of the Pythagoreans who were dedicated to quarrelling with the *mousikoi* by rejecting perception completely, and presenting reason as a self-sufficient criterion in its own right. But these people are altogether refuted by the fact that they accept something perceived at the beginning, and then forget about it.[11]

Both these groups of Pythagoreans accept something on the basis of sense-perception at the outset of their inquiry,[12] and then proceed by means of reasoning alone. But there is a significant difference. The second group, who conveniently "forget" their initial reliance on perceptual evidence, seem to be attempting the task set by Plato (*Resp.* 531a–c), where he criticizes the Pythagoreans for studying audible sounds and proposes a metaphysically oriented harmonics concerned with numbers alone. Probably, then, the "Pythagoreans" in Ptolemaïs' second group are post-Platonic theorists, whose work combined Plato's ideas with those of the earlier Pythagoreans (from the Hellenistic period onwards, many purportedly Pythagorean writings and reports about Pythagoreanism contain features that in fact originate in the Platonist tradition). By contrast, "Pythagoras and his followers" do not conceal their use of sensory evidence at the beginning, and they explain *why* human hearing is not competent to criticize reason's conclusions. It is only – so far as we are told – because it is inaccurate. This suggests that their conclusions apply to a subject-matter on which perception cannot be trusted because of its inaccuracy, but on which it *could* authoritatively pronounce if its judgments were both precise and reliable. In that case the insights of reason must illuminate the very same things as are vaguely grasped by the senses; reason analyses the mathematically "correct" musical systems to which human practices approximate.

This conclusion does not rule out that their purposes, just like those of the second group, were primarily metaphysical or cosmological. Ptolemaïs' comments could well apply to Pythagoreans of the fifth century, before

[10] Ptolemaïs *ap.* Porph. *Harm.* 23.25–31, repeated at 25.25–26.1. See Chapter 20, section 3 below.

[11] Ptolemaïs *ap.* Porph. *Harm.* 25.9–14.

[12] At 23.13–17 Porphyry gives examples of these propositions: that there are concordant and discordant intervals, that the octave amounts to a fourth combined with a fifth, that the interval of a tone is the difference between a fifth and a fourth. The examples may be quoted or paraphrased from Ptolemaïs, but may be taken directly from the introduction and propositions 12–13 of the Euclidean *Sectio canonis*.

the mathematical-metaphysical project and the one concerned with "real" music had been conceptually distinguished. The early Pythagoreans did not posit two separate domains, one described by mathematics and another accessible to the senses. The philosophical tools by which they were later separated were provided by Plato.[13]

4. Harmonics and metaphysics in Pythagoreanism

Central to the Pythagorean metaphysical enterprise is the notion of a concord, defined as a phenomenon in which two different notes mingle together so intimately that neither is perceived in its own right; we hear only an undifferentiated blend of the two, and from the two different things comes a perfect unity. Musically coordinated patterns of notes such as a well-formed scale also bring unity out of diversity or opposition,[14] and musical structures were regarded as paradigm examples of the "harmonious" integration of difference and contrariety. They exemplify such integration more perfectly than anything else readily accessible to us, and harmonics had discovered the key to their mathematical relations; hence this science became a crucial element in Pythagorean cosmological research. Aristotle's statement of the Pythagoreans' manifesto, "the elements of number are the elements of all things, and the whole heaven is *harmonia* and number,"[15] encapsulates the central role of harmonics in their metaphysics.

The combination of the musical with the metaphysical in Pythagorean harmonics is evident in the work of Philolaus (late fifth century), especially in fr. 6.[16] The universe is constituted by two sorts of items, "limiters" and "unlimiteds." Since they are

> neither alike nor of the same race, it would have been impossible for them to be organized together if *harmonia* had not come upon them, however it arose. Things that were alike and of the same race had no need of *harmonia* as well; but things that were unlike and not of the same race nor equal in rank had to be locked together by *harmonia*, if they were to be held together in a *kosmos*.

So far there is no guarantee that the bonding factor, *harmonia*, has either mathematical or musical characteristics; the word *harmonia* can refer to any "fitting-together" of separate items. But Philolaus also asserts "all things

---

[13] See especially Huffman 2005: 57–64, 84–7, 423–5.   [14] Cf., e.g., Pl. *Symp.* 187a–e.
[15] Arist. *Metaph.* 986a1–3.
[16] The passage printed as the second paragraph of DK 44B6 is quoted separately by our sources. In Huffman 1993 it is fr. 6a.

that are known have number; for it is impossible for anything to be thought of or known without this" (fr. 4); and the second paragraph of fr. 6 (fr. 6a) defines *harmonia* in simultaneously musical and mathematical terms. I cannot pursue its details here,[17] but the gist is straightforward. What Philolaus now calls *harmonia* is the interval of an octave, structurally integrated by relations between the notes inside it. He refers to its notes and its most significant intervals in the language of musicians. But his emphasis is on the intervals' definitions as ratios, 2:1 for the octave, 3:2 for the fifth, 4:3 for the fourth, and 9:8 for the tone, the interval by which a fifth exceeds a fourth. His system corresponds to a familiar musical scale to which an instrument's strings could be simply and reliably tuned, but his description is designed to bring out the remarkable symmetry of its mathematical form.

Philolaus' work is a fine example of the Pythagorean fusion of metaphysical motivation with attention to musical phenomena. But it raises an important question. Let us agree that musical structures display well-integrated mathematical patterns of organization, and that these may exemplify the modes of organization that integrate the constituents of the universe. But why are certain systems of numbers well integrated while others are not? What are the principles that Philolaus' *harmonia* obeys and that give it its special status? Plato complains that the Pythagoreans neglected these questions; they failed "to investigate which numbers are concordant with one another and which are not, *and in each case why*" (*Resp.* 531c).

5. What mathematical principles govern *harmonia*?

Evidence connected with the work of Archytas shows, however, that early Pythagoreans investigating harmonics *did* propose principles of the relevant kind.[18] Archytas describes what he calls the "three means in music," where a "mean" inserted between two numbers links the three terms in one of three forms of mathematical proportion: arithmetic, geometric and subcontrary or "harmonic" (fr. 2); and these means had already been deployed in a musical context by Hippasus, a century earlier.[19] His connection of the means with music is straightforwardly justifiable: if the ratio between two terms is that of a double octave (4:1), their geometric mean divides the interval into two octaves; the arithmetic mean between terms in the ratio

---

[17] For details, rather different interpretations, and differing views about related material in Boethius see Huffman 1993: 145–65, 364–74; Barker 2007: 263–86.
[18] For recent studies of Archytas and his harmonic theories see Huffman 2005; Barker 2007: 287–307.
[19] See Huffman 2005: 164–74.

of an octave divides it into a fifth and a fourth; the harmonic mean between the same terms does so too, but reverses the two intervals' order.[20]

I argue elsewhere that Archytas also applied a "principle of proportionality" to the construction of complete scales; the term representing each note of the scale (apart from its boundaries) must be a mean between two others in the same scale. The hypothesis, based on a study of the "divisions of the tetrachord" attributed to Archytas by Ptolemy, needs immediate qualification. As Huffman has demonstrated, empirical observation also played a significant part in his analyses; Archytas was not doing exercises in pure mathematics. He was trying to show that the patterns of relations used by musicians can be described in mathematical terms and conform to mathematical principles; but he could not do this without first listening carefully to the intervals to which musicians tuned their strings, and observing the procedures by which they did so.[21] Only then could he devise systems of ratios that conformed to intelligible mathematical rules and were also persuasive representations of attunements in actual use.[22]

Archytas' objectives and methods help to explain Plato's criticisms of Pythagorean harmonics in the *Republic* (530d–531c). He complains that their version of the science is not purely "rational"; they measure the relations between notes that we hear, and neglect questions about "concordant" relations between numbers as such. Huffman rightly contends that Archytas is his principal target, and that Archytas analyses "real world" musical systems by methods involving empirical observation.[23] Neither of Ptolemaïs' types of Pythagorean harmonics is sufficiently empirical to encompass Archytas' work.

But given that principles governing relations between numbers were also involved in Archytas' analyses, why does Plato imply that he identified no such principles? Perhaps the point is that the empirical strand in Archytas' thought prevented him from finding principles that would authorize *only* the system or systems of which pure reason would approve.[24]

---

[20] The sequence 6, 12, 24, where 12 is the geometric mean between 6 and 24, gives a pair of octaves, each in the ratio 2:1. The arithmetic mean between 6 and 12 is 9; 12:9 = 4:3, the ratio of the fourth, and 9:6 = 3:2, that of the fifth. The harmonic mean between 6 and 12 is 8; 12:8 = 3:2, the ratio of the fifth, and 8:6 = 4:3, that of the fourth.

[21] Some intervals, for instance, were tuned in two steps. In the first the musician needed to recognize only concordant intervals (fifths and fourths), which the ear can identify with great precision. In the second he adjusted the relations very slightly, to achieve the effect he sought. The adjustment is so small that listeners who have not observed the procedure are unlikely to notice it.

[22] For Archytas' divisions see Ptol. *Harm.* 1.13 (DK 47A16). Cf. Huffman 2005: 402–8; Barker 2007: 292–302.

[23] Huffman 2005: 41–2, 83–5.   [24] Cf. Huffman 2005: 423–5.

Certainly it turns out that none of Archytas' three divisions of the tetrachord corresponds to the one that Plato espouses in the *Timaeus*.

6. Degrees of concordance

Let us return to the musical concords. The octave, fifth and fourth are all concordant by Greek standards; but Pythagorean theorists argued that they are not equally so. In *Harmonica* 1.6 Ptolemy criticizes a curious procedure, which he attributes to the Pythagoreans, for establishing which are more concordant and which are less. Porphyry, in his commentary on the passage, describes the procedure more dispassionately, adding the valuable information that it was used by "some of the Pythagoreans, as Archytas and Didymus record."[25] This means that the account that he and Ptolemy read was written by Didymus (probably first century AD), who was retailing information from a work of Archytas (fourth century BC). There is no reason to doubt the attribution to Archytas; hence the account records a procedure used by Pythagoreans earlier than or contemporary with him, though not necessarily one he employed himself.

Briefly, the procedure is this. Take the "foundations" (*pythmenes*) of the ratios of the concords (that is, take them in their lowest terms, e.g. 4:3 for the fourth). Then subtract a unit from each term and add the remaining numbers; and the smaller the total resulting, the more concordant the interval. The totals for the octave (2:1), fifth (3:2) and fourth (4:3) are 1, 3 and 5 respectively; hence the octave is the most concordant and the fourth is the least. The procedure is purely arithmetical and treats degrees of concordance as arithmetically determined, but it is undeniably odd, not least because the subtraction of the units seems unnecessary. The order of precedence will be the same if it is omitted (the totals will then be 3, 5 and 7). A clue to the thought behind it may lie in the words which refer to the paired units and the totals; the former are the "similars" (*homoia*), the latter the "dissimilars" (*anhomoia*). Perhaps the *homoia* represent the element that the notes of any concord have in common, while the quantities finally compared measure the extent to which they differ. Since the total formed by the *homoia* is always the same, it can be put aside when their relative concordance is being assessed.

The sameness of the *homoia* in every concord suggests that the notes' concordance is constituted by what they have in common; they "blend" in

---

[25] Ptol. *Harm.* 13.23–15.2; Porph. *Harm.* 107.15–8.21. Porphyry's comments on Ptolemy's critique continue to 112.3.

virtue of their similarity, but their dissimilarities ensure that they do not
blend completely. "Similarity" and "dissimilarity" play that role in Plato's
account of concordance at *Timaeus* 80a; sounds "sometimes travel discor-
dantly because of the dissimilarity [*anhomoiotēs*] of the movement they set
up in us, sometimes concordantly because of its similarity [*homoiotēs*]." But
Plato's discussion gives little more help in interpreting the Pythagoreans'
procedure. His line of thought has an implicit mathematical dimension of
its own, but nothing connects it directly with their procedure apart from
the terminological resonances.[26]

Crude though it may be (Ptolemy spells out some of its mathematical absurdities), the procedure has affinities with a more sophisticated
mode of reasoning about concords, which Ptolemy also attributes to the
Pythagoreans.[27] First, equal numbers go with notes of equal pitch and
unequal numbers with notes of unequal pitch, those that define some
interval. Second, intervals fall into two classes, concords and discords,
and the former class is "finer," *kallion*. Similarly, numerical ratios fall
into two classes, "epimerics" (*epimereis*) on the one hand and "epimorics"
(*epimorioi*) and multiples (*pollaplasioi*) on the other.[28] The latter class is
"better," *ameinōn*, because the terms of its ratios stand in "simple" relations
to one another and can be straightforwardly compared. The smaller term
in a multiple ratio is a "simple part" of the greater (e.g., in the ratio 2:1 it
is one half of the greater, in 3:1 it is one third, and so on, not a fraction
such as *three*-sevenths or *four*-ninths); in an epimoric ratio such as 4:3 the
difference between the terms is a simple part of each term in the same sense.
Ratios of the former class, epimeric ratios such as 7:3, are "worse," because
3 is not related to 7 in any such clear and simple way. The Pythagoreans
infer that the "better" class of ratios should be assigned to the "finer" class
of intervals, and thereby reach the principle that all concords must have
ratios that are either multiple or epimoric.[29]

We thus have a distinction between finer and less fine intervals, corre-
lated with a distinction between better and worse ratios. Ptolemy asserts

[26] Long ago I suggested an explanation of the procedure which links it to the theory of pitch
propounded in the *Sectio canonis*. The hypothesis provides it with an intelligible basis, but I shall
not pursue it here. See Barker 1989: 35 n. 29.

[27] Ptol. *Harm*. 1.5, 11.1–12.7. With one important reservation Ptolemy approves of this argument,
unlike the procedure discussed above.

[28] A multiple ratio is one in which one term is a multiple of the other, and has the form mn:n. An
epimoric ratio is such that the greater term is equal to the other plus a unit fraction of the other,
and in its lowest terms always has the form n+1:n. An epimeric ratio, in this and related texts, is
any ratio that is neither multiple nor epimoric.

[29] The principle first appears explicitly in the Euclidean *Sectio canonis*. But the principle is probably
older, since the work is a systematization of propositions in earlier mathematical harmonics.

that assigning the ratio 2:1 to the octave makes excellent sense, "since the octave is the finest of the concords and the double is the best of the ratios, the former because it is nearest to the equal-toned [i.e., most like a unison], the latter because it makes the excess [the difference between the terms] equal to that which is exceeded" (*Harm.* 11.21–4). The implication is that the nearer this "excess" (*hyperochē*) is to being equal to the smaller term, the better the ratio will be. Thus, in the case of the ratio 2:1, the excess of 2 over 1 is 1, which is equal to the smaller term. The ratio 3:2 is not as "fine" as the ratio 2:1, because the excess of 3 over 2 is again 1, but this is not equal to the smaller term, 2, but differs from it by 1. Although Ptolemy was not a Pythagorean and criticizes the Pythagoreans for various errors, his approach to harmonics owes much to theirs and he will return to these ideas in *Harmonica* 1. 7, where the Pythagoreans' account of the concords becomes the starting-point for his own (cf. *Harm.* 15.18–27).

As we emerge from Ptolemy's discussion of the concords of the fifth and the fourth with their ratios firmly identified as 3:2 and 4:3 respectively, we find that the same principle applies when we move beyond the concords to the "melodic" intervals, those that can form individual steps of a scale. These too must have epimoric ratios, ones smaller than that of the fourth (no interval smaller than the octave has a multiple ratio), and an interval is "more melodic" than another if the difference between the two terms is "closer to equality" with the lesser term. Thus after the ratios of the primary concords, 2:1, 3:2, 4:3, the melodic intervals, in descending order of melodic excellence, will be 5:4, 6:5, 7:6 and so on (*Harm.* 16.12–21). There are no compelling reasons for attributing to Pythagoreans of any date this extension of the "closeness to equality" principle beyond the concords, or for saddling them with the doctrine that melodic intervals must have epimoric ratios (though Ptolemy tries to father this rule on Archytas in *Harm.* 1.13).[30] But Ptolemy's thesis is recognizably a development of theirs, and the order of diminishing excellence in which he places all musical intervals is precisely the one that would emerge from an extension of the Pythagorean procedure attacked in *Harmonica* 1.6.[31]

---

[30] As we shall see later, a common "Pythagorean" scale includes a non-epimoric interval; and one of Archytas' systems includes two, as Ptolemy complains in *Harm.* 1.13–14; cf. Huffman 2005: 420–3. On the correlation between musical fineness and mathematical excellence which Ptolemy attributes to the Pythagoreans, see Barker 1994; on the passages of *Harm.* 1.5 and 1.7 we have been discussing cf. Barker 2000: 54–87, cf. Solomon 2000: 16–18, 22–4; Raffa 2002: 287–302, 310–13.

[31] For other allegedly Pythagorean ways of assessing relative concordance see Boethius *Fundamentals of Music* 2.18–19.

7. The conflict between reason and perception: Pythagoreans vs. Aristoxenians

The principle that a concord's ratio must be either multiple or epimoric has a significant consequence: the interval of an octave plus a fourth (which sense-perception, according to Aristoxenus, Ptolemy and many others, unquestionably recognizes as a concord) cannot really be concordant. Its ratio, 8:3, fulfills neither condition. This is just one example of the conflict that can occur, as Ptolemaïs tells us, between Pythagorean theory and the evidence of our ears, and between the Pythagorean and Aristoxenian styles of harmonics. Should we follow our senses or the mathematical rule? Aristoxenus insisted that the business of harmonics is with the phenomena presented to our hearing, conceived in the manner in which they are presented. The main points of dissension are neatly brought out in the *Sectio canonis* attributed (insecurely) to Euclid, written, as I believe, around the beginning of the third century BC.[32] Later theorists, including Ptolemy and Porphyry, represented it as a fundamental document in Pythagorean theory.

The *Sectio canonis* contains an introduction and twenty propositions, each (with a few exceptions) set out in the form of a theorem. The first nine propositions are purely arithmetical; the others purport to demonstrate truths about musical relations on the basis of the conclusions of the first nine. But arithmetical conclusions cannot be the only premises on which these demonstrations depend, and the writer also introduces a few very basic facts drawn from sense-perception: a fifth and a fourth taken together make an octave, for instance, and the octave, fifth and fourth are concords. (In this he resembles "Pythagoras and his successors" as Ptolemaïs describes them, perhaps with this treatise in mind.) The principle that a concord's ratio must be epimoric or multiple also plays a fundamental role in his argumentation. Given these preliminary assumptions, the theorems' reasoning is almost impeccable.[33]

Aristoxenus and other empirically minded theorists had argued that tones can be divided in half into semitones and that the fourth consists of two and a half tones, the fifth of three and a half tones and thus the whole octave of six. Proposition 3 of the *Sectio* contains the argument

---

[32] On problems to do with the date and authorship of the treatise see especially Barbera 1991: 3–62. For a different view see Barker 2007: 362–410, especially 362–70.

[33] Unfortunately the complex proposition 11, whose conclusions are essential premises for many of the later ones, involves a logical error and is not valid. See, e.g., Barbera 1991: 155 n. 44; Barker 2007: 386–7.

that underpins a series of refutations of these conclusions of the empirical theorists. It proves that no epimoric ratio can be divided into two or more sub-ratios all of which are equal. A marginally different version is transmitted by Boethius (*Fundamentals of Music* 3.11), who attributes it (almost certainly correctly) to Archytas.[34] Then, once the interval of a tone has been assigned the epimoric ratio 9:8 (proposition 13), it follows immediately that it cannot be divided in half, or into thirds, quarters and so on (proposition 16). Proposition 18, proving that the pair of intervals at the bottom of an enharmonic tetrachord cannot be equal, works on the same basis. Proposition 14 demonstrates that the octave is smaller than six tones, since the ratio between the first term and the last in a sequence of six 9:8 ratios is greater than 2:1. Proposition 15 shows that, given this result, the fifth must be smaller than three and a half tones and the fourth smaller than two and a half. Later theorists in the mathematical tradition regularly repeat the refutations in the *Sectio canonis*, frequently claiming Pythagorean origins for them, though they seldom show any understanding of the Archytan proof in proposition 3.[35] These mathematically based contradictions of empirically grounded contentions mark a major faultline between the Pythagorean and Aristoxenian traditions, as theorists of the fourth century BC and later periods construed them.

8. The "Pythagorean" diatonic and Plato's *Timaeus*

The last two propositions of the *Sectio canonis* explain how to construct the "division of the *kanōn*" reflected in its title, describing a method for determining the successive positions of the bridge dividing the monochord's string which will produce the notes and intervals of a two-octave scale.[36] They use only the ratios established in earlier propositions, those of the concords and the tone. Hence all the individual scalar steps constructed are either tones or instances of the small interval, slightly smaller than a half-tone, which remains in the concord of a fourth when two tones have been subtracted from it. The writer does not name this interval or calculate its ratio, which is 256:243; but the ratio was already known to Plato, and probably to earlier writers in the Pythagorean tradition. Plato describes it

---

[34] See, e.g., Knorr 1975: Ch. 7; Barbera 1991: 58–60. Boethius' immediate source is probably Nicomachus.

[35] See, e.g., Theon of Smyrna 53.8–16, 69.17–70.6; Nicomachus *Harmonic Handbook* 12. 263.18–264.5 Jan; Panaetius *ap.* Porph. *Harm.* 65.21–67.10.

[36] The two-octave range was reckoned to be "complete" by most theorists from the fourth century onwards. Earlier theorists (e.g., Philolaus) worked within the compass of a single octave.

as something "left over" (*Ti.* 36b), and it was later called the *leimma* or "remainder."

Each octave consists of two tetrachords (fourths) joined in the middle by an interval of a tone. Every tetrachord in the system described in the *Sectio* contains two tones in the ratio 9:8, together with the *leimma*. Greek scales fell into three classes (diatonic, chromatic and enharmonic) depending on the positions of the two notes inserted into the fourths. In terms of this classification the system in the *Sectio* is diatonic, and because of its central role in later Pythagorean harmonics, it is sometimes called the "Pythagorean diatonic."[37] There are two main reasons for its prominence. One is that it can be constructed by moves involving concords alone.[38] Secondly, and very importantly, it derived weighty authority from its use by Plato in the *Timaeus* (34b–36d). Plato constructs a system of ratios that in musical terms gives a diatonic scale spanning four octaves plus a major sixth. But the numbers he gives as the terms of the ratios do not represent audible pitches; they refer to lengths along a strip of the non-material substance from which the universe's animating principle, the World-Soul, is made. The system describes the structure through which the Soul's parts are coherently organized and united. Despite its clear musical connotations, Plato's description includes no musical language, and no explicit reference to anything audible. It is presented as a purely mathematical construction, guided by mathematical principles and considerations alone, notably by applications of the three kinds of mean Archytas had identified. It thus exemplifies the kind of harmonics imagined in the *Republic* (531c), a science concerned only with numbers and not at all with sounds, and has close affinities with the approach that Ptolemaïs attributes to "those of the Pythagoreans who were dedicated to quarrelling with the *mousikoi*."

One might object that she describes these Pythagoreans as accepting certain things on the basis of perception at the outset of their project (though they later "forget" the fact), whereas Plato introduces nothing from the auditory domain. But Plato's silence on this point is misleading. It can be no coincidence that his system corresponds so exactly to the diatonic scale of the Euclidean division of the *kanōn*, familiar also from

---

[37] It is probably already implicit in the *harmonia* of Philolaus (Archytas' diatonic is different). By following methods slightly adapted from those of the *Sect. can.* and presupposing only the ratios of the concords and the tone, one can also construct a "chromatic" scale; see Thrasyllus *ap.* Theon of Smyrna 87.4–93.9. It is rarely mentioned elsewhere.

[38] The tone is constructed through moves of a fifth and a fourth; the *leimma* is what is left after the construction of two tones within the fourth. See, e.g., *Sect. can.* proposition 17; Aristox. *El. harm.* 55.3–56.13 Meibom = 68.10–70.2 Da Rios.

musicians' tuning practices.[39] Perhaps the construction's initial steps can be justified on mathematical grounds alone, though we might wonder why it is based on applications of the means used, according to Archytas, in music. But that cannot be said of the procedure by which terms are inserted between all numbers related to one another in the ratio 4:3, the ratio of a fourth. Plato gives no mathematical reasons for dividing each of these ratios into three sub-ratios (corresponding to the three intervals inside each tetrachord), or for assigning two of them the ratio of the tone, 9:8, leaving 256:243, the *leimma*, to complete the total. Only musical experience can have prompted these aspects of his construction – though Plato (or rather, his Pythagorean spokesman Timaeus) has omitted to mention the fact.[40] Plato was certainly aware of his construction's musical character; in later parts of the *Timaeus* he exploits, to good effect, the fact that the organization of the World-Soul (and of the human soul in its perfect condition) is reflected in human music.[41]

The *Timaeus* plays a major part in later Pythagorean harmonics, since many later expositions and discussions of the subject are embedded in studies of the World-Soul's musical structure. The tradition of commentaries on this part of the *Timaeus* began in the early Academy itself, in writings by Xenocrates and his pupil Crantor, and continued unabated through the Hellenistic and Roman periods. The most significant surviving examples include works by Plutarch, Theon of Smyrna (who incorporates substantial passages from studies by Thrasyllus and Adrastus), Calcidius (in Latin) and above all the indefatigable Proclus, who discusses its mathematical and metaphysical interpretation at enormous length and in minute detail, arguing extensively for or against the views of his predecessors, and thus giving us the names and some of the opinions of several other such commentators.

Most of these commentators would have regarded themselves as Platonists rather than Pythagoreans. But in the Roman period the distinction was blurred; and though few writers were seduced by the rumor that Plato had plagiarized the *Timaeus* from a Pythagorean source,[42] they thought

---

[39] It does so unproblematically in its first two octaves. Difficulties arise in the divisions of the remainder because Plato does not explicitly fill all the gaps.

[40] This might be because the divine Craftsman is not an inhabitant of the world of sense-perception, which is not yet recognizable at the time (if it is a "time") of this process. But Plato – unlike the Craftsman himself – must have drawn on musical experience when constructing the system he attributes to the divine artificer.

[41] See particularly *Ti.* 47c–e, 80b. On relations between music and the soul in Plato see Pelosi 2010.

[42] One exception is Nicomachus, who clearly aligns himself with the Pythagoreans, and refers to the *Timaeus* construction as that of "Timaeus of Locri, whom Plato also followed" (*Harm.* II, 260.16–17 Jan). The essay *On the Soul of the Universe and on Nature*, attributed to Timaeus of Locri, is notoriously spurious.

of its harmonic construction, with some justice, as a direct development of Pythagorean ideas, which Plato had induced to reveal significant truths about the cosmos and the soul. Arguments continued for centuries about the details of its structure, the numbers that best exemplify its sequence of ratios, the symbolic meanings of these numbers, the form of the diagrams which could display the relations it involved, the mathematical principles governing it, the nature of its musical counterparts and much more; and these controversies went hand in hand with changes in the metaphysical interpretations assigned to the construction and its ingredients, as the profile of Platonism in general evolved. It would be impossible to do justice to these intricate discussions here.[43]

9. Nicomachus and, finally, Pythagoras

No survey of Pythagorean harmonics would be complete without a glance at Nicomachus (early second century AD), the only avowedly "Pythagorean" author of a treatise in harmonics that survives complete.[44] This little "handbook" is presented as a letter to an unnamed "noble lady"; it claims to be no more than a hasty introduction to the discipline, and promises a much fuller account at a later date. We know that the longer work was written, since it was extensively paraphrased in Latin in Boethius' *De institutione musica* in the early sixth century.[45] It seems to have been primarily mathematical, and I shall not consider it here.

The organization of the *Harmonic Handbook*'s twelve chapters is unusual and puzzling. The excursus on the different conformations of sound in music and in speech falls naturally into place as the first topic (Ch. 2); Aristoxenus, whose account Nicomachus paraphrases (though he attributes it to the Pythagoreans), had adopted the same strategy. But he then moves directly (Ch. 3) to a discussion of a version of the famous harmony of the spheres, which Nicomachus describes as "the first music among perceptible things," that of the sun, moon and planets, a system of seven notes formed by two conjoined tetrachords, falling short of the octave by a tone, described in moderately technical terms that have not been explained. Chapter 4 offers a confused and generalized summary of Pythagorean acoustic theory,

---

[43] Readers with ample stamina and an appetite for details should study Cherniss 1935 and Baltzly 2009. See also Chapter 20 below.
[44] Greek text in Jan 1895: 237–65, English translation and commentary in Levin 1975; Barker 1989: 245–69.
[45] See especially Bower 1989. Aspects of Nicomachus' harmonic theories also appear in his *Introduction to Arithmetic*. See also Chapter 20 below.

explaining how different types of instrument produce higher and lower pitches and concluding "all these things are ordered by number." Chapters 5 to 7 celebrate the supposed achievements of Pythagoras. Boiled down to its essentials, what we are told the great man did was to devise a way of completing the octave,[46] and to discover the ratios of the concords and the intervals of a diatonic scale. Chapters 8 (on the *Timaeus* scale) and 9 (on Philolaus' discussion of the octave *harmonia*) are apparently intended to confirm the credentials of Pythagoras' scale and its ratios, though it is not clear how they do so; and Ch. 10 explains how the concords' ratios can be found and confirmed on a monochord or with different lengths of a pipe. The last two chapters abandon dealings with ratios and are irrelevant to Pythagorean theory.

It is a quirky and sometimes baffling piece of writing. Nicomachus seems careless about the details and organization of the harmonic doctrines he sets around the central theme of Pythagoras' genius. Boethius and many medieval writers treat him with great respect, but modern scholars (especially historians of mathematics) have consistently dismissed him as unintelligent, unoriginal and unaware of current advances in the disciplines he discussed. It is hard to disagree. The main virtue of all his work, and of the *Handbook* in particular, is precisely that it was *not* written by a scientific or literary giant, a Ptolemy or a Plutarch. It gives us some insight into the strange mental world of an intellectually more or less "average" individual obsessed by the intricacies of Pythagorean "lore and science."

Its best-known passage is its account of Pythagoras' discovery of the ratios of the concords and the tone (Ch. 6), wrapped up in the story of the "harmonious blacksmith." As Pythagoras walked past a smithy, plunged in thought, he noticed that the sounds made by the hammers on the anvils formed the concords of the octave, fifth and fourth, and the interval by which the latter two differ, the tone. He weighed the hammers precisely and found that the intervals were in direct proportion to the weights. Then he went home and attached metal lumps weighing the same as the hammers to perfectly identical strings suspended from a rod; and he discovered that the notes produced when the strings were plucked were in the same musical relations as those he had heard in the smithy. A string weighted by a body twice the weight of the body attached to another sounded an octave higher, and so on. But this is pure fiction. The pitches of sounds made by hammers

---

[46] This was not done by simply tacking another note on at the top, but by inserting the interval of a tone between the two tetrachords of the planetary scale, constructing the form of the octave that the theorists treat as fundamental. Nicomachus' description of this "insertion" (in Ch. 5), however, is complex and confusing.

on anvils depend mainly on the properties of the anvil, not the weight of
the hammer-head; and the ratios between pitches emitted from strings to
which weights are attached do not correspond directly to the ratios of the
weights.

The story is a myth, and the belief that Pythagoras discovered the ratios
of the concords has no foundations. Indeed, no Pythagorean *discovered*
them; they were already well known to instrument makers, as many sources
record, especially to makers of wind instruments.[47] Nor is there any good
reason for crediting Pythagoras with the invention of an octave structure
that was commonplace throughout the Greek world. There is in fact no
solid evidence that he contributed anything to the science of harmonics, or
even envisaged such a discipline.[48] The real pioneer was probably Hippasus
(see n. 3 above), the first Pythagorean to make the musical ratios the object
of mathematical and empirical research; and it was Philolaus, fifty years
later, who first integrated these researches into Pythagorean metaphysics.
In its classical form Pythagorean harmonics culminated in Archytas' subtle
fusion of mathematical reasoning and empirical observation; Ptolemy's
judgment that he was "of all the Pythagoreans the most dedicated to the
study of music" seems amply justified.[49] Its fundamental doctrines were
encapsulated and systematized around 300 BC in the *Sectio canonis*, which
also highlights substantial issues on which it conflicts with the propositions
of empirical harmonics. By the early fourth century, perhaps already in the
fifth, it was making its mark on speculations outside the Pythagorean orbit;
it figures prominently in the work of Plato and Aristotle, who make liberal
use of its musical mathematics while severely criticizing some of the ways
in which the Pythagoreans applied it.

Most writings in Pythagorean harmonics after the fourth century BC were
heavily influenced by Plato's *Republic*, with its rejection of empirical considerations and its insistence on the authority of reason, and especially by the
cosmological and psychological implications of his musical construction of
the World-Soul in the *Timaeus*. One of the Pythagorean approaches that
Ptolemaïs describes seems nevertheless to preserve a pre-Platonic character,
privileging reason over perception but still focused – at least in part – on

---

[47] They are much less relevant to the manufacture of stringed instruments such as the lyre; even on
    the monochord (unknown at this date), irregularities in the string's thickness are likely to cause
    difficulties (cf. Ptol. *Harm.* 1.8). This may explain why early accounts of Pythagorean experiments
    with instruments (e.g., Archytas fr. 1) always mention wind instruments but say nothing about
    strings.
[48] The supposition that he did probably originates with Xenocrates; see fr. 87 Isnardi Parente.
[49] Ptol. *Harm.* 30.9–10.

the analysis of audible music; and so too do the Pythagoreans discussed by Ptolemy and Porphyry. But this does not prove that there were still Pythagoreans of this sort at work in the later periods. The date of Ptolemaïs herself may be as early as the third century, and Ptolemy's and Porphyry's evidence seems to come almost entirely from Archytas and the *Sectio canonis*. For an authentic "late Pythagorean" we must turn, perhaps regretfully, to Nicomachus.

CHAPTER 10

The Pythagoreans and Plato

John Palmer

1. *Gorgias*

The ancient tradition's tendency to depict Pythagoras as a major source of Plato's philosophy complicates the question of what influence early Pythagoreanism actually had on its development. With Pythagoras himself having written nothing and the works of Philolaus and Archytas surviving only in a few fragments and testimonia,[1] Pythagoreanism as Plato would have known it remains obscure. Fortunately, Aristotle's treatment of the Pythagoreans has facilitated its reconstruction.[2] Although he also remarks on the relation between the Pythagorean and Platonic principles, this chapter will concentrate on the recognizable uses of Pythagorean material in Plato's own writings.[3] Of course, the fact that Plato's uses of the Presocratics tend to be more or less transformative, coupled with the poor state of our evidence for early Pythagoreanism, makes it difficult to determine in some instances how much of what is implicit in his uses may properly be regarded as Pythagorean. Still, one may identify Plato's more important uses of Pythagorean ideas, provided one is more careful than the ancient tradition (and some modern historians) about where one detects them. Not every mention of mathematics, for example, signals a debt to the Pythagoreans, for many mathematicians of Plato's day were not Pythagoreans. Likewise, although the doctrine of metempsychosis was central to early Pythagoreanism, Plato's association of it with the mystery cults and their initiatory rituals in both the *Meno* and later the *Laws*

---

[1] All most usefully collected and analyzed in Huffman 1993 and 2005.

[2] Aristotle's account of Pythagoreanism provides the touchstone for the effort in the initial chapter of the landmark Burkert 1972a to distinguish the movement's actual influence on Plato from the Pythagoreanizing speculations among his pupils. See also Horky 2013a, Ch. 1.

[3] Huffman 2008e: 284–91, argues that Arist. *Metaph.* 1.6.987a29–31, standardly regarded as marking Plato's debt to the Pythagoreans, actually marks his relation to the broader Presocratic tradition while signaling Aristotle's strategy of presenting Plato's theory of principles via contrast with the Pythagoreans.

(*Meno* 81a–b, *Leg.* 9.870d–e) likely indicates that he did not regard it as originating with Pythagoras. Similar caution should be extended to the detection of Pythagorean elements in the eschatological myths of the *Gorgias*, *Phaedo*, *Republic* and *Phaedrus*, for their background is broader and Plato develops his material in a creative manner that makes it difficult to identify definitively any material as a source.

The Pythagoreans' influence on Plato figures most deeply in the way he understood them as advocating a vision of value, goodness and well-being that he found amenable and highly adaptable to his own purposes as he began to range beyond his Socratic inheritance. The Socrates of the *Gorgias* and *Republic* differs from the Socrates of earlier dialogues in having a much more definite conception of what is properly good or beneficial for humans as such and thus of what constitutes human well-being. The Pythagorean trappings of this conception suggest that Plato's encounters with the Pythagoreans after Socrates' death influenced the development of his ethical thought during this period. The *Gorgias'* substantive account of goodness is articulated in a remarkable passage that portrays Socrates as responding to his own questions (*Grg.* 506c–8a). All things are good, Socrates asserts, due to the presence of their particular excellence or *aretē*, and this they have in virtue of organization (*taxis*), correctness (*orthotēs*) and the skill (*technē*) that bestows them, all of which result in the order (*kosmos*) proper to each thing that makes it good (*Grg.* 506c–e). A soul with its proper order (*kosmos*) is better than a disordered one since such a soul is orderly (*kosmia*) and self-controlled (*sōphrōn*). Thus a self-controlled soul is a good one, contrary to what Callicles has claimed (*Grg.* 506e–7a). The psychologically well-ordered and self-controlled person will possess all the other virtues, so that he will be completely good, doing whatever he does well and admirably, and thus be blessed and happy (*eudaimōn*) (*Grg.* 507a–e, cf. 503d–4e). By contrast, the Calliclean individual constantly endeavoring to satisfy his undisciplined appetites proves incapable of friendly feeling toward man or god because he is incapable of community (*koinōnia*) (*Grg.* 507e).

Plato has Socrates put this view in a cosmic perspective:

> Wise persons say, Callicles, that community, friendship, orderliness, self-control and justice hold together heaven and earth and gods and men, and for this reason they speak of this whole world as a cosmic order [*kosmos*], my friend, and not as disorder or indiscipline. I think, though, that you fail to pay attention to these things, clever though you are, and that you fail to notice that geometrical equality [*hē isotēs hē geōmetrikē*] has great power among both gods and men, for you neglect geometry. (*Grg.* 507e6–8a8)

The doxographer Aëtius reports that Pythagoras first called the world a *kosmos* because of the order (*taxis*) apparent within it (Aët. 2.1.1). Although the historical accuracy of the report has been doubted, and this very passage has been suspected as its ultimate source, it is virtually certain that the wise persons here referenced as describing the world as a *kosmos* are in the first instance Pythagoreans (even if the reference may extend more broadly). Plato's praise of geometrical equality here bears particular comparison with Archytas' account of the beneficial power of calculation:

> Once calculation [*logismos*] was discovered, it stopped discord and increased concord [*homonoia*]. For greed [*pleonexia*] ceases once it is present and equality [*isotas*] prevails. For by means of calculation we will seek reconciliation in our dealings with others. Through this, then, the poor receive from the powerful, and the wealthy give to the needy, both in the confidence that they will have what is fair [*to ison*] on account of this. (Archyt. fr. 3.6–10, after Huffman)

The great power Plato claims for geometrical equality among both gods and men is precisely along these lines. Plato introduces the crucial point that the same principles of order governing the cosmos and responsible for its order and goodness may likewise govern human relations and, as Socrates has emphasized earlier in his catechism, even the individual's relations with himself.

The fragments of Aristoxenus' *Pythagorean Precepts* preserved in Stobaeus and Iamblichus[4] represent the Pythagoreans as teaching that "organization [*taxis*] and proportion [*summetria*] are fine and beneficial, while lack of organization and lack of proportion are base and harmful" (Aristox. fr. 35 Wehrli *ap.* Stob. *Ecl.* 4.1.49). Absence of governance (*anarchia*) is the greatest evil, for human desires are so prone to excess that a combination of divine, parental and legal oversight is required to hold them in check, the results being self-control (*sōphronismos*) and organization (*taxis*) (Aristox. fr. 33 Wehrli *ap.* Iambl. *VP* 174). Aristoxenus also reports a fairly elaborate Pythagorean account of desire, defined as "a certain concentration and impulse of the soul with an appetency for filling [*plērōsis*] or the presence of sensation, or for an emptying [*kenōsis*], absence, or not experiencing sensation" (Aristox. fr. 37 Wehrli *ap.* Stob. *Ecl.* 3.10.66; cf. Iambl. *VP* 205). The three principal types of faulty or bad desire are indecorum (*aschēmosunē*), lack of proportion (*asummetria*) and inappropriateness (*akairia*), for either the desire itself is indecorous, disgraceful and servile, or else it is more

---

[4] Huffman 2006 and 2008b have sought to rehabilitate this text as a reliable source for Pythagorean ethics during the late fifth to early fourth centuries BC.

intense and of longer duration than proper, or it occurs when and where it should not. Implicit in this classification is the view that properly governed desire will be decorous, proportionate and appropriate. The parallels between the *Precepts* and the view of human goodness and rational self-control outlined in Socrates' catechism are numerous enough to suggest its specifically Pythagorean background.

Earlier in the *Gorgias*, Callicles had ridiculed Socrates' suggestion that individuals capable of governing their own appetites and pleasures might properly be regarded as superior and worthy of governing others. Callicles' view is that human excellence (*aretē*) consists in giving one's appetites rein to expand as they may and satisfying them by all possible means (*Grg.* 492d, cf. 491e). Callicles thinks no naturally superior individuals – the tyrants or potential tyrants he has in view – should subject themselves to the constraints of moderation and justice. Callicles' stance closely parallels the position ascribed in Aristoxenus's *Life of Archytas* to Archytas' acquaintance Polyarchus:

> Nature, whenever it speaks with its own voice, commands us to follow pleasures and says this is the course of a sensible man. But to resist and enslave the appetites belongs neither to one who is intelligent, nor to one who is fortunate, nor to one who understands the constitution of human nature. A strong sign of this is that all men, whenever they obtain power sufficiently extensive, are carried towards bodily pleasures and regard them as the goal of their power. (Archytas A9.11–18 [Aristox. fr. 50 Wehrli] *ap.* Ath. *Sophists at Dinner* 545a–b)

Polyarchus holds up as exemplars the Persian kings and the tyrants everywhere who use their power to pursue ever more extravagant pleasures. Only with the lawgivers who adamantly opposed those bent on having more and more (*pleonexia*), he says, were justice, temperance and self-control praised as virtues and excessive enjoyment denounced as "greed."

Although Callicles' and Polyarchus' positions are roughly similar, the responses attributed by Plato to Socrates and by Aristoxenus to Archytas run along different lines. While Socrates bases his response on arguments denying the identity of pleasure and the good (*Grg.* 495c–500b), Archytas catalogues the wicked or shameful acts to which the unrestrained pursuit of bodily pleasure leads and stresses especially how our desire for pleasure opposes the best part of our soul, namely, the intellect (Archytas A9a *ap.* Cic. *Sen.* 12.39–41). While such considerations feature in Plato's critiques of pleasure elsewhere, Socrates prefaces his response to Callicles by reporting how he once heard a wise man say the following: we are not now actually alive but dead, the body (*sōma*) is our tomb (*sēma*), and the soul's desiring part is susceptible to persuasion (*Grg.* 493a). This wise man expanded this last point by referencing "an ingenious storyteller [*muthologos*], maybe a Sicilian or Italian," who called the desiring part a "jar" (*pithos*) since it is persuadable (*pithanos*) and foolish people (*anoētoi*) "uninitiated" (*amuētoi*), which the wise man understood to mean that in foolish persons the soul's desiring part is undisciplined and improperly sealed, like a leaky jar (*Grg.* 493a–b). The storyteller also described how in Hades the uninitiated carry water with sieves into leaking jars, which the wise man explained represented foolish persons' souls (*Grg.* 493b–c, cf. *Resp.* 363d). Socrates then develops this story via an image "from the same school" representing the self-controlled as someone who fills his jars with valuable things and needs not keep filling them since they do not leak and the undisciplined person as someone whose leaky jars always require filling lest he suffer great pain (*Grg.* 493d–4a).

While an air of Pythagoreanism seems to pervade the passage, even if identification of any of the sources Socrates references as specifically Pythagorean has proved elusive, there are definitely parallels between the treatments of desire here and in the *Pythagorean Precepts* and in Archytas' response to Polyarchus. More significant is the passage's division of the soul into a part housing desires and a part capable of persuading and controlling it. In the Socratic psychological model of earlier dialogues, the soul is not represented as divided in this way but instead as possessing a unitary faculty of judgment. In *Republic* 4, Plato presents this Socratic model as one alternative when he introduces the question of the soul's structure:

> It is difficult to tell whether we do each of these things with *the same part* or with *three distinct parts*: do we learn with one, get angry with something else in ourselves, and desire with a third the pleasures of sustenance, sex, and the like, or do we act with the entire soul whenever we pursue each of these things? (*Resp.* 4.436a8–b2)

There he opts, of course, for the view that the soul has distinct parts. But a view of the soul as comprising distinct parts already features in the *Gorgias*, where it is closely connected to the dialogue's substantive conception of the good insofar as the organization and order responsible for excellence of character are tantamount to the control of the soul's appetitive part by the part capable of governing it.[5] Not only are there Pythagorean overtones in the *Gorgias*' conception of order as cause of the soul's excellence, there are

---

[5] See further Dorion 2012.

also Pythagorean parallels for this related conception of the parts of the soul.

Cicero reports a twofold division of the soul as going back first to Pythagoras and then to Plato:

> One part they make a participant in reason, the other devoid of it. In the part sharing reason they locate tranquility, that is, a calm and peaceful stability, while in that other part they locate the disordered movements of anger and desire, which are opposed and inimical to reason. (Cic. *Tusc.* 4.5.10, cf. Posidonius *ap.* Gal. *On the Opinions of Hippocrates and Plato* 5.6.43.1)

Not only does Archytas' response to Polyarchus (also reported by Cicero) emphasize the opposition of intellect and desire, Archytas argued for its absolute character by pointing out that someone experiencing maximal bodily pleasure could accomplish nothing via reason (*ratio*) or deliberation (*cogitatio*) (Cic. *Sen.* 12.41). As for the opposition between anger and reason, Cicero tells an anecdote recorded by several ancient authors designed to illustrate Archytas' self-possession in the midst of anger. When Archytas returned home (from serving, as other versions say, as general in a Tarentine campaign) only to find that none of his orders for the management of his estate in his absence had been followed, he told his steward that he would have beaten him to death by now if he were not angry (Cic. *Rep.* 1.38.59). Cicero's comment makes the relevant point: "Archytas clearly considered anger, when at variance with reason [*ratio*], as it were an insurrection against the mind's rule, and he wished it to be checked by deliberation [*consilium*]." There is also evidence for a Pythagorean division of the psychological faculties in a fragment of Philolaus' *On Nature*, where the head and brain are associated with *nous* or intellect, the heart with *psuchē* and *aisthēsis* or sensation, the navel with growth, and the genitals with reproduction (Philolaus fr. 13). Here "*psuchē*" does not designate the whole soul but some particular psychological faculty, though precisely which faculty is unclear. Carl Huffman has suggested that it refers to an emotional faculty.[6] An equally plausible hypothesis, with Pythagorean parallels, would be that *psuchē* is for Philolaus the faculty of the affective states more generally, including the active appetitive states as well as passive states of emotion. This hypothesis squares well with Cicero's report that the Pythagoreans located "the disordered movements of anger and desire" in the part of the soul distinct from reason as well as with the evidence just adduced regarding Archytas' view of the opposition between intellect and both desire

---

[6] Huffman 2009: 24–6, improving on Huffman 1993: 212. He finds further evidence for this suggestion in Herodotean usage.

and anger. Philolaus, of course, distinguishes four psychological faculties, rather than two (or three), but the difference is essentially immaterial given that the distinction between the faculties of the distinctively human intellect and the affective states shared with animals will be most germane to the explanation and assessment of human behavior.

2. *Phaedo*

Plato's engagement with the Pythagoreans in the development of his psychology continues on a different plane in the *Phaedo*, a dialogue normally regarded as one of his most "Pythagorean." Socrates' final conversation and his death are here recounted by his pupil, Phaedo, to Echecrates, a prominent member of the Pythagorean exile community in Phlius; and Socrates' interlocutors, the Thebans Simmias and Cebes, are said to have spent time with Philolaus (*Phd.* 61d6–7).[7] The dialogue's discussion of the prohibition against suicide, its ascetic conception of philosophy as a kind of purification, and most importantly its exploration of the soul's immortality and the teachings regarding its fate after death all have strong Pythagorean overtones. Throughout one sees Plato intent on developing, rather than simply adopting, certain Pythagorean ideas in a more rigorously philosophical manner of his own. When Socrates asks whether Cebes and Simmias heard of the prohibition against suicide while with Philolaus, Cebes responds affirmatively but requests an explanation: "Why then do people say it is not right for a person to kill himself, Socrates? [. . .] I did in fact hear Philolaus, during the time he spent with us, and certain others as well, say that one must not do this. But I have never heard anything clear from anyone on the topic" (*Phd.* 61e5–9). What is taken from Philolaus is simply the prohibition. Socrates takes it upon himself to determine its grounds. First he mentions the doctrine of certain "sacred [*sc.* Orphic] writings" that humans are in a sort of prison while the soul is embodied and must not release themselves or try to escape (*Phd.* 62b, cf. *Crat.* 400c). Calling this doctrine "grand and not easy to fathom," Socrates concentrates on the kernel of truth he finds in it, namely, that the gods are watching over us and that we humans are among their belongings (*Phd.* 62b5–9). From these points he then constructs his first rationale for the prohibition, namely, that the gods would not want their belongings to do away with themselves (*Phd.* 62b–c). While Philolaus is characterized as having no

---

[7] Although some have regarded this detail as sufficient indication of their Pythagorean affiliation, Cebes and Simmias are not otherwise identified as Pythagoreans in this dialogue or elsewhere in the tradition.

clear rationale for his prohibition, Socrates is made to manufacture one that would presumably appeal to a Pythagorean. The Orphic view that the body is the soul's prison would presumably do so, and the kernel of truth Socrates finds in this mystic doctrine features in the *Pythagorean Precepts* as the primary source of the external governance human beings require to flourish: the Pythagoreans, we are there told, learned from Pythagoras himself that our need of governance should make us ever mindful that the divine watches over and protects the course of human life (Aristox. fr. 33 Wehrli = Iambl. *VP* 174–5).

The same dynamic governs Plato's treatment of the soul's immortality. Here, too, Socrates rationalizes a fundamental Pythagorean doctrine in an amenable manner that yet goes well beyond anything the Pythagoreans actually taught. Although the doctrine of the soul's immortality is a cornerstone of Pythagoreanism, Plato focuses more directly on the key issue of whether the soul is of such a nature that it can survive separation from the body and be ultimately indestructible. Cicero touches on the essential point: "Plato reportedly went to Italy to meet with the Pythagoreans, and while there he made acquaintance with Archytas and Timaeus, among others. From them he learned all the doctrines of the Pythagoreans, and he not only agreed with Pythagoras regarding the immortality of the soul *but also provided reasons to support this doctrine*" (Cic. *Tusc.* 1.17, emphasis mine). Plato's analysis of the soul's nature begins in earnest with the set of mutual implications between indestructibility, partlessness and immutability at the beginning of the affinity argument (*Phd.* 78b–c) and continues through the final argument in response to Cebes, which establishes that life is itself a necessary attribute of soul (*Phd.* 105c–e, cf. 100b). What soul's essential nature is, in virtue of which life belongs to it as a necessary attribute, remains an outstanding question in the *Phaedo*. The *Phaedrus* and *Laws* will identify this essential nature as being a self-mover. The argument for the soul's immortality at *Phaedrus* 245c–246a based on this identification is superior to the *Phaedo*'s arguments precisely because it proceeds synthetically from a specification of the nature or essence of soul.

Evidence in Aristotle suggests the Pythagoreans to some small degree anticipated Plato's conception of the soul as a self-mover. In his survey of views on the soul, Aristotle associates the Pythagoreans and Plato with the broader class of thinkers identifying the soul as the source of movement:

> What the Pythagoreans say seems to imply the same thing, for some said the motes in the air are soul, while others said it is what moves them. They

mention these because they are seen moving continuously, even in perfectly calm conditions. Those who say soul is what moves itself also tend to this position; for all these suppose movement is most proper to soul and, while all other things are moved by the soul, it is moved by itself. (Arist. *de An.* 1.2.404a16–24)

The juxtaposition of this Pythagorean view with the Platonic conception of soul as self-mover may be a typically Aristotelian barb. Plato's view is more nearly anticipated in Alcmaeon's own "affinity argument" for the soul's immortality, reported by Aristotle further on, according to which the soul is immortal because of its resemblance to the heavenly bodies in respect of ceaseless movement (Arist. *De an.* 1.2.405a29–5b1). Although the Pythagorean notebooks known to Alexander Polyhistor contain the view that the soul is a detached portion of the aether and therefore immortal (Diog. Laert. 8.28, cf. 8.26), the nearest analogue of Alcmaeon's view in pre-Platonic Pythagoreanism is Hippasus of Metapontum's reported view that the soul is fiery (Aët. 4.3.4). In the end there is little evidence indicating that the early Pythagoreans seriously consider what the soul would have to be to experience the transmigration taught by Pythagoras. As with Philolaus' prohibition against suicide, so with the Pythagorean doctrine of the soul's immortality: Plato would have been justified in feeling that the members of the school provided no clear rationale for this worthy view.

The *Phaedo* itself might be thought to provide relevant evidence given that Simmias' articulation of his worry about Socrates' initial arguments has sometimes been thought to reflect a Pythagorean view of the soul as a *harmonia*.[8] In a *reductio* of the affinity argument's analogical reasoning, Simmias objects that one could argue in similar fashion that the *harmonia* or tuning of a lyre continues to exist after the lyre's own destruction (*Phd.* 85e–86a). He then endorses a view of the soul as a blending (*krasis*) and *harmonia* of opposites such as hot and cold and dry and moist properly mixed in due measure (*Phd.* 86b–c). The late Roman Neoplatonist Macrobius explicitly states that Pythagoras and Philolaus said the soul was a *harmonia* (Macrob. *In Somn.* 1.14.19). When Aristotle takes up this same theory in *On the Soul* 1.4, however, he does not mention the Pythagoreans, whose views on the soul he has just discussed (*De an.* 1.3.407b21–4, cf. 1.2.404a16–20), but treats it as a generally popular idea:

Still another view of soul has been passed down, one regarded by many as no less convincing than those thus far mentioned, seeing as it has rendered account of itself, as if to public examiners, in public and open discussions,

[8] See Gottschalk 1971 for a survey of the evidence for this theory and its adherents.

namely, that the soul is a *harmonia*, a blend [*krasis*] or compound [*sunthesis*]
of contraries from which the body is composed. (*De an.* 1.4.407b27–32)

Aristotle evidently has in his sights the same view Simmias advances in
the *Phaedo*, and his first criticism of this view, that a *harmonia* cannot
be, as the soul evidently is, a principle of change (*De an.* 1.4.407b34–8a1),
replicates a principal line of argument in Socrates' response (*Phd.* 94b–
5a). The fact that Aristotle does not associate the *harmonia* theory with
the Pythagoreans obviously trumps Macrobius' attribution. The *Phaedo's*
mention of Philolaus' sojourn with Simmias and Cebes at Thebes is all
the later tradition would require to attribute the view of the soul Simmias
espouses to Philolaus. That the view is not ascribed to Philolaus or any other
Pythagorean prior to Macrobius might therefore be thought surprising,
were it not for the obvious fact that the idea that the soul is a *harmonia*
cannot be squared with the Pythagorean doctrine of the soul's immortality.

A view more plausibly regarded as Pythagorean in fact features in
Socrates' criticism of Simmias' *harmonia* theory, namely, the view that
good souls display *harmonia* while bad souls lack this quality (*Phd.* 93c3–
10). To highlight Simmias' category mistake, he asks whether those who
say the soul is a *harmonia* will say that a good soul has yet another *harmonia*. The point is that *harmonia* is not the soul's essence but rather its
good-making quality. Given the Pythagorean trappings of Socrates' view
in the *Gorgias* that the order (*kosmos*) proper to each thing makes it good
and, more specifically, that a properly ordered soul is best since it is orderly
(*kosmia*) and self-controlled (*sōphrōn*), Plato might well expect the view
that virtue and goodness belong to the soul possessing *harmonia* to be
recognized here as the genuinely Pythagorean view.

In the *Gorgias* the orderly soul was one whose rational part governs
its appetitive part. The *Phaedo* takes a more ascetic, yet still recognizably
Pythagorean, stance by characterizing the body and its desires as evil and
as an obstacle to the soul's obtaining the proper object of its own desires,
the truth (*Phd.* 66b5–7). The body, Socrates says, fills us with lusts, desires,
fears and all sorts of nonsense, "so that, as it is said, its influence really
and truly makes it impossible for us to think anything at all" (*Phd.* 66c5–
6). So Archytas replies to Polyarchus that someone experiencing maximal
bodily pleasure could neither think clearly about anything nor accomplish
anything via reason or deliberation (Cic. *Sen.* 12.41). Socrates follows with
another criticism against pleasure also made by Archytas: the body with
its desires is the ultimate cause of war, faction and strife (*Phd.* 66c5–7,
cf. Cic. *Sen.* 12.40). Socrates and Archytas share the view that the bodily

desire for pleasure is so thoroughly inimical to the intellect's desire for truth that physical pleasure should be regarded as outright contemptible and not merely as something to be moderated and kept within bounds. "Nothing is so detestable and so pernicious as pleasure," Archytas concluded, "since when very intense and prolonged it extinguishes the whole light of the soul" (Cic. *Sen.* 12.41). Socrates similarly concludes that the true philosopher will withdraw his soul from association with the body and thus seek its purification (*Phd.* 67a, cf. 67c–d). The ascetic idea that the philosopher seeks to purify his soul lest its bodily association impede fulfillment of the intellect's desire for truth is particularly strong here in the *Phaedo*. It is somewhat more typical of Plato, as evidenced by both the *Gorgias* and the *Republic*, to regard the soul's role as regulating bodily desires to ensure that they find fulfillment in a moderate manner without becoming dominant. The *acusmata's* emphasis on various means of purification,[9] plus the imperative to purify the soul implicit in the doctrine of metempsychosis, certainly suggest Pythagorean influence in the *Phaedo's* more ascetic outlook. However, the complex conception of the soul as having as its own proper desire for apprehension of truth, of this desire as the source of genuine virtue, and of the consequently purificatory role of philosophical inquiry are more purely Platonic. Although a Pythagorean version of these ideas is glimpsed in Archytas' response to Polyarchus, it may well be that Plato influenced Archytas rather than the other way around.

3. *Republic*

The *Phaedo's* novel idea that pursuit of the soul's proper desire for truth is the source of genuine virtue forms an important complement to the view that *harmonia* makes the soul virtuous and good. One who most values what is in fact most valuable, namely, apprehension of the truth, will value other things properly as well and thus be disposed to act and react properly in all situations. In arguing that the true lover of wisdom will possess each virtue in its genuine form (*Phd.* 68c–9b), Plato strikes a different chord than in the *Gorgias*, where he had argued that the psychologically well-ordered and self-controlled person will possess all the other virtues (*Grg.* 507a–e). In the *Gorgias* he had focused on reason's control of the body's irrational desires, while here in the *Phaedo* he emphasizes reason's impulse to fulfill its own proper desire. These two views coalesce in the *Republic*. There the remarks regarding moderation or self-control, prior

---

[9] See Chapter 6.

to the division of the soul into a rational and two irrational parts, closely parallel the ethical views of the *Gorgias*. Moderation is said to resemble a *sumphōnia* and *harmonia* (*Resp.* 4.430e3–4, cf. 431e7–8) and to be "a kind of order [*kosmos*] and control over specific pleasures and desires" (430e6–7). Moderation continues to be characterized in these terms subsequent to the division as well: a person is said to be moderate due to the friendship (*philia*) and *sumphōnia* among these parts (*Resp.* 4.442c10–11). This psychological concord, this literal "unanimity," is likewise central to the overarching virtue of justice, in which each part of the soul performs its proper function:

> [The just individual] well disposes what really is his own, rules himself, puts himself in order, is friend to himself, and harmonizes the three parts, just like the three terms in a musical scale, the high, middle and low notes [*hōsper horous treis harmonias atechnōs, neatēs te kai hupatēs kai mesēs*], plus whatever others happen to be between them. He binds these together until, from having been many, he becomes completely one, moderate and harmonious. (*Resp.* 4.443d3–e2)

This statement effectively reprises the view ascribed to the Pythagorean wise men in the *Gorgias*, except here the more tightly structured harmonic proportion now stands in for the geometric, and the emphasis is on the internal order of the individual soul rather than on the relations between heaven and earth and gods and men. At the same time the passage develops the *Phaedo*'s suggestion that *harmonia* makes the soul good. The focus here on *harmonia*'s specifically musical character indicates that Plato still regards this conception of well-being as broadly Pythagorean.

The *Phaedo*'s more ascetic view also finds expression in the *Republic*, with the *Phaedo*'s argument that the true lover of wisdom possesses each virtue in its genuine form being recast in *Republic* 6. There Socrates argues that one whose desires incline toward the sciences (*pros ta mathēmata*) cares only for the pure pleasures of the soul, relinquishes bodily pleasures, and is consequently moderate, high-minded, courageous and just (*Resp.* 6.485d–6b). Plato's emphasis elsewhere on rational self-governance as producing the soul's internal harmony and thus as the source of genuine virtue might appear in tension with his emphasis on the rational soul's pursuit of its proper desire for truth as virtue's source. Plato recognizes, however, that the notion of rational self-governance is normatively inert without some end apart from itself to serve as its principle. He finds this principle in reason's proper function of understanding. On his view, valuing most highly truth and understanding results in the proper valuing of all else that is tantamount to rational self-governance. How Plato's engagement with the Pythagoreans informed various aspects of this view, including, in particular, its understanding of reason's proper function, is perhaps clearest in *Republic* 7.

In the educational program of the guardians Plato envisions an important role for the mathematical sciences of arithmetic, geometry, astronomy, and harmonics. Socrates echoes Archytas' designation of these as sister sciences (*mathēmata [. . .] adelphea*, Archyt. fr. 1.7) when he endorses the idea that astronomy and harmonics are sister sciences (*adelphai [. . .] epistēmai*) and specifically attributes this view to "the Pythagoreans" (Pl. *Resp.* 7.530d).[10] Plato also calls for introducing "stereometry" or solid geometry into the curriculum after (plane) geometry and before astronomy (*Resp.* 7.528a–e). To this field Archytas made an early and momentous contribution by solving the famous problem of doubling the cube. Plato's remarks on the science of harmonics likewise have the Pythagoreans in view. Although in describing the program he thus gestures toward the Pythagoreans and Archytas in particular, Plato believes that they failed to recognize the ultimate purpose of mathematical study. He regards it as especially useful in shifting the intellect's focus from the mutable entities encountered in perception to the immutable entities only it can apprehend. Plato's description of how calculation (*logistikē*) and arithmetic lead toward truth already implies criticism of Pythagorean mathematical practice and, perhaps, of Archytas in particular, given the preeminence he accorded the mathematical science of ratio and proportion he called "logistic" (*logistikē*) and his emphasis on its practical applications (Archyt. frs. 3, 4). Plato proposes that guardians-to-be study *logistikē* "not as amateurs do [*sc.* for practical purposes] but persisting until they see the nature of numbers with the intellect itself" (*Resp.* 7.525c1–3). His rebuke of those who think the mathematical sciences of calculation concern "the visible or tangible bodies that have numbers" (525d7–8) may well seem a criticism of the Pythagoreans, since Aristotle reports that they did not regard number as existing separately or independently from perceptible substances (Arist. *Metaph.* 13.6.1080b16–20; cf. 1.6.987b29–33). If this report is accurate, then all Plato's remarks in *Republic* 7 about mathematics' ultimate utility in lifting the intellect to contemplate its proper objects will be tinged with such criticism.[11]

---

[10] Plato's only explicit mention of "the Pythagoreans." His only mention of Pythagoras contrasts him with Homer as establishing a way of life bearing his name (*Resp.* 10.600b3–5). Since Plato also mentions Philolaus in the *Phaedo* and alludes to him in the *Philebus*, alludes specifically to Archytas here in the *Republic*, and draws fairly extensively upon Pythagorean ideas in these and other dialogues, the single mentions of Pythagoras and the Pythagoreans in the dialogues hardly reflect the depth of his engagement.

[11] Cf. Aristotle's echo of Plato's criticism at *Metaph.* 1.9.989b29–90a8.

Plato nevertheless appreciates that Pythagorean harmonic theorists approached their subject in a more scientific fashion than their empiricist rivals, whose attempts to determine the smallest interval aurally he evidently disdains (*Resp.* 7.530e–1a). He still finds fault, though, with how the Pythagoreans "look for the numbers in these audible concords, but they do not ascend to problems, to examining which numbers are concordant, which are not, and why each is so" (*Resp.* 7.531c1–4).[12] Archytas' view that pitch varies according to the speed with which sounds move from their source (Archytas fr. 1) is susceptible to this criticism in that it identifies a quantifiable feature of heard sound or "audible concords" with which the ratios known to define the major intervals could be associated.[13] Plato would have likewise regarded Archytas' division of the tetrachord as suspect insofar as it was based on actual musical practice. Certain aspects of Archytas' harmonics, however, were more purely mathematical and thus more aligned with Plato's program. Ptolemy says Archytas undertook "to preserve what is in accordance with reason, not only in connection with the concords but also in the divisions of the tetrachords, on the grounds that commensurability between the differences is intrinsic to the nature of melodic intervals" (Ptol. *Harm.* 30.9–13, trans. Barker). Ptolemy means that Archytas recognized that the numerical ratios defining not only concordant but also melodic musical intervals must be either multiple, as in the 2:1 ratio defining the octave, or "superparticular" (*epimorios*), as in the ratios 3:2 and 4:3 defining, respectively, the perfect fifth and the perfect fourth. (The difference between the two terms in superparticular ratio is a factor of the lesser term; all such ratios reduce to the general form n+1:n.) If Archytas' harmonic theorizing forged into such purely mathematical terrain, then he was doing just what Plato prescribes for properly scientific harmonics: focusing on the relations among the numbers defining musical intervals and determining the principles that account for these numbers themselves being concordant. That Archytas developed a mathematical proof of the theorem that there is no mean proportional, or geometric mean, between terms in superparticular ratio,[14] which entails that no interval defined by a superparticular ratio can be divided into equal sub-intervals, suggests that he was fully capable of engaging in the purely mathematical analysis Plato envisages in *Republic* 7. Plato may well be paying Archytas a compliment

---

[12] On this passage see Barker 1978 and Ch. 9 of this volume.

[13] Plato's own explanation at *Ti.* 67a–c and 80a–b of why concordant intervals are pleasing is nevertheless along these lines.

[14] Archytas *ap.* Boethius *Fundamentals of Music* 3.11 Friedlein; this theorem becomes proposition 3 in the Euclidean *Sectio Canonis*.

by having Socrates anticipate the day when harmonics would ascend to the treatment of the purely mathematical problems at its core that Archytas in fact came to investigate in his treatment of superparticular ratios.[15]

Plato's review of the mathematical sciences in *Republic* 7 concludes with Socrates' remark that the ascent to purely mathematical problems in harmonics is ultimately useful in the search for Beauty and the Good (*Resp.* 7.531c6–7). Harmonics would seem a particularly fruitful field for reflecting on the nature of beauty, for in music there is a stark difference between sounds that are beautiful, which is to say harmonious and concordant, and ones that are not, which is to say unharmonious and discordant. Successful determination of what *makes* certain sounds harmonious and concordant might properly be expected to constitute significant progress toward understanding the nature of beauty. Plato almost certainly would have viewed the mathematical analyses in harmonics pursued by contemporary Pythagoreans as making a major contribution to this project, to the extent that they identified in abstract terms the measured and proportionate relationship among sounds as the beauty-making property. This analysis is particularly useful because it can be readily extended to other domains. In the visual arts, for example, the standard aspect ratios, or proportional relations between width and height of an image, are superparticular because these are found the most pleasing to the eye. It is precisely the point of developing a purely mathematical analysis that it should so generalize. Harmonics likewise provides a basis for apprehending the general nature of goodness as unity (as Plato understands it), in that concordant notes blend to become one whereas discordant notes remain ununited. What enables the notes to form a unity is, technically speaking, that the mathematical terms of the corresponding ratio are commensurate, as they are in the multiple and superparticular ratios of concordant and melodic intervals. Here we have a prime example of the connection between mathematical order and goodness. It is reflected in a discussion of Pythagorean principles recorded in Ptolemy's *Harmonics* 1.5, which classes concords as more beautiful than discords, and the multiple and superparticular ratios associated with concords as *better* than others because their terms are related in mathematically simple ways. Either the smaller term is a "simple part" or

---

[15] On Plato's attitude toward Archytas, see more generally Lloyd 1990 and Huffman 2005: 32–42. Both question the once-common view that Archytas provided a model for the *Republic*'s philosopher-king. This view figures centrally in the historical reconstruction of Plato's interactions with the Pythagoreans in Morrison 1958, which proposes that the founding of the Academy and the composition of the *Republic* were direct outcomes of Plato's visit to Italy in 388/387 BC. See also Mathieu 1987.

integral factor of the larger, as in the multiple ratio 2:1 defining the octave, or the difference between them is a simple part, as in the superparticular ratios 3:2 and 4:3 defining the fifth and the fourth.

Whether or not the Pythagorean analysis Ptolemy reports can be attributed to Archytas, as some have plausibly suggested,[16] any Pythagorean contemporary with or prior to Plato, including Pythagoras himself, would have assigned positive value to the ratios represented in the *tetractys* defining the harmonious and concordant musical tones of the octave, the fifth and the fourth. This much is already implicit in the *acusmata*: "What is the most beautiful thing? *Harmonia*"; "What is the oracle at Delphi? The *tetractys*, which is the *harmony* in which the Sirens sing" (that is, contains the pattern of the most beautiful music). The Pythagoreans also called the *tetractys* the "source of ever-flowing nature" because they understood its ratios as underlying the beauty not only of musical harmony but also of the cosmos as a whole (cf. Sext. Emp. *Math.* 7.94–5). The vision of the beautiful order of the cosmos itself as based upon mathematical principles deeply attracted Plato. It underpins not only the Pythagorean view of astronomy and harmonics as sister sciences, which Plato endorses, but also the Pythagorean idea of a celestial harmony that Plato incorporates into the myth of Er (Arist. *Cael.* 2.9; cf. Pl. *Resp.* 10.617b). Understanding the mathematical basis of beauty and goodness in the study of harmonics and astronomy is for Plato an inherently good activity, furthermore, not only because it fulfills the intellect's proper desire for truth, but also because he envisions basing our own rational self-governance on the same sort of principles that govern the natural world and are responsible for its beauty and goodness. Although there are intimations of such a view in the *Republic*,[17] it finds its fullest expression in the *Philebus* and *Timaeus*.[18]

4. *Philebus* and *Timaeus*

The *Philebus* takes up the conflict between those like Philebus who regard pleasure as unequivocally good and the source of human happiness and those like Socrates who regard knowledge and understanding as such.

---

[16] See Barker 1994, the conclusions of which are conjecturally endorsed by Burnyeat 2000: 52–3. For a more skeptical view, see Huffman 2005: 426–7. See also Barker 2010 and the comments in Huffman 2010b.

[17] Plus one notoriously obscure application in the account at *Resp.* 8.546b–c of the "geometrical number" governing human procreation. The mathematics of the passage and its connections to Pythagorean number theory are well discussed in Ehrhardt 1986, while Crickmore 2006 seeks to establish its connections to Pythagorean musical theory.

[18] For fuller exploration of this view see Carone 2005: Chs. 2–5.

Plato seeks to settle this conflict by employing an analytical apparatus adapted directly from Philolaus. In an evident enough reference to his principles of limiters (*perainonta*) and unlimiteds (*apeira*) (Philolaus frs. 1, 2), Plato introduces the idea that "whatever is said to be is from one and many, possessing innately in itself limit [*peras*] and unlimitedness [*apeiria*]" as a gift to humanity from some Promethean figure (*Phlb.* 16c5–10). These principles he first applies to the intelligible forms in accordance with his method of collection and division, saying that one must not merely posit and seek to apprehend in each case the single form (*idea*) with its indefinitely multiple instances but also how many specific forms that generic form contains (*Phlb.* 16d–e).[19] Socrates' plan is to analyze pleasure and knowledge via the Philolaan principles to show they are unified genera containing a determinable number of species and thus avoid the conceptual confusion typically exploited in eristic disputation (*Phlb.* 18e–19b). He first, however, extends the analytical apparatus by identifying the combination of unlimited and limit as a third principle and the cause of their combination as a fourth (*Phlb.* 23c–d). This extension makes the metaphysical schema applicable to the mutable entities of the natural world. So Philolaus, with no conception of intelligible entities, had posited limiters, unlimiteds and their combinations (if not the causes of these) as the principles of natural entities: "Nature in the cosmos was harmonized from both unlimiteds and limiters, both the cosmos as a whole and everything in it" (fr. 1, cf. frs. 2 and 6).[20] The unlimited Plato characterizes as "the more and less" and as in itself without any determinate quantity (*Phlb.* 24a–5a).[21] Limit Plato defines as "all that is related as number to number or measure to measure" (*Phlb.* 25a–b) and as what makes opposites "commensurate and harmonious by imposing a definite number on them" (25d–e). Plato's adaptation of Philolaus' principles of

---

[19] Plato states that there is no knowledge of the unlimited multitude of things absent apprehending them as entities of some type and that expert apprehension requires location of their type within the systematic division of the broader genus that defines a field of inquiry (*Phlb.* 17e). Similarly, if less perspicuously, Philolaus had declared, "there will not be anything that will know if all things are unlimited" (Philolaus fr. 3). In stressing the need to identify the *number* of each genus (*Phlb.* 16d, 17d–e, 18a–b, 18c, 19a), i.e. the number of species into which it divides, Plato seems intent on preserving something of Philolaus' view that "all things that are known have number" (fr. 4, cf. fr. 6).

[20] The *Philebus'* adaptations of Philolaus' principles are well discussed in Meinwald 1998, 2002 and Huffman 2001. While there is no good evidence in the "middle-period" dialogues suggesting Pythagorean inspiration for the Platonic Forms hypothesis, the *Philebus* certainly shows Plato's interest in employing Pythagorean principles to ground the hypothesis, by accounting for the Forms' existence in terms of the interaction of *peras* and *apeiron*.

[21] Plato came to call this "the Indefinite Dyad" in his oral teaching within the Academy. See Arist. *Metaph.* 1.6.987b25–7; cf. Hermodorus *ap.* Simpl. *in Phys.* 247.30ff.

limiters and unlimiteds here in the *Philebus* is among his most significant uses of Pythagorean material, given its intimations of Plato's "unwritten doctrines," how his pupils in the Academy would themselves cast their *Prinzipienlehre* as an extension of Pythagoreanism, and the effect their doing so would have on the Pythagoreanism of later antiquity.

Since whatever in this adaptation pertains to intelligible reality apparently goes beyond any Pythagorean views Plato himself would have known, we may concentrate here on how the Pythagorean conceptual apparatus is applied in the *Philebus* to the task of specifying how the best human life is something other than a life of unrestricted pleasure. Much as the *Gorgias* identified organization (*taxis*), correctness (*orthotēs*) and the skill (*technē*) that bestows them as the principles of beneficent ordering (*Grg.* 506c–e), so limit in the *Philebus* plays an analogous role. After several examples of limit's various functions in producing bodily health, harmonious musical structures and good weather patterns (*Phlb.* 25e–6b), Socrates turns to how limit makes the soul good. Aphrodite herself, he says, "recognizes how excess and the overabundance of our wickedness allow for no limit in our pleasures and their fulfillment, and she therefore imposes law [*nomos*] and organization [*taxis*] as a limit on them" (*Phlb.* 26b7–10, after D. Frede). What this means becomes clearer as Socrates applies his Pythagorean schema to the analyses of pleasure and knowledge. Pleasure he classifies as an unlimited because it admits of more and less, a move the hedonist Philebus readily endorses since he believes unrestricted enjoyment is good (27e–8a). When he turns to the less straightforward classification of wisdom, knowledge and intelligence, Socrates introduces the unanimous view of the wise (*hoi sophoi*) that "intelligence [*nous*] is king for us of both heaven and earth" (28c6–7) and that, "just as our predecessors would say, intelligence and a wondrous wisdom organize and govern" the whole universe (28d5–9). The view attributed to the wise here recalls that attributed to the wise at *Gorgias* 507e–8a, though his emphasis here on his predecessors' near-unanimous agreement indicates that Socrates takes "the wise" to include Pythagoreans and non-Pythagoreans alike. The early atomists, whose view of the universe as ruled without reason by random chance Socrates rejects (*Phlb.* 28d5–7), are the obvious exception to the consensus view regarding the cosmic operation of some divine intelligence. Even against most of the rest who regarded the cosmos as rationally organized and governed, though, Plato could legitimately register the complaint leveled against Anaxagoras in the *Phaedo*, that despite his grand talk of *Nous* as cause of all things, his actual accounts of the world's origin and operation fail to reference it as such. In Pythagoreanism, by contrast, Plato would have found the means for explaining the operation of Intelligence as a cause in the cosmos, even if they spoke little of the cause itself, by describing in mathematical terms the relations of proportion and harmony that order and regulate its population and their behaviors. The crucial insight that the natural world operates according to mathematical principles of harmony and order was represented, however crudely, early in the Pythagorean tradition in the mystical figure of the *tetractys*. Sextus reports that the Pythagoreans credited discovery of the *tetractys* to Pythagoras himself and called it "the fount of ever-flowing nature" on the grounds that the entire cosmos is organized according to the *harmonia* or system of three concords whose proportions are represented in the *tetractys* (Sext. Emp. *Math.* 7.95). From early on, then, the Pythagoreans manifested a more profound interest than is evident among the earlier Greek philosophers in the particular principles ordering and regulating the cosmos. This interest is likewise manifest in the fragments of Philolaus' book: his cosmology assigns harmony the special role of fitting together limiters and unlimiteds in an ordered fashion to produce the cosmos's population (Philolaus fr. 6), and he finds the model for this cosmological harmony in the Pythagorean diatonic scale (fr. 6a).

What enables Plato finally in the *Timaeus* to undertake the teleological cosmology envisaged in the *Phaedo* is in large measure what he understood as the Pythagorean insight that mathematical principles of order and harmony serve as ultimate sources of beauty and goodness in the world. Timaeus articulates the fundamental explanatory principle toward the beginning of his account of the demiurge's creation:

> For having wished all things to be good and nothing bad, so far as possible, and yet so discerning the entire visible realm to be not at peace but moving in a discordant and unorganized manner [*plēmmelōs kai ataktōs*], god reduced it to order [*taxis*] from its condition of disorder [*ataxia*], since he regarded order as altogether better than its opposite. (Pl. *Ti.* 30a2–6)

The three mean proportions, arithmetic, geometric and harmonic, said to have been discovered by Pythagoras himself and featuring in the work of Philolaus and Archytas, play prominent roles in the ensuing accounts of how the demiurge fashioned this well-ordered cosmos. First, in explaining why god created its body from four primary elements, Timaeus provides an elaborate account of why the two additional elements of air and water were necessary to bind together fire and earth (which were required to make things visible and tangible). This account adduces the basic mathematical fact that there are two mean proportionals, or geometric means, between two "solid" or cube numbers (*Ti.* 31b–2c), e.g., 64 and 512 between

8 (2^3) and 4096 (16^3), since 8:64 = 64:512 = 512:4096. Plato introduces the mathematical machinery because the good result of unity, concord (*homologia*) and friendship (*philia*) among the elements is achieved by their being bound together in this most orderly and structured of ways.

Other quasi-Pythagorean teleological explanations feature prominently in the *Timaeus*, most notably in the account of the demiurge's creation of the World-Soul that soon follows.[22] The complex account of the World-Soul is intended to account for its rational capacity by describing it as compounded out of being, sameness and difference (the concepts fundamental to all rational judgments) and to account for the harmonious order with which it regulates the motion of the seven heavenly bodies known to Plato (the moon, sun, Mercury, Venus, Mars, Jupiter and Saturn) by dividing them into seven lengths, comprising a series of doubles proceeding from the unit (1) through the first even number (2), its square (4) and its cube (8), and a series of triples proceeding from the unit (1) through the first odd number (3), its square (9), and its cube (27), these two series being the two primary geometric progressions (*Ti.* 35b–c). The demiurge then inserts additional sections into these double and triple intervals in two mean proportions, one harmonic and one arithmetic, between each interval's extremes; this procedure produces in each case three new intervals in the ratios 3:2, 4:3, and 9:8, the ratios, respectively, of a perfect fifth, a perfect fourth, and a tone (*Ti.* 36a). His final step is to fill in all the intervals of the ratio 4:3 with tones in the 9:8 ratio, leaving in each case an interval of the ratio 256:243 (*Ti.* 36b). Although Plato neither names nor alludes to any of the Pythagoreans here, the passage is nevertheless one of his most obvious uses of Pythagorean mathematics and harmonics, for the division of each octave is identical with the diatonic scale described by Philolaus (fr. 6a).[23] Its elaborately complex and yet mathematically structured proportion and harmony serve to make the World-Soul not merely good, but "the best creation of the best of intelligible and eternal things" (*Ti.* 37a1–2, trans. Lee). Just as Pythagorean as the mathematics involved in

[22] Although one might suppose the subsequent account of the physical structure of the five elements, earth, water, air, fire and aether, in terms of the five regular solids to likewise reflect a Pythagorean inheritance, the evidence for attributing discovery of the Platonic solids to Pythagoras (e.g. Aët. 2.6.5) is one of the clearer instances of the tradition's retrofitting Pythagoras to become Plato's "source." While for the geometrical construction of the solids Plato likely owed more to Theaetetus than to any Pythagoreans (cf. schol. in Euc. 13.1, pp. 654.3ff. Heiberg and the discussions in Waterhouse 1972 and Sachs 1917), Plato indicates at *Ti.* 48b (cf. 53c) that the physical theory connecting the elements with the solids is original with himself.

[23] Good overviews of the Pythagorean musical mathematics involved in the World-Soul's construction are to be found in the discussion and commentary on Philolaus fr. 6a in Huffman 1993: 145–65 and in Barker 2007: 318–23.

its construction is the association of mathematically describable order, proportion and harmony with its goodness. In these most important stretches of the *Timaeus'* description of the demiurge's rational ordering to create a cosmos or ordered world system, Timaeus may be regarded not only as achieving the *Phaedo's* vision of teleological cosmology but also as carrying out the program implicit in the *Gorgias'* description of the view of those wise persons who say that community, friendship, orderliness, self-control and justice hold together heaven and earth, through the power of geometric equality (*Grg.* 507e–8a).

The ordering of the cosmos in the *Timaeus* has a further teleological dimension beyond making the cosmos itself good. In the midst of describing how the demiurge set the moon, sun and five planets in the seven orbits of the circle of difference, Timaeus says the demiurge placed the sun in the second orbit to shine throughout the heavens and thus make it possible for creatures such as ourselves to acquire *knowledge of number* from observing the heavenly bodies' uniform and regularly recurring motions (*Ti.* 39b–c). For this purpose, he says, night and day were created, along with the month (the period of the moon's orbit), the year (that of the sun's orbit), as well as the more obscure periods defined by the orbits of the other heavenly bodies. Timaeus returns to this important point in concluding his account of the demiurge's work:

> The sight of day and night, the months and returning years, the equinoxes and solstices, has caused the invention of number, given us the notion of time, and made us inquire into the nature of the universe; thence we have derived philosophy, the greatest gift the gods have ever given or will give to mortals. [. . .] The cause and purpose of god's invention and gift to us of sight was that we should see the revolutions of intelligence [*nous*] in the heavens and use their untroubled course to guide the troubled revolutions in our own understanding [*dianoēsis*], which are akin to them, and so, by learning what they are and how to calculate them accurately according to their nature, correct the disorder of our own revolutions by the standard of the invariability of those of god. The same applies again to sound and hearing, which were given by the gods for the same end and purpose. [. . .] All audible musical sound is given us for the sake of harmony, which has motions akin to the orbits in our soul, and which, as anyone who makes intelligent use of the arts knows, is not to be used, as is commonly thought, to give irrational pleasure, but as a heaven-sent ally in reducing to order and harmony any disharmony in the revolutions within us. (*Ti.* 47a4–d7, trans. Lee)

This magnificent statement regarding the cosmos's densely teleological order is Plato's ultimate articulation of the vision broached in the *Gorgias* and carried through into the *Republic*'s view of the philosopher's contemplation of what is permanently organized, orderly, rational and thereby just in the world itself in order to imitate it in his own person (*Resp.* 6.500b–c). The *Timaeus*' statement is saturated with elements Plato understood to be broadly Pythagorean: the fundamental importance of number and mathematics to the natural philosophical inquiries from which philosophy itself developed together with the view that the ultimate purpose of scientific inquiry, wherein one aims to understand the principles responsible for the order and goodness of the cosmos, is to make the same principles active in the governance of one's own self.

The *Philebus*' analysis of the relation between pleasure, knowledge and goodness via Philolaan principles concludes with a comparable vision likewise combining numerous elements figuring in Plato's earlier uses of Pythagorean ideas. Intense bodily pleasures are excluded from the best human life because they are inimical to reason's proper activity of theoretical understanding (*Phlb.* 63d–4a). In the mixture of genuine pleasures and such understanding Socrates sees "an incorporeal order beautifully governing an ensouled body" (*Phlb.* 64b7) and, in this order, finds goodness itself coming into view. For, he says, the value and worth of any mixture is due to the measure and proportion that make it a genuine mixture and that are particularly associated with beauty and excellence of character (*Phlb.* 64d–e, cf. 51e, 53b). In the final ranking of goods, the fourfold classification of principles adapted from Philolaus can be seen to recur. Socrates' assignment of the highest value to everything associated with measure (*Phlb.* 66a) recalls his earlier specifications of the nature of limit in terms of what makes disparate items commensurate and harmonious by imposing number upon them (*Phlb.* 25d–e). In ranking next in order of value what is proportionate, beautiful, complete, etc. (*Phlb.* 66b), Socrates recurs to the mixtures of limit and unlimited, that is, the things that have measure or limit. Likewise, in assigning intellect (*nous*) and reason (*phronēsis*) to the third order of value (*Phlb.* 66b), he recurs to the cause of these things having their measure or limit (cf. *Phlb.* 30c). Reason is what makes things good in the lesser sense of introducing into them the measure and limit primarily responsible for their being good. To the fourth rank of value Socrates assigns the sciences and arts, by which he apparently means the pure or properly philosophical varieties of arithmetic, geometry and so on, together with dialectic, which aim neither at practical utility nor merely at understanding this world's mutable entities but instead at the truth itself and understanding of what is immutable (*Phlb.* 55c–9d). The conception here of the value of the pure sciences evidently recalls the treatment of the same subject in *Republic* 7.

Their ranking fourth in the order of value is due not only to their vital presence in the mixture that constitutes the good life but also to the role they play in the human intellect's apprehension, through understanding the natural world, of the principles of measure and limit that it will apply in the ordering of the person. The fifth rank, finally, goes to the genuine pleasures that are the other element in the mixture. Implicit in this ranking yet again is the idea that coming to understand the order, proportion and harmony that are responsible as limiting principles for the natural world's beauty and goodness may lead to the embodiment of these same principles in the rational self-governance of the human microcosm that constitutes the best way of life. The evidence for early Pythagoreanism is such that we can no longer determine precisely how much of the inspiration for this vision Plato drew from Pythagorean sources. However, enough information has survived about the Pythagoreanism Plato knew, and in particular about the achievements of Philolaus and Archytas, that we may still appreciate some of the ways it influenced the conception of beauty, goodness and human well-being that Plato developed in moving beyond his Socratic inheritance.

CHAPTER II

Aristotle on the "so-called Pythagoreans": from lore to principles

Oliver Primavesi

1. Introduction

Aristotle's reports on the philosophy of the "so-called Pythagoreans" are among our earliest sources for the history of Pythagoreanism. According to Aristotle, these Pythagoreans championed both a theory of principles (ἀρχαί) in which numbers (or the elements of numbers) play a fundamental role, and an astronomical system in which not only the five ordinary planets, the sun and the moon, but also the earth itself and even an additional counter-earth orbit around a central fire. The purpose of this chapter is to analyze the most comprehensive account of the Pythagorean theory of principles in Aristotle's extant work: the first part of *Metaphysics* A5.[1]

Aristotle's treatment of "the so-called Pythagoreans" is distinguished from the rest of *Metaphysics* A by a feature which previous scholarship has tended to underrate: the focus here is on the intellectual development of the Pythagorean school.[2] Aristotle's sketch of this development, however, is based on a much fuller treatment, which Aristotle had included in his monograph on the Pythagoreans.[3] Whereas the monograph itself is now lost, Alexander of Aphrodisias, in commenting upon our chapter of the *Metaphysics*, supplies ample additional information gathered from the monograph.[4] This evidence should be used in order to supplement the picture emerging from an analysis of *Metaphysics* A5.

---

[1] For a recent discussion of the Pythagorean section of *Metaphysics* A5 as a whole see Schofield 2012; for a complementary treatment of the Pythagorean section of *Metaphysics* A8 see Primavesi 2012b; a critical discussion of Aristotle's picture of Pythagorean philosophy in general is provided by Burkert 1972a: 28–52 and by Huffman 1993: 57–64. See also Zhmud 2012b: 434–7.

[2] By contrast, even in the case of the Academy, Aristotle remains content to present the influences to which Plato was exposed in his youth; cf. *Metaph.* 987a29–b7.

[3] Rose 1886 fr. 190–205; Heitz 1869 fr. 106–22.   [4] Alexander *In Metaph.* 38.8–41.15 Hayduck.

2. Aristotle's introductory section (985b23–6)[5]

[b23] Ἐν δὲ τούτοις καὶ πρὸ τούτων
οἱ καλούμενοι Πυθαγόρειοι [b24] τῶν
μαθημάτων ἁψάμενοι πρῶτοι ταῦτα
προῆγον καὶ [b25] ἐντραφέντες ἐν
αὐτοῖς τὰς τούτων ἀρχὰς τῶν ὄντων
ἀρχὰς [b26] ᾠήθησαν εἶναι πάντων.

Contemporaneously with these
thinkers and before them, the so-called
Pythagoreans, once having taken up
the mathematical disciplines, were the
first who continuously advanced these
and who (in consequence of their
familiarity with them) came to believe
that the principles of these (of the
mathematical disciplines) are the
principles of all things.

b24 ταῦτα α : ταῦτά τε β | προῆγον α : προήγαγον β ‖ 25 τῶν ὄντων ἀρχὰς α :
om. β

Aristotle reports that the research activity of the Pythagoreans was both contemporaneous with and anterior to the thinkers examined before. The latter
certainly include the Atomists Leucippus and Democritus, whom Aristotle
has treated at the end of the preceding Chapter 4;[6] in addition, the reference might arguably include two further post-Parmenidean philosophers
of the fifth century discussed earlier in the same chapter,[7] viz. Empedocles
and Anaxagoras.[8] In either case, Aristotle indicates that the Pythagoreans
were active over a considerable period of time – over the greater part or
even the whole of the fifth century, which raises the expectation that the
main verb to which the indication is linked expresses a continuous activity
("they were advancing the *mathēmata*"), not a momentary one.[9]

It is less clear why Aristotle designates the Pythagoreans as "the *so-
called* Pythagoreans" (*hoi kaloumenoi Pythagoreioi*): does the qualification
"so-called" imply reservations with regard to the appropriateness of the label

---

[5] The Greek text and the critical apparatus of A5 will be based on my edition of *Metaphysics* A
throughout; cf. Primavesi 2012a: 482–3. The two versions by David Ross (1908 and 1928) served as
starting-points for the English translation.

[6] *Metaph.* 985b6–22. [7] *Metaph.* 984b32–5b4.

[8] Alexander discusses the extension of the reference in the following terms (37.6–12): "He says concerning the Pythagoreans that some of them were before Democritus and Leucippus, while others
were at the same time. Or 'contemporaneously with these thinkers and before them' refers not only
to Democritus and Leucippus but also to all the natural philosophers mentioned before. For they
were older than some of these and at the same time as others." Mansfeld and Primavesi 2011: 147 favor
the second option. One cannot, in any case, include Hesiod, who was discussed at the beginning of
Ch. 4.

[9] Note that προῆγον, the reading of the α-text, suits the extended period of time indicated by ἐν
δὲ τούτοις καὶ πρὸ τούτων far better than the β-reading προήγαγον, although the latter has been
preferred by editors since Bekker. For a general assessment of the comparative reliability of the α-text
and of the β-text and for a warning against an editorial case-by-case eclecticism, see Primavesi 2012a:
409–58.

Pythagoreioi, and if so, on what grounds are these reservations based?[10] It seems best to postpone the discussion of this point until we are in a position to see more clearly on what kind of sources Aristotle's account may be based.

It is the Pythagoreans' work on the *mathēmata* and the consequences they derived from it, which are presented as their main contribution to philosophy. Now in Aristotle's terms, *mathēmata* are clearly not limited to "mathematics" in the modern sense;[11] rather, they cover the whole curriculum presented in Book 7 of Plato's *Republic*, viz. not only arithmetic and geometry (plane and solid), but also musical theory[12] and astronomy,[13] the latter two being labeled by the Pythagoreans as "sister sciences," according to Plato.[14] Furthermore, the canon of four kindred *mathēmata* was defined already by the Pythagorean Archytas of Tarentum.[15] Therefore, it is virtually certain that Aristotle's remark on the Pythagoreans' work on *mathēmata* is meant to refer to the canon as a whole.

We will conclude that Aristotle's statement according to which the Pythagoreans "were bringing forward the *mathēmata*" does not just indicate that they introduced mathematics into philosophy, as Jonathan Barnes suggested,[16] but that they achieved progress within the realm of the four *mathēmata*,[17] and *thereby* prepared the ground for their own philosophy according to which the principles of the mathematical disciplines are the principles of everything there is.[18] The priority which Aristotle claims for the Pythagoreans cannot plausibly be referred to their initial step, i.e., getting in touch with the mathematical disciplines in the first place,[19] but must rather be seen to point to what they made of it later, i.e. to the

---

[10] Cherniss 1935: 385: "it has been suspected that by 'the so-called Pythagoreans' Aristotle meant to indicate that the doctrines in question were not those of genuine Pythagoreans but had in one way or another been fathered on the old sect. The use of the phrase, however, does not imply this subtlety." For a more balanced account see Burkert 1972a: 30 with n. 8.

[11] For this reason, it is potentially misleading to render μαθήματα by "mathematics" in our passage, as, for instance, Ross 1908, Ross 1928, Barnes 1982: 380 and Schofield 2012: 143 have done.

[12] *Metaph.* 997b21.   [13] *Metaph.* 989b32–3; *Metaph.* 1073b3–5.

[14] Plato *Resp.* 530d (= Archytas fr. 1E; Huffman 2005: 109).

[15] Huffman 2005: 103; Archytas fr. 1A, lines 4–7. Previous doubts concerning the best source for and the authenticity of that fragment are no longer upheld; cf. Cassio 1988: 139: "the only reliable basis for establishing the text of Archytas' fragment is Porphyry; and there should be no further doubts on its authenticity"; Burkert 1998: 311 agrees.

[16] Barnes 1982: 380–1 with n. 13 (p. 630). Barnes' interpretation of προάγω would seem to require one of the expressions quoted by LSJ s.v. προάγω I 3: προάγειν εἰς τὸ φανερόν, προάγειν εἰς τὸ πρόσθεν, προάγειν εἰς φῶς etc. Furthermore, Barnes' interpretation seems to presuppose the dubious β-reading προήγαγον, since putting pure mathematics on stage could be scarcely conceived of as a *continuous* activity.

[17] Cf. LSJ s.v. προάγω I 5 and Schofield 2012: 143–4.   [18] Cf. Schofield 2012: 143 n. 7.

[19] Ross 1928. Similarly Schofield 2012: 143, whose argument in n. 7, however, is unconvincing: it does not seem possible to restrict the priority claim to the period in which the thinkers treated in

advancement of these disciplines,[20] and, perhaps, also to the theory of principles based on that advancement.[21]

We now turn to the next passage where Aristotle will indicate what he considers to have been the intermediate steps – the additional "premises," as it were – between the initial act of "taking up the *mathēmata*" and the fully fledged Pythagorean theory according to which "the principles of the *mathēmata* are the principles of all things." With one notable exception, each and every proposition of the passage takes the form of ascribing a certain opinion to the (so-called) Pythagoreans. So it seems unlikely that Aristotle is quoting or paraphrasing a *continuous* Pythagorean argument that would have stated not only the individual opinions but also the logical connections between them. For in that case, it would have sufficed to mention the Pythagorean provenance of the whole argument once and for all. It rather seems to be the case that Aristotle presents a set of individual Pythagorean opinions and beliefs as stages of a historical development the *rationale* for which he, Aristotle, has discovered himself.[22] In other words: we are dealing with a piece of historiographical reasoning, which claims that some of the opinions attributable to the so-called Pythagoreans actually *caused* the coming-to-be of other opinions equally well attributable to them.

3. The development of the Pythagorean theory of principles (985b26–986a3)

(I) ἐπεὶ δὲ τούτων οἱ ἀριθμοὶ φύσει [b27] πρῶτοι,

(I) But since within these (the *mathēmata*) the numbers are by nature the first,

(II) ἐν δὲ τοῖς ἀριθμοῖς ἐδόκουν θεωρεῖν ὁμοιώματα [b28] πολλὰ τοῖς οὖσι καὶ γιγνομένοις (μᾶλλον ἢ ἐν πυρὶ καὶ γῇ [b29] καὶ ὕδατι) –

(II) and in the numbers they thought they saw many resemblances to things that are and come to be (more than in fire, earth and water) –

Ch. 4 were active, since Aristotle has just defined the temporal relationship between the Pythagore-ans' activity and fifth-century philosophy by means of the twofold expression "*contemporaneously with* these thinkers and *before* them."

[20] Ross 1908. Cf. Barnes 1982: 630 n. 13 (to p. 381): "*prōtoi* is often taken with *hapsamenoi*: that gives quite the wrong sense." See also Mansfeld and Primavesi 2011: 147.

[21] Grammatically speaking: πρῶτοι in b24 belongs with what follows (ταῦτα προῆγον καὶ [. . .] ᾠήθησαν) rather than with what precedes (τῶν μαθημάτων ἁψάμενοι).

[22] Cf. Alexander 37.18–19 Hayduck: "Having said that it was because of their familiarity with the mathematical disciplines that the Pythagoreans thought that the principles of these were the prin-ciples of all things, he says in what follows what reasoning they used to come to this conclusion." Schofield 2012: 145: "He is not content just to report their theory, but offers what looks like a diagnosis of how they constructed it."

(IIa) ὅτι τὸ μὲν τοιονδὶ τῶν ἀριθμῶν πάθος δικαιοσύνη [ᵇ30] τὸ δὲ τοιονδὶ ψυχὴ καὶ νοῦς, ἕτερον δὲ καιρὸς καὶ τῶν ἄλ-[ᵇ31]λων ὡς εἰπεῖν ἕκαστον ὁμοίως,

(IIa) that such and such a structural feature of numbers is "justice," such and such a structural feature "soul" and "intellect," a different one "due season," and almost each of the rest similarly;

(IIb) ἔτι δὲ τῶν ἁρμονιῶν ἐν ἀριθ-[ᵇ32]μοῖς ὁρῶντες τὰ πάθη καὶ τοὺς λόγους, –

(IIb) but also observing, in numbers, the structural features and ratios of attunements

(II') ἐπεὶ δὴ τὰ μὲν ἄλλα [ᵇ33] τοῖς ἀριθμοῖς ἐφαίνετο τὴν φύσιν ἀφωμοιῶσθαι πᾶσαν

(II') since, then, everything else seemed, in its whole nature, to be made to resemble the numbers

(I') οἱ [986ᵃ1] δ' ἀριθμοὶ πάσης τῆς φύσεως πρῶτοι,

(I') and the numbers (seemed) primary in the whole of nature,

(III) τὰ τῶν ἀριθμῶν στοι-[ᵃ2]χεῖα τῶν ὄντων στοιχεῖα πάντων εἶναι ὑπέλαβον

(III) they supposed the elements of number to be the elements of all things

(IV) καὶ τὸν [ᵃ3] ὅλον οὐρανὸν ἁρμονίαν εἶναι καὶ ἀριθμόν·

(IV) and the whole heaven to be an attunement and number.

26 ἐπεὶ δὲ] ἐπεὶ γὰρ temptavit Alexander 37.20–21 ‖ 27 τοῖς ἀριθμοῖς **α** : τούτοις **β** ‖ 30 ψυχὴ καὶ νοῦς **α** : ψυχὴ τε καὶ νοῦς **β** ‖ 32 ἐπεὶ δὴ Christ Ross Jaeger : ἐπειδή **α β** Bekker Bonitz ‖ 33 ἐφαίνετο **α** : ἐφαίνοντο **β** | πᾶσαν] πάντα temptavit Bonitz 1849: 78 cl. Al. 38.2 ‖ ἀφωμοιῶσθαι **γ** edd. : ἀφομοιῶσθαι **β** : ἀφομοιωθῆναι **α** ‖ 986a2 εἶναι ὑπέλαβον **α** : ὑπέλαβον εἶναι **β**

The first thing to note is that Aristotle's definite account of the Pythagorean theory of principles,[23] namely the end-point of his historiographical reconstruction, differs in important ways from the preliminary account given at the end of the introductory section.[24] First, the "principles [ἀρχαί] of the *mathēmata*" and the "principles of all things" of the preliminary account have been replaced by "elements [στοιχεῖα] of *number*" and "elements of all things" in the first half of the definite account (= proposition III).[25] It is clear from a subsequent remark that the "elements of number" are *even* (ἄρτιον) and *odd* (περιττόν), and that these, in turn, are qualified as unlimited (ἄπειρον) and limited (πεπερασμένον), respectively.[26] The question is, however, why these "elements of number"

---

[23] *Metaph.* 986a1–3: "(III) They supposed the elements of number to be the elements of all things (IV) and the whole heaven to be an attunement and number."

[24] *Metaph.* 985b25–6: "They came to believe that the principles of the mathematical disciplines are the principles of all things."

[25] For στοιχεῖον as *a kind of* ἀρχαί cf. *Metaph.* 1013a20–3.

[26] *Metaph.* 986a17–19. According to *Physics* 203a15–18 the Pythagoreans justified these equations by setting out odd and even numbers as patterns of pebbles. See Burkert 1972a: 33 with n. 27.

are not introduced in the preliminary version of the account. Furthermore, the second half of the definite account (= proposition 4), on the whole heaven being an attunement and number, is not prepared for by the preceding argument. One gets the impression that the version of the theory that is initially associated with the Pythagoreans' interest in the *mathēmata* (as described in the introductory section 985b23–6) might not be quite the same as the version that Aristotle presents as the end-point of the development. This impression is confirmed when we examine the fairly complex structure of Aristotle's historiographical reconstruction as a whole (985b26–6a3). The basic scheme is the transition from two initial premises, one systematical, one doxographical:

| 985b26–7: | (I) | Numbers are by nature primary. |
| 985b27–9: | (II) | In numbers the Pythagoreans thought to observe more resemblances to things than in fire, earth and water. |

to the twofold conclusion which we have already mentioned:

| 986a1–2: | (III) | They believed the elements of number to be the elements of all things. |
| 986a2–3: | (IV) | They believed the whole heaven to be an attunement (*harmonia*) and number. |

Between the initial premises and the final conclusion, however, Aristotle has inserted two further items. The first item is a bipartite set of examples (IIa/IIb) which illustrates the kind of observations by which the Pythagoreans were induced to assume, as reported in premise II, that there are many resemblances between numbers and things:

| 985b29–31: | (IIa) | (Arithmology): they thought to see that the structural features (*pathē*) of certain numbers each correspond to a certain concept, like "justice," "soul and intellect," or "due season" (*kairos*). |
| 985b31–2: | (IIb) | (Musical ratios): they observed that the structural features (*pathē*) and ratios of attunements (*harmoniai*) consist in numbers. |

The second item is a restatement of the two initial premises in reverse order and in modified form:

| 985b32–3: | (II') | Everything else seemed, in its whole nature, to be made to resemble the numbers. |
| 985b33–986a1: | (I') | Numbers seemed primary in nature as a whole. |

Due to the reversal just mentioned, the two versions of the second premise (II and II') *frame* the examples (IIa and IIb), which confirms that these examples are more immediately related to the Pythagoreans' assumption on resemblances, which was reported in the second premise. Having inserted these examples, Aristotle restates both initial premises (II and I) in a way which makes them claim much more than the initial versions,[27] as can be shown by comparing both versions of either premise. We begin with premise (II), on resemblances between numbers and other things. Its initial version (II) ascribes to the Pythagoreans no more than a series of observations: they thought that in numbers they saw more resemblances to things than in the so-called elements (fire, earth and water) assumed by ordinary naturalists – which situates the Pythagoreans in the larger context of Presocratic philosophy.[28] The revised version (II'), by contrast, ascribes to them a *general hypothesis*, in which the initial observations have been transformed on three counts:

- What was initially presented as the observation of many resemblances in numbers to things is now described as a subordination in the opposite direction: the other things are now assumed to be made to resemble numbers.
- Whereas numbers were initially judged to show relatively more resemblances to things than fire, earth and the like, the subordination of things to numbers is now perceived as the essential feature of things, which governs their whole nature.
- The scope has been extended in that the subordination to numbers applies to all things (τὰ μὲν ἄλλα = "all other things").

In the case of premise (I) the difference between the two versions is, at first glance, less conspicuous but by no means less fundamental: the initial version of premise (I) is not a doxographical proposition but a systematical one: the statement of the primacy of numbers is not presented as just being held by the Pythagoreans but as being true.[29] By contrast, the revised version (I') of the premise should be regarded as a doxographical assertion about the Pythagoreans. For it comes immediately after and in close connection with the revised version of the *second* premise (II'), which contains, in 985b33,

---

[27] Note that the restatement of the two premises is introduced not only by the causal conjunction (ἐπεί) already employed in the initial statement of them, but also by an additional particle (δή): this may just mark the resumption of the main argument after the end of the parenthesis (cf. Bonitz 1870 s.v. δή, 172b23–5), but it may also indicate that the initial premises are now being modified in consequence of the examples presented within the parenthesis (cf. Bonitz 1870 s.v. δή, 172b37–9).

[28] Cf. *Metaph.* A 5; 987a9–11: "Down to the Italian school, then, and apart from it, the others have treated these subjects – i.e. the causes – in a rather one-dimensional way [μοναχώτερον]."

[29] *Metaph.* 985b26–7: ἐπεὶ δὲ τούτων οἱ ἀριθμοὶ φύσει [b27] πρῶτοι ("Since of these the numbers are by nature the first"). Syntactically speaking, we are dealing with a nominal clause here, in which no verbal predicate can be supplied ascribing the proposition to a specific thinker or school.

the verbal predicate "it seemed" (ἐφαίνετο);[30] therefore, it seems perfectly legitimate, even natural, to assume an ellipsis of the corresponding plural "they seemed" (ἐφαίνοντο) in (I').[31] This is also suggested by a comparison of the *contents* of (I') with that of its predecessor (I). The crucial point here is the interpretation of the demonstrative pronoun "of these" (τούτων) in the first version (I): "since *of these* the numbers are by nature the first." Since the reference point for the pronoun must in any case be sought in the preceding introductory section,[32] there are four possibilities:

- The principles of all things (τῶν ὄντων ἀρχὰς [. . .] πάντων), mentioned in b25–6.
- All things (τῶν ὄντων [. . .] πάντων), mentioned in b25–6.
- The principles of the *mathēmata* (τὰς τούτων ἀρχὰς), mentioned in b25.
- The *mathēmata* themselves, mentioned in b24 and referred to by ταῦτα in b24 and by τούτων in b25.

Schofield refers the demonstrative pronoun "of these" (τούτων) to "all things," his reason being that the *revised* version of the first premise (I'; 985b33–986a1), which clearly states that numbers are primary of *nature as a whole*, should express the same proposition as the initial version of that premise.[33] But since the revised version of the second premise (= II': 985b32–3) also makes a far stronger claim than its initial version (985b27–9), it is certainly possible that the same holds for the two versions of the first premise, too.

Furthermore, in 985b26–7 Aristotle would scarcely have presented the initial version of the first premise (I) as an objective truth had he taken it to mean that numbers are by nature the first among everything there is or the first among its principles: that view is too far from anything he might consider reasonable. By contrast, it is quite plausible to ascribe to him the innocent view that numbers are by nature the first

---

[30] *Metaph.* 985b32–986a1: (II') ἐπεὶ δὴ τὰ μὲν ἄλλα τοῖς ἀριθμοῖς ἐφαίνετο τὴν φύσιν ἀφωμοιῶσθαι πᾶσαν (I') οἱ δ' ἀριθμοὶ (*scil.* ἐφαίνοντο) πάσης τῆς φύσεως πρῶτοι.

[31] Note also that, in the premise coming first (II'), the β-reviser of the *Metaphysics* has replaced the α-reading ἐφαίνετο (985b33) by the plural ἐφαίνοντο, as if he wanted to make sure that the verbal predicate is fit to serve as a common predicate to both premises II' and I'.

[32] *Metaph.* 985b24–6: "[The Pythagoreans] having taken up the *mathēmata*, were the first who continuously advanced these and who came to believe that the principles of these are the principles of all things [τῶν μαθημάτων ἁψάμενοι πρῶτοι ταῦτα προῆγον καὶ . . . τὰς τούτων ἀρχὰς τῶν ὄντων ἀρχὰς ᾠήθησαν εἶναι πάντων]."

[33] Schofield 2012: 144 n. 8: "The reprise at 985b33–986a1 ('and numbers were primary in the whole of nature') makes clear what Aristotle had in mind. Alexander gets it right." As to Alexander, cf. *In Metaph.* 37.21–2 Hayduck.

among the *mathēmata* (or, for that matter, among the principles of the *mathēmata*).[34]

Finally, referring τούτων (985b26) to *mathēmata* also makes more sense in view of Aristotle's historiographical reconstruction as a whole. For if the initial version of premise (I) were already claiming that numbers are by nature the first of all things, then the subsequent elaboration of the two premises up to and including the revised version of the first premise (I') would be quite pointless, since the final result of that elaboration (I') would amount to a mere repetition of its starting point (I). So it seems that the *initial* version of premise (I) was restricted to the primacy of numbers within the *mathēmata* or within the principles of the *mathēmata*.[35] For the same reason, we must take the much stronger revised version (I': 985b33–986a1: numbers are primary of *nature as a whole*) to state a Pythagorean tenet, not Aristotle's own view on numbers, in other words: we must indeed assume an ellipsis of "they seemed" (ἐφαίνοντο) in I'.

We have now established that both the conclusion of Aristotle's argument (i.e. the account of the Pythagorean theory of principles) and its two premises are stated twice, and that in all three cases the second version makes stronger, or more comprehensive, or more precise claims than the first one. The obvious question is whether these modifications are at all warranted:

(1)   Do the examples of *resemblances* (IIa and IIb) that are inserted after the first statement of both premises justify the subsequent modification of these premises?

(2)   Does the revised set of premises (985b32–986a1: II' + I') bear out the ensuing revised account of the Pythagorean theory (986a1–983), and, in particular, the replacement of "principles of *mathēmata*" by "elements of number," *viz.* by odd (limited) and even (unlimited)?

These questions seem difficult to answer since the resemblances (985b29–32: IIa–IIb), which obviously play a pivotal role in the unfolding of the argument, are only indicated obliquely. A little further down, however, Aristotle will state a straightforward reason for the brevity of his report on the Pythagoreans in chapter A5: he has offered a more detailed discussion

---

[34] It is true that in *Metaphysics* A, Aristotle does not presuppose the results of the later books of the *Metaphysics*; the state of the art in first philosophy is rather represented by Plato's theory of principles. But this does not mean that Aristotle subscribes uncritically to views he does not hold.

[35] Huffman 1993: 179. Note also that, since the *mathēmata* themselves have been addressed by means of corresponding demonstrative pronouns already in the introductory section (ταῦτα in 985b24 and τούτων in 985b25), the reference of the pronoun in question is most likely to be once more to the *mathēmata* themselves.

elsewhere;[36] and as Alexander specifies, Aristotle is referring here to *On the Heavens* and to his monograph on the doctrines of the Pythagoreans.[37]

In *On the Heavens*, the treatment of the Pythagoreans is restricted to their theory on the heavens, which is to say on the *harmonia* of the spheres[38] and on celestial bodies and the central fire.[39] It follows that *if* Aristotle provided more detailed information on Pythagorean arithmology and musical theory *at all*, he must have done so in his monograph on the doctrines of the Pythagoreans, now lost. Since Alexander offers, in his commentary on our passage, a very detailed account of the resemblances (both arithmological and musical), and since he indicates his source repeatedly by inserting expressions such as "he [Aristotle] says,"[40] his source must be Aristotle's monograph, not, of course, for every terminological detail, but for the doxographical substance.[41] It is precisely the testimony provided by Alexander, which will enable us to assess the function of the resemblances in Aristotle's historiographical reconstruction as outlined in *Metaph.* A5.

4.   The resemblances: Alexander's report on Aristotle's monograph

4.1.   *Pythagorean arithmology*

Alexander's summary of Aristotle's monograph supplements the brief reference to the arithmological treatment of justice, soul/intellect and due season (*kairos*) (*Metaph.* A5) in various ways: in Alexander, the list of concepts is fuller, we are told the number which corresponds to each concept, and there is a detailed description of the structural features which, according to Aristotle's account, suggested the correspondence in the first place. Alexander summarizes Aristotle's treatment of (a) *justice*, (b) *due season/Athena*, (c) *marriage*, (d) *intellect/ousia* and (e) *opinion/motion/addition*. It seems

---

[36] *Metaph.* 986a12–13.   [37] Alexander *In Metaph.* 41.1–2.
[38] *De caelo* 290b12–1a6.   [39] *De caelo* 293a18–b30.
[40] Alexander *In Metaph.* 38.10: ἐδήλωσε; 38.21: φησί; 40.18: ἐδείκνυε; 41.5: προείρηκε.
[41] The extent to which Alexander, in his commentary on *Metaph.* A5, is drawing on Aristotle's monograph, was underestimated by the two nineteenth-century collectors of fragments of lost Aristotelian writings, *viz.* Rose (who thought all lost works of Aristotle to be spurious anyway) and Heitz; cf. Rose 1863: 207–8 (fr. 13 = 188), Heitz 1869: 74–5 (fr. 14 = 120), and Rose 1886: 162 (fr. 203). The truth was seen by Wilpert 1940: 371–6 (cf. his Greek text on pp. 387–9) and put to use by David Ross in his collection of select Aristotelian fragments, cf. Ross 1955: 138–41 (fr. 13); see also Burkert 1972a: 29 with n. 5 and 166 n. 4.

sufficient to examine sections (a)–(c), since these illustrate the full range of approaches covered by the arithmology of Aristotle's Pythagoreans.[42]

4.1.1. *"Justice" and the square numbers 4 and 9*

τῆς μὲν γὰρ δικαιοσύνης ἴδιον ὑπολαμβάνοντες εἶναι τὸ [11] ἀντιπεπονθός τε καὶ ἴσον, ἐν τοῖς ἀριθμοῖς τοῦτο εὑρίσκοντες ὄν, διὰ τοῦτο [12] καὶ τὸν ἰσάκις ἴσον ἀριθμὸν πρῶτον ἔλεγον εἶναι δικαιοσύνην· τὸ γὰρ [13] πρῶτον ἐν ἑκάστῳ τῶν τὸν αὐτὸν λόγον ἐχόντων μάλιστα εἶναι τοῦτο ὃ [14] λέγεται.

τοῦτον δὲ οἱ μὲν τὸν τέσσαρα ἔλεγον, ἐπεὶ πρῶτος ὢν τετρά-[15]γωνος εἰς ἴσα διαιρεῖται καὶ ἔστιν ἴσος (δὶς γὰρ δύο), οἱ δὲ τὸν ἐννέα, ὅς [16] ἐστι πρῶτος τετράγωνος ἀπὸ περιττοῦ τοῦ τρία ἐφ᾽ αὑτὸν γενομένου.

For since they assumed that retribution and equality is a property of justice, and found that this was in numbers, they therefore said that the first equal-times-equal number is justice; for they thought that in every case the first of the things that have the same formula is in the highest degree that which it is said to be.

But some of them said that this number is 4, since, as the first square number, it is divided into equals and is itself equal (for it is twice 2), while others said that it is the number 9, which is the first square number produced from an odd number (3) multiplied by itself. (Alexander *Commentary on the Metaphysics*, henceforward *In Metaph.* 38.10–16)

11 εὑρίσκοντες (O)] εὕρισκον versio altera (LF) ‖ 15 ὅς OMS : ὃ A ‖ 16 τετράγωνος Bonitz cf. vers. alt. (LF) : στερεός OAS

The Pythagoreans could have remained content to claim that the structural feature (*pathos*) of square numbers "retribution and equality," is to be identified with "justice":[43] this is what one would have expected in view of the brief sketch in *Metaph.* A5. But Alexander's report clearly says that Aristotle attributed to the Pythagoreans the equation of the first square number *itself* with "justice" (38.12). This squares with the additional premise according to which a structural feature (*pathos*) common to an ordered series of objects belongs in the highest degree to the first item (38.12–14), which would have been quite pointless if the Pythagoreans equated a structural feature common to *all* square numbers with "justice." Finally,

---

[42] We will supplement Hayduck's *apparatus* with (and, if necessary, change his Greek text according to) readings from both the Laurentianus 85.1 (O = "*Oceanus*"), on which see Harlfinger 1975: 18–20, and from the Latin translation by Sepúlveda 1527 (S), which is based on four Greek manuscripts not all of which seem to be extant.

[43] In the *Nicomachean Ethics* (1132b 21–3), Aristotle actually states that the Pythagoreans defined "justice" as retribution (ἀντιπεπονθός).

the closing remark according to which it was disputed whether the first square number is 4 or 9 (38.14–16) clearly shows that what Aristotle actually found in his source was not an abstract reference either to "square number" or even to "the first square number", but a debate between adherents of 4 and adherents of 9. So what his Pythagoreans actually claimed is partly "the number 4 *is* justice" and partly "the number 9 *is* justice." But Aristotle did not leave the matter at that; all the extra premises featured in the summary rather indicate that he analyzed the Pythagoreans' claim by reconstructing their reasoning along the following lines:

(1)   The Pythagoreans found that an essential structural feature of square numbers is the retribution and equality that obtains between their two factors.

(2)   They assumed that a structural feature common to an ordered series of objects belongs in the highest degree to the first item of that series.

(3)   They inferred that it is the *first* square number, which is distinguished by the highest degree of "retribution and equality."

(4)   On the other hand, they assumed "retribution and equality" to be the property of "justice."

(5)   By consequence, they *equated* the first square number with "justice."

(6)   It was, however, disputed, whether the first square number is 4 or 9.

(7)   Accordingly, the number to be equated with "justice" was 4 according to some Pythagoreans, and 9 according to others.

In order to understand the competition between 4 and 9, and, in particular, the absence of 1 from the list of candidates, we must realize that both in Pythagorean arithmology and for Aristotle 1 does not count as an ordinary number but, as Aristotle puts it in *Metaphysics* N, as the basic measure unit for numbers.[44] Since "one" is not regarded as a number, it is not regarded as a square number either. The alternative between the first square number produced from an *even* number – 4 – and the first square number produced from an *odd* number – 9 – reminds us of Aristotle's reference to the "elements of number" *viz.* to "odd and even," in *Metaph.* A5, 986a1–2.

4.1.2. "Due season," "Athena" and 7

The arithmological procedure as hinted at in *Metaph.* A5, 985b29–31 starts from certain structural features of numbers and relates these features to concepts: the arithmological treatment of "justice" has just provided an example for this procedure; another example ("Athena") will be provided at the end of the section on 7. But before that, two other types of arithmological

---

[44]   *Metaph.* 1087b 33–4 + 1088a4–8 with Annas 1976: 117.

interpretation are illustrated. There is a more empirical approach in which the procedure goes in the opposite direction: one starts by observing in the external world (for instance, in human life) a certain structural feature, a *pathos*, which can be related to a certain number – the internal structural features (*pathē*) of that number being irrelevant this time. Furthermore, the arithmological interpretation of a certain concept, once established, may receive *additional* confirmation by further research into the significance of the number in question within another branch of the *mathēmata*, for instance, in astronomy.

(i) Seven = *kairos* ("due season") I: the periods of human life

καὶ-[17]ρὸν δὲ πάλιν ἔλεγον τὸν ἑπτά· δοκεῖ γὰρ τὰ φυσικὰ τοὺς τελείους καιροὺς [18] ἴσχειν καὶ γενέσεως καὶ τελειώσεως κατὰ ἑβδομάδας, ὡς ἐπ' ἀνθρώπου. [19] καὶ γὰρ τίκτεται ἑπταμηνιαῖα, καὶ ὀδοντοφυεῖ τοσούτων ἐτῶν, καὶ ἡβάσκει [20] περὶ τὴν δευτέραν ἑβδομάδα, καὶ γενειᾷ περὶ τὴν τρίτην.

They said, again, that the number 7 is *kairos* ("due season"), for natural things seem to have their seasons of completion, both of birth and of maturity, according to [periods of] 7, as in the case of a human being. For it is born 7 months after conception, and cuts his (second) teeth after the same number of years,[45] and reaches puberty at about the end of the second period of 7 years, and grows a beard at about the end of the third. (Alexander *In Metaph.* p. 38.16–20)

18 ἑβδομάδας (O)] ἑβδομάδα versio altera (LF) ‖ ἀνθρώπου (O)] ἀνθρώπου τοῦτο ὁρᾶται versio altera (LF) ‖ 19 ἐτῶν OAS : μηνῶν Ascl., cf. vers. alt. (LF) ‖ ἡβάσκει] ἡβάσις O

Observing the stages of the development of a human being may yield a subdivision of the human life span into *periods of equal duration*: in this case, the *number* of the years making up one such period acquires arithmological significance. The subdivision into seven-year periods, which is mentioned in our passage,[46] goes back to Solon, who assumed there to be ten such periods (fr. 27 West);[47] the remark referring to the date of birth is based on

---

[45] For the seventh year as the time of the second teeth see ps.-Hippocrates, *De octimestri partu* 82–3 Grensemann = 171 Joly.
[46] See further Zhmud 2012b: 397.
[47] The arrangement in periods of seven appears also in Ch. 5 of the first part (Chs. 1–11) of the ps.-Hippocratic treatise *De hebdomadibus* (text: West 1971a); but the date of that part is disputed: whereas West favors a fifth-century date at least for the cosmological system that forms the nucleus (West 1971a: 383–4), Mansfeld considers it, for linguistic and other reasons, to be late Hellenistic (Mansfeld 1971, 229–31); more recently, he has ascribed it to a *Jewish* author in Alexandria (Mansfeld 1989a: 185).

the view of Greek doctors that births are possible from the seventh month onwards but that the tenth month is safest and best for births.[48] There was an alternative tradition that credited Pythagoras with a subdivision of human life into four twenty-year periods.[49]

(ii) Seven = *kairos* (due season) II: the sun

καὶ τὸν ἥλιον [21] δέ, ἐπεὶ αὐτὸς αἴτιος εἶναι τῶν καρπῶν, φησί, δοκεῖ, ἐνταῦθά φασιν ἱδρῦ-[22]σθαι καθ᾽ ὃ ὁ ἕβδομος ἀριθμός ἐστιν, ὃν καιρὸν λέγουσιν· ἑβδόμην γὰρ [23] αὐτὸν τάξιν ἔχειν τῶν περὶ τὸ μέσον καὶ τὴν ἑστίαν κινουμένων δέκα σω-[39,1]μάτων·

κινεῖσθαι γὰρ μετὰ τὴν τῶν ἀπλανῶν σφαῖραν καὶ τὰς πέντε τὰς [2] τῶν πλανήτων· μεθ᾽ ὃν ὀγδόην τὴν σελήνην, καὶ τὴν γῆν ἐννάτην, μεθ᾽ [3] ἣν τὴν ἀντίχθονα.

But (according to Aristotle) also the sun, since it seems itself to be the cause of the fruits, is said by them to be situated where the number 7 is, which they call *kairos* (due season); for they say that the sun occupies the seventh place among the ten bodies that move around the centre, or hearth.
For the sun, they say, moves after the sphere of the fixed stars and after the five spheres of the planets; after it is the moon, eighth, and the earth, ninth, and after the earth the counter-earth. (Alexander *In Metaph.* 38.20–9.3)

21 καρπῶν (O)] καιρῶν perperam Ascl.[50] ‖ φησί (O)] φύσει coni. Bonitz ‖ 2 ὃν O Ascl. : ἣν A ‖ ὀγδόην] ὄγδοον O

The arithmological identification of 7 as *kairos* ("due season") – already established in the previous section – can be confirmed by astronomy. Observation of the heavenly bodies leads to the impression that they are arranged in an ordered sequence, according to the distance which obtains between each of them and the center of the universe. Thus, each heavenly body can be assigned a number provided that the direction of counting is defined (from the periphery to the center of the universe or the other way round). If one starts from the periphery, the first place will be taken by the

[48] See ps.-Hippocrates *De octimestri partu* 82–3, 90–1, 96–7 Grensemann = 174, 164–5, 169–70 Joly. For Empedocles' cosmogonical explanation of the fact that children are born in the seventh and tenth month see Mansfeld and Primavesi 2011: 480–1 and 546–9.

[49] Diog. Laert. 8.10; Diod. Sic. 10.9.5.

[50] The reading of Asclepius presupposes the use of καιροί in the sense of ὧραι, which is not attested in pre-Hellenistic Greek: LSJ s.v. καιρός III 2 a) does not offer any pre-Hellenistic evidence for that meaning; the inscription *IG* XIV.1018, listed there, is from AD 370; according to the Atticist lexicon of Moeris, the use of the word in addition with "of the year" is not Attic (Moeris ω 6, p. 155 Hansen: ὥρα ἔτους Ἀττικοί· καιρὸς ἔτους Ἕλληνες). Therefore, Hayduck's preference for καιρῶν is mistaken.

sphere of the fixed stars, places two to six by five planets (Saturn, Jupiter, Mars, Mercury and Venus),[51] and in seventh place we have the sun. The position of the sun brings us back to the arithmological identification of 7 as *kairos* ("due season"): the fact that the sun takes *seventh* place in the cosmos squares surprisingly well with the fact that it makes *fruits* ripen; in other words brings about their *kairos* ("due season").[52]

It is irrelevant, for that argument, how many more heavenly bodies follow suit *after* the sun if one continues to count inwards. But in Aristotle's presentation the centripetal way of counting, which guarantees the sun seventh place, appears closely connected with the system of Philolaus of Croton in which all heavenly bodies, including the sun and the earth, orbit around a central fire (ἑστία, "hearth") and in which the sun is followed in eighth place by the moon, in ninth place by the earth and, especially, in tenth place and closest to the central fire, by the so-called "counter-earth."[53] And yet the centripetal counting of the heavenly bodies that affords the sun with seventh place can equally well be performed within the ordinary geocentric system, and the connection of this counting method with the system of Philolaus seems to be a secondary construction by Aristotle himself.[54] For there was also a *centrifugal* way of counting,[55] and it is *this* method which is explicitly ascribed to Philolaus by Aëtius,[56] whereas the centripetal way, by contrast, is even reported to have run counter to the assumptions of the mathematical branch of the Pythagorean school.[57] *Mathematikoi* such as Philolaus, or so it seems, counted from the center to the periphery.

(iii) Seven = Athena

ἐπεὶ δὲ οὔτε γεννᾷ τινα τῶν ἐν τῇ δεκάδι ἀριθμῶν ὁ [4] ἑπτὰ οὔτε γεννᾶται ὑπό τινος αὐτῶν, διὰ τοῦτο καὶ Ἀθηνᾶν ἔλεγον αὐτόν.

Now since the number 7 neither generates any of the numbers in the decade nor is generated by any of these numbers, they called it "Athena."

---

[51] For the order of the planets see Burkert 1972a: 300.

[52] In *Metaph.* 990a22–3, Aristotle classes the *kairos* ("due season") – along with *doxa* (opinion) – among the concepts which take a certain place in the heavens in accordance with the corresponding number.

[53] See Huffman 1993: 231–8. Within *Metaph.* A5, this system is referred to in 986a6–12.

[54] Cf. Huffman 1993: 287–8.

[55] Alexander *In Metaph.* 74.12–13 Hayduck; see Burkert 1972a: 40 with n. 64.

[56] Huffman 1993: 238 (Text 8 = DK A17): "Philolaus the Pythagorean [puts] fire in the middle, for this is the hearth of the whole, but the counter-earth second, and third the inhabited earth."

[57] Alexander *In Metaph.*, *versio altera* of 38.21 (ἐπεί) – 39.3 (ἀντίχθονα) Hayduck, lines 3–4. On the schism of the Pythagoreans into *acusmatici* and *mathematici* in general see Burkert 1972a: 192–208.

[5] ὁ μὲν γὰρ δύο τὸν τέσσαρα καὶ ὁ τρία τὸν ἐννέα καὶ τὸν ἒξ καὶ ὁ τέσσαρα [6] τὸν ὀκτὼ καὶ ὁ πέντε τὸν δέκα γεννᾷ, γεννῶνται δὲ ὁ τέσσαρα καὶ ὁ ἒξ [7] καὶ ὁ ὀκτὼ καὶ ὁ ἐννέα καὶ ὁ δέκα· ὁ δὲ ἑπτὰ οὔτε τινὰ γεννᾷ οὔτε ἔκ [8] τινος γεννᾶται· τοιαύτη δὲ καὶ ἡ Ἀθηνᾶ ἀμήτωρ καὶ ἀεὶ παρθένος.

For the 2 generates the 4, the 3 generates both the 9 and the 6, the 4 generates the 8, and the 5 generates the 10, and the 4, the 6, the 8, the 9, and the 10 are generated; but the 7 neither generates any number nor is generated from any; so too Athena is motherless and forever a virgin. (Alexander *In Metaph.* 39.3–8)

8 γεννᾶται (O)] τῶν ὑπὸ τὴν δεκάδα add. Ascl. ‖ καὶ ἀεὶ παρθένος (O)] om. Ascl.

If one takes into consideration all possible binary multiplications of two numbers[58] the product of which remains within the first decade, one will observe that the numbers 2, 3, 4 and 5 operate as factors, and the numbers 4, 6, 8, 9 and 10 as products: $2 \times 2 = 4$; $2 \times 3 = 6$; $2 \times 4 = 8$; $3 \times 3 = 9$; $2 \times 5 = 10$. The number 7, by contrast, will display the feature (*pathos*) of appearing neither as a factor nor as a product. If we address the multiplication of numbers metaphorically as the bringing forth of offspring by way of copulation of two partners then we may say that, within the first decade, only the number 7 has neither a child nor a mother. This structural feature, however, is shared by the goddess Athena, who is not only a virgin forever, but also motherless (having sprung from the head of her father Zeus). Therefore, Aristotle's Pythagoreans called the number 7 "Athena."[59] If we allow for the metaphorical correspondence between multiplication and procreation, the argument squares with the arithmological model described in *Metaph.* A5 as closely as the section on "justice"; it may be set out as follows:

(1)   The Pythagoreans observed that an essential structural feature (*pathos*) of the number 7 is that, within the first decade, it operates neither as a factor nor as a product.

(2)   They metaphorically labeled this structural feature as "having neither child nor mother."

(3)   Drawing on that metaphor, they ascribed the same structural feature to the goddess Athena.

(4)   Accordingly, they called the number 7 "Athena."

---

58 "Of two *numbers*," that is to say: of two factors not including the "one," since the latter does not count as a number, as we have seen.

59 For the connection between numbers and gods cf. the parallels assembled in Burkert 1972a: 467 n. 9.

A *part* of this argument is ascribed also to the Pythagorean Philolaus, who is reported to have called the number 7 "motherless" (ἀμήτωρ).[60] What is *not* attested to for Philolaus, however, is the designation of the number 7 as "childless" (which presupposes that one considers the first decade only), let alone as "Athena"[61] (which presupposes both motherlessness *and* childlessness).

4.1.3. "Marriage" and the number 5

γά-[9]μον δὲ ἔλεγον τὸν πέντε, ὅτι ὁ μὲν γάμος σύνοδος ἄρρενός ἐστι καὶ θή-[10]λεος, ἔστι δὲ κατ' αὐτοὺς ἄρρεν μὲν τὸ περιττὸν θῆλυ δὲ τὸ ἄρτιον, [11] πρῶτος δὲ οὗτος ἐξ ἀρτίου τοῦ δύο πρώτου καὶ πρώτου τοῦ τρία περιττοῦ [12] τὴν γένεσιν ἔχει· τὸ μὲν γὰρ περιττὸν ἄρρεν αὐτοῖς ἐστιν, ὡς εἶπον, τὸ [13] δὲ ἄρτιον θῆλυ.

They called the number 5 "marriage" because marriage is the coming together of male and female, and according to them male is the odd and female the even, and 5 is the first number generated from the first even number, 2, and the first odd number, 3; for as I said, the odd is, in their view, male, and the even female. (Alexander *In Metaph.* 39.8–13)

As we have already seen, 2 counts as the first even number and 3 as the first odd. The sum of both numbers, the number 5, counts as the first combination of them, since the product of them, the number 6, comes later. Furthermore, all even numbers count as female, all odd as male.[62] In view of the paradigmatic character always enjoyed by the first item in an ordered series, we may say that the number 5 is the combination *par excellence* of the female *par excellence* with the male *par excellence*.

The pivotal role of even and odd in the arithmological analysis of the number 5 is clearly relevant for Aristotle's concluding remarks on the "elements of number," namely on "odd" and "even" (*Metaph.* A5, 986a1–2). Furthermore, the ascription of female and male gender to even and odd numbers makes more sense than one would think: when numbers set out as patterns of pebbles (ψῆφοι)[63] are divided into two, in even numbers an empty middle space seems to open up ready to conceive, whereas in odd numbers a procreative middle part seems to remain.[64] In a sense, then,

---

[60] DK 44B20, see Huffman 1993: 334–9.   [61] *Pace* Burkert 1972a: 249.

[62] See the table of contraries, traced back to "other" Pythagoreans by Aristotle (*Metaph.* 986a22–6): it includes both odd–even and male–female.

[63] See Burkert 1972a: 33–4, who compares these arrangements with "the sort of thing we are familiar with from dice or dominoes."

[64] Plutarch, *De E ap. Delphos* 8; 388AB. The explicit attribution to the Pythagoreans of calling the number 5 "marriage" follows in 388C. On Plutarch's acquaintance with Aristotle's monograph see Burkert 1972a: 29 n. 5.

even the ascription of gender to numbers expresses a structural feature, a *pathos*; accordingly, the arithmological interpretation of the number 5, too, can be set out in a way closely corresponding to the model described in *Metaph.* A5:

(1) The Pythagoreans observed that it is an essential structural feature (*pathos*) of the number 5 to be the first combination of the first even number – 2 – and the first odd number – 3.

(2) They regarded being female as a structural feature of all even numbers, being male as a structural feature of all odd numbers.

(3) They assumed that a structural feature common to an ordered series of objects belongs in the highest degree to the first item of that series.

(4) They inferred that the first even number, 2, is the female *par excellence*, and the first odd number, 3, the male *par excellence*.

(5) They inferred also that the number 5 is the combination *par excellence* of the female and the male.

(6) On the other hand, they observed that "marriage" is essentially the combination of female and male.

(7) Accordingly, they identified the number 5 with "marriage."

4.2.   The Pythagorean discovery of musical ratios

It remains to examine Alexander's report on the second type of resemblance briefly hinted at in *Metaph.* A5 (985b31–2): "the numerical structural features [*pathē*] and ratios of attunements [*harmoniai*]." Before doing so, however, it will be useful to clarify the concept of *harmonia*. The literal meaning of the word ἁρμονία is "tuning, attunement": the tuning of a stringed instrument, for instance, determines the pitch of each string, and the intervals between them. As a technical term of musical theory, *harmonia* can often be translated as "mode" which refers to the specific series of intervals that characterize the various *scales* of Greek music.[65] Hence, the scales made up of certain intervals may themselves be labeled as *harmoniai*. Now, potentially, all tones of a certain scale are there at the same time in any tuned instrument, but the tones of a scale are mostly struck one after the other in ancient Greek music: as a melody (in which, of course, the choice and sequence of the tones vary). The simultaneous execution of divergent tones (*heterophony*), by contrast, which played only a subordinate role in ancient music,[66] is not denoted by *harmonia*.[67] Therefore, it is misleading

---

[65] Cf. West 1992: 177–9.   [66] For the evidence on ἑτεροφωνία in general see West 1992: 205–7.
[67] See LSJ s.v. ἁρμονία, IV.

to translate the musical *terminus* ἁρμονία as "harmony" (= "synchronous consonance of several tones"), since the Pythagorean discovery to which we will now turn was about the mathematical ratios underlying musical intervals as such.

ἀλλὰ καὶ τὰς ἁρμονίας κατ᾽ ἀριθμόν [20] τινα ὁρῶντες συγκειμένας καὶ τούτων ἀρχὰς ἔλεγον τοὺς ἀριθμούς· ἡ μὲν [21] γὰρ διὰ πασῶν ἐν διπλασίῳ ἐστὶ λόγῳ, ἡ δὲ διὰ πέντε ἐν ἡμιολίῳ, ἡ δὲ [22] διὰ τεσσάρων ἐν ἐπιτρίτῳ.	But seeing that the intervals (*harmoniai*), too, are composed according to particular numbers, they said that numbers are the principles of these intervals as well; for the octave is in the ratio 2:1, the fifth in the ratio 3:2, the fourth in the ratio 4:3. (Alexander *In Metaph.* 39.19–22)

19–20 ἀριθμόν τινα (O)] ἀριθμούς τινας Ascl. ‖ 20 ἔλεγον (O)] ἐπρέσβευον Ascl.

According to this report, the Pythagoreans traced back the three basic intervals of Greek musical scales – octave (διὰ πασῶν), fifth (διὰ πέντε), and fourth (διὰ τεσσάρων)[68] – to the three most basic numerical proportions. An experimental proof was provided, according to Aristotle's pupil Aristoxenus,[69] already in the early fifth century BC by the Pythagorean Hippasus of Metapontum: Hippasus is reported to have found out that striking four brazen discs of the same diameter the thicknesses of which stand in a proportion of 12:9:8:6 brings about a "certain consonance" (συμφωνίαν τινά). Since "with free-swinging circular metal plates of the same diameter, the vibration frequencies are directly proportional to their thickness,"[70] such discs can indeed produce the perfect intervals mentioned in Alexander's summary: octave (12:6 = 2:1), fifth (12:8 = 3:2), and fourth (12:9 = 4:3). We may note that the musical ratios accounting for the fifth and the fourth are ratios of numbers which differ by one, namely combinations of even and odd: 3:2 and 4:3.[71] In order to see the relation between the musical ratios and Aristotle's argument as a whole, it is vital to remember that according to Aristotle, in the *musical* theory of the Pythagoreans, as opposed to (some of) their arithmological interpretations, the resemblance between numbers and things was not demonstrated by pointing out that the structural feature of a certain number is present in a certain

---

[68] On the structure of Greek scales see West 1992: 161–4.
[69] Aristox. fr. 90 Wehrli.   [70] Burkert 1972a: 377.
[71] Cf. Huffman 1993: 190 on ἀρτιοπέριττον and Burkert 1972a: 439 on the ἐπιμόριος λόγος. The octave, in other words the ratio 2:1, is, of course, a special case in that the one is in itself considered to be ἀρτιοπέριττον.

concept, but rather in the opposite way, *viz.* by pointing out that the structural features and ratios of the musical intervals in question are present in numbers.[72] With this difference in mind, we can set out the mathematical interpretation of musical intervals as follows:

(1)   The two different tones which each musical interval consists of can be produced by two different musical devices, be it two different brazen discs, two different strings or other.

(2)   The Pythagoreans observed that it is an essential structural feature of intervals that the relevant difference between the two musical devices involved is usually an obviously quantitative one, which can readily be expressed by a mathematical ratio.

(3)   They observed that the three basic intervals of the Greek scales – octave, fifth and fourth – correspond to the three most elementary mathematical ratios: 2:1, 3:2, and 4:3 respectively.

(4)   They inferred that numbers are the principles of musical intervals, too.

5.   Conclusion: what is wisest? number[73]

Aristotle reconstructs the development that led the Pythagoreans from their initial interest in the *mathēmata* to the assumption that the elements of number, odd and even, are the elements of all things. His first move is to ascribe to the Pythagoreans a close acquaintance with numbers, which he traces back to a prolonged research into the *mathēmata*. What he has in mind here is illustrated by Alexander's summary of Aristotle's monograph: in this work, Aristotle seems to have shown how the oracular sounding identity-claims like "7 is Athena" or "5 is marriage" which he ascribed to early Pythagoreanism were meant to be decoded.

One way of doing so was to disclose structural features (*pathē*) in numbers which lend themselves to conceptual interpretations; the fact that even and odd played a fairly important role among these features helps to understand the introduction of the "elements of number" (even and odd) in the conclusion of Aristotle's overview.[74] But in other cases, among which the system of heavenly bodies and the analysis of musical ratios figure most prominently, the procedure goes in the opposite direction: structural features (*pathē*) of natural or cultural phenomena turn out to be numerical ones; here, the advancement of the *mathēmata* ascribed to the

[72] *Metaph.* A 5, 985b31–2.   [73] Iambl., *VP* 82; 47.17 Deubner.   [74] *Metaph.* 986a1–2 (III).

Pythagoreans is most evident. This aspect is taken up in the last part of Aristotle's conclusion, about the Pythagoreans' contention that the whole heaven is *harmonia* and number.[75]

In both types of arithmological interpretation, however, the blunt equations of numbers and concepts cannot be severed from the fairly sophisticated arguments about similarities and structural features which are meant to support them, so that it would be premature to divide the elements of Aristotle's story up among different let alone conflicting versions of Pythagorean philosophy.[76] It seems more plausible to interpret the apparent tension between the equations and the arguments from a *pedagogical* point of view: the enigmatic identity-statements serve as provocative set conclusions starting from which the disciple must try to find his way back to suitable premises, using the structural features as middle terms. In the resulting deductions, there will be both nuanced analytical propositions (serving as premises from which one can deduce the conclusion) and blunt identity-statements (the set conclusions to which the deduction returns).

One element of the story told in *Metaph.* A5, however, does not emerge either from the propositions in that chapter or from the arguments preserved by Alexander: the characterization of the elements of number (even and odd) as "unlimited" (ἄπειρον) and "limited" (πεπερασμένον) respectively.[77] Now according to Philolaus, the universe as a whole and all things in it are composed of "unlimiteds and limiters" (ἐξ ἀπείρων τε καὶ περαινόντων).[78] Since we have already seen Philolaus' astronomical system feature prominently in Aristotle's reconstruction,[79] it is fairly obvious that the reference to "unlimited and limited" in *Metaph.* A5 indicates that Aristotle's evidence for the Pythagorean contention that the elements of number are the elements of all things is in fact Philolaus' theory of "unlimiteds and limiters":[80] this theory seems to be the end point of the development as reconstructed by Aristotle.

---

[75] *Metaph.* 986a2–3 (IV).

[76] *Pace* Cherniss 1935: 386: "but the account he gives of this doctrine is [...] self-contradictory, for he represents it as identifying numbers and physical objects, as identifying the *principles* of number with the *principles* of existing things, and as making things *imitate* numbers."

[77] *Metaph.* A5, 986a17–19. See also *Phys.* 203a13–15.

[78] Philolaus DK 44B1; see Huffman 1993: 93–101 and 37–53.

[79] See Alexander *In Metaph.* 38.20–9.3 (discussed above). Furthermore, Aristotle will come back to Philolaus' astronomical system in *Metaph.* A5, 986a6–12, where he criticizes the introduction of the counter-earth as being motivated by the Pythagoreans' wish for the perfect number of ten heavenly bodies.

[80] It is another question whether Philolaus himself made the connection explicit between "unlimiteds and limiters" and "even and odd," which seems at least plausible: Huffman 1993: 73–4.

The identification of the end-point, in turn, helps to see the purpose of Aristotle's generalizations of his premises in the course of his argument: the arithmological exercises which Aristotle regards as the starting-point of the development were inevitably confined to individual cases, whereas Philolaus' theory of "unlimiteds and limiters" explicitly claims universal validity.

On the other hand, the theory of Philolaus, too, had to be adjusted a bit in order to render the development more plausible. For as Carl Huffman has shown, Philolaus' "unlimiteds and limiters" cannot simply be identified with "even and odd"; rather, they operate on more than one level, whereas the more precise contrarieties such as "even and odd" or what later came to be called "matter and form"[81] are just single applications of that comprehensive pair of principles. Huffman has also emphasized that the role of number in Philolaus is rather epistemological than ontological.[82]

It is hard to see why Aristotle, in *Metaph.* A5, should have gone to the trouble of devising these generalizations and adjustments unless the need to account for a transition from archaic Pythagorean arithmology to Philolaus' theory of principles was imposed on him by solid evidence on both. But whereas it seems widely agreed that Aristotle knew Philolaus' book, it is not easy to imagine that this book contained also a detailed account of traditional Pythagorean arithmology.[83] Yet Huffman hesitated to admit of further sources.[84] In this context, however, it is helpful to keep in mind that Aristotle's lost monograph also contained *other* items which belong with the more traditional branch of the Pythagorean school and which are equally unlikely to have been included in Philolaus' book: an account of the legend of Pythagoras according to which the founder of the school was an incarnation of the Hyperborean Apollo,[85] and a section on old-fashioned Pythagorean precepts and riddles, the so-called *acusmata* or *symbola*.[86] It is particularly noteworthy that the *acusmata* collected in Aristotle's monograph are often provided with an explanation (just as the arithmological examples reported by Alexander). Given that for the

---

[81] Just as Aristotle had reduced "unlimiteds and limiters" to "even and odd", Jonathan Barnes reduced them to "matter and form"; cf. Barnes 1982: 388: "to apply a limiter to an unlimited is to give specific shape or form to a mass of unformed stuff."

[82] Philolaus DK44 B4; see Huffman 1993: 172–99 and 64–74.

[83] This is not to deny that Philolaus can occasionally refer to features like the number 7 being "motherless" (DK 44B20: ἀμήτωρ), as we have seen.

[84] Huffman 1993: 58–9.   [85] Rose 1886: 153–6 (fr. 191); Heitz 1869: 68–70 (fr. 107).

[86] Rose 1886: 157–9 (fr. 194–6); Heitz 1869: 70–3 (fr. 110–13).

acusmata Aristotle has drawn on a source other than Philolaus,[87] it seems plausible to assume that the arithmological riddles and solutions which we have been concerned with were transmitted by the same source.[88]

The assumption that the material on which Aristotle's reconstruction is based goes back to two different and even fairly heterogeneous Pythagorean sources also explains why Aristotle calls the subject of this reconstruction the philosophy of the "so-called Pythagoreans": Aristotle might have felt comfortable calling the *acusmata* Pythagorean, but he recognizes that Philolaus introduces some quite new material. Although this material is in a sense a development of earlier ideas, he has some hesitations about calling these new developments "Pythagorean." Since, however, he recognizes that many people describe it thus, he uses the phrase "so-called Pythagoreans."

We conclude that Aristotle has attempted to present the arithmological speculations attested to in his sources on early Pythagoreanism and the theory of principles by Philolaus as different stages in the intellectual development of one and the same school – by reconstructing a gradual transition from one to the other.

---

[87] A possible source is the *Explanation of Pythagorean Symbola* by Anaximander of Miletus (the younger), which is attested to by the *Suda* entry α 1987 (I.179 Adler) and which can be dated to around 400 BC; see Burkert 1972a: 166 with n. 2.

[88] We are building here on a remark by Burkert 1972a: 477: "One cannot help recognizing how closely this number symbolism is connected with the realm of the *acusmata*."

CHAPTER 12

Pythagoreanism in the Academic tradition: the Early Academy to Numenius

John Dillon

1. Introduction

Whatever may be said about Plato himself, there can be no doubt that Pythagoras and the Pythagorean tradition were major influences on his successors. Indeed, it may be claimed that the lineaments of what was to become the movement denominated in modern times "Neopythagoreanism" was given its impetus by the work of such figures in particular as Xenocrates and Heraclides of Pontus, though to a considerable extent also by Plato's immediate successor Speusippus. If we ask what are the salient characteristics of this intellectual movement or tendency in later Greco-Roman culture, I would propose the following: Neopythagoreanism is a branch of Platonism that emphasizes the role of number in the cosmos and which regards Pythagoreanism as the origin of this emphasis. Neopythagoreans thus show devotion to what they chose to regard as the basic principles of the Pythagorean philosophical system, the One and the Indefinite Dyad, although these principles are, in fact, Platonic. Neopythagoreans were Platonists and not themselves directly affiliated to anything that could be described as a Pythagorean "school," although a few of them may also have followed to varying extents the Pythagorean way of life, or *bios*.

2. The Old Academy: Speusippus

If we turn first to Plato's nephew and successor Speusippus, we find, in his admittedly exiguous remains, some significant traces of "Neopythagoreanism." His adoption of the One and Multiplicity (*pléthos*) as first principles need not be regarded as in itself "Pythagorean," as it is simply an adaptation of Plato's "unwritten" doctrine of principles (itself, of course,

This survey inevitably draws heavily on my previous treatments of this topic in *The Middle Platonists* and *The Heirs of Plato*, though a number of issues present themselves to me differently now.

indebted to the Pythagorean tradition), but in a passage preserved by Proclus in his *Commentary on the Parmenides* (Book 7 38.32–40.7 Klibansky), Speusippus attributes his system of first principles to "the ancients," by which he undoubtedly means the Pythagoreans. Here is the passage in context:

> For if the first One participated in Being in some way, although it is higher than Being and produces it, it would be a one which took over the mode of reality which belongs to Being. But it is not *a* one, and it is the cause not just of Being but of everything, though of Being before the rest. And if everything must participate in its cause, there must be a "one," other than the simply One, in which Being participates; and this "one" is the principle of Beings. This is also what Speusippus says, presenting his views as the doctrines of the ancients:

> "For they (sc. the Pythagoreans) held that the One is higher than Being and is the source of Being; and they delivered it even from the status of a principle. For they held that, given the One, in itself, conceived as separated and alone, without other things, with no additional element, nothing else would come into existence. And so they introduced the Indefinite Dyad as the principle of beings."

> So he too testifies that this was the opinion of the ancients about the One; it is snatched up beyond existence, and next after it comes the Indefinite Dyad. Here too, then, Plato proves this One to be beyond the existent and beyond the unity that is in the existent and beyond the whole One Being. (Translations mine unless otherwise noted)

This constitutes a good example of Platonist practice in their appropriation of the Pythagorean tradition. Speusippus himself places his first principle, the One, firmly "above" Being,[1] whereas such a distinction would not have occurred to the original Pythagoreans.

That a Pythagorizing tendency pervaded Speusippus' metaphysics is further indicated by his treatise *On Pythagorean Numbers*, a summary of the contents of which is preserved in the rather mysterious Neoplatonic compilation, the *Theology of Arithmetic* (without much plausibility attributed

---

[1] This is plain not only from the present passage, but from the text preserved in Ch. 4 of Iamblichus' *On Common Mathematical Science* (15.5ff. Festa), which I would agree with Philip Merlan (1960) in identifying as substantially Speusippan, despite demurrals from some weighty authorities, such as Tarán, in his edition of the fragments of Speusippus (1981: 86–107), Isnardi Parente, in her edition (1980), Steel (2002) and Zhmud (2012b). While admitting that certainty cannot be attained on this question their objections do not outweigh the remarkable concordance of this text with what we know of Speusippus' distinctive metaphysical scheme, and with no other known thinker. I have developed my arguments at greater length in Dillon 1984. Steel and Zhmud are skeptical about the passage in Proclus' *Commentary on the Parmenides* as well, though with even less justification, in my view. Burkert (1972a: 63) interpreted both passages as I do.

to Iamblichus, but certainly later than him, and probably dependent on him). The title of Speusippus' work is interesting, for a start, as one of the topics dealt with was the five Platonic figures of the *Timaeus*, which are not, properly speaking, numbers, but plainly the whole mathematical system of the Pythagoreans is being included – and Timaeus is being regarded, for the purpose, as an accredited spokesman for Pythagoreanism.

On the account given (82.13ff. De Falco), the first half of the book comprised the following:

> In the first half of the book, he very elegantly expounds linear numbers, polygonal and all sorts of plane numbers,[2] solid numbers, and the five figures which are assigned to the elements of the universe, discussing both their individual attributes and their shared features, and their analogousness and correspondence. (tr. Waterfield, slightly modified)

There are a number of interesting features here. First Speusippus is said to discuss "the five figures which are assigned to the elements of the universe," whereas we will recall that in the *Timaeus*, Timaeus rather coyly assigns the dodecahedron to "the universe as a whole" (*epi to pan*, 55c), presumably because of difficulties perceived in mutual interchange between the triangles composing the dodecahedron and those of the other figures. Speusippus' colleague Xenocrates, however, had no such inhibition, assigning the dodecahedron to the fifth element composing the heavens, the aether (normally regarded as an innovation of Aristotle), which is not, after all, interchangeable with the other elements. It would seem from this evidence that Speusippus did the same, while attributing the doctrine to the Pythagoreans.

Then there is the problem as to whether we are to take the last phrase, which speaks of "individual attributes" (*idiotētes*) and "shared features" (*koinotētes*), "analogousness" (*analogia*) and "correspondence" (*antakolouthia*), as referring only to the five regular solids (which might seem more relevant), or to the various types of number mentioned before them – or both. It would seem most reasonable to take them as referring to both. This suggests that Speusippus gave a fairly full account of the traditional Pythagorean characters of each of the numbers from 1 to 9, together with what features some of them shared with others, and this would have

---

[2] In this connection, Leonard Tarán (1981: 263) notes that Speusippus, like Nicomachus after him, regards triangular and pentagonal numbers as plane numbers, whereas Euclid (*Elem.* 7 Def. 17) makes a distinction between polygonal and plane numbers. For Speusippus, 2 is the first linear number, 3, as triangle, the first plane number, and 4, as pyramid, the first solid number, whereas for Euclid 4 is the first plane and 8 the first solid. In this, Speusippus is probably nearer to the mathematics of such figures as Archytas and Philolaus, but we cannot be sure.

been an opportunity to list the various traditional Pythagorean identifications of features of the world with numbers. But Speusippus could well also have discussed such topics as the *idiotēs* of the triangles that make up the cube (cf. *Ti.* 55b–c), which render earth non-exchangeable with the other elements, as well as the analogies and correspondences between the various classes of numbers and the Platonic figures. We may assume, then, that every sort of property of and relationship between the numbers from 1 to 9, and the figures corresponding to them, were discussed in this part of the work, and the whole fathered on the Pythagoreans.

The description of the contents continues as follows:

> Next, in the remaining half of the book, he goes on to deal with the Decad, which he shows to be the most natural [*physikōtatē*] and perfective [*telestikōtatē*] of existent things, because it is, in itself, and not based on our conceptions, or because we postulate that it happens to be so, a sort of productive form [*eidos ti technikon*] of the finished products in the world, and set before the god who created the universe as a completely perfect paradigm.

Overall, what Speusippus seems to be doing is to give a Pythagoreanizing gloss to the metaphysics of Plato's *Timaeus*, the Decad being identified with the Paradigm of the creation myth. If we consider details of terminology, the adjective *physikōtatē* (most natural) would seem to denote that the Decad is the fundamental principle behind all the phenomena of nature, while the rare adjective *telestikōtatē* (perfective) indicates, as does *technikon* (productive) below, that it is the agent responsible for bringing all things to realization. As for the use of the rather loaded Platonic term *eidos,* it is not clear if it is to be taken in the fully technical sense of "Form," or simply in the sense of "sort" or "type," but I see no compelling reason not to take it in its technical sense. If so, however, we must observe that this *eidos* is given an active, demiurgic role in the universe, and thus the description of it as being "set before the god who is the creator of the universe" must be taken as figurative language based on the *Timaeus* myth, which, as we know,[3] Speusippus maintained should not be taken literally. The Decad thus emerges as the sum-total of the arithmetical products of the union of Monad and Dyad, as well as a dynamic creative principle, along the lines of a rational World-Soul, which is probably what Speusippus (and Xenocrates) saw as the de-mythologized active principle at work in the *Timaeus.*

---

[3] Cf. fr. 61b Tarán.

3.   The Old Academy: Xenocrates

We may now turn to Speusippus' successor as head of the Academy, Xenocrates of Chalcedon, who must share with Speusippus the honor of being the founder of "Neopythagoreanism." First of all, a number of personal anecdotes give evidence of Pythagoreanizing tendencies. We have, for instance, the curious tale of his St. Francis-like sheltering of a sparrow that flew into his bosom while fleeing from a hawk (Diog. Laert. 4.10). More substantial, perhaps, is the report (Diog. Laert. 4.7) that, because of his extreme trustworthiness, the Athenians exempted him from taking an oath when giving evidence in court. Now Pythagoreans notoriously did not take oaths (Diod. Sic. 10.9), and a plausible basis for this otherwise rather improbable story – after all, what is the problem, for an honest and reliable man, in taking an oath? – would be that Xenocrates asked to be excused from taking an oath on Pythagoreanizing grounds, and this concession was granted him. He is also reported to have allotted one hour in the day to silent meditation (Diog. Laert. 4.11), which could be seen as a Pythagorean trait – according to the later tradition it was a Pythagorean practice to review the previous day's events at the end of the day (Diog. Laert. 8.22) or before arising in the morning (Diod. Sic. 10.5).

So there is some evidence of Xenocrates' adopting certain features of the Pythagorean *bios* in his personal life. How does this play out in his philosophy? First of all, he adopts, as does Speusippus, the Pythagoreanizing first principles of Plato's "unwritten doctrines," the Monad and the Dyad, though for him the Monad – unlike Speusippus' One – is explicitly an intellect.[4] It is in his terms for the second principle, the Dyad, however, that one may discern Pythagorean resonances. Apart from the epithets *plēthos*, "Multiplicity" (in agreement with Speusippus) and *apeiria*, "Unlimitedness" (derivable from the *Philebus*), we also find him bestowing on it a rather poetical term, replete with Pythagorean overtones, *to aenaon*, "the Everflowing." Aetius, our doxographic source for this information (1.3.23), says that Xenocrates was "by 'everflowing,' alluding to Matter, by reason of its multiplicity [*aenaon tēn hylēn ainittomenos dia tou plēthous*]." However, it is possible that there is more than one dimension to this term. No doubt there is on the one hand a reference to the famous Pythagorean Oath, in which the Tetraktys is described as a "fount containing the roots of Nature ever-flowing [*physis aenaos*]"; but there is also the intriguing possibility that Xenocrates is indulging in some thoroughly Platonic (and Pythagorean)

---

[4] Aët. 1.7.30 p. 304 *DG* = fr. 15 Heinze/213 Isnardi Parente.

word-play, and taking *aenaon* to contain the terms *a-en*, "not-one," and *a-on*, "not-being." At any rate, *aenaos* is a distinctively Pythagorean term (Burkert 1972a: 72, 186).

There may be more to be derived from this bald doxographic notice. If Xenocrates is making an allusion to the Pythagorean Oath, may he not also be invoking the concept of the *tetraktys*, the sequence of the first four numbers, which, when combined together, make up the Decad? As we have seen, Speusippus was much intrigued with this Pythagorean concept and it is hardly conceivable that Xenocrates was not also. For Speusippus, the *tetraktys* symbolized the totality of numbers, and, through the sequence of point, line, surface and solid, which he associated with it, of geometrical figures, which make up the Paradigm of the *Timaeus*; for Xenocrates, I would suggest, it must have done the same. Xenocrates' first principle is a Monad, but it is also, as we have seen, an intellect, and an intellect, after all, must *think*; thus, it must have contents.

We may adduce here a further doxographic notice, admittedly from a rather late source, Favonius Eulogius, fifth-century-AD author of a commentary on Cicero's *Dream of Scipio*, but a man who was able to draw much of his information from Cicero's contemporary, Varro, and there is no reason to doubt the substantial accuracy of his testimony. He declares that it was the view of Xenocrates that "Number is Intellect and God [*estque numerus animus et deus*], for there is nothing else but what is subject to Number" (fr. 16 Heinze/214 Isnardi Parente). This is simply stating, in a compressed and oversimplified way, what must have been the doctrine of Xenocrates, that the divine Intellect, though itself characterized as a monad, comprehended within itself the totality of number, symbolized by the *tetraktys* (which equates to the Paradigm of the *Timaeus*), and it is in accordance with this that it fashions the world.

Thus, a highly mathematized vision of the world emerges. We learn from Plutarch, apropos the generation of the soul in the *Timaeus* (*De procreatione animae* 1012d–e) that Xenocrates took the first product of the Monad and the Dyad to be Number – by which we may understand the totality of natural numbers, which (or at least combinations of which) are to be identified with the traditional Platonic Forms – and that Soul emerges as a secondary product of these, by the addition of Sameness and Otherness, which between them generate both self-motion and the ability to move others, the salient characteristics of Soul. The inspiration behind this seems clearly Pythagorean, even though many specifics may have been added from the Academic tradition. It is a system that provokes the deep disapproval of Aristotle, as attested by many passages of Books M and N of the *Metaphysics,* of which the following may be selected as representative (1086a6–11):

> Others (sc. Xenocrates), wishing to preserve both Forms and numbers, but not seeing how, if one posits these (sc. the Monad and the Dyad) as first principles, mathematical number can exist beside form-number [*eidētikos arithmos*], identified form-number with mathematical number – but only in theory, since in practice mathematical number is done away with, because the hypotheses which they proposed are of a peculiar nature [*idiai*] and not mathematical.

We can observe here, albeit from a thoroughly jaundiced perspective, the strongly Pythagoreanized version of Plato's doctrine that Xenocrates is propounding.

If we descend, next, to the level of the physical cosmos, we can observe the influence of Pythagorean musical theory in a remarkable triadic division of the cosmos, which Plutarch says Xenocrates favored: "Xenocrates calls that Zeus who is in the realm of what is invariable and identical [in this context, presumably, the realm of the fixed star] 'topmost' (*hypatos*), but 'nethermost' (*neatos*) he who is below the Moon" (*Platonic Questions* 1007ff. = fr. 216 Isnardi Parente). It is odd that Plutarch does not mention a median (*mesos*) Zeus, especially as the reference occurs in a context where he is comparing the three parts of the Platonic soul in the *Republic* to the three traditional pitches on the Greek musical scale, *hypatē, mesē* and *nētē*, so we must assume that Xenocrates in fact postulated a third deity associated with the heavenly realm. The aspect of this testimony that is particularly interesting, however, is the musical analogy. The cosmos is for Xenocrates held together by Pythagorean-style harmony: the lower Zeus (or Hades), while in a way antithetical to the higher Zeus, is yet a necessary component of the great musical scale that is the universe, and does his bit to hold it together.

We find more on Xenocrates' Pythagoreanizing theory of harmonics in Porphyry's commentary on Ptolemy's *Harmonics.*[5] In explaining the Pythagorean doctrine of harmonics, Xenocrates sets out, first, an analysis of types of motion (*kinēsis*), and then, when he has identified sound as a species of motion in a straight line, he presents it as consisting of a sequence of sound-atoms, each occurring at a given instant, but giving the impression of a continuous flow. These observations are merely presented incidentally

---

[5] *In Ptol. Harm.* 30.1ff. Düring (= fr. 87 Isnardi Parente). Porphyry gives his primary authority here as a certain Heraclides (perhaps Heraclides of Pontus, but see Barker 1989: 230) in his *Introduction to Music,* and he is quoting Xenocrates as giving the doctrine of Pythagoras, which is significant.

to an exposition of Pythagorean harmonic theory, but they may be taken as forming part of a coherent theory of perception on Xenocrates' part, which thus has its roots in Pythagorean doctrine.

In the sphere of ethics, the only feature of Xenocrates' position which exhibits a specifically Pythagorean quality is his approval of vegetarianism. In *On Abstinence* (4.22 = fr. 252 Isnardi Parente), Porphyry notes that Xenocrates laid claim to the legendary culture hero Triptolemus as the originator of laws enjoining abstinence from the slaughter and consumption of animals, though Porphyry presents him as expressing doubt as to what exactly Triptolemus' motivation was in laying down his injunction, "Do no harm to animals." Whatever Triptolemus' motivations, it would seem from this report that Xenocrates was himself opposed to the slaughter of animals, and probably for the Pythagorean reason that "it is a terrible thing to kill one's kindred." We also have a report from Plutarch (*The Eating of Flesh* 996a–b = fr. 53 Isnardi Parente) of his making a remark showing a sympathy with vegetarianism: "The Athenians punished a man who had flayed a ram while it was still alive; yet, in my opinion, he who tortures a living creature is no worse than he who slaughters it outright."

Whether we can identify Xenocrates, together with Speusippus, as the substantial founders of Neopythagoreanism depends on the weight that one is prepared to place on the various pieces of evidence that have been assembled here. It would indeed be enlightening to know the contents of his work (or works!) entitled *Pythagoreia* (Diog. Laert. 4.13), but unfortunately we have no definite indications of its contents. It is probable that his various attested works on mathematics – *On Numbers*, *On Geometry* (in two books), *On Dimensions*, and a further work *The Theory of Numbers* (if it is not the same as the first one listed here) – exhibited Pythagorean sympathies. Certainly Aristotle portrays him, indignantly, as introducing "peculiar theories of his own" into the science of mathematics, in a passage (*Metaph.* 1090b21ff.), which refers immediately to the relating of the numbers composing the *tetraktys* to the various dimensions, but more generally to the "Pythagoreanizing" of mathematics.

4. The Old Academy: Heraclides of Pontus

If Speusippus and Xenocrates established the doctrinal parameters of later Pythagoreanism, it is to another, rather idiosyncratic, member of the Old Academy that must go the honor of contributing significantly to the later life-myth of Pythagoras, namely Heraclides of Pontus. Heraclides (*c.* 385–320 BC), joined the Academy from his native Heraclea Pontica in the mid

360s, and was entrusted with the management of the school during Plato's
third visit to Sicily, in 361/360, since Speusippus and Xenocrates accompanied Plato on that mission. Though he composed numerous treatises
as well, his chief contribution to Neopythagoreanism comes through a
number of his dialogues, which were set in the past and featured both
Pythagoras himself and other Pythagoreans. In one dialogue, the *Abaris*,
Pythagoras is presented as conversing with the Hyperborean Abaris, and
perhaps revealing certain personal details about himself. We have a report
(Diog. Laert. 8.4–5 = fr. 89 Wehrli) that he represented Pythagoras as
giving an account of all seven of his previous incarnations, starting with
Aethalides, son of Hermes. Abaris would certainly be a suitable recipient of
such information, though the report cannot be ascribed to the *Abaris* with
certainty.[6] Certain elements of this tale may precede Heraclides (e.g. the
choice by Aethalides of a boon from his father, that in future incarnations
he would remember his previous ones, or his incarnation as the minor
Trojan warrior Euphorbus), but Heraclides does seem to be the figure that
put all this together and transmitted it to posterity.

Another dialogue, *On the Things in Hades*, featured the report of a
character called Empedotimus of Syracuse,[7] who, while resting in the
noonday from a hunt, had an out-of-body experience, which involved an
interview with Hades and Persephone themselves, and, by their courtesy,
a vision of "the whole truth about the souls (in Hades) in a series of direct
visions" (fr. 95 Wehrli). One feature of his revelation is a tripartite division
of the universe, the highest realm being that of the fixed stars, ruled over
by Zeus, while an intermediate realm, that of the heavens, is ruled over by
Poseidon, and the lowest, sublunar realm, which we inhabit, is ruled over
by Pluto/Hades – a scenario not unlike that attributed to Xenocrates, and
exhibiting similarly Pythagorean overtones.

The dialogue about which we know most, however, is entitled *On the
Woman Who Stopped Breathing*. This featured Empedocles and his revival
of a woman who had suffered some sort of seizure (which may have involved
her soul leaving her body, and acquiring some vision of the other world,
which was then recounted); various anecdotes involving Pythagoras were
introduced into the work – perhaps as tales recounted at a banquet, which
Empedocles gave for his friends in the aftermath of his achievement. The

---

[6] The identification was first made by Corssen 1912a: 28. For a stimulating but idiosyncratic account
of the importance of Abaris for Pythagoreanism see Kingsley 2010.

[7] Presumably a name compounded from Empedocles and Hermotimus of Clazomenae, both notably
shamanistic figures.

most notable was an exchange between Pythagoras and Leon, the tyrant of Phlius,[8] concerning the origin of the concept of "philosophy":

> Pythagoras, as Heraclides of Pontus, a pupil of Plato and one of the most learned of men, writes, is said to have visited Phlius, and to have spoken learnedly and eloquently with Leon, the ruler of the Phliasians. Leon, admiring his genius and eloquence, asked him what class of wisdom he professed;[9] but he replied that he knew no wisdom, but was rather a wisdom-lover [*philosophos*]. Leon wondered at the novel term and asked what *philosophoi* were, and how they differed from other men, whereat Pythagoras replied that life seemed to him like the gathering when the great games were held, which were attended by the whole of Greece. For there some men sought to win fame and the glory of the crown by exerting their bodies, others were attracted by the gain and profit of buying and selling, but there was one kind of man, the noblest of all, who sought neither applause nor profit but came in order to watch, and wanted to see what was happening and how: so too among us, who have migrated into this life from a different life and mode of being, as if from some city to a crowded festival, some are slaves to fame, others to money; but there are some rare spirits who, holding all else as nothing, eagerly contemplate the universe. These he called "wisdom-lovers," for that is what *philosophos* means, and as at the festival it most becomes a gentleman to be a spectator without thought of personal gain, so in life the contemplation and understanding of the universe is far superior to all other pursuits.

This story does not necessarily originate with Heraclides, but, once again, he does seem to have been the chief vehicle of its dissemination to later generations.[10] It becomes a fundamental text for the role, not just of the Pythagorean philosopher, but also of any philosopher, in society. All in all, we can observe in Heraclides a literary rather than a philosophical interest in Pythagoras, but this does not exclude his having philosophical sympathies with Pythagoreanism as well.

There is one interesting item of doctrine in which Heraclides may be building on Pythagorean sources, and that is his theory of the diurnal rotation of the earth, as an alternative explanation of the apparent motion of

---

[8] Reported by Cic. *Tusc.* 5.3.8ff. (= fr. 88 Wehrli). Cicero is not specific as to the provenance of this story, but Diogenes Laertius reports (1.12 = fr. 87 Wehrli) that it was to be found in *On the Woman Who Stopped Breathing*.

[9] "Qua maxime arte confideret." The Greek original of *ars* here is doubtless (see Gottschalk 1980: 23n.) *sophia* (wisdom), which is needed for the word-play with *philosophos*.

[10] Following Burkert's influential article (1960) most scholars regard the story of Pythagoras' invention of the term "philosophy" as a Platonizing literary fabrication, as indeed is suggested by its presence in one of Heraclides' clearly fictional dialogues. Riedweg (2005: 90–7) has, however, recently defended the story as largely historical. For a critique of Riedweg see Huffman 2008b: 207–8.

the heavenly bodies (frs. 104–8 Wehrli). Philolaus had postulated the revolution of the earth around a central fire (DK 44A16). Rejecting that bizarre postulate, Heraclides proposed the concept of rotation round its own axis. It is possible, however, that in advancing this theory, he has as predecessors two obscure fourth-century Pythagoreans, Hicetas and Ecphantus (DK 50 and 51) – if these are not indeed, as some have suggested, merely figures in some dialogue of Heraclides![11]

5.   The post-Hellenistic and early Imperial Period

I pass over the period of the New Academy, as being a stage of the Platonist tradition in which no sign of a devotion to Pythagoreanism or the memory of Pythagoras manifests itself to our gaze. Even the first stage of revived dogmatism within the tradition, initiated by Antiochus of Ascalon (as a revived "Old Academy") shows no sign of a renewed interest in Pythagoreanism, being, if anything, most closely allied to Stoicism.[12]

However, outside the ambit of the Academy, by the first century BC, a body of pseudo-Pythagorean works began to be produced; indeed, some have suggested that these works arose in part because Pythagoreanism had been banished from the New Academy.[13] These works were forged in the names of prominent Pythagoreans such as Archytas, and prominent intellectuals not usually regarded as Pythagoreans, such as Hippodamus, but also of largely unknown figures such as Callicratidas, Metopus and Theages. A tendency running through these works is plainly to reclaim for the Pythagorean tradition key elements of the doctrines of the later philosophical schools, Platonist, Peripatetic and Stoic, in all three of the accredited spheres of philosophy, logic, ethics and physics (see further Chapter 15). In the first century BC the learned Alexander Polyhistor (see further below and Chapter 17) utilized a pseudo-Pythagorean document entitled *Pythagorean Notes* (Diog. Laert. 8.24–35), which presents a system involving simply a Monad, from which arises an Indefinite Dyad, in contrast to the more traditional Neopythagorean pair of Monad and Dyad. There was also a revival of interest in Pythagoreanism in "official"

---

[11]   Gottschalk 1980: 44–5 rejects the suggestion that Hicetas and Ecphantus were fictional characters in a dialogue of Heraclides. See also Burkert 1972a: 341 and Chapter 4 section 9 above.

[12]   See the comprehensive survey of Platonic doctrine according to Antiochus in Cicero's *Acad. post.* 19–32.

[13]   Burkert 1961: 236. Kalligas 2004 argues that the re-emergence of Aristotle's exoteric writings in the first century BC spurred Pythagorean forgeries.

philosophical circles dating to the mid first century BC, in the person of a younger friend of Cicero's, Publius Nigidius Figulus (See Chapter 16).

6. Eudorus

To see the revival of Pythagoreanism in the Platonist tradition, however, we must turn our attention to Alexandria, in the latter half of the first century BC. Here we find Eudorus, who may or may not have been a pupil of Dion, who was in turn a pupil of Antiochus. However, if there is some such connection, it does not betoken any great degree of doctrinal affinity, apart from a common concern to reassert Platonism as a dogmatic philosophy. For Eudorus, however, this involves not just a return to the doctrines of the Old Academy, as in the case of Antiochus, but a return to the wisdom of Pythagoras – itself, however, not necessarily more than an extrapolation of the "Neopythagoreanism" of the Old Academy.

We have, preserved by the Neoplatonist Simplicius (*In Phys.* 181.10–30 Diels), a most interesting report of Eudorus' account of the "Pythagorean" system of first principles:

> The Pythagoreans postulated on the highest level the One as a first principle [*archē*], and then on a secondary level two principles of existent things, the One and the nature opposed to this. And there are ranked under these all those things that are thought of as opposites, the good under the One, the bad under the nature opposed to it. For this reason these two are not regarded as absolute first principles by this School; for if the one is the first principle of one set of opposites and the other of the other, then they cannot be common principles of both, as is the (supreme) One.

Eudorus goes on to make this supreme One the causal principle of Matter as well as of all created things, and to call it the supreme God. Further on again, he gives the name of "Unlimited Dyad" to the principle opposed to the second One, and finally calls the second One "the Monad." Interestingly, while he characterizes the supreme One as a "principle" (*archē*), he describes the secondary pair rather as "elements" (*stoicheia*).

Now there can be no question of this system corresponding to anything in ancient Pythagoreanism, but it is nonetheless interesting for that.[14] It would seem to be an extrapolation, either by Eudorus himself or some

---

[14] See on this the useful discussion of Kahn (2001: 94–9).

pseudo-Pythagorean text,[15] of the system of Limit and Unlimited propounded by Plato in the *Philebus* (16c–30e), together with the Good, and/or the One of the *Parmenides*. The "cause of the mixture" of *Philebus* 27c may also be in play here, regarded as a separate principle superior to the other two. If Eudorus in fact assumed, as do many modern interpreters, that the "Prometheus" of *Philebus* 16c who brought the art of division down from the gods is a reference to Pythagoras, then he might well feel that he was justified in making such an extrapolation.[16]

In the area of ethics, or more precisely as to the question of the purpose of life, or *telos*, Eudorus also exhibits Pythagorean influence. Antiochus had accepted the Stoic *telos* of "living in conformity with Nature," as we see from such a text as Cicero *On Ends* 5. Eudorus turns back instead to the *telos* of "assimilating oneself to God" (*homoiōsis theōi*), derived from Plato, *Theaetetus* 176a, but with an explicit reference back to Pythagoras:

> Socrates and Plato agree with Pythagoras that the *telos* is assimilation to God. Plato defined this more clearly by adding "according as is possible" [*kata to dynaton*], and it is only possible by the exercise of wisdom [*phronēsis*], that is to say, as a result of virtue. (Stobaeus 2.49.8–12 Wachsmuth)[17]

We may note here how Pythagoras is brought in as the originator of the definition, with Plato portrayed as agreeing with him, and amplifying him somewhat, by the addition of "according as is possible."

Even in the area of logic, one might discern in Eudorus' attack on Aristotle's *Categories* (of which traces are preserved in Simplicius' *Commentary on the Categories*) a Pythagoreanizing note. If we could assume that the pseudo-Pythagorean "Archytas," *Concerning the Whole System [of Categories]* (Περί τοῦ καθόλου λόγου), which purports to be the "original" behind Aristotle's treatise, precedes and was available to Eudorus, then such moves as ranking Quality before Quantity, directly after Substance (Simpl. *On the Categories*, henceforward *In Cat.*, 206.10ff.) could be seen as derived from "Archytas" – but the influence could just as well be the other

---

[15] One such source might be "Archytas," *On First Principles* (19.3–20.17 Thesleff), which presents a very similar system, but we cannot be certain of the date of this document, and so in which direction the influence is flowing.

[16] On the identification of this Prometheus with Pythagoras see Huffman (1999a: 11–17), who argues that Plato did not intend Prometheus to be understood as Pythagoras.

[17] This is one of a series of passages tacked on to the end of a summary of Eudorus' ethics by Arius Didymus (Stob. 2.42.7ff. Wachsmuth) but, since Arius tells us that Eudorus went through the whole field of philosophy *problēmatikōs*, that is, by arranging his subject matter into *problēmata*, or controversial topics, and this is one such, I would take it as very probable that this is Eudorus.

way around.[18] From another passage (*In Cat.* 174.14ff.), it would seem that Eudorus himself favored the Old Academic categories of Absolute (*kath' hauto*) and Relative (*pros ti*), but even here there may be a connection to pseudo-Pythagorean texts, if we take into account the employment of these categories in such a text as "Callicratidas" *On Happiness in the Home* (103.12–13 Thesleff).

7. Philo

In Eudorus, then, we may discern a fairly strong injection of "Pythagoreanism," derived chiefly from Neopythagorean pseudepigraphic sources, into the Stoicized mix inherited from Antiochus, and which then passes on into the Middle Platonist bloodstream. The first discernible beneficiary of this, however, is not properly speaking a Platonist, but the Platonizing Jewish philosopher Philo – like Eudorus, a native of Alexandria, and flourishing in the generation after him (*c.* 20 BC – 45 AD). Philo was born into one of the leading Jewish families of Alexandria, and plainly received an excellent Greek education, which he puts to good use in the creation of his "grand design," which is to prove that philosophy, that cherished jewel in the crown of Greek culture, was actually the achievement of Moses. In the transmission of this wisdom to the Greeks, Pythagoras is, for Philo, a key figure. The scenario with which Philo is necessarily working[19] involves the tradition of Pythagoras' protracted "study tour," at the start of his career, around the Eastern Mediterranean, absorbing the wisdom of various ancient systems, such as that of the Chaldaeans, or Magi, and that of the Egyptians, but also including, for Philo, a period of study on Mt. Carmel with "followers of Moses." Pythagoras thus becomes the conduit for the transmission of the "Mosaic" system of philosophy to the Greeks, and the founder of "Greek" philosophy, which his followers in due course passed on to Plato and his followers.

What features of Philo's system may be identified as distinctively "Pythagorean"? First, let us consider his system of first principles. Philo is,

---

[18] As is indeed argued by Thomas Szlezák in his edition of the work (1972). On the relation between Eudorus and pseudo-Pythagorean texts see Chapter 15 below.

[19] I say "necessarily," but I am conscious that Philo never explicitly mentions this scenario. We only know of it from a much later source, Iamblichus (*VP* 14), where, to complicate the issue further, we are told that Pythagoras studied with "the descendants of Mochos, the prophet and natural philosopher," and this "Mochos" (despite plainly being a variant of "Moshe") takes on something of a life of his own in Greek tradition (cf. Strabo 16.757); but the legend of Pythagoras' absorbing Jewish wisdom on his travels must go back at least into the Hellenistic era to some patriotic Jewish historian, such as Demetrius or Eupolemus.

of course, strictly monistic in his concept of the deity, and it might seem as if there is no place in his system for either the Pythagorean opposition between Monad and Dyad, or the particular innovation on this developed by Eudorus; but such assumptions are not entirely justified. Certainly, Philo does not wish to postulate a secondary creative principle that would in any way be independent of God, but he does at various points recognize a role for something corresponding to the Neopythagorean-Platonic Dyad, whether as matter or as "maternal" creative principle, while maintaining its complete subordination to God as Monad.

In his treatise *On the Creation* (8–9), he speaks as follows of Moses' conception of the universe:

> Moses, however, had not only reached the very summit of philosophy, but had also been instructed in the very many and most essential doctrines of nature by means of oracles. He recognized that it is absolutely necessary that among existing things there is an activating cause [*drastērion aition*] on the one hand, and a passive [*pathēton*] on the other, and that the activating cause is the absolutely pure and unadulterated intellect of the universe, superior to excellence and superior to knowledge and even superior to the Good and the Beautiful itself. But the passive, which of itself was without soul and unmoved, when set in motion and shaped and ensouled by the intellect, changed into the most perfect piece of work, the cosmos. (Tr. Runia, slightly modified)

This constitutes a good example of the extent to which Philo is prepared to go in recognizing another, secondary principle in the universe, and, as we can see, that is not very far. We have here, then, a Stoicizing Platonist modification of the Neopythagorean pair of Monad and Dyad, with perhaps a distinctive enhancement of the Monad as being "above" excellence (*aretē*) and knowledge (*epistēmē*), and even the Good and the Beautiful; but even this, while concordant with Philo's view of the Deity, could be derived from Speusippus' doctrine of the One as being superior to such characteristics as goodness and beauty in virtue of the fact that it bestows these characteristics on the rest of existence, and so cannot possess them itself, at least in the same sense.

The dyadic principle, however, is to be found in Philo in a different manifestation to the material one, and that is in the guise of God's Wisdom (*Sophia*), a concept that Philo can derive from Hebrew Wisdom literature, but which he can also assimilate to the Neopythagorean Dyad, at least in the form that it appears in the *Pythagorean Memoirs* summarized by Alexander Polyhistor. There, the Dyad "arises out of the Monad as matter for the Monad, which is Cause," and from their union arise, first, numbers, and then, in sequence, all other things (Diog. Laert. 8. 25). At *On Drunkenness* 30–1, we find, apropos the various meanings of the terms "father" and "mother," the following:

> For example, we will say most correctly that the Creator [*dēmiourgos*] who has made our universe is the "father" of that which he has made, while its "mother" is the knowledge [*epistēmē*] of the Creator, through consorting with whom – though not in the manner of men – he sowed the seed of creation. She receives the seed of God, and, at the term of her pregnancy, brings forth her only son, which is our sensible universe.

So God, as the Monad, requires some sort of "female" principle in order to generate anything further, whether the form-numbers, or, ultimately, the physical universe, and the least threatening form that this other principle can take for Philo is God's Wisdom, as emanating from himself. Philo has absorbed the Neopythagorean Indefinite Dyad into his monistic system, with the help of the Jewish concept of God's Wisdom.

In other respects too we can observe the influence of Neopythagoreanism on Philo. First, at one level down from the supreme principles, corresponding to the Platonic Forms, we find a strong influence of Pythagorean number-mysticism. That the Forms are to be viewed as numbers becomes clear from such passages as *Who Is the Heir* 156, where God is described as employing all numbers and all forms in bringing the world to completion. That Philo is familiar with the peculiar values attached by the Pythagoreans to the *tetraktys*, and to all the numbers up to 10, becomes plain from his exposition of the six days of creation in *On the Creation* 13–88, leading up to his excursus on the 7. He in fact composed a special treatise *On Numbers*, which has not survived.[20]

Pythagorean influence may also be detected in Philo's ethical theory, probably through the medium of pseudo-Pythagorean texts. His theory is influenced by Antiochian Platonism, notably in his adoption of the concept of happiness as dependent on the aggregation of all three classes of good, external, bodily and psychic – though, of course, with greatest weight given to the last. This doctrine is duly attributed to Moses, but in *Questions on Genesis* 3.16 we find the following: "This doctrine was praised by some of the philosophers who came afterwards, such as Aristotle and the Peripatetics. Moreover, this is said to have been the legislation of Pythagoras." What we may postulate here is some "Pythagorean" treatise

---

[20] Alluded to, e.g., at *On the Creation* 52; *Moses* 2.115. See in this connection the useful discussion in Runia 2001: 5–9, Staehle 1931 and Moehring 1995.

appropriating the Aristotelian ethical system for Pythagoras, such as that of "Hippodamus" *On Happiness* (94.7–7.15 Thesleff).

Philo's doctrine of the virtues is much influenced by Stoic terminology but a distinctively Pythagorean element manifests itself in *On the Special Laws* 4.230–1, where Philo praises the virtue of justice:

> For the mother of Justice is Equality [*isotēs*], as the masters of natural philosophy (sc. the Pythagoreans) have handed down to us, and Equality is light unclouded, an intelligible sun, if the truth be told, just as its opposite, Inequality, in which one thing is exceeded by another, is the source and fount of darkness.

Here justice is linked to equality in a distinctively Pythagorean way (Arist. *Magna Moralia* 1182a11–14; Alexander *In Metaph*. 38.10) and Equality and Inequality are then linked with Light and Darkness which appear in the Pythagorean table of opposites (Arist. *Metaph*. 986a25–6).

Even in the realm of logic, Pythagorean influence appears, perhaps mediated through Eudorus. When listing the categories at *On the Decalogue* 30, Philo, like Eudorus, gives us the order "Substance –Quality – Quantity," which Eudorus, as we have suggested, may have derived from pseudo-Archytas. In the case of the Aristotelian categories of "when" and "where," identified with Time and Place, Philo is actually truer to "Archytas" than is Eudorus, in putting them at the end of the list, whereas Eudorus ranks them immediately after Quantity.[21]

8. Plutarch

Philo, then, shows in every aspect of philosophy how pervasive Pythagorean influence had become in the emerging amalgam that is "Middle" Platonism. To see how this influence develops further, we may turn to the major figure in the Platonist tradition from the later part of the first century AD, Plutarch of Chaeronea.[22] Plutarch would never be regarded as being on the "Neopythagorean" wing of Platonism in the Imperial Age, represented by the figures of Moderatus of Gades, Nicomachus of Gerasa and Numenius of Apamea, but there is no question that he knew a good deal about Pythagoreanism, and in various important respects exhibits influence from that quarter.

[21] For Philo and pseudo-Pythagorean writings see Chapter 15.

[22] I note here the presence, earlier in the century, of the Pythagoreanizing Platonist, Thrasyllus, court philosopher to the Emperor Tiberius, who established the present (tetralogic) format of the Platonic corpus. His "Pythagoreanism" seems to manifest itself primarily in astrology and musical theory – though Porphyry (*Life of Plotinus* 20) testifies that he wrote on the first principles of Pythagoreanism.

We may first of all focus on a detail that he provides about his "intellectual pre-history" in his dialogue on *The E at Delphi*. There (387ff.), he portrays himself as, in his youth (around 66–67 AD), "devoting myself to mathematics with the greatest enthusiasm, although I was destined to pay all honor to the maxim 'Nothing in Excess' when I joined the Academy." This, in the context, seems to betoken an ironic confession of excessive enthusiasm for Pythagoreanizing numerology, which he moderated later. Even the more mature Plutarch, however, exhibits traits that may be identified as Pythagorean.

In metaphysics, we can regard as Neopythagorean his postulation of a pair of supreme principles, the One and the Indefinite Dyad, though there is nothing un-Platonic about this. However, at *The Obsolescence of Oracles* 428ff., we find a starkly dualist scenario presented, which is compatible with the oldest Pythagorean traditions, which emphasize the principles of limit and unlimited (i.e., Philolaus fr. 1):

> Of the supreme principles, by which I mean the One and the Indefinite Dyad, the latter being the element underlying all formlessness and disorder, has been called Limitlessness [*apeiria*]; but the nature of the One limits and contains what is void and irrational and indeterminate in Limitlessness, gives it shape, and renders it in some way tolerant and receptive of definition.

This pair of principles turns up at various places in Plutarch's works, attributed to a wide range of authorities, including Zoroaster and various Presocratic figures (e.g., *Generation of the Soul* 1024d–5d; *Isis and Osiris* 370c–1a – where "the Pythagoreans" are included). Pythagoras is not included in the list given in the *Generation of the Soul* passage, but elsewhere, at 1012e, we find the information that "Zaratas" (whom Plutarch does not seem to identify with Zoroaster!) was a teacher of Pythagoras, and called the Indefinite Dyad the mother of Number, the One being its father.[23]

In ethics, particularly in the essay *On Moral Virtue*, we can, I think, discern some Pythagorean elements overlaying a basically Peripatetic system. When Plutarch turns, at 444ff., to discussing the precise sense in which virtue is said to be a "mean," he selects a distinctively Pythagorean one, as is attested by its presence in various pseudo-Pythagorean writings:

---

[23] The connection between Zaratas and Pythagoras goes back to Aristoxenus (fr. 13). See Chapter 13 below and Zhmud 2012b: 88–91 for a different view.

But it is a mean, and is said to be so, in a sense very like that which obtains in musical sounds and harmonies. For there the mean, or *mesē,* a properly-pitched note like the *nētē* or *hypatē,* escapes the sharpness of the one and the deepness of the other.

In various pseudo-Pythagorean treatises, such as "Archytas," *On Law and Justice* (33.17 Thesleff), "Metopus," *On Virtue* (119.28 Thesleff), and "Theages," *On Virtue* (190. 1–14 Thesleff), we find virtue described as a "harmonizing" (*harmonia, synharmogē*) of the irrational by the rational soul, which would seem to indicate an overlaying by Plutarch of Neopythagorean influence on a basically Aristotelian substratum.

9.   The second-century Neopythagoreans: Moderatus

In general, however, Pythagoreanism is not a dominant feature of Plutarch's thought, despite the considerable knowledge he shows of it in such works as the *On the Sign of Socrates,* the *Life of Numa,* and elsewhere.[24] Far different is the case with the "Neopythagorean" Platonists mentioned above, Moderatus, Nicomachus and Numenius. These do not constitute anything like a school, and indeed Numenius shows himself to be radically at odds with Moderatus, but they do have enough in common to be characterized as a tendency.

Moderatus, at the turn of the first century AD, may have lived a Pythagorean life, since Plutarch (*Table-Talk* 727b) labels him a Pythagorean and presents his follower Lucius as living a life according to the Pythagorean *symbola.* Moderatus comes across as a rather strident "Pythagorean," who, in his work *Lectures on Pythagoreanism* (Porph. *VP* 48–53) claims that the Platonists have appropriated for themselves all that was best in Pythagorean doctrine, leaving for the school itself all that was superficial or frivolous. It is, then, somewhat ironic that Moderatus' distinctive system of first principles appears to be inspired by, if anything, an interpretation of the "three kings" of the *Second Platonic Letter* and the first three hypotheses of the second part of the *Parmenides:*[25]

> It seems that this opinion concerning matter was held first among Greeks by the Pythagoreans, and after them by Plato, as indeed Moderatus tells us. For he (sc. Plato), following the Pythagoreans, declares that the first One is above Being and all essence, while the second One – which is the

---

[24] E.g. *Table-Talk* 8.7–8, where he discusses Pythagorean dietary habits.

[25] Reported by Simplicius (*in Phys.* 230.34ff. Diels), who quotes Porphyry's treatise *On Matter.* See on this the seminal article of Dodds (1928).

truly existent [*ontōs on*] and the object of intellection [*noēton*] – he says is the Forms; the third – which is the soul-realm [*psychikon*] – participates in [*metechei*] the One and the Forms, while the lowest nature which comes after it, that of the sense-realm, does not even participate, but receives order by reflection [*kat' emphasin*] from those others, Matter in the sense-realm being a shadow cast by non-being as it manifests itself primally in quantity [*to poson*], and which is of a degree inferior even to that.

The last sentence here is ill-expressed and consequently obscure, but the overall scheme presented is clear enough and most interesting. As Dodds argues, Moderatus' scheme is best explained as an interpretation of the first three hypotheses of Plato's *Parmenides* – though there is influence from the *Second Letter* (itself probably a Neopythagorean forgery) as well. Moderatus' view presumably is that the metaphysical system adumbrated in the *Parmenides* is one of those features "stolen" by Plato from the Pythagorean tradition.

The same would go for the *Timaeus*, which is the dominant influence behind a further report on the doctrine of Moderatus subjoined by Porphyry to the above passage. There he speaks of a *heniaios logos* ("unitary reason-principle") which, "wishing to produce from itself the generation of beings, by withdrawing itself [*kata sterēsin hautou*], made room for Quantity [*posotēs*], by depriving itself of all its own *logoi* and forms." It is not clear whether Porphyry is here referring to Moderatus' first or second One, but it seems better on the whole to take it as the latter.[26] In this way, Moderatus' second One, generating its counterpart, the "dyadic" Quantity, by a sort of "self-withdrawal," would correspond to Eudorus' secondary pair of Monad and Dyad, and to Numenius' second God, to which we will come presently. The second One will thus be described correctly as the *logos*, or projection, of the first.

It is at the level of this second One that a "material" element comes into existence, in the form of Quantity – not, as Porphyry specifies, "Quantity as a Form, but in the sense of privation, weakening, dispersion and severance." Here we can see the use being made of quantity as a metaphysical concept, and the reason why Eudorus should have wished, like "Archytas," to rank the category of Quantity third, after Quality, in his list of categories. This Quantity is the Indefinite Dyad under another title, projecting its "shadow" right down to the lowest point on the scale of being, Matter proper, forming the substratum of the physical realm.

---

[26] We must recall that the Monad of the system relayed by Alexander Polyhistor generates a Dyad out of itself; but that is a simpler scenario than we have here.

Moderatus' doctrine of the soul – his third "One" – is what one would expect from a Pythagoreanizing Platonist. According to Iamblichus (*On the Soul* 4–5: 364 Finamore and Dillon), Moderatus declared the soul to be number, as comprising all the ratios (*logoi*), and thus functioning in the body as an attunement (*harmonia*), "as being a mean and conjunction in beings and lives and the generation of all things" – a definition that owes much to both Speusippus and Xenocrates, as well as to the Pythagorean tradition represented by Philolaus.

10. The second-century Neopythagoreans: Nicomachus

We may turn next to Nicomachus of Gerasa, who seems to be active in the first half of the second century AD, slightly later than Moderatus. His surviving contributions are chiefly in the areas of mathematical and musical theory. Two of his works are extant, and were very popular in later antiquity, *Introduction to Arithmetic* and *Manual of Harmonics,* while of two others, *The Theology of Arithmetic* and the *Life of Pythagoras,* considerable fragments remain in later works, the anonymous *Theology of Arithmetic* (possibly based on a compilation by Iamblichus),[27] and the *Lives of Pythagoras* composed by Porphyry and Iamblichus.

Despite his importance in the area of ancient mathematics, Nicomachus' philosophical position is less distinctive than either that of Moderatus or of Numenius.[28] He does interestingly connect the early Pythagorean principles of Philolaus, limit and unlimited, with his basic system of Monad and Indefinite Dyad (*Introduction to Arithmetic* 2.18.4). The Monad produces the Dyad later by a process of "self-doubling," with as their product a *Logos,* to which he gives the epithets "creative" and "seminal" in which are contained the sum-total of Forms, themselves envisaged as numerical entities.[29] We have intimations of a process of "procession and return," characteristic later of the philosophy of Plotinus. Nicomachus (*Theology of Arithmetic,* henceforward *Theol. Ar.,* 19.5ff.) uses sexual imagery ("emission," "reception" and "restitution"), with the Dyad described, interestingly, as a sort of "turning point" (*kamptēr*), where the flow of existence from the Monad turns back again to the Monad (*Theol. Ar.* 9.4ff.). The World-Soul Nicomachus associates with the Hexad (*Theol. Ar.* 45.6ff.) and characterizes

---

[27] There is also an epitome preserved in Photius' *Bibliotheca* 187, which is most useful as a check on passages not explicitly attributed to Nicomachus in the anonymous *Theology of Arithmetic.*

[28] For a more detailed account of his philosophy, see Dillon 1977: 352–61 and Kahn 2001: 110–18.

[29] All this is derivable from the introduction to the *Introduction to Arithmetic,* amplified by Bishop Photius' summary of his *Theology of Arithmetic.*

as the "Form of Form," since it is its nature to mold the formlessness of Matter. This it does by imposing harmony on opposites (45.13ff.), receiving Forms from the *Logos* and projecting them upon Matter as harmony and number.

In the sphere of ethics, Nicomachus adopts the Peripatetic doctrine of virtue as a mean but gives it a Pythagorean twist by associating it closely with mathematics. At *Introduction to Arithmetic* 1.14.2, he brings it into a discussion of perfect numbers, and at 1.23.4 he sums up his discussion of arithmetical relations by remarking that this investigation teaches us the primacy of the beautiful and definite and intelligible nature over its opposite, and how the former must order the latter, even as the rational part of the soul orders the two irrational parts, spirit (*thymos*) and desire (*epithymia*), and derives from this imposing of "equality" or equilibrium (*apisōsis*) the so-called ethical virtues. This doctrine, we may note, resembles that of Plutarch in his essay *On Moral Virtue* (see section 8 above).

Nicomachus is also notable for his extensive use of Pythagorean writings, both genuine and spurious, thus providing evidence for their availability in his time. Between the *Introduction to Arithmetic*, the *Manual of Harmonics*, and the *Theology of Arithmetic*, he adduces works of Philolaus and Archytas, Androcydes (*On the Symbols*), Eubulides, Aristaeus and Prorus (*On the Hebdomad*). He also, as we have noted, had an active interest in the life-myth of Pythagoras.

11. The second-century Neopythagoreans: Numenius

The last of our three Neopythagoreans of the second century, Numenius of Apamea, is a major figure in the development of later Platonism, to the extent that a figure such as Plotinus in the next century had to be defended against charges of simply plagiarizing Numenius (Porphyry *Life of Plotinus* 17). He seems much more comfortable than Moderatus appears to be with identifying himself as a Platonist as well as a Pythagorean. He describes Plato as "not better than the great Pythagoras but perhaps not worse either" (fr. 24 Des Places). He reveals strong views on the nature of Platonist orthodoxy by launching an attack on the Platonist credentials of the skeptical New Academy in *On the Unfaithfulness of the Academics to Plato* (frs. 24–5 Des Places). His other main work, a treatise in dialogue form *On the Good* (of which extensive passages are preserved by Eusebius, who regularly describes Numenius as a Pythagorean), sets forth his own system. Like Moderatus, and unlike Nicomachus, we can see evidence in Numenius of a hierarchy of principles. For a succinct summary of his system, albeit a slightly polemical one, we may turn, not to the verbatim passages, but to Proclus (*Commentary on the Timaeus* 1.303.27ff.):

> Numenius proclaims three gods, calling the first "Father," the second "Creator,"[30] and the third "Creation"; for the cosmos, according to him, is the third god. So, according to him, the Demiurge is double, being both the first god and the second, and the third god is the object of his demiurgic activity. (fr. 21 Des Places)

Numenius, then, like Moderatus, propounds a triad of divinities, influenced, no doubt, by the Platonic *Second Letter* (312e), as well as by an interpretation of the first two hypotheses of the *Parmenides*. The first god, or "Father," is a self-directed Intellect, rather on the lines of Aristotle's Unmoved Mover (frs. 11–13, 16, 19), identified also as the Good and the One, which stimulates the second god to creativity by acting as a focus for his contemplation (fr. 18). What we do not find, however, at the highest level, is any mention of a Dyad, but that appears, in fr. 11, as Matter, which causes the division of the second god, while being brought to order by him.

This is all a creative development of the Neopythagorean heritage, influenced no doubt to some extent by Moderatus; but Numenius differs strongly from Moderatus in the degree of his dualism, as becomes clear from an extended report from Calcidius (*In Tim.* Chs. 295–9 = fr. 52), where Numenius criticizes those Pythagoreans who postulate that the "indefinite and immeasurable Dyad was produced by the Monad withdrawing from its own nature and departing into the form of the Dyad – an absurd situation!" Numenius' own view, which he ascribes to Pythagoras himself, is that the Dyad constitutes an independent "evil" principle coeval with the Monad, which it can only bring to some sort of order, but never entirely subdue. Moreover, Numenius was noted for postulating, not just an irrational part of the soul, but two souls, the second being a material one, deriving from the Dyad (frs. 44; 52), which accentuates the tension within the human being, and increases the urgency of escape from the body.

12. Conclusion

The influence of Pythagoreanism of one form or another on Platonists from Speusippus in the Old Academy to Numenius in the later second century AD can be seen to be pervasive, though never forming more than

---

[30] Here giving a creative interpretation of *Ti.* 28c, taking the "father" and the "creator" mentioned there to refer to different entities.

one element in the mix, along with Aristotelianism and Stoicism. Only in the case of Moderatus, however, do we observe any signs of tension between the two traditions; in general, Platonist thinkers were content to see Pythagoras and the Pythagoreans as worthy forerunners of their system, and Pythagoras himself and his circle as suitable models for a way of life.

CHAPTER 13

The Peripatetics on the Pythagoreans

Carl A. Huffman

1. Introduction

Aristotle's students in the Peripatos (active 350–280 BC) are exceptionally important sources for the history of Pythagoreanism. Although none of their treatments of Pythagoreanism survive, numerous excerpts are found in later authors such as Iamblichus and Porphyry. Only one book devoted to Pythagoreanism had been written earlier than those of Aristotle and his students: Anaximander of Miletus' lost treatise on the Pythagorean *symbola* (*c.* 400 BC – Burkert 1972a: 166).[1] The early Peripatos increased this number tenfold. Aristotle himself wrote two books on the Pythagoreans and three on Archytas (Huffman 2005: 583–4). Aristotle's pupil Aristoxenus contributed another five: *The Life of Pythagoras, Pythagoras and His Associates, The Life of Archytas, On the Pythagorean Life* and *The Pythagorean Precepts*. No other Peripatetic devoted an entire work to the Pythagoreans, but Dicaearchus and Clearchus made Pythagoras and Pythagoreans prominent examples in their *On Modes of Life*. Moreover, the early Peripatos included the Pythagoreans in its grand surveys of accomplishments in the sciences. None of these survive, but they were again important sources for the later doxography. The most striking characteristic of these works (Theophrastus' *Physical Opinions*, Meno's *Collection of Medical Views* and Eudemus' *Histories of Arithmetic, Geometry, Astronomy* and *Theology* as well as his *Physics*) is their universal failure to mention Pythagoras himself, always referring instead to the Pythagoreans as a group or to specific Pythagoreans such as Archytas or Philolaus. Pythagoras does appear in the works on biography and ways of life by Aristoxenus and Dicaearchus as well as in a later anecdote of Hieronymus of Rhodes (290–230 BC). The Peripatetic view of Pythagoras mirrors the split in the tradition that was present in the

---

[1] It is possible that Xenocrates wrote *Things Pythagorean* (Diog. Laert. 4.13) before the Peripatetic writings. Speusippus' *On Pythagorean Numbers* (fr. 28 Tarán) may also have been earlier but was probably not historical in approach.

earliest sources: Aristoxenus (and Chamaeleon who is probably dependent on him) follow Empedocles in being overwhelmingly positive, whereas Dicaearchus and Hieronymus are heirs to Heraclitus' bitter critique. In terms of amount of material, the Peripatetics put greatest emphasis on the way of life of Pythagoras and later Pythagoreans. Accordingly I will spend the bulk of the chapter on these topics, after first surveying the Peripatetic view of their contribution to the sciences.

2. Theophrastus

Theophrastus succeeded Aristotle as head of the Lyceum in 322 and remained until 287. He certainly referred to the Pythagoreans in his contribution to the Peripatetic survey of human knowledge, the *Physical Opinions*, which systematically collected early Greek views about the natural world. There is, however, only one doubtful mention of the Pythagoreans in its surviving fragments. In a passage preserved by Simplicius, Empedocles is described as an admirer of Parmenides and "even more of the Pythagoreans" (*DG* 477 = FHS&G 227A). Diogenes Laertius (8.55) ascribes the same report to Theophrastus, in identical language, but he does not mention the Pythagoreans, who were thus probably not in the text of Theophrastus but added by Simplicius (*DG* 477).

There remain only two references to the Pythagoreans in Theophrastus, both in his *Metaphysics*. At 11a27 Theophrastus reports, "Plato and the Pythagoreans make the distance [sc. between the good and the things of nature] great but hold that all things wish to imitate the good" (Burkert 1972a: 62 n. 57). He adds that they both make an opposition between the One and the Indefinite Dyad, which is surprising, because Aristotle emphasizes that these were Platonic and not Pythagorean principles (*Metaph.* 987b25–7). Burkert argues that Theophrastus is here agreeing with Plato's immediate successors in the Academy and rejecting Aristotle's interpretation (1972a: 66). In the later doxography, Aëtius (first century AD) assigns Plato's principles to Pythagoras himself. While many scholars assume that the Pythagorean doxography was rewritten in the first century BC under the influence of Neopythagoreanism, which accounts for this glorification of Pythagoras and the Pythagoreans (*DG* 181; Zeller 1919: 1.1.467ff.), Burkert suggests that the glorification of Pythagoras in Aëtius derives from Theophrastus (1972a: 63). However, Theophrastus does not assign these Platonic views to Pythagoras himself as does Aëtius. Moreover, it is impossible to securely identify genuinely Theophrastan material in Aetius (Runia 2008: 38).

The second reference to the Pythagoreans in the *Metaphysics* is a famous report about Eurytus, for which Theophrastus cites Archytas as the source, although he does not explicitly call either a Pythagorean (6a15–6b5). Theophrastus praises Eurytus for not simply identifying first principles and then failing to explain how the cosmos developed from those principles. Eurytus went beyond identifying numbers as first principles by setting out pebbles to show that "this was the number of man and that of horse." Some scholars suppose that Theophrastus' praise was ironic, since Eurytus' procedure seems so naive (Burkert 1972a: 47 n. 107), but nothing in his language suggests irony and Eurytus is cited in support of a view that Theophrastus is championing (Laks and Most 1993: 43; Gutas 2010: 304).

Immediately after praising Eurytus, however, Theophrastus goes on to criticize "those who posit the One and the Indefinite Dyad" for not doing what Eurytus did. Thus Theophrastus did not include Eurytus among those Pythagoreans whom he presents at 11a27 as anticipating Plato in adopting the One and the Dyad. This is puzzling, since the Academic view that Theophrastus seems to embrace traces Plato's views back to Pythagoras himself. This presentation of Pythagoras as the master metaphysician would surely imply that other Pythagoreans adhered closely to his teachings. There is thus a tension in Theophrastus. On the one hand, he presents the Pythagoreans and Plato as adopting a common theory of principles that presumably goes back to the master Pythagoras. On the other hand, Theophrastus presents Eurytus as promulgating a metaphysics that is to some degree independent of the master.[2]

3. Eudemus and Meno

Like Theophrastus Eudemus never wrote a work exclusively devoted to the Pythagoreans, but he mentions them in five fragments from his histories of arithmetic, geometry and astronomy and in three fragments from his *Physics*. Additional texts about the Pythagoreans in the later tradition can, with more or less plausibility, be traced back to Eudemus. Methodologically, however, it is necessary to start with texts that explicitly name Eudemus and only then consider possible expansions of the evidence.

Proclus (fifth century AD), in his commentary on Book 1 of Euclid, preserves two fragments from the *History of Geometry*, in which Eudemus

---

[2] In harmonics Theophrastus argues against the Pythagorean view that differences in pitch are quantitative. He may be arguing against a general approach rather than the Pythagoreans in particular (*FHS&G* 716; see Barker 2007: 411–36). Nonetheless, his arguments make the best sense if he had Archytas in mind (Barker 2007: 420).

reports that the Pythagoreans originated the proofs that became propositions 32 and 44 of Euclid (frs. 136–7 Wehrli). Presumably also in the *History of Geometry*, Eudemus presented Archytas' solution to the duplication of the cube (A14 Huffman), which Eutocius (sixth century AD) cites as from Eudemus. The only surviving fragment from the *History of Arithmetic* asserts that for the Pythagoreans "the ratios of the three concords (the fourth [4:3], the fifth [3:2] and the octave [2:1]), in their lowest terms, turn out to belong to nine; for two and three and four are nine" (fr. 142 Wehrli). The addition of parts of ratios to reach a significant number (9) is reminiscent of Aristotle's reports of Pythagorean emphasis on significant numbers (*Metaph.* 986a8–12) and of Archytas' account of earlier Pythagorean harmonic theorists (A17 Huffman), so these Pythagoreans belong to the fifth century.

One fragment of *The History of Astronomy* refers to the Pythagoreans: they were the first to give the "correct" order of the planets (fr. 146 Wehrli). This report matches the system of Philolaus, in which the ordering of the planets from the earth outward agrees with the standard ordering in Eudemus' day (A16 Huffman). Zhmud argues that, since Eudemus refers to Pythagoreans in the plural, he cannot be referring to Philolaus and is referring to an earlier Pythagorean system (2006: 258; 2012b: 337). However, there is no direct evidence for a Pythagorean astronomical system before Philolaus. So the most reasonable supposition is that Eudemus is following Aristotle's universal practice of assigning Philolaus' system to the Pythagoreans as a group. Aristotle describes only one astronomical system, that of Philolaus.[3] The ascription of the system to Philolaus makes excellent sense in terms of the history of Greek knowledge of the planets. There is no trace of a system including the canonical five planets in either Anaxagoras or Empedocles. This would be puzzling, if there was a Pythagorean system prior to Philolaus which had already done so, but makes sense, if it was only with Philolaus that the five planets appear in the correct order (Burkert 1972a: 308–21).

Finally in his *Physics* Eudemus refers to Pythagoreans three times. He joins the Pythagoreans to Plato as maintaining that motion belongs in the class of the indefinite (fr. 60 Wehrli). Eudemus, however, distinguishes Plato (and probably these Pythagoreans) from Archytas, who argued that

[3] Zhmud (1998b: 249 n. 20) counters that Aristotle refers to Pythagoras' study of the heavens in the *Protrepticus* but this is not Aristotle but Iamblichus (see n. 7 below). He also notes that nothing in Aristotle's account of the Pythagorean harmony of the spheres (*Cael.* 290b12–1a28) suggests that he was thinking of Philolaus (2012b: 344). This is true, but there is also no indication that he is thinking of any other specific system either.

motion was not to be identified with the uneven or the unequal as Plato supposed but was rather caused by them (A23 Huffman). The context suggests that Eudemus is thinking of the Pythagoreans who put forth the table of opposites. Elsewhere in his *Physics* Eudemus reports that the Pythagoreans thought events repeated themselves, not just things that are the same in form, such as the seasons, but particular things. He illustrated this by saying to his students that, according to the Pythagoreans, the exact same conversation he was having with them would be repeated so that "I [i.e. Eudemus] will speak to you [again] holding my staff thus" (fr. 88 Wehrli). Eudemus also reports Archytas' famous argument that the universe is unlimited: Archytas has us imagine him at the supposed limit of the universe and asks whether he would be able to extend his staff farther or not (A24 Huffman).

There are several striking things about these eight references to the Pythagoreans. First, Eudemus never mentions Pythagoras. Second, over a third of the references are to Archytas. Third, all other references are to the Pythagoreans as a group. Fourth, Pythagorean interests are wide ranging: geometry, arithmetic, harmonics, astronomy, motion, as well as the spatial and temporal nature of the cosmos. Fifth, the Pythagoreans are cited for specific contributions to a given area of thought and are not presented as the founders of any discipline.

It is likely that three other accomplishments assigned to the Pythagore-ans in Proclus' commentary and in the scholia to Euclid also go back to Eudemus, even though he is not identified as the source: a theorem not found in Euclid which shows that only three polygons can fill the space around a point (Proclus *Commentary on Euclid* 304.11), the construction of the first three regular solids (*Scholia on Euclid* 654.3), and the entirety of Book 4 of Euclid (*Schol. Eucl.* 273.3).[4] In light of all this information, how, then, did Eudemus view the Pythagorean contribution to geometry? It is hard to reach firm conclusions because we only have fragments of his work. Nonetheless, Proclus was very interested in the Pythagoreans and probably had access to all of Eudemus' *History of Geometry* (Zhmud 2006: 184). Thus, in his commentary on Book 1 of Euclid's *Elements*, he is likely to have reported all that Eudemus said about them that was relevant at least to that book (Burkert 1972a: 450–1). If this is so, Eudemus thought

---

[4] Burkert 1972a: 450. Zhmud argues that passages in Nicomachus and Iamblichus, which ascribe the discovery of the first three means to Pythagoras, go back to Eudemus (2006: 172–4). That Eudemus discussed this topic seems likely. Both Nicomachus and Iamblichus, however, have the habit of ascribing discoveries to Pythagoras that were not his. Zhmud is right that Iamblichus' detailed account is more likely to reflect Eudemus' words. Iamblichus, however, does not assign the discovery to Pythagoras but rather to "the mathematicians of his time." If this reflects Eudemus' language, he again avoids ascribing the mathematical discovery to Pythagoras himself.

that the Pythagoreans contributed only two of the forty-eight propositions in Book 1, although he makes them responsible for all of Book 4,
just as he makes Eudoxus responsible for Book 5. Eudemus' Pythagoreans emerge as playing an important but not a dominant role in Greek
geometry.

Such is also the view of the Pythagoreans that emerges from Proclus'
brief overview of Greek geometry in the prologue to his commentary on
Euclid, an overview that most scholars ascribe to Eudemus. Here, Thales is
the first geometer and the first *Elements* of geometry belongs to the Ionian
mathematician Hippocrates of Chios (*c.* 430 BC). The Pythagoreans are
neither the first geometers nor the first to establish geometry as a science.[5]
Pythagorean accomplishments in geometry begin in the last quarter of the
fifth century after the work of Hippocrates, rather than in the first half
(Burkert 1972a: 449–54). This chronology makes particular sense in the
case of Pythagorean work on the regular solids, since Theaetetus, who was
not a Pythagorean, finished their work by completing constructions of the
last two regular solids in the first part of the fourth century. Eudemus'
presentation of Archytas mirrors his view of the Pythagoreans as a whole.
He preserves Archytas' brilliant solution to the problem of doubling the
cube and in the overview of geometry (Procl. *in Eucl.* 66.15–18) says that
Archytas helped to increase the number of theorems and to bring them
into a more scientific order. Nonetheless, Archytas is just one of three
geometers dominant in Plato's time, along with Leodamas of Thasos and
Theaetetus, neither of whom was a Pythagorean. Archytas himself is not
called a Pythagorean, probably because Eudemus saw nothing particularly
Pythagorean about his mathematics.

The pivotal text supporting this interpretation of Eudemus' presentation
of the Pythagoreans is a text that, upon careful examination, turns out not
to be by Eudemus at all. These are the lines devoted to Pythagoras in
Proclus' overview of early Greek geometry:

> Following these men [sc. Thales and Mamercus], Pythagoras transformed
> the philosophy concerned with it [sc. geometry] into a form of liberal
> education, reviewing its principles from a higher perspective and investig-
> ating its theorems in an immaterial and (purely) intellectual way. He, indeed,
> also discovered the study of irrationals and the construction of cosmic
> figures. (*in Eucl.* 65.15–21)

[5] Zhmud follows van der Waerden in supposing that Eudemus used a Pythagorean mathematical
compendium that preceded Hippocrates' *Elements* and that contained the basis for Euclid 1–4
(2006: 195–6; 2012b: 279). This compendium is a construct of modern scholarship based solely on
indirect arguments. Its existence is extremely unlikely given Eudemus' failure to mention it in his
overview of geometry.

Most scholars recognize that parts of Proclus' history of geometry are later insertions that cannot go back to Eudemus (Zhmud 2006: 179–90; 2012b: 263–4). There are strong arguments that this entire passage about Pythagoras is such an insertion (Burkert 1972a: 409–11). The language and thought in line 4, "in an immaterial and intellectual way [ἀΰλως καὶ νοερῶς]" is Neoplatonic rather than Peripatetic; ἀΰλως (immaterial) is a common word in Proclus but unparalleled in the time of Eudemus. There is also good evidence both that Pythagoras did not make the discoveries attributed to him in the last line (the fourth and fifth regular solids [cosmic figures] were only discovered by Theaetetus in the fourth century – *Schol. Eucl.* 654.3) and also that Eudemus did not think that he did, so that the last line is also likely to be due to Proclus (Zhmud 2006: 180–1).

Does the remaining assertion that "Pythagoras transformed the philosophy of geometry into a form of liberal education" belong to Eudemus? If so, this would be the sole case in which Eudemus refers to Pythagoras himself. On the other hand, if these two lines are as much an insertion as the other three, then Pythagoras is not mentioned at all in Eudemus' overview of the history of geometry, which is powerful evidence that Eudemus, who had studied the evidence carefully, did not regard Pythagoras as an important geometer. It is almost certain that the lines are, in fact, also an insertion; they appear word for word in Iamblichus' *On Common Mathematical Science* (70.1–3 Festa "Pythagoras transformed the philosophy concerned with the sciences into a form of liberal education"). Proclus relies heavily on this work elsewhere (Festa in his edition of Iamblichus notes over ten cases, which amount to ten to fifteen percent of the text). Proclus often paraphrases, but there is also word for word repetition (e.g. Proclus 24.27–5.1 and Iamblichus 57.22–3) so that there can be little doubt that Proclus got these lines about Pythagoras from Iamblichus as well. We might try to save the passage for Eudemus by supposing that Iamblichus and Proclus were drawing on a common source (Zhmud 1997: 135–6), but the passage in Iamblichus comes right at the beginning of a section, which is precisely where Iamblichus typically provides transitional sentences of his own composition.[6] We must conclude that Eudemus made no mention of Pythagoras in his overview of Greek geometry and that Proclus inserted a reference to Pythagoras of his own composition drawing partly on Iamblichus.

---

[6] Burkert 1972a: 410–11. Iamblichus' mention of geometry becoming a form of liberal education in the transitional sentence at the beginning of Ch. 23 is picked up by his reference to liberal learning in the body of the chapter, so it is "out of the question that Iamblichus just happened to quote Eudemus in the transitional sentence" (Burkert 1972a: 410 n. 58).

Eudemus' failure to mention Pythagoras in his histories of the sciences and his focus on Pythagoreans of the time of Philolaus (*fl.* 430 BC) and later coincides with the other evidence for the Peripatos. His teacher Aristotle followed exactly the same practice.[7] What survives of the final contribution to the Peripatetic survey of the sciences, Meno's *Medical Collection,* known through its reflection in the medical papyrus *Anonymus Londiniensis,* similarly makes no mention of Pythagoras. Meno identifies two types of explanations of diseases, those that explain them in terms of residues and those that explain them in terms of the elements that constitute the body. Among the latter type Meno includes Philolaus' explanation of the origin of the body from the hot and of diseases from bile, blood and phlegm (Huffman 1993: 289–306). The account is detailed enough to suggest that Meno had access to Philolaus' book. Meno identifies Philolaus as from Croton but does not call him a Pythagorean. If not for Meno we would have no idea that Philolaus contributed to medical theory.

4. Dicaearchus

Dicaearchus, writing at the same time as Theophrastus, Eudemus and Meno, focuses not on Pythagorean contributions to the sciences but rather on the life of Pythagoras himself. None of his references to Pythagoras is ascribed to a specific work, and they probably come from *On Lives.* This work focused on types of lives (e.g., the contemplative life) and used incidents from the lives of particular individuals to illustrate them (Fortenbaugh 2007: 72 and White 2001: 197–8). Indeed, no life of any individual philosopher is ever assigned to Dicaearchus and an anecdote about Plato is cited as from Book 1 of *On Lives* rather than from a *Life of Plato* (Momigliano 1993: 71).

Four fragments of Dicaearchus mention Pythagoras. Two long fragments are preserved in Porphyry's *Life of Pythagoras* (second century AD). The first (fr. 40 Mirhady = Porph. *VP* 18–19) describes the remarkable impact of Pythagoras' arrival in Croton, before discussing the difficulty of knowing

---

[7] Zhmud (2006: 196; 2012b: 259–60) cites fr. 191 as evidence that Aristotle ascribed mathematical work to Pythagoras ("Pythagoras devoted himself to mathematics and numbers"), but these words occur before Aristotle is quoted and come from the source, Apollonius. Similarly Zhmud cites fr. 20 of Aristotle's *Protrepticus* as evidence that Aristotle regarded Pythagoras as devoted to abstract contemplation (2006: 196; 2012b: 56). However, in Iamblichus the same story is told first about Pythagoras and then about Anaxagoras producing a strange repetition. The story about Anaxagoras is found in Aristotle's *Eudemian Ethics* (1216a11) and thus may well also have been in his *Protrepticus,* but there is no mention of Pythagoras in the *Eudemian Ethics* so the doublet about Pythagoras must be an insertion by Iamblichus (Burkert 1960: 167–9).

what his beliefs were and circumspectly summarizing what little can be ascribed to him.[8] The second (fr. 41a Mirhady = Porph. *VP* 56–7; cf. Diog. Laert. 8.40) describes the attack on the Pythagoreans in southern Italy, Pythagoras' flight from Croton because of these attacks and his eventual death in Metapontum. A third recounts briefly and satirically Pythagoras' supposed reincarnations (fr. 42 Mirhady = Gellius 4.11.14). A final brief reference suggests that Plato's philosophy was a combination of Lycurgus, Socrates and Pythagoras (fr. 45 Mirhady = Plut. *Table Talk* 719a–b).[9]

At first sight it is hard to discern a coherent theme in Dicaearchus' presentation. The account of Pythagoras' arrival (fr. 40) seems positive in its recognition of his wide impact in southern Italy. Jaeger (1948: 452) argued that Dicaearchus' presentation of earlier philosophers was colored by his emphasis on the practical life in contrast to Theophrastus who championed the contemplative life (fr. 33 Mirhady = Cic. *Att.* 2.16.3). Following Rohde (1901: 110), he maintains that Dicaearchus regarded Pythagoras as "the ideal picture of the practical life as he himself taught it" (Jaeger 1948: 456). This has been the dominant view. Kahn asserts that Dicaearchus respected Pythagoras "as a moral guide and social reformer" (2001: 68). White similarly argues that Dicaearchus regarded Pythagoras as an epochal figure, although for different reasons than Jaeger (2001: 210–14). On the other hand, Dicaearchus' account of the attacks on the Pythagoreans and Pythagoras' flight to Metapontum (fr. 41a) has a clearly negative implication, since no city is willing to receive him. Most problematic of all is Dicaearchus' report that in one of his incarnations Pythagoras was the beautiful prostitute Alco (fr. 42). Burkert (1972a: 139) and Wehrli (1967: 53) rightly regard it as "sarcastic" and "derisive" but do not reconcile it with the apparently positive fr. 40.

The key to the puzzle is found in careful reading of Dicaearchus' account of Pythagoras' arrival. Pythagoras influenced not just the leaders of Croton but also the young men, the boys and the women, not to mention the

---

[8] Wehrli included only Porph. *VP* 18 as a fragment of Dicaearchus, but Mirhady is right to include section 19. Dicaearchus is named as the source at the beginning of section 18, there is no break in train of thought between sections 18 and 19, and Porphyry does not cite a new source until the beginning of 20. Moreover, although Burkert (1972a: 122–3) says that the issue "cannot be definitely decided by philological means," he gives compelling arguments to show that the circumspect tone about the doctrines of Pythagoras in section 19 is much more plausible for Dicaearchus in the fourth century than for any author in the later tradition.

[9] Plutarch's speaker Florus presents Plato as mixing "Lycurgus in with Socrates no less than Pythagoras, as Dicaearchus thought." Jaeger (1948: 459) argues convincingly that Plutarch would not single out Dicaearchus for the common view that Plato combined Socrates and Pythagoras and is asserting that Dicaearchus thought Plato combined all three.

leaders of surrounding non-Greek communities.[10] Iamblichus, writing over 600 years later, provides the text of the four speeches given at Croton, but these are a fabrication of the later tradition. If they had existed in Dicaearchus' time, he could hardly have claimed, as he does in fr. 40, "no one can say securely what he said to his associates" (Burkert 1972a: 115 n. 38). Dicaearchus emphasizes that Pythagoras' success resulted from his initial effect on the elders: "after he had influenced the council of elders with many fine arguments, he made addresses suitable for their age to the young, when bidden by the councilors, and after this to the children gathered in groups from the schools, then to women, when an assembly of women was created for him" (tr. Mirhady). The last case is presented as a climax since, although Mirhady does not translate it, καί is used to indicate that "even" an assembly of women was created for him.

The key is the word used to describe Pythagoras' impact on the elders, ψυχαγωγέω. It is relatively rare, appearing only about twenty times in the whole fourth century. Plato uses it three times, Aristotle only once. It does not have the bland sense of "influence" that Mirhady assigns to it. It denotes the action of influencing the soul, but it has a strong connotation of magic and usually refers to an appeal directed solely to the emotions. It consists of two parts ψυχή, which can refer to the spirit that escapes at death and exists as a ghost in the underworld or to the soul that governs our actions in life, and ἄγω, which has the basic sense of "leading." In its earliest uses it refers to the literal "leading up," or "conjuring" of souls from Hades. Aeschylus wrote a play about Odysseus' visit to the underworld to consult the shades of the dead, which was called, ψυχαγωγοί, "Ghost raisers" (tr. Sommerstein, Loeb). Aristophanes plays on this original sense of the word, when the chorus in *The Birds* (1555) reports that unwashed Socrates "conjures" (ψυχαγωγεῖ – tr. Henderson, Loeb) spirits in the underworld like Odysseus. Aristophanes is referring to Socrates' persuasive effect on the souls of men, while at the same time evoking the magical associations of raising the dead. The three uses in Plato describe the irrational part of the soul as "bewitched" (*Ti.* 71a6, tr. Bury, Loeb) by the use of images and refer to evil men who "charm" the souls of many of the living just as they claim "to charm" the dead (*Leg.* 909b2–3).[11]

If we give ψυχαγωγέω the force suggested by these parallels, Dicaearchus' description of Pythagoras takes on a quite different tone.

---

[10] A fragment of Antisthenes (V A 187 *SSR*) confirms the tradition that Pythagoras gave speeches tailored to the different groups.

[11] In Xenophon (*Mem.* 3.10.6.4) and Aristotle (*Poet.* 1450a33) there is an emphasis on an appeal to emotion but the ties to magic are less clear.

He emphasizes Pythagoras' incredible charisma but the use of ψυχαγ-ωγέω portrays him as employing illegitimate appeals to the emotions to "beguile" and "bewitch" his audience. This led the elders of Croton to allow him to speak to all levels of society and, most remarkably, even to the women. There is a touch of scandal in Dicaearchus' emphasis here, which continues in the emphasis on his popularity with non-Greeks in the area. Pythagoras has particular appeal to two groups that traditionally represent the "wild" aspect of the world that the Greeks see themselves as civilizing, women and foreigners. Dicaearchus' subsequent emphasis on Pythagoras' secrecy fits this presentation of Pythagoras as a sorcerer of sorts. The sobriety of Dicaearchus' report of Pythagoras' beliefs and its freedom from the exaggerations of the later tradition is striking. It seems likely to be an accurate account of the evidence available to the Peripatos. Accuracy should not be confused with approval, however. Dicaearchus lists four doctrines that can be ascribed to Pythagoras: the immortality of the soul, its transmigration into other animals, the kinship of all ensouled beings and the theory that events repeat themselves according to certain cycles. Three of these doctrines focus on the soul, which Dicaearchus has portrayed Pythagoras as "conjuring." Dicaearchus stresses the revolutionary nature of these doctrines, emphasizing that Pythagoras first introduced them into Greece. Dicaearchus did not believe in an immortal soul, so he may be underlining how radical these ideas were (frs. 13–32 Mirhady).[12]

Dicaearchus' account of the attacks on the Pythagoreans in the second long fragment (41a) makes more sense in light of this emphasis on Pythagoras as a charismatic charlatan. In particular it explains the behavior of the Locrians, who did not allow Pythagoras to even enter their city-state but sent elders to meet him "at the borders of their territory." The elders treat him with kid gloves. They acknowledge his wisdom and cleverness and try to appease him by offering any necessary supplies but send him away. Their insistence that they "have no complaint with their own laws" betrays their fear of his ability to overturn their traditional practices. The hostility that pursues him everywhere he goes flows from this ability to revolutionize society. Dicaearchus highlights this point by reporting that

---

[12] Clearchus, a contemporary of Dicaearchus (Moraux 1950), also wrote *On Modes of Life* (Bollansée 2008) but differed from him in believing in an immortal soul. He presents the Pythagorean Euxitheus as saying that men's souls were imprisoned in their bodies for punishment and that they should never try to escape life before old age, since it is only then that they can be confident that their masters are releasing them (fr. 38 = Athenaeus 157c). Euxitheus is likely to be fictitious, since he is mentioned nowhere else (Burkert 1972a: 124). Plato alludes to the view ascribed to Euxitheus in the *Phaedo* (62b) and *Cratylus* (400c), but he treats it not as Pythagorean but as belonging to the mysteries.

even in his time the people of the region referred to turmoil in this period as the "revolutions in the time of the Pythagoreans."

Dicaearchus' account of Pythagoras' incarnations now makes sense. His rebirth as the beautiful prostitute Alco fits particularly well with Dicaearchus' emphasis on Pythagoras' bewitching of Croton. Just as a prostitute beguiles a man into abandoning societally sanctioned behavior, so Pythagoras used meretricious charms to disrupt society. Dicaearchus may have thought that Plato was like Pythagoras in his ability to charm readers into abandoning traditional customs for radical innovations such as those proposed in the *Republic*, including an expanded role for women (fr. 45). Dicaearchus' sarcasm about Pythagoras and his appeal to women may be echoed in the later Peripatetic Hieronymus (290–230 BC). He reported that Pythagoras saw Homer and Hesiod being punished in Hades because of what they had said about the gods. He also saw men who were not willing to have sex with their own wives being punished. To this Hierony-mus added the remark, "it was particularly on account of this that he was honored by those in Croton" (fr. 50 = 42 W = Diog. Laert. 8.21). Burkert argued that a descent to Hades belonged to the earliest stratum of evidence for Pythagoras but that this account of Hieronymus was satirical (1972a: 155–61). The final remark alludes sarcastically to the gratitude of the women of Croton for getting their sex lives back.[13]

5. Aristoxenus

Aristoxenus, like Dicaearchus, focused on the Pythagorean way of life, but his portrait of Pythagoras was overwhelmingly positive. He was more informed about Pythagoreanism than any other Peripatetic. He grew up in the Greek city of Tarentum (375–350 BC), when the Pythagorean Archytas (430–350 BC) was its dominant figure. In addition, he used his father, Spintharus, a contemporary of Archytas, as a source (fr. 30). Aristoxenus took a Pythagorean teacher, Xenophilus, after immigrating to Athens, around 350. He associated with four Pythagoreans from Phlius, a city-state near Corinth, whom, along with Xenophilus, he calls the last of the Pythagoreans (fr. 19). Despite this intimate knowledge of Pythagoreanism, Aristoxenus made no attempt to keep it alive and joined Aristotle's school. Moreover, in developing his own great contribution to ancient philosophy,

---

[13] Others see no irony in the passage. It indicates Pythagoras' strictures about blasphemy and adultery, for which he was praised in the later tradition (Wehrli 1967: 41; Iambl. *VP* 48–50). Attempts to show that Hieronymus derived his account from Heraclides are dubious (Burkert 1972a: 103; Gottschalk 1980: 119–21).

music theory, he rejected the Pythagorean approach.[14] Thus Aristoxenus combines an insider's knowledge of Pythagoreanism with the independence of someone who had moved beyond it. Aristoxenus is the first Peripatetic to write biography. The unique importance of the example of the master in Pythagoreanism may have led him to begin by writing the life of Pythagoras and then go on to Archytas and non-Pythagoreans such as Socrates and Plato (Momigliano 1993: 75).

According to the standard view of Aristoxenus' presentation of the Pythagoreans, he is reliable about chronology and the main actors (von Fritz 1940: 31). He gives the only coherent account of the end of the Pythagoreans (fr. 18) by correctly distinguishing two different revolts against them (Riedweg 2005: 104). On the other hand, his intimate connections with the last generation of Pythagoreans suggest that he is presenting their view of Pythagoreanism. His bias in their favor may have led him to downplay the extent of the opposition to the Pythagoreans in southern Italy (von Fritz 1940: 27–30; Burkert 1972a: 115 n. 42). Some scholars emphasize that he presents all Pythagoreans in an uncritical way as "ideal" leaders and thinkers (Zhmud 2012a: 229). Thus, Archytas was never defeated in battle (fr. 48). Still others suggest that the seeds of the later extreme idealization of Pythagoras are already present in Aristoxenus' presentation of Pythagoras as a culture hero like Prometheus, who provides the Greeks with their first weights and measures (fr. 24; Burkert 1972a: 415). The idealization is most obvious in Aristoxenus' emphasis on the rational side of Pythagoreanism and his attempt to remove any trace of superstition (Lévy 1926: 44–9; Wehrli 1967: 55; Burkert 1972a: 200–5; Riedweg 2005: 37; Zhmud 2012a: 224–30). Aristoxenus accepts only the *mathematici* as true Pythagoreans and rejects the *acusmatici*, who focused on the ritual taboos involved in the way of life (Burkert 1972a: 200). The Pythagoreans that he identifies as "the last" are rather the last *mathematici*; he ignores later *acusmatici* such as Lycon or Diodorus of Aspendus (Burkert 1972a: 204–5, Riedweg 2005: 106). Some scholars welcome Aristoxenus' rationalization and his denial that the Pythagorists of comedy and other radical ascetics such as Diodorus of Aspendus and Lycon are real Pythagoreans (Zhmud 2012a: 224, 228). Most scholars think that Aristoxenus' main flaw is not that he invents evidence (Kahn 2001: 70 is the exception) but rather that he is very selective in what he accepts, so that his account is not fanciful but partial (Burkert 1972a: 107–8). This picture of Aristoxenus as a strong Pythagorean

---

[14] See Chapter 9 above.

partisan is further supported by his supposed malicious presentation of non-Pythagoreans such as Socrates and Plato (Kahn 2001: 70–1).[15]

Although this view of Aristoxenus is widespread, it is open to serious criticism. It emphasizes fr. 25, in which Aristoxenus denies that Pythagoras prohibited beans or practiced vegetarianism. It rejects other fragments and testimonia, however, because they contradict the picture of Aristoxenus as rationalizing Pythagoreanism. To evaluate Aristoxenus properly two principles need to be followed: (1) We should accept all material directly ascribed to him unless it involves obvious impossibility. (2) We should assign to Aristoxenus only what is directly ascribed to him or what is very tightly connected to what is directly ascribed to him. A number of passages have been assigned to Aristoxenus because they are in the general context of something directly attributed to him, even though it is common knowledge that many of our sources combine material from different sources in a mosaic fashion. Thus, all fragments and testimonia ascribed to Aristoxenus' works on the Pythagoreans by Wehrli (frs. 11–41 and 47–50) should be accepted, whereas some scholars have tried to exclude frs. 12–13 (Zhmud 2012b: 88–91). On the other hand, Wehrli in many cases includes too much of the surrounding material as belonging to Aristoxenus, when this is quite doubtful. Thus, only lines 3–4 of fr. 12, lines 1–6 of fr. 13, lines 9–10 of fr. 17, lines 5–41 of fr. 18, and lines 8–34 of fr. 31 are likely to reflect what Aristoxenus wrote.

Using this approach to the evidence, a different picture of Aristoxenus' account of Pythagoreanism emerges. He was not trying to remove all the non-rational aspects of Pythagoreanism or to distance himself from the *acusmatici*, who emphasized religious ritual and the way of life; he was rejecting radical ascetics such as Diodorus of Aspendus and the Pythagorists of Middle Comedy, who were unwashed and unkempt. He wanted to get rid of the image of Pythagoreans as "low-class tatterdemalions" (Burkert 1972a: 200). Aristoxenus was not alone in rejecting figures such as Diodorus of Aspendus (cf. Timaeus in Athenaeus 163e) and Lycon (DK 57A4) and was probably right to do so. His attempt to distinguish between true and false Pythagoreans may have led him to develop a list of genuine Pythagoreans. At the end of *On the Pythagorean Life*, Iamblichus gives a catalogue of Pythagoreans without citing his source, but Aristoxenus has long been recognized as the most likely candidate (Huffman 2008e: 297–9). Iamblichus' catalogue has undoubtedly been altered somewhat in transmission, but its core may go back to Aristoxenus' *On Pythagoras and*

---

[15] See n. 28 below.

his Associates (Zhmud 2012a: 241). The list excludes the radical ascetics, but it is not simply a list of *mathematici* such as Philolaus and Archytas either. The vast majority of the names appear nowhere else. It is thus likely that they were not figures who contributed to mathematics or cosmology but rather *acusmatici* who emphasized the way of life.

A series of texts emphasize the religious and mythic aspects of Pythagoreanism. These texts concern the master himself rather than later Pythagoreans, so that for Aristoxenus Pythagoras appears to have been a far more religious figure than his successors. First, Aristoxenus agreed with Aristotle and Theopompus in presenting Pythagoras as of Tyrrhenian stock, from one of the islands that the Athenians seized (fr. 11 = Diog. Laert. 8.1). The island in question is Lemnos, whose inhabitants "were called Tyrsenoi by the Greeks and thus identified with the Etruscans" and who were conquered by the Athenians in the late sixth century; it was precisely for religious mysteries dedicated to gods called the Kabeiroi that the Lemnians were known (Burkert 1985: 281). Thus, Aristoxenus subscribes to a story of Pythagoras' origin designed to show that from the beginning Pythagoras had access to secret religious knowledge (Wehrli 1967: 49). Second, Aristoxenus reports that Pythagoras' rebirths occurred at 216-year intervals (fr. 12), so that he clearly assigns the religious doctrine of metempsychosis to him.[16] Third, a series of three testimonia assign Pythagoras teachers whose view of the world has a strong religious and mythic component.

Pythagoras took most of his ethical teachings from Themistoclea, a priestess from Delphi (fr. 15 = Diog. Laert. 8.8). Wehrli argued that this was an attempt to rationalize the presentation of Pythagoras by replacing stories identifying him as the Hyperborean Apollo with the more mundane idea that he studied with a Delphic priestess (1967: 51). Yet, while some traditional wisdom, including aphorisms like "know thyself," is ascribed to Delphi, it above all gave advice on religious cult (*OCD* s.v. "Delphic Oracle"). Associating Pythagoras with the Delphic priestess thus surely suggests that his ethical views were based on religious authority and may explain the large amount of ritual material in the *acusmata*, such as the practices of sacrificing and entering the temple barefoot and not wearing rings with depictions of gods (Iambl. *VP* 84–5, probably from Aristotle). Aristoxenus (fr. 14 = Diog. Laert. 1.118) also reports that Pythagoras buried

---

[16] Fr. 12 explicitly cites Aristoxenus and four others as authorities for the 216-year cycle. The explanation of the cycle that follows is a compilation, in which it is impossible to distinguish Aristoxenus' contribution (Burkert 1972a: 139 n. 108). However, the mixed provenance of the explanation is insufficient grounds for rejecting the explicit report that Aristoxenus assigned the 216-year cycle to Pythagoras.

Pherecydes of Syros on the island of Delos, and this piety suggests that Pherecydes was one of his teachers. Certain aspects of Pherecydes' thought anticipate later rational cosmologies, but the most obvious points of contact are with Hesiod, and both Orphic and Near Eastern theogonies.[17] His theogony/cosmogony begins with the triad of Zeus, Chronos and Cthonie. The tie to Pherecydes thus suggests that, when it came to cosmology, Aristoxenus put Pythagoras in the company of Hesiod (as did Heraclitus in fr. 40) as more of an expert on the gods than a rational cosmologist. Finally, Aristoxenus reports that Pythagoras visited the Chaldaean Zaratas and learned from him a cosmology that began from a father principle and a mother principle (fr. 13).[18] This cosmology also appeals to some of the opposites typically used in Presocratic cosmologies such as the hot and the cold, but the focus is clearly on the initial male and female principle, so this is a cosmology that still bears the marks of basic principles that are persons and hence typical of myth. Thus, Aristoxenus' presentation of Pythagoras' birth and education, far from portraying him as "a stranger to all superstition and everything supernatural" (Lévy 1926: 44), emphasized his affinity for mystery religion (fr. 11), his expertise in religious ritual and the fate of the soul after death (frs. 15 and 12), and his penchant for cosmology of a mythic bent (frs. 13–14).

This emphasis on the religious dimension of Pythagoras' thought is not in conflict with fr. 25, which itself has previously unnoticed connections to religion. The goal of fr. 25 is not to rationalize Pythagoras but to set

---

[17] On Pherecydes, see Granger 2007.

[18] Zaratas is probably another name for Zoroaster. Zhmud (2012b: 88–90) rejects this fragment for four reasons none of which is compelling. First, he argues that it undercuts Aristoxenus' rationalization of Pythagoras, but this begs the question of whether Aristoxenus is, in fact, engaged in such rationalization. Second, he follows Zeller's (1919: 1.1.385 n. 1) argument that, since the second part of what Wehrli prints as fr. 13 mentions the prohibition on beans, the fragment cannot be by Aristoxenus, since he famously denies that Pythagoras had such a prohibition (fr. 25). However, Wehrli himself recognizes that what he prints as fr. 13 is a compilation of sources (1967: 51) and while material after line 6, including the prohibition on beans, does not go back to Aristoxenus, this in no way shows that the first six lines do not. Third, the standard dating for Zoroaster by Aristoxenus' contemporaries such as Aristotle (fr. 34 = Plin. *HN* 30.3) places him 6000 years before the time of Plato and hence Aristoxenus could hardly have thought that Pythagoras met him. However, disagreements about the dating of Zoroaster have been rife both in antiquity and in the modern world. Since Aristotle's dating seems to depend on a theory of cosmic cycles (Jaeger 1948: 133–5) rather than any documentary evidence, there is no impossibility in supposing that Aristoxenus disagreed with him. Until quite recently modern scholars have accepted a sixth-century date for Zoroaster, perhaps under the influence of Aristoxenus (Kingsley 1990). Fourth, Zhmud argues that, since elsewhere in Hippolytus, the source for fr. 13, the Platonic One and Indefinite Dyad, which the Neopythagoreans assigned to Pythagoras, are identified as father and mother, the presence of the father and mother here in fr. 13 indicates that it is a Neopythagorean forgery. However, the One and the Dyad are not mentioned in fr. 13. Burkert regards fr. 13 as authentic (2004: 115).

the record straight. There is, in fact, no unambiguous evidence ascribing the prohibition on beans to Pythagoras until the third century;[19] the
clear evidence for Empedocles' prohibition (fr. 141 DK – "Wretches, utter
wretches, keep your hands away from beans") may have been illegitimately
transferred to Pythagoras. Aristoxenus' frustrated attempt to clarify matters on the basis of his Pythagorean sources may explain his tendentious
addition that beans were, in fact, Pythagoras' favorite vegetable because
they "smooth" the bowels.[20] The same point also applies to vegetarianism.
The earliest and best evidence that we have for the Pythagorean way of life,
Aristotle and the *acusmata*, show that Pythagoras only forbade the eating
of certain types of meat. The Pythagoreans accepted animal sacrifice (as
is shown by the *acusma*: "What is most just? To sacrifice" – Iambl. *VP*
82) and probably reconciled it with metempsychosis on the assumption
that human souls did not enter animals that were to be sacrificed (Burkert
1972a: 181–2). Aristoxenus' further assertion that Pythagoras ate kids and
piglets is not more tendentiousness, but rather reflects religious scruples.
Suckling pigs and kids are the most important sacrificial animals in the
mysteries (Burkert 1972a: 182), and it may be that Pythagoras appealed to
a myth to justify this practice, since Ovid has his Pythagoras say that the
pig and the goat are justly sacrificed for crimes that they committed in
the golden age (*Met.* 15. 115). Aristoxenus also said that Pythagoras ate all
animals except plough oxen and rams (fr. 29a = Diog. Laert. 8.20). Thus,
Pythagoras banned eating these two animals, as well as certain parts of
other animals, such as the womb and heart (Aristotle fr. 194) but thought
that other types of animals could be eaten, if they had been accepted by the
gods in sacrifice.[21] Middle Comedy presents the Pythagorists as strict vegetarians but, as might be expected in comedy, these plays seize upon extreme
ascetics, whose Pythagorean credentials Aristoxenus calls into question.

Aristoxenus' focus in most other fragments is also on the Pythagorean
way of life. The Pythagoreans regularly ate bread and honey; those who
always ate it for lunch lived free from disease (fr. 27). The Pythagoreans
purified the body through medicine (undoubtedly medicine that emphasized correct diet) and the soul through music.[22] They were particularly
concerned about the proper way to correct bad behavior through admonitions, which they called "retunings," and emphasized never punishing
in anger. Archytas refused to discipline slaves who had mismanaged his

---

[19] See further Huffman 2012a.   [20] See further Huffman 2012a.
[21] See further Huffman 2012a.   [22] See Provenza 2012.

estate, because he had become angry (fr. 30).[23] They were remarkably loyal to their friends and did not give in to tears and lamentations. Phintias was accused by the tyrant of Syracuse, Dionysius I, of plotting against him and sentenced to death. Phintias calmly turned to setting his affairs in order and had his friend Damon take his place for the day. Neither Pythagorean shows any consternation at the situation; Damon willingly takes the place of Phintias and Phintias keeps his word and returns to face his fate (fr. 31). In *Laws of Education* (fr. 43), Aristoxenus recounted Xenophilus' advice that one's son will be best educated if he is born in a well-governed city; from the same work comes the dictum "not all things should be said to all people." This might refer to Pythagorean secrecy (Burkert 1972a: 179) but, given the work from which it comes, others more plausibly interpret it as advising a teacher not to teach the same things to children as to adults (Zhmud 2012a: 247–8).

Aristoxenus also connects Pythagoras to number. In fr. 23, he reports that Pythagoras "most of all valued the pursuit of number [τὴν δὲ περὶ τοὺς ἀριθμοὺς πραγματείαν] and brought it forward, taking it away from the use of traders." Some have assumed that by "valuing and bringing forward the pursuit of number" Aristoxenus means that Pythagoras "turned arithmetic into a theoretical science,"[24] but the passage suggests something different. A participial phrase explains the meaning: Pythagoras brought forward numbers by "likening all things to numbers." Aristoxenus says nothing about Pythagoras developing mathematical proofs or an elements of arithmetic; Pythagoras, finding all things susceptible to numerical analysis, took numbers away from traders and brought them forward to solve philosophical and other problems. Two fragments provide examples. First, the 216-year cycle for rebirths (fr. 12) demonstrates the role of number in metempsychosis. Second, the emphasis on number may explain the puzzling report in fr. 24 (Diog. Laert. 8.14) that Pythagoras first introduced measures and weights to the Greeks. Rather than turning Pythagoras into another Prometheus (Burkert 1972a: 415), Aristoxenus' words mean that Pythagoras was the first to introduce *standardized* weights and measures

---

[23] Chamaeleon, a generation younger than Aristoxenus, reported that the Pythagorean Cleinias, if he ever found himself becoming angry, would play the lyre. When asked why, he replied that he was "calming himself down" (fr. 4 = Ath. 623ff., cf. Ael. *VH* 14.23). Wehrli assigns this anecdote to his *Protrepticus*, so it may have been an example of the role of music in the good life. Chamaeleon may be drawing on Aristox. fr. 30.

[24] Zhmud 2006: 219; cf. 2012b: 261. In the *Elementa Harmonica* Aristoxenus does use πραγματεία to mean "science" in some passages but he more frequently uses it in the less formal sense of "study," "inquiry" or "pursuit." (See Barker 1989 for these translations.) In fr. 23 "science" cannot be what is meant because Pythagoras is said to take it away from the traders and it is implausible to suppose that they had a "science" of number.

to Croton. Croton became generalized to "the Greeks" in the course of transmission.

Although Aristoxenus presents the Pythagoreans in a uniformly positive light, he stopped far short of hagiography. The tone can be seen in the longest fragment, his account of the last days of Pythagoras and the Pythagoreans (fr. 18 = Iambl. *VP* 248–51). The blame for the uprisings against the Pythagoreans is placed squarely on Cylon, who persecuted the Pythagoreans, because Pythagoras refused to admit him to the society in light of his vicious character. However, Aristoxenus does not turn Pythagoras into a martyr or assign him a miraculous death. His report is startlingly bare: in the face of Cylon's persecution Pythagoras "withdrew to Metapontum and is said to have ended his life there." Similarly Aristoxenus praises the nobility of the Pythagoreans in dealing with the persecution and says that the last Pythagoreans "maintained their original customs and studies, although the school was failing, until preserving their nobility to the end, they disappeared." Nonetheless, he does not attempt to hide the failure of the society.

Aristoxenus' restraint can be instructively contrasted with a description of Pythagoras' activities, which has sometimes been mistakenly ascribed to him. Fr. 17 derives from Porphyry's *Life of Pythagoras* (21–2). In Chapter 20 Porphyry identifies his source as Nicomachus. Nicomachus' tone is hagiographical. He reports that by a single lecture Pythagoras won over more than 2000 men and that they and their families received "commandments from him as if they were divine covenants" (tr. Hadas). In Chapter 21 the extravagant praise continues. On his arrival in Italy he found the cities enslaved to one another and freed them all. The famous lawgivers Charondas and Zaleucus are presented as his pupils even though they lived long before Pythagoras.[25] Simicus abandons his tyranny immediately upon hearing Pythagoras. At this point in Porphyry's account appears the sentence "To Pythagoras there came, as Aristoxenus says, Lucanians and Messapians and Peuctians and Romans." The quotation of Aristoxenus is

---

[25] Frtiz (1940: 20) following Mewaldt (1904: 34) argued that the mention of Charondas and Zaleucus shows that Aristoxenus is already the source here, because the two lawgivers are also called pupils of Pythagoras in fr. 43 of Aristoxenus. However, the ascription of the report about Zaleucus and Charondas to Aristoxenus is just as suspect in fr. 43 as it is here in fr. 17. Chapters 15 and 16 of Diogenes Laertius in which fr. 43 appears are clearly a combination of several sources. Diogenes quotes from Aristoxenus' *Laws of Education* and the material from Aristoxenus is clearly marked by its form: two brief apothegms very much like "laws of education." The surrounding historical narrative, including the mention of Zaleucus and Charondas, comes from a different source.

limited to this single sentence,[26] following which Porphyry continues to quote Nicomachus, as is clear from the hagiographical tone: "He utterly destroyed discord, not only among his associates but also among their descendants for many generations and in general from all the cities in Italy and Sicily, both within the cities and between the cities." The incredible claim that Pythagoras removed all conflict from Italy and Sicily cannot come from Aristoxenus, since it contradicts his own account of the tumultuous last days of the Pythagoreans (fr. 18).[27] Thus, fr. 18 and Aristoxenus' other reports on the Pythagoreans have a positive tone that is probably due to a bias in favor of his Pythagorean friends, but Aristoxenus' account is not hagiography and is, on the whole, likely to be reliable.[28]

Stobaeus preserves seven fragments from *The Pythagorean Precepts* of Aristoxenus. Several of them match, word for word, passages in Iamblichus' *On the Pythagorean Life*, for which Iamblichus provides no source. Thus other passages in *On the Pythagorean Life* are also likely to come from *The Pythagorean Precepts*. Taken together the fragments from Stobaeus and Iamblichus provide more text than all of the other fragments of Aristoxenus' works on the Pythagoreans combined.[29] The *Precepts* record what "they" (i.e. the Pythagoreans as a group rather than Pythagoras himself) "say" or "think" on how human beings should live their lives. The obvious suggestion is that these precepts represent what Aristoxenus learned from the last of the Pythagoreans, including his teacher Xenophilus. They ought to provide invaluable evidence for the Pythagorean way of life in the fourth century. However, they have been neglected because many scholars think that, in order to glorify the Pythagoreans, Aristoxenus tampered with the evidence by incorporating Platonic and Aristotelian ethical views into them

[26] Burkert notes that Iamblichus quotes the whole passage without the sentence and that it is quoted by itself in both Iamblichus and Diogenes Laertius, which suggests that it circulated in compendia as a one line assertion that was of interest because of the mention of the Romans (1972a: 119 n. 60).

[27] Wehrli followed von Fritz in regarding all of Chapters 21 and 22 as from Aristoxenus because Aristoxenus elsewhere reported that Pythagoras fled the tyrant Polycrates, because he did not think it appropriate for a free man to endure despotism (fr. 16 = Porph. *VP* 9). Von Fritz (1940: 20) argues that this theme of Pythagoras as a "bringer of freedom" can be seen in Chapters 21 and 22. This similarity cannot, however, overcome the contradiction in tone and content between the presentation of Pythagoras in Chapters 21 and 22 and in Aristoxenus fr. 18. Von Fritz says that the contradiction is just "seeming," but his only attempt to remove it is to say that the assertions in Chapters 21 and 22 must be taken *cum grano salis*. This is in effect to say we should ignore the contradiction.

[28] Attacks on Aristoxenus as a source have been supported by reference to his supposed scurrilous attacks on Socrates and Plato, but recent scholarship suggests that here too Aristoxenus' account is more reliable than is usually supposed (Schorn 2012, Huffman 2012b, Dillon 2012).

[29] Besides frs. 34–7 and 39–41, which are preserved by Stobaeus, the following sections of Iamblichus' *On the Pythagorean Life* are likely to come from the *Precepts*: 101–2, 174–6 (fr. 33 W), 180–3, 200–13 (205–6 = fr. 38 W) and 230–3. See Burkert 1972a: 101 n. 17. I am currently at work on an edition of the *Precepts*.

(Rivaud 1932: 784; Wehrli 1967: 59; Burkert 1972a: 107–8; Zhmud 2012a: 234).

This standard view is unlikely to be true, however. The *Precepts* undoubtedly show similarities to the ideas of other philosophers, and in particular to Plato, but it is not the distinctive ideas that are claimed for the Pythagoreans (e.g., the tripartite soul or holding wives and children in common). Instead the similarities are all of a more general sort. The *Pythagorean Precepts* and Plato espouse moral views that arise from a shared conservative moral outlook that can be found in many other authors as well. Thus the *Precepts* assert that "there is no greater evil than anarchy" (fr. 35) and passages in Plato express a similar sentiment (*Leg.* 942d), but the exact same view is ascribed to Creon in the *Antigone* (672). The *Precepts* say that people should abide "by the customs and laws of their fathers even if they should be somewhat worse than those of others" (fr. 34) and Plato similarly emphasizes that stability can be more important than correctness (*Leg.* 634e), but even closer are the words of Cleon in Thucydides: "a city will be stronger if it employs worse laws that are fixed than good laws that have no authority" (3.37.3).[30] There is then no good reason to doubt that the *Precepts* are what they *prima facie* appear to be, the moral teachings of fourth-century Pythagoreans.[31]

The *Precepts* show that fourth-century Pythagoreanism maintained continuity with the *acusmata*; however, the heterogeneous combination of dietary restrictions and cultic taboos has been replaced with "the lineaments of a rational, clearly articulated ethic, oriented towards practical needs."[32] The *Precepts* are based on the principle that human beings are by nature *hubristic* (fr. 33). This is a development of the *acusma*: "What is said most truly? That human beings are wicked" (Iambl. *VP* 82). It follows that the greatest evil is indeed anarchy (fr. 35), the lack of anything to restrain this inherently evil human nature. Human nature is explored further through a definition of desire and an examination of its varieties

---

[30] Zhmud (2012a: 234) supports the traditional view by arguing that the *Precepts*' statement that education only reaches its goal if the student pursues the subject voluntarily and not under compulsion "unmistakably draws on Plato's socio-pedagogical principles." He quotes *Resp.* 536d–e "Nothing that is learned under compulsion stays with the mind." However, the issue of whether students should be forced to learn or not has been around as long as people have tried to educate the young; it is hardly a novel idea of Plato that compulsion does not lead to good results. The general idea is already present in Theognis: "everything compulsory is grievous" (472). Aristotle quotes this proverbial wisdom three times, although he ascribes it to the poet Evenus (*Metaph.* 1015a30, *Rhet.* 1370a10, *Eth. Eud.* 1223a31).

[31] For a full defense of authenticity see Huffman 2008b.

[32] Burkert 1972a: 107. Burkert regards this rational ethic as Aristoxenus' construction, but his description is still accurate even if it, in fact, belongs to the Pythagoreans themselves.

(fr. 37). The *Precepts* then sets out a series of constraints on human action beginning with a belief in the gods and followed by respect for parents and the laws. Appropriate rules are suggested for a number of aspects of human life including education and procreation, where what is precocious is to be avoided at all costs (fr. 39). The Pythagoreans promulgated a theory of luck to explain why it is that despite our best efforts we do not succeed, while others who make less effort are successful (fr. 41). The *Precepts* bring together a number of traditional ideas into a coherent whole based on a few central principles. The impact of fourth-century Pythagoreanism was seen not in innovations in ethical theory but in the lives of individual Pythagoreans, who followed the *Precepts* and to whom Plato refers in the *Republic* (600b).

6. Conclusion

The conflict between Dicaearchus' and Aristoxenus' presentation of Pythagoras shows that there was no single interpretation of Pythagoreanism among Aristotle's successors in the Peripatos. Certainly Theophrastus, Eudemus and Meno reveal that Pythagoreans, if not Pythagoras himself, made important contributions to a wide range of sciences, although they did not play the decisive or foundational role assigned to Pythagoreanism in the later tradition. Since Aristoxenus had clear ties to the last generation of Pythagoreans, there has been some tendency to accept Dicaearchus' version of Pythagoreanism as a less biased view. However, the savageness of Dicaearchus' satire of Pythagoras has not often been fully appreciated, while Aristoxenus' bias has been overstated. Certainty is impossible, but Aristoxenus' account, although idealized, is better informed and probably comes closer to the truth than what is found in Dicaearchus.

CHAPTER 14

Pythagoras in the historical tradition: from Herodotus to Diodorus Siculus

Stefan Schorn

1. Introduction

Taking a look at the preserved works of classical historiography, which for the most part focus on political and military history, we get the impression that Pythagoras and Pythagoreanism were of rather marginal interest to historians.[1] The picture changes considerably when we take into account works that are preserved in fragments and, at the same time, apply a broader concept of historiography by including, among others, biography, universal history, local history and doxography (i.e. history of philosophy).[2] Then the following picture emerges: Pythagoras, the Pythagorean way of life and the history of the Pythagorean communities played a prominent role in biographies from the fourth century BC onwards, when the first work titled *Life* was written by Aristoxenus. Furthermore, Pythagorean politics in southern Italy and even the life of Pythagoras seem to have been a regular topic of universal history. The earliest examples of this genre from which fragments of this sort have been preserved are excerpts from Book 10 of Diodorus' *Library* and Justin's epitome of Pompeius Trogus' *Philippic History* (20.4), which both contain important chapters on Pythagoras' life and work in Magna Graecia. We may suppose the existence of such chapters in many other works of this type, for example in Ephorus' *Histories*, although no such fragments have been preserved.[3] Even more information

This contribution is a result of the research project "Hellenistic Biography: Antiquarian Literature, Gossip or Historiography? Fragmente der Griechischen Historiker Continued. Part IV," financed by Onderzoeksfonds KU Leuven. I would also like to thank Gertrud Dietze and Carl Huffman for checking my English.

[1] There are good recent chapters on the historiographical tradition of Pythagoras and Pythagoreanism to which the following sketch owes a lot: Burkert 1972a: 97–109; Muccioli 2002 (the most comprehensive modern account); Zhmud 2012b: 9–77.

[2] On the necessity of applying a broad concept of historiography when dealing with Pythagoreanism, see Muccioli 2002: 341.

[3] Cf. Burkert 1972a: 105.

must have been contained in local histories and histories of the Greek west, all preserved in only fragmentary state or completely lost. We can conclude this on the basis of the fragments of Timaeus' *Histories* that deal with Pythagoras and his students. It is likely that in the works of Antiochus and Philistus of Syracuse among others this topic was treated as well, although we do not have a single fragment.[4] Even in mythography Pythagoras was mentioned as is shown by Neanthes' *Collection of Myths* and maybe also in cultural history, if Dicaearchus' fragments on Pythagoras stem from his *Life of Greece*.

It was also the fourth century BC that saw the first works of doxography. Pythagorean doctrine found its way into the general works of doxography, but as early as Aristotle we also encounter monographs on Pythagorean doctrine. Doxographical information was also transmitted by biographies and, to a smaller extent, historiography. Doxographical sections, rarely attested in biographies of other philosophers, seem to have been frequent, already in Hellenistic times, in those of Pythagoras, and probably most accounts of the successions of philosophers (*Diadochai*), which all contained a section on Pythagoras as the founder of the "Italian line," were bio-doxographical.[5]

In addition, Pythagoras and his (real and alleged) students were topics of philosophical fiction (e.g., Heraclides Ponticus' *On the Woman Not Breathing*; Aeschines' *Telauges*) and rhetoric (e.g., Isocrates' *Busiris*). These works were later used by historians and biographers. Finally the chronographical literature deserves to be mentioned (Eratosthenes, Apollodorus of Athens), where information on Pythagoras and other philosophers was regularly included because its authors usually had a concept of history that included literature and philosophy as well.[6]

There was communication and exchange between all these and many other literary genres. Thus, although in the following I limit myself, for practical reasons, to historiography in a stricter sense, this does not mean that these works form a distinct group, clearly separable from others, with characteristics of its own.

---

[4] Cf. Burkert 1972a: 105; Muccioli 2002: 396. Lycus of Rhegium (*FGrHist* 570F15), the author of *On Sicily* (fourth to third centuries BC), may have dealt with Pythagoras' origin but in the fragment in question the historian's name is the result of conjecture; Jacoby *ad loc.* is skeptical whereas Muccioli 2002: 393 accepts it.

[5] I try to show this in Schorn 2013; see, e.g., Alex. Polyh. fr. 9 Giannattasio Andria.

[6] Eratosth. *FGrHist* 241F11 with Geus 2002: 327–8; Apollod. *FGrHist* 244F339 with Jacoby *ad loc.* and Jacoby 1902: 215–27.

2. Herodotus

The earliest historian who mentions Pythagoras is Herodotus, who refers to him and Pythagorean doctrine in two problematic passages.[7] In addition, there are other passages where he may allude to them. In his report on Egyptian customs in Book 2, he mentions the Egyptians' use of linen garments to which he adds (2.81.1–2):

> When they enter sanctuaries or when they are buried, however, they never wear wool, for to do so would offend their religious sensibility. (2) This agrees with the ritual practices called Orphic and Bacchic, which are in reality Egyptian and Pythagorean [ὁμολογέει (*codd. DTRSV*, ὁμολογέουσι *codd. PM*) δὲ ταῦτα τοῖσι Ὀρφικοῖσι καλεομένοισι καὶ Βακχικοῖσι, ἐοῦσι δὲ Αἰγυπτίοισι καὶ Πυθαγορείοισι], for the participants in these rites also find it religiously offensive to be buried in woolen garments, and there is a sacred story concerning this. (tr. Purvis, modified)[8]

One group of manuscripts transmits a short version of the first sentence of § 2: "They agree in this with the so-called Orphics and Pythagoreans, for the participants . . . " (ὁμολογέουσι δὲ ταῦτα τοῖσι Ὀρφικοῖσι καλεομένοισι καὶ Πυθαγορείοισι [*codd. ABC*]).[9] Although no definite decision is possible, the arguments for the long version, accepted by most scholars, seem to be stronger.[10]

Thus Herodotus believes that the Bacchic and Orphic rites have been imported from Egypt. In addition the equation of Pythagorean with Egyptian shows that he thought Pythagoras to have brought this knowledge from Egypt. He therefore must have known the tradition, attested from Isocrates on (*Bus.* 28), of the philosopher's trip to Egypt.[11] Further, for Herodotus Bacchic rites and Orphism are identical with or based on Pythagorean doctrine. Whether Pythagoreanism did, in fact, exert a strong influence

---

[7] This chapter is much indebted to Burkert 1972a: 123–33; 155–61; Riedweg 2007: 76–9.

[8] Here and in the following I am drawing freely on Purvis' translation of Herodotus.

[9] For the transmission of the text see Rosén's Teubner edition (1987); cf. Bernabé 2005: 219 = *PEG* T650.

[10] See Burkert 1972a: 127–8; cf. Dodds 1951: 169 n. 80; cf. Graf 1974: 92–3 n. 60; Makarov 1999 (*non vidi*); Riedweg 2007: 77; Bernabé and Hernández Muñoz 2010: 85–6. The long version with ὁμολογέουσι appears in the editions of Hude ³1927; Rosén 1987; the long version with ὁμολογέει in: Giangiulio 2000: Vol. 1, 7 = T9; Bernabé 2005: 219 = *PEG* T650; cf. also Riedweg 2007: 77; the fullest collection of literature is in Bernabé 2005: 219 note to T650. For the short version see Zhmud 2012b: 224–6; cf. Wilamowitz 1931–1932: Vol. 2, 189 n. 1; Rathmann 1933: 52–5; Linforth 1941: 38–50; Casadio 1991: 128–9 n. 23; Casadesús 1994.

[11] Thus e.g. Burkert 1972a: 128; Riedweg 2007: 77; Graf and Johnston 2007: 159; differently Zhmud 2012b: 224 n. 77.

on Bacchic rites and Orphism remains controversial.[12] What is sure is that there was doctrinal overlap (belief in life after death or metempsychosis) and both Orphics and Pythagoreans led an ascetic life (the first as full, the latter as full or partial vegetarians) and abstained from beans. Herodotus must also have noticed this overlap. According to Ion of Chios Pythagoras published poems under the name of Orpheus.[13] This may reflect the same tradition that we find in Herodotus.[14]

Unlike most modern scholars, Herodotus also believes in a strong Egyptian influence on Pythagoras. Apart from the text under discussion, this can be seen in two other passages where Pythagoras' name does not appear. First, Herodotus claims that the Egyptians believed in metempsychosis and that their priests were not allowed to eat beans.[15] This is wrong, but has been correctly explained as a projection of Pythagorean practice onto Egypt.[16] Herodotus must have believed that Pythagoras had found all his doctrines in Egypt and had this view confirmed by Egyptians or Greeks who lived in Egypt by asking leading questions until he got his prejudices confirmed, as he often did. The ban on woolen clothes in Bacchic rites and Orphism and Pythagoreanism in our passage is in all likelihood connected with metempsychosis.[17] It was a small step to conclude from the same custom in Egypt to the same belief. Second, in 2.123.3 he adds to his discussion of Egyptian metempsychosis that "there are certain Hellenes – some who lived earlier, some later – who have adopted this theory as though it were their own; I know their names but shall not write them down" (tr. Purvis). The "earlier Greeks" are most likely to be Pythagoras and his followers, the later ones Empedocles and others.[18] Herodotus thus seems to have started from some real similarities between Egyptian and Pythagorean customs. Since, as a basic principle, he regarded Egypt as a major source of Greek religious beliefs and cults, priority had to be given to the land on the Nile.[19] In combination with the assumption that Pythagoras travelled to Egypt and that he was the author of some Orphic poems he developed the theory of

---

[12] See Chapter 1, section 3 and Chapter 7, section 1 above.   [13] DK 36B2 = fr. 116 Leurini.
[14] Cf. Burkert 1972a: 129–30; Riedweg 2007: 77; Graf and Johnston 2007: 159; West 1983: 7–15.
[15] Hdt. 2.123.2–3, 2.37.
[16] Cf. e.g., Burkert 1972a: 126, 128, 158; Riedweg 2007: 77. On the genesis of the misunderstanding, see Lloyd 1975–1988: Vol. 1.57–8, Vol. 3.59–60.
[17] Cf. e.g., Zhmud 2012b: 234.
[18] Thus Riedweg 2007: 77; Lloyd and Fraschetti 1999: 343; cautious Burkert 1972a: 126 with n. 38; differently Casertano 2000: 204–5.
[19] On Egypt as the main source of Greek religion in Herodotus see, e.g., Harrison 2000: 182–207.

dependence that we can read in 2.81 and "found" more similarities by leading questions.[20]

It is noticeable that in 2.81 there is no criticism of Pythagoras and in 2.123.3 he leaves the Greeks he accuses of plagiarism unnamed. Both of these features are best explained by the fact that, when writing, Herodotus was living in Thurii where many influential Pythagoreans resided, whom he did not want to offend.[21]

In the last section to be discussed here, Pythagoras himself is mentioned, and the context is again life after death (4.94–6). In connection with the conquest of the land of the Getae, Herodotus describes their belief in immortality: They assume that after death they come to the *daimōn* Salmoxis. But Herodotus has also heard a different story from the Greeks living at the Hellespont and the Pontus. Salmoxis, they claim, had actually been the slave of Pythagoras on Samos. After being manumitted he became rich and returned to his home country. As the Getae were poor and simple-minded whereas Salmoxis was familiar with Ionian lifestyle and more sophisticated manners through his commerce with the Greeks and Pythagoras, "who was not the worst wise man [σοφιστής] among the Greeks," he built a banqueting hall where he entertained the élite of the country. "He taught them that neither he nor they, his drinking companions, nor their descendants would die, but that they would come to a place where they would live on and have all good things" (tr. Purvis). At the same time he constructed an underground room where he hid away at a certain moment. Considered dead by his comrades, he came back after three years, which made them believe in his teachings. Herodotus though is skeptical about this story and does not want to decide if Salmoxis was a man or a local *daimōn*. "However," he adds, "this Salmoxis lived many years before Pythagoras."

Things are complicated by the fact that Hermippus (third century BC; *FGrHist* 1026F24) tells a very similar story about the way Pythagoras deceived the Crotoniates. The connection between the two stories has been explained in different ways.[22] One group of scholars holds that Hermippus has transferred Herodotus' story about Salmoxis to his teacher

---

[20] Cf. Mora 1986: 111–17. If, however, the short version is correct, Herodotus does not attest dependency of Orphism and Bacchic rites on Pythagoras nor essential influence of Egyptian customs on them but only agreement on one single custom.

[21] See, e.g., Burkert 1972a: 126; Riedweg 2007: 78.

[22] Important recent interpretations are by Burkert 1972a: 155–61; Gottschalk 1980: 117–18; Hartog 1980: 102–25; Bollansée 1999a: 263–76 (on *FGrHist* 1026F24); Riedweg 2007: 78–9; Taufer 2008: esp. 132–4, 144–6; Zhmud 2012b: 41–3; cf. Corcella, Medaglia and Fraschetti 1999: 307.

Pythagoras.[23] This view was contradicted by Burkert, who showed that Hermippus' story presupposes a story of a "real" descent (*katabasis*) to Hades with Pythagoras as a protagonist, which is parodied by Hermippus.[24] Independent sources show that Salmoxism was a mystery cult restricted to the nobles that promised a happy life after death.[25] The status of its founder alternates in the sources between god and human, and a cave on a mountain as his abode seems to have played an important role.[26] The obvious similarities with Pythagoreanism explain why the Greeks made Salmoxis the apprentice of Pythagoras.

So what did the northern Greeks think of Pythagoras? In any case, he was obviously well known to them.[27] Did they consider him an imposter too? This is possible,[28] since public opinion about secret societies to which the majority does not belong is usually negative. But they may also have claimed that Pythagoras was really able to perform descents to Hades (*katabaseis*), whereas his pupil only pretended to do so and perverted Pythagoras' doctrine. In addition, Pythagoras is called here one of the foremost σοφισταί (wise men), a word that has positive connotations in the two other passages where Herodotus uses it. However, this characterization may have been an addition of Herodotus to the story and not part of the story his informants told.[29] So Herodotus does not make clear the attitude of the northern Greeks to Pythagoras.

What about Herodotus' own attitude? His opinion of the Salmoxis cult seems to have been negative.[30] Why does he report gossip that he considers chronologically improbable? His motivation to do so may have been the striking fact that here, too, Pythagoras was presented as the spiritual father of a mystery cult – just as in the case of Orphism and Bacchic rites according to Herodotus' own theory. Does he want to cast a negative light on him by linking him to Salmoxis? Many interpreters do indeed think so,[31] but the use of the word *sophistes* seems to speak against it. On the other hand, he

---

[23] Corssen 1912a: 22–5 and other scholars listed by Bollansée 1999a: 265 n. 104; Zhmud 2012b: 218 n. 51.

[24] Burkert 1972a: 155–61; cf. Riedweg 2007: 79. In later tradition we read of meetings of Pythagoras and his disciples in subterranean chambers on Samos; see Burkert 1972a: 155 n. 197; Bollansée 1999a: 268 n. 118.

[25] For the following see Taufer 2008. He postulates for Salmoxis also a "real" *katabasis*, as does Gottschalk 1980: 118. Possibly the Salmoxians also practiced vegetarianism (see Taufer 2008: 135, 155); differently Marcaccini 1998.

[26] See esp. Bollansée 1999a: 270–1.

[27] Cf. Burkert 1972a: 158; Riedweg 2007: 79; Zhmud 2012b: 195 n. 104.

[28] Soph. *El.* 62–4 seems to allude to such an allegation; see Burkert 1972a: 161; Riedweg 2007: 79.

[29] This is Zhmud's (2012b: 42) view.   [30] Cf. Harrison 2000: 166–8, 216–17.

[31] E.g., Bichler 2000: 91–3; Riedweg 2007: 79.

seems to consider Pythagoras a plagiarist. So the evidence is ambiguous. Obviously Herodotus does not want the reader to make out his opinion. It seems as though he does not dare to express his repudiation.

3.   The fourth and early third centuries

The fourth century saw a remarkable output of works on the life and teachings of Pythagoras and the history of the Pythagorean communities. Authors of that period were the last who were able to gather authentic historical information among the last Pythagoreans or the inhabitants of areas where oral traditions survived.[32] Early historiographical works on the Pythagoreans were often written by philosophers who had various thematic focuses.[33] The Academics Xenocrates and Speusippus wrote works on Pythagorean philosophy[34] as did Aristotle with his *On the Pythagoreans*, which also dealt with biographical and historical aspects.[35] It is remarkable that he presents Pythagoras as a wonder-worker. This tendency is also strong in the works of Heraclides Ponticus. He too, wrote *On the Pythagoreans*, and Pythagoras played a role in his philosophical dialogue *On the Woman Not Breathing* and probably in *Abaris*.[36] In the latter two works Pythagoras seems to have been part of a literary fiction. For all aspects of Pythagoreanism, the various works of Aristoxenus (*Life of Pythagoras*, *On Pythagoras and His Followers*, *On the Pythagorean Way of Life*, *Pythagorean Sayings*) and the fragments of Dicaearchus (no title transmitted, maybe from *Life of Greece* or *On Lives*) are of special importance. They show a much soberer picture of Pythagoras than Aristotle and Heraclides and focus on his political activity. Both authors used oral traditions, Aristoxenus the reports of a certain group of Pythagoreans, Dicaearchus those of a different group of Pythagoreans and/or non-Pythagoreans living in southern Italy.[37]

At the same time historians discovered the Pythagoreans. In the first half of the century, Anaximander of Miletus (the Younger) wrote an *Interpretation of Pythagorean Symbola* (*FGrHist* 9T1), of which nothing is preserved. To the same period belongs Andron of Ephesus' *Tripod*, a

---

[32] Cf. Zhmud 2012a: 228–9.
[33] For the following see esp. Muccioli 2002: 342–92 to whom I am deeply indebted; cf. von Fritz 1963: 172–9; Zhmud 2012b: 61–70.
[34] Speusippus fr. 28 Tarán = 122 Isnardi Parente; Xenocrates fr. 2 [13] Isnardi Parente.
[35] Fr. 190–205 Rose; on this work see Muccioli 2002: 372–3 and Chapter 11 above.
[36] Fr. 84–6, 149 etc. Schütrumpf; on this author, see Muccioli 2002: 371–2.
[37] Cf. von Fritz 1963: 173–9; Vattuone 1991: 217–31; Muccioli 2002: 373–92; Zhmud 2012b: 63–7; 2012a; Chapter 13 in this volume.

biographical or anecdotal work.[38] In one fragment he discusses the identity of Pythagoras' teacher Pherecydes (*FGrHist* 1005F4; assigned), another (fr. 3) shows that he had talked about Pythagoras' prophecies. It is interesting to see that the thread of tradition that emphasizes the miraculous side of Pythagoras was not limited to the works of philosophers. Theopompus of Chios deserves special attention. He wrote about Pythagoras in Book 8 of his *Philippica*, which contained a long digression on marvels.[39] Porphyry claims that he transferred the wonder stories told by Andron about Pythagoras to Pherecydes (*FGrHist* 115F70 = Andron, *FGrHist* 1005F3). In another fragment he calls Pythagoras an Etruscan (fr. 72), as does Aristoxenus (fr. 11a Wehrli), and in still another he associates Pythagorean doctrine with aiming at tyranny (fr. 73). This all suggests an account of a certain length. Unlike most of the above authors, who were in various degrees favorable to Pythagoras, with Theopompus we encounter an early authority, who represents the tradition hostile to the philosopher, to which authors like Aristoxenus and Dicaearchus seem to have responded.

Aristotle, Aristoxenus, Dicaearchus and Heraclides are usually regarded as the most important sources for the study of Pythagoreanism, together with Timaeus who wrote some years later. But the latter is, in Burkert's words, "the greatest unknown" and thus deserves special attention.[40]

4. Timaeus

In his *(Sicilian) Histories*, Timaeus of Tauromenium (*c.* 360/350 – after 260) described the history of the Greek west from mythical times until the death of Agathocles (289/288) in at least thirty-eight books.[41] Modern scholars have called him the "Herodotus of the West," because he did not limit himself to political-military history but was also interested in geography, mythology, cultural history and other aspects of life.[42] This explains why there was a long digression on the Pythagoreans in (part of?)

[38] On Andron, see Bollansée on *FGrHist* 1005; Muccioli 2002: 369.
[39] On this section and Pythagoras within it, see Shrimpton 1991: 15, 17–18; Burkert 1972a: 17–18; cf. Muccioli 2002: 369–70.
[40] Cf. Burkert 1972a: 103. Note also his evaluation of the sources.
[41] For Timaeus Jacoby's commentary on *FGrHist* 566 is still fundamental; important contributions are Brown 1958; Pearson 1987; Vattuone 1991 and 2002; good introductions in Meister 1990: 131–7; Lendle 1992: 211–18.
[42] "Herodotus of the West," in Murray 1972: 210; cf. Meister 1990: 135; Marincola 2001: 109; Baron 2009: 24–5.

Books 9–10 of his work. We do not have enough fragments of these books to define precisely the period treated there, but they seem to have covered the late sixth to early fifth centuries, the period that comprised the lifetime of Pythagoras and the heyday of Pythagorean influence in southern Italy. The importance of the movement and Timaeus' notorious local patriotism may explain its length.[43] Only a few fragments on Pythagoras survive, but some more on Empedocles are preserved, which may help reconstruct Timaeus' picture of Pythagoreanism, since he regarded Empedocles as a direct disciple of Pythagoras.[44]

FGrHist 566F13 (from Book 9) describes the origin of the Pythagorean community and the rules of admission to it.[45] The young men who wanted to live together with Pythagoras were obliged to practice community of goods.[46] In addition, they had to keep silence for five years, listening to the words of the master without seeing him, and were only admitted to his presence after an examination. Timaeus seems to present this sympathetically as proof of the seriousness of Pythagorean education. Fr. 14 (from Book 9) also is related to the strict rules of admission and the exclusiveness of Pythagorean knowledge. It reports that Empedocles was a disciple of Pythagoras (on the chronological implications see below), but was excluded from the community on account of λογοκλοπία ("stealing of words or thoughts"), as was Plato.[47] In addition, Empedocles is said to have praised Pythagoras in some of his verses (which are quoted). It is usually assumed that Timaeus disapproved of Empedocles' behavior. However, the other fragments show an encomiastic depiction of this man who, in Timaeus' *Histories*, appears as a champion of democracy.[48] To be sure, even if the general evaluation was positive, he could have critiqued individual acts,[49] but stealing and publishing Pythagoras' doctrine is a serious offense. So I wouldn't exclude the possibility that Timaeus interpreted the deed as a democratization of knowledge. This would at the same time imply reservations concerning the elitist character of Pythagoras' esoteric doctrine. At

[43] Cf. Jacoby on *FGrHist* 566F13–17 (Vol. IIIB Commentary [Text] 550–2) *pace* Vattuone 1991: 114.

[44] The reason for this imbalance is that Timaeus is only used twice for additional information in Diogenes Laertius' *Life of Pythagoras*, while he is one of the main sources in his *Life of Empedocles*; cf. Centrone 1992: 4186–7.

[45] Cf. Vattuone 1991: 213–14. I do not accept all parts of Vattuone's interpretation of this fragment.

[46] Here and in the following I am drawing freely on Hicks' translation of Diogenes Laertius.

[47] For the reference to Plato as part of the Timaeus fragment, see, e.g., Vattuone 1991: 215 n. 30. Jacoby on fr. 14 remains doubtful.

[48] Fr. 2, 134, cf. 132; cf. Vattuone 1991: 117–19.

[49] That is Vattuone's (1991: 117 n. 97, 215) explanation of the inconsistency; cf. Jacoby, *FGrHist* IIIB Kommentar (Noten) 326 n. 197.

any rate, Timaeus is, after Aristotle, the earliest testimony to the secrecy of part of the Pythagorean doctrine and to the existence of two different groups of Pythagoreans.[50] In general, however, the fragments point to a positive attitude towards Pythagoras without a special bias.[51] This is shown by the verses of Empedocles that Timaeus quotes (DK 31B129), and by the fact that he seems to have defended Pythagoras against Heraclitus' allegation of being the inventor of rhetorical tricks (fr. 132; no book number). Text and context of the latter fragment are uncertain,[52] but the statement may be part of a defense of Pythagoras against the accusation of aiming at tyranny (see above on Theopompus).[53] The names of four goddesses given by Pythagoras to women according to age (fr. 17 from Book 10) may come from the same context as the parallel report in Iamblichus (*VP* 56) where it is part of Pythagoras' speech to the women of Croton that made them more pious and less attracted to luxurious clothes. If this contextualization is correct, Timaeus also knew of a third (and lowest) stage of instruction by Pythagoras, the one open to everyone.

Fr. 131 (no book number) reporting the honors paid to Pythagoras' daughter and the philosopher himself shows that he was highly esteemed in Croton for a long time. But according to fr. 44 (cf. 45; no book numbers), Croton fell victim to luxury after the victory over Sybaris (510). This must have happened before the anti-Pythagorean revolution, which shows that Timaeus cannot have spoken of a Pythagorean dominance in politics and customs during a long period of Crotonian history. I would not exclude the possibility that there were also critical remarks on the Pythagoreans and on Pythagoras himself concerning the later years of his stay in Croton. If Iamblichus *VP* 254–64 goes back to Timaeus, the relationship between Pythagoreans and Crotoniates deteriorated in the course of time due to an increasing exclusivity of the brotherhood, which an author like Timaeus may have assessed critically. Timaeus' excursus went far beyond the lifetime of Pythagoras himself. In fr. 16 (Book 9) he pokes fun at Diodorus of Aspendos, a cynicizing Pythagorist of his own time, and denies his having

---

[50] See Burkert 1972a: 192, 179 n. 96, 454; Pearson 1987: 114; cf. Vattuone 1991: 215 with n. 28. Whether Timaeus regarded Empedocles a novice or a full member at the time of his exclusion is not clear.

[51] Cf. Burkert 1972a: 104; Vattuone 1991: 210–27; Muccioli 2002: 397; Zhmud 2012b: 69; but Pearson 1987: 116 remains reserved. At any rate the picture was not encomiastic: see Jacoby on fr. 13–17 (*FGrHist* IIIB Kommentar [Text] 550–1). I do not follow Vattuone (1991: 112–21, 210–27) who assigns to Pythagoras a crucial role within the historiographical concept of Timaeus as embodiment of a "wisdom of the West" nor can I detect any influence of Empedocles' concept of love and strife on Timaeus' philosophy of history.

[52] See Jacoby on fr. 132; Vattuone 1991: 216. [53] Cf. Vattuone 1991: 216, cf. 210–13; 2002: 211.

been a student of Pythagoreans. This critique may also be significant for Timaeus' conception of Pythagoreanism.[54]

In these fragments Timaeus shows no interest in Pythagorean philosophy that goes beyond the general ethical advice given to all citizens,[55] but he may have dealt with it if he described Pythagoras' teaching to his students (cf. fr. 9),[56] and it is often stressed that they are free from miraculous traits.[57] But both characteristics may be accidental. We should not forget that Timaeus did not refrain from ascribing to Empedocles a ritual that can be characterized as "shamanistic" (fr. 30 from Book 18).[58]

We do not know much about Timaeus' sources.[59] He was famous for his zeal for collecting books, but he was surely not the armchair scholar Polybius wants us to believe he was. Generally he also made use of documents and oral sources. If he ever returned to Italy from exile, he may have collected local traditions there, and if the Echecrates (fr. 12 [10, 7–8]), whom in another context he once refers to as his source, is the Pythagorean from Locri or his descendant, he may have been his informant on the Pythagoreans as well.[60] In fr. 6 he polemicizes against Heraclides Ponticus' version of Empedocles' death (fr. 94 Schütrumpf). Thus it does not seem hazardous to assume that he was familiar with all written sources on Pythagoras available in Athens, had knowledge of oral traditions from his time in Italy and perhaps consulted informants from this region.

Many scholars have attempted – in vain – to reconstruct Timaeus' full account of Pythagoras by means of *Quellenforschung* (source criticism). Nevertheless there are some passages in the preserved texts where it is reasonable to assume the use of Timaeus. Yet a caveat is needed: in none of them are we likely to have pure Timaeus. These texts may include material from other sources and their authors have surely reworked what they found in Timaeus.[61] These texts are:[62] (1) Justin 20.4. This is an excursus

54 On the range of the excursus, see Jacoby on fr. 13–17 (*FGrHist* IIIB Kommentar [Noten] 551); on the fragment as a source of Timaeus' concept of Pythagoreanism, see Riedweg 2007: 139; cf. Burkert 1972a: 202–4.
55 Cf. Brown 1958: 50; Pearson 1987: 42; somewhat differently Muccioli 2002: 397.
56 I owe this suggestion to Carl Huffman.   57 Thus, e.g., Lévy 1926: 59; Zhmud 2012b: 69.
58 Differently Vattuone 1991: 120; cf. 2002: 210. On the shamanistic character, see Burkert 1972a: 154.
59 On his possible sources, see Jacoby on fr. 13–17 (*FGrHist* IIIB Kommentar [Text] 552); Pearson 1987: 48; Muccioli 2002: 347–8, 396; Vattuone 1991: 213 n. 23.
60 Thus Jacoby, *FGrHist* IIIB Kommentar (Noten) 316 n. 66; Brown 1958: 49–50; Muccioli 2002: 396. Pearson 1987: 100–1 remains skeptical.
61 Cf. e.g., Jacoby on fr. 13–17 (*FGrHist* IIIB [Text] 551 with IIIB [Noten] 325–6 n. 193); Pearson 1987: 113.
62 For arguments, see Burkert 1972a: 104–5 n. 35–7; Radicke 1999: 148–54; Muccioli 2002: 397–8; Zhmud 2012b: 69–70 n. 35 (with literature and other passages).

on Pythagoras and is the most important text. It includes his travels, arrival at Croton, three speeches, the revolt, his departure to Metapontum and death; (2) Iambl. *VP* 37–57. This includes his three speeches. The intermediate source is Apollonius;[63] (3) Iambl. *VP* 71–2 discuss criteria for admission; (4) Iambl. *VP* 254–64 describe the revolution. The intermediate source is Apollonius (*FGrHist* 1064F2); (5) On Polybius and Strabo see below.

Much ink has been spilt over the reconstruction of Timaeus' chronology. Scholars are probably right in assuming that it was superior to that of many other authors of the fourth century, as Timaeus was renowned for his interest in chronology[64] and dealing with Pythagoreanism in the context of a general history of the west, which means that he had to take historical reality more into account than biographers and philosophers.[65] Unfortunately, the only chronological indication found in the named fragments is that Pythagoras was the direct teacher of Empedocles. The latter's birth was generally dated to the beginning years of the fifth century,[66] so that we can assume that Timaeus must have had a late chronology of Pythagoras, unlike, e.g., Eratosthenes, because in his account the philosopher must have died after 480. All other elements of his chronology are doubtful. Everything depends on which anonymous texts one is willing to assign to Timaeus.[67]

5. Neanthes of Cyzicus[68]

Neanthes of Cyzicus, a historian who lived ca. 360/350 – after 274, is known to have written works titled *On Famous Men*, *Collection of Myths According to Cities*, *Hellenica*, *On Mysteries* and *Yearbooks* (of Cyzicus?). Like his contemporary Timaeus, he studied in Athens under the Isocratean Philiscus of Miletus so that the two historians may have known each other. The fragments show that he wrote biographies of Pythagoras and Empedocles, whom, like Timaeus, he regarded as a Pythagorean (*FGrHist* 84F26,

---

[63] Usually identified with Apollonius of Tyana; see J. Radicke on *FGrHist* 1064; differently Staab 2007: Apollonius Molon. See Chapter 16 in this volume.

[64] This is even admitted by his enemy Polybius (12.11.1 = *FGrHist* 566T10); cf. Diod. Sic. 5.1.3 = T11; on Timaeus' attention to chronology, see Pearson 1987: 44–8; Vattuone 2002: 223–4.

[65] Cf. von Fritz 1963: 177, 180; Brown 1958: 127 n. 30; Vattuone 1991: 212.

[66] Cf. Schorn 2007: 129 with references.

[67] For various interpretations, see von Fritz 1940: 33–67; 1963: 179–85 (with literature); Pearson 1987: 114–15; Burkert 1972a: 111 n. 7; cf. Jacoby, *FGrHist* IIIB (Noten), 326 n. 198.

[68] In this section I am summarizing part of Schorn 2007 with a few corrections and additions. A different picture of Neanthes is found in Zhmud 2012b: 67–8.

28). As fr. 29a shows, the biography of Pythagoras (and thus probably of Empedocles) was part of *Collection of Myths According to Cities*, not of *On Famous Men*, as one might suppose,[69] and there is no reason to doubt the transmitted text. He may have written about them in *On Famous Men* too, but there is no evidence for that.[70]

I once characterized his biographical approach as historical or periegetical. Unlike many other biographers he was not a philosopher but a historian who travelled the Greek world in order to gather information for his various historiographical works. Many of his stories are, as a consequence, local oral traditions related to buildings and places where persons he writes about had lived. Some fragments show that Neanthes mentioned the names of his local informants. Furthermore, he extensively read and quoted extant literature often adding to or correcting the information he found there. Burkert was therefore right when he characterized his work as a handbook.[71] Neanthes' fragments on Plato show the tendency to present him as a human being and to demystify the picture of the philosopher, whereas he told extravagant stories about Heraclitus and others. But in the latter cases he may just have reported existing traditions without endorsing them, a practice we can discern in some of the more literal fragments. He had a special interest in chronology and seems to have been more concerned about the basic facts of a life than the character of a person.[72]

Fr. 29a (the only one with the book title) discusses the origin and education of Pythagoras.[73] Neanthes considers him a Syrian from Tyre whose father, a merchant, had been naturalized in Samos. Pythagoras, he relates, was educated by the Chaldeans in Tyre, and later by Pherecydes and Hermodamas. In addition to this he mentions a different tradition that made him an Etruscan. The parallel tradition in fr. 29b shows that in all likelihood he referred to the versions of Aristoxenus, Aristotle and Theopompus in the course of the discussion of Pythagoras' origin. He himself was later used by Hippobotus, who appropriated all the material gathered by Neanthes on this question.[74] Fr. 32 probably belongs to the same context as fr. 29. There Neanthes and Asclepiades of Cyprus (probably Neanthes' source) describe the origin in mythical times in Syria of

---

[69] Zhmud 2012b: 68 assigns the biographies of the Pythagoreans to *On Famous Men*.

[70] For Neanthes' biography, literary production and the question of the work in which he wrote about the Pythagoreans, see Schorn 2007: 115–19, 132–5.

[71] Burkert 1972a: 102; cf. Centrone 1992: 4185–6. I was too cautious in Schorn 2007: 148.

[72] For a general characterization of Neanthes as a historian, see Schorn 2007: esp. 151.

[73] On fr. 29 see Schorn 2007: 135–6.

[74] On Hippobotus as a reader of Neanthes, see Schorn 2007: 136 n. 124 with reference to Burkert 1972a: 102 n. 27.

a meat diet and animal sacrifice. The fragments are interrelated because fr. 32 seems to have explained the reason for Pythagoras' vegetarianism by linking it to his Syrian origin and education. I would not exclude the possibility that fr. 32 prompted the digression on Pythagoras.[75] That might explain why Neanthes dealt with Pythagoras in a work on myths without forcing us to conclude that he regarded him as some kind of mythical figure.[76]

Neanthes' crucial role as an intermediary can also be seen in the fragments in Diogenes Laertius that relate to the "Pythagorean" Empedocles. Here we are able to see that he systematically quoted, corrected and added to the reports of Timaeus.[77] Immediately after Timaeus' version of Empedocles' exclusion from the Pythagoreans Diogenes adds that, according to Neanthes (fr. 26), Pythagorean teaching was public until the time of Philolaus and Empedocles, but after Empedocles had divulged this doctrine in his poems a law was made that excluded poets (ἐποποιοί) from instruction and Plato was also excluded on account of this law. Although this text is not totally clear (why a law if teaching was public? Plato was not a poet), we can clearly see the dialogue between the two authors. This also becomes obvious in the same passage with regard to Empedocles' Pythagorean teacher. Neanthes opposes Timaeus, who sees this teacher as Pythagoras himself, and declares that the letter of Telauges, which stated this view, is untrustworthy, i.e. a forgery.[78] According to him, Empedocles had a Pythagorean teacher but not the master. One reason why he thought so and, as a consequence, athetized the letter of Telauges must have been that he advocated a different chronology of Pythagoras from that of Timaeus according to which such a relationship was impossible.[79] This can be seen from fr. 33, which comes from the *Theology of Arithmetic*,[80] and attributes to the Pythagoreans Androcydes and Eubulides and to Aristoxenus, Neanthes and (again) Hippobotus the report that Pythagoras was reborn every 216 years. He was born as Euphorbus and was later a contemporary of, among others, Polycrates and Cambyses. The latter made him a prisoner of war when he conquered Egypt and brought him to Babylon where he was initiated into the local mysteries. He died at the age of eighty-two. We cannot be sure that every source reported everything we read in this passage, but if the chronology in the fragment is

---

[75] For a separate study of this fragment see Schorn 2009.
[76] But a different interpretation is also possible; see Schorn 2007: 132–5.
[77] This was seen by Bidez 1894: 61–7; cf. Schorn 2007: 128–32; Centrone 1992: 4186 with n. 15.
[78] Incidentally, this is the earliest text that mentions a ps.-Pythagorean work; cf. Zhmud 2012b: 68.
[79] I leave aside another fragment on Empedocles where he reacts to Timaeus (fr. 28).
[80] Cf. Burkert 1972a: 139 n. 108; Schorn 2007: 129–30, 136.

also Neanthes', the synchronism with Polycrates probably means that he dated Pythagoras' acme to 532/531; this fits deportation under Cambyses (conquest of Egypt 525). Pythagoras thus died in 490/489 and cannot have been Empedocles' teacher. So it seems that Neanthes followed Aristoxenus' chronology (fr. 16 Wehrli).[81] It would be interesting to know if he took the reincarnations seriously. If the chronology is his, which is possible because Pythagoras' places of residence in this fragment are compatible with Neanthes' reconstruction of the philosopher's youth in fr. 29, he obviously did not oppose Pythagoras' reincarnation as Euphorbus on chronological grounds.

Neanthes also wrote about the anti-Pythagorean revolt (fr. 30). It has been suggested that his version is chronologically unsound, but that is not correct.[82] For in fr. 30 the report that Pythagoras was on Delos at the time of the attack does not go back to him. Neanthes probably owes the long fragment with the story of Myllias and Timycha (fr. 31; Neanthes is again quoted along with Hippobotus) to a local Pythagorean tradition. It shows that his account was not limited to Pythagoras himself.[83]

We have no clear evidence for Neanthes' attitude towards Pythagoras. If the fragments are not misleading, it was his goal to reconstruct the dates and facts of the man's life but he was not interested in his philosophy. What makes Neanthes important is his function as an intermediary who collected information in literature (historiography, biography and philosophy) and supplemented it by oral traditions. Through Hippobotus and other compilers his views and information from his authorities entered the biographies of Pythagoras that have come down to us.[84]

6. From Neanthes to Diodorus

From the third to the first centuries BC Pythagoras remained a favorite topic of biography and was on occasion mentioned in historiography.[85] Duris of Samos, in the *Yearbooks of Samos*, defended the Samian origin of the philosopher,[86] and Polybius and Strabo mentioned him in the context of the history of the western Greeks, possibly drawing on Timaeus.[87] In biography the life of the philosopher became the playground of Hellenistic literati with as a consequence a tendency towards more spectacular

---

[81] On the complicated calculation, see Jacoby 1902: 215–27; Schorn 2007: 129–30, 136; differently Laqueur 1907.

[82] I disagree with Musti 1989 and 1990; see Schorn 2007: 137–8.   [83] Cf. Schorn 2007: 124–6.

[84] Cf. Schorn 2007: 138, 151.   [85] A sketch of this period in Muccioli 2002: 393–4, 398–402.

[86] *FGrHist* 76F23; cf. fr. 62; Muccioli 2002: 393–4; Landucci Gattinoni 1997: 209–10, 216, 218, 249–51.

[87] Polyb. 2.39.1; Strabo 6.1.12–13 with Zhmud 2012b: 69 n. 35.

stories. Pythagoras was now more often the man of wonders and new "historical" facts were made up, sometimes by transferring anecdotes from others to Pythagoras or by combining and reinterpreting existing data (cf. the Hermippus fragment in section 2 above). New information also came from the ps.-Pythagorean literature. Authors where this description applies are, among others, Hieronymus of Rhodes, Hermippus and Satyrus.[88] Biographical information in works describing successions of philosophers (*Diadochai*) and similar works does not seem to have been very different.[89] Nevertheless all these authors used (and sometimes quoted) their predecessors and in this way preserved valuable material. The doxographical information in the *Diadochai* must sometimes have been remarkable as is shown by the long Pythagorean doxography in Alexander Polyhistor, coming from the *Pythagorean Notes*.[90]

7. Diodorus

Diodorus of Sicily's *Library*, a universal history covering the period from the beginning of the world until 60/59 BC, was written *c.* 60–30 BC.[91] Although its author claims to have travelled widely in order to collect historical information, his work is for the most part a compilation of existing books. It is likely that Diodorus, for extensive portions of his work, used one main source that he supplemented with one or sometimes several secondary sources. In addition he adapted his sources to his own language and style and added some moralizing interpretations.[92]

Book 10, which originally covered the period from 528/525 (?) until 481, contained a long section on the life of Pythagoras and the history of Pythagoreanism as a part of the history of the western Greeks.[93] The book is not preserved in its entirety but there are ample quotations in the *Constantinian Excerpts*, a collection of excerpts on various topics commissioned by Constantinus Porphyrogenitus. Compared to the situation

---

[88] Hieronymus of Rhodes fr. 50 White; Hermippus, *FGrHist* 1026 F21–7 with Bollansée 1999a: 233–97; 1999b: 44–52; Satyrus fr. 10–11 Schorn with Schorn 2004: 24, 358–68.

[89] Sotion fr. 23–4 Wehrli with Wehrli 1978: 55–7; Sosicrates fr. 17 Giannattasio Andria with Giannattasio Andria 1989: 111–14; Hippobotus fr. 12–14, 18–19 Gigante; Philodemus: *PHerc.* 1508, edited with commentary by Cavalieri 2002.

[90] Alex. Polyh. *FGrHist* 273F93 = fr. 9 Giannattasio Andria with Giannattasio Andria 1989: 129–43. See also Chapter 17, section 5 below.

[91] On the following see especially the excellent characterization of Diodorus by Meister 1990: 171–81, which summarizes the author's previous research on this historiographer.

[92] See Meister 1990: 176–81 on the various theories about Diodorus' use of sources and his own contributions.

[93] Cf. Cohen-Skalli 2012: 166–9.

of other fragmentary authors this manner of preservation has the great advantage that these excerpts are often long literal quotations with essentially no intervention in the text.[94] Within one thematic collection of excerpts (*Excerpts on Virtues and Vices/on Sayings* etc.) the excerptor keeps the sequence of the excerpted text so that we can often get an impression of its structure. By a lucky chance Diodorus' programmatic statement, which followed the chapter on the Pythagoreans, has been transcribed. There Diodorus explains that the function of biography within historiographical works is to provide portraits of virtue and vice in order to motivate men to act virtuously. Thus the section on Pythagoras and his followers must have been inserted as an example of outstanding virtue.[95] A disadvantage of the transmission in the *Constantinian Excerpts,* however, is that the selection of texts is one-sidedly focused on passages with an ethical impact.[96]

In addition to the fragments of Book 10, Pythagoras is mentioned occasionally in the preserved books of Diodorus.[97] I will focus here on the long excursus in Book 10, but I cannot discuss all twenty-four fragments in detail. They show that the work contained a description of Pythagoras' life. If fr. 3 is the beginning of the biography, as it seems, it focused on his time in Italy. Diodorus dealt with Pythagoras' origin (fr. 3) and Pherecydes' burial (fr. 4), mentioned Pythagoras' journey to Egypt (fr. 11), the recognition of Euphorbus' shield (fr. 9–11) and the honors paid to him by the Crotoniates (fr. 23).[98] We may add that a passage in Book 12 (12.9.2–6) deals with the origin of the war between Croton and Sybaris and highlights the role Pythagoras played in this context. The history of the school after Pythagoras is represented by the description of the revolt in Croton and, as its consequence, the flight of Lysis and Archippus as well as the former's relation to Epaminondas, and especially by the anecdotes that illustrate the teaching of Pythagoras through the behavior of his followers (fr. 6, 13, negatively 16). Verse quotations livened up the text (fr. 11, 13). It is worth mentioning that Diodorus explained the revolt as a consequence of envy (fr. 24). It is astonishing how much text in a work that usually focuses on politics and war is devoted to Pythagoras' teaching. His ethics, of which he is presented as the ideal teacher, was given ample space (esp. fr. 3, 12, 16–18, 20–4), while miraculous aspects (apart from the Euphorbus story,

---

[94] On this and the following, see Cohen-Skalli 2012: xxxii–xxxvi.
[95] Diod. Sic. 10 fr. 27 Cohen-Skalli with Cohen-Skalli 2012: 170–4, 379–81 n. 53. In the following I use Cohen-Skalli's new numbering of the Diodorus fragments of Book 10.
[96] Cf. Cohen-Skalli 2012: 166–7.   [97] E.g., 1.69.4, 1.96.2, 1.98.2, 8.14.1, 12.9.4, 15.39.2, 16.2.3.
[98] The references are from Cohen-Skalli 2012: 177–8.

fr. 9–11) are absent. That his political activity is largely reduced to the general education of the citizens (fr. 3, 6.1–6, 24.2, 26) must be due to the interests of the excerptor. Other fragments are concerned with Pythagorean friendship (fr. 5–6, 14–15), vegetarianism (fr. 9, 11–12) and other characteristics of the community (fr. 7–8). They all illustrate Pythagorean ethics as well.[99]

Diodorus' chronology seems to have been sound and in line with Aristoxenus. He dated Pythagoras' acme, and probably also his transfer to Croton, to 533/532.[100] Given the early place of fr. 4, he probably had him bury Pherecydes long before the anti-Pythagorean revolt.[101] He dated this conflict to the time after Pythagoras, which fits his statement that Lysis escaped the fire and became Epaminondas' teacher.[102]

Diodorus' main source in the Pythagorean section of Book 10 is still debated, and is difficult to identify. Cohen-Skalli has recently made a case for Timaeus, but he is not a likely candidate because Diodorus and Timaeus disagree in most cases.[103] It was observed long ago that there is some agreement with fragments of Aristoxenus and that some passages look like reworkings of Aristoxenus' text.[104] Thus an author who drew on Aristoxenus (but as well on others) is likely to be Diodorus' source. He cannot be dated early (fourth century BC), as has been suggested,[105] because there are passages in which the *Tripartitum* has been used, a ps.-Pythagorean text written under the name of the master in the late second century BC. As Diels saw, both Diogenes Laertius and Diodorus use the same source in which this pseudepigraphon was already used, a text that expanded the *Tripartitum* with illustrative anecdotes.[106] Furthermore a

---

[99] See Cohen-Skalli 2012: 178–80 for a systematic discussion of the topics.

[100] Diod. Sic. 10 fr. 3 (ἐγνωρίζετο); cf. Aristox. fr. 16 Wehrli (Polycrates); cf. von Fritz 1940: 25–6. For details, see Schorn (forthcoming).

[101] Aristox. fr. 14 Wehrli does not show how this author dated the event; von Fritz 1940: 8–10 is not compelling.

[102] A date after Pythagoras is shown by τοὺς μετ᾽ ἐκεῖνον in Diod. Sic. 10 fr. 24; cf. Aristox. fr. 18 Wehrli (with literal reminiscences); cf. Zhmud 2012b: 147 n. 40 for the identity of the two accounts; Cohen-Skalli (2012: 378 n. 50) seems to see an agreement with Aristotle fr. 75 Rose and Satyrus fr. 11 Schorn; but Aristotle and Satyrus are incompatible: see Schorn 2004: 364–8 for Satyrus and add Aristotle fr. 191. Aristoxenus/Diodorus may have followed Aristotle.

[103] Cohen-Skalli 2012: 177–81 and her commentary, *passim*. I will deal with the question in Schorn (forthcoming).

[104] See for references Schwartz 1903a: 679; Lévy 1926: 87: a reworked version of Aristoxenus with additions; similarly Mewaldt 1904: 47–52 (fundamental); von Fritz 1940: 22–6, Meister 1967: 39; De Sensi Sestito 1991: 137 with n. 58; Zhmud 2012b: 72.

[105] Thesleff 1961: 109 (not later than the fourth century BC); cf. Zhmud 2012b: 72.

[106] Diod. Sic. 10 fr. 17–19, 21–2. Diels 1890 followed by Delatte 1922a: 166–8; Cohen-Skalli 2012: 178–9 with n. 47 (misleading), 375–6 n. 40–1; differently Zhmud 2012b: 72 n. 47. On the *Tripartitum* see the literature in Huffman 1993: 14 n. 22.

quote from Callimachus points to a later author, as also might the dating
by Olympiads and Athenian archons.[107] Schwartz thought that Diodorus
here used the same source as for his narrative on the Seven Sages in Book
9, but that is not convincing.[108] The source will have been some late
biographer of the second or first century. In the account of the origin
of the war between Croton and Sybaris in Book 12 (12.9.2–6), in which
Pythagoras plays a central role, Timaeus may well have been Diodorus'
source.[109]

---

[107] Diod. Sic. 10 fr. 11 and 3.

[108] Schwartz 1903a: 678–9, followed by Meister 1967: 39. De Sensi Sestito 1991: 140–3 thinks of
Posidonius. There are some remarkable similarities between the information on the Seven Sages
and Pythagoras in Diodorus and Satyrus (see Schorn 2004: 56) but not enough to think of
dependence. Both may sometimes follow the same tradition. For other identifications proposed by
scholars, see Delatte 1922b: 167; Cohen-Skalli 2012: 179 n. 47, 375 n. 40 (she thinks of Aristoxenus
which cannot be right).

[109] Thus, e.g., Zhmud 2012b: 69 n. 35 with references; for Ephorus: De Sensi Sestito 1991: 131–3.

CHAPTER 15

The pseudo-Pythagorean writings

Bruno Centrone

1. Preliminary considerations

After the disappearance of the original society in the fourth century BC, Pythagoreanism survived only sporadically, mostly through individual personalities who continued to lead a Pythagorean way of life; the very existence of actual Pythagorean communities prior to the first-century BC revival is highly conjectural. What is well attested instead is a cultural interest in Pythagorean teachings, as evidenced by the writing of apocrypha, a phenomenon that gradually grew to impressive proportions. The apocryphal sources that have reached us by far outnumber the few fragments that can claim to belong to early Pythagoreans. This apocryphal literature is extremely varied and includes philosophical treatises, collections of precepts and sayings, and short poems such as the famous *Golden Verses* attributed to Pythagoras himself.

According to Zeller's hypothesis, which dominated scholarship for a long time, this literature has its roots in the Pythagorean revival that occurred in Alexandria in the first century BC. Later studies, however, came to view this material under a different light, rejecting the hypothesis of a common origin and dating.[1] Pythagorean forgeries were already circulating by the third century BC, and the production of apocrypha extended over a long period of time. Such varied material reflects the heterogeneous character of Pythagoreanism: originally a way of life (*bios*),[2] it later acquired the features of a philosophical doctrine, initially thanks to Philolaus and Archytas but then largely through the influence of the Academy and the doxographical tradition.

---

[1] Zeller 1919: 3.2.123. On pseudo-Pythagorean literature in general see Burkert 1961 and 1972b; Thesleff 1961 and 1972; Moraux 1984: 605–83; Centrone 1990: 13–44 and 2000b; Macris 2002 (on Iamblichus and pseudo-Pythagorean literature).
[2] Huffman 1993: 10–12.

Several factors explain the origins of this apocryphal literature, whose spread was initially favored by the lack of any writings by Pythagoras himself. Mere profit-seeking can hardly account for the emergence of such detailed philosophical literature. One crucial factor is Plato's controversial attitude towards Pythagoreanism. Although in the Platonic dialogues Pythagoras and his followers are only expressly mentioned twice,[3] the *Timaeus* was long considered a dialogue of Pythagorean inspiration and a veiled reference to Pythagoras was also detected in the *Philebus* (16c).[4] What is most significant, however, is the Academics' firm belief in an essential continuity between Pythagorean and Platonic doctrines. The authority of the label "Pythagorean" led Plato's disciples to project onto ancient Pythagoreanism doctrines they themselves had developed. This kind of ideological distortion blurred the differences between Platonism and Pythagoreanism, which are clearly illustrated in Aristotle's account – however partial it may be.[5] The aim of the Academics was to secure the *imprimatur* of authority for their doctrines, thereby enforcing the idea of continuity between the two schools. Pythagoreanism thus became inextricably entwined with Platonism and came to exercise a far wider influence than its actual standing should have permitted. Its image was mainly determined by this connection to Platonism rather than by the doctrines actually professed by genuine Pythagoreans such as Philolaus and Archytas. Thus, in later ages it became difficult to determine reliable criteria by which to distinguish original Pythagorean ideas from Academic accretions.

2.   The Writings of "Pythagoras"

A basic distinction within the ps.-Pythagorean corpus can be drawn between writings attributed to Pythagoras himself or members of his family and writings that bear the names of other Pythagoreans. There are only scanty and very heterogeneous fragments of the first group, which are thus unlikely to have a common origin. Criticism concerning the authenticity of writings bearing the name of Pythagoras began very early and led to sharply differentiated positions, as is shown by a passage in Diogenes Laertius' *Life of Pythagoras* (8.6–8). According to Diogenes (or to his source, who may be Neanthes of Cyzicus (third century BC[6])), some "absurdly"

---

[3] Pl. *Resp.* 530d and 600b.   [4] Burkert 1972a: 83–96.
[5] Burkert 1972a: 15–83; for a different view see Zhmud 2012b: 415–56.
[6] See Burkert 1972a: 102, 225 n. 34; Centrone 1992: 4185–6.

insisted that Pythagoras left no writings.[7] In order to prove the contrary, Diogenes adduces a quotation from Heraclitus (= DK B129), which he considers to be directed against the grandiloquent beginning of Pythagoras' *On Nature* ("Nay, I swear by the air I breathe, I swear by the water I drink, I will never suffer censure on account of this work"). Pythagoras, in fact, Diogenes continues, wrote three books, *On Education*, *On Politics* and *On Nature* (the so-called *Tripartitum*), whereas another book that passes as his work should be attributed to Lysis, the Pythagorean, who escaped the persecutions against the sect and fled to Thebes (*c.* 450 BC).

All this seems to indicate that the upholders of the authenticity of the *Tripartitum* regarded another text circulating at that time under Pythagoras' name as spurious. The latter is possibly to be identified with the *Pythagorean Notes* (*Hypomnēmata*) preserved by Diogenes Laertius (8.24–33) from an excerpt in Alexander Polyhistor. An apocryphal letter that has come down to us in two different versions under Lysis' name[8] does indeed report that Pythagoras entrusted "notes" (*hypomnēmata*) to his daughter Damo, forbidding her to divulge them; Damo in her turn passed them to her daughter Bistala with the same instruction. The same did not happen with a certain Hipparchus, who in the letter is reproached for having divulged the Pythagorean doctrines. Whether or not these notes must be identified with the excerpt from Alexander Polyhistor, as Burkert argues, the letter served the purpose of guaranteeing the authenticity of the *Pythagorean Notes*, which can be dated to the third century BC.[9] The latter must then be distinguished from the *Tripartitum* in Ionic prose, from which Diogenes quotes some precepts concerning sexual pleasure, drinking and eating, and the ages of human life (8.9–10). The tradition concerning the publication by Philolaus of three books that were later purchased by Plato (Satyrus in 3.9) similarly served the purpose of corroborating the authenticity of the *Tripartitum*, which was therefore forged before 200 BC.[10]

Heraclides Lembus (*c.* 167 BC), whose *Epitome* of Sotion's *Successions of Philosophers* is mentioned soon after by Diogenes, lists other works of Pythagoras, among them *On the Universe* (περὶ τοῦ ὅλου) in verse

---

[7] A comparison with other passages in Diogenes Laertius (7.163) suggests the identification of these critics with Sosicrates. But the polemic is already found in Neanthes.

[8] Hercher *Epistolog. Graec.* 601 and Iambl. *VP* 75–8 (=III.14–14.12 Thesleff); see Burkert 1961. I cite the pseudo-Pythagorean writings according to page and line numbers in Thesleff's edition (1965).

[9] For a different dating of the letter (first to second century AD) see Städele 1980: 212ff.

[10] Burkert 1961: 17–28; 1972a: 218–38.

and a *Sacred Discourse*. Concerning the first work, we are informed that Callimachus (fr. 442 Pfeiffer = Diog. Laert. 9.23) rejected the attribution to Pythagoras of an astronomical poem which dealt among other things with Venus, claiming the identity of the evening star and the morning star: a discovery attributed to Parmenides elsewhere. There existed, then, in the third century BC a poem on natural philosophy circulating under Pythagoras' name, which is perhaps to be identified with the work mentioned by Heraclides.[11]

But maybe the most famous among the writings attributed to Pythagoras is the *Sacred Discourse* (*Hieros Logos*), which scholars have variously tried to reconstruct, although with questionable results.[12] The case here is more complicated. The thesis that Pythagoras himself published a written *Sacred Discourse* rests on shaky ground and must be rejected.[13] Forgeries of later ages, however, are well attested. Heraclides Lembus (Diog. Laert. 8.7 = *FHG* fr. 8 Müller) quotes the initial hexameter of a *Sacred Discourse* ("Young men, come reverence in quiet all these words"). A few scattered verses from this poem are to be found in the sources along with the famous *Golden Verses*, one of which is already quoted by Chrysippus (*ap.* Gell. 7.2.12 = *SVF* II 1000), and it has been supposed that all this material belongs to the *Sacred Discourse*. From the latter must be distinguished a *Sacred Discourse* in Doric prose (164–6 Thesleff) mentioned by Iamblichus and other Neoplatonists, the content of which is mainly concerned with arithmology. The hypothesis of a *Sacred Discourse* in Latin, on the basis of a passage in Iamblichus (*VP* 152–6), is rather dubious.[14]

In the third and second century BC there were other apocryphal writings in circulation under Pythagoras' name; among them, a cosmological book that presupposes a knowledge of Eratosthenes' work and can be dated between 200 and 160 BC.[15] Cato's reference (*On Agriculture* 157) to a kind of cabbage that he calls *brassica Pythagorea* shows that he is relying on a book on magical-therapeutic virtues of plants, which is repeatedly mentioned and used by Pliny (*On the Effect of Plants* = 174.25–7.11 Thesleff). According to Pliny (*HN* 24.159), others attributed it to Cleemporus the Physician. This work should also be dated at the latest to the first half of the second century BC.[16]

---

[11] Burkert 1972a: 307
[12] Delatte 1915: 3–82; Rostagni 1924. The testimonies in question are Thesleff 1965: 158.7–68.12.
[13] See Hdt. 2.81 and Burkert 1972a: 219.
[14] See 167.1–8.12 Thesleff, and Burkert's objections (1962a: 764).
[15] Burkert 1961: 28–43.   [16] Burkert 1961: 239–40.

3. Doric treatises by other "Pythagoreans"

As for the writings bearing the names of other Pythagoreans, a group of philosophical treatises, whose doctrinal content mainly consists of a mix of Platonic and Aristotelian doctrines, form a rather homogeneous corpus within the apocrypha.[17] Shared features of these works include their dialect – an artificial language reproducing the most characteristic elements of Doric – and their overall style. A few rare exceptions aside, the forgers were successful in their work and these treatises came to be regarded as authentic. Among those which have an established manuscript tradition we find ps.-Timaeus' *On the Nature of the World and the Soul*, from which Plato supposedly drew most of the doctrines presented in the *Timaeus*; ps.-Archytas' *Concerning the Whole System* [sc. of Categories] (Περὶ τῶν καθόλου λόγων), which commentators held to be the source behind Aristotle's *Categories*; and ps.-Ocellus' *On the Universe*. Some writings are only preserved in fragments transmitted by Stobaeus and Simplicius, most of them under the name of Archytas. Others bear the names of ancient – and otherwise little-known – Pythagoreans that also appear in Iamblichus' catalogue, while other names appear nowhere else. Others still are ascribed to leading personalities that were made members of the society, sometimes regardless of historical plausibility, as in Hippodamus' case. Pythagoras' name is absent from this corpus. The authors of our corpus probably adhered to the view that he had left no writings, but the absence of his name also reflects the well-established notion of the underlying doctrinal unity of Pythagoreanism: it was widely believed that all Pythagorean tenets could be traced back to the founder himself. The allegedly different authors of the treatises, in fact, seem to rely on a single coherent system, whose tenets are applied to different domains. An author's membership in the school was proof in itself of the soundness of his doctrines, even if his name was otherwise unknown. To further support these treatises' claim to antiquity, some of them were even attributed to women (Phyntis and Periktione): female membership in the society had been a distinctive feature of original Pythagoreanism.

Despite their remarkable homogeneity, the dates and places of origin of the treatises remain highly controversial. The proposed dating has swung

---

[17] The treatises that are my particular focus are those attributed to Archytas, Aresas, Aristaeus, Damippus, Diotogenes, Eccelus, Ecphantus, Euryphamus, Eurytus, Hippodamus, Callicratidas, Clinias, Crito, Metopus, Ocellus, Onatas, Pempelos, Perictione, Philolaus (*On the Soul*, 150–1), Phintys, Sthenidas, Theages and Timaios. Possibly to the same group belong Brotinus, Bryson, Dios, Hipparchus, and also Charondas' and Zaleucus' *Prefaces to the Laws* in Stobaeus. A partial translation is found in Guthrie 1987.

erratically between the fourth century BC and the second AD;[18] as for
their geographical provenance, candidates are Rome, where Pythagoreanism exercised several different kinds of influence, southern Italy, the area
where one might expect the Pythagorean tradition to have been maintained, and Alexandria, a pulsating cultural centre where an interest in
Pythagoreanism is attested in authors such as Eudorus and Philo.[19] The
doctrinal content of these writings bears few traces of early Pythagoreanism
and has led the majority of scholars to view them within the framework of
Middle-Platonism,[20] a problematic historiographical category.

The basic material betrays a scholastic origin: the subjects discussed
are presented in a plain and schematic way, with a marked tendency
towards classification and systematization. Expositions tend to be pedan-
tic, and often consist of monotonous enumerations of cases. Yet, in order
to strengthen these works' claim to antiquity, their authors did not limit
themselves to attaching Pythagorean labels to preexisting material. Along
with the Doric dialect, at times they also employ an ornate and magnilo-
quent style, replete with rare or poetic words; some minor devices, such as
the use of examples with suitably Pythagorean contexts (e.g., Tarentum in
ps.-Archytas 22.29), further suggest that these texts represent intentional
forgeries. Moreover, the fragments from this corpus clearly reveal an intention to cover all fields of knowledge by devoting entire treatises to specific
subjects. It is possible to reconstruct a single systematic theory to which
all these writings refer; the alleged inconsistencies between them are in fact
only apparent. Although these texts are not conceptually sophisticated,
what is noteworthy is the authors' effort at systematization, behind which
a unitary project is detectable.

4. The pseudo-Pythagorean "system"

The existence of a single coherent system behind the pseudo-Pythagorean
writings is confirmed by numerous internal parallels concerning basic

[18] Thesleff 1961 proposed an earlier chronology for the apocrypha, dating most to the fourth and
third century BC, although many of his arguments are questionable; Burkert 1972b opted for a more
wide-ranging chronology, tracing some of the treatises (ps.-Ecphantus') back to the time of the
Severi (second century AD). Most scholars tend to narrow down the time frame to between the first
century BC and the first century AD, see Baltes 1972: 20–36 for ps.-Timaeus; Szlezák 1972: 13–26 for
ps.-Archytas' *Categories*; Moraux 1984: 606–7; Centrone 1990: 41–4 for the *Ethica*. Harder 1926:
31–3; 110–11; 149–53 dated ps.-Ocellus to the second century BC. For the political treatises see below,
n. 47–8.

[19] See Thesleff 1961 (southern Italy); Burkert 1972b (Rome); Centrone 1990 (Alexandria).

[20] Dörrie 1963: 271; Baltes 1972: 20–1 *passim*; Szlezák 1972: 13–19; Moraux 1984: 606–7; Centrone
1990: 16–30.

doctrines. Their authors clearly sought to discover the same structure at work in all complex realities. The idea of a pseudo-Pythagorean "system" is suggested by the very centrality of the notion of *systama* in the treatises. A *systama* is a complex structure, comprised of many different parts, which, while different or even opposite to one another, are brought together under a common rule (103.21–3; 49.15–21). The whole universe may thus be viewed as a complete system articulated into different sub-systems: world, city, family, individual and individual soul. The *logos* too is a *systama*, the system of thought and speech categories impressed by God upon man (44.7–10). These systems entail an analogy between microcosm and macrocosm, whereby each system imitates the one above it.

The same golden rule governs the functioning of all the systems: the better ought to rule and direct, the worse ought to be governed and obey, while intermediate entities will both govern and be governed. When the various parts are not well-balanced with a view to the common good, the result is a badly functioning system. The perfect functioning of a system consists in the harmonization of its parts, described by means of a recurrent musical metaphor of Pythagorean flavor: every lyre requires equipment, harmonization and touching (86.15–27; 99.18–22; 104.3–7); in plain terms, a preparation of the various parts, their mutual adaptation, and the smooth running of the system. This schema is applied to the political community, to the family and to the individual's life as well.

5. The doctrine of principles and logic

The above-mentioned system is based on a doctrine of principles, which stretches back to the early Academy and in which all allegedly Pythagorean elements appear to be mediated by the Platonic tradition. This theory of principles (see ps.-Archytas *On Principles* 19.5–20.17) provides the background for all the treatises, finding application in every domain.

> There are two principles of reality, the one containing the series [συσ-τοιχία] of ordered and determined things, the other containing the series of unordered and undetermined things. (19.5–7)

This arrangement in two series (συστοιχίαι) possibly represents a Pythagorean bequest, although Academic influences are already visible in the ancient table of opposites, whose authors Aristotle distinguishes from the "so-called Pythagoreans" (*Metaph.* 986a22–6).

The first principle provides order and is beneficent in nature; the second, being maleficent, causes ruin and dissolution. This "Manichean" opposition is defined in Aristotelian terms as between form (μορφώ), the cause of things being this-something (τόδε τι), and matter, which in a Stoic fashion is here called ὠσία, the underlying substrate that receives form. Since matter cannot participate in form by itself, because opposites are in need of harmonization, a third principle must be posited to bring them together. This principle is a moving cause, which impresses form upon matter according to numerical ratios. It is first in power and self-moving, and "must be not merely *nous*, but something better: but it is clear that such an entity is what we call God" (20.13–14). So the original two principles become three and the orientation becomes strongly monistic. The doctrine of God as superior to *nous* may be traced back to the *Eudemian Ethics* (1248a27–9),[21] where Aristotle takes it for granted that only God could be superior to the intellect. However, Aristotelian hylomorphism is here fitted into the Academic scheme of two metaphysical principles, to which a demiurgical God is added.

A similar scheme operates in ps.-Timaeus: the author sets out the two causes, intelligence and necessity, which Plato only introduces relatively late in the *Timaeus*, at the very beginning of his work (205.5–9), thus assigning them paramount importance. The former cause belongs to the nature of the good and is called God; the latter is related to the powers of the elements. Here too hylomorphism plays a prominent role, since reality consists of three components: form, matter and their offspring, sensible objects (205.5–10; 24.17–19). Form is everlasting, unmoved, and indivisible; it is the pattern and belongs to the nature of the Same/Identical; matter, though eternal, is not unmoved; though formless in itself, it receives every kind of form and belongs to the nature of the Other. Unlike ps.-Archytas, ps.-Timaeus considers God to be identical to *nous*. However, in his paraphrase of two well-known passages in Plato's dialogue (*Ti.* 30a; 52c) the author presents a new triadic scheme in which God is set above the two principles: before the world came into existence, there were only form, matter and God, the demiurge of the Good:

> the deity, being good – on seeing that matter receives form and is altered in every way but without order – found the necessity of organizing it, altering the undefined to the defined, so that the differences between bodies might be proportionally related. (206.13–17)

[21] Moraux 1984: 633 n. 148.

In spite of the superficial divergence between the two texts, both rely on the same metaphysical pattern. Moreover, the fluctuation between equating God with *nous* and assigning him the most prominent position as the supreme principle is typical of Middle Platonism. Ps.-Timaeus transposes Aristotelian hylomorphism into Platonic terms, equating Forms with Ideas and matter with the "space" (χώρα) of Plato's *Timaeus*; the Form-matter opposition is fitted into the two-principle scheme, while adding God to ensure their mutual interaction.

Metopos' *On Virtue* (120.3–12) provides a glimpse at the process of categorial reduction that is attested for the ancient Academy. Here "the right mean" (δέον) and its opposite, whose species are excess and deficiency, stand to each other as the equal to the unequal and the ordered to the unordered; both are reduced to the limited and the infinite, which are the original pair of principles in early Pythagoreanism. Our authors generally speak of these principles as "natures" rather than using the more common "One/Monad" and "Dyad," and this usage possibly reflects an archaizing tendency.[22] Other traces of a Pythagorean-oriented doctrine of principles can be found in a fragment from Callicratidas (103.11–18): the Monad is the generating and limiting, the Dyad the generated and limited. The basic Academic categories absolute–relative (καθ'αὐτό–πρός τι) turn up again with reference to the odd–even couple: odd belongs to the nature of being *per se*, even to the nature of the relative. The attempt to exhaustively reduce of all reality to the above principles clearly emerges in Damippus' *On Wisdom and Good Fortune* (68.19–69.19): the parts of the soul (rational/irrational), those of the universe (ever-moving/ever-passive [ἀεικίνατον–ἀειπαθές]) and those of the polis are traced back to two natures: the limiting and rational principle of order, and the indeterminate and irrational principle deprived of order.[23]

These various hints at a theory of principles point to a single, coherent system. The most striking parallel is provided by Eudorus, a crucial figure for any attempt to philosophically frame the pseudo-Pythagorean writings.[24] Seeking to revive original Pythagoreanism by emphasizing its continuity with Plato and Aristotle, Eudorus presents a theory of principles of Academic origin as a genuine account of ancient Pythagorean doctrines (Simpl. *in Phys.* 181.10–30). According to him, the "Pythagoreans" posited two levels of principles: the One as supreme principle and, on a secondary level, the One which is called monad (μονάς), along with the

---

[22] Pl. *Phlb.* 24e4; Arist. fr. 47.   [23] See also Eurytus 88.11–19.
[24] On the relationship between Eudorus and the pseudo-Pythagorean writings see Theiler 1965; Dillon 1977: 117–21; Bonazzi 2005: 152–60; 2007; 2013b.

nature opposed to it. The supreme One is identified with the "God above" and properly called "principle" (ἀρχή), whereas the One and the Dyad are called "elements" (στοιχεῖα) and receive different appellations: ordered, limited, knowable, male and odd, as opposed to unordered, unlimited, unknowable, female and even.

The doctrine of a third principle above this basic couple, which later became a distinctive tenet of Middle Platonism, was an unprecedented idea whose origins are hard to trace.[25] However, a comparison between Eudorus and ps.-Archytas reveals striking similarities: both make God a supreme entity above the two "Pythagorean" principles, which both strikingly call "natures," assigning them axiological value.[26] Some differences persist: the pseudo-Pythagorean writings do not call the supreme principle One; nor does the distinction between principle (ἀρχή) and element (στοιχεῖον) play any role. However, the similarities are more than superficial: Eudorus' doctrine probably emerged from exegesis of the *Timaeus* and is grounded in passages that underline the necessity of proceeding from the "elements" to superior principles (*Ti.* 48b–e); the notion of God as the supreme principle naturally followed from this. Eudorus thus answered Aristotle's criticism that Plato failed to account for the most important factor: the divine and efficient principle.[27] Now, in the pseudo-Pythagorean writings the introduction of a principle above the traditional pair serves this very purpose: God acts as a moving cause that explains the interaction between form and matter. A convergence between Eudorus and the pseudo-Pythagorean writings is at work here; it is more difficult to ascertain whether Eudorus is attributing his own ideas to Pythagoreans, or whether he is borrowing from already existing apocryphal literature. Whatever the case, the attempt to reconcile Plato and Aristotle is typical of the pseudo-Pythagorean writings, and this makes their attribution to Eudorus' circle a plausible – if unprovable – hypothesis.

As is common in the Platonic tradition, when it comes to logic the pseudo-Pythagorean treatises mainly rely on Aristotle's *Categories*, which provided a conceptual apparatus capable of competing with that of the dominant Hellenistic schools. While ps.-Archytas' writing on categories largely depends on Aristotle, some of the topics it examines reveal that its author was familiar with the exegesis of the early commentators.[28] This suggests the first century BC as a *terminus post quem* for the treatise. The existence of a distinct work by ps.-Archytas, *On Opposites* (15.3–19.2),

[25] Mansfeld 1988: 98–103.   [26] Bonazzi 2005: 152–60.
[27] Bonazzi 2005: 139–52.   [28] Szlezák 1972: 13–19; Moraux 1984: 609–10.

dealing with topics related to but going beyond the ten categories (known as the *postpredicamenta*), also reflects Andronicus of Rhodes' (70–20 BC) separate treatment of the last chapters of the *Categories* (Simplicius *On the Categories* 379.3 –12).

At the beginning of this work the ten categories are defined as "the universal *logos*, by which man acquires an exact knowledge of reality" (22.8–12). *Logos* is the system constituted by thought (meanings) and speech (signifiers); the categories are the universal meanings of Being. The author is here taking a stand with regard to the much debated issue of what the object (σκοπός) of the categories might be, whether words or things. In ps.-Archytas' *On Wisdom* (44.8–13) the universal *logos* is said to encompass both the genera of Being and the meanings of speech, names and verbs: the categories are interpreted as the genera of Being and the universal system of thought and speech. This solution reconciles the two opposing views mentioned above, by following the path paved by Boethus of Sidon. Remarkably, this *logos* is imprinted by God; in ps.-Archytas' *On Intelligence* Form is defined as an "impression/imprinting" (τύπωσις) of things qua things-that-are (38.10–12). A comparison between the two treatises shows also that the doctrine of categories fits within a theological framework, which is paralleled in other pseudo-Pythagorean writings. A distinctive Pythagorean feature, along with the *tetraktys* and the table of oppositions, is the emphasis given to ten as the number of categories: ten is the number of the whole, as well as of the extremities of the body (32.18–20). The analogy between microcosm and macrocosm, which is typical of the pseudo-Pythagorean writings, is clear here; human *logos*, just like the body, mirrors the cosmic order.

Ps.-Archytas deals with other *topoi* of the later debate on the categories, such as their order: a problem to which Aristotle attached little importance. Ps.-Archytas' exposition endeavors to justify the logical order of the categories (23.17ff.). First comes substance (*ousia*), which underlies all other categories; then quality, for no substance can be unqualified; quantity follows, since any sensible substance must have body and size; and then come the remaining categories. The substance–quality–quantity succession has parallels in Eudorus and Philo of Alexandria. Ps.-Archytas' order coincides with Philo's in *On the Decalogue* 30,[29] and both authors emphasize the simultaneous applicability of the categories to one and the same subject. The justification offered both by ps.-Archytas and Eudorus for the proposed order is also similar. Eudorus is probably the common source of

---

[29] Mansfeld 1992: 67.

ps.-Archytas and Philo,[30] and all this strengthens the hypothesis of the proximity of the pseudo-Pythagorean writings to Eudorus' circle.

Particularly interesting is the notion that non-substantial categories only apply to the sensible world (30.17–31.5), whereas the first category includes both intelligible and sensible substances: quality, quantity, etc. do not apply to the Form of Man, which is indivisible and unmoved, but only to the individual man as sensible substance. Only the first category (τί ἐστι) applies to intelligible substance. The categorial system exhausts the whole of reality, including intelligible substance, although it only applies in its entirety to the sensible world (22.31–3.2). Ps.-Archytas presupposes the much-debated question of the relationship between intelligible substance and the categories. His position, however, differs from the criticism advanced by some commentators on Aristotle, and later developed by Plotinus, according to which the categories *in their entirety* do not apply to intelligible substance.[31] Ps.-Archytas is not criticizing Aristotle; his aim is to integrate the categories into a Platonic system: he places the distinction between intelligible substance, which has the features of the Platonic Form, and sensible substance within the categorial system. By putting intelligible substance in the first Aristotelian category, ps.-Archytas again shows his proximity to Eudorus, who probably superimposed the Academic absolute–relative distinction (καθ' αὑτό–πρός τι) on Aristotle's categories.[32]

6. Theology

Pseudo-Pythagorean theology too is steeped in Platonic and Aristotelian doctrines. Some specific theses are strikingly reminiscent of the pseudo-Aristotelian *On the Cosmos* (*De Mundo*), as well as of Philo and the Jewish tradition. While the only work expressly devoted to theological issues is ps.-Onatas' *On God* (139.1–40.24), the treatises as a whole reveal a unitary theology. God is the Supreme Being, superior even to the two highest principles. As the nature of the good, however, he has a place in the table of oppositions (205.7–8). This apparent inconsistency can be explained: since the second principle is defined as evil, God is naturally assigned a position opposite to it.

As the cause of cosmic harmony, God is the most honorable thing; he is the king of the cosmos, with whom he is bound by a relationship of friendship (φιλία). God is invisible and can only be grasped by the

[30] Szlezák 1972: 17.
[31] See Mansfeld 1992: 64–7, and the correct reconstruction in Chiaradonna 2009: 93–107.
[32] Bonazzi 2013b.

intellect; his powers (δυνάμεις) and his works are, however, visible to all (139.7–11). The distinction between God's substance (*ousia*) and his powers plays an important role in ps.-Aristotle's *On the Cosmos*, where it serves to reconcile God's transcendence with his action in the world.[33] The God of the pseudo-Pythagorean writings does intervene in the world, but occupies a lofty position that reveals his transcendence.

Overt polemics against monotheism do not prevent our authors from acknowledging a divinity superior to all others: there exists a multiplicity of gods, but above it is one Supreme God. The other gods are the celestial bodies, whose movements follow the first God (139.11–140.5). The anti-monotheistic polemic is probably directed against those who denied the divinity of the stars. The relationship between the supreme God and the other gods is analogous to that between a general and his soldiers in conformity to the usual pattern: the better rules, the worse obeys – for without the assistance of the superior, the inferior could not act properly.

God, who is self-sufficient, is not a synthesis of soul and body but is the soul, or *phronēsis*, of the Universe (84.4–6; 139.6–7). From his incorporeality it follows that his virtue, unlike that of man, is free from any passion, and that his power is inexhaustible. God has no need of good fortune, but is naturally good and happy (ps.-Euryphamus 85.17–20; ps.-Hippodamus 95.9–13). His untiring action as a mover ensures the eternity of the world (ps.-Aristaeus 52.21–3). In Platonic fashion, God is a demiurge, who impresses form upon matter (19.21–20.14; 206.11–17). Unlike Aristotle's God, he acts directly on matter as the active principle acting on the passive (26.8–10). God's action towards human beings is providential. God has made only man capable of law and justice (ps.-Aresas 49.8–11); he has given him the appropriate instruments and desires for the perpetuation of his race, in order for him to participate in immortality as far as possible (ps.-Ocellus 135.13–18).

Here the parallels with Philo and the Old Testament become noteworthy:[34] God has molded man and his body, impressing upon him a superior principle, the *logos*, by which he gains knowledge of good and evil (85.22–5), rising to contemplate the highest heavens. Man, weighed down by the earth, could not lift himself up from his "mother," if not by a divine inspiration that allows his superior part, the *nous*, to glimpse its sacred parent, who is otherwise impossible to contemplate (ps.-Ecphantus 79.2–7). God's ultimate unknowability and man's condition as an exile

---

[33] Ps.-Arist. *Mund.* 397b16–30; Moraux 1984: 639 n. 176.
[34] See Delatte 1942: 179–80; Burkert 1972b: 49–53; Centrone 1990: 233–4.

on earth recall Philo's doctrines, which are deeply rooted in the Jewish tradition.[35]

The authors' effort to harmonize basic Platonic and Aristotelian views is manifest: God is described in terms that fit the Aristotelian conception of the first mover moving the heaven of the fixed stars (139.11–40.5) and the thesis that God embraces the universe can be regarded as genuinely Aristotelian.[36] Yet God's direct action upon the world and his providential care for man is distinctly Platonic, while more specific features are strikingly reminiscent of Philo and the Jewish tradition. All this fits the Alexandrian milieu well.

7. Cosmology

Along with ps.-Timaeus, the most renowned cosmological treatise is ps.-Ocellus' *On the Universe*, first mentioned by Varro (Censorinus 4.3). The cosmos is here defined as the "consummate and perfect system of the universal nature": a system comprehending all things within itself (127.11–14). The corresponding expression, "the whole and the all" (τὸ ὅλον καὶ τὸ πᾶν), is expressly justified: the word "cosmos" was coined as a result of its being adorned (διακοσμηθείς) with all things. In fact this expression, which occurs in Aristotle (*Cael.* 278b20–1; *Ph.* 212b16–17), reflects anti-Stoic polemics: the Stoics used to distinguish the "whole" (ὅλον), i.e. the cosmos, from the "all" (πᾶν), the "all" being the sum of the cosmos and the void that surrounds it.[37] Instead, according to ps.-Ocellus, there is nothing outside the cosmos.

Ps.-Ocellus argues for the eternity of the universe at length. The universe cannot be corrupted by an external cause, since there is nothing outside it and its power could never be overcome by any internal force (128.15–24). Ocellus' terminology recalls Plato's description of his Forms: the universe subsists always constant, unvarying and self-identical (127.2–3). According to ps.-Aristaeus (52.21–3), any principle is by definition ungenerated, complete in itself, and immortal, and what is immortal must be "untiring"; such is God, who uninterruptedly moves the universe. The universe itself, therefore, must be eternal. The thesis of eternity, borrowed from Aristotle, is brought into accordance with Plato by allegorical interpretation of the *Timaeus*, a reading that goes back to the early Academy. According to ps.-Timaeus, heaven was only generated in word (λόγῳ γενέσθαι, 206.11):

[35] Cf. e.g., Philo *On the Creation* 71; *On the Change of Names* 7, 15; *On the Special Laws* 1.41–8. On this particular point see Calabi 2008: 202–5.
[36] Arist. *Ph.* 267b6–9; Moraux 1984: 638–9.   [37] Sext. Emp. *Math.* 9.332 = *SVF* 2.524.

a remarkable point of contact – even in terms of the language used – with Eudorus,[38] who was probably the first, after centuries, to restore this ancient allegorical interpretation.[39]

Also borrowed from Aristotle is the division of the cosmos into two regions: the superlunary, a celestial region in perpetual motion (ἀεικίνητον, or ἀεὶ θέον, 134.3–4; 150.19–21), governs the sublunary, which is always subject to corruption. The cosmos, as the work of the divine intelligence, is the outcome of the harmonization of these two parts. Once again, an Aristotelian doctrine is adapted to the Academic two-principle scheme: the ever-moving belongs to the limiting nature, the ever-passive to the undetermined (68.21–5).

8. Ethics

The blending of Platonic and Aristotelian doctrines is particularly noticeable in ethics.[40] Aristotelian elements are almost invariably integrated within the Academic theory of principles. On account of his rationality, man is the only terrestrial being capable of virtue and happiness (85.15–17; 94.9–12); his virtue and happiness, however, differ from those of God, who, being self-sufficient, is intrinsically good and happy. Virtue is the perfection of a thing's nature (116.23–17.2); for man it is the harmonization of the rational and irrational parts of the soul, both of which may be traced back to the first principles (33.15–16; 103.3–13). The perfect accord is established when the rational part governs and the irrational is governed and the latter follows the former without constraint (117.19–20; 190.11–12). When the irrational part obeys with reluctance, the result is endurance and continence, "half-perfect virtues" that are always accompanied by pain. When the irrational part, instead, prevails on the rational, vice is produced; but if the rational part is overcome by constraint, the result is incontinence and softness/effeminacy, which are "half-vices," for in this case reason is unwilling (117.16–23; 192.21–3.4).

Ethical virtue is defined as "the habit of what ought to be" (δέον), consisting in the right mean between excess and defect of passion, which is the stuff of virtue. In this respect, virtue is a mean, but insofar as it is a perfection, it is an extreme (cf. Arist. *Eth. Nic.* 1107a6–8). The right mean and its opposites are traced back to the superior principles of the limited and the unlimited. A coherent development of this conception is

[38] Plutarch *On the Generation of the Soul* 1013a; Baltes 1972: 47–50; Bonazzi 2013a.
[39] Baltes 1976: 85; Dörrie-Baltes 1987: 332–4; Bonazzi 2013.
[40] On the ethical treatises see Centrone 1990 and Thom 2008.

the doctrine of metriopathy. In an overt polemic against Stoic positions, ps.-Archytas claims that:

> Their boasting of impassivity enervates the noble element of virtue, if one withstands death, pains, poverty as "indifferents" [ἀδιάφορα] and not-evils, for the latter are easy to defeat. One should therefore practice metriopathy, so as to avoid both insensitivity and over-sensibility to pain. (41.13–18)

Virtue does not remove the passions from the soul, but brings them into harmony with its rational part. Ps.-Archytas' *On Law* (33.17–18) seems to be at variance with metriopathy: the author claims that virtue turns the soul away from pleasures and pains, leading it to quietude and impassivity. However, the contradiction is only apparent: this kind of impassivity (ἀπά-θεια) is not complete elimination of the passions, but avoids an excess of pathos. Ps.-Archytas' terminology (ἀρεμίαν καὶ ἀπάθειαν) echoes ancient Academic formulations (cf. Arist. *Eth. Eud.* 1222a4–5; *Eth. Nic.* 1104b24–5), or possibly the views of the historical Archytas.[41] It is not Stoic ἀπάθεια that is at stake here: ps.-Theages, who openly favors metriopathy, employs an analogous formulation (τὰ πάθεα ἐξαιρέονται, 192.18).[42] Hence it is reasonable to conclude that our authors unanimously share the metriopathic ideal of the Platonic tradition.

Specific virtues are assigned to the parts of the soul, according to a traditional scheme (practical wisdom (*phronēsis*): rational part; courage: spirited/irascible part; temperance (*sōphrosynē*): appetitive part; justice: harmony of the parts; 118.7–13; 190.19–25). The authors variously consider *phronēsis* or justice (190.26–1.2) as the supreme virtue. *Phronēsis* as the virtue of the rational part is defined as "knowledge of the human goods and of happiness" (11.20–1), or "a critical habit of discerning (good and evil)" (118.9–10). It is traced back to the principle of order, whereas good fortune (εὐτυχία) belongs to the irrational and disorderly nature (68.4–18). *Phronēsis* governs human life by balancing the limiting element and the unlimited in one's actions; she is the leader and mother of all other virtues (69.14–15). Elsewhere justice is called the "mother and nurse" (78.1) of the other virtues. Far from pointing to internal inconsistencies, this variance reflects a widespread tension, which can be traced back to Plato himself.

A strong Aristotelian influence is found in the doctrine of choice (προαίρεσις), which results from desire (ὄρεξις) and thought (διάνοια) and represents, along with "reason" (λόγος) and "ability" (δύναμις), an

---

[41] Huffman 2005: 603.
[42] A contradiction has been seen by Burkert 1972b and Moraux 1984: 662 n. 285. Thus there is no need to emend the text, as proposed by Becchi 1992: 114–15, followed by Thom 2008: 76 n. 19.

essential component of virtue. These components are assigned to the parts of the soul: reason to the rational part, ability to the irrational, and choice, which is composed of thought and desire, to both of these parts (117.2–12). The mutual entailment of the virtues is only hinted at by ps.-Archytas' claim that the various virtues do not stand in opposition to one another, but are in perfect accord (42.19–20).

The ultimate good is happiness (εὐδαιμονία), defined as the "perfection and completion of human goods" (87.6–7), or the "perfection of the human life as a system of actions" (95.5–7). Happiness consists in the use of virtue accompanied by good fortune (12.4–6; 87.10; 94.18; 95.11). The pseudo-Pythagorean writings adopt a clear position on the role of good fortune and the relationship between virtue and happiness: virtue is not sufficient for happiness, although it is necessary. However, good fortune is good only for the virtuous man who possesses *phronēsis*, whose role is to govern events belonging to chance (68.3–18). Unlike virtue, good fortune can be excessive making one too bold; therefore it is harder to bear than misfortune (13.7–29). Vice is sufficient for infelicity, whereas virtue by itself only precludes unhappiness (40.19–20). It is then possible to distinguish between happiness, not-unhappiness and outright unhappiness (10.30–11.2). Happiness, unlike virtue, can be lost at any moment (9.2–3).

The importance of good luck for happiness follows from the role of the body in human life: virtue (ἀρετή) and good fortune (εὐτυχία) are parts of life, the former insofar as man is endowed with a soul, the latter insofar as he has a body (87.7–9). The body is an instrument of the soul and a part of man. Corporeal and external goods are therefore parts of life (86.23–4); good fortune consists in possessing these goods, whose appropriate use depends on virtue. Unlike virtue, good fortune does not depend on us, yet it enables us to fulfill our purposes (11.31–2; 87.13–15). This position entails rejection of Stoic rigor regarding bodily and external goods. Ps.-Archytas (9.25–10.20) divides goods into goods of the soul and bodily and external goods. Some goods, such as happiness, are desirable in themselves, while others, such as physical exercise, are desirable in view of something else. Virtue belongs to a third genus: what is desirable both in itself and in view of something else. The inferior goods attend to the superior as "bodyguards" (δορυφόροι): friendship, glory and wealth serve both body and soul; health and strength, the soul; the cardinal virtues, the mind (*nous*); the mind, God (11.12–17). In order for them to be properly goods, they must be oriented towards the divine. Ps.-Archytas' position is very close to a *locus classicus* of Plato's *Laws* (631b–d): noteworthy parallels are the orientation of all goods towards the hegemonic reason (*nous*), and the prominent role of wisdom (*phronēsis*), which in the *Laws* is the first among the divine goods.

Even more striking are the parallels with Philo. Particularly significant is the application of the bodyguard metaphor to the hierarchical ladder of the goods, attributed by Philo (*On Drunkenness* 201) to unnamed philosophers, who divided the goods into three classes, each class serving the one above it. As this application of the bodyguard metaphor is unparalleled elsewhere, it is likely that Philo was directly acquainted with ps.-Archytas' treatise.

Assimilation to God (ὁμοίωσις θεῷ) as the goal of human life, which is typical of Middle Platonism, is not found in the pseudo-Pythagorean writings in just these terms. An analogous prescription is rather provided: the traditional Pythagorean command to follow the divine (85.27–8; 95.21). The knowledge of divine things is the principle of human happiness (119.25–6). The good man who follows the Gods is happy, but he who follows mortal things is doomed to unhappiness (95.21–2; 224.8–12). The more specific issue of the imitation of God is dealt with in the treatises on kingship, where the possibility of assimilation to God is mediated by the king; the practice of virtue and the search for wisdom enable humans to imitate God in his self-sufficiency.

With regard to the much-debated question of the best form of life, our authors suggest it is a mixed form, which combines the contemplative and the active life (42.5–19). Reason has two parts, the practical, which leads man to politics, and the theoretical, which aims at the contemplation of the universe. Mind (*Nous*) maintains a balance between these two for the sake of happiness, which coincides neither with a practical life that would exclude science, nor with mere contemplation removed from praxis. Ps.-Archytas solves the tension by defining intellectual activity as "praxis" and recalling the overall harmony of the virtues: a fair-flowing life will bring together the principles of virtue and the divine law of cosmic harmony.

While rising from the earth to contemplate heavenly things requires divine assistance, pursuing virtue or vice is within man's power: it depends on his will and deliberate choices, although this capacity was given him by God himself (85.21–6.1; ps.-Crito 109.5–16). This position recalls Jewish doctrine found in Philo, which aims at reconciling the belief that all comes from God with the existence of evil and human freedom.[43]

---

[43] Philo *On the Creation* 73–5, 149; *On the Unchangeableness of God* 48; *On the Sacrifices of Abel and Cain* 106; *On the Decalogue* 176–7.

When it comes to ethics, it is difficult to distinguish distinctive Pythagorean features. While no traces of the *acusmata* tradition are discernible, it is possible to draw some parallels with Aristoxenus' *Pythagorean Sayings*, which however contain much Academic and Peripatetic material.[44] One Pythagoreanizing feature (also found in Xenocrates and many other authors) is the strong predilection for triadic divisions: there are three parts of the soul; three causes of evil (vice, incontinence and bestiality: 118.13–14);[45] three components of virtue (reason, power and choice: 117.2–3), which has three psychological causes: desire, fear and shame that are produced, respectively, by reason, law and customs (100.14–17; ps.-Clinias 108.13–16).

The very presence of treatises attributed to women (Phyntis and Periktione) can be regarded as a Pythagoreanizing feature. Despite the important role of women in the ancient Pythagorean society, the pseudo-Pythagorean writings assign them a subordinate position. The basic duties of women concern the household and the family, though their participation in politics is not excluded. Though the virtues are common to both sexes, in performing her duties woman must particularly exhibit temperance (*sōphrosynē*), which is regarded as a typically female virtue.[46]

9. Politics

The political thinking of the pseudo-Pythagorean writings is found in treatises expressly devoted to the subject, although evidence is scattered throughout the corpus.[47] While the most renowned treatises are those on kingship, politics is also the subject of ps.-Hippodamus' *On the Republic*, largely inspired by Plato's *Republic*, and ps.-Archytas' *On Law*, which some have regarded as authentic.[48] While the kingship treatises extol monarchy, ps.-Hippodamus prefers aristocracy, and ps.-Archytas champions a mixed constitution. Despite these apparent inconsistencies, closer examination reveals a single systematic theory in the political sphere as well.

[44] Centrone 1990: 38–41.
[45] Cf. Arist. *Eth. Nic.* 1145a16; *Mag. Mor.* 1200b4–6. On triadic divisions in early Pythagoreanism, see Chapter 7 in this volume.
[46] See Periktione 144.23–5.6; Phyntis 152.5–19.
[47] The dating of the kingship-treatises ranges between the third century BC (Goodenough 1928; Thesleff 1961; Aalders 1975, with some reservations) and the first or second century AD (Delatte 1942; Burkert 1972b). The Hellenistic monarchies and the Roman empire have been seen as the most favorable contexts for the production of texts extolling kingship; yet, there are no compelling reasons for assuming a connection with historical reality, see Centrone 2000c and below.
[48] Johnson 2008. See the discussion in Huffman 2005: 600; *On Law* has mostly been dated to the Hellenistic period, see Goodenough 1928: 59; Thesleff 1961: 112, 114; Aalders 1968: 13–23; 1975: 27–38.

Our authors show few distinctively Pythagoreanizing tendencies and are instead substantially indebted to the Platonic tradition, although the borrowings from Aristotelianism are not insignificant. The political community arises because men are not self-sufficient (86.11–14). According to the hierarchical ordering of the various systems, the *polis* is a complex whole that imitates the system above it, the cosmos (72.19–23). The *polis* should be self-sufficient like the cosmos, having in itself the cause of its subsistence (35.8–12). Thus the political community ought to reproduce the harmony of the cosmos. In a perfectly organized *polis* the better element governs and the inferior obeys, while the intermediate classes obey the superior and govern the inferior. A distinction is made between despotic rule, serving only the ruler's interest, protective (ἐπιστατικά) rule, aiming at the good of the subject, and political rule, which pursues the common advantage (105.10–23). This distinction of Aristotelian origin[49] is applied to the monarchical ideal and connected to the authors' theological views. The *polis* imitates the cosmos, whose ruler, God, acts in order to produce the overall good. The friendship (φιλία) that should rule in the polis imitates cosmic harmony (81.21–2). This doctrine underlies the treatises on kingship, kingship being an imitation of the divine (θεόμιμον πρᾶγμα; 73.28; 75.15–16; 102.11–12; Sthenidas 187.9–188.13):

> Of things which naturally deserve honor, God is the best, but of things on earth and human the best is the king [. . .] who has a power which is not liable to render an account of itself, and who himself, as living law [νόμος ἔμψυχος], takes the form of God among men. (ps.-Diotogenes 72.18–23)

Ps.-Ecphantus gives particular prominence to this doctrine. Although like other men in his bodily features, the king has been fashioned by God after his own image. Being proximate to God, the king is almost an exile on earth, a stranger descended from heaven. His virtues are the work of God himself, for man, oppressed by earthly matter, becomes capable of contemplating God only through divine inspiration (79.1–7; 80.1–7). God governs the world through no other intermediaries but the king; by offering himself as a model, he makes the latter yearn to imitate him. Since God is good, imitating him amounts to practicing the good (82.17ff.). The king assimilates himself to God in self-sufficiency and benevolence towards his subjects: to them he is like a shepherd to his flock, and a father to his sons. Like God, the king fills his subjects with a desire to emulate him. The king is thus an intermediary, making it possible for the rest of humanity

---

[49] Arist. *Pol.* 1278b30–9a16. However, the idea that the same form of government is appropriate for different types of community derives from Plato (*Plt.* 259b–c; *Leg.* 690a).

to achieve a mediated assimilation to God. The doctrine of assimilation to God (ὁμοίωσις θεῷ) thus becomes inseparable from its political dimension.

Of paramount importance is the description of the sovereign as living law (33.6–10; 71.19–23; 72.18–23). Just as God is the cause of cosmic harmony, the law is the cause of overall concord (124.19–20). If the law is embodied by the sovereign, kingship becomes the ideal form of government. But one might wonder whether the notion of "living law" (νόμος ἔμψυχος) implies that the king is the source of the law, or simply that he embodies the already existing law by ensuring its efficacy. In fact, the supremely just king conforms to the law, without which there can be no justice (71.20). So, we are faced with the question of the relation between the kingship-treatises and ps.-Archytas' *On Law*, where the law also seems to be assigned primacy; ps.-Archytas advocates a mixed constitution– monarchy being only one of its components – and this has prompted the hypothesis of a different origin of the treatises. It seems possible, however, to identify a common orientation for these authors.

According to ps.-Archytas (33.3–10), by observing the law, the king becomes "lawful" (νόμιμος), the ruler "compliant" (ἀκόλουθος), the subject free, and the whole community happy. The law would thus appear to possess absolute primacy, entailing a subordinate position for the king. Ps.-Archytas himself, however, distinguishes living law (the king) from lifeless law (written law), which should conform to nature and be useful to the social community. This will occur if the law imitates the just by nature, which assigns to each according to his merits, and pursues not private advantage but public interest. The primacy of the law, then, does not entail the preeminence of positive law at the expense of the king, and ps.-Archytas argues that in some happy cases the king might be the source of the law. The primacy of the law, as the primacy of the just by nature, remains valid even in a monarchy in which a virtuous king is held to be the "living law." Moreover, the features of the ideal ruler listed by ps.-Archytas largely overlap with those of the king: he will be knowledgeable, lawful, benevolent towards his subjects and concerned with the common good (36.2–11).

The mixed constitution advocated by ps.-Archytas is based on the distinction of three forms of justice (aristocratic, democratic and oligarchic-tyrannical), which are respectively associated with the traditional Pythagorean proportions (subcontrary, geometric and arithmetic; 34.3–14). The best constitution combines democracy, oligarchy and aristocracy, here associated with kingship. The author's endorsement of a mixed consti-tution presupposes that the mutual check of political forces can prevent abuses; this danger, however, would not exist in the case of a virtuous king – a possibility ps.-Archytas too contemplates, as witnessed by his definition of the king as "living law." Thus a mixed constitution seems to represent only a second-best solution.

A possible way of reconciling the apparent inconsistencies between ps.-Archytas and the kingship treatises is found in ps.-Hippodamus' *Republic* (97.16–102.20); following the Platonic model, the *polis* is divided into three groups: counselors, auxiliaries and artisans. Although this system is based on the rule of an aristocracy, ps.-Hippodamus also favors a mixed constitution, which combines kingship, aristocracy and democracy; at the same time, kingship, since it imitates divine rule, is extolled as the ideal form, aristocracy only coming second. Since, however, kingship can easily degenerate into *hubris*, it should be introduced only where it is advantageous to do so in a city. Democracy is a just form, inasmuch as all citizens are part of the community, but it should be employed with caution, due to the irresponsibility of the mob. Aristocracy is generally preferable, since it permits the alternation of offices (102.10–20).

It is possible, then, to trace a single fundamental orientation in these treatises: kingship is ideally the best form, but also the most difficult to realize; in the absence of a virtuous sovereign as living law, a more realistic perspective prevails, which favors positive law and a mixed constitution. The diverse outlooks in the distinct treatises reflect a tension already present in Plato (*Plt.* 301a–e; 302e; *Leg.* 875c–d): if by divine decree a wise king were to rule, he would be the source of law and monarchy would be the best constitution; otherwise monarchy will degenerate into tyranny, and it is then preferable that the laws have full authority. Hence the predilection is for a mixed form combining monarchy and democracy, which still represents only a second-best alternative.

The preference for monarchy mirrors the monistic tendency of the pseudo-Pythagorean writings: since God is the supreme principle of the universe, the ideal form of government, which imitates God's rule, must be monarchy. The authors' overall attitude does not reflect any concrete historical reality but derives from theoretical reflection. Despite a variety of influences, the political treatises are essentially of Platonic inspiration.

10. Conclusions

As the foregoing analysis has shown, the content of the pseudo-Pythagorean writings results from a blending of Platonic and Aristotelian doctrines, which is typical of Platonism, beginning in the first century BC. Platonic doctrines are mostly mediated by the Academic tradition, which profoundly shapes the basic orientation of the treatises towards systematization and classification. The theory of principles plays a fundamental role in all spheres of knowledge, but its very formulation contains innovative elements, which make the pseudo-Pythagorean system more than simply a repetition of early Academic doctrines. The Aristotelian doctrines are integrated within a Platonizing system: Aristotle's hylomorphism is thus interpreted in the light of the doctrine of Ideas – identified with Aristotelian Forms – and traced back to the two fundamental principles. The same reduction of Aristotelian notions to two principles occurs in cosmology, ethics and politics.

The question of the purpose of these Pythagorean forgeries is intimately tied to that of their authors' conception of themselves. Whether the treatises attest to a clear awareness on the authors' part of their own Pythagorean identity is perhaps the most intractable problem. Some typical features of the Pythagorean way of life are absent from the treatises (e.g., metempsychosis), but other features usually reputed to be Pythagorean give them a Pythagoreanizing flavor: the importance assigned to the all-pervading triads and to the number 10, as well as to musical metaphors and to the concept of harmonization. Nonetheless, this sort of mysticism of numbers is also found in some Platonists and the pseudo-Pythagorean treatises ultimately belong to the tradition of Platonism. Their authors' adoption of the mask of ancient Pythagoreanism certainly entails a firm belief in a deep continuity between Pythagoreanism and Platonism, of the sort that is typical of the Platonic tradition. The attribution of Platonic and Aristotelian doctrines to ancient Pythagoreanism might have favored the reshaping of a strong Pythagorean identity at the expense of both Plato and Aristotle, yet the forgers in no way intended to convey the impression that Plato and Aristotle were plagiarists.

It is preferable then to describe the authors of the apocrypha as Pythagoreanizing Platonists, who considered themselves to be heirs to the Pythagorean tradition, with a firm belief in the continuity between Pythagoras, Plato and Aristotle.[50] The composition of apocrypha bearing the names of Pythagoreans settled problems which were current at the time by suggesting that a solution was already available in the doctrines of ancient Pythagoreanism: ps.-Archytas' treatise on categories in some cases

---

[50] See the Pythagorean succession in Phot. *Bibl.* 249, 438b17–19, where Plato and Aristotle are listed as the ninth and tenth successors of Pythagoras in the school.

addresses objections which Aristotle's opponents had raised against his doctrine. The appeal to an authoritative philosophical tradition made it easier to take a stand against views of the Hellenistic schools. Although explicit Stoic influence is limited to terminology, a strong polemical bias against Stoicism is clearly detectable (although, for obvious reasons, Stoicism could not be explicitly mentioned as a target).

Yet there is more to it. The hypothesis that the production of Pythagorean apocrypha may have originated in Eudorus' circle remains an intriguing possibility. The doctrine of principles attributed by Eudorus to otherwise unknown "Pythagoreans" displays impressive similarities to that of ps.-Archytas; further remarkable parallels are found in the order of the categories and its justification, as well as in the inclusion of the intelligible substance (*ousia*) in the first category. Distinctive features of Eudorus' reading of the *Timaeus*, such as the allegorical interpretation of the generation of the cosmos and the choice of number 384 as a starting-point – in order to avoid fractions – in the division of the cosmic soul[51] are unfailingly found in ps.-Timaeus. Broadly speaking, both Eudorus and the pseudo-Pythagorean writings aim to reconcile Platonism and Aristotelianism by tracing them back to Pythagoreanism. Both possibly sought to erect a philosophical system capable of answering topical questions through particular interpretations of Plato and Aristotle and/or by reference to early "Pythagorean" texts.

Correspondences and connections between Pythagoreanism and Judaism have been repeatedly noted since antiquity, starting with Flavius Josephus (*Jewish Antiquities* 15.371). Influences from the Jewish tradition and the Old Testament and affinities with the *New Testament* household codes have also been detected in our treatises.[52] Hints in this direction are provided by the numerous parallels with Philo[53] which can be drawn with regard to fundamental doctrines, such as the conception of divinity: God is envisaged as the supreme cause of the universe, which he tirelessly supervises;[54] he stands to the latter as the king stands to the *polis*.[55] Unlike man, God is self-sufficient, perfectly virtuous and happy.[56] God is

---

[51] Eudorus followed Crantor: Plut. *On the Generation of the Soul* 1020c; Baltes 1972: 23, 79–82.

[52] Burkert 1972b; Balch 1992.

[53] See also Goodenough 1932; 1938: 45–54, 94–100; Delatte 1942: 150–1, 235–8, 264–5.

[54] Cf. Philo *Who Is the Heir* 156–7; *On the Cherubim* 87–90; *On the Sacrifices of Cain and Abel* 40 (ἀκάματον, cf. ps.-Aristaeus 52.21–2).

[55] Philo *On Abraham* 71; *On Joseph* 29, 69–70; *On the Creation* 19, 143; *Allegorical Interpretation* 3.98; *On the Cherubim* 127; *On the Special Laws* 1.14, 34.

[56] Philo *On the Sacrifices of Cain and Abel* 40; *On the Change of Names* 183–4, 258; *On the Unchangeableness of God* 52; *On the Cherubim* 86; *On Abraham* 202–3; *On the Special Laws* 1.209; 2.53–4.

the archetype of man, whom he molded after his own pattern, impressing upon his soul a trace of the cosmic *logos*, which in turn is an image of the divine *logos*. *Nous* is the divine part of man, and the human mind is shaped in conformity with the ideal archetype, the cosmic *logos*.[57] Thus with respect to the rational part of his soul, man participates in God's immortal nature. This transmission takes the (biblical) form of an inspiration, of a divine breath, which enables man to rise from the earth and contemplate God, whose nature is hard to grasp; thus only a few men – the king in ps.-Ecphantus' account – can look upon God directly. Man, the only living being capable of gaining knowledge of good and evil, is free to choose between virtue or vice by way of προαίρεσις, thereby receiving praise or blame for his actions.[58] While some of these views belong to the common tradition of Platonism, others enable us to draw more precise parallels that reinforce the idea of a common milieu for Philo and the pseudo-Pythagorean writings.

II. Chronology

If the thesis of a substantial homogeneity of the treatises is well founded, the hypothesis of different datings should be abandoned. The wild fluctuation in the chronology proposed by scholars is due to an attempt to situate specific doctrines in a historical context; yet the scholastic character of these writings undercuts such an approach; the divergent views seem to derive from theoretical reflection, and hardly reflect any concrete historical situation. This applies particularly to the political treatises, which, despite appearances, display a remarkable homogeneity. Moreover, it is hard to believe that the philosophical milieu favoring the production of these writings might have occurred at moments centuries apart. It seems equally improbable that authors might have sought to imitate, in different historical contexts, writings that do not distinguish themselves for any depth of thought. On the other hand, as we have seen, it is highly probable that the authors' overall project involved the production of an exhaustive corpus of treatises to cover all fields of knowledge. Decisive evidence suggests a period ranging from the first century BC to the first century AD as the most likely.[59] Varro knows ps.-Ocellus' *On the Universe*; ps.-Archytas' writing on the categories clearly presupposes Andronicus' edition; and the use of Aristotle's esoteric works, particularly in the ethical treatises, is more than

---

[57] Philo *Allegorical Interpretation* 1.19; 2.4; 3.96, 100; *On the Creation* 20, 24–5, 69, 139, 146; *Who Is the Heir* 231–2; *The Worse Attacks the Better* 83.
[58] See above n. 35 and 43.   [59] See above n. 18.

just conjectural.[60] As the evidence above has shown, the treatises are very close to the Alexandrian milieu of the first century BC in which Eudorus and Philo operated.

[60] The dating of Diotogenes' *On Kingship* in the first century BC is confirmed by an analysis of Papyrus Bingen 3, see Andorlini and Luiselli 2001; for ps.-Ecphantus see Calabi 2008: 185–215.

CHAPTER 16

Pythagoreans in Rome and Asia Minor around the turn of the common era

Jaap-Jan Flinterman

1. Introduction

Given the state of the evidence, studying the history of Pythagoreanism is often harsh training in recognizing our ignorance. The situation may look less bleak for the Roman world during the centuries around the turn of the era, but this impression is deceptive. Admittedly, we do have a considerable body of evidence for people credited with Pythagorean beliefs and a Pythagorean lifestyle. On closer inspection, however, much of this information turns out to be dubious. To mention just one example, most information about the first-century-AD Pythagorean philosopher Apollonius of Tyana comes from a heavily fictionalized biography written in the third century by the Athenian sophist Philostratus. Most scholars doubt whether Philostratus' *Life of Apollonius* can be used with any confidence as evidence for the historical Apollonius. Moreover, the non-Philostratean evidence probably gives us access to second-century traditions about the Cappadocian sage rather than to the first-century historical figure. This complicated evidential situation is not unrepresentative: there is evidence for the posthumous reputations rather than for the views and practices of the historical figures concerned, and although one can argue that their life and work offered a starting-point for the development of such reputations, it is not a foregone conclusion that this was provided by conscious Pythagoreanism.

In addition, during the centuries around the turn of the era "Pythagorean" was a label with diverging connotations, not all of them positive. Its denotation was, of course, "an adherent of a set of doctrines going back to the sixth-century BC philosopher Pythagoras." Quite often, however, this denotation was combined with or even superseded by the connotation "meddler in the supernatural." One of the recurring questions in this chapter will be what earned someone the label of "Pythagorean"; in answering that question, doctrine will turn out to be of secondary importance. Nor was Pythagoreanism predicated on membership of an organization.[1] The claim that Pythagoreanism was an organized movement in Rome around the turn of the common era cannot be easily substantiated; the available evidence can be better reconciled with Pythagoreanism being a matter of individual choice and individual practice – which, of course, does not exclude contacts between kindred souls and the passing on of ideas through successive generations. Such individual choices should be understood against the background of the availability among the educated of knowledge of Pythagorean views in general and of (pseudo-)Pythagorean literature in particular.

The geographical and chronological focus of this chapter will be on the city of Rome from the Late Republic up to and including the Julio-Claudian period, and on Asia Minor in the first and second centuries AD. In the case of Rome, both people to whom the label "Pythagorean" was applied and other members of the educated elite with an interest in Pythagoreanism will be discussed. As for Asia Minor, two men who in our evidence are presented as not just following Pythagorean precepts, but as consciously modeling their public image after Pythagoras, will be the center of attention: Apollonius of Tyana and Alexander of Abonouteichos. Both received biographical treatment, laudatory in the former case, defamatory in the latter. The contrast may serve to illustrate the controversies provoked by the activities of people labeled "Pythagoreans" in our evidence.

A relatively uncontroversial variety of Pythagoreanism can be found in the *Golden Verses*, a collection of precepts in seventy-one lines of poetry of uncertain date and origin. Although the most recent editor has argued for a date *c.* 350–300 BC (Thom 1995: 35–58), we have to wait until *c.* 100 AD for a quotation exceeding one line and until *c.* 200 for the first reference by name (Thom 1995: 13–17). The ethical guidelines that constitute the first part of the *Golden Verses* (1–49) would have been acceptable to most philosophical schools, but the self-examination prescribed in 40–4 was considered specifically Pythagorean around the middle of the first century BC (see below in section 2). Moreover, the second part (49–71), presenting the rewards awaiting those who organize their lives in accordance with the precepts, refers to dietary rules contained in texts of unclear provenance called *Purifications* and *Deliverance of the Soul* (67–9), and it culminates in a promise of apotheosis in afterlife (70–1). Missing from the *Golden Verses*, however, are two characteristics of quite a few self-styled Pythagoreans

---

[1] See Kingsley 1995: 329: "The so-called Neo-Pythagoreans of the first century BC onwards [...] appear as a rule to have been strikingly individualistic."

around the turn of the common era: a fascination with magical lore and a claim to superhuman status in this life.

2. Pythagoreanism in Rome

2.1. Around the middle of the first century BC: Nigidius Figulus, Vatinius, Varro, Cicero, Sextius

The Roman senator P. Nigidius Figulus (*c.* 100–45 BC) is often mentioned in connection with an alleged revival of Pythagoreanism during the first century BC.[2] The evidence for this appraisal of Nigidius is the characterization of him by Cicero, in the proem of his translation of Plato's *Timaeus*:[3]

> In my judgment [*sic iudico*], after those noble Pythagoreans whose school was to some extent extinguished after having flourished for several centuries in Italy and Sicily, it was Nigidius who arose as the one to restore it [*hunc extitisse, qui illam renovaret*].

This is hardly solid evidence for Nigidius' Pythagorean leanings, let alone for his alleged role in reviving Pythagoreanism. There is ambiguity in Cicero's wording about Nigidius' achievement. The subjunctive in the relative clause, *qui illam renovaret,* may suggest a potential rather than an actual result:[4] the clause does not need to mean more than that the multifaceted talents of Nigidius, who was dead by the time Cicero wrote these words, had justified the expectation that he would restore Pythagoreanism to its ancient glory. In addition, the proem to the translation of the *Timaeus* is the mise-en-scène of a dialogue rather than a contribution to the history of philosophy. Apparently, Cicero wanted to use his translation in the framework of a dialogue of his own, Nigidius Figulus cast in the role of spokesman of Pythagorean views.[5] In characterizing the *dramatis personae* of a dialogue Cicero may have had no qualms about foisting upon them views that their historical counterparts did not share. Admittedly, he seems to have preferred not to assign roles in such a way that the result was out of character (*Att.* 13.16.1). Still, he was aware that his ascriptions could raise a few eyebrows among the people concerned (*Fam.* 9.8.1), and it seems

---

[2] On Nigidius see Kroll 1936; Della Casa 1962, with Thesleff 1965b; Schmidt 2000.

[3] Cic. *Ti.* 1. I owe a great debt of gratitude to Lidewij van Gils, Lecturer in Latin at the Vrije Universiteit, Amsterdam, for discussing this passage with me. Of course the views expressed here are my sole responsibility.

[4] See for consecutive *qui* + subjunctive after *est, exstitit, exstiterunt* etc. Kühner and Stegmann 1971 2.303 (§ 194.8.c).

[5] See, e.g., Rawson 1985: 291; Musial 2001: 359 with n. 51; Lévy 2003: 95–100.

imprudent to accept the proem of the *Timaeus* as unequivocal evidence of Nigidius' views.[6]

The proem to Cicero's translation of the *Timaeus* is not the only evidence for Nigidius' Pythagoreanism. In a speech *Against Vatinius*, held in 56 BC, Cicero accuses his opponent of necromancy. He points out that Vatinius calls himself a Pythagorean and that he uses the sage's name to cloak hideous practices (*Against Vatinius* 14). Commenting on this passage, the *Scholia Bobiensia* refer to people meeting at Nigidius' house; they thought of themselves as Pythagoreans (*Pythagorae sectatores*), but detractors portrayed them as an unsavory set (*factio minus probabilis*). In the pseudo-Ciceronian *Invective against Sallust*, a rhetorical exercise, the historian is accused of having become an associate "in Nigidius' sacrilege club" (*sodalicium sacrilegi Nigidiani*, tr. Shackleton-Bailey).[7] A final piece of information about Nigidius, probably derived from Suetonius' *On Famous Men*, can be found in Jerome's *Chronicle*, where Nigidius is labeled "Pythagorean and magician," *Pythagoricus et magus*.[8]

It is tempting to identify the disreputable company mentioned in the scholium with the "sacrilege club" of the *Invective* and to present this conflation as evidence for a Pythagorean congregation led by Nigidius. But a rhetorical declamation and a commentary from late antiquity constitute a flimsy base for the hypothesis of organized Pythagoreanism at Rome; if it is at all necessary to think in such terms, a circle of variable size and composition is a more economical hypothesis than a "powerful religious sect."[9] Still, the entry in Jerome's *Chronicle* and the scholium suffice to demonstrate that the memory of Nigidius as a Pythagorean lived on under the Empire. Moreover, Jerome's labeling of Nigidius as *Pythagoricus et magus* and the scholium's characterization of the people frequenting his house suggest that his image as a Pythagorean involved dabbling in the occult. This combination may hold the key to an understanding of what earned Nigidius his reputation as a Pythagorean.

Of Nigidius' writings only fragments have survived. Indisputable indications for Pythagorean leanings are missing from these scanty remains:

---

[6] On history and fiction in Cicero's dialogues see Leeman and Pinkster 1981: 90–1; on *Att.* 13.16.1 and *Fam.* 9.8.1 cf. Lintott 2008: 326–7.

[7] *Scholia Bobiensia in Vat.* 14 (146.9–12 Stangl); [Cic.] *Against Sallust* 5.14. On the *Invective* as a rhetorical exercise see Novokhatko 2009: 15–16. The use of *Against Sallust* 5.14 as evidence for a *sodalicium* led by Nigidius Figulus is questioned by Santangelo 2011.

[8] Jerome *Chronicon* p. 156[l] Helm = Suet. *De viris illustribus* fr. 85 Reifferscheid.

[9] E.g., Kroll 1936: 202; Liebeschuetz 1979: 130: "This man's house became a meeting-place of men interested in Pythagoreanism." Rawson 1985: 94: "some sort of society." Contrast with these modest reconstructions Carcopino's (1926: 195–202) "'loge' pythagoricienne," Ferrero's (1955: 287–310) "setta nigidiana," and Lehmann's (1997: 300) "puissante secte religieuse avec ses chapelles ou loges."

metempsychosis, vegetarianism, musical theory and numerology are absent, as is the name of Pythagoras.[10] Pliny the Elder, however, mentions Nigidius repeatedly in contexts where he also refers to the *Magi*. When mentioning, for example, the sedative properties of a tick taken from the left ear of a black dog, he refers to the *Magi* (*HN* 30.82–3). He adds that according to Nigidius dogs will avoid for a whole day the presence of a man who has extracted a tick from a pig (*HN* 30.84 = fr. 128 Swoboda).[11] Matthew Dickie argues that in passages such as these Nigidius himself referred to "the *Magi*."[12] Moreover, he has demonstrated that for Pliny "the *Magi*" are the authorities appealed to in works ascribed to Pythagoras and Democritus on the magical properties of stones, plants, and animals.[13] That Pythagoras had travelled to the East and owed his wisdom to exotic sages was widely believed in the Hellenistic period.[14] Democritus, who was often portrayed as a Pythagorean philosopher,[15] was credited with similar journeys.[16] In the tradition exploited and criticized by Pliny, what Pythagoras and Democritus were supposed to have learnt from the *Magi* was magical lore (*HN* 24.156 and 160; 25.13). The best-known representative of this tradition is Bolus of Mendes, the second-century-BC author of a pseudo-Democritean *Cheirokmēta* ("Things wrought by hand").[17] Another example is the work on the magical properties of plants ascribed to Pythagoras by Pliny (*HN* 24.159). The remains of Nigidius' writings suggest that it was his adherence to this pseudepigraphic Pythagorean and Democritean tradition which earned him the label *Pythagoricus et magus*.[18] This fits in quite well with part of Cicero's characterization of Nigidius (*Ti.* 1; cf. Dickie 1999: 170): "an assiduous investigator of those matters which nature seems to have hidden." Nigidius' adherence to this tradition may not only explain his posthumous reputation as a Pythagorean but also attest to conscious Pythagoreanism on his part.

[10] Thesleff 1965b: 47; Rawson 1985: 291.
[11] For similar lore see Plin. *HN* 29.69 (= fr. 126 Swoboda); *HN* 29.138 (= fr. 127 Swoboda); cf. Rawson 1985: 182; Dickie 1999: 171–2.
[12] Dickie 1999: 172, referring to Serv. *Comm. in Ecl.* 4.10 (= fr. 67 Swoboda). Dickie 2001: 168–75 is a condensed version of Dickie 1999.
[13] Dickie 1999: 172–6. [14] See e.g., Cic. *Fin.* 5.87; Clem. Al. *Strom.* 1.15.66.2; Diog. Laert. 8.3.
[15] Duris of Samos *FGrHist* 76F23 = Porph. *VP* 3; Thrasyllus *ap.* Diog. Laert. 9.38.
[16] Cic. *Fin.* 5.50 and 87; *Tusc.* 4.44; Clem. Al. *Strom.* 1.15.69.6; Hippol. *Haer.* 1.13.1; Diog. Laert. 9.34–5; Ael. *VH* 4.20.
[17] Columella 7.5.17; Vitr. 9.praef.14; Plin. *HN* 24.160; cf. Kingsley 1994: 5–9; Dickie 1999: 177–89; and now Węcowski 2012.
[18] Rawson 1985: 182 with n. 69; Dickie 1999: 176–7; Kahn 2001: 140–1.

The fragments of Nigidius' works also display a strong interest in different varieties of divination.[19] His posthumous fame was primarily that of a skilled astrologer (Luc. 1.639–72; Suet. *Aug.* 94.5; cf. Cassius Dio 45.1.3–5). Referring to Varro, Apuleius (*Apol.* 42.7–8) tells how by incantations Nigidius successfully brought some boys into a divinatory trance. Divination had the reputation of being a favorite Pythagorean pastime (e.g., Cic. *Div.* 1.5). Nigidius probably saw his intellectual work in this field as fitting in with Pythagorean convictions. If the story told by Apuleius was indeed borrowed from Varro,[20] Nigidius also ventured into the practical side of private divination. Thus, the application of the label *magus* by Suetonius may also have referred to Nigidius' interest in divinatory theory and practice.[21]

Nigidius was not the only Pythagorean among Cicero's contemporaries. As we saw above, in 56 BC the orator accused P. Vatinius of using the name of Pythagoras to cover up his crimes (*Against Vatinius* 14). The *Scholia Bobiensia* add the information that Cicero in a speech *For Vatinius*, given two years later, put a much more positive spin on Vatinius' Pythagoreanism.[22] That Vatinius considered himself a Pythagorean is, therefore, certain. His case attests both the possibility of conscious Pythagoreanism among the Roman elite around the middle of the first century BC and the risks to one's reputation entailed by such a choice.

For Aulus Gellius (4.16.1) Nigidius Figulus and M. Terentius Varro (117–28 BC) had been "the most learned men of Roman stock." The name of Pythagoras, which is so conspicuously absent from the fragments of Nigidius' writings, regularly crops up in Varro's, and a predilection for Pythagorean notions is certainly present in what remains of his oeuvre.[23] In Book 5 of *The Latin Language* (5.11), the fourfold division of the subject matter, the origin of words, is introduced by a reference to the idea that reality is built out of opposing principles, a notion which the author explicitly ascribes to Pythagoras. That the introduction by Varro, in the preceding passage (5.8–9), of the notion of the king as name giver also betrays Pythagorean influence is harder to substantiate,[24] even if one is

---

[19] Rawson 1985: 310–11; MacIntosh Turfa 2006: 174–5.

[20] On the story's Varronian origin see Cardauns 1960: 45–50.

[21] On the meaning of *magus* in Latin prose after Pliny see Rives 2010: 65–6. The term *magus* cannot be taken as reflecting contemporary, i.e. first-century-BC, usage. The label *magus* may well have been welcomed by Nigidius himself.

[22] *Scholia Bobiensia in Vat.* 14 (146.8–9 Stangl).

[23] Cardauns 2001 and Sallmann 2002 offer convenient starting-points for Varronian studies. Varro's dates of birth and death: Burgess 2002: 31; Varro and Pythagoreanism: Lehmann 1997: 299–314.

[24] That Varro's conception of the king as namegiver was inspired by Pythagoreanism is maintained by Lehmann 1997: 304–7 and Cardauns 2001: 32, following Boyancé 1975 and 1976: 141–5. For

prepared to admit that in Book 8 the phrase "those who first imposed names upon things" (8.7) may echo the *acusma* that "the wisest is number, second is the one who gave names to things."[25] *On the Principles of Numbers* was presumably devoted to Pythagorean numerology.[26] More numerological lore could be found in Book 1 of the *Sevens*, a collection of 700 portraits of famous men. In its preface Varro emphasized the cosmological, biological and cultural importance of the number 7 (Gel. 3.10). One of the subjects dealt with in this numerological exposition was embryology, a topic Varro also discussed in his *Tubero on Human Birth*, where he gave an account of Pythagorean views on gestation.[27]

In addition to the evidence from Varro's own writings, an external piece of information should be taken into account. According to Pliny (*HN* 35.160), Varro "was interred in the Pythagorean style, in leaves of olive, myrtle, and black poplar." Myrtle was sacred to Demeter and to the gods of the Underworld, and according to Homer's Circe the black poplar was prominent in Persephone's sacred woods, near the entrance of the Underworld.[28] The names of Demeter and Persephone are reminiscent of "Orphic" mysteries, and the symbolic presence of these goddesses at Varro's funeral suggests that the antiquarian had high expectations for the destination of his final journey. Varro's last wish seems to attest a commitment going beyond a merely intellectual interest.

That an interest in Pythagoras and Pythagoreanism was hardly an idiosyncrasy is apparent from the oeuvre of Cicero. A chauvinistic touch is recurrent in passages about Pythagoras and Pythagoreans. The philosopher and his followers demonstrate that Italy was not devoid of indigenous intellectual accomplishments: Pythagoras and the Pythagoreans were "almost fellow-countrymen of ours" (*incolae paene nostri*), and in earlier times they were called "Italian philosophers" (*Sen.* 78).[29] Pythagoras is repeatedly mentioned as an exemplary philosopher (e.g. *Tusc.* 3.36, 4.55 and

---

criticism of Boyancé's ideas on this issue see Blank 2012: 284–6; on *The Latin Language* 5.8–9 also Schröter 1963; Piras 1998: 57–71.

[25] Ael. *VH* 4.17 (cf. Cic. *Tusc.* 1.62; Iambl. *VP* 82 and 56); Boyancé 1975: 109 with n. 7.

[26] The work is mentioned by Jerome *ep.* 33.2; cf. Rawson 1985: 162.

[27] Censorinus *De Die Natali* 9–11; cf. Mansfeld 1971: 190–1 n. 198; Rawson 1985: 161–2.

[28] On Pythagorean burial customs (inhumation, no cremation) see Boyancé 1937: 135–6; Cumont 1943: 114–15; Bollansée's commentary on *FGrHist* 1026F22; on Bacchic funerary rituals Graf and Johnston 2007: 158–63. For attempts to explain the leaves of myrtle, olive and black poplar see Rohde 1925 Vol. 1: 226–7 n. 3; Cumont 1942: 11–12; Cumont 1943: 115 n. 1. Olive and myrtle used for funerary purposes: e.g., Callim. *Ia.* 4.49–56 and Artem. 4.57 for the olive; Eur. *El.* 324 and 512 for the myrtle. Myrtle sacred to Demeter: Schol. S. *OC* 681; Artem. 1.77 (85.13–16 Pack); to Demeter and the *chthonioi*: Schol. Ar. *Ran.* 330. Black poplars: *Od.* 10.510.

[29] Huffman 2005: 21: " a conscious attempt on the part of the Romans to claim Pythagoreanism as a native Italian philosophy." See also Burkert 1961: 238–9. "Italian philosophers": e.g., Arist. *Metaph.* 987a10 and 31; 988a26.

5.30), together with Socrates, Plato and Democritus. Pythagoras was the man who had coined the word "philosopher,"[30] and Plato was intellectually indebted to Pythagoreanism.[31] The tradition that Numa had been a disciple of Pythagoras is, on the other hand, repeatedly refuted with chronological arguments.[32] But the possibility that Pythagoreanism had at least some impact on Rome during the Early Republic is acknowledged, and the story that Numa had been a disciple of Pythagoras explained as a misunderstanding resulting from clear vestiges of Pythagorean influence on Roman customs (*Tusc.* 4.2).

As far as Pythagorean doctrine is concerned, Cicero offers mostly brief references, for example to the notion that the universe originates from numbers and mathematical principles (*Academica* 2.118; cf. *Tusc.* 1.20); to the immortality of the soul (*Tusc.* 1.38; *Sen.* 78); as well as to the preference for bloodless sacrifice (*Nat. D.* 3.88) and the notorious taboo on beans (*Div.* 1.62 and 2.119). In the field of ethics Pythagorean friendship is a recurrent topic,[33] and the orator is, naturally, interested in Pythagorean involvement in politics (*De or.* 3.139; *Off.* 1.155). The music of the spheres is mentioned and attributed to Pythagoras in *On the Nature of the Gods* (3.27); it receives an extended description in the *Dream of Scipio* (*Rep.* 6.18–19).[34]

In *On Old Age* (38) the main speaker says that, in order to exercise his memory, he follows the Pythagorean practice of recalling every evening everything said, heard or done during the day; according to Diodorus Siculus (10.5.1) the Pythagoreans used to do so every morning with everything experienced during the preceding day. In its evening variant this practice is also attested for Cicero's contemporary Quintus Sextius.[35] But whereas Cicero's Cato uses it as a method for memory training, explicitly mentioning its Pythagorean character, Sextius advised it as a road to moral improvement without referring to its origin (Sen. *Dial.* 5.36). In fact, Diodorus Siculus and Cicero offer the earliest securely datable characterizations of this practice as Pythagorean.[36] Sextius also advocated vegetarianism, although his abstention from meat resulted from frugality rather than a belief in metempsychosis (Sen. *Ep.* 108.17–19). One did not have to share

---

[30] *Tusc.* 5.8–9 = Heraclid. Pont. fr. 88 Wehrli; cf. Diog. Laert. 1.12 = Heraclid. Pont. fr. 87 Wehrli; Riedweg 2002: 120–8.

[31] Cic. *Rep.* 1.16; *Fin.* 5.87; *Tusc.* 1.39.   [32] Cic. *Rep.* 2.28–9; *De Orat.* 2.154.

[33] *Fin.* 2.79; *Tusc.* 5.63; *Off.* 1.56 and 3.45; *Amic.* 88.

[34] Boyancé 1936: 104–15. On the harmony of the spheres see Burkert 1972a: 350–7; Huffman 1993: 279–83.

[35] On Sextius see Dingel 2001; Kahn 2001: 92–3.

[36] Moral self-examination can also be found in the *Golden Verses* (40–4), but these are of uncertain date, see section 1 above.

basic Pythagorean doctrines in order to appreciate Pythagorean precepts as ethical guidelines.

The presence of Pythagoras and Pythagoreanism in Cicero's oeuvre confirms that Roman intellectuals around the middle of the first century BC were interested in and had access to a broad range of Pythagorean ideas. This interest and access can be partially explained by the fact that Pythagoreanism had not been an unknown phenomenon in the Middle Republic. The pseudo-Pythagorean and pseudo-Democritean tradition that was central to Nigidius' Pythagoreanism was known in Rome in the first half of the second century BC.[37] Ennius referred in the opening lines of his *Annals* to the doctrine of transmigration, claiming that he was an incarnation of Homer's soul.[38] The legend of Numa's discipleship of Pythagoras must reach back to the third century BC at the latest.[39] According to Pliny, a statue of Pythagoras was erected in the comitium during a Samnite war (late fourth or early third century BC).[40]

The palpable Roman interest in Pythagoreanism around the middle of the first century BC thus did not appear from thin air. The increased access to Hellenistic intellectual life during the period starting with the Mithridatic wars, however, no doubt contributed to a widening of the circle of Romans interested in Pythagoreanism and to a deepening of their familiarity with Pythagorean doctrine as well.[41] Conversely, existing Roman interest may have stimulated Greeks staying in Rome to write on Pythagorean topics.[42] The grammarian Alexander of Miletus was imprisoned during the first Mithridatic war (89–85 BC) and brought as a slave to Rome. He received freedom and citizenship from Sulla, stayed in Rome, and earned a reputation for learning that gained him the epithet "Polyhistor."[43] Among his numerous works were *Successions of Philosophers* and *On Pythagorean Symbols*. In the former he presented a summary of doctrines he claimed to have found in "Pythagorean notebooks" (*Pythagorika hypomnēmata*).[44] John Dillon (1977: 117–18) suggested that Nigidius Figulus may have been taught by Alexander. But it is not easy to find common ground between Nigidius' Pythagoreanism and Alexander's notebooks. Besides, Alexander

---

[37] Cato *Agr.* 157; cf. Plin. *HN* 20.78, and see Burkert 1961: 239–40; Kahn 2001: 88.
[38] Enn. *Ann.* fr. 1.2–10 Skutch; cf. Skutch 1985: 147–67; Burkert 1961: 243–4.
[39] Burkert 1961: 237; Gruen 1990: 162–70; Humm 1996: 340–5.
[40] Plin. *HN* 34.26; cf. Plut. *Num.* 8.20, and see Burkert 1961: 237 with n. 2; Gruen 1990: 161; Humm 1996: 345–50. Pliny does not specify which Samnite war he has in mind.
[41] Rawson 1985: 7–12 and 39–40.   [42] Rawson 1985: 292–3.
[43] Schwartz 1894; Rawson 1985: 69–70.
[44] See, e.g., Burkert 1961: 26–8; Burkert 1972a: 53; Kahn 2001: 79–83; Long 2013; Chapter 17 below.

is not mentioned by any contemporary Roman source,[45] and his paraphrase of the "Pythagorean Notebooks" does not seem to have made a large impact in Rome during the first century BC.[46] Of course it is highly likely that there were more Greek intellectuals who catered for Roman interest in Pythagoreanism.[47]

2.2. Augustan and Julio-Claudian Rome

Varro made his final journey in 28 BC, three years after the Battle of Actium that made Octavian sole ruler of the Roman world. We owe this information to Jerome (*Chronicon*, p. 164ᵃ Helm) who, in the preceding entry of his *Chronicle* (p. 163ᵏ Helm), tells us that in the same year Octavian expelled from Rome and Italy Anaxilaus of Larissa, "Pythagorean and magician" – the label also given to Nigidius Figulus. The Larissaean worked in the pseudo-Democritean tradition that was also central to the senator's Pythagoreanism.[48] To Anaxilaus' intellectual legacy belonged a collection of conjuring-tricks (παίγνια), at least part of which were probably attributed to Democritus.[49] About the reason for his expulsion from Rome one can only speculate. Five years earlier, in 33 BC, astrologers and magicians (*goëtes*) had been expelled (Cassius Dio 49.43.5). Suspicion of potentially subversive private divination probably played a decisive role, both during the tense period before Actium and in the year preceding the constitutional settlement of 27 BC.[50] But some people may have considered Pythagoreanism a threat to conventional religion.[51]

This did not stop prominent Augustan poets from using Pythagorean material. The drowned man introduced as speaker in one of Horace's odes addresses first Archytas, and then appeals to a passing sailor for burial.[52] The emphasis of the apostrophe to Archytas is on the inevitability of death and the baneful consequences of immortality, points that are illustrated by allusions to mythical stories as well as to Pythagoras' alleged claim that he once had been the Trojan hero Euphorbus.[53] This claim, which served to

---

[45] Rawson 1985: 62.   [46] Long 2013.

[47] That this might also result in additions to pseudepigraphic literature is suggested by the case of King Juba II of Mauretania, who was educated in Rome in the third quarter of the first century BC and who became an avid collector of Pythagorean texts. According to Olympiodorus (*CAG* 12.1, p. 13), his willingness to invest in this hobby encouraged the production of forgeries; cf. Thesleff 1961: 54–5.

[48] See for Anaxilaus Dickie 1999: 165–8.

[49] Irenaeus *Against Heresies* 1.7.1; cf. Plin. *HN* 28.181; 32.141; 35.175. The παίγνια Δημοκρίτου (*PGM* VII 167–86) are an offshoot of this tradition.

[50] Liebeschuetz 1979: 135–6; cf. Kienast 1999: 266 n. 192a.   [51] Gordon 1999: 261.

[52] Hor. *Carm.* 1.28; cf. Huffman 2005: 19–21.

[53] On which see Burkert 1972a: 138–41; Riedweg 2002: 17.

prove the doctrine of metempsychosis, is rejected by the speaker: Archytas may have thought Pythagoras "no mean authority on nature and truth," but "one night waits for all of us and the path of death must be trod once and for all" (14–16, tr. Huffman). In Augustan Rome poetic use of Pythagorean materials did not require sympathy with Pythagorean ideas.

Ovid's *Metamorphoses* offer an even more spectacular example of poetic use of Crotonian wisdom. Book 15 contains 404 lines of oratory by Pythagoras (75–478), embedded in a speech by an elderly inhabitant of Croton (12–478) to Numa during a visit of the future king to the city (7–8). Ovid's Pythagoras makes a passionate plea for vegetarianism and against animal sacrifice (75–142). Claiming divine authority (143–5), the sage expounds the doctrine of metempsychosis (156–72), adducing it as an argument against the consumption of meat (173–5). The change implied in metempsychosis is taken as paradigmatic for the permanent mutation to which all beings are subject (165: *omnia mutantur*), and this law of universal metamorphosis is phrased in Heraclitean terms (178: *cuncta fluunt*).[54] Among the examples given is the way in which the four elements evolve from and into each other (237–51). In his peroration the speaker returns to the plea for vegetarianism (456–78), warning against the risk of eating a body that has held a relative's soul (459–62). This warning is strongly reminiscent of Empedocles (DK 31B137), and the four elements mentioned in 237–51 are Empedoclean as well (DK 31A33 and B6).[55] The notion that the elements evolve from and into each other is, on the other hand, definitely un-Empedoclean and has an Heraclitean ring (e.g., DK 22B31 and 90). The upshot of the Presocratic cocktail served by Ovid's Pythagoras is the variability of being. The idea that the speech offers an interpretative key to *Metamorphoses* as a whole seems to be out of favor.[56] Few will be inclined to accept the speech as evidence of the poet's philosophical conviction,[57] but it certainly attests the familiarity of Ovid and his intended audience with the "Italian philosophy," its founding father, and some of its central tenets.[58]

---

[54] Cf. DK 22A6; Galinsky 1998: 321.

[55] On Empedoclean material in the speech of Ovid's Pythagoras see Hardie 1995: 205 with n. 7.

[56] It is dismissed by Little 1970, who offers a useful survey of older scholarship. Segal 1969: 292 perceives "touches of exaggeration bordering on parody" in the Pythagoras section; Galinsky 1975: 104–6 maintains that Ovid created with Pythagoras' speech "a foil to his own *Metamorphoses* [. . .] intentionally monotonous, dreary, and long-winded," a view restated in Galinsky 1998: 331–4.

[57] As was Carcopino 1963: 59–170 ("L'exil d'Ovide, poète pythagoricien"), who also explained Ovid's exile from his alleged Pythagoreanism.

[58] See also Boyancé 1939: 39–43, pointing out the concordance between the myth about the origin of animal sacrifice in Ov. *Met.* 15.111–14 and Aristoxenus' statement (fr. 25 Wehrli = Gell. 4.11.6) that Pythagoras ate very young pigs and tender kids.

During the reign of Tiberius, Seneca was instructed by his teacher Sotion, a follower of Sextius, about the advantages of abstention from meat. Sotion argued that vegetarianism was beneficial regardless of one's persuasions. Believers in metempsychosis would not run the risk of consuming a parent's incarnation, while people skeptical about Pythagorean doctrine would profit by curbing their extravagance (Sen. *Ep.* 108.17–21). Inspired by Pythagoras (*Ep.* 108.17), Seneca heeded Sotion's admonitions for a year, only returning to his former ways when vegetarianism came under suspicion as emblematic of an interest in foreign superstition (*Ep.* 108.22).[59]

A treatment of Pythagoreanism at Rome during the Julio-Claudian period would be incomplete without mentioning the ongoing discussion about the subterranean basilica discovered in 1917 near the Porta Maggiore.[60] One of the hypotheses about this enigmatic building is that it was a meeting-place of a Pythagorean congregation. The great proponent of this theory was Jérôme Carcopino (1926; 1956: 1–82). He drew arguments from the stuccoes decorating the basilica's walls and ceilings,[61] especially the representation of Sappho's leap from the Leucadian rock. As evidence for the Pythagorean character of this representation he adduced a passage from Pliny's *Natural History* (22.20) on the aphrodisiacal properties of the white variant of the plant *eryngium*, which are illustrated by the report that "on account of this Phaon was loved by Sappho." Pliny adds that the subject gave rise to a lot of idle speculation, not only by the *Magi*, but also among Pythagoreans. In Carcopino's interpretation, it was Pliny's contention that magicians and Pythagoreans speculated about Sappho's love for Phaon (resulting in her leap into the sea).[62] However, since the passage may just as well, if not better, be understood as implying nothing more than that *Magi* and Pythagoreans were fascinated by the plant's aphrodisiacal properties, it does not warrant Carcopino's conclusion.[63] While the possibility that the iconography of the stuccoes lends itself to Pythagorean exegesis remains,[64] for the time being it seems advisable to consider the issue undecided and

---

[59] Presumably in 19 AD, when Jews and worshippers of Isis were expelled from Rome. On this expulsion see Rutgers 1994: 60–5.

[60] North 2012 is the most recent contribution and offers good bibliography.

[61] For the date (first half first century AD) of the decorations see North 2012: 38–9.

[62] Carcopino 1926: 382–3; 1956: 14–23.

[63] Hubaux 1928; cf. Hubaux 1930: 187–94; André 1958; Latte 1960: 341 n. 1; North 2012: 54–5. Unfortunately, the passage from Pliny is still sometimes referred to as support for the alleged Pythagorean character of the basilica, see, e.g., Sauron 1994: 606, 609, and 614–15.

[64] See North 2012: 52–3 and 58–9.

not to adduce the underground basilica as evidence for Pythagoreanism at Rome.

3. Pythagoreanism in Asia Minor

3.1. Apollonius of Tyana

A few years before Seneca decided to resume meat consumption, a youth from Cappadocian Tyana adopted an uncompromisingly Pythagorean way of life. He abstained from all animal products, renounced wine and let his hair grow long (Philostr. *V A* 1.8). When he had reached manhood, he decided to abjure sex as well (*V A* 1.13.3), and he observed the five-year period of silence required from aspiring Pythagoreans (*V A* 1.14–15). The young man's name was Apollonius, and we owe this information to an eight-book *Life of Apollonius of Tyana*, written, probably in the 220s or 230s, by the Athenian sophist Flavius Philostratus.[65] The asceticism practiced by Philostratus' Apollonius is in line with conceptions of the Pythagorean life during the first centuries AD.[66] Among the rewards for those who follow the Pythagorean way of life pride of place is, in the *Life of Apollonius*, taken by privileged access to the divine, clairvoyance and the faculty of foreknowledge (*V A* 1.32.2; 6.11.6).[67] As presented by Philostratus, Apollonius is in no way inferior to Pythagoras himself (*V A* 1.2.1). He is credited with a number of miraculous feats that are strongly reminiscent of the Pythagoras legend, e.g., bilocation (*V A* 4.10.1) and communicating with animals (*V A* 1.20.3, 4.3.1 and 6.43.2). The semi-divine status that is part and parcel of the Pythagoras legend is in the *Life* reserved for the protagonist: Apollonius' disciple Damis recognizes that his master's nature is "divine and superhuman."[68]

This portrayal of Apollonius as a latter-day Pythagoras is conveyed in a rich and sophisticated narrative. Apollonius' conversion to Pythagoreanism takes place in the Cilician city of Aegae, where as a youth he finds hospitality in the sanctuary of Asclepius. Despising a settled existence, he roams

---

[65] The best translation of the title, Τὰ ἐς τὸν Τυανέα Ἀπολλώνιον, is *On Apollonius of Tyana*. I see no harm in sticking to the traditional designation. My references are to the books, chapters, and sections of the edition by C.P. Jones in the Loeb Classical Library (2005).

[66] Flinterman 2009a: 157–63, pointing out parallels in Ovid, Seneca, Plutarch, Juvenal, Lucian and Apuleius. The evidence for full-blown celibacy in common conceptions of Pythagoreanism is thin though: a remark by Clement of Alexandria (*Strom.* 3.3.24.1) allows the inference that celibacy was considered an ideal by at least some Pythagoreans; cf. Flinterman 2009a: 161–2.

[67] Flinterman 2009a: 163–9.

[68] *V A* 7.38.2; cf. Flinterman 2009a: 170–5; Van Uytfanghe 2009.

the southern part of Asia Minor and Syria. In the 40s AD, he journeys
to Mesopotamia, Iran and eventually India, where for four months he
enjoys the company of Indian sages. According to Philostratus, Pythagoras'
wisdom originated from India, so Apollonius here taps the very sources
of Pythagoreanism.[69] Apollonius' youth and Eastern travels are covered in
the first three books of the *Life*. Books 4 to 6 deal with his peregrinations
through the Mediterranean world. He heals the sick, casts out demons,
suppresses an outbreak of the plague, predicts the future, and even brings
a young woman back to life. In addition, he instructs the citizens of Greek
cities how they ought to live together as well as, during the Year of the
Four Emperors (69 AD), advising the new emperor Vespasian about the
correct way to exercise monarchic power. With Vespasian and his oldest
son Titus he is on friendly terms, but he clashes with the last ruler of
the Flavian dynasty, the tyrannical emperor Domitian. The story of the
resulting conflict, the dramatic climax of the *Life*, is told in Books 7 and
8. It culminates in a trial before the emperor, who has to acquit the sage,
whereupon Apollonius miraculously disappears from the courtroom. A few
years afterwards, he ascends to heaven from the sanctuary of the Cretan
goddess Dictynna.[70]

The extent to which this remarkable account can be taken as evidence
for the historical Apollonius is, unfortunately, very limited.[71] To begin
with, Philostratus presents the *Life* as a text with an apologetic purpose:
he wants to defend the protagonist against the accusation of being a magician, portraying him instead as a Pythagorean philosopher endowed with
exceptional wisdom and superhuman abilities (*V A* 1.2). This fits in with
the fact that the *Life* was commissioned by Julia Domna, the widow of
Septimius Severus and the mother of his successor Caracalla (*V A* 1.3.1);
to a certain extent, Philostratus' work reflects the interest in and devotion
to Apollonius of members of the Severan dynasty (*V A* 8.31.3; Cassius Dio
77.18.4). Moreover, there is a scholarly consensus that the *Life of Apollonius*
belongs to "that zone between truth and fiction that is so bewildering to the
professional historian,"[72] and that the historical value of the information

---

[69] *V A* 3.19–20; 6.11.13; cf. Flinterman 1995: 86–7.

[70] On Apollonius' ascension see Flinterman 2009b.

[71] Bowie 1978 is the fundamental study of the traditions on Apollonius; see also Flinterman 1995:
52–88; Francis 1995: 86–97; Schirren 2005: 1–9.

[72] The phrase is borrowed from Momigliano's (1993: 46) characterization of Socratic literature. See,
on the *V A* as fiction, e.g., Bowie 1978: 1663–7; Holzberg 1986: 25–6; Billault 2000: 105–26; Schirren
2005: 38–50. There is also an almost complete scholarly consensus that "Damis" – the disciple of
Apollonius whose memoirs Philostratus claims to have had access to – is a literary fiction, see esp.
Bowie 1978: 1653–71; Anderson 1986: 155–73 and Flinterman 1995: 79–88 disagree.

it offers should not be taken for granted unless external confirmation can be found.

Non-Philostratean evidence does exist,[73] but it has its problems, dating being one of them. The oldest securely datable evidence is the implicit characterization, in Lucian's *Alexander the False Prophet*, of Apollonius as a *goēs*, a meddler in the supernatural; Lucian wrote his *Alexander* after the death of Marcus Aurelius in 180 AD.[74] Presumably in the first half of the second century a certain Moeragenes wrote *Memorabilia of Apollonius, Magus and Philosopher*, in four books.[75] Philostratus disqualifies the now lost work of Moeragenes as a source of information about Apollonius; probably it was the standard account when he wrote the *Life*. The title suggests that Moeragenes presented Apollonius as both a *magus* and a philosopher, a combination at odds with Philostratus' apologetics, but which corresponds to the positive content given to the term *magus* in two letters ascribed to Apollonius (*Epp. Apoll.* 16 and 17). If not authentic, these letters may well represent a pre-Philostratean tradition on Apollonius, which is the closest we may be able to get to the Tyanean sage. The addressee of both letters is the Stoic philosopher Euphrates, who is the archenemy of the main character of the *Life* (e.g., *V A* 5.39) and who also appears in conflict with Apollonius in the fragment of Moeragenes' *Memorabilia* preserved in Origen's *Against Celsus* (6.41).[76] Both for the epistolographer and for Moeragenes, Pythagoreanism seems to have been a philosophical label under which the roles of philosopher and *magus* could be combined. This combination is strongly reminiscent of the characterization of Nigidius Figulus and Anaxilaus in Jerome's *Chronicle*: *Pythagoricus et magus*.

In a few cases we can be reasonably sure that miraculous feats described in the *Life* were part of local traditions. A prime example is the liquidation of a plague demon in the theater at Ephesus (*V A* 4.10). The same story is also told by Lactantius (*Div. inst.* 5.3), who probably drew independently on the same tradition as Philostratus (Bowie 1978: 1687). In the case of the Syrian city of Antioch, the focus of local tradition was on *telesmata*, "talismans," put up by Apollonius against the north wind, scorpions and gnats (Malalas *Chronographia* 10.51 Thurn). In the Byzantine and Arab world Apollonius enjoyed a widespread posthumous reputation as a manufacturer of talismans.[77] Although the evidence for talismans ascribed to

---

[73] The *testimonia* are collected in the third volume of Jones's Loeb (2006).
[74] Lucian *Alex.* 5; cf. Robiano 2003. *Alexander* completed after 180 AD: *Alex.* 48.
[75] Title: Origen *C. Cels.* 6.41; four books: Philostr. *V A* 1.3.2; cf. Bowie 1978: 1673–80.
[76] Pre-Philostratean origin of letters to Euphrates: Bowie 1978: 1676–78.
[77] Dulière 1970; Speyer 1974: 56–61; Dzielska 1986: 99–127.

Apollonius does not emerge before the early fourth century, it seems plausible that this part of his posthumous reputation belonged to an earlier tradition that was disregarded by Philostratus.[78]

Healing abilities are part of Apollonius' miraculous powers both in the *Life* and in the extra-Philostratean tradition. In this capacity Apollonius is linked to Asclepius. As we saw above, the protagonist of the *Life* lives as a youth in the sanctuary of the healing god at Aegae. As "servant and companion" of Asclepius (*VA* 1.12.1) he plays the part of a freelance religious middleman: he advises both priests and worshippers, and Asclepius is "glad to cure the sick with Apollonius as his witness" (*VA* 1.8.2, tr. Jones). For Apollonius' stay in the Asclepieum at Aegae Philostratus refers to a work of a citizen of this city, Maximus (*VA* 1.12.2). Opinions differ on the question whether Maximus' work ever existed outside the pages of the *Life*,[79] but even if Philostratus would have referred to a fictional source, a link with Asclepius is also suggested by an Apollonian letter to Euphrates in which the epistolographer compares himself with the god (*Epp. Apoll.* 8.2).

The evidence adduced so far attests the reputation of Apollonius as a charismatic sage and miracle-worker, a man endowed with supernatural powers suggestive of his superhuman nature. This suggestion is also present in the Apollonian letters: again in a letter addressed to Euphrates, the epistolographer claims that "[t]he most wise Pythagoras, too, belonged to the class of *daimones*" (tr. Penella), probably implying that the same is true of himself.[80] Apollonius is presented or he presents himself not just as a conscious Pythagorean, but even more as a conscious imitator of Pythagoras. But what about substantial writings attesting Pythagorean thought?

Of the writings attributed to Apollonius which (may) have been fragmentarily preserved, there are two deserving attention. The first of these is *On Sacrifices*, a work twice mentioned by Philostratus (*VA* 3.41 and 4.19). More importantly, a passage is quoted by Eusebius (*Praep. Evang.* 4.13) and paraphrased by Porphyry (*Abst.* 2.34). The fragment refers to the highest, fully transcendent deity, to whom one should not sacrifice or even pray; with this first and greatest god only voiceless communication through the Mind (*Nous*) is possible. This train of thought bears a close resemblance to theological speculations of Neopythagorean philosophers such as

---

[78] Speyer 1974: 58; *pace* Dzielska 1986: 123–4.

[79] The reality of Maximus' work is accepted by Bowie 1978: 1684–5; Graf 1984/1985. Differently: Schirren 2005: 2–5.

[80] *Epp. Apoll.* 50, with Penella 1979 *ad loc.* Apollonius as a superhuman being in the Apollonian letters: Macris 2006b: 315–16.

Moderatus and Numenius, whose thinking was characterized by a "strong transcendental tendency" and a "stress on the ineffability of God" (Dillon 1977: 383). The fragment may be authentic, but proof is impossible.[81]

On Sacrifices is among the works attributed to Apollonius in the lexicon known as the *Suda* (A 3420: Τελεταὶ ἢ περὶ θυσιῶν); also listed by the lexicographer is a *Life of Pythagoras* (Πυθαγόρου βίος). Whether a book containing the doctrines of Pythagoras mentioned by Philostratus (*V A* 8.19–20) can be identified with the biography listed in the *Suda* is controversial.[82] That Apollonius wrote a biography of Pythagoras seems to be confirmed by references to a work by *an* Apollonius in Porphyry's *Life of Pythagoras* (*VP* 2) and Iamblichus' *On the Pythagorean Life* (*VP* 254). Erwin Rohde (1901) argued that about one quarter of Iamblichus' work could be assigned to the biography of Pythagoras ascribed to Apollonius of Tyana by the *Suda*. Burkert (1972a: 100–1) accepted a light version of Rohde's hypothesis. More recently, Rohde's edifice has come under attack.[83] The assumption that the Apollonius referred to by Porphyry and Iamblichus must be Apollonius *of Tyana* has been questioned: although the identification of the Apollonius mentioned by the Neoplatonist biographers with the Tyanean sage has some plausibility, it is hardly certain. In addition, the arguments for the ascription of large portions of Iamblichus' work to one and the same source have been challenged.

Both *On Sacrifices* and the *Life of Pythagoras* are problematic evidence for the historical Apollonius: *On Sacrifices* because we cannot exclude the possibility that it was a pseudepigraphic text, composed in order to broaden the image of Apollonius as a Pythagorean philosopher by foisting upon him some appropriate metaphysics; and the *Life of Pythagoras* because we cannot be sure that the Apollonius referred to by the Neoplatonist biographers was Apollonius of Tyana and because attempts to reconstruct this hypothetical biography fail to carry conviction. The remaining evidence, especially letters addressed to Euphrates and a fragment of Moeragenes' *Memorabilia of Apollonius*, portrays Apollonius as a man endowed with supernatural abilities. Probably he understood himself as a Pythagorean philosopher, but his Pythagoreanism may have been a legitimization of his reputation as a miracle-worker more than anything else.[84]

---

[81] On Περὶ θυσιῶν see Dzielska 1986: 136–41 and 145–51; Kahn 2001: 144–5. Both tend to accept the work as authentic.

[82] Contrast Bowie 1978: 1672 n. 77 with Anderson 1986: 301.

[83] Gorman 1985; Staab 2002: 228–37; Staab 2007; cf. Flinterman 1995: 77–9; Flinterman 2009a: 172–3 n. 115.

[84] See Bowie 1978: 1685–8 and 1691–2; cf. Flinterman 1996: 90.

3.2.   Alexander of Abonouteichos

According to Philostratus, Apollonius was during the larger part of his public life accompanied by disciples.[85] One of these disciples appears in Lucian's *Alexander the False Prophet*. As a youth Alexander of Abonouteichos was allegedly taught by a man from Tyana who had been a follower of "the infamous Apollonius." Lucian gives an unflattering description of Alexander's Tyanean teacher: he was an expert in all kinds of magical spells and incantations, attracting clients wishing to harm their enemies and to fulfill their sexual or material desires. He also claimed, however, to be a physician (*Alex.* 5), which nicely fits in with Apollonius' reputation as a healer.

If we are to believe Lucian, Alexander of Abonouteichos became the founder and prophet of an oracle in his hometown, on the south coast of the Black Sea. The god speaking through the oracle was a new manifestation of Asclepius in the shape of a big snake with (partly) human facial features. The oracle was a huge success, drawing visitors from far and wide, including members of the imperial aristocracy. Its founder became rich and famous, and the modest town of Abonouteichos expressed its new self-esteem as the site of a major oracular shrine by changing its name to Ionopolis, "City of Ion" (*Alex.* 58). The prophet of the New Asclepius presented himself as a Pythagorean, professing the doctrine of metempsychosis (*Alex.* 34 and 43). He even claimed to be "like Pythagoras" (*Alex.* 4: Πυθαγόρᾳ ὅμοιος), displaying a golden thigh (*Alex.* 40).[86]

As portrayed by Lucian, Alexander was a charismatic individual of Pythagorean persuasion who became the founder of a major religious institution. This should suffice to earn him a place in the history of Pythagoreanism. Scholars have pointed out that the importance of the cult of Glycon and the change of name of Abonouteichos find confirmation in numismatic and iconographic evidence, and Lucian has clearly taken care of the prosopographical and chronological plausibility of his account.[87] Unfortunately, the only evidence for Alexander's role in the cult and its foundation is Lucian's defamatory biography. In recent scholarship there is a tendency to consider the description of Alexander's role as largely a literary construct and even to doubt the prophet's historicity.[88]

---

[85] E.g., *VA* 1.16.3–4 and 8.24; cf. Petzke 1970: 182–3.

[86] On the Pythagoreanism of Lucian's Alexander see Macris 2006b: 319–20.

[87] Robert 1980: 393–421; Jones 1986: 133–48; Flinterman 1997; Chaniotis 2002; on Glycon's iconography see Petsalis-Diomidis 2010: 14–41.

[88] Elm von der Osten 2006: 154; Bendlin 2011: 242–3.

Even if Alexander's existence or his role as the oracle's founder cannot be taken for granted, Lucian's account is still important for our purpose. His portrayal of Alexander as a youth paints, for all its malicious fiction, a largely plausible picture of a pair of travelling Pythagorean miracle-workers, a master and his disciple. For the fact that such figures were active in Early Imperial Asia Minor, we have the testimony of the second-century oneirocritic Artemidorus of Daldis. In his *Interpretation of Dreams* (2.69) he mentions Pythagoreans (*Pythagoristai*) among the representatives of competing and, in his opinion, worthless divinatory disciplines. In quantity, this is a very modest testimony in comparison with Lucian and Philostratus. In quality, however, it is excellent evidence. Artemidorus was engaged in a polemic against real rivals, whose activities are amply attested (Bilbija and Flinterman 2006: 259–64). That such figures were not averse to diversify into activities such as healing and that they earned a reputation for miracle-working along the way seems plausible. In short, alertness to the risks involved in extracting historical information from literary texts such as the *Life of Apollonius* and *Alexander* should not result in elimination of the Pythagorean miracle-worker from the Early Imperial scene. Like the "Pythagoreans and magicians" in first-century-BC Rome they deserve a place in the history of Pythagoreanism.

CHAPTER 17

Diogenes Laertius' Life of Pythagoras

André Laks

1. Introduction

We know very little about Diogenes Laertius as a person. One recent hypothesis is that his surname refers to his birthplace (the city of Laerte in Caria or Cilicia), but other interpreters prefer to think – on the basis of a controversial indication in his text – that he was born (and lived) in Nicaea in Bithynia;[1] it is also generally admitted on the basis of the scanty and mostly negative internal evidence that he lived and worked at the beginning of the third century AD: the last philosophers he mentions are Sextus Empiricus (active *c.* 190 AD) and his disciple Saturninus, and the most recent source he refers to is Favorinus of Arelate.[2] This approximate date helps us appreciate the chapter he devotes to Pythagoras at the beginning of Book 8 of his *Lives* (as I shall abbreviate the work known as *Lives and Opinions of Eminent Philosophers*),[3] for it allows us to relate Diogenes' treatment of Pythagoras to two philosophical movements deeply indebted to Pythagoreanism, i.e. Neopythagoreanism and Neoplatonism.

Neopythagoreanism, which goes back to the first century BC,[4] must have still been vigorous during Diogenes' lifetime. Thus, the fact that his own presentation of Pythagoras does not appear to be indebted to Neopythagoreanism is certainly significant, even if *what* this is significant of is more difficult to assess. Geographical marginality is probably not a good

---

[1] For the city of Laerte, cf. Masson 1995. Mansfeld 1986: 300ff. defends Reiske's old interpretation of the expression "our Apollonides" (Ἀπολλωνίδης . . . ὁ παρ' ἡμῶν) in 9.109 as meaning "our compatriot." Apollonides was from Nicaea.

[2] Cf. Diog. Laert. 9.116. Diogenes Laertius had dealt in the final section of Book 7 – now lost – with twenty Stoic philosophers after Chrysippus down to Cornutus and Seneca (first century AD). Favorinus of Arelate, born *c.* 80 AD, belongs to the first half of the second century AD (cf. below n. 20). On the dating see also Jouanna 2009.

[3] This title is itself an abbreviation of that which is transmitted (with minor variations) in two manuscripts, *Lives and Thoughts [gnōmai] of Those Who Are Famous in Philosophy and of the Opinions [areskonta] of Each School [hairesis]*.

[4] Neopythagoreanism is a somewhat flexible term. See Kahn 2001: 94ff. and Chapter 12 above.

explanation, because Diogenes' erudite work suggests – even if his actual sources are certainly fewer that those which are quoted – that he had access to a major library, perhaps that of Alexandria. It may also be that Diogenes Laertius was simply not interested in contemporary developments and more specifically that the Pythagoras of Neopythagoreanism, who is hardly more than a Platonizing-Aristotelianizing doctrinaire, was not especially attractive to him. As a matter of fact, one of Diogenes' interests lies – as the title of his work indicates – in the *person* of any given philosopher. As for Neoplatonism, which was to take Pythagoras as its philosophical hero and did also pay a great deal of attention to his life (both of Plotinus' most famous successors were to deal with the subject, Porphyry in his *Life of Pythagoras* and Iamblichus in his *On the Pythagorean Way of Life*), a Diogenes writing at the beginning of the third century could not know of it (Plotinus, its founder, was born in 205). This does not mean that there is not, between Diogenes' *Life of Pythagoras* and the writings of Porphyry and Iamblichus, much in common: first, the three works draw directly or indirectly on a number of common sources – as a matter of fact, the comparison of the three lives sometimes helps illuminate passages that Diogenes Laertius' handling of his sources makes obscure;[5] second, they all belong to a cultural context deeply marked by a religious, spiritual and intellectual confrontation between paganism and Christianity. In this respect, it is significant that Diogenes' book is roughly contemporary with Philostratus' *Life of Apollonius of Tyana* (which we know was written in 217) – a work which, like the Neoplatonic *Lives of Pythagoras* (and some passages in Diogenes' own *Life of Pythagoras*), depicts the thaumaturgic powers, legendary deeds and miracles of the "divine man" (θεῖος ἀνήρ) Pythagoras – thus making him appear as a competitor of Jesus.[6]

The *Life* itself is an odd book, a product of late erudite Hellenistic scholarship, extremely heterogeneous, full of quotations (explicit or not), and often lacking visible, or for that matter any kind of organization. This explains why reading Diogenes may mean – and has in fact often meant – reading him for the sources he quotes and uses, especially since he frequently happens to be the only author to preserve them. This natural tendency to exploit Diogenes' work rather than read it "for itself" has been enhanced on the one hand by a disciplinary orientation towards *Quellenforschung*

---

[5] See for example Delatte 1922b: 241ff. on the first version of Pythagoras' death in Diog. Laert. 8.39.

[6] Cf. Momigliano 1987: 169–73. It has been suggested that Diogenes' vindication of the Greek origins of philosophy is directed against Clement of Alexandria (Canfora 1994). On θεῖος ἀνήρ and Philostratus, see Bieler 1935, Du Toit 1997, Schirren 2005, Demoen and Praet 2009 and Chapter 16 above.

("inquiry about sources") and, on the other hand, by a strongly deprecia-
tive judgment on Diogenes' own capacities and achievement.[7] Progressive
awareness of the fact that part at least of the strangeness of Diogenes' book
may come from our own expectations as to what historiography should be
has led some scholars at least (mostly in recent times) to minimize Diogenes' shortcomings and to try to understand better his procedures and
intentions.[8]

Given the nature of his work, it is in any case difficult to talk about
Diogenes without talking about his sources. I shall do this (section 3) after
having reviewed the content of Book 8 and explained its place within
Diogenes' work (section 2). I shall then comment about some specific
features of Diogenes Laertius' picture of Pythagoras (section 4), give an
analysis of the extended report about his (alleged) doctrines which, as I
read it, plays a central function in the overall construction of the book
(section 5) and eventually raise the problem of Diogenes' attitude towards
Pythagoras (section 6).

2. Diogenes' chapter on Pythagoras: place and content

Diogenes' book falls into two parts, in agreement with a view about the
development of Greek philosophy presented in the prologue of his work.
According to this scheme, which Diogenes inherits from Hellenistic philosophical historiography but which ultimately goes back to Aristotle, Greek
philosophy is divided throughout its history into two philosophical "lin-
eages" or "successions."[9] The model is the political successions (διαδοχαί)
of emperors, each philosopher inheriting in turn from his predecessors the
direction of an ideally ongoing philosophical school (even if the philosophical empire may split at some point and generate ramifications and there
also are some independent kingdoms).[10] The "Ionic" succession, which

---

[7] See the typical assessment in Lévy 1926: 88ff., a propos the specific case of Pythagoras' legend:
"[Diogenes'] chapter about Pythagoras [. . .], an invaluable collection (in spite of its obvious
shortcomings) of relatively early documentation (all of the primary sources quoted antedate the
Roman period) has provided us a great part of the material presented thus far, but he hardly has
anything more to teach us" (my translation).

[8] The most important are Mejer 1978 and Gigante 1986 (cf. esp. p. 47). These studies have been
influential (cf. the subtitle of Schirren's 2005 book: *The Ancient Philosophical Life as a Symbolic
Form*; on Diogenes' *Life of Pythagoras*, see pp. 127–37).

[9] The presentation of Greek philosophy in terms of "successions" goes back to Sotion (most probably
to be dated in the first quarter of the second century BC, cf. Mejer 1978: 63 n. 11). Aristotle, talking
about Pythagoreans, speaks of "the Italic philosophers" (οἱ Ἰταλικοί, see esp. *Metaphysics* A5, 987a9).

[10] See n. 11.

begins with Anaximander, owes its name to the fact that Miletus, birth-place of Anaximander and his master Thales, is located in Ionia, while the name "Italic" given to the second lineage, comes from the fact that it is in Italy – and not in Samos, where he was born – that Pythagoras "practiced philosophy for the longest period" (1.13). At a certain point, the geographical reference loses its meaning: in the case of the Ionic succession, at the latest when Anaxagoras or his pupil Archelaus, the master of Socrates, brings Ionian philosophy to Athens (cf. 2.16). Thus Books 2 to 7 follow the so-called Ionic succession down to Clitomachus, Chrysippus and Theophrastus (three Hellenistic philosophers active during the third century BC), while Books 8 to 10, starting with Pythagoras, follow the so-called Italic succession down to Epicurus.[11] So when Pythagoras' life opens at the beginning of Diogenes' Book 8, we are back to the second origin, so to speak, of Greek philosophy. This may be important for assessing Diogenes' appreciation of Pythagoras – a topic to which we shall return later. For in the prologue of his book Diogenes, defending rather vigorously the idea that philosophy is a distinctively Greek achievement without any "barbaric" antecedents,[12] put forward as one of his arguments that "its very name ['philosophy'] prevents it from being a barbarian designation" (1.4). Thus, Diogenes may have been sensitive to the tradition (which he mentions as early as 1.12) according to which "the first to have used the name 'philosophy,' and for himself, that of 'philosopher,' was Pythagoras." The fact that this indication is taken up and fleshed out in our book (8.8) would of course be more significant, had Diogenes himself made the link between the two passages, which he does not – a good example of the difficulties which confront the reader of his *Lives*.

Typically, a Diogenian *Life* contains sections about the philosopher's origin, his education, his discoveries (each item of the list being typically introduced by the standard formula "he was the first to discover that . . . "), a number of anecdotes about his life and sayings (or "apothegms"), his books, his doctrine, his death, as well as a list of his homonyms. All these components are present in Diogenes' *Life of Pythagoras*, but the chapter, perhaps more than usual, is uneven and presents by any standard a fair number of structural problems –some isolated, some more serious.[13] These may be accounted for in a variety of ways (authorial distraction if not stupidity, the unfinished state of the work, textual corruption and disturbances due to the transmission). On the other hand, it should be

---

[11] Book 9 presents a complication in that Heraclitus and Xenophanes are presented as "isolated" thinkers (σποράδην, 9.20, announced twice in 8.50 and 91).

[12] This is at least the common reading of the prologue.   [13] See Delatte 1922a: 5–15.

kept in mind that juxtaposition and association are typical Diogenian procedures. Whether we have to deal with disorder or with parataxis must be decided, or at least pondered, case by case.

Diogenes begins with some information concerning Pythagoras' origins, his family and his education (1–3; 42–3 contain further indications about Pythagoras' family), which is followed by an alleged self-report on Pythagoras' previous lives (4–5). This section belongs in some sense to Pythagoras' biography – it is, so to speak, an autobiographical piece of evidence – but it evidently also refers to Pythagoras' doctrine of reincarnation, of which it gives so to speak a personal testimony. Then comes an important section about Pythagoras' writings (6–8a), followed by the paragraph on the origin and meaning of the term "philosophy," to which I have already alluded (8b). The next sections are heterogeneous and deprived of any identifiable logical sequence. However, moral, religious and behavioral precepts, which are the topic of 9–10, 17–21a, and 22–3, provide a kind of thread. They even directly lead to the extended and central doxographical section given in 24b–34, if indeed the latter is meant to provide (as I shall suggest below) a theoretical justification for the Pythagorean mode of life and the very practice of imparting precepts. Further rules of conduct are, in any case, enumerated at the end of the report (33, which is immediately completed in 34–5 by yet another set of precepts taken from Aristotle's work about the Pythagoreans). Interrupting the enumeration of precepts, we find in 11a a short section on Pythagoras' thaumaturgic deeds (briefly taken up in 14a, and then in 21, which deals with Pythagoras' *katabasis*, i.e. "descent to the nether world"), then a longer section on Pythagoras as a "first inventor" in various fields such as geometry, music, astronomy, dietetics and psychic transmigration (11b–14a, also with some internal disorder), then a notice on secrecy and the transmission of Pythagoras' doctrine (15–16), which, while related to the former discussion about his writings, also prepares in some sense for the doxographical section beginning in 25, since the latter is supposed to be a "record" (ὑπομνήματα: "notes taken for remembering") of Pythagoras' doctrine. The shaping of what follows the doxographical report is simpler to account for, even if it also contains at least one anomalous piece (the section on Pythagoras' family, 42–3) and its final part is disordered. We first get quotations from a series of authors who deride Pythagoras and the Pythagorean way of living (36–8, which are obviously related to the precepts), and then various reports about Pythagoras' death, aspects of which are connected to the question of his divinity (39–41, to be completed by 44a on the question of the age at which he died). An unusually long section devoted to Diogenes' quoting of his own epigrams on Pythagoras (four of them are reproduced), 44b–5a, is followed by some chronological remarks about Pythagoras' life and the longevity of his school (45a–6). The ensuing paragraph on homonyms is somewhat atypical in that it includes some detailed information about the other men named "Pythagoras" as well as "our" Pythagoras (46b–9a). The chapter closes with the quotation of an alleged letter of Pythagoras – evidently pseudepigraphic – addressed to Anaximenes (one of the first representatives of the Ionian school).

3. Diogenes' sources for his *Life of Pythagoras*

The material presented above evidently stems from a number of different sources. The identification of Diogenes' sources has played an important role in the heyday of *Quellenforschung*; indeed, it may be seen, *mutatis mutandis*, as a counterpart in a more arid field of the so-called "Homeric question": what are the previous components of the epic poems that the tradition attributes to a single author called Homer and how are they pieced together? Diogenes quotes a great number of sources in the course of his work, some of them with regularity. It is admitted that Diogenes' overall knowledge is not firsthand, and that his quotations come from some intermediaries, although scholars differ widely about the number and identity of these. While nineteenth-century philologists tried to identify a few main sources,[14] there have also been attempts to make Diogenes a respectably widely read scholar.[15] The problem – which is tightly linked with that of the source of any given source(s), and also, in the case of his chapter on Pythagoras, of the sources of Porphyry's *Life of Pythagoras* (and to a certain extent with those of Iamblichus' *On the Pythagorean Way of Life*) – is so intricate that there is no chance of settling it definitively. Nevertheless, it is important to sort out and to characterize the different bits and pieces of which Diogenes' (or for that matter Porphyry's and Iamblichus') exposition is made up: for it is crucial to deciding, among other things, whether the picture of Pythagoras as a thaumaturge and his "legend" go back to ancient sources or are based on forgeries developed in the later tradition. Thus, it is a relief to see that, thanks to renewed and numerous scholarly efforts, at least a broad picture of the story emerges, even if many specifics are doomed to remain obscure or controversial.[16]

---

[14] Nietzsche, to take the first of a long series, argued in the first study he dedicated to Diogenes Laertius that Diocles of Magnesia and Favorinus were two of his major sources. On Nietzsche's Diogenian studies, see Barnes 1986.

[15] Thus Mejer 1978: 41ff.

[16] Rohde 1901 (on Iamblichus' sources); Delatte 1922b; Lévy 1926; Burkert 1972a: 101ff.; Centrone 1992: 418ff.; Zhmud 2012b: 72–7.

Some of Diogenes' sources have (directly or indirectly) shaped the over-all conception of his book. Thus he often quotes (or uses) authors of "successions" (all of them belong to the second and first century BC) such as – in roughly chronological order – Sotion, Hippobotus, Heraclides Lembus, Sosicrates, Alexander (Polyhistor), Iason, Antisthenes, Nicias of Nicaea and Philodemus.[17] The lists of homonyms come from Demetrius of Magnesia;[18] many of the stories about the deaths of philosophers go back to Hermippus of Smyrna[19] and he often draws on Favorinus of Arelate.[20] But there are also specific sources for each book, school or author, which often are of apologetic or for that matter polemical nature. In the case of Pythagoras' life, a number of such important sources are identifiable, whether Diogenes names them or their identity may be deduced from parallel texts in Porphyry, Iamblichus or other parts of Diogenes' book.[21] These are, following again a rough chronological order: Aristotle (*On the Pythagoreans*), Aristoxenus (*On Pythagoras and His Associates*), Heraclides Ponticus (*Abaris*), Neanthes (*On Famous Men*, now currently dated at the end of the fourth century BC), Timaeus of Tauromenium (*Histories*, third century BC), Sosicrates (*Successions*, second century BC), Alexander Poly-histor (*Successions*, first century BC), and an anonymous source, which may be reconstructed on the basis of a parallel between a series of passages in Diogenes Laertius and Hesychius of Miletus.[22]

A number of these authors are dealt with in other parts of this vol-ume, and I shall say more below about Alexander Polyhistor's doxograph-ical extract. Here I shall only note: (1) that most of the material about Pythagorean precepts may be traced back to our most ancient source:

---

[17] Sotion, Sosicrates and Hippobotus are quoted in Diogenes' *Life of Pythagoras* (7, 8, 43). On authors of *Successions*, see Kienle 1961 and Mejer 1978: 62–74.

[18] On whom see Mejer 1978: 38ff.

[19] Quoted in 41. On Hermippus' (second half of the third century BC) biographical work, see Wehrli 1974: 102–6.

[20] Diogenes' chapter has four quotations from Favorinus' *Memoirs* and *Miscellaneous History*: 12, 15, 47 and 48 (on Favorinus, see Amato's 2005/2010 edition).

[21] Among others the chapter on Empedocles, who is classified as a Pythagorean and whose *Life* follows that of Pythagoras (see Bidez 1894).

[22] Most of the sources named by Diogenes Laertius in Book 8 are known only through him (cf. Zhmud 2012b: 72). Aristoxenus, who is one major source for Pythagoras' life in general, is quoted at 8, 14, 15, 20, 21, cf. 46. Neanthes (see Chapter 14, section 5 above), who is mentioned three times in the *Life of Empedocles* (8.55, 58, 72), is identified by Lévy (1926: 62) as the source of 8.39 on the basis of a parallel with Porphyry's *Life of Pythagoras* 55; the problems about Neanthes' identity and chronology are documented in Fuentes González 2005a. Timaeus (see Chapter 14, section 4 above) is an important source for Diogenes' *Life of Empedocles* and is mentioned twice in the chapter on Pythagoras (10 and 11 = fr. 13b and 17 *FGrHist* 566). One of the clearest presentations of most of the sources for Pythagoras' life remains that of Lévy 1926, even if later studies must be consulted for an up-to-date presentation of each author. On Diogenes' anonymous source see Burkert 1972a: 101ff.

Aristotle's *On the Pythagoreans*, an important fragment of which Diogenes is also the only one to preserve in 35;[23] (2) that Heraclides Ponticus (listed as a disciple of Plato), is presented as launching the long-lived "Pythagoras legend" about Pythagoras' travels and thaumaturgical deeds; (3) that there is, from early on (Aristoxenus), a recognizable if diversified critical reception of that legend. Two prominent examples featuring in Diogenes Laertius are Hermippus' ironical description of Pythagoras' alleged *katabasis* in 8.41, which reads like a parody of Heraclides' narratives,[24] and passages deriving from Timaeus of Tauromenium, who reported, in Books 9 and 10 of his *Histories*, rationalistic explanations of a number of fabulous stories linked to Pythagoras and Empedocles.

4. Some specific features of Diogenes' portrayal of Pythagoras

Contrary to Porphyry's and Iamblichus' works on Pythagoras and the earlier Platonic tradition they incorporate, Diogenes' *Life* is not clearly oriented towards an apologetic goal, nor is it easy to see, on the basis of most of his reports, where exactly his interests lie. One can nevertheless make a few observations. Diogenes, for example, does not seem to be especially interested in the internal organization of Pythagoras' school nor in its (arguably remarkable) history. He does mention, for sure, that it survived "nine or ten generations" and gives the names of the last ("ancient") Pythagoreans (one of them is Xenophilus, 46);[25] but he does not have much to say about the political vicissitudes of the school, even if, talking about Pythagoras' death (39), he mentions the burning of the house of Milo, which was the meeting place of the Pythagorean community in Croton.[26] By the same token, it is striking that he does not mention the distinction between *mathematici* and *acusmatici* – especially since he certainly is interested in the question of doctrinal secrecy, publicity and writing.[27] For Diogenes does mention the tradition – also reflected in the prologue (1.16) – which denied that Pythagoras had ever written any book – an assertion directed against the attribution to Pythagoras of the so called *Tripartitum* (*On Education*, *On Politics* and *On Physics*).[28]

---

[23] Fr. 195 Rose.   [24] See Chapter 14, section 2 above and below, n. 79.   [25] Cf. below, n. 55.
[26] On the event and the chronological confusion implied here, see Burkert 1972a: 115–17 and Chapter 5 in this volume.
[27] According to Zhmud 2012b: 186ff. the distinction comes from a source (Nicomachus) that Diogenes did not use; however, if it goes back to Aristotle as Burkert argues (1972a: 196; 1998: 315), Diogenes would probably have been aware of it.
[28] Diogenes himself seems to endorse this attribution at the end of 6, and it is probable that it is also presupposed by the story about the publication of those books by Philolaus in 15 ("Down to the time of Philolaus it was not possible to acquire knowledge of any Pythagorean doctrine, and Philolaus

Many further observations about what Diogenes selects and what he leaves out (or is not aware of) could be added. But if we want to detect an overall interest in Diogenes' *Life of Pythagoras*, we must certainly locate it in the Pythagorean *mode of life*[29] as reflected in the long lists of religious and ethical precepts which, as already noted, are found in a number of sections. A closer look at the material will be useful, both because it is worthwhile in itself and because it points to an important (and as far as I can judge, previously unnoticed) structural principle in Diogenes' otherwise rather chaotic *Life of Pythagoras*.[30]

A first series of three precepts, which are said to come from the aforementioned books (most probably the "pedagogical" one), occurs at the beginning of 9 (I shall call it A).[31] They concern prayer (we should not pray on our own behalf, because we do not know what is useful for us), sobriety and moderation in diet, and sex (the right time to practice it is winter, not summer). Then we get in 17 (B) a series of precepts called *symbola* ("signs of recognition" or "watchwords"). The meaning of *symbolon* – originally a fragment of a coin allowing the identification of the possessor of the other half – is illustrated by the introductory phrase: "when he found his own watchwords adopted by anyone, he would immediately take to that man and make a friend of him" (end of 16).[32] Seventeen of them are quoted in a row,[33] before a rational explanation is provided for five of them (the first four, and then the last one: we can spot here the epitomator at work) in 18 (B').[34] This group is immediately followed in 19–20 by a short series

alone brought out those three celebrated books which Plato sent a hundred minas to purchase"). The *Tripartitum* was already known to Satyrus (*c.* 200 BC). The story about Plato's buying these books features also in Diogenes' *Life of Plato* (3.9). In 8.6, Diogenes quotes the beginning of Pythagoras' alleged *Physics*; in 8.9, he announces a summary of the general content of the books (although he only quotes some precepts, see below) and in 8.14 we find a further a misplaced indication probably coming from the same "writing" (γραφή) about the interval – 216 years– between two incarnations. Cf. also 8.55, which 8.15 might have followed in the source (Neanthes). On this (intricate) topic, see Diels 1890, Delatte 1922b: 159–68, Lévy 1926: 70–7, Thesleff 1965a: 170 (in the apparatus), and Burkert 1961 and 1972a: 223–7.

29 This is correctly emphasized by Schirren 2005: 130.

30 See below, section 5. For more discussion of the Pythagorean *symbola/acusmata* see Chapter 6 above.

31 Sections 9–10 are paralleled with some variations in Diodorus of Sicily, 10.9.3–5, which obviously draws from the same source as Diogenes.

32 On the original meaning of *symbola* as "passwords," cf. Burkert 1972a: 176. They are called *acusmata* in Iamblichus.

33 "Don't stir the fire with a knife, don't step over a yoke, don't sit down on a bushel, don't eat a heart, don't help to unload a burden but to load it, always keep your bed-clothes tied up, don't carry around a god's image on a ring, wipe out the traces of the pan in the ashes, don't wipe a seat with a torch, don't urinate turned towards the sun, don't walk outside the highway etc." (Translations, if not otherwise indicated, are taken from Laks and Most forthcoming.)

34 Here are the five explanations given: "Don't stir the fire with a knife" meant for him don't arouse the anger or the swelling pride of the great. "Don't step over a yoke": that is, don't step over the bounds of equity and justice. "Don't sit down on a bushel" is the same as: have a care for the

of dietary prohibitions (C1), which almost imperceptibly points towards a description of Pythagoras' own behavior in daily life and of his (exceedingly gentle) character. This section, which is interrupted by the (anomalous) section on Pythagoras' *katabasis*, continues in 22–3 (C2) with a second long series of precepts, this time of an ethical and not ritualistic nature.[35] Some further recommendations then pop up at the end (33) of the central doxographical report (D), which are then immediately completed by a literal quotation of Aristotle fr. 195 Rose (E). The latter, like the B/B' section, presents a number of ritual precepts followed by their exegesis.

It will already have become obvious to the reader that the Pythagorean precepts are very heterogeneous.[36] As a matter of fact, three parameters must be taken into account here. First, a classification preserved in Iamblichus, but certainly going back to Aristotle, tells us that *symbola* are answers given to three kinds of different questions: What is a given thing? What is most of some given quality? How must we behave?[37] The overwhelming majority of *symbola* quoted in Diogenes Laertius' chapter belong to the third category: this is why we can use "precepts" to refer to them. However, it should be noted that at the end of section D a few representatives of the first category – we would call them definitions, not precepts – and even one of the second, evaluative category, are added to (and partly mixed with) "practical" *symbola* or precepts properly speaking.[38] Second, one can distinguish, among these precepts, two broad categories: some of them are

future too, for a bushel is the ration for a day. By "not eating a heart" he meant not wasting your soul away in troubles and pains. By saying "when you go abroad don't turn around at the frontier," he admonished those who are departing from life not to hold passionately onto life nor to be guided by the pleasures of this life. It is generally admitted that Diogenes' sections 17 and 18 derive from Androcydes, a Hellenistic Pythagorean writer (first century BC?) who wrote a book entitled *On Pythagorean Symbols*; but Anaximander of Miletus' book *Interpretation of Pythagorean Symbols* (*c.* 400 BC), which Aristotle must have used, already contained some rational-moralizing interpretations of ritual and superstitious prohibitions (cf. Burkert 1972a: 166ff.; Zhmud 2012b: 171ff., 192ff.).

35 Here is the first half of the series: " He is said to have advised his disciples as follows: Always to say on entering the house: Where did I trespass? What did I achieve? And what duty did I leave unfulfilled? To forbid sacrificial victims to be offered to the gods, and to worship only at an altar unstained with blood. Not to call the gods to witness, for one should try to make oneself trustworthy. To honor their elders, thinking that what is earlier in time is more honorable; for in the world sunrise is [sc. more honorable] than sunset, in human life the beginning than the end, and in all organic life birth than death. And to honor gods before demi-gods, heroes before men, and among men especially their parents; and to behave with one another in such a way as not to make friends into enemies, but to turn enemies into friends; to consider nothing to belong only to themselves. To come to the aid of the law, to wage war against lawlessness."

36 On the heterogeneity of Pythagorean *symbola*, see Burkert 1972a: 173; Zhmud 2012b: 192ff.

37 Cf. Iambl. *VP* 82. The Aristotelian provenance is secured by the overlap between the *acusmata* (= *symbola*) that Iamblichus goes on quoting and the (fuller) list we find in the fragment from Aristotle quoted by Diogenes Laertius (cf. Burkert 1972a: 167–8).

38 Here is an extract from Aristotle's fragment (I have printed in italics definitional and evaluative *symbola*): "Do not eat a white rooster, because it is holy to the Month and a suppliant; and the latter

conspicuously tied to ritual, which also means that their significance is (as a rule) opaque, while others are ethical, sometimes commonsensical, recommendations or exhortations.[39] Both kinds are represented in Diogenes Laertius. Ritual precepts are to be found essentially in B and E, prudential ones in A, C and D. The third parameter, which is related to the bi-partition just mentioned, is that ritual precepts are at times followed by an explanation (normally introduced by a γάρ-clause, "for . . . "), at times, not. This explanation, in turn, may be read as a justification or as an interpretation – sometimes, as both. Whether these explanations, or at least some of them, are part of the original or more archaic version of the precepts or represent later rationalizations is not an easy question. In any case, two points seem obvious: first, the kind of rationale that was put forward in order to explain the meaning of opaque precepts has varied through time; second, ethical precepts, which are (or are supposed to be) rational by themselves, do not need (in principle) specific justification – indeed, they may themselves function as an explanatory item.[40]

Thus Diogenes Laertius, in the paragraphs discussed so far, provides us with rich material concerning the history of the rationalization – both within and outside the school – of *specific* Pythagorean precepts. But we also find in Diogenes' chapter another, *global*, kind of justification for the precepts, one that suggests that (some version of) the Pythagorean way of life is grounded in the explanation of the cosmos as a whole. This is the crucial function of the long doxographical report taken from Alexander Polyhistor, or so I shall suggest.

5. Alexander Polyhistor and the *Pythagorean Notes*[41]

The last item of the precept section I called C2 is dedicated to one of Pythagoras' most celebrated prohibitions together with one of its possible rational explanations: "Abstain from beans because they are flatulent and

---

is characteristic of those who are good; and it is holy to the Month, for it indicates the hours. [. . .] *And of geometrical figures, the most beautiful is the sphere among solids, and the circle among plane figures. Old age and everything that decreases are similar; and growth and youth are the same thing. Health is the persistence of the form, disease its destruction.* Salt should be brought to table to remind us of what is right; for salt preserves whatever it finds, and it arises from the purest sources, sun and sea."

[39] This kind of precept presents some affinity with Aristoxenus' *Pythagorean Precepts* and may indeed go back to him; Diels 1890: 466ff.; Delatte 1922b: 167ff.; Huffman 2006.

[40] See the explanatory part of the precepts quoted above, n. 34.

[41] The ὑπομνήματα, here translated *Notes*, are, according to Burkert's characterization (1961: 26ff.), "Notes without any literary claim, meant for internal usage, not for publication." Other current renderings of this difficult word are *Memoirs*, *Commentaries* and *Notebooks*.

partake most of the breath of life; and besides, it is better for the stomach if they are not taken, and this again will make our dreams in sleep smooth and untroubled" (24). This is immediately followed by: "Alexander in his *Successions of Philosophers* says that he found in the *Pythagorean Notes* the following tenets as well." Diogenes then goes on quoting in full (perhaps with some occasional cuts or modifications) the report he found in Alexander (25–33).[42] It is obvious that this report constitutes the official "opinions" section of the chapter on Pythagoras. There is something striking about the way this report is introduced, for in other *Lives*, the corresponding section usually begins with the formula: "His [the philosopher in question] opinions are as follows...," without indication of source.[43] Is Diogenes implicitly telling us that in Pythagoras' case, it is important to authenticate the source? In any case, the report excerpted by Alexander and copied by Diogenes is itself a sample of (early) pseudo-Pythagorean literature.[44] But it is a quite unusual sample, in respect of its chronology as well as of its content. As far as dating is concerned, Alexander Polyhistor provides a *terminus ante quem* (first half of the first century BC); on the other hand, the doctrines attributed to Pythagoras reflect a number of post-Academic and Hellenistic influences. Thus, the text must have been written sometime between the end of the fourth century and the second/first century BC. This fairly extended timespan happens to correspond with an important gap in our information about the survival of the Pythagorean school and the transmission of its doctrine. Diogenes' excerpt provides a glimpse of how things may have developed between the extinction of the school and the Roman Renaissance.[45]

In spite of some isolated difficulties (especially in the paragraphs devoted to the soul), the text breaks up into a series of clearly distinguishable units. It progressively displays, in a synthetic manner, a complete picture of reality, metaphysical, cosmological and practical. We are led from the principles to the elements (25a); from the elements to the world (25b–6); from earth (26) and stars (27) to life (28); from the soul, which is to say the principle of life, to physiology and sensation (28) and embryology (29); and, last but

---

[42] Alexander of Miletus, surnamed Polyhistor because of his vast learning, lived in Rome in 82 – *c.* 35 BC under Sulla (for further information, see Schwartz 1894). He was, among many other works, the author of a treatise entitled *On Pythagorean Symbols* (FGrHist 273F94). The quotation of Aristotle's fr. 195 in 34–5 may or may not stem from Alexander himself.

[43] On this feature of Diogenes' excerpting practice, see Mejer 1978: 4–7.

[44] Burkert (1961: 26ff.) put forward the hypothesis that the *Pythagorean Hypomnēmata* are to be identified with the *hypomnēmata* mentioned at the end of the pseudepigraphic *Letter to Lysis*, whose subject is the public dissemination of Pythagoras' doctrines (*contra*, see Thesleff 1972: 78, and Du Toit 1997: 234 n. 83).

[45] The following paragraphs build on Laks 2013.

not least, from further considerations about the soul (its parts, in 28 and 30a, its properties and above all its immortality, in 30b–2) to the final series of ethical considerations and ritual precepts (32–3) to which I have already alluded.

In their treatment of this piece, scholars have mostly been led – just as in the case of Diogenes Laertius as a whole – by the two traditional and interrelated questions raised by *Quellenforschung*: chronology and sources. These questions are certainly relevant and have yielded some important results, but one should also be aware that the interpretive procedures their treatment requires tend to obfuscate one central feature of the *Pythagorean Notes*. This is because they consider the text to be nothing more than a gathering of *heterogeneous* units of different provenance and doctrinal coloration. An influential view identifies three independent sections: (1) The first paragraph, which attributes to Pythagoras a (apparently already Neopythagorean) version of the Academic doctrine of derivation according to which duality (the "Dyad"), taken as equivalent to matter, is derived from the One, which is the origin of everything; then from the One and the Dyad derives the series point, line, surface, and perceptible and elementary bodies (25). (2) A section (26–30) coming from a scientific work, whose author would be "a Pythagorean doctor from the fifth century" belonging to the Sicilian school, and presenting traces of Presocratic philosophy (such as Diogenes of Apollonia) as well as authentic Philolaic elements. (3) Three paragraphs of "theological content" (30–3) and of indeterminate source.[46] In another influential study, Festugière observed that the summary, at least as far as 26–30 are concerned, in essence follows the structure of Aëtius' doxographical handbook. This leads him to distinguish five sections: (1) 25a, corresponding to Aëtius I.3 (On the principles); (2) 25b–27a, corresponding to Aëtius II.1–31 (On the world, the sky, the stars, the sun, and the moon); (3) 26, corresponding to Aëtius III.10 (On earth); (4) 27b–28a, corresponding to Aëtius V.3–5, 15–18, 19–21, 23 (On semen and embryology); (5) 28b–31, corresponding to Aëtius IV.2–16 (On the soul, the sensations, vision, hearing, etc.).[47] This means recognizing in the text at least some formal homogeneity. But this formal homogeneity does not have any real counterpart as far as contents are concerned. Most metaphysical and physical tenets are, according to Festugière, of Academic and Aristotelian origin, and the physiological section, because of its terminology and the

---

[46] Cf. Wiersma 1942: 99ff. The quotations come respectively from p. 109, 108 and 107 (my translation). See also Centrone 1992: 4193ff.

[47] Festugière 1945: 376. He does not consider the final section (31–3), however, on which see below.

function it attributes to *pneuma*, depends on Diocles of Carystus' medical works.[48]

The degree to which the report betrays Stoic influence is disputed. The occurrence of such terms as προνοεῖσθαι and εἱμαρμένη (27) do not say much, because they can be of Platonic as well as of Stoic origin. But the role devoted to *pneuma* and the importance played by the hot (θερμόν) may be felt to owe much to Stoicism.[49] It will be tempting to conclude, in this case, that the Platonizing (and possibly Neopythagorean) monism of the doctrine of principles had been permeated by a Stoicizing worldview.

Now, there is little doubt that the Pythagorean doctrine Alexander's excerpt offers us is filtered extensively by post-Academic and Hellenistic terminology and ideas. Hence Zeller's characterization of the text as the product of an "eclectic" Pythagoreanism is entirely fitting.[50] But once this is recognized two problems arise. One may ask, first, whether Alexander's extract shows at least traces of pre-Platonic Pythagoreanism; and one may try to characterize the kind of Pythagoreanism we have to deal with here.

As far as the first question is concerned, the relevant passages are, proceeding from the most promising down to the more dubious:

(1)   The ritual precepts correspond to well-attested ancient material.[51]

(2)   The table of opposites mentioned in 26, and especially the occurrence within it of the pair light–obscurity has some claim to derive from ancient Pythagoreanism.[52] This is equally true of the "proportions due to harmony" (οἱ τῆς ἁρμονίας λόγοι) mentioned in relationship with the formation of the human embryo (29) and more generally of harmony considered as a widely applicable principle (33).

(3)   The physiological section of the *Notes* (28–31), for all its Hellenistic background, could at some level reflect Philolaus' medical interests

---

[48] In 31, veins, arteries and *neura* are said to be the bonds of the soul. The distinction between veins and arteries is Hellenistic, and if *neura* refers to "nerves" (in 28 the term must refer to sinews), the *terminus post quem* for the section on the soul will be Erasistratus. Hence Festugière suggests that the section on the soul reflects Diocles of Carystus' doctrine either directly or through Erasistratus (1945: 419–28).

[49] Zeller (1919: 3.2.103 and 107) took the *Notes* to show strong Stoic influence. Subsequent research rather tended to minimize it, but see Mansfeld 1971: 98–103.

[50] Zeller 1919: 3.2.107 and 108. It has been widely accepted (see most recently Long 2013).

[51] "There is little in our text so far that can be identified as specifically Pythagorean. But the final section on morality and religion suggests that the connection of this very eclectic treatise with the name of Pythagoras is not altogether arbitrary" (Kahn 2001: 82).

[52] Cf. Journée 2012: 298ff.

(which were revealed by the publication of the papyrus known as the *Anonymus Londinensis* by Diels in 1893).[53]

(4) The intriguing tripartition of the soul in 30 into νοῦς (here to be interpreted as "comprehension"), φρένες ("intelligence") and θυμός ("emotion") obviously does not correspond to the Platonic division, since the νοῦς represents here a faculty of discrimination common to animals and human beings, whereas the φρένες refer to the intellectual (and immortal) part. The tripartition could thus take up a genuinely Pythagorean view.[54]

(5) It has been argued that the geocentric conception of the world at the end of 25–6, which strikingly conflicts with Philolaus' theory of a central fire and thus seems to depend on Plato and Aristotle, could in fact reflect an anti-Philolaic but still old Pythagorean doctrine.[55]

(6) The curious doctrine of the three species of ether (the pure, healthy and superior one; the cold and unhealthy one, which is air; the thick one, which is liquid) could have ancient credentials.[56] One could also argue that the importance and functions attributed to the warm (τὸ θερμόν), which, as we have seen, have often been considered as reflecting Stoic doctrine, are in fact of pre-Platonic origin, and may even reflect Philolaic interest in fire and heat.[57]

The hope of recovering ancient Pythagorean (and more generally Pre-socratic) material in the *Pythagorean Notes* relies on two assumptions. The first is that pre-Platonic Pythagoreanism is much more diverse than the picture Aristotle gives of it suggests.[58] The second insists that a late *formulation* does not imply that the corresponding *content* be equally late.[59] Both points are important and well taken; on the other hand, their application

---

53 Wellmann 1919: 227 (cf. Huffman 1993: 292 "It is a good reminder of the inadequacy of our sources to point out that, if not for the discovery of the *Anonymus Londinensis*, we would never have known that Philolaus dealt with medical topics at all").

54 Cf. Delatte 1922b: 222ff. Tripartition is not attested, however, for ancient Pythagoreanism.

55 At *Phaedo* 108c6, Plato's Socrates declares that he has been persuaded by "someone" (ὑπό τινος πέπεισμαι) to adopt a geocentric worldview. This is usually referred to Anaximander, but Wellmann suggested that this might also be the view defended in the circle of Athenian (that is, not Italic) Pythagoreans, and more specifically by Xenophilus, a contemporary of Plato (Wellmann 1919: 242–5; cf. Delatte 1922b: 204ff.). This hypothesis is not supported by any evidence.

56 Cf. Boyancé 1967: 205 (*contra* Festugière 1945: 393, who thinks that the passage depends on Plato's doctrine of the three forms of air at *Timaeus* 58d1–4).

57 Wellmann 1919: 228–31; Delatte 1922b: 212; Boyancé 1967; *contra*: Mansfeld 1971: 98–103. On the question, see also Solmsen 1957. For the centrality of the hot in Philolaus' thought, cf. Huffman 2007.

58 The point has been made in particular by Wellmann 1919: 242ff. On the diversity of ancient Pythagoreanism, or rather Pythagoreans, see Zhmud (2012b: 137ff.).

59 Delatte 1922b: 235.

in particular cases is often delicate. The skeptical stance on this matter has been well formulated by Burkert: "surely there is much ancient there, but incorporated in a post-Platonic system, in the way Epicurean and Stoic physics also have incorporated 'Presocratic' physics."[60] Given the nature of the material, there is, as a matter of fact, little chance that identification of genuine Pythagorean tenets can rely, in the majority of cases, on more than the interpreter's personal inclinations or prejudices.

What, then, about the kind of Pythagoreanism that is directly reflected in Alexander's eclectic report? One might start from the crucial point that moral and ritual recommendations round off the exposition.[61] This point is supported not only by the overall structure and dynamic of the report itself but also by the function it plays within Diogenes Laertius' chapter on Pythagoras (i.e., articulating Pythagoras' (mode of) life on the one hand and his doctrine on the other hand). We have already seen that this section is perhaps the only part of the summary whose content goes back to pre-Platonic Pythagoreanism. But no less important is that these precepts, considered within the framework of Alexander's report, appear to be the goal of the whole development. The fact is that there are a number of points in the cosmological and psychological doctrine that may be seen, at least retrospectively, as preparing the ground for the final moral doctrine and its concretization through a series of precepts. The link is provided by the idea of *purity*. Precepts suppose purification,[62] and the world is also divided into pure and impure. This is already the case, for example, with the characterization of the spring as healthy and the autumn as unhealthy in 26, and the ensuing opposition between the lower regions where mortal things live and perish in the grip of an unhealthy and immobile atmosphere and upper regions which are always moving, pure, and healthy, where things are immortal and hence divine (end of 26 – one is of course reminded of the final myth in Plato's *Phaedo*); then you get in 28 the idea of the soul differing from simple life in as much as it is a fragment of the divine aither (ἀπόσπασμα αἰθέρος),[63] so that the divide between the mortal bottom and the immortal top appears to be not insuperable after all. The soul's special

---

[60] Burkert 1961: 26 n. 5 (my translation).

[61] One shortcoming of Festugière's analysis is that he only considers the three first sections on principles, world and soul, "because they are the most important" (1945: 372 n. 6).

[62] "We should worship the gods and the heroes, but not in the same way: the gods always with reverent silence, in white robes, and after purification [ἀγνεύοντας], the heroes starting at noon. Purification [ἀγνεία] is by purgings, baths, and lustrations, and by keeping pure from [καθαρεύειν ἀπό . . .] death and birth and all pollution, and abstaining [ἀπέχεσθαι] from meat and flesh of animals that have died, red mullets, black-tailed fish, eggs and animals born from eggs, beans, and the other things prescribed also by those who perform mystic rites in the temple" (33).

[63] One wonders whether this refers to human or animal soul.

cosmological status creates the condition for a code of moral conduct that can easily be seen as a kind of purification. Confirmation of this is given in the properly psychological section, where one reads that the φρόνιμον (which must be proper to human beings, as opposed to the νοῦς, which is shared by all animals) is immortal (ἀθάνατον, 30). There is also, in the same paragraph, the witty, and in some sense beautiful, idea that the bonds of the soul, when the latter is in full force and acts by itself, are not the veins, arteries and *neura*, but its reasonings and *deeds* (ἔργα). The latter word is important, because, without precluding intellectual achievements, it also draws attention for the first time to the practical dimension that will become prominent towards the end of the text. Soul is a principle of action. This moral train of thought then becomes fully explicit in 32, where it is said that "he [sc. Pythagoras] says that the most important thing in the domain of human affairs is the act of persuading the soul either in the direction of the good or in the direction of evil" – an interesting formulation, which implies not only that it is good to comply with the recommendations that follow, but also that the very imparting of those recommendations is in itself the most important action of which one might conceive. Read in this way, the last section of the text follows or at least flows from an elaborate metaphysical, cosmological and psychological construction that begins with the One and ends with the soul.

Now, if the point of the piece taken as a whole is, as I have just argued, the very *articulation* of the connection between moral precepts and explicative account, we are confronted with a genuinely Pythagorean problematic, which may be traced back to the classical and possibly even the archaic period. In the well-known passage of his *On the Pythagorean Way of Life* deriving from Aristotle,[64] the beginning of which I have already mentioned,[65] Iamblichus writes the following about Pythagorean precepts (the *acusmata*):

> In some cases a reason why we should [act in a certain way] is added (for example, one ought to have children in order to leave behind another in the place of oneself to worship the gods), but in other cases there is no explanation. And some of the added explanations seem to have been attached from the outset [ἀπ᾽ ἀρχῆς], others later [πόρρω]. For example, not to break bread, because it is not advantageous for judgment in Hades.[66]

Iamblichus (that is Aristotle) goes on to say that the "likely explanations which have been added about such matters are not Pythagorean,

---

[64] With some possible interventions, cf. Zhmud 2012b: 303 n. 62.
[65] See section 4 above.   [66] Iambl. *VP* 86.

but were devised by some outside the school trying to give a likely reason." The reference must be to Anaximander the Younger's *Interpretation of the Pythagorean Symbola*,[67] but it is important to recognize that Iamblichus (Aristotle) distinguishes those later, and implicitly illegitimate additions, from older ones (ἀπ᾽ ἀρχῆς), whose legitimacy is not denied. If this is true, then explanation and justification *as such* may well have been part and parcel of ancient Pythagorean precepts.[68] This would be hardly surprising, given the nature of these utterances, which cry out for justification and rationalization. But it does shed light, I think, on the *Pythagorean Notes*, whose function, read against this background, is to provide both a specific instance and a remarkable extension (given the nature and the scale of the explanation) of a traditional preceptual γάρ-clause: it is because the universe is as it is that we should behave as Pythagoras demands.[69] In other words, the *Pythagorean Notes* would be not only a testimony of an *eclectic* Pythagoreanism, but also of an eclectic *Pythagoreanism*.[70] Whether this specific brand of Pythagoreanism reflects the existence of an actual Pythagorean community in the dark age of Pythagoreanism, or is the result of purely scholarly activity (and both views have been upheld),[71] cannot be decided on the basis of the available information.

6. The problem of Diogenes' attitude towards Pythagoras

Although much of the research about Diogenes is directed towards his sources, there also have been attempts to capture Diogenes' "personality," his literary character and philosophical inclinations.[72] It has been thought, for example, that he was attracted towards Epicureanism (because of his praise of Epicurus in Book 10 and the way he quotes him at length), or Skepticism (because of a wrongly interpreted reference to the skeptical philosopher Apollonides of Nicaea, but also because of his overall non-committal attitude), or else some mild form of Platonism (because his

---

[67] See above, n. 34.

[68] See Thom 2013, who rightly and crucially corrects Burkert's (1972a: 174) mistranslation (respectively "ideally suitable" and "far-fetched") of ἀπ᾽ ἀρχῆς and πόρρω in Iamblichus' text.

[69] Cf. Riedweg 2008: 66ff. "Over time individual Pythagoreans strove to give maxims that proceeded chiefly from the religious ritualistic thought and that seemed increasingly old-fashioned a more intellectual meaning that corresponded to contemporary philosophical discussion." (Cf. already Zeller 1923: 3.2.107.)

[70] Huffman 2013b provides powerful support for the reading suggested here by showing that and how the question of the relationship between cosmology and way of life already arises in early Pythagoreanism.

[71] The two positions are Kahn's 2001: 83 and Long's 2013.

[72] On Diogenes' personality, see Schwartz 1903b: 760ff.; Delatte 1922b: 34–40; Mejer 1978: 46.

book is dedicated to a lady who was interested in Plato).[73] As far as his
Life of Pythagoras is concerned, it has been observed that there are sections
in Diogenes' chapter that reflect a critical "attitude" towards Pythagoras and his followers. Was Diogenes himself hostile to Pythagoras? This
interpretation would fit well with the idea that Diogenes kept away from
contemporary forms of Pythagoreanism;[74] but there is also evidence for
the opposite view.

There are three critical sections in Diogenes' *Life of Pythagoras*. First,
immediately following Alexander Polyhistor's doxographical report, is the
series of quotations stemming from satirical and comic authors (36–8). Diogenes begins by quoting three passages, one from Timon of Phlius' *Satires*
(Σίλλοι) and two from Xenophanes[75] which mock various personal features of Pythagoras: while Timon sneers at Pythagoras' pomposity (σεμνο-
πρέπεια) and charlatanism,[76] Xenophanes targets what I take to be his
sentimentality.[77] Diogenes goes on saying that Pythagoras was also mocked
in Cratinus the Younger's comedy *The Pythagorizing Woman*. The four quotations from fourth-century-BC comic authors which follow – one from
another of Cratinus' plays, *People from Tarentum*, one from Mnesimachus'
Alcmaeon, and two from Aristophon's *The Pythagorist* – are all related to
the Pythagorean community: Cratinus sneers at the initiation newcomers
must undergo in order to get into the circle; Mnesimachus and Aristophon
at the ritual and vegetarian diet as well as the Pythagoreans' shabbiness and
filth.[78] The second critical section is the ironical-rationalistic explanation
of Pythagoras' alleged *katabasis* taken from Hermippus in 41.[79]

---

[73] Epicurus: 10.9; Apollonides of Nicaea: 9.109; the woman interested in Plato: 3.47.

[74] See above, section 1, and below, n. 81.

[75] The association of Xenophanes, the father of the satirical genre "Silloi," and Timon, author of a
      parody of philosophers called *Silloi*, is worth noticing.

[76] "But although Timon too gets a dig in at Pythagoras' great dignity in his *Silloi*, nonetheless he did
      not neglect him, saying, 'and Pythagoras, inclined to magical opinions / Hunts after humans, a
      whisperer of lofty speech'" (fr. 58 di Marco).

[77] The first fragment reads: "Now I will pass over to another story, and I shall show the path." It is
      usually taken to belong to the same context as the second one (cf. DK 21B7) and to be quoted for
      the purpose of identification. The second fragment ("And they say that when he was once passing
      by a puppy that was being mistreated / He took pity and said these words: / 'Stop beating it, since
      this is truly the soul / Of a dear friend, which I recognized upon hearing it cry out'") happens to be
      our oldest testimony about Pythagoras' doctrine of transmigration (see Burkert 1972a: 120ff.). But
      Diogenes does not seem to quote it to illustrate this point.

[78] Cratinus, frs. 6 and 7 K-A; Mnesimachus, fr. 1 K-A; Aristophon, frs. 12 and 13 K-A.

[79] "When Pythagoras arrived in Italy, he constructed a little room underground and told his mother
      to note and write down on a writing-tablet whatever happened and when and then to send it down
      to him until he came back up. His mother did this. After some time, Pythagoras came back up
      withered and looking like a skeleton, then he went to the assembly and said he had gone to Hades,
      and he even read out to them what had happened. They were so affected by what he said that

Finally, there are the epigrams in 44–5, in a section which is atypical not only for its length, but also because only the last epigram of the series bears on the philosopher's death (as is usually the case in other chapters), while the first three mock the Pythagorean mode of life. The first epigram makes the point that eating animals which are dead does not amount – by definition – to eating beings with souls, so that it does not contradict Pythagoras' prohibition (mentioned in 13). The second epigram discloses the contradiction of letting others do what one thinks to be an injustice, namely eating flesh – an allusion to Pythagoras' recommended diet for athletes, which included meat (cf. 12).[80] The third (somewhat overstretched) one reflects the undoubtedly serious difficulty of reconciling metempsychosis and personal identity, illustrated by the relation between Pythagoras and Euphorbus (cf. 4). The last one interestingly takes up a recurrent feature in various versions of Pythagoras' death, which, in a typical way for ancient biographies, relates it to a central doctrinal item: just as Thales dies from heat and thirst (Diog. Laert. 1.39; the revenge of fire against water, which Thales had elected as his philosophical principle), and Heraclitus from hydropsy (9.3; the revenge of water against Heraclitus' fire), Pythagoras dies not only because of the hatred accumulated against his sectarian organization (the vengeance of the jealous and the excluded), but because in the course of escaping their attack, he wants to avoid crossing a field of beans – the revenge of the prohibited vegetable, so to speak (cf. 19, 24, 34, and the death narratives in 39 and 40).

For all their intrinsic criticisms, however, these negative testimonies hardly tell us anything about Diogenes' own position. This is not even the case with Diogenes' own epigrams, if we accept that witty maliciousness is inherent in epigrams considered as a literary genre.[81] After all, other passages suggest or at least are compatible with a positive assessment of Pythagoras' philosophical achievements. I have already mentioned that Diogenes' report about the coinage of the term "philosophy" by Pythagoras (8) would lend support to his views about the Greek origin of philosophy

they wept and wailed and believed that he was divine, so that they even entrusted their wives to him in the hopes that they would learn something from him; and these were called Pythagorean women" (Hermippus, fr. 20 Wehrli). An ironical exploitation of Pythagoras' *katabasis* has also been recognized by Burkert in Hieronymus of Rhodes' report in 21 (1972a: 155ff.).

[80] We know that there are contradictory reports on Pythagoras' ban on eating flesh. The situation obviously evolved in time. See Burkert 1972a: 180–3. The mention of a pugilist named Pythagoras in the homonyms section (47) may be related.

[81] Contrast Gigante 1986: 39, commenting on Diogenes' epigrams: "the irony towards some beliefs of the Pythagorean system or attitudes [. . .] seem to me to be a sure indication, if not of hostility, at least of a distance. Diogenes is immune to the Neopythagorean fanaticism of his time" (my trans.). See also Chapter 18, section 3 below.

so vigorously expressed at the beginning of his work.[82] By the same token, Pythagoras' piety, made evident by the long series of precepts that play such a crucial role in his chapter, may have spoken directly to the heart of Diogenes, who, in his prologue again, rejected the claim that Orpheus – rather than Musaeus or Linus – was the first Greek philosopher precisely because of his impiety.[83] Last but not least, Pythagoras' theoretical discoveries in the field of mathematics and astronomy make him both an equal and a rival of Thales. In the end, the chapter does not yield clear evidence as to Diogenes' personal attitude towards Pythagoras and his school.[84] As often happens with the contradictory evidence that Diogenes is happy to provide his reader, it is up to us to raise questions and to make up our own minds.

---

[82] See section 2 above.   [83] See Diog. Laert. 1. 5.
[84] Compare Diogenes' procedure in Book 10, where he directly opposes to the many stories defaming Epicurus the contrary, apologetic tradition that he clearly prefers.

CHAPTER 18

Porphyry's Life of Pythagoras

Constantinos Macris

In memory of Alain Segonds (1942–2011)

1. Introduction

For centuries, Porphyry's *Life of Pythagoras* (Πυθαγόρου βίος, *Vita Pythagorae* = *VP*) and Iamblichus' *On the Pythagorean Way of Life* have conveyed idealized pictures of Pythagoras that continued to be "canonic" down to the nineteenth century. These two works remain, along with Book 8, §§1–50 of Diogenes Laertius' *Lives and Doctrines of the Eminent Philosophers*, the three main sources for scholarly efforts to establish, with great pains and little certitude, a few basic historical facts pertaining to Pythagoras' life, and, more confidently, to reconstruct the process of the creation of his legend.[1]

It is not a coincidence that, like the two other fully preserved lives of Pythagoras, Porphyry's text comes from the third century AD, a period of (Neo)-Pythagorean revival when interest in Pythagoras was at its peak. Given Porphyry's dates (234 – *c.* 305 AD), the *VP* should be placed somewhere between Diogenes (first half of the third century) and Iamblichus (end of the century or early fourth, a few years before or after Porphyry's edition of Plotinus' *Enneads*, *c.* 301), and more precisely after Porphyry's joining the school of Plotinus in Rome in 264 (see below n. 14).

Unlike Iamblichus' *On the Pythagorean Life*, which gives a full and systematic account of Pythagoras' biography and the Pythagorean way of life, as the first of Iamblichus' ten-book sequence *On Pythagoreanism*, Porphyry's *VP* is *not* an independent work – a monograph of sorts on Pythagoras, or part of a larger project devoted to Pythagoreanism. Instead, like Diogenes' Book 8, it is just one chapter of a broader *History of Philosophy* (Φιλόσοφος ἱστορία, *Historia philosophica* = *HP*) in four books, of which

---

[1] On the distinction between historical facts and fiction about Pythagoras, see Riedweg 2008: 1–41 vs. 42–97. On the sources about Pythagoras' legend, see Lévy 1926.

only a few fragments have been preserved.[2] Apparently, in the course of transmission this chapter was detached from the whole and circulated separately, although Cyril of Alexandria in the early fifth century, and even Ibn Abī Uṣaybiʿa in the thirteenth, still quoted the *VP* as belonging to Book 1 of the *HP* (207T–207aT). The independent manuscript tradition of the *VP* – no doubt due to the continuous interest in Pythagoras during the Byzantine period – ensured its privileged fate: out of the whole *HP*, only this chapter has survived as an extensive text – although the degree to which it can be considered complete in its present state is uncertain.[3] The exceptional preservation of the *VP*, however, should not make us forget that Porphyry's aim was not to focus exclusively on Pythagoras, but to present him as an integral part of a larger picture of Greek philosophy. Consequently, before examining the *VP* we should look at the *HP* as a whole in order to find out how Pythagoras' biography fitted into this ambitious work.

2. Porphyry's *History of Philosophy*

One of the aspects of the *HP* that immediately catches our attention is its essentially antiquarian, scholarly, and at the same time compilatory and derivative character. Like Diogenes' *Lives*, the *HP* offers the reader a wide range of material on ancient Greek philosophers, collected from various sources, and puts great emphasis on chronology.[4] This way of proceeding is perfectly in tune with the tastes of a polymath such as Porphyry, a "bookish" scholar and "indefatigable source-hunter" (Barker 2000: 61) who wrote on a multitude of subjects.[5] His astonishing erudition was displayed in such diverse works as *On Abstinence from Animal Food* and the *Commentary* on Ptolemy's *Harmonics*.[6]

From Hellenistic times four types of literature were available to those interested in the history of philosophy (Mejer 1978: 60–95): (1) "Doxographies," i.e. collections of opinions (δόξαι, *placita*) of particular philosophers

---

[2] Frs. 193F–224F (fragments of Porphyry's works are cited from Smith 1993); see the translations with commentary by Segonds 1982 and Sodano 1997. For an introduction with bibliography, see Zambon 2012. Four books: 193T (from the *Suda*); cf. also 3aT, 4T, 194aT and 194cT.

[3] Its beginning in a dry manner resembling a dictionary entry and breaking off in the middle of a sentence are clear indications that the text of the *VP* was damaged at both the beginning and the end.

[4] See 200F–202F, 204F, 209F; cf. also 225T. John Malalas cites it as Φιλόσοφος χρονογραφία (199T). Other sources may cite it as "the *Chronicle*."

[5] See the impressive list of his writings in Goulet *et al.* 2012: 1300–11.

[6] Compare the oracular pronouncement "Divinely inspired is the Syrian (*scil.* Iamblichus), learned is the Phoenician (*scil.* Porphyry)" (6T).

systematically arranged according to topics (Mansfeld and Runia 1997: 323–7). (2) Works *On the Schools* [*of Philosophy*] (Περὶ αἱρέσεων), dealing with the teachings of the philosophical schools or of a specific school (Mejer 1978: 74–5), such as Iamblichus' compendium *On Pythagoreanism* (Macris 2009b). (3) *Successions* (Διαδοχαί), whose aim was to establish master–pupil relations among philosophers, arranging their biographies in successions, from Thales to the Hellenistic schools.[7] (4) *Lives* (Βίοι), i.e. biographies of individual philosophers and/or descriptions of philosophical ways of life. To which of these types does Porphyry's *HP* belong?

In the absence of a formal statement on the author's part (which the lost proem might have contained), one must rely on the evidence of ancient readers. Eunapius (198T) compares the *HP* to Sotion's *Lives* (or rather *Successions*) *of Philosophers* (a purely biographical work; cf. (3) above), and Theodoret (195T–197T) to Aëtius' and ps.-Plutarch's *Placita* (cf. (1)), pointing out that what distinguished it from them was the combination of *both* doxography *and* biography – a fact confirmed by the *VP* itself as well as by other fragments of the *HP*.[8] This was Porphyry's originality in his reader's eyes.[9] Porphyry may have been following the ancient conception of philosophy as being expressed not only in doctrines but also in character (ἦθος) and way of life, which offer concrete examples of philosophy "in action." However, he was also concerned with purely documentary and historical issues.[10]

Porphyry probably organized his material in roughly chronological order by individual philosophers, i.e., neither by schools of thought (as in Diogenes) nor by philosophical themes or questions (as in the doxographies). We know that Pythagoras appeared in Book 1, along with Homer and Hesiod, the Seven Sages, Thales and Pherecydes (200F–207bT); Socrates was discussed in Book 3 (210F–218F), and Plato in Book 4 (219F–223F). So we can reasonably assume that Book 2 examined Presocratics and Sophists, such as Empedocles (208F), Gorgias (209F) and a few others.[11]

---

[7] E.g., Hippobotus' Φιλοσόφων ἀναγραφή or Philodemus' *Index of Philosophers*; cf. Engels 2007.

[8] For the *VP*, see section 3 below; for the *HP*, the surviving fragments about Socrates are biographical, whereas the ones about Plato deal with doctrines.

[9] Diogenes also has exactly this combination; Theodoret does not mention him since his work was practically unknown until Byzantine times (the notable exception being the Iamblichean Sopatros in the fourth century).

[10] The title may mean *History of Philosophy* or *Inquiry into Philosophy*. See also Zhmud 2002: 290–2. Athanassiadi 1999: 39 envisages the same possibilities about Damascius' Φιλόσοφος ἱστορία, more widely known as the *Life of Isidore*.

[11] One should add the fragments on Solon and Zeno of Elea discovered by Rosenthal 1937 in Arabic sources (cf. Sodano 1997: 142–53). By contrast, the Porphyrian origin of some unattributed doxographical passages in Eusebius (Smith 1988; cf. Sodano 1997: 131–41) is by no means certain,

A crucial step in understanding the *HP*[12] is to stress that the work ended, and indeed culminated, with Plato.[13] In itself this need not imply that Plato occupied the center of the stage or that the *HP* aimed at giving a genealogy of his thought. However, Porphyry's *History of Philosophy* is first and foremost the work of a convinced Platonist, whose project was determined by a decidedly Neoplatonic point of view.[14] From such a perspective, the entire history of early Greek philosophy turns out to be nothing more than a preparation for the true, that is, Platonic, philosophy, whereas the period between Plato and Plotinus seems full of errors, misunderstandings and sterile disputes unworthy of a genuine philosopher's attention.[15] Such a provocative view goes a long way in explaining why Porphyry did not include the Hellenistic schools in his *HP*: he thought that between Plato and Plotinus there was no proper philosophy worth mentioning.[16]

For his account of the pre-Platonic tradition Porphyry appears to have proceeded by highlighting key figures. To use an Empedoclean simile, he must have tried to advance from one mountain peak to the other, downplaying what lies between (DK 31B24). The selection of Pythagoras and Socrates as "peaks" was natural, given that, already at the time of Aristotle (*Metaph.* 987a29ff.) and Dicaearchus (fr. 41 Wehrli = 45 Mirhady), Plato was regarded as the heir of both – a view shared also by Numenius and later by Proclus.[17]

and that of long sections of Al-Shahrastani's *Book of Sects* (an *idée fixe* of Altheim and Stiehl 1954 and 1961) is doubted by Segonds 1982: 172–6, and sharply criticized by De Smet 1998: 20–2; cf. Hugonnard-Roche 2012: 1465–6.

[12] For the following considerations see Segonds 1982.

[13] Clearly stated in 198T, where Porphyry's attitude is revealingly contrasted with Sotion's, who, despite living many centuries before Porphyry, "seems to have descended" later than Plato.

[14] A fact that supports a post-Plotinian dating of the *HP*, as also do the metaphysics and ontology attributed to Plato in it; see Segonds 1982: 166 and 190–1; Zambon 2012: 1330–1.

[15] Porphyry's approach may have been influenced by Numenius (frs. 24–8 Des Places, cf. O'Meara 1989: 10ff.) and reflected in Proclus' *Platonic Theology* (1.1 pp. 6.16–7.8 Saffrey and Westerink).

[16] Unless it was in accord with Plato – a qualification that might allow the inclusion of Aristotle in the *HP*, given that Porphyry thought that the Stagirite agreed with his master on all crucial issues; see Karamanolis 2006: 243–330. If the expression "[Porphyry] finished with Plato *and his time period*" (my italics) used in 198T is interpreted literally, Porphyry may have discussed Plato's successors, including Aristotle. So Porphyry's work was not unaffected by the *Successions* literature, and must have given at least a few hints about the philosophers' legacy. A passage at the end of the *VP* (59ff.), where the Master's biography is followed by anecdotes about his followers, encourages us to think along similar lines.

[17] See Burkert 1972a: 94 with n. 47; Numenius fr. 24 Des Places; Proclus *In Tim.* Vol. 1 7.19–8.4 Diehl. Porphyry's approach might be modeled on that of Dicaearchus, who "tried to chart the evolution of philosophy by highlighting a series of epochal figures" (White 2001: 195), namely the Seven Sages, Pythagoras, Socrates and Plato.

3. The *Life of Pythagoras*[18]

Now that we have a clear picture about the place of the *VP* within the framework of the *HP*, it is time to turn to the *VP* itself. Like the *HP* in its entirety, Porphyry's biography of Pythagoras is a scholarly piece of work. It has the following well-articulated structure:[19]

(1)   Origin and family of Pythagoras (§§1–5).
(2)   Education: Greek masters and travels to the Orient (§§1, 2, 6–8, 11–12).
(3)   The "Helladic" period: educational activity on Samos, visits to Delphi and Crete, departure for Italy in reaction to Polycrates' tyranny (§§9–11, 13–17).
(4)   Public activity in Italy (§§18–31):
    (i)   Educational: speeches given in Croton, acquisition of followers (including women), teaching, foundation of a school (the ὁμακοεῖον) (§§18–20).
    (ii) Political: foundation of the Magna Graecia, lawgiving, liberation of cities from tyranny, elimination of civil strife (§§21–2).
    (iii) Miracle-working (§§23–31).
(5)   Way of life (διαγωγή) (§§32–6).
(6)   Content of Pythagoras' teaching and philosophy (§§37–53):
    (i)   Moral exhortations (§§38–45):[20]
       (a)   expressed in a detailed and comprehensive way (§§38–41a);
       (b)   formulated in a symbolic way: *symbola* and taboos followed by allegorical and other explanations (§§41b–45a).
    (ii) Training of the mind through mathematics and number philosophy (§§45b–52):
       (a)   transition: necessity of purification for recollection; Pythagoras' capacity for recalling his previous reincarnations (§45b);
       (b)   the role of mathematics in purification and pedagogy: preparation of the mind for contemplation of the intelligible realm (§§46–7);

[18] Standard edition: Des Places 1982. Commentaries: Sodano and Girgenti 1998; Macris 2001; Staab 2002: 109–34. Briefer studies: Philip 1959; Edwards 1993; Clark 2000; Macris and Goulet 2012.
[19] For detailed accounts of the structure, see Sodano and Girgenti 1998: 40–123; Macris 2001: 50–6; Staab 2002: 118–21.
[20] On this section, see Hüffmeier 2001.

     (c)   numbers as an educational device; specimen of Pythagorean number philosophy: the one, the dyad, the triad and the decad (§§48–52).

(7)   Pythagoras' death, the end of his school and the Pythagoreans (§§53–61):

     (i)   Reasons for the disappearance of the Pythagorean school (§53).

     (ii)   The end of Pythagoras and the early Pythagoreans: Cylon's anti-Pythagorean conspiracy; diverging versions about Pythagoras' death; the diaspora of the Pythagoreans and the preservation of Pythagoras' teaching (§§54–8).

     (iii)   Anecdotes illustrating the way of life of individual Pythagoreans (§§59–61).

The Greek text of the *VP* stops here, in the middle of a sentence, but Ibn Abī Uṣaybiʻa preserves a fragment in Arabic probably deriving from the lost final paragraphs of the *VP*, which deals with a further theme:

     (iv)   Pythagoras' and other Pythagoreans' genuine writings, which are cautiously distinguished from later forgeries circulating under their names.[21]

This is a simple and clear plan reflecting only limited effort on Porphyry's part to integrate the collected material into a new synthesis or to embed it in a unified narrative. It is, in reality, just a well-ordered and reasoned juxtaposition of elements found in earlier sources without further elaboration or rhetorical amplification. The situation is not at all comparable to what we find in *On the Pythagorean Life*, where Iamblichus rewrote and considerably rearranged the excerpts drawn from his sources, embroidered them rhetorically, and submitted them to a compositional structure of his own invention put at the service of a specific philosophical project (see Chapter 19, sections 1 and 5, below).

    Although Porphyry was not unfamiliar with the genre of philosophical biography (cf. Zambon 2004) – after all, he is also the author of the *Life of Plotinus* – when he wrote the *VP*, which concerns a philosopher of the distant past, he relied on earlier testimonies. Thus his own voice is rarely heard in the *VP*; it is replaced by the constant reference to other authorities, in the biographical sections at least.[22] His authorial interventions

---

[21] For translations and commentaries, see van der Waerden 1965: 862–4; Macris 2001: 381–4 and 2002: 113–14 with n. 159–65; Huffman 2005: 616–18; Cottrell 2008: 532–6. Cottrell envisages the possibility that this fragment, in which Archytas features prominently, derives from Book 4 of the *HP*, which may have included a *Life* of Archytas.

[22] In the doxographical part, by contrast, some passages could come from Porphyry's own hand: §19: the doctrines on the soul brought to Greece by Pythagoras; §§46–7: the account of the preparatory role of mathematics; §53: some aggressive remarks about Plato, Aristotle and their pupils.

are minimal, their primary function being to provide the necessary transitions between the various items or to introduce his sources to the reader; he only rarely inserts remarks of his own. In such a situation, the only way to uncover Porphyry's personal view about Pythagoras is to consider: (i) his choices of sources (also paying attention to his evaluation of them); (ii) the kind of evidence he selected, and more precisely the specific items he considered important to transmit; and (iii) the general attitude he adopted as a historian of philosophy and as a biographer of Pythagoras.

Let us start with the sources. In the *VP*, Porphyry names no fewer than fifteen authors. It is clear, however, that most are not direct sources that Porphyry had on his desk when composing, but just authorities cited in his sources.[23] Scholars have concluded that no more than four sources were used directly by Porphyry, with only minor disagreements about the extent of the quotations.[24] These sources are, in order of appearance:

(1)   A handbook, the author and title of which are not mentioned (§§1–9, 15, 18–19).

(2)   Antonius Diogenes' fantastical novel, *Unbelievable Things beyond Thule* (§§10–17, 32–44).[25]

(3)   Nicomachus' *Life of Pythagoras* (§§20–31, 54–61).[26]

(4)   Moderatus' ten-book *Collection of Pythagorean Doctrines* (§§48–53).[27]

Among these sources, (1) the handbook provided evidence of biographical and historical nature and has much in common with late authors with antiquarian interests such as Diogenes Laertius and Clement of Alexandria;[28] (2) the novelist Antonius Diogenes is a source peculiar to Porphyry, quoted because of a narrative he reported about Pythagoras' life, allegedly deriving from the latter's adoptive brother Astraeus (a fictional character); (3) Nicomachus, from whom the account about Pythagoras' miracles

---

[23]   On the distinction between sources used directly and authorities referred to or quoted indirectly, see Goulet 1997.

[24]   See Burkert 1972a: 98–100 and Sodano and Girgenti 1998: 40–123.

[25]   Stephens and Winkler (1995: 101–57) also include *VP* 45 and 54–5. On the diverging views on Antonius Diogenes' portion in the *VP*, see Macris 2001: 198–9; Zhmud 2012b: 74 n. 54.

[26]   *FGrHist* 1063F1 and F3. Only the author's name is given by Porphyry, but the provenance of the fragments from a biography of Pythagoras seems most probable. Radicke only prints *VP* 20–31 and 57–61 as fragments, but also accepts (1999: 125–6 and n. 13) the Nicomachean origin of *VP* 54–5, and even of *VP* 1–9, 18–19 and 56–7. Sodano (1998: 83) limits the portion attributable to Nicomachus to *VP* 20–31 and 54–61. See also Zhmud 2012b: 75 n. 59.

[27]   Ten books (and not eleven as in Des Places 1982): O'Meara 1989: 23 n. 52; Macris 2001: 59 and 341–2; Staab 2002: 78 n. 173. For the suggestion that §53 should be attributed to Porphyry, see below n. 70.

[28]   It could be comparable, e.g., to Sosicrates' and Sotion's *Successions of Philosophers* or to Favorinus' *Miscellaneous History*, three of Diogenes' customary direct sources, also quoted in his chapter on Pythagoras.

derives, is an important direct source of Iamblichus, too, used extensively in *On the Pythagorean Life* and in the rest of his *On Pythagoreanism*; (4) Moderatus – also peculiar to Porphyry – is the source of the brief exposition of Pythagorean number theory.

There are twelve authorities and works cited indirectly (from the handbook and Nicomachus): Neanthes' of Cyzicus *Collection of Myths According to Cities*, cited as *Mythica* (§§1–2, 55b, 61); Apollonius' *On Pythagoras* (more probably a vague reference than an exact title, §2); Duris' *Samian Annals* (§3); Timaeus' of Tauromenium *Histories* (no title is given by Porphyry) (§4); Lycus' *Histories* (§5); Eudoxus' *Tour of the Earth* (§7); Antiphon's *On the Life of Those Who Excelled in Virtue* (§7–8); Aristoxenus' *On the Pythagorean Way of Life* (§§9, 21–2, 54–5a, 59–61); Dionysophanes (§15); Dicaearchus' *On Lives* (no title given) (§§18–19, 56 and 57); Aristotle's *On the Pythagoreans* (no title given) (§41b); and Hippobotus' *On the Schools of Philosophy* or *Catalogue of Philosophers* (no title given) (§61).

From this listing it is clear that Porphyry uses sources and authorities that seem reliable to him for different reasons: their historical character; their accurate knowledge of the local history of Samos (Duris) and/or Italy (Timaeus, Lycus), and more precisely of some *realia* related to Pythagoras' activities in these two places; their specialization in philosophical biography (Dicaearchus, Antiphon, Hippobotus); their primary or exclusive focus on Pythagoras and his school in (some of) their writings (Aristoxenus, Aristotle); or their (Neo-)Pythagorean philosophical affiliation (Moderatus, Nicomachus) – supposedly guaranteeing an insider's view.

Prominent among the sources of the *VP* are Aristotelian-Peripatetic and Neopythagorean authors, who inform Porphyry's views in his other treatises too. About the authors belonging to the first category, Aristoxenus in particular was known to Porphyry both as a biographer (he is the main source for the *Life of Socrates* in the *HP*)[29] and as a specialist on harmonic science (extensively and regularly used throughout the *Commentary* on Ptolemy's *Harmonics*), whereas Dicaearchus' *Life of Greece* is quoted in *On Abstinence* (4.2ff. = frs. 47–66 Wehrli), and Aristotle himself is, of course, perfectly familiar to Porphyry, who not only wrote commentaries on the Stagirite's works, but also played a decisive role in introducing him into the Neoplatonic philosophical curriculum.

In such a serious and scholarly context the inclusion of a novel in the basic tetrad of the *VP*'s direct sources comes as a surprise. Porphyry justifies

---

[29] He is referred to explicitly only in 211F, 213F and 215aF, but he is certainly the source of most of the fragments on Socrates (see below and n. 38).

his recourse to it by explaining that it furnished a complete and precise account that he judged worth quoting (§10). This is true: Antonius Diogenes' continuous narrative contains a colorful description of Pythagoras' everyday life as well as information about a more obscure period of his life, namely his childhood and early years on Samos and his travels to other places in Greece and the Orient. But perhaps Porphyry considered it even more valuable because of its Pythagorean character (see below and n. 69).

Porphyry's direct sources are relatively recent, dating from the first and second century AD. Thus what we get by reading the *VP* is basically the Middle Platonic version of Pythagoras that was current a century or two earlier than Porphyry. At the same time, the accounts reproduced in these sources are often based, implicitly or explicitly, on earlier reports going back to the fourth century BC or more generally to the Hellenistic period. This is especially the case with the material drawn from the handbook, but also with material from Nicomachus, who used Aristoxenus, Hippobotus-Neanthes and probably paradoxographical sources as well. In this way Porphyry also provides us with access to some aspects of the Hellenistic Pythagoras, who is partly the traditional, "canonical" Pythagoras of the vulgate, familiar to the layman with no special interest in, or affiliation to, the Pythagorean tradition, and partly a rather *recherché* Pythagoras, the protagonist of rarely recounted bizarre stories and fanciful anecdotes known only to the connoisseurs.

The salient features of the Middle Platonic Pythagoras reflected in the *VP*, accepted by Porphyry and transmitted to his Neoplatonic posterity, are the following: Pythagoras is the quintessential Sage of old, the prototype of the divine man. His homeland and citizenship are disputed in much the same way as those of Homer, and traditions are reported about his links with Syria and his being a son of the god Apollo. For his education, he not only sat at the feet of the Homerids and the first Greek thinkers (Pherecydes, Anaximander), but also drew his wisdom and scientific knowledge directly from their ultimate, i.e., Oriental, sources, which are Egyptian, Chaldean, Phoenician and Iranian, but also Arabian and Jewish. A champion of virtue and a contemplative ascetic himself, he was also a master of allegorical symbols, physiognomonics and music therapy. He was most of all active as an educator, a teacher of ethics and morality, and as a lawgiver. He introduced to humanity such inspiring ideas as the harmony of the spheres and the universal kinship of all living beings and promoted the ideal of friendship and the practice of communal property among his followers. His figure is shrouded in religious mystery: he was taught by the Delphic Pythia in person, initiated by the Dactyls in the high mountains of Crete where Zeus was born and nurtured, and taught the principles of all things by Zaratas (= Zarathustra). In his ability to perform miracles of various kinds Porphyry's contemporaries could instantly recognize a *theios anēr* (divine man): the model imitated by miracle-workers like Apollonius of Tyana – and the pagan equivalent of Jesus.[30] Moreover, the Pythagoras of the *VP* is presented as providing Platonists with both an ascetic way of life and a set of doctrinal elements of major importance, such as the belief in the immortality and transmigration of the soul and the preparatory role of mathematics in the soul's striving to purify itself and ascend to the intelligible realm.

This version of Pythagoras contains the germs of later developments. However, it should be stressed that, contrary to a widespread opinion,[31] Porphyry's Pythagoras is *not yet* the full-blown Neoplatonic Pythagoras launched by Iamblichus. He is not conceived as a privileged soul sent to humanity for its salvation after having contemplated the Ideas in the region above the heaven described in the *Phaedrus*; he is neither an Orphic initiate nor a link in the "golden chain" of philosophical transmission going from Orpheus to Plato; he is not presented as the incarnation of the Platonic cardinal virtues; and he is not a master of theurgy. The similarities between the versions of Pythagoras found in Iamblichus and Porphyry are simply due to their use of a common source, Nicomachus, who almost two centuries earlier (*c.* 100 AD) promoted (rather than created) the image of Pythagoras the "divine sage" – already current during the first century. In this sense it is legitimate to say that the *VP* does no more than perpetuate a Middle Platonic or Neopythagorean Pythagoras, thus making clear once more the extent of Porphyry's indebtedness to his pre-Plotinian predecessors.[32]

On the other hand, the Hellenistic inheritance is also present in what is after all a work of erudition; it is evident not only in the kind of sources used in the *VP*, but also in the generally "objective," pluralistic and "encyclopedic" stance adopted by Porphyry, in his tendency to reproduce documentary evidence verbatim, his "flair" for rarities, and his predilection for obscure details and mysterious stories. In spite of his affinity for Pythagoras, Porphyry apparently prefers to be as all-inclusive as possible rather than to have a "formative" impact upon the reader (as does, e.g.,

---

[30] On "The Rise of the Friends of God" in late antiquity, see Brown 1978: 54–80 and 118–25; on "The Pagan Holy Man," Fowden 1982; on the role played by the example of Pythagoras in this process, Macris 2006b.

[31] See, e.g., Philip 1959; Zhmud 2012b: 9: "*Porphyry* and Iamblichus . . . *created* the image of Pythagoras the 'divine sage'" (my italics).

[32] Such indebtedness is confirmed in many other fields; see Zambon 2002.

Plutarch in his *Lives*) or to engage in composing a well-rounded biopic novel (like Philostratus in his *Life of Apollonius of Tyana*) or a systematic and "programmatic" account (similar to that of Iamblichus). These features of the *VP* could well have been criticized by Iamblichus and later Neoplatonists, as revealing, e.g., a philologist lost in an infinite plurality and diversity of details (μερικώτερον), and hesitant (ἐνδοιάζει) to adopt one biographical or doxographical version to the detriment of another, rather than a philosopher who attains an all-embracing and unified view (ἐποπτικώτερον).[33] Even to modern eyes Porphyry's narrative has sometimes appeared "so diffuse and eclectic as to represent a Pythagoras who, in many respects, is no Pythagorean."[34] The lack of a unifying, systematic presentation is also patent in the doxographic part: here we find, e.g., nothing similar to the so-called *Pythagorean Memoirs* transmitted by Alexander Polyhistor and preserved by Diogenes Laertius, which give a brief but full account of the Pythagorean doctrines concerning first principles, cosmology, psychology, the body, embryology and ethics (see Chapter 17, section 5, above).

However, even if Porphyry's primary concern was not to produce an encomium of Pythagoras, it is the positive aspects that prevail in the philosopher's portrait, and what emerges as a whole is an empathetic narrative reflecting a respectful and even admiring attitude towards a sage who was enveloped in the aura of the extraordinary. Here the comparison with Diogenes' apparently neutral, but at times negative, dismissive and ironic account of Pythagoras' life is revealing.[35] The *VP*, by contrast, is devoid of any mockery, ridiculing anecdotes, polemical tone, maliciousness or enmity. Moreover, Porphyry wholeheartedly reproduces encomiastic elements from earlier authors (Empedocles,[36] Dicaearchus, Antiphon, Apollonius, Antonius Diogenes) as well as bits of a more "flowery" hagiographical

---

[33] For the opposition between φιλόλογος and φιλόσοφος, used by Plotinus for Porphyry's former master Longinus, see Pépin 1992, and for the μερικώτερον versus the ἐποπτικώτερον attitude, underlining the contrast between Porphyry and Iamblichus, Pépin 1974. For Porphyry's hesitations (ἐνδοιάζει), see Iamblichus *On the Soul* fr. 6, 30.10–12 Finamore and Dillon; Eunapius *Lives of Philosophers and Sophists* IV 2.6, p. 10. 7–10 Giangrande.

[34] Edwards 2006: 89, having in mind instances in the *VP* where meat is presented as an indispensable part of the athlete's regimen (contrary to Pythagorean vegetarianism) or where Pythagoras, distressed by the ruin of the Pythagorean community in Metapontum, decides to die from starvation (contrary to the Pythagorean prohibition of suicide).

[35] See especially the epigrams composed by Diogenes himself and his fondness for providing satirical accounts of Pythagoras' presumed descent into Hades and of his belief in metempsychosis, as well as verses drawn from Middle Comedy making fun of the ascetic Pythagoreans of the fourth century BC. (See Chapter 17, section 6, above for a different view of Diogenes' attitude.)

[36] For Empedocles' testimony on Pythagoras transmitted by Porphyry via Nicomachus, see Macris and Skarsouli 2012.

discourse (e.g., in the long passage from Nicomachus about Pythagoras'
miracle-working), thus endorsing the glorifying and sanctifying tone used
in the sources.[37]

The contrast with Porphyry's attitude to Socrates is astonishing. In the
HP he presents him as prone to anger, lacking in education, intemperate
and such a slave to his sexual drive that he had two women in his life at the
same time (210–217F).[38] Even if by doing this Porphyry was simply keeping
his promise (212F) to pick out both what was praiseworthy and what was
blameworthy in earlier accounts about Socrates, one can be certain that he
did not (and could not, in the context of Neoplatonic ethics, or even of
common late antique morality) present Socrates as a moral *exemplum* to
the readers of the *HP*.[39] Such a role was no doubt reserved for the ascetic
Pythagoras, the paragon of virtue *par excellence*.

A word must be said here about Porphyry's attitude toward his sources.
In his philosophical treatises, he does not hesitate to formulate criticisms
of other thinkers (e.g., of Iamblichus, on theurgy) or to engage in polemics
(e.g., against Christianity). In the *VP*, however, he rather uncritically
accepts the accuracy of "traditional" accounts transmitted by what he
considers precise (§10, 36, 55), ancient and trustworthy sources (§23) without challenging their historical veracity or legendary features. Rare are the
instances where he distances himself from what he reports, and even when
he does so, it is only because his direct source did it before him (§27).
As for the expressions of caution recurring in the passage about miracle
stories extracted from Nicomachus, they alternate with assertions about the
high quality of the sources and the unanimous testimony of the witnesses
(§27–8), and in fact prove to be part of a make-believe strategy characteristic of ancient paradoxography.[40] So although Porphyry was familiar with
philological criticism and fond of disentangling issues of chronology and
authenticity,[41] the extravagant biographical material about Pythagoras did
not arouse any suspicions in him and was reproduced uncut[42] – we even

---

[37] Porphyry's positive attitude to Pythagoras is also visible in other works. In his *Homeric Questions on
the Odyssey* (1.1.1 and 10), Porphyry praises Pythagoras' πολυτροπία, i.e. his pedagogic sensitivity in
adapting his discourse to different audiences: children, women, adolescents and adult aristocrats.
On the Antisthenian or Porphyrian paternity of this passage, see Luzzatto 1996: *passim*, esp. 342–6
and 356–7; Brancacci 1996 (esp. 401ff.) and 2002.

[38] For Porphyry's dependence on Aristoxenus in his chapter on Socrates (and arguments against the
standard view of Aristoxenus as a biographer), see Schorn 2012; Huffman 2012b.

[39] See Rangos 2004: 470–2, who gives a full account of Porphyry's Socrates.

[40] See Schepens and Delcroix 1996: 386–9.   [41] See Macris 2002: 111–12, with n. 155–6.

[42] Not only that, but when, in one of his *Lessons in Philology* (408F), Porphyry discussed the attribution
to Pythagoras or to Pherecydes of four miraculous stories serving to highlight their prowess as seers,
he defended the version featuring Pythagoras as being the original.

have the feeling that the most mysterious aspects of Pythagoras' legend strongly attracted Porphyry, whose insatiable curiosity for myth, religion and rituals surfaces several times in his works. Similarly, the 280 books of Pythagoras and other Pythagoreans supposedly collected by Archytas and distinguished from forgeries "put in the mouth of Pythagoras and circulating under his name" were considered by Porphyry as genuine and "beyond suspicion" – a fact that seems to indicate (if the late report in Arabic is accurate) that "he accepted essentially all of what we regard as the pseudo-Pythagorean treatises . . . as genuine."[43]

Such an attitude does not merely reflect the under-development of the historical-critical method in Porphyry's time or the propensity of ancient scholarship to accumulate interesting pieces of information rather than to establish their antiquity and authenticity. It shows that, as a Platonist full of sympathy and admiration for Pythagoras and the Pythagorean tradition, Porphyry was attached to it and not eager to question its foundations or scrutinize its sources in a critical way. Having no awareness of the constructed character of this tradition, he regarded it as an authentic and undifferentiated whole going back to Pythagoras himself and did not try to distinguish successive strata within it. This is particularly clear in the doxographic part of the *VP*, where more "archaic" oral sayings (§41b), moral exhortations, either direct (§§38–41a) or "symbolic," followed by allegorical explanations (§42), portions of the *Golden Verses* (§40) and Platonizing theories about mathematics (§§46–7) and numbers (§§48–52) are all attributed to Pythagoras himself and taken as the original teachings of early Pythagoreanism. Porphyry's attitude here poses the question of the exact nature of his relation to Pythagoreanism, to which we now turn.

4. Porphyry and Pythagoreanism[44]

In the first lines of the treatise *On Abstinence from Animal Food* Porphyry reminded his comrade Firmus Castricius, who had abandoned the vegetarian diet and "reverted to consuming flesh," that they had *both* shown respect (εὐλάβεια), in the past, "for those men, at once ancient and god-fearing, who pointed out the way," and later accuses him of "spurning the ancestral laws of the philosophy to which he was committed" (1.2.3). This has

[43] Huffman 2005: 617. In the part of the *VP* extant in Greek, Porphyry quotes from the *Golden Verses* (§§20 and 40) and refers to the Pythagorean *Notebooks* (§§7 and 58) and to the "preserved" writings of members of Pythagoras' family (§4), but he categorically asserts that there were no writings of Pythagoras himself (§57). For ambiguities in Porphyry's attitude toward the Pythagorean pseudepigrapha, see Macris 2002: 98 n. 85 and 111–14.

[44] See Taormina 2012: 109–12.

rightly been taken as an unmistakable allusion to Porphyry's commitment to the way of life introduced by Pythagoras and adopted by the Pythagoreans, if not to his membership in a Pythagorean "conventicle" in Rome. The latter, maximal interpretation is not compelling, given the rhetorical exaggeration involved in a protreptic passage the purpose of which was to convert Castricius back to his earlier convictions. The former, minimal one, however, points to the practice of vegetarianism (at least optionally) among the members of the narrower circle of Plotinus' students in Rome.

This is not sufficient to make Porphyry, or Plotinus and his more committed pupils, Pythagoreans (or rather Neopythagoreans) pure and simple, but it shows how widespread was a philosophical asceticism of Pythagorean inspiration in some of the Platonic schools of the time.[45] Although *On Abstinence* fervently advocates a universal approach to vegetarianism embracing a whole range of Greek and oriental sages and nations and does not confine itself to a defense of Pythagoreanism, it is the "Pythagorean" version of asceticism that is displayed not only in the idealized portrait of the true philosopher sketched in that treatise but also in the *Life of Plotinus* as depicted by Porphyry. Thus both the ideal of the philosopher and its embodiment in real life exhibit a considerable number of "Pythagorean" features,[46] as also do the moral exhortations addressed to his wife Marcella in a letter stuffed with Neopythagorean gnomic utterances inviting her to adopt an ascetic and contemplative life. All these elements confirm Porphyry's enthusiasm as a Platonist and a puritan for a tradition that was so much preoccupied with the pollution of the soul and its liberation from the body.

It is not surprising that exactly this is recognized in the *VP* as Pythagoras' major contribution to philosophy. According to Porphyry (§§46–7), the aim of Pythagoras' philosophy was to purify the mind and to release it from its bodily fetters and bonds, setting it entirely free. Through mathematics and concepts (θεωρήματα), which lie on the border between corporeal and incorporeal realities, Pythagoras trained the mind to progressively turn itself away from the sensible world, and guided it gently toward the contemplation of "the things that truly are," i.e., of the intelligible, eternal realities akin to it – a real blessing for humans, adds Porphyry. He then rushes immediately to provide an alternative account of the general epistemic and pedagogical function of numbers, drawn from Moderatus (§§48–9a). The

---

[45] See Meredith 1976; Finn 2009: 27–32; and on vegetarianism Sfameni Gasparro 1987–1989. This trend began already in the early Academy with Xenocrates (Diog. Laert. 4.6–11); cf. Isnardi Parente 1985; Macris 2009b: 154, and Chapter 12, section 3 above.

[46] O'Meara 1989: 28–9 with n. 75–9. For the *Life of Plotinus*, see also Staab 2002: 134–43.

latter maintained that the Pythagoreans resorted to numbers for the sake of pedagogical clarity (εὐσήμου διδασκαλίας χάριν), in order to overcome the difficulty in conceiving and giving a clear account of the primary reasons (*logoi*), the incorporeal Forms, and the first principles. He compared their device to those of the geometers and the grammarians: just as written letters represent the spoken sounds of the language, and as geometric diagrams and drawings illustrate the ideal geometric shapes, so the numbers are used to represent the Forms (cf. Kahn 2001: 106). In this way Porphyry appropriated mathematical Pythagoreanism as preparation of the human mind for grasping higher, immaterial Reality, namely the Platonic Forms – exactly as it is suggested in Book 7 of Plato's *Republic*.

This pedagogic project does not seem to be just a theoretical desideratum for Porphyry. We know that he not only wrote about the importance of the cycle of the seven liberal arts (ἐγκύκλια μαθήματα) as preparatory to philosophy and as constituting the first stage in the soul's striving to ascend,[47] but he was also actively involved in the study of at least two sciences of the *quadriuium*, i.e., music and astronomy:[48] he wrote a *Commentary* on Ptolemy's *Harmonics* and an *Introduction* to Ptolemy's *Tetrabiblos*, both still extant, and probably also an *Introduction to the Study of Astronomy* (attested in the *Suda*). Archytas' statement (fr. 1; cf. Pl. *Resp.* 530d6–9) about the close relationship between the four mathematical "sister" sciences, in a fragment that Porphyry quoted extensively in his *Commentary* to Ptolemy, certainly encouraged him to do so.

Another core tenet of Platonism, namely the belief in the immortality and transmigration of the soul, is plainly acknowledged in the *VP* (§19) as a personal contribution of Pythagoras, in a passage so remarkable for its precision and concision that it is worth quoting in full:

> What [Pythagoras] used to say to his associates, no one can tell for certain, since they observed no ordinary silence. Nonetheless the following became universally known: first, (1) that he held the soul to be immortal; next, (2) that it changes into other kinds of living beings; in addition, (3) that events that have happened once recur again periodically, and nothing is ever absolutely new; and finally, (4) that all animate things that come into being should be regarded as belonging to the same family (ὁμογενῆ).

---

[47] See *HP* 224F. Augustine's *De ordine* 2 (esp. Ch. 10.28ff.), where the same idea is developed, may be essentially Porphyrian in content according to Hadot 2006: 101–36 (see also O'Meara 1989: 29 n. 79; Zambon 2002: 55).

[48] For the Pythagoreanizing background to the Neoplatonists' interest in music, see O'Meara 2005a and 2007.

Pythagoras seems to have been the first to introduce these doctrines into Greece.[49]

Porphyry refers many times, in passing, to this theory,[50] although it seems that he discussed and rejected the metempsychosis of humans in animal bodies.[51] In doing so he was probably following the Neopythagorean Cronius, author of a work *On Rebirth*, who also rejected this point of the theory by means of an allegorical interpretation.[52]

This brings us to the issue of the pervasive influence of Middle Platonic thinkers with Pythagoreanizing tendencies on Porphyry and the *VP*. The most important among them is Numenius of Apamea. Porphyry relied on him (and on Cronius) very heavily in the treatise *On The Cave of the Nymphs*, to an extent much greater than the explicit references reveal; Numenian themes in fact permeate Porphyry's thought throughout his work: for example, the appreciation of "alien wisdom,"[53] the allegorical exegesis of Homer,[54] and the doctrines pertaining to dreams, hypostases, matter and the origin of evil.[55] This explains why Porphyry was unable to escape from the accusation of servile dependency on Numenius,[56] like Plotinus earlier.[57] Second comes Moderatus, who, apart from being extensively quoted in the *VP*, also provides the basis for Porphyry's interpretation of Plato's *Parmenides* and (the pseudepigraphic-Neopythagorean) *Letter II* (312e) as expositions of a tripartite theology.[58]

Even Plotinus, whose ties with Pythagoreanism seem quite loose to us,[59] explained, according to his Athenian colleague Longinus,[60] the

---

[49] *VP* 19 = Dicaearchus fr. 40 Mirhady (not in Wehrli), translation inspired by those of Mirhady, Kirk, Raven and Schofield, Guthrie and Barnes. The attribution to Dicaearchus is not certain; see Zhmud 2012b: 157 and n. 81, who argues that this paragraph is due to Porphyry.

[50] For the Pythagoreanizing elements present in his doctrine of the soul, see Taormina 2012: 110–12.

[51] See Deuse 1983; Smith 1984; Castelletti 2006: 305–21; see also Helmig 2008.

[52] Nemesius of Emesa *On the Nature of Man* 2.117, p. 35.2–5 Morani.

[53] Clearly echoed in the section of *VP* about Pythagoras' travels to the Orient (§§1–2, 6–8 and 11–12): "For it was from his peregrination [πλάνη] among these peoples that Pythagoras acquired the greatest part of his wisdom." See also Numenius frs. 1a–1c; 8.9–13; 30.5–6, with O' Meara 1989: 13.

[54] Like Numenius and other Neopythagoreans (Lamberton 1986), Porphyry considered the "old theologian" Homer a philosopher in his own right. See the treatise *On the Cave of the Nymphs*, the fragments of *On the Styx*, and the title of his lost treatise, *On the Philosophy of Homer*.

[55] See Waszink 1966; Zambon 2002: 171–250; and Numenius' dismissal of the skeptical Academy and the Hellenistic schools noted above p. 384 with n. 15.

[56] See Proclus *Commentary on the Timaeus*. vol. 1 77.22–3 Diehl.

[57] *Life of Plotinus* 17.1–3. For Numenius and Moderatus see Chapter 12, sections 11 and 9 above along with Fuentes González 2005b and Centrone and Macris 2005.

[58] See 236F. *Pace* Dodds 1928, Moderatus' views are reinterpreted in a Neoplatonic sense, and not faithfully transmitted by Porphyry and/or Simplicius; see Hubler 2011.

[59] See Bonazzi 2000; O'Meara 2005b; Taormina 2012: 103–9.

[60] Porph. *VP* 20.71–6; see also 21.6–9. See Menn 2001.

"Pythagorean and Platonic principles" in his courses, and he did so with more clarity and precision than any of his predecessors, based on the writings of the Neopythagoreans Numenius, Cronius, Moderatus and Thrasyllus, who were also regularly read in his "seminars."[61] Such activity of Plotinus is confirmed at least as far as his treatise *On Number* is concerned.[62] The high esteem in which Plotinus' school held Pythagoras is shown in the oracle of Apollo probably issued by Amelius and reproduced by Porphyry in the *Life* of his master (22.54–7), where it is proclaimed that after death, Plotinus' soul will rejoin the company of Plato and Pythagoras in the heavens. The same esteem, as well as the will to make Plotinus appear more Pythagorean, is reflected in Porphyry's arrangement of the latter's treatises in six sets of nine (three nines, then two, then one: an ascending simplicity), the *Enneads* ("ninefolds"), according to "Pythagorean" arithmological considerations.[63]

Porphyry's thorough knowledge of the Pythagoreanizing trends of his time required a substantial "Pythagorean" library, like those of his masters Longinus in Athens and Plotinus in Rome, or like that of their contemporary Origen in Alexandria, which contained Numenius, Cronius, Moderatus, Nicomachus, "and the most highly esteemed (ἐλλόγιμοι) among the Pythagoreans," along with the Stoics Chaeremon and Cornutus.[64] The abundant use of Pythagorean sources in many of Porphyry's works shows that he had indeed access to such a library.[65] In addition to Numenius, Cronius and Moderatus, already discussed above, we find references to or quotations from Empedocles, who is invoked in *On Abstinence*, together with Pythagoras, as a defender of vegetarianism; Apollonius of Tyana (*On Abstinence, On the Styx*); a Neopythagorean gnomology (*Letter to Marcella*);[66] an anonymous "theologian" (*On Abstinence*), etc. A most impressive collection of Pythagorean sources, opinions and quotations is displayed in Porphyry's *Commentary* to Ptolemy's *Harmonics*, where a long fragment of Archytas is quoted in Doric (Huffman 2005: 103–8), as well as Thrasyllus[67] and two music theorists that provide precious information on the distinctions between "schools of harmonics" in antiquity, which is

[61] Porph. *VP* 14.10–14. [62] See Slaveva-Griffin 2009: esp. 42ff.

[63] See O'Meara 1989: 29 n. 79; Slaveva-Griffin 2008 and 2009: 131–40. From a passage of *On Abstinence* (2.36.1) it is clear that Porphyry allowed also for a theology of numbers and geometrical figures (cf. Macris 2009a: 34–5).

[64] Eusebius *Ecclesiastical History* 6.19.8 = Porphyry *Against the Christians* Book 3 fr. 39.

[65] Porphyry's "Pythagorean" library might be usefully compared to that of Iamblichus; see Macris 2002: 88–91 and 92–109.

[66] See Rocca-Serra 1971; Sodano 1991.

[67] *In Ptol. Harm.* 12.21–8 Düring. Tarrant (1993: 108–47) suggested that the ideas expounded in the immediately following epistemological excursus of *In Ptol.* 12.29–15.28 are derived from Thrasyllus; but see also the skeptical comments of Gerson 1994.

to say Didymus (first century AD), also author of a work *On Pythagorean Philosophy*,[68] and Ptolemaïs of Cyrene (first century BC – first century AD), the author of a *Pythagorean Musical Elements* (cf. Macris 2012 and Chapter 9 above). To these predominantly first- and second-century AD Neopythagorean authors we must add Nicomachus and Antonius Diogenes, who are two out of the four direct sources for the *VP*.[69]

Even more noteworthy is that Porphyry decided to give space in the *VP* (§53) to some aggressive Neopythagoreans who had both a strong identity and "imperialistic" tendencies towards the other schools of philosophy, and lived close to Porphyry's time, probably just before the time of Moderatus, who seems to be the source here.[70] He lets them express their own view about the history of their tradition, and its appropriation and hijacking by other philosophers, in particular Plato, Aristotle and their pupils in the Academy and the Lyceum.[71]

5. Conclusion

We can confidently conclude that reading Porphyry's *VP* gives us access to the state of Pythagoreanism in the first centuries AD and to its views of Pythagoras and the Pythagorean tradition. Porphyry displays the uniformly positive attitude towards Pythagoras that is found in Middle Platonism and does not temper that attitude with reports from the negative tradition about Pythagoras, which Diogenes Laertius, who is largely free from the influence of Middle Platonism, includes. Nonetheless, Porphyry's idealized version differs in important ways from that which Iamblichus later presents. Furthermore, given the scholarly and compilatory character of the *VP*, Porphyry also provides glimpses into the shipwreck of Hellenistic literature – a crucial stratum in understanding and reliably reconstructing the development of the Pythagoras legend.

---

[68] Clem. Al. *Strom.* 1.16.80.4.

[69] For Nicomachus see Chapter 12, section 10 above and Chapter 20, section 2 below as well as Centrone 2005. As for Antonius, there are numerous "Pythagorean" aspects in his novel, even in the parts that do not deal with Pythagoras himself, whereas the Pythagorean material proper occupied a central position in it. See Merkelbach 1962: 225–33; Fauth 1978; Reyhl 1969: 121; Stephens 1996: 677–8. The practice of collecting and recounting incredible stories (Iamblichus *On the Pythagorean Way of Life* 138–9, 143 and 148) had a great philosophical significance for the pious (Neo-)Pythagoreans; it invited them to believe in the unbelievable, because everything is possible for the gods.

[70] For the diverging views about the attribution of this passage to Moderatus or to Porphyry himself, see Macris 2002: 112 n. 157 and Staab 2002: 214 n. 525.

[71] On *VP* 53 see Centrone 2000a: 153–6; Kahn 2001: 105; Macris 2002: 111–12; 2009b: 147–8 and 149–50 with n. 43; Staab 2002: 214–16.

CHAPTER 19

Iamblichus' On the Pythagorean Life *in context*

Dominic J. O'Meara

1. Introduction

Iamblichus' work *On the Pythagorean Life* is the most extensive and richest source of information on Pythagoras and his school to have reached us from antiquity. The work itself is based, directly or indirectly, on a wide range of earlier sources, themselves no longer surviving, and presents us with a generous mix of clearly fictional tales attached to the legend of Pythagoras and information which seems to be more reliable. This mix has been the object of philological research which began in earnest with a major article published in 1871–1872 by Erwin Rohde, research which has tended to approach Iamblichus' work as if it were little better than a jumble of materials of varying value which need to be sorted out in order to get to what might be of use in reconstructing early Pythagoreanism. In the process, Iamblichus himself, his intentions as author of the work and his stature as a philosopher have been eclipsed and ignored. The contempt shown for him as the author of the text (Rohde spoke of the text as a "piteous patchwork")[1] was matched by the contempt shown in histories of philosophy for the later Neoplatonic philosophy of which Iamblichus was a major figure, a philosophy believed to have capitulated to irrationality and magic, a decadent ending to Greek philosophy.[2]

In more recent times, however, beginning in the second half of the twentieth century, new approaches have emerged. A considerable amount of work has been done on Iamblichus and on later Neoplatonic philosophy, which allows us to see beyond the attitude of ignorant prejudice of

---

I am greatly indebted to Carl Huffman and Constantinos Macris for their generous questions and suggestions.

[1] "Das klägliche Flickwerk," Rohde 1901: 113. By "Flickwerk" Rohde means, not a bad repair job, but a patchwork (127, 151). The degree of hostility towards, and contempt for, Iamblichus and his work shown by Rohde throughout his analysis (e.g., "a ridiculous botched piece of work of exceeding ignorance" ["lächerliches Machwerk äusserster Unwissenheit"], 143) is quite remarkable.

[2] For an example of this, equal in virulence to that shown by Rohde, see Rohde's contemporary A. von Harnack 1931: 1.820 (first edition 1885).

earlier accounts. And Iamblichus' work *On the Pythagorean Life*, beginning with an essay published by Michael von Albrecht in 1966, has been
taken seriously as a text in its own right, with specific philosophical purposes, a structure corresponding to these purposes and a context, that of
Iamblichus' ambitions as a philosopher at the turn of the third century AD.
In what follows I would like to review some of the results of these new
approaches, coming back later to the question of Iamblichus' use of earlier
sources, as seen in the light of a new approach.

2. *On the Pythagorean Life*: part of a larger project

On the Pythagorean Life (henceforth '*VP*') is usually published in modern
times,[3] in the Greek text and in translation, as if it were a separate work. This
suggests that the work stands by itself and can be treated and discussed
as such. However, if we look at the Greek manuscript from which our
other Greek manuscripts of the *VP* derive, Laurentianus 86.3 (manuscript
F, dating to the fourteenth century), we find that the manuscript gives a
table of contents (*pinax*)[4] in which the *VP* features as the first of nine *logoi*
(discourses, texts) by Iamblichus *On Pythagoreanism*.[5] The manuscript lists
the nine parts of the whole as follows:

   (I)   *On the Pythagorean Life*
   (II)   *Protreptic to Philosophy*
   (III) *On General Mathematical Science*
   (IV)   *On Nicomachus' Arithmetical Introduction*
   (V)   *On Arithmetic in Physical Matters*
   (VI)   *On Arithmetic in Ethical Matters*
   (VII) *On Arithmetic in Theological Matters*
   (VIII) *On the Geometry of the Pythagoreans*
   (IX)   *On the Music of the Pythagoreans*

It is likely that the table of contents omits a last, tenth part of the work,
which would have dealt with Pythagorean astronomy.[6] The manuscript
continues, after the table of contents, with the chapter headings (*kephalaia*)
of the *VP*, introduced as the chapter headings of the "first *logos*, about the
Pythagorean life," with the text of the *VP* and then with that of the
following three *logoi*, the *Protrepticus*, *On General Mathematical Science*
and *On Nicomachus' Arithmetical Introduction*, the first two preceded by

---

[3] With the exception of Romano 2006.   [4] Reproduced in Nauck 1884: xxxiv.
[5] On the title of the whole (*Peri tēs Puthagorikēs haireseōs*), which I propose to translate as *On
   Pythagoreanism*, see O'Meara 1989: 32–3.
[6] See O'Meara 1989: 33.

their chapter headings.[7] The following five *logoi*, as listed by the table of contents, are missing. What appears to have happened is that the text of Iamblichus' work *On Pythagoreanism* was divided into two volumes (or *codices*), of which the second was lost or ceased to be copied sometime after the eleventh century.[8] And so we now can read only parts I to IV of the whole, of which the *VP* is part I.

A first glance at the table of contents already suggests that the work as a whole reflects a systematic plan. Pythagoreanism is treated first in terms of the Pythagorean life and then in terms of Pythagorean philosophy, starting with philosophy in general and continuing with what Iamblichus clearly thought to be distinctive of Pythagorean philosophy, mathematics, beginning with general mathematical science and continuing with the specific sciences, arithmetic, geometry, music (and probably astronomy), of which the first (and highest) science, arithmetic, is discussed in its importance for physics, ethics and theology. The work as a whole is characterized, in its earlier parts (see below, section 5), by a strong protreptic purpose – we are being exhorted to engage ourselves in Pythagoreanism – and shows a clear pedagogic progression, going from the more familiar and common to the more difficult and what is more specific to Pythagoreanism. Iamblichus himself on occasion gives indications of the protreptic and pedagogic structure of the work.[9] A consequence of this structure is that we may expect that what is more specific and technical in Iamblichus' interpretation of Pythagoreanism would have emerged in the later parts of the work, in particular in parts V, VI and VII.

However, the presence of Iamblichus' philosophical interpretation can already be felt both in the general plan of the work, which uses a division of sciences characteristic of the later Neoplatonic curriculum (physics, ethics, theology), and in the first parts of the work, for example in details of Iamblichus' account of Pythagoras in the *VP*. To see this we might begin with the opening chapter of the *VP*, which the chapter headings of manuscript F suggest ("*proemium* on the philosophy of Pythagoras")[10] opens the work *On Pythagoreanism* as a whole:

---

[7] The chapter headings probably go back to Iamblichus himself; the chapter headings of part III are quoted by Syrianus in the early fifth century (see O'Meara 1989: 35 and especially Macris 2004: 2.11–20 for a full listing of ancient *kephalaia*).

[8] When Michael Psellos made his excerpts from parts V–VII (see O'Meara 1989: 53–60). Assuming the work originally had ten parts, the two *codices* would have corresponded to a tetrad (parts I–IV) and to the rest of the decade (parts V–X).

[9] O'Meara 1989: 34.

[10] *VP* 1.1. The chapter headings are conveniently translated by Clark 1989 and by Dillon and Hershbell 1991 at the beginning of their translations of each chapter.

All right-minded people, embarking on any study of philosophy, invoke a god. This is especially fitting for the philosophy which takes its name from the divine Pythagoras (a title well deserved), since it was originally handed down from the gods and can be understood only with the gods' help. Moreover, its beauty and grandeur surpass the human capacity to grasp it all at once [*exaiphnēs*]: only by approaching quietly, little by little, under the guidance of a benevolent god, can one appropriate a little. Let us then, for all these reasons, invoke the gods to guide us [. . .] And after the gods we shall take as our guide the founder and father of the divine philosophy, first saying a little about his ancestry and country.[11]

Invoking, in the spirit of Plato's *Timaeus* (27c), the help of the gods at the start of this undertaking, Iamblichus speaks of the "divine" philosophy named after Pythagoras as so exceeding human capacities that it cannot be grasped "all at once" (Pl. *Symp.* 210e), but must be approached step by step, under the guidance of the gods, who "handed it down," and of Pythagoras, its founder.

The connection between the gods, the divinely revealed philosophy and Pythagoras becomes clearer as we read on and find:

But no one who takes account of this birth and of the range of Pythagoras' wisdom could doubt that the soul of Pythagoras was sent to humankind from Apollo's retinue and was Apollo's companion or still more intimately linked with him.[12]

Iamblichus has just told the story of Pythagoras being born when his mother was impregnated by Apollo (as Plato's mother would later be, according to ancient biographies), a story which Iamblichus rejects, replacing its bodily genealogy with the "ancestry" of Pythagoras' soul: its origins in the "retinue" of Apollo, a "companion" of the god in the god's heavenly progress as described in Plato's *Phaedrus* (253b). In the myth of the *Phaedrus*, souls that accompany the gods and share in the vision of the transcendent Forms fall from this vision and find themselves in bodies. Pythagoras' soul, however, does not fall: it is "sent down" to humans, bringing divine wisdom. We can link these ideas with the theory of immaculate souls which Iamblichus developed in other works, in particular in his *De anima*, according to which there is a special sort of soul which does not lose its purity on descent to the body and descends in the body to purify, perfect and save the material world, whereas other souls descend on account of

---

[11] *VP* 5.4–6.5. I cite Clark's translation, here and in what follows, sometimes slightly modified. All references to the *VP* are to the page and line numbers of Deubner's edition. However, more general references will sometimes be given to chapters ("Ch.") of the text.

[12] *VP* 7.27–8.4.

moral failure and in view of punishment and purification.[13] Iamblichus' theory of different sorts of descended souls relates to the attempt to integrate the positive, perfective mission given to soul in Plato's *Timaeus* with the negative, punitive function of the descent of soul in the *Phaedrus*. It is a theory that provides a framework for understanding Pythagoras' divinity, his relation to the gods, the divine origin of his knowledge, and his special status and mission among humans.

There are other such souls. Plotinus, for example, had mentioned not only Pythagoras, but also Plato among those who had been able to contemplate transcendent intelligible being and to communicate the metaphysical knowledge that this brought. Plotinus even suggests that by doing philosophy, we, as souls, can return to this vision, as he did.[14] We might wonder then how Iamblichus' Pythagoras relates to these other souls, what indeed makes him and his philosophy of such interest as to call for the composing of such a large work as that of *On Pythagoreanism*.

3. The battle over Plato's legacy

In about 300 AD, Porphyry, who had probably been Iamblichus' teacher, published his biography of Plotinus and edition (the *Enneads*) of Plotinus' writings, about thirty years after Plotinus' death. Porphyry tells us (*Life of Plotinus* 24.6–11) that he "followed the example of Apollodorus of Athens, who collected the works of Epicharmus the comedian in ten volumes, and Andronicus the Peripatetic, who classified the works of Aristotle and Theophrastus according to subject." Like Andronicus, Porphyry also discussed in his biography of Plotinus the order of Plotinus' writings. These writings he ordered in six groups of nine, divided in three *codices* (*Ennead* I–III; IV–V; VI) and arranged in a progression going from ethics (*Ennead* I) to physics (*Ennead* II–III) and culminating in theology (*Ennead* IV–VI). The comparison of Porphyry's editorial work with Iamblichus' work *On Pythagoreanism* is evident: both works present philosophical curricula, pedagogies of the soul leading through the philosophical disciplines, prefaced by the life of the author of the philosophy to be studied, a portrait sufficiently impressive and inspiring in the wisdom it suggests to incite us to read on. And, of course, both works have a numerological structure (in Porphyry's edition of Plotinus: 6×9; in Iamblichus' *On Pythagoreanism*: $4 + 6 = 10$). But what conclusions can we draw from this comparison?

---

[13] See O'Meara 1989: 38–9.   [14] Plotinus, *Enn.* 5.1.8–9 with 4.8.1.

It has been suggested that Porphyry published his life and works of Plotinus, so late after Plotinus' death, in reaction to the new circumstances represented by the increasing strength and success of the philosophical school founded by Iamblichus in Apamea.[15] Porphyry may have been reacting to the challenge represented by Iamblichus' school and indeed Porphyry gives to the figure of Plotinus in his biography divine credentials, supernatural powers and Pythagorean traits that could certainly compete with the Pythagoras of Iamblichus' *VP*. However, it does not seem to be possible to be sure about the order of priority: Porphyry reacting, in his biography and edition of Plotinus, to Iamblichus' *On Pythagoreanism*, or the reverse. Certainly, the two philosophers quite frequently wrote in reaction to each other, the best-known example being Iamblichus' *De Mysteriis*, a response to Porphyry's *Letter to Anebo*.[16] Whatever the order of priority, we might at least consider Porphyry's Plotinian edition and Iamblichus' Pythagorean curriculum as representing two competing positions in a wider debate, which could be described as the battle over Plato's legacy.

Without going any further back, we can take note of some phases of this conflict in the second century AD, when the systematic teaching of Plato sometimes led to recourse to Aristotelian and Stoic ideas. Such contamination of Plato's teaching was vigorously attacked by Numenius of Apamea, who traced the increasing infidelity and betrayal of Plato's philosophy back to the skeptical phases of the Academy. In Numenius' view, a return had to be made to the pure, authentic teaching of Plato, the essence of which was due to Pythagoras, whose ancient wisdom could be identified with the wisdom of other ancient barbarian peoples.[17] Numenius' polemic with contemporary adulteration of Platonic philosophy can be compared with the position taken by another Platonist of the second century, Nicomachus of Gerasa, who also regards Platonism as essentially Pythagorean and who extols Pythagoras as having initiated scientific knowledge among the Greeks.[18] Plotinus was suspected of Pythagorizing by his contemporaries and accused of plagiarizing Numenius.[19] If Plotinus does indeed do homage to Pythagoras, as we have seen, and if Porphyry emphasizes Pythagorean traits in his biography of Plotinus, Pythagoras in general is not a major presence in Plotinus' writings: Plotinus regards himself as interpreting Plato, who expresses with greater clarity truths obscurely and partially indicated by Pythagoras.[20]

---

[15] Saffrey 1992.   [16] See Taormina 1999.   [17] Evidence summarized in O'Meara 1989: 10–13.
[18] O'Meara 1989: 15–16.   [19] Menn 2001 and Porph. *VP* 18.3.   [20] Plotinus, *Enn.* 4.8.1.21–6.

In publishing the *Enneads*, Porphyry presumably adhered to Plotinus' reading of Plato and wished to promote it beyond the circle of those who might once have heard Plotinus. Iamblichus, however, in a radical development of the options taken before him by Numenius and Nicomachus, advocates a return to the ancient wisdom that inspired Plato, that of Pythagoras. True Platonism is Pythagoreanism; the true legacy of Plato is Pythagorean.[21] To see this more clearly we need to look beyond the work *On Pythagoreanism* and consider other parts of Iamblichus' philosophical production.

4. Pythagoreanism in Iamblichus' other works

Does *On Pythagoreanism* have no relevance to Iamblichus' own work as a philosopher, nearing degree zero in terms of his presence as a philosopher, perhaps the product of a youthful immaturity that would be left behind? If we consider what little is left of Iamblichus' serious (presumably mature) philosophical work, his commentaries on Aristotle and on Plato, we can see that his interest there in Pythagorizing philosophy is just as strong. I shall mention here very briefly the main evidence.

We are best informed about Iamblichus' commentary on Aristotle's *Categories*, since it is extensively used by Simplicius in his commentary on the text. From Simplicius we learn that it was Iamblichus' (misguided) view that Aristotle's text is inspired by a similar text attributed to Archytas. Aristotle, according to Iamblichus, takes his theory from the Pythagorean author, and when he differs from him, he deviates and must be corrected.[22] There are indications that Iamblichus adopted the same approach with regard to Plato's *Timaeus*, supposed (falsely) to be inspired by a related text by Timaeus of Locri. Here indeed Plato's Pythagoreanism was most evident and Plato's fidelity to Pythagoreanism could be shown.[23]

---

[21] There are few references to Plato in the *VP* (see in particular 74.17–21), but a massive appropriation of Platonic dialogues as Pythagorean in the second part of *On Pythagoreanism* (the *Protrepticus*); see O'Meara 1989: 40–2; Staab 2002: 449. It is sometimes suggested that Iamblichus' *VP* promotes the figure of Pythagoras as a pagan reaction and response to the figure of Christ. The suggestion is old (see Lurje 2002: 253 n. 91; Staab 2002: 34) and could be described as an historian's variant on the theme of theological polemicists that pagan Greek philosophy was inspired by the Bible. If superficially suggestive, the idea is unproven (see for example Staab 2002: 279, and the contrasting essays by Du Toit and Dillon in von Albrecht, Dillon, George, Lurje and Du Toit 2002: 275–301). One should also note that, at the time of the *VP*, pagan philosophers, in their social standing and liberty, were not yet a threatened (reactionary) minority, and that *VP* is not a separate text, but part of a larger project, of which account must also be taken in interpreting the purpose of the *VP*.

[22] O'Meara 1989: 96–7.   [23] O'Meara 1989: 9 with n. 31.

Plato' *Timaeus* was one of the dialogues which Iamblichus chose as part of his Platonic curriculum, which was made up of a first cycle of ten dialogues and a second cycle of two. The decade began with the *Alcibiades*, considered as a monad implicitly containing all that would come after it,[24] and the second cycle, made up of the *Timaeus* and *Parmenides*, reminds us of a pair of first principles, the Dyad and the One, surpassing all else. Not only does this curriculum look Pythagorean in its structure: Iamblichus also invokes "Pythagorean" hermeneutical principles in the interpretation of individual dialogues in the curriculum.[25]

It might be of interest to add that the use made of Pythagorean and pseudo-Pythagorean authors in parts I–III of *On Pythagoreanism* – Philolaus, Archytas, Brontinus and others – suggests a sustained effort to collect a large body of Pythagorean literature of which we may still find traces in the Pythagorean authors quoted in Stobaeus' anthology. Stobaeus seems to be using, in part at least, collections of texts (including Iamblichus and Porphyry) deriving from Iamblichean schools, and the Pythagorean excerpts preserved in his anthology may have in part the same origin.[26]

Perhaps enough has been said to warrant our going back now to the first part of *On Pythagoreanism*, the *VP*, so that, taking its author's philosophical intentions seriously, we might attempt to see how these intentions are expressed in the composition of the work.

5. The compositional structure of the *VP*

A considerable amount of work has been done in more recent studies on the compositional structure of Iamblichus' *VP*, work suggesting that this structure is far from irrational or crude.[27] I would like here to summarize some results of this research, with a view to dealing with the question as what the purpose might be that is intended by this compositional structure.

It seems that the *VP* can be articulated into three main sections enclosed by introductory and concluding material:
- General introduction to *On Pythagoreanism* (Ch. 1).
- Part I: Pythagoras' ancestry, upbringing, travels, life and activities in Samos and in Italy (Chs. 2–11).
- Part II: Pythagorean education (*paideia*), as practiced by Pythagoras (Chs. 12–27).

---

[24] O'Meara 1989: 98.   [25] O'Meara 1989: 98–9.

[26] See Piccione 2002; Macris 2002: 88–106 (on Iamblichus' "bibliothèque pythagoricienne").

[27] See especially Staab 2002 (who gives a plan at 478–87), Lurje 2002: 238–42 and Macris 2004: 1.1–99; also von Albrecht 1966: 257–64; Dillon and Hershbell 1991: 26–9; Brisson and Segonds 1996: xvii.

- Part III: six Pythagorean virtues, taken individually, exemplified and communicated by Pythagoras (Chs. 28–33).
- Concluding matters (Chs. 34–6).

In the following, I would like to comment briefly on each of these parts of the work, without attempting to give a full analysis of the structure of each part.

(i)   General introduction

This part has already been discussed above (section 2).

One might also note Iamblichus' statement that Pythagoreanism has long been neglected, "hidden from view by unfamiliar doctrines and secret symbols, obscured by misleading forgeries" (5.16–19). The theme of long neglect suggests the project of a new revival that makes Pythagorean doctrine more accessible. This revival involves rescuing Pythagorean philosophy from falsification through forgeries. Porphyry, in his *Life of Pythagoras* (Ch. 53), also refers to a disappearance of Pythagorean philosophy, due to its obscurity and to falsifications in reports by others, which had brought this philosophy into disrepute. For Iamblichus, the attempt to revive Pythagorean philosophy as the origin and essence of Platonism will then require that attention be given to what would constitute a body of *authentic* Pythagorean documents, as distinguished from illegitimate productions: how is this distinction to be made? The question concerning the body of authentic Pythagorean literature is a recurrent theme in the *VP*.[28]

(ii)   Part I

At the beginning of his *Life of Plotinus*, Porphyry says that Plotinus "could never bear to talk about his race or his parents or his native country" (1.3–5). Iamblichus, however, has much to say about these subjects with regard to Pythagoras (*VP*, Ch. 2), also dealing with Pythagoras' education among the Greeks and the Barbarians (Phoenicia, Egypt, Babylon) (Chs. 2–4). The account continues with Pythagoras' return and teaching

---

[28] In *VP* 15.17 and 139.11–13 Iamblichus mentions falsely attributed texts; in 50.10 additions made by non-Pythagoreans; in 82.1–2 and 85.20–2 what he takes to be the authentic *Sacred Discourse* (by Pythagoras or as good as by him); in 88.13–89.7 the literary qualities of Pythagorean writings; and Philolaus' books in 109.9–10. Given that Iamblichus was very active in promoting what we consider today to be pseudo-Pythagorean texts, we may be surprised that he shows any interest at all in the question of authenticity. But his "authenticity" would not have been ours. Doctrinal and literary criteria of authenticity, as he saw them, would have been pertinent, as well as indications which he would have found in his sources about suspect texts.

activity in Samos (Ch. 5), followed by his move to Italy and teaching there
(Chs. 6–11), and includes a large section purporting to give the edifying
sermons given by Pythagoras to the young men, the ruling citizens, boys
and women of Croton (Chs. 8–11).

(iii)   Part II

This part begins (Ch. 12) with Pythagoras as having been the first to call
himself a "philosopher" and with Pythagoras' definition of philosophy as
the striving after knowledge (*theōria*), in particular wisdom (*sophia*) as the
science (*epistēmē*) of primary, divine and unchanging realities (32.17–21).[29]
Then Iamblichus writes: "Concern for education [*paideia*] is beautiful
too, working with Pythagoras for the moral improvement [*epanorthōsis*]
of humanity" (32.21–2). The relation between Pythagorean "philosophy"
and "education" seems to be the following: philosophy, on the one hand,
includes a wide range of sciences such as medicine, music, physics, astronomy, mathematics, theology, of which the last, as the science of eternal and
divine being represents the culmination, corresponding to the strong orientation of Pythagoreanism to assimilation to the divine;[30] education, on
the other hand, represents the communication of these sciences, as revealed
by Pythagoras, to humanity, with a view to moral improvement and gradual divinization. The following chapters of Part II are largely devoted to
this education offered by Pythagoras, dealing for the most part with its
preliminary, preparatory stages: the education of animals (Ch. 13); recol-
lection of earlier lives (Ch. 14); education of the senses through music (Ch.
15); purification of the soul (Ch. 16); stages in the education of Pythagoras' pupils (Chs. 17–18); various methods of instruction (Chs. 19–25); and
Pythagorean political education (Ch. 27).

(iv)   Part III

The transition to this part is clearly marked: "From now on let us no longer
deal with everything in common [*koinōs*], but divide his actions [*erga*]
according to the particular [*kat'idian*] virtues" (75.25–6). The progression
from the common to the particular is a general compositional feature
of *On Pythagoreanism*. Here, it involves a more differentiated treatment of

---

[29] Iamblichus is inspired here by Nicomachus' (Platonic) definition of philosophy and science; see
  also *VP* 89.23–90.11 and Nicomachus *Introduction to Arithmetic* 1.5–3.9.
[30] *VP* 37.10–11 (assimilation); 50.18–20 (repeated at 77.16–19); the range of sciences communicated by
  Pythagoras is indicated in Ch. 29.

Pythagoras' virtues, as manifested in his actions and as taught in his school. The four cardinal virtues are covered (Ch. 29: wisdom; Ch. 30: justice; Ch. 31: moderation; Ch. 32: courage), enclosed by the virtue of piety, placed at the beginning (Ch. 28), given the priority of the divine in Pythagoreanism, and by that of friendship, placed at the end (Ch. 33). For it is through friendship that we return to god.[31]

(v)   Concluding chapters (Chs. 34–6)

These chapters deal with a variety of topics, including differing accounts of the suppression of the Pythagorean community in Italy and a unique and impressive catalogue of ancient Pythagoreans.[32]

More fine-grained analyses of the structure of *VP* have been offered elsewhere.[33] But perhaps this general articulation is sufficient for the purpose of discerning Iamblichus' intention in giving the work this structure.

A start might be made by comparing the structure with compositional guidelines given by ancient manuals of rhetoric for the production of various types of work. It is not so much that we should expect the structure of Iamblichus' *VP* to conform slavishly to such guidelines – Iamblichus was no mean rhetorician himself – but rather that these guidelines may help provide a background against which the structure of the *VP* can be placed and compared. The lists of topics to be treated, as given at the end of *VP* Ch. 1 and in the chapter heading of Ch. 2 (ancestry, fatherland, upbringing, education) – and the artful renunciation of such a list at the beginning of Porphyry's *Life of Plotinus* – correspond to guidelines given in ancient manuals of rhetoric for the writing of *encomia*, speeches of praise in honor of a hero, or prominent person. Such speeches, having dealt with the upbringing of the hero, would then, according to the guidelines, cover the virtues of the hero and the actions stemming from these virtues. We might thus distinguish the topics into three groups: birth and upbringing; virtues; actions. In each of these groups, testimonies would be collected so as to extol the hero, thus distinguished by noble birth, by outstanding personal qualities and by remarkable deeds.[34] Such speeches of praise may appear to correspond to what might be described today as "biography," but of course their purpose is not to speak of the life of the individual, but

---

[31] *VP* 128.24–9.4; see Staab 2002: 432, 458, 477.
[32] On this catalogue see Zhmud 2012a: 236–44 and Huffman 2008e: 297–9. See also Chapter 4, section 1, and Chapter 13, section 5 above.
[33] See above n. 27.   [34] See in general Pernot 1993.

to extol the individual as exemplifying in his (or her) life what is deemed praiseworthy and admirable by the speaker and his public.

The *VP*, in its structure, appears, then, to correspond in various respects to the genre of the *encomium*. Besides the list of topics already noted, we can find other indications of this in the text. Iamblichus refers, for example, in dealing with Pythagoras' virtues, to the deeds (*erga*) stemming from these virtues (75.26). Indeed it has been suggested that Iamblichus is inspired more specifically by a particular *encomium*, that written by Xenophon in honor of the Spartan king Agesilaos.[35] If we read the *VP* as an *encomium*, our expectations must be different from those we would have in reading a modern biography. We must expect the collection of everything that may serve to magnify Pythagoras in one way or another; we will find nothing that does not. The magnification relates to what Iamblichus and his public consider to be exemplary, admirable and divine in Pythagoras. But what purpose does such an *encomium* serve?

The *VP* does not, it seems, fit perfectly into the mold of ancient *encomia*. The three groups of topics we can distinguish in the guidelines given by rhetorical manuals – birth and upbringing, virtues, and deeds – are replaced in the structure of the *VP* by three sections dealing with birth and upbringing, Pythagorean education, and virtues. The theme of the deeds stemming from the hero's virtues is not absent, as we have seen, but it is as if a second section, on Pythagorean education, has been inserted between the topics of upbringing and virtues, Pythagoras' deeds being absorbed into the second and third sections. Iamblichus' work, then, does not conform completely to the standard format of *encomia*: is this just the liberty he is taking with rhetorical conventions?

I would like to suggest referring in this regard to another rhetorical genre. Not only could heroes, demons and gods be the subjects of speeches of praise: other subjects could be taken, for example cities (such as Alexandria), or sciences. In the latter case, the science to be praised, according to the manuals of rhetoric, could be presented in a series of topics corresponding to the praise of a hero: thus, to the praise of a hero in terms of birth and upbringing, virtues and deeds would correspond the praise of a science in terms of its inventor or founder (*archēgos*), its practice (*askēsis*) and its use or utility (*chreia, ōpheleia*).[36] The praise of a science, in late antiquity, can be found in particular in the *prolegomena* that were produced as introductions to the study of various sciences and of philosophy.[37] The student beginning

35 Staab 2002: 443–5; see von Albrecht 1966: 263 n. 50.   36 See O'Meara 2010.
37 See Mansfeld 1994 and 1998.

the study of, say, astronomy, would be introduced to the science and encouraged to study it by preliminary remarks on the founder(s) of the science, on its practice and on its utility: the *encomium* of the science serves to introduce, inspire, motivate the student at the beginning of a course of study. Iamblichus himself uses the format of the *encomium* of a science elsewhere in *On Pythagoreanism*, notably in part III (*On General Mathematical Science*), where he deals with Pythagoras (along with Thales) as founder (*archēgos*) of mathematics (Ch. 21); with the practice of mathematics (Ch. 22) and its utility (Ch. 23).[38] So also is Pythagoras more generally, at the beginning of the *VP*, the founder (*archēgos*) of divine philosophy (6.3), the discoverer and transmitter of a wide range of sciences spanning the different levels of reality, and the benefactor (*euergesia*) of humanity (3.30).[39] The topics of the practice and utility of a science, in this case Pythagorean philosophy, are not treated separately in the *VP*, but they are present throughout the work.[40]

Seen against the background of the rhetorical genres of the praise of a hero and the praise of a science, we can suggest that the *VP* functions as a *prolegomenon* to the study of Pythagorean philosophy, in which Pythagoras' divine mission to humanity is praised as introducing the knowledge which this mission revealed. This knowledge, especially in its higher reaches, mathematics and theology, is barely sketched in the *VP*: a fuller introduction to the practice and utility of Pythagorean philosophy will be given in the following volumes, the *Protreptic*, *On General Mathematical Science*, and the volumes on the specific mathematical sciences and on the relations between arithmetic and physics, ethics and theology. The *VP*, in this regard, provides preliminary information, not only on Pythagoras and his school, but also on the preparatory stages of a Pythagorean education and on the virtues that are required of the student, prior to access to the higher, theoretical life of mathematics and theology.[41] The *VP* established Pythagoreanism as a philosophical school (*hairesis*) in its own right, having a divine founder, a distinctive way of life and an ancient history[42] and it sketches the beginnings of a philosophical education that continues and progresses in the following parts of *On Pythagoreanism*.

---

[38] O'Meara 2010: 62.   [39] See Macris 2004: 2.277–89.   [40] See for example, 2.31; 38.12; 91.19.
[41] The virtues, as described in the *VP*, correspond in general to the lower (ethical and political) levels of virtue in the Iamblichean hierarchy of virtues; see Staab 2002: 463–71 and Lurje 2002: 244–6, as against von Albrecht 1966, who found the full hierarchy of virtues in the *VP*.
[42] See Macris 2009b. The documentation of the early history of Pythagoreanism in the *VP* serves to establish the ancient credentials of Pythagoreanism as a philosophical school, the final proof being the catalogue of ancient Pythagoreans given in the last chapter.

It has been suggested that the *VP* and the work *On Pythagoreanism*, which it opens, may have been conceived as a course of public lectures designed to prepare students for access to the philosophical curriculum of Iamblichus' school.[43] Certainly the first three parts of *On Pythagoreanism*, being heavily protreptic and introductory in nature, could well have provided suitable material for public lectures (and perhaps not just for these). However, the following parts of the work appear to be less suited to this use and more appropriate for the purposes of a more technical instruction and study, since they provided, it seems, manuals for the four mathematical sciences, as well as demonstrations of the use of arithmetic in physics, ethics and theology. We could add that these later, more technical parts of *On Pythagoreanism* include manuals for the mathematical sciences not to be found in the corpus of the works of Aristotle and Plato, but which ought to be part of an education in true, i.e. Pythagorean, philosophy. Perhaps the whole work can be considered as a sort of handy two-volume *vade mecum* for the modern (fourth century AD!) Pythagoreanizing Platonist, for reading, studying and teaching.

6. Back to Iamblichus' sources in the *VP*

If a nineteenth-century male philologist such as Rohde could show such contempt for patchworking, what academic today would show such disrespect for this art? Having sketched above the way in which Iamblichus constructed his patchwork, let us look now at the patches, at the materials used by Iamblichus in composing the *VP*.

Rohde argued that Iamblichus did little more than tear scraps taken from two earlier texts, which he clumsily sewed together to produce the *VP*. The two texts were a life of Pythagoras by Nicomachus of Gerasa and one by Apollonius of Tyana. In Rohde's view, the *VP* is made up of alternating bits taken from Nicomachus and from Apollonius, with perhaps some additional material. Rohde consequently goes through the *VP*, attempting to identify the sections taken from Nicomachus or from Apollonius. This is of importance since, Rohde believes, Nicomachus conveys valuable earlier sources, in particular Aristoxenus (hence the references to Aristoxenus in

---

[43] Staab 2002: 41, 195–6, 446. Staab sees in the many repetitions of certain passages in the *VP* an indication of its character as lectures to be given orally (222–4). Such repetitions are common, not only within the *VP*, but also between the successive parts of *On Pythagoreanism*. They are perhaps not necessarily linked specifically to the needs of oral delivery, but may reflect more generally a practice of re-using materials in different contexts as documenting different themes, as von Albrecht has suggested (1966: 262–3).

the *VP*), whereas Apollonius is extremely unreliable and pretty worthless. Rohde furthermore holds that Iamblichus is using Nicomachus directly, and not just on the basis of the Nicomachus quotations in the *Life of Pythagoras* included by Porphyry in his *Philosophical History*. All of Rohde's claims have since been contested, while remaining extremely influential.[44] I shall limit myself here to some comments on the major issues.

The claim that Iamblichus uses Nicomachus directly, rather than through Porphyry's *Life of Pythagoras*, seems correct.[45] Nicomachus, as a Pythagorizing Platonist, was in any case an important author for Iamblichus, as we can see in part IV of *On Pythagoreanism* (*On Nicomachus' Arithmetical Introduction*), and Iamblichus could easily have drawn information directly from Nicomachus, even if he was aware (as he probably was) of the Nicomachus quotations in Porphyry's *Life of Pythagoras*. What is not clear, however, is the identity of the text(s) of Nicomachus used by Iamblichus: a life of Pythagoras? Other lost works? A number of works by Nicomachus?[46] The loss of such texts makes it difficult to answer these questions. It also appears, when comparing passages common to Porphyry's *Life of Pythagoras* and the *VP* that appear to have Nicomachus as origin, that Iamblichus rearranged and elaborated at some length, in the light of his own philosophy, passages which appear in a simpler form in Porphyry.[47] It thus looks as if Iamblichus, far from crudely stitching scraps together, restructured them considerably and re-embroidered them. Hardly patchworking! More an extensive re-weaving.

Rohde's claim that a large part of the *VP* is taken from a life of Pythagoras by Apollonius of Tyana, since lost, is, however, fairly dubious. The attribution of such a work to Apollonius of Tyana is far from solid, and there is a good chance that the Apollonius Iamblichus names as a source is not Apollonius of Tyana.[48] Rohde's identifications of sections of the *VP* as authored by Apollonius of Tyana can consequently be regarded as speculation, or even fantasy.

The claim that Iamblichus used only two (main) sources for his patches (further evidence of Iamblichus' mediocrity!) is not persuasive, if we take the trouble to look a little further in *On Pythagoreanism*, in parts II and III, where we find that Iamblichus has incorporated material from a wide

---

[44] Useful reviews of research since Rohde are to be found in Burkert 1972a: 98–101; Staab 2002: 217–37.
[45] See Burkert 1972a: 98–9; Staab 2002: 224–8 provides a critique of arguments against this claim.
[46] Iamblichus also uses Nicomachus' *Harmonic Handbook* (*Encheiridion*) in *VP* Ch. 26.
[47] For some examples see Staab 2002: 262–5; O'Meara 2007. In unpublished research Huffman has shown Iamblichus' very extensive rewriting of passages of Plato's *Republic* in *On General Mathematical Science*.
[48] See Staab 2002: 229–37; 2007.

range of texts. I have indicated above (section 4) that Iamblichus may have undertaken to assemble a library of *Pythagorica*, which may have included, for example, texts attributed to Philolaus and Archytas. Nicomachus referred to these two Pythagorean authors and quoted them. But Iamblichus, inspired by Nicomachus, could also have sought out and used texts attributed to the two Pythagoreans. The same may be true of Aristoxenus: here too Iamblichus could have followed Nicomachus' lead and made use of Aristoxenus' *Pythagorean Precepts*, a text of which excerpts would be preserved later in Stobaeus' anthology.[49] Iamblichus himself refers to Aristoxenus' *On the Pythagorean Life*,[50] perhaps using Nicomachus, or perhaps Aristoxenus himself. It would be desirable to undertake a comparative study of the Pythagorean authors and sources used by Nicomachus, Iamblichus and Stobaeus, as this may reveal more of the Pythagorean library that Iamblichus, following Nicomachus, seems to have assembled, a library that is attested also in the writings of Iamblichus' philosophical successors, Syrianus and Proclus.

Among other sources that have been suggested for the *VP* is the first-century-AD Pythagorizing Platonist Moderatus of Gades, who wrote a (lost) multi-volume work on Pythagoreanism.[51] Iamblichus himself quotes from Pythagoras' *Sacred Discourse*,[52] Aristotle's (lost) books on Pythagorean philosophy (*VP* 18.12–13), from a letter by the Pythagorean Lysis,[53] from Androcydes *On the Pythagorean Symbols*,[54] and from Hippobotus and Neanthes.[55] Some of these he may have used directly, others indirectly, through intermediary sources such as Nicomachus.

At any rate, the range of possible sources used by Iamblichus in the *VP* and the degree to which he reworked these sources ought not to be underestimated[56] and some caution must be exercised with regard to the extent to which one can hope to succeed in recovering these sources. At best, particular sections of the text can be analyzed synchronically, in terms of their organization, their relation to other parts of the *VP* and of *On Pythagoreanism* and to Neoplatonic philosophical ideas in general, and

---

[49] See Burkert 1972a: 101; Dillon and Hershbell 1991: 25; Staab 2002: 221; 2003: 155–7. In unpublished research Huffman argues that Iamblichus is using a different recension of Aristoxenus' text (also used by Ocellus Lucanus) than that found in Stobaeus.

[50] *VP* 125.18.   [51] Mentioned in Porph. *VP* 48; see Staab 2002: 451.

[52] *VP* 82.12.   [53] See Staab 2002: 309–10.

[54] *VP* 81.11–12; see Burkert 1972a: 167; Androcydes is quoted by Nicomachus *Introduction to Arithmetic* 6.11–15.

[55] *VP* 104.24; on Neanthes and Hippobotus see Burkert 1972a: 102 and Schorn in Chapter 14, section 5, above.

[56] See Staab 2003 for further discussion.

diachronically, in relation to information that we have from other sources concerning earlier periods in the history of Pythagoreanism.[57]

7. A very brief look forward

Iamblichus' ambition to revive Pythagoreanism as a way of life and as a philosophy was largely successful, both in later ancient Neoplatonism and after. Syrianus, head of the Platonic school of Athens in 432–437, adopted Iamblichus' views on the importance of Pythagoras in the history of philosophy, on the nature of Pythagorean philosophy and its relation to Platonism. He recommends Iamblichus' treatise *On Pythagoreanism* in his *Commentary on Aristotle's Metaphysics*, where he quotes from the chapter headings of part III of the treatise and also makes use of parts IV, V and VII.[58] Syrianus' pupil and successor, Proclus, shows a comparable enthusiasm for Iamblichean Pythagoreanism in an early work, the *Commentary on Plato's Timaeus*. However, Proclus came to adopt a more sober attitude in his other work, emphasizing the clarity and scientific character of Plato's dialogues as compared to the somewhat enigmatic revelations of the Pythagoreans. An interesting example is provided by the first prologue of Proclus' *Commentary on Euclid*, where, in rewriting part III of Iamblichus' *On Pythagoreanism*, Proclus substituted (the original) passages from Plato (Plato is named) for the (supposedly) Pythagorean authorities that had been used by Iamblichus. However, these differences are more of emphasis than of substance. Pythagoras' importance in Greek philosophy remains, for Proclus, what it had been for Iamblichus: Pythagoras is a divine soul, who revealed knowledge for the salvation of human souls. And Proclus' Platonism is profoundly Pythagorean (as interpreted by Iamblichus) in the way in which, in his interpretation of Plato, mathematical principles, as models and images, permeate all reality, from the physical world, through the soul, to transcendent first causes.[59] It would seem that essentially the same view of Pythagoreanism prevailed among the last members of the schools of Athens and Alexandria in the sixth century, Damascius, Simplicius, Ammonius, Philoponus, and others.[60] Through their works and especially through those of Proclus, Iamblichus' revival of Pythagoreanism would reach the philosophers and mathematicians of the Renaissance.

---

[57] See the commentaries on the *VP* in Staab 2002 and in Macris 2004 (on *VP* Chs. 1–6).

[58] See O'Meara and Dillon 2008: 9 and more generally on Syrianus' relation to Iamblichean Pythagoreanism O'Meara 1989: Ch. 6.

[59] See O'Meara 1989: Chs. 7–10.   [60] See O'Meara 2013 for a preliminary survey.

CHAPTER 20

Pythagoras and Pythagoreanism in late antiquity and the Middle Ages

Andrew Hicks

1. Introduction and overview

> Pitagoras, id est non indigens interrogationis vel interrogationis cumulus. ΠΥΘΟΣ enim interrogatio, ΑΓΟΡΑ cumulus.

> Pythagoras, i.e., one who needs no questioning, or the culmination of questioning. For ΠΥΘΟΣ means questioning, ΑΓΟΡΑ means culmination.[1]

This creative etymology, variations on which are employed by Carolingian scholars to annotate (or "gloss") mentions of Pythagoras in both Boethius' *Fundamentals of Music* (*De institutione musica*) and Martianus Capella's *On the Marriage of Philology and Mercury* (*De nuptiis Philologiae et Mercurii*), neatly encapsulates the medieval use of Pythagoras. In line with a tradition long established in the late ancient Latin texts that provided exclusive access to "Pythagorean" teachings, the medieval Pythagoras functioned as a "first principle": to invoke his authority was to invoke *the* icon of Greek wisdom traditions. This gloss's etymological assertion of Pythagorean authority resonates with late ancient and medieval accounts of Pythagoras and the Pythagoreans on multiple levels. First, it well accords with the method of instruction ascribed to the Pythagoreans. According to Boethius, "it was customary for the Pythagoreans, whenever Master Pythagoras said something, that no one thereafter dare to challenge his reasoning; rather the reasoning of the teacher was their authority" (*Inst. mus.* 1.33 [223.4–7 Friedlein]; cf. Valerius Maximus 8.15.ext.1). By the twelfth century, this account of the Pythagorean method of instruction (*Pythagorica doctrina*) had codified into a supposed imposition of seven years of silence "according to the number of the seven liberal arts" (as Hugh of St. Victor explains:

---

[1] *Glossa Maior in institutionem musicam* (Bernhard and Bower 1993–2011: Vol. 1, 61 [*ad Inst. mus.* 1.1]); cf. John Scottus Eriugena *Annotationes in Marcianum* (Lutz 1939: 203.10 [*ad De nupt.* 9.923]); Remigius of Auxerre *Commentum in Martianum* (Lutz 1965: 323.25 [*ad De nupt.* 9.923]).

Didascalicon 3.3), during which Pythagorean disciples were allowed only to listen and believe; not until the eighth year were they allowed to broach questions (William of Conches *Dragmaticon* 1.1.3).[2] Second, it echoes the common view of Pythagoras as both the inaugurator of the Greek philosophical tradition and its consummate practitioner, a view exemplified by Boethius' equation of "Pythagorean knowledge" (*scientia Pythagorica*) with "perfect teaching" (*perfecta doctrina*: *On the Categories* 160B; see Ebbesen 1990: 387–91; Asztalos 1993: 379–88), a loftier mode of philosophizing suited only to those who have already mastered the beginning and intermediate stages of philosophy.

Closely connected to Boethius' invocation of *scientia Pythagorica* as the highest mode of philosophizing is a third level of Pythagorean authority, namely the philosophical (and theological) method ascribed to Pythagoras by (*inter alios*) Proclus: the mathematical and analogical mode. Although Proclus, as O'Meara has highlighted (1989: 148–9), parts ways with Iamblichus' Pythagorean Platonism by subordinating Pythagorean "analogic" theology to the more scientific or "dialectical" theology of Plato, he nonetheless valorizes a tradition that became closely linked to the Pythagoreans throughout late antiquity and the Middle Ages: the veiling of sacred doctrine through the use of symbolic and analogic discourse. As Proclus has it in his commentary on Euclid's *Elements*:

> Hence, Plato teaches us anew many wonderful doctrines about the gods through mathematical forms, and the philosophy of the Pythagoreans using these as screens conceals the secret doctrine of their teachings about the gods. For, such is the whole *Sacred Discourse*, as is the *Bacchae* of Philolaus, and the whole manner of Pythagoras' instruction about gods. (*Commentary on Euclid* 22.9 Friedlein; tr. Huffman 1993: 417–18)

The details of Proclus' account and application of Pythagorean theology need not detain us here.[3] More to the point is the close connection between Pythagorean science and a veiled presentation of its truths, a point elaborated upon several times by Proclus in his Platonic commentaries (e.g., *Commentary on the Timaeus*, henceforth *In Tim.* 1.29.31ff. Diehl; *Commentary on the Republic* 1.73.11ff. Kroll) and presented to the Latin West through Macrobius' famous account of the philosophical use of mythical narrative (*narratio fabulosa*), similitudes (*similitudines*) and analogies (*exempla*) in his *Commentary on the Dream of Scipio* (1.2.9–21). According

---

[2] In ancient sources, the period of silence imposed upon Pythagorean neophytes ranges from "no less than two years" (Aul. Gell. 1.9.4) to the widely reported five years (e.g., Diog. Laert. 8.10).
[3] See Gritti 2007 and Steel 2007.

to Macrobius, philosophers employ a mythic narrative to discuss the soul, airy or aethereal powers, or the other gods, but when they turn their pen upon the Platonic triad – τἀγαθόν, νοῦς and ἰδέαι (the Good, Mind and Ideas) – myth is inappropriate, and they can take recourse only in similitudes and analogies, this last being a direct echo of Proclus' "Pythagorean" ὅμοια (similitudes) and εἰκόνες (images), to which Proclus adds σύμβολα (symbols) (on which see Dillon 1990). When Macrobius draws his comments to a close by enumerating the ancient philosophers that employed an analogic mode of theologizing, Pythagoras heads the list (which includes Empedocles, Parmenides, Heraclitus and Timaeus). In the twelfth century, the Macrobian account of *narratio fabulosa* coalesced into a flexible doctrine of philosophical myth and allegory, known as "veils" or "concealments" (*integumenta* or *involucra*: on which see Bezner 2005), which at least one medieval commentator on the *Timaeus* ascribes to Pythagoras: "But theologians speak with veils [*integumenta*] when they discuss the airy and aethereal powers and the World-Soul. Pythagoras is said by many to have been the leader of this view" (BnF lat. 8624: 18r).

Joost-Gaugier has deemed the Middle Ages an age of "New Pythagoreanism," but this is a misleading characterization.[4] If anything, medieval Pythagoreanism arises from a reification and simultaneous iconization of a particular strain of late ancient (Neo-)Pythagorean speculation. For it was the "mathematical Pythagoreanism" of Nicomachus (and, indirectly, Iamblichus and Proclus: see O'Meara 1989) that most captured the medieval imagination and thereby overshadowed (though did not eliminate entirely) some of the more diffuse Pythagorean contributions in ethics and ontology. In turn, it was *this* Pythagoras and "Pythagorean" speculation that was subsequently inherited and enriched by Renaissance philosophers and humanists. Late ancient and medieval authors themselves inherited and embellished upon a Pythagoras credited with an increasingly illustrious list of discoveries and inventions, most of which were closely connected to the late ancient "mathematicalized" Pythagoreanism: the science of music,[5] the monochord,[6] arithmetic and the science of numbers,[7] the abacus,[8]

---

[4] Joost-Gaugier 2006: 116.

[5] E.g., Boethius *Inst. mus.* 1.10–11; Cassiod. *Inst.* 2.5.1; Isid. *Etym.* 3.16.1. See Münxelhaus 1976, McKinnon 1978.

[6] E.g., Diog. Laert. 8.12; Gaudentius 341.12; Aristides Quintilianus 3.2; Boethius *Inst. mus.* 1.11; Guido of Arezzo *Micrologus* 20. See Creese 2010.

[7] E.g., Isid. *Etym.* 3.2.1; Eriugena *Periphyseon* 3 652A; Hugh of St. Victor *Didascalicon* 3.2. See Heath 1921: 1.65–117.

[8] The so-called "table of Pythagoras" (*mensa Pythagorea*) of the ps.-Boethian *Ars geometrica* (396.7–16 Friedlein), which is held aloft by a personification of Arithmetic in Alan de Lille's *Anticlaudianus* (3.288). On the ps.-Boethian *Geometry*, see Folkerts 1981.

Venus and the computation of planetary distances,[9] even the discipline of philosophy, for which Pythagoras was said to have coined the very term *philosophia*.[10]

Numerous passages in late ancient Latin sources – e.g., Boethius' claim in the *Consolation of Philosophy* that Lady Philosophy had daily exhorted him to that Pythagorean maxim: ἕπου θεῷ ("Follow God": 1.4.38)[11] – suggested that a reconciliation of Pythagorean authority with Christian thought was not entirely out of the question. Within Pythagorean ethics, the maxims of "Sextus Pythagoreus," translated in the fourth century by Rufinus of Aquileia, enjoyed a wide circulation in Christian circles (despite Jerome's protestations against the work's presumed Christianity: *Ep.* 133.3). One of these maxims found its way into the Rule of St. Benedict (no. 145: "a wise man is distinguished by the brevity of his words"; see Chadwick 1959).[12] Moreover, the mathematical speculation of the Neopythagoreans, which developed the original Pythagorean idea according to which "all is likened unto number" (e.g., Nicomachus, *Introduction to Arithmetic* 1.4.2, 1.6.1; Theon of Smyrna, *Mathematics Useful for Reading Plato* 17.25–18.2 Hiller; cf. Arist. *Metaph.* 1.5, 985b24ff.), was transmitted to the Middle Ages through the "Pythagorean" arithmologies of Calcidius (*In Tim.* 35–8), Macrobius (*In Somn.* 1.5–1.6) and Martianus Capella (*The Marriage of Philology and Mercury*, henceforward *De nupt.* 7.732–42). This mathematical speculation played a central role in the formulation of a Christian Neoplatonism consonant with the oft-cited scriptural testimony that God "hath ordered all things in measure, number, and weight" (*omnia mensura et numero et pondere disposuisti*: *Wisdom of Solomon* 11:20).[13] However, several points of doctrine attributed to Pythagoras – most notably, the doctrine of metempsychosis (on which see Maaz 1998) – strongly conflicted with Christian teaching.[14] Hence, medieval authors were wont to pick and choose their way through Pythagorean teachings, accepting what they found useful but casting aside what they found reprehensible. As John of Salisbury explains: "When the Pythagoreans teach us about innocence, frugality, and contempt for the world, we should listen to them; when they

---

[9] E.g., Plin. *HN* 2.37, 2.83; Martianus *De nupt.* 8.882–3; Eriugena *Periphyseon* 3 715BC.

[10] E.g., Augustine *C.D.* 8.2; Boethius *Inst. mus.* 2.2; Isid. *Etym.* 8.6.2; etc. See Riedweg 2005: 90–7.

[11] Cf. Apul. *On Plato* 2.23; Hierocles *In carmen aureum* 23.11; Iambl. *VP* 86, etc.

[12] For a résumé of other suggestive but tenuous connections between Pythagoreanism and Christian monastic practices, see Jordan 1961.

[13] E.g., Cassiodorus makes the connection explicit at *Inst.* 2.4.1 (cf. *Variae* 1.10.3), as does Claudianus Mamertus *De statu animae* 2.3. Cf. Eriugena *Periphyseon* 3 652A. On Eriugena's "metaphysics of number" generally, see Jeauneau 2007.

[14] See Chapter 21 below.

force souls that have ascended into the heavens back into the bodies of beasts, even Plato must be refuted [*iuguletur uel Plato*], for on this point he followed Pythagoras too closely" (*Policraticus* 7.10).

Despite abundant testimony to the continuity of Pythagorean thought across the Middle Ages, we cannot speak of medieval "Pythagoreanism(s)" in the same way that we can of medieval Platonism(s) and medieval Aristotelianism(s). Accounts of Pythagoras and the ancient Pythagoreans are largely consigned to doxographical contexts; they belong not to contemporaneous debates but rather to an imagined history of philosophy and philosophical thought. But if Pythagoreanism *per se* was no longer a viable strain of thought, it was precisely within the history of philosophy that Pythagoreanism gained considerable traction. It was not a question of what Pythagoras "really" thought – though medieval authors were optimistic about the recoverability of Pythagorean thought[15] – but rather a question of how to deploy appropriately the Pythagorean inheritance within the new cultural and philosophical contexts of (largely) Christian patterns of thought.

It must also be stressed that much of what circulated under Pythagoras' name has little or nothing to do with the "historical" Pythagoras. The Pythagoras and Pythagoreanisms I shall discuss are *not* those of modern historians of philosophy, but, as already noted, of an imagined history of philosophy inherited and embellished by medieval authors. (Nor is this imagined history solely the product of the medieval imagination: the available evidence had already been tampered with for generations.) In vain would we search amid the copious medieval testimony of Pythagoras and the Pythagoreans for "authentic" Pythagorean fragments, though some of the surviving *testimonia* are of considerable, if second- or third-hand, antiquity (e.g., the citations of Eubulides and Hippasus at *Inst. mus.* 2.19; the paraphrases from Philolaus and Archytas at *Inst. mus.* 3.5–8 and 3.11, respectively; the Numenian positions articulated by Calcidius at *In Tim.* 256; etc.). Rather, the medieval Pythagoras was deeply conditioned by the late ancient overwriting (aptly characterized by Riedweg [2005: 128] as a "palimpsest") of Pythagorean positions with what is essentially

---

[15] E.g., both Calcidius (*In Tim.* 136 [177.2 Waszink]) and Macrobius (*In Somn. Scip.* 1.6.41) accept the *Golden Verses* as authentically Pythagorean; Adelard of Bath claims that Pythagoras "wrote down his findings" (*officio stili usus est*), lest they be lost to posterity (Burnett 1998: 54); Hugh of St. Victor attributes to Pythagoras a work entitled *Methen tetrados*, which he describes as "a book on quadrivial teaching" (*Didascalicon* 3.2), a claim perhaps resulting from a misreading of Martianus *De nupt.* 2.107 (via Remigius *Comment. in Mart.* 44.20 [Lutz 1962: 150]); finally, the *Turba philosophorum* (translated into Latin in the twelfth century from Arabic) posed as a "first-hand" account of a gathering of philosophers presided over by Pythagoras (on which see Ruska 1931).

late Platonic doctrine (cf. O'Meara 1989: 16): in the memorable phrase of Apuleius, "Plato Pythagorized in many respects" (*Plato pythagorissat in plurimis: Florida* 15.25; cf. Aët. 2.6.6), which eventually transforms – through the medium of Augustine (e.g., *Against the Skeptics* 3.17.37) and others – into a simple, factual statement by William of Conches: "Plato was a Pythagorean" (*Dragmaticon* 2.5.4; cf. *Glosae super Platonem* 12.18). It was this Platonizing Pythagoreanism (Bonazzi, Lévy and Steel 2007) that deeply colored the primary late ancient Latin accounts of Pythagoras (Calcidius, Macrobius and Boethius) that in turn formed the essential foundation for Pythagoras' medieval *Nachleben* ("afterlife").

This chapter cannot encompass the full sweep of late ancient and medieval invocations of Pythagoras and the Pythagoreans (a book-length treatment remains a desideratum), which, ideally, would include Byzantine (e.g., Photius, Michael Psellus, Bryennius, Plethon), Arabic (e.g., Arabic translations of commentaries on the Pythagorean *Golden Verses* attributed to Iamblichus and Proclus) and Arabo-Persian traditions (e.g., Avicenna, Suhrawardī, Quṭb al-Dīn Shīrāzī). Nonetheless, space limitations do not allow for consideration of non-Latin texts. Nor will this chapter march chronologically through a litany of citations and mentions of Pythagoras and the Pythagoreans, for in later periods the sources quickly reduce, and the repetition of already familiar themes and passages would quickly become tedious. To give but one instance, the tradition of the *Life of Pythagoras* continued unabated in the medieval encyclopedic tradition, but the lives were not based upon the two extant Greek lives by Porphyry and Iamblichus (neither of which was available in Latin translation until the Renaissance). Instead, the life of Pythagoras was reconstituted through an increasingly standardized cento of passages drawn from various ancient historians and church fathers (e.g., Cicero, Seneca, Valerius, Solinus, Justin, Jerome and Augustine). Lives in this vein are included in John of Salisbury's *Policraticus* (7.4), Vincent of Beauvais's *Speculum historiale* (3.24–6), John of Wales's *Compendiloquium* (3.6.2) and (ps.-)Walter Burley's *The Lives and Habits of the Philosophers* (on the last, see Prelog 1990).[16] Instead, this chapter will survey some of the broad themes in the late ancient and medieval use of Pythagoras and the Pythagoreans beginning with a summary of

---

[16] Joost-Gaugier overstates considerably the originality of (ps.)-Burley's biography: it is not the first "original biography of Pythagoras" in centuries, nor does (ps.)-Burley's observation that Pythagoras' house became a shrine (*templum*) after his death evince any connection to Diogenes Laertius (8.15), much less that (ps.)-Burley had access to a "partial or complete translation" nearly a century before the first documented Latin translation (Joost-Gaugier 2006: 73). (Ps.)-Burley has this on the authority of Justin, *Epitome* 20.4.17–18, and this had been part of the life tradition at least since John of Salisbury's *Policraticus* (7.4).

Pythagoras' quadrivial legacy (20.2), followed by a resume of (20.3) the
music-theoretical heritage of *Pythagoras musicus* (cf. Cassiod. *Var.* 1.45);
and (20.4) the natural philosophical heritage of *Pythagoras physicus* (cf.
Eusebius-Jerome *Chronicon* Olymp. 62 [Helm 1956: 104b.12]).

2. Boethius and the Pythagorean division of mathematics

The "first fruits" (*primitiae*) of Boethius' intellectual labors, the *Fundamentals of Arithmetic* (*De institutione arithmetica*), is a loose translation of
Nicomachus of Gerasa's *Introduction to Arithmetic*, which Boethius seems
to have undertaken early in his career. Following Nicomachus, Boethius
begins the *Fundamentals of Arithmetic* with an account of philosophical
knowledge from the standpoint of ontology. He declares that the objects
of philosophy (*sapientia*) are "what exist and have been allotted their own
immutable substance," which are *not* subject to quantitative, qualitative or
substantial change. These then are "qualities, quantities, forms, greatnesses
[*magnitudines*], smallnesses [*paruitates*], equalities [*aequalitates*], habitudes,
acts, dispositions, places, times, as well as anything that is found in
some way united to bodies."[17] While these themselves are incorporeal
and immutable, through their participation in bodies and the contagion of
changeable things they necessarily share in bodily, material flux. Boethius'
abridgment of this passage in *The Fundamentals of Music* (2.2 [227.20–8.2
Friedlein]) makes explicit what is only implied in his first handling of this
Nicomachean material: that this is a fundamentally Pythagorean ontology,
which serves as a prelude to a Pythagorean division of mathematics (cf.
Procl. *In Euc.* 35.16ff. Friedlein).

Fully in accord with what Proclus explicitly deems a Pythagorean classification of the mathematical sciences (as does Boethius himself at *Inst. mus.*
2.3), Boethius divides the objects of mathematics into discrete quantity
(*multitudo*, τὸ ποσόν) and continuous quantity (*magnitudo*, τὸ πηλίκον).
Each of these has a second bipartition, which combined, constitute the
four mathematical sciences. Arithmetic is the science of multitude in itself
(*per se*, καθ᾽ ἑαυτό), whereas music is the science of multitudes in relation to each other (*ad aliquid*, πρὸς ἄλλο); geometry is the science of
immobile magnitudes (*immobilis*, ἐν μονῇ καὶ στάσει), but astronomy is
the science of magnitudes in motion (*mobilis*, ἐν κινήσει καὶ περιφορᾷ).[18]
The order, moreover, is not arbitrary, as the four mathematical sciences

---

[17] *Inst. ar.* 1.1 (9.8–22 Oosthout and Schilling). Cf. Nic. *Intr. ar.* 1.1.3 (2.21–3.3 Hoche). See O'Meara
1989: 16–18.
[18] *Inst. ar.* 1.1 (10.31–11.43 Oosthout and Schilling) = Nic. *Intr. ar.* 1.3.1–2 (6.1–7 Hoche).

are not, strictly speaking, co-ordinate. Rather, they demonstrate a clear order of priority, which takes the tidy form of two parallel priorities – the absolute (arithmetic) is prior to the relative (music) just as stasis (geometry) is prior to motion (astronomy) – nested within the single overarching priority of arithmetic to the other mathematical sciences.[19] Famously, Boethius deemed these four mathematical sciences the *quadrivium*, that "fourfold road that must be traversed by those whom a more excellent soul leads away from the senses inborn within us to the greater certainties of understanding."[20]

In the prooemium to the *Fundamentals of Music* (*De institutione musica*), Boethius' second mathematical treatise and likewise an interpolated translation of a (no longer extant) musical treatise by Nicomachus, Boethius sets out a further division of music: cosmic music (*musica mundana*), human music (*humana*) and music as constituted in instruments, including voice (*quae in quibusdam constituta est instrumentis*: *Inst. mus.* 1.2 [187.18–23 Friedlein]).[21] Cosmic music concerns the harmonic structures and periods of the celestial bodies, the delicate balance of the four elements, and the cyclical succession of the seasons (*Inst. mus.* 1.2 [187.23–188.26 Friedlein]). Human music comprises the harmonic structures governing the human soul, the human body, and the relations between soul and body (*Inst. mus.* 1.2 [188.26–189.5 Friedlein]). And instrumental music encompasses the numerical laws that govern the sonorous sounds arising from instruments and voices (*Inst. mus.* 1.2 [189.5–12 Friedlein]). It remains uncertain whether Boethius found this division already articulated in Nicomachus or whether it is of his own devising. The little evidence there is suggests the latter, for despite the wide influence of Nicomachus' mathematical works on the commentaries and treatises of the (Greek) Neoplatonists, there exists no direct Greek parallel to Boethius' division (cf. Bower 1978: 44–5). Moreover, at *Fundamentals of Arithmetic* (*Inst. ar.*) 1.2, Boethius lists three numerically based realities in support of the assertion that number was the primary exemplar in the mind of the world's creator: the elements, seasons and heavenly motions (14.2–6 Oosthout and Schilling). While this list strongly anticipates the parts of cosmic music enumerated at *Inst. mus.* 1.2 (187.25–6 Friedlein), significantly, it has no literal analogue in Nicomachus, for the parallel passage, *Introduction to Arithmetic* 1.6.1

---

[19] *Inst. ar.* 1.1 (12.73–14.130 Oosthout and Schilling) = Nic. *Intr. ar.* 1.4–5 (9.5–11.23 Hoche); cf. O'Meara 2005a: 134–5.

[20] *Inst. ar.* 1.1 (11.64–6 Oosthout and Schilling).

[21] Cf. Cassiod. *Inst.* 2.5.2; Isid. *Etym.* 3.23.2; Adelard of Bath *De eodem et diuerso* (Burnett 1998: 54) creatively attributes this classification directly to Pythagoras.

(12.11–12 Hoche), offers the longer and more generic list "time, motion, the heavens, stars, and all sorts of revolutions."

In short, the prefaces to the mathematical works project a "seamless continuum between the mathematical sciences and philosophy in all of its other manifestations" (Magee 2010: 798). In fact, Nicomachus presents the division of mathematics as a division of philosophy, insofar as Pythagoras (in Nicomachus' account) first properly defined σοφία as the science of "true being," i.e., "those things which always continue uniformly and the same in the universe and never depart even briefly from their existence" (2.10–13 Hoche), and in support, he cites (3.19–4.4 Hoche) *Timaeus* 27d (a citation that was clearly standard within the tradition; cf. Numenius fr. 7; O'Meara 1989: 10–16). Boethius, in distilling Nicomachus' first few chapters into his own prooemium, tones down the broader claims and suppresses the Timaean citation; however, mathematics clearly still holds a paradigmatic role, and Boethius maintains the strongly (Neo-)Pythagorean commitment to the numerical basis of reality.

3.   Pythagoras *musicus*: perception and reason

Undoubtedly the most important of Boethius' "Pythagorean" legacies is his presentation of Pythagorean music theory in the *Fundamentals of Music*. As Klaus-Jürgen Sachs has rightly highlighted, "Boethius' teaching concerning *sensus* and *ratio* is among the most frequently cited topics from the *De institutione musica*" (Sachs 1991: 171), and Boethius' presentation of the "Pythagorean" position largely defined the discipline of music theory for at least a millennium. In short, Boethius' Pythagoreans steer a middle course (*medio quodam feruntur itinere*: *Inst. mus.* 1.9 [195.27–6.1 Friedlein]) between perception (*sensus*) and reason (*ratio*), between, that is, Plato's criticism that the Pythagoreans were too concerned with the audible realm (*Resp.* 531a1–3) and Ptolemy's complaint that the Pythagoreans were excessively theoretical and "did not follow the impressions of the hearing even in those things where it is necessary for everyone to do so" (*Harm.* 1.2).

Pythagorean hesitations about the reliability of perception are of central concern to Boethius from the very outset of his treatise. It may be effortless, Boethius claims, to recognize that we somehow employ sensation for the perception of sensibles, but the precise nature of that sensation, as both activity and content, is a matter of dispute (*Inst. mus.* 1.1 [179.2–8 Friedlein]). Boethius' first example of the problem is not hearing, but vision, which remained for Boethius, as for the entire ancient tradition, the paradigmatic sense. But Boethius generalizes the epistemological and ontological problems inherent in vision to all sense-perceptible objects. And the stakes are apparently higher with regard to the "judgment of the ears" (*arbitrium aurium*), for

> the faculty of hearing [*uis aurium*] strives to comprehend sounds [*sonos captat*] in such a way that it not only forms judgments about them and recognizes differences between them, but even more often it is delighted if their measure be sweet and well joined, or it is distressed if they strike the sense as ill-arranged and unconnected. (*Inst. mus.* 1.1 [179.16–20 Friedlein])

Although sight may offer the paradigm of sensation, hearing is yet the most valuable (if vulnerable) sense, insofar as it offers the most direct route to instruction or knowledge (*nulla enim magis ad animum disciplinis via quam auribus patet*: 181.1–2 Friedlein), a claim analogous to the Aristotelian stance on the superiority of hearing for the acquisition of knowledge (*Sens.* 437a10). Hearing, moreover, is the very origin of (at least central aspects of) the discipline of music (*Inst. mus.* 1.9 [195.18–19 Friedlein]; cf. Arist. *De an.* 432a7–8). But if hearing is a necessary first principle (*Inst. mus.* 1.9 [195.17–18 Friedlein]), it alone is not sufficient; perception serves rather as a kind of exhortation or admonition to the reasoning faculty to flesh out the occasionally confused and specious perceptions of the ears. The sustained argument of 1.9, ostensibly articulating the position of the Pythagoreans, makes the point clear: the judgment of the ears is blunt (*obtusa*), and without the support of reason, it has no sure judgment, no comprehension of truth. But Boethius stops short of denying aural criteria (*iudicium aurium*) any role whatsoever within Pythagorean harmonics. In fact, the very phrase *iudicium aurium* (e.g., *Inst. mus.* 1.33 [223.24–5]; 1.28 [220.2–3 Friedlein]) allows for the perceptual judgment of sensibles within the domain of perception (which thus cannot be entirely passive).

A crucial passage that points in this direction – a passage that momentarily bridges the seemingly unbridgeable gap between perception and reason – occurs at 2.18, wherein Boethius ranks the consonances "according to the Pythagoreans" on the basis of their merit and measure. The diapason (the octave, 2:1) graces the top of the list, but the argument for its excellence is grounded in perception, and strikingly so. In a passage that has puzzled modern expositors, Boethius writes:[22]

> The consonance whose property sense perception [*sensus*] apprehends more readily ought to be classified as the primary and most pleasant [*prima*

---

[22] Surprisingly, Sachs omits this passage from his synopsis of the "most important quotations from the *De institutione musica* concerning the criteria" (Sachs 1991: 171–5).

suavisque] consonance. For everything is apprehended through sense perception to be such as it is in itself [*quale est enim unumquodque per semet
ipsum, tale etiam deprehenditur sensu*]. If, therefore, the consonance that consists in the duple ratio is better known to everyone [*cunctis*], then there can
be no doubt that the octave is the first of all consonances and is surpassing
in merit, because it comes first in cognition. (249.22–9 Friedlein)

This crucial passage seems *prima facie* to break ranks with the Pythagoreans.
So to keep Boethius from marching out of step, Bower (1989: 72–3, followed
by Meyer 2004) translates both instances of *sensus* as "critical faculty."
"Boethius, or his Pythagorean source," Bower argues, "is obviously not
arguing that 'as every single thing is in itself, so it is perceived by the sense';
to do so would blatantly contradict the basic tenet of Pythagorean thought
that the senses are unreliable" (1989: 73). Bower's worry is justified,[23] but
the trajectory of Boethius' argument is perhaps less obvious than Bower
suggests. Would Boethius have deployed *sensus* in such a loaded context if
he did not actually intend to bring sense perception into play? Nor does the
supposition of an unspecified "critical faculty" clarify matters much. What
is this critical faculty? And on what grounds and with what sort of data
does it facilitate critique? This critical faculty is also, presumably, not yet
fully cognitive, since Boethius had a perfectly good set of terms (*cognitio,
intellectus*, etc.) had he intended to make such a claim. So this critical
faculty, as postulated in Bower's translation, must somehow fall vaguely
between sense perception and cognition, and it unduly complicates the
stages in the intellectual process. While the translation "critical faculty"
deftly sidesteps any seemingly "blatant contradiction" with Pythagorean
orthodoxy, it fails to offer a cogent alternative.

There are two hints – one lexical, the other contextual – that Boethius
here intends *sensus* as sense perception. Lexically, Boethius' use of the adjective "pleasant" (*suavis*) is neither innocent nor otiose; rather, it deliberately
evokes Boethius' definition of consonance, which is consistently couched
in aesthetic terms that trade on an irreducibly sense-perceptible property: "pleasantness" (*suauitas*).[24] A consonance, to cite but one instance
of Boethius' repeated definitions, is "a mixture of high and low sounds
pleasantly [*suauiter*] and uniformly falling upon the ears" (1.8 [195.6–8
Friedlein]).[25] Hence, the pleasantness of a consonance is first and foremost

---

[23] E.g., in Book 5, an (incomplete) paraphrase of Ptolemy's *Harmonics*, Boethius is more careful: "the
sense observes [*advertit*] a thing as indistinct [*confusum*] and nearly to be such as is the object it
senses" (5.2 [352.7–8 Friedlein]).

[24] On Boethius' use of *suavis*, see Hentschel 2000: 24–5.

[25] Compare 4.1 (302.2–4); 5.7 (357.13–14); 5.11 (361.10–12) Friedlein; cf. Nicomachus *Harmonic Handbook* 12 (262.1–4 Jan).

a feature of its perception. Contextually, this passage functions explicitly[26] as a transition from the fundamentally arithmetical concerns of 2.1–17 – the theory of ratios and means – to the fundamentally musical concerns of 2.18–30 – the connection between ratios and consonances, namely which ratios correspond to which musical intervals. This chapter thus inaugurates a discussion of "how the Pythagoreans proved that the musical consonances are associated with the ratios discussed above," and this transition thus seeks to bridge the gap between Boethius' definition of consonance, which is dependent upon sense perception, and arithmetical ratios, which are understood through the application of reason (cf. Hentschel 2000: 29–32). The octave, the sense-perceptible manifestation of the ratio 2:1, is not just the simplest mathematical ratio; it is also, in a more basic way, readily apprehended to be such through perception. The point is simple: who would deny that the octave sounds consonant? It is as easily recognized as such by any reasonable listener as a shape is recognized by a reasonable observer to be a square or a triangle (cf. *Inst. mus.* 1.1). Notably, Augustine makes an identical point at *On the Trinity* 4.2, observing that even untrained listeners (*imperiti*) recognize the "consonance of one to two." Boethius is not, however, claiming that a listener would know from perception alone the real nature of consonance any more than a casual glance would reveal the mathematical nature of a triangle or square. Rather, perception captures some distinguishing feature (*proprietas*), and it is in this limited sense that we should read Boethius' (overstated) claim that "everything is apprehended through sense perception to be such as it is in itself."

Nor is this claim as radically contradictory to (Boethius' presentation of) Pythagorean thought as it might seem. It well concords with Boethius' earlier claim that the Pythagoreans "investigate certain things only by the ear," which include, he continues, the measuring of consonances, although the precise calculations of how the consonances differ among themselves is entrusted only to reason, the judge and ruler over subservient perception (*Inst. mus.* 1.9 [196.1–7 Friedlein]). Similarly, early commentators on Pythagorean harmonics emphasize the foundational role of perception in establishing the basic nature of consonance, even if reason ultimately plays a trump card in some special cases (e.g., the eleventh, see Barbera 1984). For instance, Ptolemaïs' *Introduction* claims that "Pythagoras and his successors [. . .] wish to accept perception as a guide for reason at the outset, to provide reason with a spark, as it were; but they treat reason, when it has set out from these beginnings, as working on its own in separation from

---

[26] Note its opening words: *sed de his hactenus* (enough about this – 249.18 Friedlein).

perception" (Porph. *In Ptol. Harm.* 25.25–30; trans. Barker 1989: 242; see Chapter 9, section 3 above). The passage in Boethius provides precisely this sort of spark; it presents an attempt to fan the spark of sensation into the fire of rational knowledge. Admittedly, Boethius is (momentarily) more optimistic about the accuracy of perceptual judgment than "orthodox" Pythagoreanism would seem to allow; nonetheless, the tension between reason and perception in Boethius' account of the "Pythagoreans" set in motion nearly a millennium of music-theoretical speculation.[27]

4. Pythagoras *physicus*: psychology and cosmology

Cambridge University Library MS Ii.3.12, a twelfth-century English copy of Boethius' *Fundamentals of Music*, bears on fol. 61*v* a famous Romanesque illumination that depicts Boethius and Pythagoras in the upper half, while Plato debates with Nicomachus in the lower half, both of whom hold a book inscribed MVSICA (on which see Knipp 2002: 376–7). Each scene is encircled by descriptive (if flat-footed) leonine hexameters. The verses dedicated to Pythagoras are as follows:

> Pythagoras physicus physicaeque latentis amicus
> Pondera discernit trutinans et dissona spernit.
> Pulsans aera probat quota quaeque proportio constat.

> (Pythagoras, the natural philosopher, friend to the hidden secrets of nature, by weighing the weights [of the hammers],[28] distinguished their differences and rejected what was dissonant. By striking bronze, he proved how many were proportional to each other.)

While this description accords well with the Pythagoras of Boethius' music treatise, Pythagoras' medieval legacy as a *physicus* or natural philosopher is primarily indebted not to Boethius but to Plato. According to an ancient tradition, Plato's *Timaeus* is an inherently Pythagorean text, insofar as Plato imitated a Pythagorean named Timaeus Locrus (the dialogue's primary interlocutor), under whose name there later circulated a spurious but widely accepted "Pythagorean" cosmology, *On the Nature of the Cosmos and the Soul.*[29] Moreover, the classification of Plato's *Timaeus* as a book on natural philosophy is attested as early as Theophrastus (Fortenbaugh,

---

[27] E.g., Jerome of Moravia *Tractatus de musica* 1.15 (Cserba 1935: 63); Jacques de Liège *Speculum musicae* 1.29 (Bragard 1955: 1.86–90); Johannes de Muris *Musica speculativa* (Meyer 2000: 138–40); Franchino Gaffurio *Theorica musice* 1.7–8 (Gaffurio 1492).

[28] See Chapter 9, section 9 above.

[29] E.g., Nicom. *Harm.* 11 (260.16–17 Jan); Procl. *In Tim.* 1.1.8–13, 1.7.18–21 Diehl; Calcidius *In Tim.* 6 and 50; on Timaeus Locrus, see Baltes 1972 and Chapter 15 above.

Huby, Sharples and Gutas 1992: 422 no. 230) and was codified within Iamblichus' Platonic curriculum (see O'Meara 2003: 62–3). Nicomachus, in the passage quoted at the end of section 2 above, cites the *Timaeus* as the key evidence for his reconstruction of Pythagorean ontology. Both Proclus and Calcidius closely follow this tradition and present the *Timaeus* as a deeply Pythagorean work on natural philosophy.[30]

We begin, then, with Calcidius, whose partial Latin translation of Plato's *Timaeus* (through 53c) accompanied by a formidable commentary was the primary conduit through which Plato (and Platonic Pythagoreanism) reached the Latin West. Near the conclusion of his doxographical account of primordial matter (*silva, hylē*), Calcidius, on the authority of Numenius, asserts that Pythagoras had called god unity (*singularitas*) and matter duality (*duitas*) (*In Tim.* 295 [297.7–10 Waszink]). The details of Calcidius' account of matter and his use of Numenius cannot be rehearsed here (for detailed commentary, see van Winden 1965), but it should be noted that this Numenian/Pythagorean claim undergirds crucial moments elsewhere in Calcidius' commentary, most notably the final remarks on the creation of the World-Soul. There, in a somewhat confused and complicated chain of inferences, Calcidius hints that unity and duality are in some way analogous to the subdivisions of primary components of the World-Soul: double substance (undivided and divided) and two-fold nature (the same and the different).[31]

Calcidius consistently describes the World-Soul in language that implies a harmonic structure: it is "analogous [*conuenire*] to number and measure" (*In Tim.* 51 [100.3–5 Waszink]), it has a "rational composition [*ratio compositionis*] akin to a musical concord [*symphonia*]" (*In Tim.* 228 [243.18–4.2 Waszink]), and it is "divided by numbers, comprised of analogies, close packed with [numerical] means, and ordered with musical ratios" (*In Tim.* 102 [153.3–4 Waszink]). Nevertheless, the implications of these numerical structures and musical ratios within the soul, in Calcidius' view, pertain more to the points of connection between the psychic and the corporeal than they do to any explicitly harmonic or musical rationale (see Reydams-Schils 2006). Thus Calcidius provided medieval scholars with a model of interpreting the Platonic soul's numerical and harmonic structure as fundamentally anagogic, a mathematical expression of a higher ontological reality. For instance, the underlying numerical structure of the

---

[30] E.g. Procl. *In Tim.* 1.1.26, 1.2.29–1.3.2 Diehl; Calcidius *In Tim.* 107 (156.2–3), 127 (170.8–12), and 272 (277.3–8 Waszink), etc.

[31] *In Tim.* 53 (101.14–102.8 Waszink); cf. Procl. *In Tim.* 2.153.17–25 Diehl (citing Aristrandus and Numenius).

World-Soul – the series 1 2 3 4 9 8 27 – is adduced by Calcidius as proof
of the *ratio* that underlies the union of soul and body (*animae corporisque
coniugium*):

> Because soul was designed to penetrate both surfaces and solids with its
> vital vigor, it was necessary that it possess powers akin to the solid [i.e., the
> cubic numbers 9 and 27] and the surface [i.e., the square numbers 4 and 8],
> insofar as like flocks with like. (*In Tim.* 33 [82.9–15 Waszink])

This last claim, "insofar as like flocks with like," Calcidius elsewhere identifies as a fundamentally Pythagorean teaching (*Pythagoricum dogma*), citing
the well-known formula "like is known by like."[32] Hence, the numerical
and harmonic structure within the World-Soul comports with the world's
body, and the similitude accounts for the ability of the soul to penetrate
bodies and to have knowledge of both the intelligible and the sensible world
(*In Tim.* 53 [102.4–8 Waszink]). Thus in Calcidius' account, the World-
Soul's harmonic structure serves ontological and epistemological ends.

Occasionally, though, the soul's harmonic structure was understood
more literally, and the thesis that the soul is or has within it harmony
gained considerable traction as a fundamentally Pythagorean position,
despite the fact that the evidence is both late and unreliable (Aristotle
famously attributes it only to "many of the wise" at *Politics* 1340b18–19).
The earliest and most famous witness to such a thesis is Plato's presentation
in the *Phaedo* (85e–86d), which although translated into Latin in the mid
twelfth century had only small circulation (Minio-Paluello 1950). Rather,
the primary conduit of the thesis was four other preeminent authorities –
Cicero, Augustine, Nemesius of Emesa and Macrobius – all of whom
transmitted a version of the harmony thesis (that none agrees as to who held
the view highlights the complexity of the tradition).[33] Cicero's summary of
views on the soul in *Tusculan Disputations* 1.10.19 attributes to Aristoxenus
the view that the soul is "a kind of tension in the body, as if in song or strings,
which is called *harmonia*" (= Aristoxenus fr. 120a). Thus, upon the death
of the body, the soul too will dissolve.[34] Augustine's *On the Immortality
of the Soul* (at 2.2 and 10.17) twice floats (without ascription) the theory
that the soul is the "harmony of the body" or "some proportioning of
the body" (*aliqua temperatio corporis*) (cf. *On the Trinity* 10.9), but he
denies the thesis, since it would force the soul to be, like shape or color,

---

[32] *Similia non nisi a similibus suis comprehendi*: *In Tim.* 51 (100.8–11 Waszink).

[33] The root of this doxographical tradition may well be Aëtius' *Placita philosophorum*, on which see
Mansfeld 1990.

[34] For a brief discussion of how this view may yet cohere with Aristoxenus' music theory generally, see
Rispoli 2009: 135–6. For Aristoxenus see Chapter 13 above.

inseparably present in the body, and thus the soul would be as mutable as the body (2.2) and could not withdraw to perceive intelligible things (10.17).[35] The *On the Nature of Man* by Nemesius of Emesa, a fourth-century Greek theologian, a work translated into Latin in the eleventh century by Alfanus of Salerno as the *Premnon physicon*, lists the view of a certain "Dinarchus," who claimed that the soul is the "harmony of the four elements" (2.4 = 24.21–2 Burkhard).[36] The arguments Nemesius mounts against "Dinarchus" are those given by Socrates against Simmias in the *Phaedo* (2.32–8 = 31.20–3.9 Burkhard). Thus, even if the *Phaedo* itself was not widely available in the twelfth century, the *Premnon physicon* – which was known and cited by William of Conches, William of St. Thierry and John of Salisbury, among others – provided a summary (albeit not entirely accurate) of its primary arguments against the harmony thesis. Yet it seems not to have been utilized in this regard until Albert the Great's *On Man* I, q.4, a.5 (as noted in Gersh 2010: 913).

Finally, and crucially, Macrobius' *Commentary on the Dream of Scipio* 1.14.19 offers a similar doxographic compendium.[37] The fourth of his collected nineteen views on the nature of the soul is that of "Pythagoras and Philolaus," who, according to Macrobius, held that "soul is harmony." Macrobius alone, and his is the latest of the *testimonia*, ascribes this view to Pythagoras (cf. Huffman 1993: 327–8; 2009: 29–34);[38] nonetheless, it was Macrobius' attribution that gained the strongest foothold among medieval mentions of the thesis (e.g., Vincent of Beauvais *Speculum Historiale* 3.26: *Pythagoras dicebat animam esse harmoniam*). Throughout his commentary, Macrobius is inclined (more so than Calcidius) to accept the numerical and musical structure of the soul, which he readily attributes to Pythagoras' influence on Plato (*In Somn.* 2.2.1). The World-Soul is, in a favored Macrobian phrase, "woven from numbers" (*contexta numeris*; 2.2.1, 2.2.14, 2.2.19); it originated from music and thus confers a musical structure upon everything that it animates, both celestial bodies and animate bodies that move in and upon the earth, air and water (2.3.11). This harmonic structure equally applies to the human soul:

> The Pythagoreans call the quaternary the *tetraktys*, and so revere it among their secrets as pertaining to the perfection of the soul that they have made a

---

[35] On the ambiguity of Augustine's *temperatio*, see O'Connell 1968: 140–2.
[36] Δείναρχος = Δικαίαρχος, a pupil of Aristotle; see Mirhady 2001: frs. 13–32. On the organization and sources of Nemesius' doxography generally, see Dörrie 1959: 111–51; Mansfeld 1990: 3076–82.
[37] For a concise survey of the source(s) for Macrobius, see Mansfeld 1990: 3073 n. 49.
[38] Claudianus Mamertus (*De statu animae* 2.3) attributes such a view to Philolaus; see Huffman 1993: 410–14.

> religious oath from it: "By him who gave the quaternary to our soul." [. . .]
> Moreover, none of the wise has doubted that the soul consisted of musical
> concords. (Macrob. *In Somn.* 1.6.41–3)

When medieval commentators encountered this passage, however, they
were (not unlike Calcidius) hesitant to follow it literally. A set of anonymous twelfth-century glosses on Macrobius (the *Glosae Colonienses super
Macrobium*) neutralizes the metaphysical implications of Macrobius' text
by interpreting the "quaternary" as the four cardinal virtues (prudence,
courage, justice and temperance) or the four stages of understanding (sense
perception, imagination, reason and intellect) (Caiazzo 2000: 15–27). Likewise, William of Conches' twelfth-century *Glosses on Macrobius* explains
the "quaternary" as the four cardinal virtues, though William appends a
second level of interpretation of a more natural philosophical bent: "The
quaternary granted being to the soul because of the four elements; for if
there were not four elements, then bodies would not exist; and if there were
no bodies, then the soul would not have its being within bodies" (*comment.
ad* 1.6.41).

This Macrobian line of "Pythagorean" speculation, that number and
harmony somehow grant being to the soul, finds culmination in a twelfth-
century commentary on Martianus Capella attributed to Bernard Silvestris.
In a survey of various views on the origin of the soul in his comment on *De
nupt.* 1.7, Bernard discusses Plato's account of the creation of souls and the
allotment of each to its own star (*Ti.* 41d–e). Although Bernard insists that,
if properly understood, Plato says nothing that would contradict catholic
doctrine, his interpretation goes so far as to claim that the soul *qua* soul
ceases to exist upon the dissolution of the bodily harmony, and his remarks
come very close to a quasi-functionalist account of the soul. The soul is
analogous (*compar*) to the proportion that obtains between the elemental
qualities within the human body. Hence,

> when the concord of these is present in the body, the soul begins to exist,
> but when that concord is dissolved, the soul ceases to exist, not because that
> immortal substance itself ceases to exist, but that substance – although the
> soul always lives – is no longer a soul. For the soul is the name of a function
> [*officium*]. And thus, when the duration of its animation is completed, it is
> no longer a soul. (*Commentary on Martianus Capella* 6.530–42 Westra)

The most famous manifestation of the harmony within the World-Soul is
the harmony of the spheres, which is a direct consequence of the World-
Soul's numerical structure. According to Calcidius, this view is entirely in
line with Pythagorean teaching:

[Plato] delineated the form of the world as an image with a likeness comparable to the sketch that he employed to depict the World-Soul; he established seven circles and separated them by musical intervals, so that, in accord with Pythagoras, as the stars rotate with a harmonic motion, they might produce musical modes in their rotation. Plato says something similar in his *Republic*, namely that a Siren resides in each individual sphere, and as each Siren spins with its sphere it produces a single mellifluous song. From these eight unequal sounds a single, concordant harmony arises. (*In Tim.* 95 [148.2–11 Waszink])

Calcidius likely knew a planetary scale, for at *In Tim.* 72 (120.1–10 Waszink), he translates ten lines of "Pythagorean" Hellenistic verse that deal with the harmony of the planets.[39] Calcidius, however, employs these verses primarily as testimony to the "Pythagorean" planetary order (as against Eratosthenes) and thereby omits the subsequent sixteen lines that present the planetary scale (as given by Theon of Smyrna, *Mathematics Useful for Reading Plato* 140.5–1.4 Hiller; see Haar 1960: 104ff.). Calcidius (or his source, Adrastus) instead envisaged a Pythagorean "harmony of the spheres" entirely in line with the Timaean World-Soul. Chapters 95 and 96 of Calcidius' commentary set forth the planetary arrangement as an intervallic series derived from the harmonic constitution of the World-Soul. Hence, Calcidius does not identify each sphere with a specific pitch in the gamut, but rather calculates the successive intervals between the spheres, enumerated in the "Egyptian" order, in accord with Plato's division of the World-Soul (*In Tim.* 95 [147.26–8.5]; cf. 73 [120.11–13 Waszink]). The distance from the earth to the moon corresponds to the soul's first division, the single portion, whereas the outermost planet, Saturn, is twenty-seven times farther than the moon from the earth and thus corresponds to the last division of the psychic substance (*In Tim.* 96 [148.12–19 Waszink]).[40] These harmonic planetary distances are visualized in an astronomical diagram that features eight concentric spheres – the earth at the center, the fixed stars (*aplanes*) at the outermost periphery – with the series 1 2 3 4 8 9 27 inscribed successively within each circle from the lunar orbit (1) to the orbit of Saturn (27).[41] This diagram found its way into copies of Boethius' *Fundamentals of Music* to gloss his description of two planetary scales

---

[39] *Sortitos celsis replicant anfractibus orbes*, etc.; see Buechner 1982: 196–7 (no. 18); cf. Theon of Smyrna, *Mathematics Useful for Reading Plato* 139.1–10 Hiller, on which see Burkert 1961: 32.

[40] Macrobius, too, formulates the *musica caelestis* as an intervallic series based upon the World-Soul (*In Somn. Scip.* 2.3.14), but he (unlike Calcidius) preserves the strict alternation of even and odd numbers (1 2 3 4 9 8 27), even though preserving this order comes at the cost of a nonsensical musical system, which amounts to 46,656:1, or fifteen octaves and a tritone!

[41] This Calcidian diagram is not included in Eastwood and Graßhoff 2004.

(*Inst. mus.* 1.27 [219.4–25 Friedlein]): a seven-note scale (unattributed but based upon Nicomachus)[42] descending from the moon (sounding the *nētē synēmmenōn*) to Saturn (the *hypatē mesōn*) with the sun holding the middle at the *mesē*, and an eight-note scale, extrapolated from Cicero's *Dream of Scipio* (5.1–2 = *Rep.* 6.18), ascending from the moon (*proslambanomenos*) to the highest heaven (*ultimum caelum* – the *mesē*).

Through the conduit of Calcidius, Macrobius and Boethius (as well as Martianus Capella *De nup.* 1.11), the theory of cosmic harmony – nearly always attributed directly to Pythagoras – became a central tenet in most medieval Neoplatonic cosmologies, though its applications demonstrate considerable conceptual variation (as discussed in Rankin 2005; Teeuwen 2007; O'Meara 2007; Ilnitchi-Currie 2008). The re-introduction of Aristotle's criticisms of the Pythagorean position in *On the Heavens* 2.9 spurred still more variation in the thirteenth century, as commentators sought to reconcile Pythagorean authority with Aristotle's refutations (see Lord 1992; Ilnitchi 2002; Rico 2005a). Often, however, Aristotle's criticisms proved decisive and the heavenly harmony fell silent, dismissed as a "Pythagorean fiction" (*Pythagoricum figmentum*: see Rico 2005b: 149–58). Famously, the music theorist Johannes de Grocheio (*c.* 1300) dismissed both "cosmic music" and "human music" (see section 2 above) as mere figments of the Pythagorean imagination, for "those who posit such divisions either make them up, wish to obey Pythagoras (or others) rather than the truth, or they are ignorant of nature and logic" (Rohloff 1943: 46.35–7). The full reawakening of the *concentus caeli* ("harmony of the heavens") awaited the pioneering translations and Pythagorean imagination of Marsilio Ficino, who again revived the Pythagorean legacy.[43]

---

[42] Cf. *Harm.* 3 (241.3–2.18 Jan) and *Excerpta ex Nicomacho* (271.16–2.8 Jan).   [43] See Chapter 21.

Pythagoras in the Early Renaissance

Michael J. B. Allen

1. Introduction

The Renaissance story of Pythagoras and Pythagorean wisdom, its religious and its scientific aspects alike, is a complicated one.[1] This is partly because leading philosophers and historians of the age read a host of later developments and assumptions back into their source materials, and thereby recreated a Pythagoras in their own image, one invested with their own enthusiasms and preoccupations. In the process they created a thinker of enormous stature, who was the founder of a number of disciplines, and a moralist and sage of such lofty grandeur that he anticipated the virtues of Christianity's greatest saints, if not of Christ himself.[2] Ralph Cudworth as late as the mid seventeenth century was not untypical when he called Pythagoras "the most eminent of all the ancient philosophers"[3] implying that his school had surpassed even the Academy and the Lyceum. This is a positive way of saying that Renaissance thinkers falsified the record in their syncretistic desire to find either a magisterial pre-Platonic thinker or a Greco-Jewish mystagogue whom they could set beside Moses and to whom they could attribute a like plenipotential wisdom and authority, especially since St. Ambrose had intimated that Pythagoras was a Jew.[4]

Underlying this impulse was the assumption that Pythagoras was part of a storied succession of ancient theologians (*prisci theologi*) that climaxed in Plato but stretched back prior to Pythagoras through Aglaophamus, Orpheus and Hermes Trismegistus to Zoroaster, and constituted a line of

---

[1] "The historian of science rediscovers Pythagoras the scientist; the religiously minded show us Pythagoras the mystic, [. . .] the anthropologist finds 'shamanism'" (Burkert 1972a: 9).

[2] Joost-Gaugier entitles her second chapter "The emergence of 'Saint' Pythagoras in the Early Renaissance" and cites a letter to Henry VIII in which Erasmus compares Pythagoras and Apollonius of Tyana to Christ himself (2009: 50).

[3] Cudworth 1678: 370. See Heninger 1974: 19.

[4] In a letter to Irenaeus, St. Ambrose identified Pythagoras as Jewish or of Jewish descent and as a follower of Mosaic teachings (*Epistle* 28, Migne *PL* 16, col. 1051B [1095B]). Ambrose's letter was widely known in the Renaissance: see Ficino's *On Christian Religion* Ch. 26 (*Opera* p. 29).

sages who had adored God by combining "marvelous wisdom and incomparable sanctity" (14.10.2) as distinct from the simple piety of unlearned men.[5] The line ran loosely parallel to that of the Hebrew prophets and bore witness to the same principal theological truths: the existence of one almighty God, who had created a harmonious world, who rewarded virtue and punished sin, who had endowed humankind with immortal souls, and who had established a beginning and an end to time, however vast the intervening duration. This ancient wisdom had been shared by Gentiles and Jews alike, however separate the traditions. For Platonizing Christians it had been perfected in Christ, who was accordingly both the Hebrew Messiah and the new Zoroaster, the culmination of what the Platonists saw as the Chaldaean-Pythagorean-Platonic wisdom.[6]

2.   The rediscovery of ancient sources and their influence on Ficino's music

One of the arresting dimensions of early Renaissance Pythagoreanism is consequent on the rediscovery of certain ancient sources. A seminal figure here is the Florentine Hellenist, philosopher and magus, Marsilio Ficino (1433–1499), whose principal work, the eighteen-book *Platonic Theology: On the Immortality of Souls* (1482), contains some fifty references to Pythagoras or the Pythagoreans, notably in Book 17, which addresses the history of the Platonic debate about the soul's status before and after it enters the body. Without exaggeration we may legitimately think of Ficino as the father of Quattrocento Pythagoreanism, albeit of a Pythagoreanism confused with, and fused with, the very Neoplatonism that was its inheretrix and daughter.[7] For instance, he describes the two greatest Neoplatonists, Plotinus and Proclus, as "followers of Zoroaster, Pythagoras and Plato" as if they were spokesmen of a unified and continuous tradition (18.9.4). Plato himself, Ficino says – and he is voicing an opinion shared by contemporaries such as Pletho, Bessarion and Filelfo – "learned about the Pythagorean wisdom, which emanated from Zoroaster, from Archytas, Eurytus and Philolaus." Having encountered a variety of philosophies on his travels, "Plato had eventually chosen the Pythagorean school before all others as being closer to the truth." He was to illuminate (*illustraret*) it in his own writings and thus he deliberately introduced Pythagoreans as spokesmen in his principal works: Timaeus of Locri, Parmenides of Elea,

---

[5] Ficino *Platonic Theology*. Cf. 6.1.7; 17.1.2 (cited by book, chapter and paragraph in the I Tatti edition).
[6] See Allen 1998: Ch. 1.   [7] Celenza 1999, 2001 (introduction) and 2002.

Melissus (whom Ficino identified with the Eleatic Stranger in the *Sophist*), and Zeno, who appears at the beginning of the *Parmenides*. From them, says Ficino, Socrates had learned what he repeated to others in the rest of the dialogues (17.4.4; cf. 2.7.1; 17.4.10) and this includes, so the Pythagoreans and Platonists had both argued, the important material in the *Sophist* on the six principal genera from which the soul is composed (17.2.4–5). Thus Socrates too, by implication, was a Pythagorean.

This Ficinian perspective is important, since the serious accounting of Pythagoras and his school in the later Middle Ages (as distinct from the accretions and obfuscations of legend) was primarily keyed to notices in Aristotle's *Metaphysics*, *Physics* and *De Caelo*, and in his late ancient commentators, especially Themistius and Simplicius. Additionally, there were notices in the Church Fathers, and, given Pythagoras' foundational role in the mathematical tradition, in Boethius, where he was trumpeted as the father of the medieval quadrivium.[8] Ficino by contrast, inspired perhaps by Cardinal Bessarion (1403–1472), first turned to Iamblichus (*c.* 250–325 AD), the eminent Neoplatonic philosopher and theurgist whose work had been virtually unknown in the Latin Middle Ages, but whom Ficino saw as the brightest star in the Neoplatonic firmament between Plotinus and Proclus.[9]

In particular he took up the four surviving Pythagorean works attributed to Iamblichus and known collectively as the *Four Books on the Pythagorean School*: namely, *On the Pythagorean Life*, *Protreptic to Philosophy*, *On General Mathematical Science*, and *On Nicomachus' Arithmetical Introduction*. In the 1460s, early in his career, he translated this quartet into Latin,[10] along apparently with Theon of Smyrna's *Mathematics Useful for Reading Plato*. These were working translations for his personal use, and there are omissions – many in the case of the *On the Pythagorean Life* – as well as passages of intermittent paraphrasing and epitomizing.[11] These newly discovered texts, stemming from what Celenza calls a fourth-century Neopythagoreanizing Neoplatonism,[12] obviously made an impact on Ficino in his formative years and he instantly realized that they were integral to the Platonic tradition.

To begin with, he was the first Renaissance thinker – though the significance of this has not been fully recognized – to read in detail and mine for

---

[8] See the copious annotation in Joost-Gaugier 2006.
[9] See Dillon 1988 and the contributions in Blumenthal and Clark 1993.
[10] For the two manuscripts, Vat. Lat. 5953 and 4530, see Gentile's entry n. 24 in Gentile, Niccoli and Viti 1984. On p. 34, he argues for a date prior even to 1464. Of the Greek MSS Ficino may have used, foremost are the Laurenziana's 86.3, 86.29 and 86.6.
[11] Gentile 1990: 73–4 and 80n; also Allen 1994: 32–3. [12] Celenza 2001: 26.

musical and medical information the most compelling of the five treatises, namely, *On the Pythagorean Life*.[13] He thus encountered its vivid descriptions of Pythagoras "whom our Plato honored [*veneratur*] in all things,"[14] of the Pythagorean communities, and of the importance the sect attributed to musical therapy. Pythagoras is depicted as a sage who had heard the music of the spheres (*Platonic Theology* 17.2.15) and dedicated himself to philosophy each morning with the singing of sacred hymns (12.1.14), having secluded himself for ten years in a kind of sustained philosophical ecstasy (13.2.2). From Iamblichus Ficino also learned that the entire Pythagorean community had daily practiced what was called "arrangement," "composition," "treatment" or "attuning" (*VP* 64, 114, 224) in order to adjust and then temper its members' individual moods, and to balance their mental attitudes by way of the beneficial use of vocal and instrumental accompaniment, especially when waking or preparing to sleep (65). Attending souls were thus profoundly attuned.[15]

Specific proof is wanting, but this Iamblichean account of Pythagorean song must have served as a model (along conceivably with Byzantine chant) for Ficino's own Orphic lyre recitals,[16] when he was, in Celenza's phrasing, "crafting his own prophetic image [...] as an Iamblichean/Pythagorean holy man"[17] and, we might add, as a psychiatrist too. After all, the purpose of the Pythagorean hymns was to cure various afflictions and diseases by singing over those who were suffering from them (*VP* 114), the Pythagorean day being lived *sub specie musicae*, suffused, that is, by healing instrumental and choral music.

Iamblichus also informed Ficino that the Orphic-Pythagorean musical instrument *par excellence* was the lyre. In his *Philebus Commentary* 1.28, Ficino claimed that Orpheus had introduced the tetrachord since, in the "Hymn to Apollo" 21–3, he attributed the god a lyre with four strings, each signifying one of the four seasons;[18] and in his introduction to Plato's *Ion* he elaborated on the notion.[19] This might in turn suggest that Ficino's

---

[13] I follow Clark 1989 in referencing the traditional section numbers of the *Vita Pythagorae* (*VP*).

[14] Ficino, *argumentum* for Plato's *Second Letter* (*Opera* p. 1531).

[15] Socrates in the *Phaedo* 85e–6d, 91c–5a, however, had famously countered the Pythagorean argument that the soul itself is a harmony born from the human "complexion" as from a lyre.

[16] Walker 1958: 3–29 (esp. 20); Walker and Gouk 1985: 17–28; 131–50; Tomlinson 1993: 84–9, 101–36; D'Accone 1994: 272–3; and Voss 2000; 2002.

[17] Celenza 2001: 21–2. But I would question Celenza's bolder claim that Ficino "helped craft a vatic sensibility in Florence, a cultural matrix where the figure of Pythagoras was one lens through which one could examine crucial intellectual issues" (26).

[18] Hymn 34. Cf. Ficino's *Platonic Theology* 2.9.7.   [19] Allen 2008a: 206–7.

Orphic lyre was a tetrachord, even though a seven-stringed instrument would seem to be ideal for imitating the harmonies of the seven planets.[20]

From Ficino's viewpoint at least, Pythagoras' musical and theological debts were unquestionably to Orpheus.[21] Iamblichus' treatise explicitly connects the two:

> Pythagoras took his inspiration from Orpheus in composing his account of the gods, which he called "holy" precisely because it was culled from the inner mysteries of the works of Orpheus (*VP* 145–6) [...] Pythagoras emulated Orpheus' interpretation and composition, and honored the gods as Orpheus did, setting up carved and bronze images. (151)[22]

For the Renaissance, the "works of Orpheus" meant the divine hymns that later antiquity had attributed to the Thracian bard, eighty-six of which have survived. Now deemed pious forgeries or imitations, the hymns were accepted as authentic exemplars of Platonic song. In the very years he was reading Iamblichus' Pythagorean treatises, Ficino translated the hymns into Latin – though the translation has not survived or at least been identified.[23] He never published them in their entirety lest they should serve, however unintentionally, to provoke or invoke the daemons, and thus to further their cult.[24]

How they were sung or performed remains a mystery. Our best clues, however, are once again the descriptions in *On the Pythagorean Life*. In other words, Ficino's conception of Orphic music must have been governed by Pythagorean music as Iamblichus describes it. Moreover, Pythagoras served in many respects as a more admirable, less controversial figure than Orpheus, given that aspects of Orpheus' myth, including his journey to the underworld, his loss of Eurydice, and his death at the hands of the Ciconian maenads, detracted from his status as an august sage and a model of courage and temperance.[25] Yet these were the very virtues that everyone admired in the Samian successor to the Thracian bard.

In sum, the revival of interest in Orpheus, his songs and the stringing of his ancient lyre, a revival initiated by Ficino in his twenties when

---

[20] See Ficino's *In Timaeum* 30 and 32 in Ficino 1576: 1453 and 1457; also Warden 1982: 93–4, who assumes, following Gafurius, that Ficino's Orphic lyre was seven-stringed.

[21] See Burkert 1972a: 162–5, with further references.

[22] This iconophilia seems odd given the emphasis on music and musical harmonies.

[23] See Klutstein 1987: 21–52.

[24] However, three correspondents, Cosimo de' Medici himself, Germain de Ganay and Martinus Uranius (Prenninger), did get to see Ficino's doctored versions of four of the hymns. We must leave aside the issue of whether Ficino thought of music itself as daemonic, or even as a succession of airy daemons transforming themselves into notes or chords. Tomlinson 1993: Ch. 4 examines earlier scholarship.

[25] For Platonic strictures on Orpheus, see Allen 2012.

he was presenting himself as a performer of Orphic song, was in many striking ways, it seems, a Pythagorean as well as an Orphic revival. At the very least, it was a conflation of the two, based on Ficino's reading of Iamblichus; for in singing or intoning an Orphic hymn, Ficino was also performing a Pythagorean musical and therapeutic exercise,[26] one that Celenza has suggested was part of a deliberate attempt to "craft" or define himself as a prophet.[27] Along with the holistic consequences of this Orphic-Pythagorean singing, came the ability to prophesy (even unintelligibly by way of glossolalia, or just in musical notes or numbers). In such moments, the singer, and perhaps his auditors, would be flooded by supernal influences, and these would enable his soul, now rendered wise, attuned and tempered, to receive like Pythagoras the gift of fore-knowledge.

3.   The Renaissance confronts Pythagorean metempsychosis

One of the most distinctive and controversial dimensions of the Pythagoras legend that Ficino, Pico and others derived from the biographical tradition stemmed not only from Iamblichus' treatise, but also from the *Life of Pythagoras* by Diogenes Laertius who flourished in the late second to early third century AD. This biography (which contains material also found in Porphyry's brief *Life of Pythagoras*) occurs in Book 8 of his *The Lives of the Eminent Philosophers*.[28] This had become newly available to the West in the Quattrocento after Ambrogio Traversari had translated it into Latin and it proved to be a rich source for Ficino and others, and notably for the lives and works of Pythagoras and Plato and the folklore surrounding them. Diogenes had no hesitation in adducing Pythagoras' claims to have lived a series of lives, and not only human lives, and to be able to remember them in detail, along with the intervening descents into the underworld, remembering in detail being the core Pythagorean exercise before rising every morning.[29] "Perpetual transmigration" was a gift, says Diogenes, given Pythagoras when he was Aethalides by his father Hermes, since he could not give him immortality itself. Hence Pythagoras' soul with its memories "was constantly transmigrating into whatever plants or animals it pleased" (8.4). Notably he had lived the life of the Trojan hero Euphorbus

---

[26] Ficino also encountered Iamblichus' claim that Pythagoras synthesized what he had learned from the Orphics, the Egyptian priests, the Chaldaeans and magi, the rites at Eleusis and other cult shrines, and from the Celts and Iberians (*VP* 151).

[27] Celenza 2001: 21–2. For Ficino and prophecy, see Allen 1994: Ch. 4, and esp. 124–42.

[28] Delatte 1922b lists all parallel passages. Whether Ficino knew Porphyry's *Life of Pythagoras* is unknown.

[29] Diog. Laert. 8.4–5; Porph. *VP* 19, 26; and Iambl. *VP* 63; cf. 165, 178.

whose wounding at the hand of Menelaus is poignantly described in the *Iliad* 17.51–66 in lines that the Samian used to sing "most elegantly" to the lyre.[30]

Ficino was confronted in short by the notion of the rational soul's transmigration not only into another body (*metensomatosis*) but more radically into the irrational soul of a non-human life (*metempsychosis*), into the souls of horses, frogs and sponges, as listed, for instance, in Erasmus' *In Praise of Folly*.[31] Ficino argues in the *Platonic Theology* 5.14.8 that the Pythagoreans and Egyptians thought: (a) that human souls are minds fallen into reason and sense; (b) that beasts' souls are our human souls fallen entirely into sense and generation; and finally (c) that plants' souls are these same souls which have fallen completely into the power of generation. They also supposed that all these souls could be returned to the higher levels. "This is what Empedocles, Timaeus, Origen and Plotinus apparently meant. But that is their concern." It was, however, everyone's concern.

Not only did Ficino confront the twin Pythagorean notions of *metensomatosis* and *metempsychosis*, but he was drawn into speculating about the cycle of lives and of deaths, deaths that are inter-lives as lives are inter-deaths. In the *Platonic Theology* 17.3.5 he engaged the argument for palingenesis. Pythagoras' soul existed for a time free of an earthly body before the birth of Pythagoras himself; then it was born into a body. Having been free, it accepted being not-free. Later it passed from having a body to not having a body. Indeed, says Ficino, "Pythagoras' soul lived inside and outside an earthly body numberless times before Pythagoras himself, so again it will live alternately outside and inside a body after Pythagoras." Furthermore, at the end of a world-cycle it will join all the other souls in donning "the various forms of bodies" in which they had been enveloped beforehand. This cyclical notion addresses the thorny problem of having to set a limit to the number of souls in almost limitless time.[32] And Ficino references here not only Zoroaster and the Hermetic *Pimander* but also Plato's own *Statesman*.

In short, the *Platonic Theology* presents Pythagoras as a soul-voyager, a philosopher who had undergone a sequence of incarnations even at times into animals and plants; and who could remember former lives. This was

---

[30] Cf. Iambl. *VP* 63 and Ov. *Met.* 15: 161.

[31] Erasmus, *In Praise of Folly* 34B, says Pythagoras lived the lives of a cock, fish, horse, frog and sponge besides those of a commoner, king, man, woman and philosopher. In antiquity Dicaearchus had already reported that he was also reborn as the prostitute Alco (fr. 42 Mirhady).

[32] *Platonic Theology* 15.7.12 refers to "this Pythagorean theme of everlasting generation," entailing apparently "an everlasting and fixed number of souls also changing bodies."

the all-defining dimension of Pythagoras' spiritual profile for Ficino, and the chief witness to his spiritual power and thus to his distinction as a teacher who could teach others to remember who and what they had been, and thus convince them of the soul's immortality. For Iamblichus claims that

> the starting point of Pythagoras' whole system of education was to [have his followers] recall the lives which they had lived before entering the bodies they happen to inhabit at the time [. . .] and he began his training of others by awakening their memory of an earlier existence. (*VP* 62–3)

Without successfully remembering his past succession of lives, a seeker could not become a disciple at all – could not become a Pythagorean. He would be floundering still in Lethean oblivion.

However integral to Pythagoras' teaching and however keyed to belief in immortality, reincarnation obviously presented a series of quandaries to Christian thinkers. Ficino took great pains indeed in the *Platonic Theology* to survey the ancient Neoplatonic tradition in order to establish – to his own satisfaction – that the vast majority of the Platonists had interpreted Plato's various references to journeys in ecstasy and after death to signify that some souls had succumbed to bestial ways perhaps, or even been imprisoned in bestial forms, but that they had not become, had not crossed over into, the souls of animals when they returned to earth. The core assumption here was that animals' souls were irrational, while men, however overwhelmed at times by wrath and desire, were nonetheless endowed with rational souls. The only Platonic philosopher whose statements were open to interpretative doubts was Plotinus, ironically so given his preeminent stature among Platonists (second only in authority to Plato himself). But even with Plotinus, Ficino scrambled to save the appearances by invoking distinctions introduced by the post-Plotinian commentators (especially by Proclus), and then reading these distinctions back into Plotinus. This is a legitimate strategy only for someone wedded to the notion of the unity of the Platonic tradition and the integrity of its wisdom. It certainly enabled Ficino to declare in the *Platonic Theology* 17.4.1 "that Pythagoras was always introducing the transmigrations of souls into his customary conversations [*consuetis confabulationibus suis*] and into his symbols."

Most importantly, Plato's own retelling of the myth of Er at the finale of the *Republic* raises the whole issue not only of reincarnation but also of transmigration.[33] Er the dream traveller is a witness to souls in the meadows

---

[33] See Ficino's *Platonic Theology* 17.3.8–9 for his interpretation of the dream of Er as well as his epitome of *Republic* 10 in his *Opera* pp. 1431–8.

of Hades choosing various future lives. He sees Orpheus selecting the life of a swan, being unwilling "to be conceived and born of a woman" (murdered as he had been by the Bacchae). He sees Ajax's soul selecting the life of an eagle, and the soul of the buffoon Thersites, the life of an ape. Ficino argues that these selections were selections of "lives" not souls, and that Orpheus, Ajax and the others did not exchange their rational souls for bestial souls, they merely lived the lives of their newly adopted non-human forms. But the alternative, more radical account that human souls transmigrate into animal even vegetal souls could never be completely dismissed,[34] and particularly since Pythagoras had insisted on our remembering our other lives. It suggests he must have elected to live as different things in the great chain of being, not because he was angry with women like Orpheus, or dragged down by his own buffoonery like Thersites; but because such a series of soul-journeys was somehow necessary. This aspect of Pythagoras' story was arguably the most challenging to Renaissance thinkers precisely because it gave rise to fundamental cosmological questions about what it is to be a seeker in a world of becoming, about our connections with other lives in an ordered and harmonious cosmos.

At this point we might bear in mind that Marinus' *Life of Proclus* 28 states that Proclus was the reincarnation of the soul of Nicomachus, having been born 216 years after Nicomachus' death.[35] This number is the cube of six – six being the first perfect number as the sum of its aliquot parts and the product of its own factors – but 216 is also the sum of the cubes of the three sides of the first perfect Pythagorean right-angled triangle, i.e. $27 + 64 + 125$. This speaks to the power of the number symbolism Ficino associated with the Pythagoreans, but it also underscores their conception of time as being numbered, indeed perfectly numbered, and of reincarnation as being calculable and not merely predictable.

Such reincarnations and soul-journeys obviously entail a belief in the immanence of the divine as well as the connectedness of humanity with all present life and with past and future time, the ties that connect us with our other selves and with all that is other in a pantheistic or panentheistic cosmos. This speaks to a notion of the "dignity of man" that is different from the anthropocentrism traditionally associated with such Renaissance

---

[34] *Platonic Theology* 17.3.10–12; 17.4.3–4; see also his *In Phaedrum* 3.25.3–6. Ficino is aware of the varying opinions.

[35] The anonymous *Theology of Arithmetic* (52.8ff. de Falco) claims, in a section on the hexad, that certain disciples of Pythagoras had declared that their master was reincarnated every 216 years. Ficino may have known this treatise and attributed it to Iamblichus, though the idea goes back to Aristoxenus (fr. 12 Wehrli).

Quattrocento humanists as Bruni, Manetti and Pico.[36] To a Pythagorean, a man was not one form but a succession of forms; and wisdom came with Proteus, with our ability to become other selves, in other creatures, at other times, assuming their various skills (*artes*) and excellences.

Though the history of engagement with reincarnation in the Renaissance awaits a definitive study, one thing is clear: the many lives of Pythagoras certainly attracted the attention of major figures like Ficino and Agrippa, Erasmus and Reuchlin; and this despite the fact that there were always, as in antiquity itself, Lucianic satirists eager to mock and lampoon the ancient vegetarian and his bean-shunning disciples. We might note that Pythagoras' succession of lives is not presented as a linear ascent from the lowliest to the most eminent – after all he went from being an aristocratic Euphorbus and Hermotimus to being a humble fisherman. It is not even clear that his rebirths went along with an increasing sapience or gradual acquisition of authority, at least until he was born as Pythagoras. Rather, he seems to have experienced a variety of lives for their own sake: to have experienced creation's plenitude and otherness (and here we might recall the famous Pythagorean table of balanced opposites). This shamanistic dimension of Pythagoras' story (and incidentally that of Empedocles after him) might suggest that he was different from Plato – more powerful certainly as a religious figure. For it links him with the roles of priest, prophet, healer and magician rather than with philosophy as such. Post-Platonic Pythagoreans were led to think of Plato as a subordinate figure in this regard, for his biography (despite its legendary accretions)[37] was less significant, less mysterious, less miraculous than his Samian predecessor's. However profound the wisdom Plato had infused into his dialogues, his life – at least as it emerges from the standard biographies including that of Diogenes Laertius – was not that of a magus, or even that of a spiritual teacher. And there is nothing in the record to suggest that Plato lived other lives, though Ficino and his fellow Renaissance Platonists toyed with the twin conceits that Plotinus was the son of Plato, and Pletho was Plato reborn.[38] It is important not to underestimate the impact of reincarnation on Christian Platonism; for the Renaissance revival of Pythagoreanism

---

[36] See Trinkaus 1970, the classic study.

[37] See Ficino's *Life of Plato*; this became a letter to Francesco Bandini (now letter 19 in his *Epistulae* 4, *Opera* pp. 763–70). It refers to Plato's tracing his descent from Neptune on both sides of his family; to bees bringing honey to his lips while he was still in his cradle; and to Socrates' dream of a fledgling cygnet sitting on his knee. But these are obviously eclipsed by the wonders associated with Pythagoras.

[38] See Wind 1968: 256–8 ("Bessarion's Letter on Palingenesis"). Wind notes that "palingenesis was a thought that fascinated the Renaissance" (1968: 257).

necessarily brought with it a revival of interest in reincarnation. Edgar Wind properly observes: "Since the Church taught the second advent not only of Christ, but also of Enoch, Elijah and Jeremiah, esoteric belief in periodic returns or restitutions, although a potential nuisance to the authorities, was not necessarily heterodox."[39]

Following on this interest in rebirth, came, predictably, a revival of interest in the various ancient notions of cyclical or epicyclical time, of temporal repetition, and of recurrence. Following on these in turn came a revival of interest in the ancient notion of the vastness of time, one that was dramatically opposed to the notion of a circumscribed linear time as it was preached by the apostles, fiercely affirmed by Augustine, and reaffirmed throughout the Middle Ages by orthodox Scholastics. One of the major contributions to this revival of interest in the vastness of time (and indeed of space) may well have been a new exposure to historical chronologies, and particularly those of the Greeks and Romans (the Pharaonic dynasties remained of course a mystery). But this new awareness was in turn accompanied by a sense that time was, from a mere human viewpoint, almost timeless, almost indeed eternal. This is in sharp contrast to the notion of time as compressed into the allotted span of three score years and ten, or as signaling the imminence of the Apocalypse and the Second Coming. Any notion, whether identifiably Pythagorean or not, of a cyclical or repeated Second Coming, or of a reincarnated or indeed a reincarnating Savior – one constituting in effect a series of Enochs or Elijahs or Jeremiahs or their avatars – would have struck the Renaissance as erroneous perhaps, but not as unreasonable or uninterpretable. The key for a devout hermeneut would be the tool of allegory, the drawing aside of "poetic veils," since this would ensure that such Pythagorean ideas, if Christianized, could be interpreted figuratively:[40] Christ must be continually reborn in men's hearts as the ancient of days that we in turn may be reborn as members of His one body.

In brief, we should not underestimate the impact that a renewed encounter with Pythagorean reincarnation made on the more adventurous Christian thinkers of the fifteenth and subsequent centuries, the Ficinos, the Postels, the Agrippas. It spurred them to reconceive the notion of men's soul-journeys up and down the ladder of being as souls with "no

---

[39] Wind goes on to note that Agrippa von Nettesheim devoted "a generous chapter" to pro-palingenesis arguments (*On Occult Philosophy* 3.41), while adducing Augustine's warning: "It is better to doubt those things that are secret than to quarrel about those things that are uncertain" (*Melius est dubitare de occultis quam litigare de incertis*).

[40] See Ficino's *Platonic Theology* 17.1.2; 17.2.11–15. But in 17.4.5 he argues that Plato was aware of but did not believe in these Pythagorean views.

fixed abode" in the universal hierarchy – to recall the famous formulations at the beginning of Pico's *Oration*. For such soul-journeys would certainly require a special consideration in any Platonic account of trial and judgment, of the afterlife, or of prenatal and postmortal existence, concepts that are integral to the whole notion of reincarnation, and indeed transmigration, and do not necessarily undermine an orthodox notion or notions of immortality.

Modern scientific, ethical or even religious objections to reincarnation, however, would not have been those of Renaissance thinkers. For them it was the problem of accommodating or reconciling the story of Christ's incarnation with the stories of Pythagoras' reincarnations, of arriving at a Christian-Pythagorean vision of rebirth which was keyed to the casting off of a previous life of sin, and a putting on of the whole armor of God. But they could only arrive at this accommodating vision by way of the mediation of Plato and his school, .the only thinkers whom Augustine had valorized as being in possession of the truths that led to Christian conversion. Hence the wheel came in a way full circle. Plato, who had commenced as a follower of Pythagoras, though not endowed with the Samian's magical and shamanic powers, emerged eventually as the preeminent ancient authority, who, by way of Augustine's endorsement, could justify a sympathetic reading of the tributary Pythagorean mysteries. Hence the significance for Ficino of Plato's choice of Pythagorean speakers.

4. Pythagorean arithmology

Let us now turn to an argument that Ficino specifically identified as Pythagorean in his *Platonic Theology* 4.1.14–16, one that focuses, not as we might expect on the Pythagorean obsession with 10, but rather on the mystery and the symbolism of 12. It can serve to introduce what the Renaissance saw as Pythagoras' mathematical, though to us it is his arithmological legacy. In elaborating on the notion of being subject to the ruling soul of a sphere, Ficino turns to the triple images of emperor, king and prince. Any creature is subordinate, he argues, to the twelve ruler-souls or kings of the twelve spheres, the realms of the four elements, the seven planets, and the fixed stars. These ruler souls are identified with the twelve deities, beginning with the goddess of the Earth: Vesta, Neptune, Juno, Vulcan, Diana, Mercury, Venus, Apollo, Mars, Jupiter, Saturn and Uranus. These deities in turn are under the imperial sway of the World-Soul traditionally identified with Jupiter (who is thus seen in a twofold capacity as emperor of all the spheres, but as king of his planetary sphere). Within each sphere are twelve ranks or orders of souls – and Ficino obviously thinks of this as an explicitly Pythagorean feature.[41] Each of the twelve orders is ruled by a soul-prince, though each order contains numberless lesser souls. When gazing up at the celestial fire, at the uranian sphere, that is, of the fixed stars, we can see these twelve princes as the twelve zodiacal animals or constellations, or rather as their principal stars.[42] At the other end of the cosmic scale we encounter under the regal soul of the Earth the twelve kinds of earthy daemons and men, kinds which Ficino distinguishes here in terms of the ways they are governed by reason, wrath, and desire, or by just two of these "faculties" in various combinations. By extrapolation therefore, each of the ten other intermediary spheres has one soul-king and twelve subordinate orders led by twelve soul-princes.[43] Thus in the air (including the aethereal air) under regal Juno dwell the twelve orders of airy daemons; and in the water under king Neptune dwell the twelve kinds of watery daemons (usually characterized as nymphs); and similarly with each of the seven planetary spheres. Thus each particular soul has its place in a hierarchy of souls, ordered by twelves, and all under the soul-emperor, the World-Soul.[44] Each pure soul, moreover, possesses mind, a Jovian mind being equally, in the formulation of the *Philebus* 30d, both a royal mind and a royal soul.

For Ficino, this whole Pythagorean argument is embodied in the *Phaedrus'* depiction at 246eff. of the cavalcade led by Zeus of the eleven deities and the accompanying host of souls across the intellectual heaven – eleven because Hestia/Vesta "remained alone in the gods' dwelling place," even though she was one of the twelve cosmic gods.[45] Ficino connects this with another motif found, not as far as we know in Pythagoras, but certainly in Orpheus, Anaxagoras, Empedocles, Heraclitus and many of the Stoics: that of a cyclical and fated combustion of the world, a combustion that is followed by a reconstitution that results in the world's re-creation. The argument of the ancients is that cyclical time is part and parcel of God's handiwork. Ficino, interestingly, raises no Christian objection to this contention,[46] since he sees the notion of restitution as the result of the finite nature of, and the internal strife within creation itself, of its deficiency of form, a deficiency that God periodically compensates. "Such," he declares, "is the vision of these men."

---

[41] Numerologically 12 has always been significant. For Ficino see Allen 1994: 71–2.

[42] *Platonic Theology* 4.1.15.   [43] *Platonic Theology* 4.1.16.

[44] *Platonic Theology* 16.6.3–4 has further elaborations.

[45] See Allen 1984: 116–21, 139–43, 148–9, and 250–3.

[46] However, he Christianizes the notion of the end of a world cycle or aeon by interpreting it as the Last Judgment in his analysis of the myth in Plato's *Statesman*. See Allen 2008b.

Later in the *Platonic Theology* 17.2.11 Ficino argues that the Pythagoreans "use mathematical figures and numbers alike in figuring forth the soul," since souls, like mathematicals, are intermediate between the natural and the divine forms. Hence the Pythagoreans have established a triangle (the *Timaeus'* "lambda" figure) with 1 at the apex and 2–4–8 down one side and 3–9–27 down the other (35b–6b) to signify the soul; the descending numbers signify the soul's parts, powers, and offices. The seven numbers signify the seven planets: Saturn at one extreme causes changes every seven years, while the moon at the other causes changes every seven days even as the fetus is perfected in the womb in the seventh month and we thereafter live through seven ages (17.2.12). According to the Pythagoreans, the soul partakes of both odd and even numbers, and linear, plane and solid numbers are introduced to illustrate how "the soul extends itself with greatest ease through the length, breadth and depth of body" (17.2.13). Most importantly, they are convinced the soul is harmoniously compounded. At 17.2.14 Ficino declares that the shaping powers of numbers and figures are at "the very summit of the Pythagorean and Platonic mystery" – the tetraktys signifying the chariot of the soul in the *Phaedrus*, which Ficino defines in the Pythagorean manner as "self-moving number" (3.1.12), even as body is "infinite plurality" (1.2.4).[47]

In attributing to the Pythagoreans a fascination with 12 and 12^2 (and eventually with 12^3), Ficino was very aware of the role played by squaring and square-rooting – the two procedures identified in Greek mathematics with the notion of a number exercising its "power" or "powers" – in orchestrating the famous Pythagorean proof determining the value of any side of a right-angled triangle when the values of the other two sides are known. Now Ficino was especially concerned here with determining the number of the starry soul host, or rather its divisions and arrangement, and he specifically looked to the Pythagoreans for a duodecimal wisdom, though there are of course significant biblical references to twelve including $12^2 \times 10^3$ as the number of the saved. He was the more emboldened to do so given Plato's own Pythagorean sorties into the numerology of 12 in the *Phaedo* 110bff.; *Timaeus* 55c; *Critias* 109b, 113b–c; *Phaedrus* 246e–7e; and obviously in the twelve books of his *Laws*, 12 being the number into which the Athenian Stranger had divided the state's capital city.

---

[47] Ficino says Xenocrates appropriated this formulation from the Pythagoreans, though he is usually credited with it.

Most importantly, Ficino asserts that 12 was "secretly venerated" in the *Republic* Book 8 in Plato's mystificatory reference to the fatal number. After years contemplating this enigma, Ficino decided in his last decade that he had mastered enough Pythagorean-Platonic mathematical wisdom, with its arcane categories, terms and strategies, to write a commentary on it (the *On the Fatal Number* of 1496). Having elaborated a number of intricate numerological arguments, he concluded that the value of Plato's fatal number had to be 12^3. Not only was 12 the sum of the three sides of the first perfect Pythagorean right triangle of 3–4–5, it was also divisible by 2, 3, 4 [and 6] and thus contained the fundamental musical ratios of 2:1 (double), 3:2 (sesquialteral) and 4:3 (sesquitertial), and hence the octave, the perfect fifth, and the perfect fourth. Moreover, as 3 × 4, twelve was a spousal number and at the same time the first and the prince of the "abundant" numbers, meaning that the sum of its factors of 6 + 4 + 3 + 2 + 1 exceeded itself (by a third as much again). As such it designated fertility. Even more significantly, he argues, 12^3 could be triply partitioned into 1000, 700 and 28, units which in turn had to be interpreted by reference to diagonal and lateral numbers. And so on.

Ficino was able to cut the Gordian knot of this fatal number only by way of consulting the mathematical treatises of Nicomachus, Theon and Iamblichus, and by mastering their terminology.[48] None of the treatises had solved Plato's most challenging crux, but together they provided Ficino with the tools to do so. It was their Pythagorean mathematical wisdom that had led him to determine the duodecimal value of the fatal number (along with the values of other numbers, fatal and nuptial, in its train), and had given him the ability to extract it from the matrix in which it was embedded: to unravel as it were Plato's mathematical equivalent to a Pythagorean *symbolum* or golden dictum. In short, the determination of the fatal number to which Plato had subordinated the lifetime of an ideal republic, was a Pythagorean triumph and the power and mystery of 1728 must have been known to the Master himself. For Ficino, it held out the prospect of determining not only the times of the great periodic cycles of astronomy, of Saturn and Jupiter's conjunctions and oppositions and those signified by various fatal and nuptial, lateral and diagonal numbers, but also of determining prophetic time itself, the time of an Isaiah, a John the Baptist, or, for a while, a Savonarola. Such a prophetic time looked

---

[48] For a comprehensive account of this Pythagorean mathematics and its categories, see Michel 1950 and 1958. There is a debt too to Boethius' mathematical treatises given their authority in the Middle Ages.

to Christ's second coming and to the perfection of all things, when the
sublunar world of 10s and the celestial realm of 12s alike would be subsumed
at last in God's hexadic time, the six days of His Creation being the perfect
sum of its parts and the product of its factors.

5. Pythagorean *symbola*

Iamblichus' *On the Pythagorean Life* also emphasizes the terse nature of
the master's sayings, his gnomic wisdom (157), and his "riddling symbols"
(227). This surely refers to the utterance of the *Symbola*[49] and the *Golden
Verses*, though the latter is, to quote Celenza, "a doctrinal poem [. . .]
coherent though gnomic," whereas the *Symbola* are "a loose configuration of apophthegmata," of "cultic taboo-precepts,"[50] originating in the
Pythagorean communities of the fifth century BC.[51] Iamblichus gives the
fullest ancient listing of the *Symbola* in his *Protreptic*, but provides another
long list in *On the Pythagorean Life* (82–7). In the latter he declares that
"the entire Pythagorean training was distinctive and symbolic, resembling
riddles and puzzles, at least in its sayings, because of its archaic style, just
like the Delphic oracles" (247). While it would be absurd to take everything
resembling a maxim in the Western tradition, everything that is succinct or
apophthegmatic, and attribute it to the influence of Pythagoras, nonetheless compactness and enigma have had signal roles to play both in wisdom
literature and in negative theology. In the sixth chapter of his commentary
on the treatise by the pseudo-Areopagite, *On Mystical Theology*, Ficino
writes that the further away the mind is from contemplating the supreme
hypostasis, the One, the more words and the more arguments it needs to
deploy. Contrariwise, the closer the mind approaches the One, the fewer

---

[49] For Renaissance commentaries on the *Symbola*, see Alberti's *Veiled Sayings*, one of his *Dinner Pieces*
(77–82 Garin); Antonio degli Agli's *Explication of the Symbola of Pythagoras* (in Swogger 1975);
Giovanni Nesi's commentary (in Celenza 2001); and the explications of Filippo Beroaldo, Erasmus,
Reuchlin and Lilio Gregorio Giraldi in the sixteenth century (Celenza 2001: 52–81).

[50] Celenza 2001: 6–7. The lists vary and we cannot assume that all the *symbola* are by Pythagoras
himself. For the testimonies see DK 58C. Various patristic works commented on various symbols:
Clement of Alexandria's *Miscellanies*, Origen's *Against Heresies*, Ambrose's letter to Irenaeus and
Jerome's *Letter against Rufinus* (this treats briefly of thirteen symbols); see Celenza 2001: 10–12 with
further references. Swogger argues that Jerome's list was at the center of what little medieval
discussion there was of the symbols in Vincent of Beauvais, Walter Burley and others (1975: 44–7).
Additionally, seven are cited in the infamous medieval magic manual, the *Picatrix*; see Celenza 2001:
12–13.

[51] Burkert 1972a: 189, traces them back to the sixth century BC and to Pythagoras himself.

the words it needs; and at the moment when it is finally enraptured, it contemplates in wordless silence.[52] This is an aspect of the Pythagorean, and later the Socratic insistence on guarded oral instruction, which is aimed at bringing the disciple to the moment when the flint is struck and the divine spark (in the famous analogy in Plato's *Seventh Letter* 341c–d) sets the mind on fire. In his *On Christian Religion* 34, Ficino even suggests that the precepts of Moses were in form of expression akin to the Pythagorean *symbola*.[53]

Pythagorean maxims are likened to the little seeds which give rise in nature to an enormous abundance (*VP* 161); for the Master's "brevity of speech conceals a boundless treasury of knowledge" (162). Take for example the saying "all things correspond to number," or "love is equality," or the articulation of the tetraktys. These golden dicta and oracular statements were so revered by his followers "that they became a form of oath" (162);[54] and they were also what Ficino admired in Plato. For along with the flowers of his Attic oratory, his often labyrinthine argumentation and refutations, and his daedal flights of myth, Plato was also the fountainhead of lapidary *sententiae*. In this regard he was a disciple of Pythagoras and of the wisdom traditions preceding him: indeed, seen through these lenses, all the ancient theologians were esteemed as the authors of golden sayings that spoke to moments when prolixity must yield to brevity. One might even argue that for Ficino it was the authority of the Pythagorean *Golden Verses* that established the sapiential dictum as Plato's own – and one thinks of the famous enigmas in the *Second* and *Sixth Letters* and of other knotty formulations that the Neoplatonic tradition, ancient and early modern, had culled from the dialogues themselves.

6. Conclusion: the apotheosis of Pythagoras

For the early Renaissance at least, Plato was not only indebted to Pythagoras as his illustrious predecessor – Iamblichus' treatise says that he lived seven generations after Pythagoras (*VP* 265) – but he was himself a Pythagorean, or rather the perfection of Pythagorean wisdom, the perfected reincarnation, figuratively at least, of the Samian himself. Hence the new age's revival

---

[52] Opera 1018.3 entitled *Quomodo Deus apparet in silentio*, and commenting on 1000C.
[53] *Opera*: 69 (*tamquam figurae quaedam Pythagoricorum simbulorum instar*). See Celenza 2001: 22–3.
[54] *Platonic Theology* 17.4.10 and 18.8.1 quote the concluding lines of the *Golden Sayings* 70–1 ("soul yearns for aether where we will become an immortal god, mortal no more") and lines 47–8 and 63–4 are quoted at 9.1.3, 11.5.3 and 14.8.2.

of Neoplatonism was also a revival of the old Neopythagoreanism of later antiquity in which the Neoplatonists had participated. It is a complicated situation, obviously, but all of a piece.

The sixteenth century saw what Christiane Joost-Gaugier characterizes as "the apotheosis of Pythagoras."[55] Particularly striking is the claim of Johannes Reuchlin (1455–1522) that the Samian "drew his stream of learning from the boundless sea of Kabbalah," and that he was uniquely able to understand the secrets of Moses and consequently could not have believed in metempsychosis. Thus he was not a purveyor of the ancient theology of the Gentiles, as he had been for Ficino but rather a mediator between Christianity and the ancient Jewish wisdom.[56] Paracelsus (c. 1493–1541) was also drawn to the notion of Pythagoras' Jewish wisdom, though he also accounted him a magus and an alchemist who had found his way to the philosopher's stone, a role already assigned Pythagoras in the Middle Ages. Two important Franciscans, the Venetian patrician Francesco Zorzi (1460–1540) and Egidio of Viterbo (c. 1469–1532), the Vicar General of the Augustinian order in Rome, championed the notion that Moses was the source of the wisdom that Pythagoras transmitted to Plato. Guillaume Postel (1510–1581) entertained the bizarre idea that the ancient French Druids had inherited Pythagoras' number symbolism and mathematical wisdom, notably his account of the five regular solids. The solids also obsessed the great Johannes Kepler (1571–1630) who looked to Pythagoras and Plato as his true "preceptors" in astronomy and cosmology.[57] To Bernardino Baldi, in the opening paragraph of his biography of Pythagoras of 1588, the Samian was "the prince of Italian philosophy," while to Reuchlin he was "the prince of *all* philosophers." Even the mocking spirit of Gianpaolo Lomazzo (1538–1600) testified to the prestige of Pythagoras: in his youthful *Book of Dreams* Lomazzo imagines the sage's soul as having just left the body of Pietro Aretino (1492–1566), the famous egotist, writer and pornographer, even as it had formerly inhabited the gorgeous body of Helen of Troy and the bodies of other sexually active and attractive women, as well as the body of an Indian ant.[58]

Nonetheless, in the age's consideration at large, as distinct from the views of various individuals, Pythagoras never eclipsed the supreme authority, intellectual and spiritual, of Plato and the Platonists. And it is Renaissance Neoplatonism that dominates our attention still as intellectual historians, not Renaissance Neopythagoreanism. This is in large part because, given

---

[55] Joost-Gaugier 2009: Ch. 3.   [56] Joost-Gaugier 2009: 43–4, and in general 108–41.
[57] Joost-Gaugier 2009: 45–55, with further details.   [58] Joost-Gaugier 2009: 52–4.

the absence of a monumental single-author oeuvre such as the Platonic dialogues, its surviving witnesses consist of tesserae, of fragmentary insights, however profound, as is the case with other Presocratics. By the same token, however, Pythagoras and his school emerged for the Renaissance as the most authoritative of the Presocratic philosophers, and as the vital link between the Athenian Academy and its luminous Ionian, Italic, Thracian, Egyptian and even Chaldaean sources.

Bibliography

Please see also the abbreviations page ix.

Aalders, G. J. D. 1968. *Die Theorie der gemischten Verfassung im Altertum*. Amsterdam: Hakkert.

1975. *Political Thought in Hellenistic Times*. Amsterdam: Hakkert.

Adler, A. 1971. *Suidae Lexicon*. Stuttgart: Teubner.

Albrecht, M. von 1966. "Das Menschenbild in Jamblichs Darstellung der pythagoreischen Lebensform," *Antike und Abendland* 12: 51–63 [repr. in Albrecht, Dillon, George, Lurje and Du Toit 2002, pp. 255–74].

Albrecht, M. von, Dillon, J., George, M., Lurje, M. and Du Toit, D. S. (eds.) 2002. *Jamblich. Pythagoras: Legende – Lehre – Lebensgestaltung*. Darmstadt: Wissenschaftliche Buchgesellschaft.

Alderink, L. J. 1981. *Creation and Salvation in Ancient Orphism*. University Park, PA: Chico, CA: American Philological Association; Scholars' Press.

Allen, M. J. B. 1984. *The Platonism of Marsilio Ficino*. Berkeley/Los Angeles: University of California Press.

1994. *Nuptial Arithmetic: Marsilio Ficino's Commentary on the Fatal Number in Book VIII of Plato's Republic*. Berkeley/Los Angeles: University of California Press.

1998. *Synoptic Art: Marsilio Ficino on the History of Platonic Interpretation*. Florence: Olschki.

(ed.) 2008a. *Marsilio Ficino: Commentaries on Plato*. Vol. 1: *Phaedrus and Ion*. Cambridge, MA: Harvard University Press.

2008b. "Quisque in sphaera sua: Plato's *Statesman*, Marsilio Ficino's *Platonic Theology* and the Resurrection of the Body," *Rinascimento* 2nd ser. 47: 25–48.

2012. "Eurydice in Hades: Florentine Platonism and an Orphic Mystery," in Caroti, S. and Perrone Compagni, V. (eds.). *Nuovi maestri e antichi testi: Umanesimo e Rinascimento alle origini del pensiero moderno*. Florence: Olschki, pp. 19–40.

Allen, M. J. B. and Hankins, J. with Bowen, W. (tr. and ed.) 2001–2006. *Marsilio Ficino: Platonic Theology*. 6 vols. I Tatti Renaissance Library. Cambridge, MA: Harvard University Press.

Allen, M. J. B. and Rees, V. with Davies, M. (eds.) 2002. *Marsilio Ficino: His Theology, His Philosophy, His Legacy*. Leiden: Brill.

Altheim, F. and Stiehl, R. 1954. *Porphyrios und Empedokles*. Tübingen: M. Niemeyer [repr. in Sezgin, F. (ed.) 2000. *Democritus, Theophrastus, Zenon, Bryson (?), Porphyrius, Themistius and Johannes Philoponus in the Arabic Tradition: Texts and Studies*. Frankfurt am Main: Institute for the History of Arabic-Islamic Science at the Johann Wolfgang Goethe University, pp. 139–82].

1961. "New Fragments of Greek Philosophers," *East and West* (n.s.) 12: 3–18.

Amato, E. (ed.) 2005 and 2010. *Favorinos d'Arles: Œuvres*, vols. 1 and 3. Paris: Les Belles Lettres.

Anderson, G. 1986. *Philostratus: Biography and Belles Lettres in the Third Century A.D.* London: Croom Helm.

Andorlini, I. and Luiselli, R. 2001. "Una ripresa di Diotogene Pitagorico, 'Sulla regalità,' in PBingen 3 (Encomio per Augusto?)," *Zeitschrift für Papyrologie und Epigraphik* 136: 155–66.

André, J. 1958. "Pythagorisme et botanique," *Revue de philologie, de littérature et d'histoire anciennes* 32: 218–43.

Annas, J. 1976. *Aristotle's Metaphysics: Books M and N*. Oxford: Clarendon.

Anton, J. P. 1992. "The Pythagorean Way of Life: Morality and Religion," in Boudouris (ed.), pp. 28–40.

Armisen-Marchetti, M. (ed.) 2001–2003. *Macrobe: Commentaire au Songe de Scipion*. 2 vols. Paris: Les Belles Lettres.

Armstrong, A. H. (tr.) 1966. "Porphyry: On the Life of Plotinus and the Order of His Books," in *Plotinus: Porphyry on Plotinus, Ennead 1*. Loeb Classical Library. Cambridge, MA: Harvard University Press, pp. 1–87.

Asztalos, M. 1993. "Boethius as a Transmitter of Greek Logic to the Latin West: The *Categories*," *Harvard Studies in Classical Philology* 95: 367–407.

Athanassiadi, P. (ed.) 1999. *Damascius. The Philosophical History*. Athens: Apamea.

2006. *La Lutte pour l'orthodoxie dans le platonisme tardif: de Numénius à Damascius*. Paris: Les Belles Lettres.

Balch, D. L. 1992. "Neopythagorean Moralists and the New Testament Household Codes," *ANRW* 26.1: 380–410.

Baltes, M. 1972. *Timaios Lokros: Über die Natur des Kosmos und der Seele*. Leiden: Brill.

1976. *Die Weltentstehung des platonischen Timaios nach den antiken Interpreten*, vol. 1. Leiden: Brill.

Baltzly, D. 2009. *Proclus on the World Soul (Proclus: Commentary on Plato's Timaeus vol. 4. Book 3, Part II)*. Cambridge University Press.

Barbanti, M., Giardina, G. R. and Manganaro, P. (eds.) 2002. *Henosis kai philia / Unione e amicizia*. Catania: CUECM.

Barbera, A. 1981. "*Republic* 530C–531C: Another Look at Plato and the Pythagoreans," *American Journal of Philology* 102: 395–410.

1984. "The Consonant Eleventh and the Expansion of the Musical Tetraktys: A Study of Ancient Pythagoreanism," *Journal of Music Theory* 28: 191–223.

1991. *The Euclidean Division of the Canon: Greek and Latin Sources*. Lincoln, NE/London: University of Nebraska Press.

Barker, A. 1978. "ΣΥΜΦΩΝΟΙ ἈΡΙΘΜΟΙ: A note on *Republic* 531C1–4," *Classical Philology* 73: 337–42.
 1984. *Greek Musical Writings I: The Musician and his Art.* Cambridge University Press.
 1989. *Greek Musical Writings II: Harmonic and Acoustic Theory.* Cambridge University Press.
 1994. "Ptolemy's Pythagoreans, Archytas, and Plato's Conception of Mathematics," *Phronesis* 39.2: 113–35.
 2000. *Scientific Method in Ptolemy's Harmonics.* Cambridge University Press.
 2006. "Archytas Unbound. A Discussion of Carl A. Huffman. *Archytas of Tarentum,*" *Oxford Studies in Ancient Philosophy* 31: 297–321.
 2007. *The Science of Harmonics in Classical Greece.* Cambridge University Press.
 2010. "Mathematical Beauty Made Audible: Musical Aesthetics in Ptolemy's *Harmonics,*" *Classical Philology* 105: 403–20.
Barnes, J. 1982 [1979]. *The Presocratic Philosophers,* rev. edn. London: Routledge & Kegan Paul.
 1986. "Nietzsche and Diogenes Laertius," *Nietzsche-Studien* 15: 16–40.
Baron, C. 2009. "The Use and Abuse of Historians: Polybios' Book XII and the Evidence for Timaios," *Ancient Society* 39: 1–34.
Becchi, F. 1992. "L'ideale della *metriopatheia* nei testi pseudopitagorici: a proposito di una contraddizione nello Ps.-Archita," *Prometheus* 2: 102–20.
Becker, O. 1936. "Die Lehre vom Geraden und Ungeraden im neunten Buch der Euklidischen Elemente," *Quellen und Studien zur Geschichte der Mathematik, Astronomie und Physik* B 3: 533–53.
Bélis, A. 1983. "Le procédé de numération du pythagoricien Eurytos," *Revue des études grecques* 96: 64–75.
Bendlin, A. 2011. "On the Uses and Disadvantages of Divination: Oracles and Their Literary Representations in the Time of the Second Sophistic," in North and Price (eds.), pp. 175–250.
Bernabé, A. 1995. "Una etimología platónica: σῶμα-σῆμα," *Philologus* 139: 204–37.
 2004–2005. *Poetae epici graeci. Testimonia et fragmenta. Pars II. Orphicorum et Orphicis similium testimonia et fragmenta.* Fasc. 1 and Fasc. 2. Munich/Leipzig: K. G. Saur.
 2008. "El mito órfico de Dioniso y los Titanes," in Bernabé and Casadesús (eds.), pp. 591–607.
 2011. "La transmigración entre los órficos," in Bernabé, Kahle and Santamaría (eds.), pp. 179–210.
Bernabé, A. and Casadesús, F. (eds.) 2008. *Orfeo y la tradición órfica: un reencuentro.* Madrid: Ediciones Akal.
Bernabé, A. and Hernández Muñoz, F. G. 2010. *Manual de crítica textual y edición de textos griegos.* Madrid: Ediciones Akal.
Bernabé, A. and Jiménez San Cristóbal, A. I. 2008. *Instructions for the Netherworld: The Orphic Gold Tablets.* Leiden/Boston, MA: Brill.
Bernabé, A., Kahle, M. and Santamaría, M. A. (eds.) 2011. *Reencarnación: la transmigración de las almas entre Oriente y Occidente.* Madrid: Abada Editores.

Bernhard, M. and Bower, C. (eds.) 1993–2011. *Glossa maior in institutionem musicam Boethii.* 4 vols. Munich: Bayerische Akademie der Wissenschaften.

Betegh, G. 2004. *The Derveni Papyrus: Cosmology, Theology, and Interpretation.* Cambridge University Press.

Betegh, G., Pedriali, F. and Pfeiffer, C. 2013. "The Perfection of Bodies. Aristotle, *De Caelo* I.1," *Rhizomata* 1.1: 30–62.

Bezner, F. 2005. *Vela Veritatis. Hermeneutik, Wissen und Sprache in der Intellectual History des 12. Jahrhunderts.* Studien und Texte zur Geistesgeschichte des Mittelalters, 85. Leiden: Brill.

Bichler, R. 2000. *Herodots Welt. Der Aufbau der Historie am Bild der fremden Länder und Völker, ihrer Zivilisation und ihrer Geschichte.* Berlin: Akademie.

Bicknell, P. 1966. "The Date of the Battle of the Sagra River," *Phoenix* 20: 294–301.

Bidez, J. 1894. *La Biographie d'Empédocle.* Ghent: Clemm [repr. 1973 Hildesheim and New York: Olms].

Bieler, L. 1935. *Theios Aner. Das Bild des "göttlichen Menschen" in Spätantike und Frühchristentum.* Vienna: Höfels.

Bilbija, J. and Flinterman, J. J. 2006. "De markt voor mantiek. Droomverklaring en andere divinatorische praktijken in de *Oneirocritica* van Artemidorus," *Lampas* 39: 246–66.

Billault, A. 2000. *L'Univers de Philostrate.* Brussels: Éditions Latomus.

Blank, D. 2012. "Varro and Antiochus," in Sedley (ed.), pp. 250–89.

Blech, M. 1982. *Studien zum Kranz bei den Griechen.* Berlin/New York: De Gruyter.

Blumenthal, H. J. and Clark, E. G. (eds.) 1993. *The Divine Iamblichus: Philosopher and Man of Gods.* London: Bristol Classical Press.

Bodnár, I. and Fortenbaugh, W. W. (eds.) 2002. *Eudemus of Rhodes.* New Brunswick, NJ: Transaction.

Böhm, F. 1905. "De symbolis Pythagoreis." Diss. Friedrich-Wilhelms-Universität, Berlin.

Bollansée, J. (ed.) 1999a. *Die Fragmente der Griechischen Historiker Continued. IV.A.3. Hermippos of Smyrna.* Leiden: Brill.

    1999b. *Hermippos of Smyrna and His Biographical Writings. A Reappraisal.* Leuven: Peeters.

    2008. "Clearchus' Treatise *On Modes of Life* and the Theme of *Tryphè*," *Ktema* 33: 403–11.

Bonazzi, M. 2000. "Plotino e la tradizione pitagorica," *Acme* 53: 39–73.

    2005. "Eudoro di Alessandria alle origini del platonismo imperiale," in Bonazzi and Celluprica (eds.), pp. 115–60.

    2007. "Eudorus and Early Imperial Platonism," in Sharples and Sorabji (eds.), pp. 365–78.

    2013a. "Eudorus of Alexandria and the 'Pythagorean' Pseudepigrapha," in Cornelli, McKirahan and Macris (eds.), pp. 385–404.

    2013b. "Pythagoreanizing Aristotle: Eudorus and the Systematization of Platonism," in Schofield (ed.), pp. 160–86.

Bonazzi, M. and Celluprica, V. (eds.) 2005. *L'eredità platonica. Studi sul platonismo da Arcesilao a Proclo.* Naples: Bibliopolis.

Bonazzi, M., Lévy, C. and Steel, C. (eds.) 2007. *A Platonic Pythagoras: Platonism and Pythagoreanism in the Imperial Age.* Turnhout: Brepols.

Bonazzi, M. and Opsomer, J. (eds.) 2009. *The Origins of the Platonic System. Platonisms of the Early Empire and Their Philosophical Contexts.* Leuven: Peeters.

Bonitz, H. 1848. *Aristotelis Metaphysica.* Pars Prior. Bonn: Marcus.

1849. *Aristotelis Metaphysica.* Pars Posterior. Bonn: Marcus.

1870. *Index Aristotelicus (Aristotelis Opera. Edidit Academia Regia Borussica. Volumen Quintum).* Berlin: Reimer.

Boudouris, K. J. (ed.) 1989. *Ionian Philosophy.* Athens: International Association for Greek Philosophy.

(ed.) 1992. *Pythagorean Philosophy.* Athens: International Center for Greek Philosophy and Culture.

Bouffartigue, J. and Patillon, M. (eds.) 1977–1979. *Porphyre. De l'abstinence.* 2 vols. (Books 1–3). Paris: Les Belles Lettres.

Bower, C. 1978. "Boethius and Nicomachus: An Essay Concerning the Sources of *De institutione musica*," *Vivarium* 16: 1–45.

(tr.) 1989. *Fundamentals of Music: Anicius Manlius Severinus Boethius.* New Haven, CT: Yale University Press.

Bowie, E. L. 1978. "Apollonius of Tyana: Tradition and Reality," in *ANRW* 2.16.2: 1652–99.

Bowie, E. and Elsner, J. (eds.) 2009. *Philostratus.* Cambridge University Press.

Boyancé, P. 1936. *Études sur le Songe de Scipion.* Limoges: Imprimerie A. Bontemps.

1937. *Le Culte des Muses chez les philosophes grecs.* Paris: de Boccard (2nd ed. 1972).

1939. "Sur la vie pythagoricienne," *Revue des études grecques* 52: 36–50.

1967. "Note sur l'éther chez les Pythagoriciens, Platon et Aristote," *Revue des études grecques* 80: 202–9.

1975. "Étymologie et théologie chez Varron," *Revue des études latines* 53: 99–115.

1976. "Les implications philosophiques des recherches de Varron sur la religion romaine," in *Atti del congresso internazionale di studi varroniani.* Vol. 1. Rieti: Centro di studi varroniani editore, pp. 137–61.

Bragard, R. 1955. *Jacobi Leodiensis Speculum musicae.* 7 vols. Rome: American Institute of Musicology.

Brancacci, A. 1996. "Dialettica e retorica in Antistene," *Elenchos* 17: 359–406.

2002. "Porfirio e Antistene: τρόπος e πολυτροπία in SSR V A 187," in Barbanti, Giardina and Manganaro (eds.), pp. 410–17.

Bremmer, J. N. 1987. "Orpheus: A Poet among Men," in Bremmer, J. N. (ed.), *Interpretations of Greek Mythology.* London/Sydney: Croom Helm, pp. 80–106.

1992. "Symbols of Marginality from Early Pythagoreans to Late Antique Monks," *Greece and Rome* 39: 205–14.

1999. "Rationalization and Disenchantment in Ancient Greece: Max Weber among the Pythagoreans and Orphics?," in Buxton (ed.), pp. 71–83.

2002. *The Rise and Fall of the Afterlife.* London/New York: Routledge.

Brisson, L. 2002. "Orphée, Pythagore et Platon. Le mythe qui établit cette lignée," in Kobusch and Erler (eds.), pp. 415–27.

Brisson, L. and Segonds, A. 1996. *Jamblique, Vie de Pythagore*. Paris: Les Belles Lettres [2nd edn. 2011].

Broadie, S. 1999. "Rational Theology," in Long (ed.), pp. 205–24.

Brown, P. 1978. *The Making of Late Antiquity*. Cambridge, MA: Harvard University Press.

Brown, T. S. 1958. *Timaeus of Tauromenium*. Berkeley/Los Angeles: University of California Press.

Buechner, K. 1982. *Fragmenta poetarum Latinorum epicorum et lyricorum praeter Ennium et Lucilium*. Leipzig: Teubner.

Burch, G. B. 1954. "The Counter-Earth," *Osiris* 11: 267–94.

Burgess, R. W. 2002. "Jerome Explained: An Introduction to His *Chronicle* and a Guide to Its Use," *The Ancient History Bulletin* 16: 1–32.

Burkert, W. 1960. "Platon oder Pythagoras? Zum Ursprung des Wortes 'Philosophie,'" *Hermes* 88: 159–77 (reprint in Burkert 2006, pp. 217–35).

1961. "Hellenistische Pseudopythagorica," *Philologus* 105: 16–43 and 226–46 (reprint in Burkert 2006, pp. 236–77).

1962a. Review of Thesleff 1961. *Gnomon* 34: 763–8.

1962b. *Weisheit und Wissenschaft: Studien zu Pythagoras, Philolaos und Platon*. Nuremberg: Hans Carl.

1968. "Orpheus und die Vorsokratiker. Bemerkungen zum Derveni-Papyrus und zur pythagoreischen Zahlenlehre," *Antike und Abendland* 14: 93–114 (reprint in Burkert 2006, pp. 62–88).

1972a. *Lore and Science in Ancient Pythagoreanism*. Tr. of Burkert 1962b by Minar, E. with revisions. Cambridge, MA: Harvard University Press.

1972b. "Zur geistesgeschichtlichen Einordnung einiger Pseudopythagorica," in von Fritz (ed.), pp. 25–55 (+ discussion, pp. 88–102) (reprint in Burkert 2006, pp. 278–98 [without the discussion]).

1977. "Orphism and Bacchic Mysteries: New Evidence and Old Problems of Interpretation," *Colloquy* 28. *The Center for Hermeneutical Studies in Hellenistic and Modern Culture* (Berkeley), pp. 1–8 (+ discussion, pp. 9–48) (reprint in Burkert 2006, pp. 37–46 [without the discussion]).

1982. "Craft versus Sect: The Problem of Orphics and Pythagoreans," in Meyer, B. F. and Sanders, E. P. (eds.), *Jewish and Christian Self-Definition*. Vol. 3: *Self-Definition in the Graeco-Roman World*. London: SMC Press, pp. 1–22 and 183–9 (reprint in Burkert 2006, pp. 191–216).

1985. *Greek Religion*. Cambridge, MA: Harvard University Press.

1998. "Pythagoreische Retraktationen: Von den Grenzen einer möglichen Edition," in Burkert, Gemelli Marciano, Matelli and Orelli (eds.), pp. 303–19 (reprint in Burkert 2006, pp. 299–316).

2003. *Die Griechen und der Orient. Von Homer bis zu den Magiern*. Munich: Beck. Revised translation of 1999. *Da Omero ai magi*. Venice: Marsilio Editori.

2004. *Babylon, Memphis, Persepolis: Eastern Contexts of Greek Culture*. Cambridge, MA: Harvard University Press.

2006. *Kleine Schriften*, III: *Mystica, Orphica, Pythagorica*, ed. Fr. Graf, Göttingen: Vandenhoeck & Ruprecht.

2011. *Griechische Religion der archaischen und klassischen Epoche*. 2nd edn. Stuttgart: Kohlhammer.

Burkert, W., Gemelli Marciano, L., Matelli, E. and Orelli, L. (eds.) 1998. *Fragmentsammlungen philosophischer Texte der Antike*. Göttingen: Vandenhoeck & Ruprecht.

Burkhard, K. (ed.) 1917. *Nemesii episcopi Premnon physicon siue ΠΕΡΙ ΦΥΣΕΩΣ ΑΝΘΡΩΠΟΥ liber a N. Alfano archiepiscopo Salerni in latinum translatus*. Leipzig: Teubner.

Burnett, C. (ed. and tr.) 1998. *Adelard of Bath: Conversations with His Nephew*. Cambridge University Press.

Burnett, C., Fend, M. and Gouk, P. (eds.) 1991. *The Second Sense: Studies in Hearing and Musical Judgement from Antiquity to the Seventeenth Century*. London: The Warburg Institute.

Burnet, J. 1930. *Early Greek Philosophy*. 4th edn. London: Macmillan.

Burnyeat, M. F. 2000. "Plato on Why Mathematics Is Good for the Soul," in Smiley, T. (ed.), *Mathematics and Necessity: Essays in the History of Philosophy*. Oxford University Press, pp. 1–81.

2005. "Archytas and Optics," *Science in Context* 18: 35–53.

Bury, R. G. (tr.) 1929. *Plato: Timaeus, Critias, Cleitophon, Menexenus, Epistles*. Cambridge, MA: Harvard University Press.

Buxton, R. (ed.) 1999. *From Myth to Reason? Studies in the Development of Greek Thought*. Oxford University Press.

Caiazzo, I. 2000. *Lectures médiévales de Macrobe. Les Glosae Colonienses super Macrobium*. Paris: Vrin.

Calabi, F. 2008. *God's Acting, Man's Acting: Tradition and Philosophy in Philo of Alexandria*. Leiden: Brill.

Canfora, L. 1994. "Clemente di Alessandria e Diogene Laerzio," in *Storia, poesia e pensiero nel mondo antico. Studi in onore di Marcello Gigante*. Naples: Bibliopolis, pp. 79–81.

Cannata, D. B., Ilnitchi Currie, G., Mueller, R. C. and Nádas, J. L. (eds.) 2008. *Quomodo cantabimus canticum? Studies in Honor of Edward H. Roesner*. Middleton, WI: American Institute of Musicology.

Capelle, W. 1906. "Zur Geschichte der griechischen Botanik," *Philologus* 69: 264–91.

1961. "Menestor Redivivus," *Rheinisches Museum* 104: 47–69.

Carcopino, J. 1926. *La Basilique pythagoricienne de la Porte Majeure*. Paris: L'Artisan du livre.

1956. *De Pythagore aux apôtres. Études sur la conversion du monde romain*. Paris: Flammarion.

1963. *Rencontres de l'histoire et de la littérature romaines*. Paris: Flammarion.

Cardauns, B. 1960. *Varros Logistoricus über die Götterverehrung (Curio de cultu deorum). Ausgabe und Erklärung der Fragmente*. Würzburg: K. Triltsch.

2001. *Marcus Terentius Varro. Einführung in sein Werk*. Heidelberg: Winter.

Carone, G. R. 2005. *Plato's Cosmology and Its Ethical Dimensions*. Cambridge University Press.

Casadesús, F. B. 1994. "Heródoto II 81: ¿órficos o pitagóricos?," in *Actas del VIII congreso español de estudios clásicos*. Vol. 2. Madrid: Ediciones Clásicas, pp. 107–11.

2011. "Pitágoras y el concepto de transmigración," in Bernabé, Kahle and Santamaría (eds.), pp. 211–32.

Casadio, G. 1991. "La metempsicosi tra Orfeo e Pitagora," in Borgeaud, P. (ed.). *Orphisme et Orphée en l'honneur de Jean Rudhardt*. Geneva: Droz, pp. 119–55.

Casertano, G. 2000. "Orfismo e pitagorismo in Empedocle?," in Tortorelli Ghidini, Storchi Marino and Visconti (eds.), pp. 195–236.

Cassio, A. C. 1988. "Nicomachus of Gerasa and the Dialect of Archytas Fr. 1," *Classical Quarterly* n.s. 38: 135–9.

Castelletti, C. (ed.) 2006. *Porfirio: Sullo Stige*. Milan: Bompiani.

Cavalieri, M. C. 2002. "La Rassegna dei filosofi di Filodemo: scuola eleatica ed abderita (PHerc 327) e scuola pitagorica (PHerc 1508)," *Papyrologica Lupiensia* 11: 17–53.

Celenza, C. S. 1999. "Pythagoras in the Renaissance: The Case of Marsilio Ficino," *Renaissance Quarterly* 52: 667–711.

2001. *Piety and Pythagoras in Renaissance Florence: The Symbolum Nesianum*. Leiden: Brill.

2002. "Temi neopitagorici nel pensiero di Marsilio Ficino," in Toussaint, S. (ed.), *Marsile Ficin ou les mystères platoniciens*. Paris: Les Belles Lettres, pp. 57–70.

Centrone, B. 1990. *Pseudopythagorica ethica. I trattati morali di Archita, Metopo, Teage, Eurifamo*. Naples: Bibliopolis.

1992. "L'VIII libro delle *Vite* di Diogene Laerzio," *ANRW* 2.36.6: 4183–217.

1996. *Introduzione a i pitagorici*. Bari: Laterza.

2000a. "Cosa significa essere pitagorico in età imperiale: per una riconsiderazione della categoria storiografica del neopitagorismo," in Brancacci, A. (ed.), *La filosofia in età imperiale*. Vol. 1: *Le scuole e le tradizioni filosofiche*. Naples: Bibliopolis, pp. 137–68.

2000b. "La letteratura pseudopitagorica: origine, diffusione e finalità," in Cerri, G. (ed.), *La letteratura pseudepigrafa nella cultura greca e romana*. Naples: Istituto Universitario Orientale, pp. 429–52.

2000c. "Platonism and Pythagoreanism in the Early Empire," in Rowe and Schofield (eds.), pp. 559–84.

2005. "Nicomaque de Gérasa," in Goulet (ed.) Vol. 4, pp. 686–90.

Centrone, B. and Macris, C. 2005. "Modératus de Gadès," in Goulet (ed.) Vol. 4, pp. 545–8.

Chadwick, H. 1959. *The Sentences of Sextus: A Contribution to the History of Early Christian Ethics*. Cambridge University Press.

Chaniotis, A. 2002. "Old Wine in a New Skin: Tradition and Innovation in the Cult Foundation of Alexander of Abonouteichos," in Dabrowa (ed.), pp. 67–85.

Chapoutier, F. 1928. "Sur la libation pythagoricienne," *Revue des études grecques* 30: 201–4.

Chemla, K. and Guo, S. 2004. *Les Neuf Chapitres: le classique mathématique de la Chine ancienne et ses commentaires.* Paris: Dunod.

Cherniss, H. 1935. *Aristotle's Criticism of Presocratic Philosophy.* Baltimore, MD: Johns Hopkins University Press (reprint 1976, New York: Octagon).

1944. *Aristotle's Criticism of Plato and the Academy.* Vol. 1. Baltimore, MD: Johns Hopkins University Press.

1945. *The Riddle of the Early Academy.* Berkeley: University of California Press.

1976. *Plutarch: Moralia.* Vol. 13, part 1. Loeb Classical Library. Cambridge, MA: Harvard University Press, pp. 133–365.

Chiaradonna, R. 2009. "Autour d'Eudore. Les débuts de l'exégèse des *Catégories* dans le moyen platonisme," in Bonazzi and Opsomer (eds.), pp. 89–111.

Chiesara, M. L. 2001. *Aristocles of Messene: Testimonia and Fragments.* Oxford University Press.

Clark, G. 1989. *Iamblichus: On the Pythagorean Life.* Liverpool University Press.

2000. "Philosophic Lives and the Philosophic Life: Porphyry and Iamblichus," in Hägg, T. and Rousseau, P. (eds.). *Greek Biography and Panegyric in Late Antiquity.* Berkeley/Los Angeles: University of California Press, pp. 29–51.

Clark, S. and Leach, E. E. (eds.) 2005. *Citation and Authority in Medieval and Renaissance Musical Culture: Learning from the Learned.* Woodbridge: Boydell.

Cohen-Skalli, A. 2010. "À propos de l'anecdote pythagoricienne de Phintias et Damon: extrait du Pseudo-Maxime, un nouveau témoin d'un fragment de Diodore," *Revue des études grecques* 123: 543–85.

2012. *Diodore de Sicile. Bibliothèque historique. Fragments. Tome I. Livres VI–X.* Paris: Les Belles Lettres.

Corcella, A., Medaglia, S. M. and Fraschetti, A. 1999. *Erodoto. Le storie. Vol. IV. Libro IV. La Scizia e la Libia.* Milan: Arnaldo Mondadori Editore.

Cornelli, G., McKirahan, R. and Macris, C. (eds.) 2013. *On Pythagoreanism.* Berlin: De Gruyter.

Corssen, P. 1912a. "Der Abaris des Heraklides Ponticus," *Rheinisches Museum* 67: 20–47.

1912b. "Die Schrift des Arztes Androkydes Περὶ πυθαγορικῶν συμβόλων," *Rheinisches Museum* 67: 240–63.

1912c. "Die Sprengung des pythagoreischen Bundes," *Philologus* 71: 332–52.

Cottrell, E. 2008. "Notes sur quelques-uns des témoignages médiévaux relatifs à l'*Histoire philosophique* (ἡ φιλόσοφος ἱστορία) de Porphyre," in Akasoy, A. and Raven, W. (eds.). *Islamic Thought in the Middle Ages.* Leiden/Boston, MA: Brill, pp. 523–55.

Creese, D. 2010. *The Monochord in Ancient Greek Harmonic Science.* Cambridge University Press.

Crickmore, L. 2006. "The Musicality of Plato," *Hermathena* 180: 19–43.

Cristiani, M., Panti, C. and Perillo, G. (eds.) 2007. *Harmonia mundi. Musica mondana e musica celeste fra Antichità e Medioevo.* Florence: SISMEL Edizioni del Galluzzo.

Cserba, S. 1935. *Hieronymus de Moravia O.P. Tractatus de Musica*. Regensburg: Friedrich Pustet.

Cudworth, R. 1678. *The True Intellectual System of the Universe*. London: Printed for Richard Royston.

Cullen, C. 1996. *Astronomy and Mathematics in Ancient China: The Zhou Bi Suan Jing*. Cambridge University Press.

Cumont, F. 1942. *La Stèle du danseur d'Antibes et son décor végétal. Étude sur le symbolisme funéraire des plantes*. Paris: P. Geuthner.

  1943. "À propos des dernières paroles de Socrate," *Comptes Rendus. Académie des Inscriptions et Belles-Lettres* 87: 112–26.

Cuomo, S. 2007. *Technology and Culture in Greek and Roman Antiquity*. Cambridge University Press.

Curd, P. and Graham, D. W. (eds.) 2008. *The Oxford Handbook of Presocratic Philosophy*. Oxford University Press.

Dabrowa, E. (ed.) 2002. *Tradition and Innovation in the Ancient World*. Cracow: Jagiellonian University Press.

D'Accone, F. 1994. "Lorenzo the Magnificent and Music," in Garfagnini, G. C. (ed.). *Lorenzo il Magnifico e il suo mondo*. Florence: Olschki, pp. 259–90.

Da Rios, R. (ed.) 1954. *Aristoxeni Elementa harmonica*. Rome: Officina Poligrafica.

De Falco, V. (ed.) 1922. [*Iamblichi*] *Theologoumena arithmeticae*. Leipzig: Teubner.

Deikmann, A. 2000. "A Functional Approach to Mysticism," in Andresen, J. and Forman, R. K. C. (eds.). *Cognitive Models and Spiritual Maps. Interdisciplinary Explorations of Religious Experience*. Special Issue of *Journal of Consciousness Studies* 7.11–12. Thorverton: Imprint Academic, pp. 75–91.

Delatte, A. 1915. *Études sur la littérature pythagoricienne*. Paris: Champion.

  1922a. *Essai sur la politique pythagoricienne*. Liège: Vaillant-Carmanne.

  1922b. *La Vie de Pythagore de Diogène Laërce*. Brussels: Lamertin.

  1932. *La Catoptromancie grecque et ses dérivés*. Liège: Vaillant-Carmanne/Paris: Droz.

Delatte, L. 1942. *Les Traités de la royauté d'Ecphante, Diotogène et Sthénidas*. Paris: Droz.

Della Casa, A. 1962. *Nigidio Figulo*. Rome: Edizioni dell'Ateneo.

Demand, N. 1976. "The Incuse Coins. A Modern Pythagorean Tradition Re-Examined," *Apeiron* 10: 1–5.

  1982. "Plato, Aristophanes, and the Speeches of Pythagoras," *Greek, Roman and Byzantine Studies* 23: 179–84.

Demoen, K. and Praet, D. (eds.) 2009. *Theios Sophistes: Essays on Flavius Philostratus' Vita Apollonii*. Leiden/Boston, MA: Brill.

De Sensi Sestito, G. 1991. "La storia italiota in Diodoro. Considerazioni sulle fonti per i libri VII–XII," in Galvagno, E. and Molè Ventura, C. (eds.). *Mito, storia, tradizione: Diodoro Siculo e la storiografia classica*. Catania: Edizioni del Prisma, pp. 125–52.

De Smet, D. 1998. *Empedocles arabus. Une lecture néoplatonicienne tardive*. Brussels: KAWLSK.

Des Places, E. (ed.) 1973. *Numénius: Fragments*. Paris: Les Belles Lettres.

(ed.) 1982. *Porphyre: Vie de Pythagore. Lettre à Marcella*. Paris: Les Belles Lettres.

Detienne, M. 1994. *The Gardens of Adonis*. Lloyd, J. (tr.). Princeton University Press.

Deubner, L. 1937. *Iamblichi de vita Pythagorica liber*. Leipzig: Teubner. [rev. edn. by Klein, U. 1975. Stuttgart: Teubner].

Deuse, W. 1983. *Untersuchungen zur mittelplatonischen und neuplatonischen Seelenlehre*. Wiesbaden: Steiner.

De Vogel, C. J. 1966. *Pythagoras and Early Pythagoreanism: An Interpretation of Neglected Evidence on the Philosopher Pythagoras*. Assen: Van Gorcum.

Dickie, M. W. 1999. "The Learned Magician and the Collection and Transmission of Magical Lore," in Jordan, D. R., Montgomery, H. and Thomassen, E. (eds.). *The World of Ancient Magic*. Bergen: The Norwegian Institute at Athens, pp. 163–93.

2001. *Magic and Magicians in the Greco-Roman World*. London/New York: Routledge.

Dicks, D. R. 1970. *Early Greek Astronomy to Aristotle*. Ithaca, NY: Cornell University Press.

Diehl, E. (ed.) 1903–1906. *Procli Diadochi in Platonis Timaeum commentaria*. 3 vols. Leipzig: Teubner.

Diels, H. 1890. "Ein gefälschtes Pythagorasbuch," *Archiv für Geschichte der Philosophie* 3: 451–72.

1882. *Simplicii in Aristotelis Physicorum libros quattuor priores commentaria*. *CAG* 9. Berlin: Reimeri.

1951. *Die Fragmente der Vorsokratiker*, ed. Kranz, W. 3 vols. 6th edn. Berlin: Weidmann.

Dignas, B. and Smith, R. R. R. (eds.) 2012. *Historical and Religious Memory in the Ancient World*. Oxford University Press.

Dillon, J. 1977. *The Middle Platonists 80 B.C. to A.D. 220*. Rev. edn. 1996 with a new afterword. Ithaca, NY/New York: Cornell University Press.

1984. "Speusippus in Iamblichus," *Phronesis* 29: 325–32.

1988. "Iamblichus of Chalcis (c. 240–325 A.D)," in *ANRW* 2.35.2: 862–909.

1990. "Image, Symbol and Analogy: Three Basic Concepts of Neoplatonic Exegesis," in Dillon, J. (ed.). *The Golden Chain: Studies in the Development of Platonism and Christianity*. Aldershot: Variorum, pp. 247–62.

2002. "Die Vita Pythagorica – ein 'Evangelium'?," in Albrecht, Dillon, George, Lurje and Du Toit (eds.), pp. 295–301.

2003. *The Heirs of Plato: A Study of the Old Academy (347–274 B.C.)*. Oxford University Press.

2012. "Aristoxenus' *Life of Plato*," in Huffman (ed.) 2012c, pp. 283–96.

Dillon, J. and Hershbell, J. (eds.) 1991. *Iamblichus, On the Pythagorean Way of Life: Text, Translation and Notes*. Atlanta, GA: Scholars' Press.

Di Marco, M. (ed.) 1989. *Timone di Fliunte: Silli*. Rome: Edizioni dell'Ateneo.

Dingel, J. 2001. "Sextius [I 1]," in *DNP* 11: 490–1.

Dixsaut, M. (ed.) 1999. *La Fêlure du plaisir: Études sur le Philèbe de Platon*. Vol. 2: *Contextes*. Paris: Vrin.

Dodds, E. R. 1928. "The *Parmenides* of Plato and the Origin of the Neoplatonic 'One'," *Classical Quarterly* 22: 129–42.

    1951. *The Greeks and the Irrational.* Berkeley: University of California Press.

    1959. *Plato: Gorgias. A Revised Text, with Introduction and Commentary.* Oxford: Clarendon.

D'Ooge, M. L. (tr.) 1938. *Nicomachus of Gerasa: Introduction to Arithmetic.* Ann Arbor: University of Michigan Press.

Dorion, L.-A. 2012. "*Enkrateia* and the Partition of the Soul in the *Gorgias*," in Barney, R., Brennan, T. and Brittain, C. (eds.). *Plato and the Divided Self.* Cambridge University Press, pp. 33–52.

Dörrie, H. 1959. *Porphyrios' "Symmikta Zetemata." Ihre Stellung in System und Geschichte des Neuplatonismus nebst einem Kommentar zu den Fragmenten.* Munich: Beck.

    1963. *Pythagoreismus. RE* 24.2: 268–77.

Dörrie, H. and Baltes, M. 1987. *Der Platonismus in der Antike.* Vol. 1. Stuttgart/Bad Cannstatt: Frommann/Holzboog.

Drozdek, A. 2007. *Greek Philosophers as Theologians: The Divine Arche.* Aldershot/Burlington, VT: Ashgate.

Dulière, W. L. 1970. "Protection permanente contre des animaux nuisibles assurée par Apollonius de Tyane dans Byzance et Antioche. Évolution de son mythe," *Byzantinische Zeitschrift* 63: 247–77.

Dunbabin, T. J. 1948. *The Western Greeks.* Oxford University Press.

Düring, I. 1932. *Porphyrios Kommentar zur Harmonielehre des Ptolemaios.* Gothenburg: Elanders.

Du Toit, D. S. 1997. *Theios Anthropos. Zur Verwendung von "theios anthrōpos" und sinnverwandten Ausdrücken in der Literatur der Kaiserzeit.* Tübingen: Mohr.

Dzielska, M. 1986. *Apollonius of Tyana in Legend and History.* Rome: L'Erma di Bretschneider.

Eastwood, B. and Graßhoff, G. 2004. *Planetary Diagrams for Roman Astronomy in Medieval Europe, ca. 800–1500.* Philadelphia, PA: American Philosophical Society.

Ebbesen, S. 1990. "Boethius as an Aristotelian Commentator," in Sorabji (ed.), pp. 373–91.

Edmonds, R. G. 1999. "Tearing Apart the Zagreus Myth: A Few Disparaging Remarks on Orphism and Original Sin," *Classical Antiquity* 18: 35–73.

    2008. "Extra-ordinary People: Mystai and Magoi, Magicians and Orphics in the Derveni Papyrus," *Classical Philology* 103: 16–39.

    (ed.) 2011. *The "Orphic" Gold Tablets and Greek Religion: Further Along the Path.* Cambridge University Press.

Edwards, M. J. 1993. "Two Images of Pythagoras: Iamblichus and Porphyry," in Blumenthal and Clark (eds.), pp. 159–72.

    2006. *Culture and Philosophy in the Age of Plotinus.* London: Duckworth.

Ehrhardt, E. 1986. "The Word of the Muses (Plato, *Rep.* 8.546)," *Classical Quarterly* n.s. 36: 407–20.

Elm von der Osten, D. 2006. "Die Inszenierung des Betruges und seiner Entlarvung: Divination und ihre Kritiker in Lukians Schrift 'Alexandros oder der Lügenprophet'," in Elm von der Osten, D., Rüpke, J. and Waldner, K. (eds.). *Texte als Medium und Reflexion von Religion im römischen Reich.* Stuttgart: Franz Steiner, pp. 141–57.

Engels, J. 2007. "Philosophen in Reihen: Die Φιλοσόφων ἀναγραφή des Hippobotos," in Erler and Schorn (eds.), pp. 173–94.

Erler, M. and Schorn, S. (eds.) 2007. *Die griechische Biographie in hellenistischer Zeit.* Berlin/New York: De Gruyter.

Farnell, L. R. 1909. *The Cults of the Greek States.* Vol. 5. Oxford: Clarendon.

Fauth, W. 1978. "Astraios und Zalmoxis: Über Spuren pythagoreischer Aretalogie im Thule-Roman des Antonius Diogenes," *Hermes* 106: 220–41.

Ferrero, L. 1955. *Storia del pitagorismo nel mondo romano (dalle origini alla fine della repubblica).* Turin: Università di Torino, Facoltà di lettere e filosofia, Fondazione Parini-Chirio.

Ferwerda, R. 1985. "The Meaning of the Word σῶμα in Plato's *Cratylus* 400 C," *Hermes* 113: 266–79.

Festa, N. (ed.) 1975. *Iamblichi de communi mathematica scientia.* Stuttgart: Teubner.

Festugière, A.-J. 1945. "Les 'Mémoires pythagoriques' cités par Alexandre Polyhistor," *Revue des études grecques* 58: 1–65 = 1971. *Études de philosophie grecque.* Paris: Vrin, pp. 371–435.

Ficino, M. 1484. *Platonis opera omnia.* Florence.

  1492. *Plotini Enneades.* Florence.

  1576. *Ficini opera omnia.* Basel: Heinrich Petri [repr. Turin 1959; Paris 2000].

Fiedler, W. 1985. "Sexuelle Enthaltsamkeit griechischer Athleten und ihre medizinische Begründung," *Stadion* 11: 137–75.

Finamore, J. and Dillon, J. 2002. *Iamblichus: De Anima.* Leiden: Brill.

Finn, R. D. 2009. "A Pythagorean Tradition?," in Finn, R. D. (ed.). *Asceticism in the Graeco-Roman World.* Cambridge University Press, pp. 27–32.

Flinterman, J. J. 1995. *Power, 'Paideia' & Pythagoreanism. Greek Identity, Conceptions of the Relationship between Philosophers and Monarchs and Political Ideas in Philostratus' Life of Apollonius.* Amsterdam: Gieben.

  1996. "The Ubiquitous Divine Man," *Numen* 43: 82–98.

  1997. "The Date of Lucian's Visit to Abonouteichos," *Zeitschrift für Papyrologie und Epigraphik* 119: 280–2.

  2009a. "'The Ancestor of my Wisdom': Pythagoras and Pythagoreanism in *Life of Apollonius*," in Bowie and Elsner (eds.), pp. 155–75.

  2009b. "Apollonius' Ascension," in Demoen and Praet (eds.), pp. 225–48.

Flower, M. A. 2008. *The Seer in Ancient Greece.* Berkeley/Los Angeles/London: University of California Press.

Folkerts, M. 1981. "The Importance of the Pseudo-Boethian *Geometria* during the Middle Ages," in Masi (ed.), pp. 187–209.

Fortenbaugh, W. W. 2007. "Biography and the Aristotelian Peripatos," in Erler and Schorn (eds.), pp. 45–78.

Fortenbaugh, W. W., Huby, P., Sharples, R. W. and Gutas, D. (eds.) 1992. *Theophrastus of Eresus: Sources for His Life, Writings, Thought and Influence*. Leiden: Brill [repr. with corrections 1993].

Fortenbaugh, W. W. and Schütrumpf, E. (eds.) 2001. *Dicaearchus of Messana: Text, Translation, and Discussion*. New Brunswick, NJ/London: Transaction.

Fortenbaugh, W. W. and White, S. A. (eds.) 2004. *Lyco of Troas and Hieronymus of Rhodes: Text, Translation and Discussion*. New Brunswick, NJ/London: Transaction.

Fowden, G. 1982. "The Pagan Holy Man in Late Antique Society," *Journal of Hellenic Studies* 102: 33–59.

Fowler, D. H. F. 1994. "The Story of the Discovery of Incommensurability, Revisited," in Gavroglu, K., Christianidis, J., Nicolaidis, E. (eds.). *Trends in the Historiography of Science*. Boston, MA: Kluwer, pp. 221–35.

Francis, J. A. 1995. *Subversive Virtue. Asceticism and Authority in the Second-Century Pagan World*. University Park, PA: University of Pennsylvania Press.

Frank, E. 1923. *Plato und die sogenannten Pythagoreer*. Halle: Niemeyer.

Frede, D. and Reis, B. (eds.) 2009. *Body and Soul in Ancient Philosophy*. Berlin: De Gruyter.

Friedlein, G. (ed.) 1867. *Anicii Manlii Torquati Severini Boetii De institutione arithmetica libri duo, De institutione musica libri quinque, accedit Geometria quae fertur Boetii*. Leipzig: Teubner.

1873. *Procli Diadochi in primum Euclidis Elementorum librum comentarii*. Leipzig: Teubner.

Fritz, K. von 1940. *Pythagorean Politics in Southern Italy*. New York: Columbia University Press.

1945. "The Discovery of Incommensurability by Hippasos of Metapontum," *Annals of Mathematics* 46: 242–64.

1960. *Mathematiker und Akusmatiker bei den alten Pythagoreern*. Sitzungsberichte der Bayerischen Akademie der Wissenschaften. Philosophisch-historische Klasse 11. Munich: Bayerischer Akademie der Wissenschaften.

1963. "Pythagoras" and "Pythagoreer," *RE* 24.1: 171–203 and 209–68.

(ed.) 1972. *Pseudepigrapha I*. Fondation Hardt Entretiens XVIII. Vandœuvres, Geneva: Fondation Hardt.

1973. "Philolaus," *RE* suppl. 13: 453–84.

Fuentes González, P. P. 2005a. "Néanthe de Cyzique," in Goulet (ed.) Vol. 4, pp. 587–94.

2005b. "Nouménios (Numénius) d'Apamée," in Goulet (ed.) Vol. 4, pp. 724–40.

Furley, D. J. 1987. *The Greek Cosmologists*. Vol. 1: *The Formation of the Atomic Theory and Its Earliest Critics*. Cambridge University Press.

Gaffurio, F. 1492. *Theorica musice*. Milan: Ioannes Petrus de Lomatio [repr. 1967 *Monuments of Music and Music in Literature in Facsimile* II/21. New York: Broude Brothers].

Gagné, R. 2007. "Winds and Ancestors: The 'Physika' of Orpheus," *Harvard Studies in Classical Philology* 103: 1–23.

Galinsky, G. K. 1975. *Ovid's Metamorphoses. An Introduction to the Basic Aspects*. Berkeley/Los Angeles: University of California Press.

  1998. "The Speech of Pythagoras at Ovid *Metamorphoses* 15.75–478," *Papers of the Leeds Latin Seminar* 10: 313–36.

Garin, E. (ed.) 1965. *L. B. Alberti: Intercenali inediti*. Florence: Sansoni.

Garnsey, P. 2005. "Pythagoras, Plato and Communality: A Note," *Hermathena* 179: 77–87.

Gemelli Marciano, M. L. 2002. "Le contexte culturel des Présocratiques: Adversaires et destinataires," in Laks and Louguet (eds.), pp. 83–114.

  2007. *Die Vorsokratiker. Griechisch–lateinisch–deutsch. Auswahl der Fragmente und Zeugnisse, Übersetzung und Erläuterungen*. Vol. 1: *Thales, Anaximander, Anaximenes, Pythagoras und die Pythagoreer, Xenophanes, Heraklit*. Düsseldorf: Artemis & Winkler.

  2009. *Die Vorsokratiker. Griechisch–lateinisch–deutsch. Auswahl der Fragmente und Zeugnisse, Übersetzung und Erläuterungen*. Vol. 2: *Parmenides, Zenon, Empedokles*. Düsseldorf: Artemis & Winkler (2nd edn. Berlin: Akademie 2013).

  2010. *Die Vorsokratiker. Griechisch–lateinisch–deutsch. Auswahl der Fragmente und Zeugnisse, Übersetzung und Erläuterungen*. Vol. 3: *Anaxagoras, Melissos, Diogenes von Apollonia, Die antiken Atomisten*. Düsseldorf: Artemis & Winkler (2nd edn. Berlin: Akademie 2013).

  2013. Gemelli Marciano, M. L. et *alii*. *Parmenide: suoni, immagini, esperienza. Con alcune considerazioni "inattuali" su Zenone* (ed. L. Rossetti, M. Pulpito). Sankt Augustin: Academia.

Gentile, S. 1990. "Sulle prime traduzioni dal greco di Marsilio Ficino," *Rinascimento* 2nd ser. 30: 57–104.

Gentile, S., Niccoli, S. and Viti, P. (eds.) 1984. *Marsilio Ficino e il ritorno di Platone*. Florence: Le Lettere.

Gersh, S. 1996. *Concord in Discourse: Harmonics and Semiotics in Late Classical and Early Medieval Platonism*. Berlin/New York: Mouton de Gruyter.

  2010. "Ancient Philosophy Becomes Medieval Philosophy," in Gerson (ed.), pp. 894–914.

Gersh, S. and Hoenen, M. J. F. M. (eds.) 2002. *The Platonic Tradition in the Middle Ages: A Doxographic Approach*. Berlin: De Gruyter.

Gerson, L. P. 1994. Review of Tarrant 1993, http://bmcr.brynmawr.edu/1994/94. 03.07.html.

  (ed.) 2010. *The Cambridge History of Philosophy in Late Antiquity*. 2 vols. Cambridge University Press.

Geus, K. 2002. *Eratosthenes von Kyrene. Studien zur hellenistischen Kultur- und Wissenschaftsgeschichte*. Munich: C. H. Beck.

Giangiulio, M. 1989. *Ricerche su Crotone arcaica*. Pisa: Scuola Normale Superiore.

  (ed.) 2000. *Pitagora. Le opere e le testimonianze*. Intro. by Burkert, W. 2 vols. Milan: Mondadori.

Giangrande, G. 1956. *Eunapius: Vitae sophistarum*. Rome: Publica Officina Polygraphica.

Giannantoni, G. 1990. *Socratis et Socraticorum reliquiae.* 4 vols. Naples: Bibliopolis.

Giannattasio Andria, R. 1989. *I frammenti delle "Successioni dei filosofi."* Naples: Arte Tipografica.

Giannelli, G. 1924. *Culti e miti della Magna Grecia.* Florence: Sansoni.

    1928. *La magna Grecia da Pitagora a Pirro: Parte Prima, Gli stati italioti fino alla costituzione della lega dei Bruzi.* Milan: Vita e pensiero.

Gigante, M. 1983. "Frammenti di Ippoboto. Contributo alla storia della storiografia filosofica," in Mastrocinque, A. (ed.). *Omaggio a Piero Treves.* Padua: Antenore, pp. 151–93.

    1986. "Biografia e dossografia in Diogene Laerzio," *Elenchos* 7: 7–102.

Gigon, O. 1987. *Aristotelis opera III: Librorum deperditorum fragmenta.* Berlin: De Gruyter.

Goodenough, E. R. 1928. "The Political Philosophy of Hellenistic Kingship," *Yale Classical Studies* 1: 55–102.

    1932. "A Neo-Pythagorean Source in Philo Judaeus," *Yale Classical Studies* 3: 117–64.

    1938. *The Politics of Philo Judaeus: Practice and Theory.* New Haven, CT: Yale University Press.

Gordon, R. 1999. "Imagining Greek and Roman Magic," in Flint, V. (ed.). *The Athlone History of Witchcraft and Magic in Europe.* Vol. 2: *Ancient Greece and Rome.* London: Athlone, pp. 159–275.

Gordon, R. L. and Marco Simón, F. (eds.) 2010. *Magical Practice in the Latin West.* Leiden: Brill.

Gorini, G. 1975. *La monetazione incusa della Magna Grecia.* Milan: Edizioni Arte e Moneta.

Gorman, P. 1985. "The 'Apollonius' of the Neoplatonic Biographies of Pythagoras," *Mnemosyne* 38: 130–44.

Gottschalk, H. B. 1968. "The *De Audibilibus* and Peripatetic Acoustics," *Hermes* 96: 435–60.

    1971. "Soul as Harmonia," *Phronesis* 16: 179–98.

    1980. *Heraclides of Pontus.* Oxford: Clarendon.

Goulet, R. (ed.) 1989–2012. *Dictionnaire des philosophes antiques.* Vols. 1–5a and b. Paris: CNRS.

    1997. "Les références chez Diogène Laërce: sources ou autorités?," in Fredouille, J.-Cl., Deléani, S., Goulet-Cazé, M.-O., Hoffmann, P., Petitmengin, P. (eds.). *Titres et articulations du texte dans les œuvres antiques.* Paris: Institut d'études augustiniennes, pp. 149–66 [repr. in Goulet, R. 2001. *Études sur les vies de philosophes de l'Antiquité tardive: Diogène Laërce, Porphyre de Tyr, Eunape de Sardes.* Paris: Vrin, pp. 79–96].

Goulet, R. *et al.* 2012. "Porphyre de Tyr," in Goulet (ed.) Vol. 5b: 1289–468.

Graf, F. 1974. *Eleusis und die orphische Dichtung Athens in vorhellenistischer Zeit.* Berlin/New York: De Gruyter.

    1984/1985. "Maximos von Aigai. Ein Beitrag zur Überlieferung über Apollonios von Tyana," *Jahrbuch für Antike und Christentum* 27–8: 65–73.

    1987. "Apollon Lykeios in Metapont," in *Acts of the 7th Congress of Greek and Roman Epigraphy.* Vol. 2. Athens, pp. 242–5.

2009. *Apollo*. London: Routledge.

2011. "Text and Ritual. The Corpus Eschatologicum of the Orphics," in Edmonds (ed.), pp. 53–67.

Graf, F. and Johnston, S. I. 2007. *Ritual Texts for the Afterlife. Orpheus and the Bacchic Gold Tablets*. London/New York: Routledge.

Graham, D. W. 1999. "Empedocles and Anaxagoras: Responses to Parmenides," in Long (ed.), pp. 159–80.

2002. "La lumière de la lune dans la pensée grecque archaïque," in Laks and Louguet (eds.), pp. 351–80.

2006. *Explaining the Cosmos: The Ionian Tradition of Scientific Philosophy*. Princeton University Press.

2013. *Science before Socrates: Parmenides Anaxagoras and the New Astronomy*. Oxford University Press.

Granger, H. 2004. "Heraclitus' Quarrel with Polymathy and *Historiê*," *Transactions and Proceedings of the American Philological Association* 134: 235–61.

2007. "The Theologian Pherecydes of Syros and the Early Days of Natural Philosophy," *Harvard Studies in Classical Philology* 103: 135–63.

Grensemann, H. 1968. *Hippokrates, Über Achtmonatskinder. Über das Siebenmonatskind (Unecht)* (= *Corpus Medicorum Graecorum* I 2.1). Berlin: Akademie.

Gritti, E. 2007. "Insegnamento pitagorico e metodo dialettico in Proclo," in Bonazzi, Lévy and Steel (eds.), pp. 163–94.

Gruen, E. S. 1990. *Studies in Greek Culture and Roman Policy*. Leiden: Brill.

Grummond, N. T. de and Simon, E. (eds.) 2006. *The Religion of the Etruscans*. Austin: University of Texas Press.

Gutas, D. 2010. *Theophrastus: On First Principles (Known as His Metaphysics)*. Leiden/Boston, MA: Brill.

Guthrie, K. S. (tr.) 1987. *The Pythagorean Sourcebook and Library*. Grand Rapids, MI: Phanes.

Guthrie, W. K. C. 1962. *A History of Greek Philosophy*. Vol. 1: *The Earlier Presocratics and the Pythagoreans*. Cambridge University Press.

1993. *Orpheus and Greek Religion: A Study of the Orphic Movement*. Princeton University Press [repr. of the 1952 edition].

Haar, J. 1960. "Musica Mundana: Variations on a Pythagorean Theme." Diss. Harvard University.

Haase, W. and Temporini, H. (eds.) 1990. *Aufstieg und Niedergang der römischen Welt* 36.4. Berlin: De Gruyter.

Hadas, M. (tr.) 1965. "*The Life of Pythagoras* by Porphyry," in Hadas, M. and Smith, M. (eds.). *Heroes and Gods: Spiritual Biographies in Antiquity*. New York: Harper and Row, pp. 105–28.

Hadot, I. 2006. *Arts libéraux et philosophie dans la pensée antique. Contribution à l'histoire de l'éducation et de la culture dans l'Antiquité*. Paris: Vrin. 1st edn. 1984.

Hagel, S. 2009. *Ancient Greek Music: A New Technical History*. Cambridge University Press.

Hankinson, R. J. 1998. *Cause and Explanation in Ancient Greek Thought*. Oxford: Clarendon.

Hansen, D. 1998. *Das Attizistische Lexikon des Moeris*. Berlin: De Gruyter.

Harder, R. 1926. *"Ocellus Lucanus": Text und Kommentar*. Berlin: Weidmann.

Hardie, P. 1995. "The Speech of Pythagoras in Ovid *Metamorphoses* 15: Empedoclean *Epos*," *Classical Quarterly* 45: 204–14.

Harlfinger, D. 1975. "Edizione critica del testo del 'De ideis' di Aristotele," in Leszl, W. (ed.). *Il "De ideis" di Aristotele e la teoria Platonica delle idee*. Florence: Olschki, pp. 15–54.

Harnack, A. von 1931. *Lehrbuch der Dogmengeschichte*. 5th edn. Tübingen: Mohr.

Harris, G. R. S. 1973. *The Heart and the Vascular System in Ancient Greek Medicine*. Oxford: Clarendon.

Harrison, T. 2000. *Divinity and History. The Religion of Herodotus*. Oxford University Press.

Hartog, F. 1980. *Le Miroir d'Hérodote. Essai sur la représentation de l'autre*. Paris: Gallimard (2nd ed. 1991; Engl. transl. J. Lloyd, *The Mirror of Herodotus. The Representation of the Other in the Writing of History*, Berkeley/Los Angeles: University of California Press, 1988).

Hayduck, M. 1891. *Alexandri Aphrodisiensis In Aristotelis Metaphysica Commentaria*. *CAG* 1. Berlin: Reimer.

Heath, T. L. 1921. *A History of Greek Mathematics*. 2 vols. Oxford: Clarendon.
   1926. *The Thirteen Books of Euclid's Elements*. 3 vols. 2nd edn. Cambridge University Press.

Heiberg, J. L. (ed.) 1886. *Euclidis opera omnia*. Vol. 5. Leipzig: Teubner.
   (ed.) 1893. *Apollonii Pergaei quae Graece exstant cum commentariis antiquis*. Vol. 2. Leipzig: Teubner.
   (ed.) 1910–1915. *Archimedis opera* (Vol. 1: 1910, 2: 1913, 3: 1915). Stuttgart: Teubner.

Heinze, R. 1892. *Xenokrates. Darstellung der Lehre und Sammlung der Fragmente*. Leipzig: Teubner [repr. 1965. Hildesheim: Olms].

Heitz, E. 1869. *Fragmenta Aristotelis*. Paris: Didot [repr. 1973. Hildesheim: Olms].

Helm, R. (ed.) 1956. *Eusebius Werke VII, Die Chronik des Hieronymus*. Berlin: Akademie.

Helmig, C. 2008. "Plutarch of Chaeronea and Porphyry on Transmigration – Who Is the Author of Stobaeus I 445.14–448.3 (W.-H.)?," *Classical Quarterly* 58.1: 250–5.

Henderson, J. (tr.) 2000. *Aristophanes: Birds, Lysistrata, Women at the Thesmophoria*. Loeb Classical Library. Cambridge, MA: Harvard University Press.

Heninger, S. K. 1974. *Touches of Sweet Harmony: Pythagorean Cosmology and Renaissance Poetics*. San Marino, CA: Huntington Library.

Henrichs, A. 2010. "Mystika, Orphika, Dionysiaka. Esoterische Gruppenbildungen, Glaubensinhalte und Verhaltensweisen in der griechischen Religion," in Bierl, A. and Braungart, W. (eds.). *Gewalt und Opfer: im Dialog mit Walter Burkert*. Berlin: De Gruyter, pp. 87–114.

Henry, P. and Schwyzer, H.-R. (eds.) 1964–1968. *Plotini opera*. Oxford: Clarendon.

Hentschel, F. 2000. *Sinnlichkeit und Vernunft in der mittelalterlichen Musiktheorie: Strategien der Konsonanzwertung und der Gegenstand der musica sonora um 1300*. Stuttgart: Steiner.

Hermann, A. 2004. *To Think Like God: Pythagoras and Parmenides. The Origins of Philosophy*. Las Vegas: Parmenides.

Hernández de la Fuente, D. 2011. *Vidas de Pitágoras*. Girona: Atalanta.

Hexter, R. and Townsend, D. (eds.) 2012. *The Oxford Handbook of Medieval Latin Literature*. Oxford University Press.

Hicks, A. 2012. "Martianus Capella and the Liberal Arts," in Hexter and Townsend (eds.), 307–34.

Hicks, R. D. (tr.) 1925. *Diogenes Laertius. Lives of Eminent Philosophers, with an English Translation*. 2 vols. Loeb Classical Library. Cambridge, MA: Harvard University Press.

Hiller, E. (ed.) 1878. *Theonis Smyrnaei expositio rerum mathematicarum ad legendum Platonem utilium*. Leipzig: Teubner.

Hinz, V. 1998. *Der Kult der Demeter und Kore auf Sizilien und in der Magna Graecia*. Wiesbaden: Reichert.

Hoche, R. (ed.) 1866. *Nicomachi Geraseni Pythagorei introductionis arithmeticae libri II*. Leipzig: Teubner.

Hölk, C. 1894. "De acusmatis sive symbolis Pythagoricis." Diss. Kiel: Fiencke.

Holzberg, N. 1986. *Der antike Roman. Eine Einführung*. Munich: Artemis.

Holzhausen, J. (ed.) 1998. ψυχή – *Seele – Anima: Festschrift für Karin Alt zum 7. Mai 1998*. Stuttgart/Leipzig: Teubner.

2004. "Pindar und die Orphik. Zu Frg. 133 Snell/Maehler," *Hermes* 132: 20–36.

Horky, P. 2013a. *Plato and Pythagoreanism*. Oxford University Press.

2013b. "Theophrastus on Platonic and 'Pythagorean' Imitation," *Classical Quarterly* n.s. 63.2: 655–91.

Hsu, E. 1999. *The Transmission of Chinese Medicine*. Cambridge University Press.

Hubaux, J. 1928. "L'herbe aux cent têtes," *Musée belge* 32: 167–76.

1930. "Une épode d'Ovide. Nouvelles recherches au sujet de la basilique souterraine de la Porta Maggiore, à Rome," in *Serta Leodiensia*. Liège: Vaillant-Carmanne; Paris: Champion, pp. 187–245.

Hubler, J. N. 2011. "Moderatus, E. R. Dodds, and the Development of Neoplatonist Emanation," in Turner, J. D. and Corrigan, K. (eds.). *Plato's Parmenides and Its Heritage*. Vol. 1: *History and Interpretation from the Old Academy to Later Platonism and Gnosticism*. Leiden/Boston, MA: Brill, pp. 115–28.

Hude, K. 1927. *Herodoti Historiae*. 3rd edn. Oxford: Clarendon.

Huffman, C. A. 1985. "The Authenticity of Archytas Fr. 1," *Classical Quarterly* 35: 344–8.

1988. "The Role of Number in Philolaus' Philosophy," *Phronesis* 33: 1–30.

1993. *Philolaus of Croton: Pythagorean and Presocratic*. Cambridge University Press.

1999a. "Limite et illimité chez les premiers philosophes grecs," in Dixsaut (ed.), pp. 11–31.

1999b. "The Pythagorean Tradition," in Long (ed.), pp. 66–87.

2001. "The Philolaic Method: The Pythagoreanism behind the *Philebus*," in Preus (ed.), pp. 67–85.

2002a. "Polyclète et les Présocratiques," in Laks and Louguet (eds.), pp. 303–27.

2002b. "Archytas and the Sophists," in Caston, V. and Graham, D. (eds.). *Presocratic Philosophy, Essays in Honour of Alexander Mourelatos*. Aldershot: Ashgate, pp. 251–70.

2005. *Archytas of Tarentum: Pythagorean, Philosopher and Mathematician King*. Cambridge University Press.

2006. "Aristoxenus' *Pythagorean Precepts*. A Rational Pythagorean Ethics," in Sassi (ed.), pp. 103–21.

2007. "Philolaus and the Central Fire," in Stern-Gillet and Corrigan (eds.), pp. 57–94.

2008a. "Alcmaeon," in Zalta, E. N. (ed). *The Stanford Encyclopedia of Philosophy (Winter 2008 Edition)*. Online at http://plato.stanford.edu/archives/win2008/entries/alcmaeon.

2008b. "Another Incarnation of Pythagoras," *Ancient Philosophy* 28: 201–26.

2008c. "Heraclitus' Critique of Pythagoras' Enquiry in Fragment 129," *Oxford Studies in Ancient Philosophy* 35: 19–47.

2008d. "The *Pythagorean Precepts* of Aristoxenus: Crucial Evidence for Pythagorean Moral Philosophy," *Classical Quarterly* 58.1: 104–19.

2008e. "Two Problems in Pythagoreanism," in Curd and Graham (eds.), pp. 284–304.

2009. "The Pythagorean Conception of the Soul from Pythagoras to Philolaus," in Frede and Reis (eds.), pp. 21–44.

2010a. "Pythagoreanism," in Zalta, E. N. (ed.). *The Stanford Encyclopedia of Philosophy (Summer 2010 Edition)*. Online at http://plato.stanford.edu/archives/sum2010/entries/pythagoreanism.

2010b. "Response to Barker," *Classical Philology* 105: 420–5.

2011a. "Archytas," in Zalta, E. N. (ed.). *The Stanford Encyclopedia of Philosophy (Fall 2011 Edition)*. Online at http://plato.stanford.edu/archives/fall2011/entries/archytas.

2011b. "Pythagoras," in Zalta, E. N. (ed.). *The Stanford Encyclopedia of Philosophy (Fall 2011 Edition)*. Online at http://plato.stanford.edu/archives/fall2011/entries/pythagoras.

2012a. "Aristoxenus' Account of Pythagoras," in Patterson, Karasmanis and Hermann (eds.), pp. 159–77.

2012b. "Aristoxenus' *Life of Socrates*," in Huffman 2012c, pp. 251–81.

(ed.) 2012c. *Aristoxenus of Tarentum: Discussion*. New Brunswick, NJ/London: Transaction.

2012d. "Philolaus," in Zalta, E. N. (ed.). *The Stanford Encyclopedia of Philosophy (Summer 2012 Edition)*. Online at http://plato.stanford.edu/archives/sum2012/entries/philolaus.

2013a. "Plato and the Pythagoreans," in Cornelli, McKirahan and Macris (eds.), pp. 237–70.

2013b. "Reason and Myth in Early Pythagorean Cosmology," in McCoy (ed.), pp. 55–76.

Hüffmeier, A. 2001. "Die pythagoreischen Sprüche in Porphyrios' Vita Pythagorae: Kapitel 36 (Ende) bis 45." Diss. Münster. Online at http://miami. uni-muenster.de [recherche].

Hugh-Jones, S. 1994. "Shamans, Prophets, Priests and Pastors," in Thomas, N. and Humphrey, C. (eds.). *Shamanism, History, and the State.* Ann Arbor: University of Michigan Press, pp. 32–75.

Hugonnard-Roche, H. 2012. "Porphyre de Tyr – III. Survie orientale – *Philosophos historia,*" in Goulet (ed.) Vol. 5b, 1464–7.

Humm, M. 1996 and 1997. "Les origines du pythagorisme romain: problèmes historiques et philosophiques," *Les Études classiques* 64: 339–55; 65: 25–42.

Ilnitchi, G. 2002. "'*Musica mundana,*' Aristotelian Natural Philosophy and Ptolemaic Astronomy," *Early Music History* 21: 37–74.

Ilnitchi Currie, G. 2008. "*Concentum celi quis dormire faciet?* Eriugenian Cosmic Song and Carolingian Planetary Astonomy," in Cannata, Ilnitchi Currie, Mueller and Nádas (eds.), pp. 15–35.

Isnardi Parente, I. 1980. *Speusippo: Frammenti.* Naples: Bibliopolis.

1982. *Senocrate-Ermodoro: Frammenti.* Naples: Bibliopolis.

1985. "Le 'Tu ne tueras point' de Xénocrate," in Brunschwig, J., Imbert, C. and Roger, A. (eds.). *Histoire et structure.* Paris: Vrin, pp. 161–72.

Jacoby, F. 1902. *Apollodors Chronik. Eine Sammlung der Fragmente.* Berlin: Weidmann.

(ed.) 1923–. *Die Fragmente der griechischen Historiker.* Berlin: Weidmann. [Abbreviated as *FGrHist.*]

Jäger, H. 1919a. "Die Quellen des Porphyrios in seiner Pythagoras-Biographie." Diss. Zurich. Chur: Sprecher, Eggerling & Co.

Jaeger, W. 1947. *The Theology of the Early Greek Philosophers.* Oxford: Clarendon.

1948. *Aristotle: Fundamentals of the History of His Development.* 2nd edn. Oxford University Press.

Jan, C. 1895. *Musici scriptores Graeci.* Leipzig: Teubner [repr. 1995].

Jeauneau, É. 2007. "Jean Scot et la métaphysique des nombres," in Jeauneau, É., "*Tendenda vela*": Excursions littéraires et digressions philosophiques à travers le Moyen Âge. Turnhout: Brepols, pp. 461–77.

Johnson, M. R. 2008. "Sources for the Philosophy of Archytas," *Ancient Philosophy* 28: 173–99.

Jolivet, J. 1993. "Les philosophes de Šahrastānī," in Jolivet, J. and Monnot, G. (eds.). *Shahrastani. Livre des religions et des sectes.* Vol. 2. Leuven: Peeters; Paris: UNESCO, pp. 14–51.

Joly, R. 1970. *Hippocrate.* Vol. 11: *De la génération, De la nature de l'enfant, Des maladies IV, Du fœtus de huit mois.* Paris: Les Belles Lettres.

Jones, C. P. 1986. *Culture and Society in Lucian.* Cambridge, MA: Harvard University Press.

(tr.) 2005–2006. *Philostratus: The Life of Apollonius of Tyana.* 3 vols. Loeb Classical Library. Cambridge, MA: Harvard University Press.

Joost-Gaugier, C. L. 2006. *Measuring Heaven: Pythagoras and His Influence on Thought and Art in Antiquity and the Middle Ages.* Ithaca, NY: Cornell University Press.

2009. *Pythagoras and Renaissance Europe: Finding Heaven*. Cambridge University Press.

Jordan, D. 1985. "A Survey of Greek Defixiones Not Included in the Special Corpora," *Greek, Roman, and Byzantine Studies* 26: 151–95.

Jordan, P. 1961. "Pythagoras and Monachism," *Traditio* 17: 432–41.

Jouanna, J. 2003. *Hippocrate: La Maladie Sacrée*. Paris: Les Belles Lettres.

2009. "Médecine et philosophie: sur la date de Sextus Empiricus et celle de Diogène Laërce," *Revue des Études Grecques* 122.2: 359–90.

Journée, G. 2012. " Lumière et nuit, féminin et masculin chez Parménide d'Elée: quelques remarques," *Phronesis* 57: 289–318.

Kahn, C. H. 1993. "Pythagorean Philosophy before Plato," in Mourelatos (ed.), pp. 161–85. 1st edn. 1974.

2001. *Pythagoras and the Pythagoreans: A Brief History*. Indianapolis, IN: Hackett.

Kahrstedt, U. 1932. "Grossgriechenland im 5. Jahrhundert," *Hermes* 53: 180–7.

Kaiser, S. I. 2010. *Die Fragmente des Aristoxenos aus Tarent*. Hildesheim: Olms.

Kalligas, P. 2004. "Platonism in Athens during the First Two Centuries AD: An Overview," *Rhizai* 1.2: 37–56.

Karamanolis, G. E. 2006. *Plato and Aristotle in Agreement? Platonists on Aristotle from Antiochus to Porphyry*. Oxford: Clarendon.

Kassel, R. and Austin, C. (eds.) 1983–. *Poetae Comici Graeci*. Berlin: De Gruyter. [Abbreviated as K–A.]

Kerkhof, R. 2001. *Dorische Posse, Epicharm und Attische Komödie*. Munich: Saur.

Kienast, D. 1999. *Augustus. Prinzeps und Monarch*. 3rd edn. Darmstadt: Wissenschaftliche Buchgesellschaft.

Kienle, W. von 1961. "Die Berichte über die Sukzessionen der Philosophen in der hellenistischen und spätantiken Literatur." Diss. Berlin: Free University of Berlin.

Kingsley, P. 1990. "The Greek Origin of the Sixth-Century Dating of Zoroaster," *Bulletin of the School of Oriental and African Studies* 53: 245–65.

1994. "From Pythagoras to the Turba Philosophorum: Egypt and Pythagorean Tradition," *Journal of the Warburg and Courtauld Institutes* 57: 1–13.

1995. *Ancient Philosophy, Mystery, and Magic*. Oxford: Clarendon.

1999. *In the Dark Places of Wisdom*. Inverness, CA: The Golden Sufi Center [repr. 2001. London: Routledge].

2010. *A Story Waiting to Pierce You: Mongolia, Tibet and the Destiny of the Western World*. Inverness, CA: The Golden Sufi Center.

Kirk, G. S. and Raven, J. E. 1957. *The Presocratic Philosophers*. Cambridge University Press.

Kirk, G. S., Raven, J. E. and Schofield, M. 1983. *The Presocratic Philosophers*, 2nd edn. Cambridge University Press.

Kleingünther, A. 1933. *Protos heuretes: Untersuchungen zur Geschichte einer Fragestellung*. Leipzig: Dieterich.

Klibansky, R. and Labowsky, C. (eds.) 1953. *Parmenides usque ad finem primae hypothesis nec non Procli Commentarium in Parmenidem, pars ultima adhuc inedita interprete G. de Moerbeka*. London: Warburg Institute.

Klutstein, I. (ed.) 1987. *Marsilio Ficino et la théologie ancienne: oracles chaldaïques, hymnes orphiques, hymnes de Proclus*. Florence: Olschki.

Knipp, D. 2002. "Medieval Visual Images of Plato," in Gersh and Hoenen (eds.), pp. 373–414.

Knorr, W. R. 1975. *The Evolution of Euclidean Elements*. Dordrecht: Reidel.

1986. *The Ancient Tradition of Geometric Problems*. Cambridge, MA: Birkhäuser.

Kobusch, T. and Erler, M. (eds.) 2002. *Metaphysik und Religion: Zur Signatur des spätantiken Denkens*. Munich/Leipzig: Saur.

Kohlschitter, S. 1991. "Parmenides and Empedocles in Porphyry's *History of Philosophy*," *Hermathena* 150: 43–53.

Kouremenos, T., Parássoglou, G. M. and Tsantsanoglou, K. 2006. *The Derveni Papyrus*. Florence: Olschki.

Kraay, C. M. 1976. *Archaic and Classical Greek Coins*. London: Methuen.

Krische, A. 1830. *De societatis a Pythagora in urbe Crotoniatarum condita scopo politico*. Göttingen: Deuerlich.

Kroll, W. 1899–1901. *Procli Diadochi in Platonis rem publicam commentarii*. 2 vols. Leipzig: Teubner.

1936. "P. Nigidius Figulus," in *RE* 17.1: 200–12.

Kühner, R. and Stegmann, C. 1971. *Ausführliche Grammatik der lateinischen Sprache*. Vol 2: *Satzlehre*. Darmstadt: Wissenschaftliche Buchgesellschaft.

Lachenaud, G. 1978. *Mythologies, religion et philosophie de l'histoire dans Hérodote*. Lille/Paris: Université de Lille III.

Laks, A. 2005. "Die Entstehung einer (Fach) Disziplin: der Fall der vorsokratischen Philosophie," in Rechenauer, G. (ed.). *Frühgriechisches Denken*. Göttingen: Vandenhoeck & Ruprecht, pp. 19–39.

2013. "The Pythagorean Hypomnemata Reported by Alexander Polyhistor in Diogenes Laertius (8.25–33)," in Cornelli, McKirahan and Macris (eds.), pp. 371–84.

Laks, A. and Louguet, C. (eds.) 2002. *Qu'est-ce que la philosophie présocratique?* Villeneuve d'Ascq: Presses Universitaires du Septentrion.

Laks, A. and Most, G. W. (eds.) 1993. *Théophraste: Métaphysique*. Paris: Les Belles Lettres.

(ed. and tr.) forthcoming. *Early Greek Thinkers*. 4 vols. Loeb Classical Library. Cambridge, MA: Harvard University Press.

Lamberton, R. 1986. *Homer the Theologian: Neoplatonist Allegorical Reading and the Growth of the Epic Tradition*. Berkeley/Los Angeles/London: University of California Press.

Landucci Gattinoni, F. 1997. *Duride di Samo*. Rome: Bretschneider.

Laqueur, R. 1907. "Zur griechischen Sagenchronographie. Excurs. Zur Chronologie des Pythagoras," *Hermes* 42: 530–2.

Latte, K. 1960. *Römische Religionsgeschichte*. Handbuch der Altertumswissenschaft 5.4. Munich: Beck.

Leeman, A. D. and Pinkster, H. 1981. *M. Tullius Cicero: De Oratore Libri III. Kommentar. Band 1: Buch 1.1–165*. Heidelberg: Winter.

Lefkowitz, M. L. 1981. *The Lives of the Greek Poets*. London: Duckworth.

Legrand, Ph.-E. 1944. *Hérodote. Histoires. Livre II. Euterpe*. Paris: Les Belles Lettres.

Lehmann, Y. 1997. *Varron théologien et philosophe romain*. Brussels: Latomus.

Lendle, O. 1992. *Einführung in die griechische Geschichtsschreibung. Von Hekataios bis Zosimos*. Darmstadt: Wissenschaftliche Buchgesellschaft.

Lesky, E. 1950. *Die Zeugungs- und Vererbungslehren der Antike und ihr Nachwirken*. Mainz: Akademie der Wissenschaften und der Literatur.

Leurini, L. 1992. *Ionis Chii testimonia et fragmenta*. Amsterdam: Hakkert.

Levin, F. R. 1975. *The Harmonics of Nicomachus and the Pythagorean Tradition*. Philadelphia, PA: American Philological Association.

2009. *Greek Reflections on the Nature of Music*. Cambridge University Press.

Lévy, C. 2003. "Cicero and the *Timaeus*," in Reydams-Schils (ed.), pp. 95–110.

Lévy, I. 1926. *Recherches sur les sources de la légende de Pythagore*. Paris: Leroux (reprint New York: Garland Publ. 1987).

Liebeschuetz, J. H. W. G. 1979. *Continuity and Change in Roman Religion*. Oxford: Clarendon.

Linforth, I. M. 1941. *The Arts of Orpheus*. Berkeley: University of California Press.

Lintott, A. 2008. *Cicero as Evidence. A Historian's Companion*. Oxford University Press.

Little, D. 1970. "The Speech of Pythagoras in *Metamorphoses* 15 and the Structure of the *Metamorphoses*," *Hermes* 98: 340–60.

Littré, É. (ed.) 1839–1861. *Œuvres complètes d'Hippocrate*. 10 vols. Paris: Baillière.

Lloyd, A. B. 1975–1988. *Herodotus. Book II*. 3 vols. Leiden: Brill.

Lloyd, A. B. and Fraschetti, A. 1999. *Erodoto. Le storie. Volume II. Libro II. L'Egitto*. Milan: Arnaldo Mondadori. 4th edn.

Lloyd, G. E. R. 1975. "Alcmaeon and the Early History of Dissection," *Sudhoffs Archiv* 59: 113–47.

1979. *Magic, Reason and Experience*. Cambridge University Press.

1990. "Plato and Archytas in the Seventh Letter," *Phronesis* 35: 159–74.

Long, A. A. (ed.) 1999. *The Cambridge Companion to Early Greek Philosophy*. Cambridge University Press.

2013. "The Eclectic Pythagoreanism of Alexander Polyhistor," in Schofield (ed.), pp. 139–59.

Longrigg, J. 1993. *Greek Rational Medicine: Philosophy and Medicine from Alcmaeon to the Alexandrians*. London: Routledge.

Lonie, I. M. 1981. *The Hippocratic Treatises "On Generation," "On the Nature of the Child," "Diseases IV."* Berlin: De Gruyter.

Lord, M. L. 1992. "Virgil's *Eclogues*, Nicholas Trevet, and the Harmony of the Spheres," *Mediaeval Studies* 54: 186–273.

Luna, C. 2001. *Trois Études sur la tradition des commentaires anciens à la Métaphysique d'Aristote*. Leiden/Boston, MA: Brill.

Lurje, M. 2002. "Die Vita Pythagorica als Manifest der neuplatonischen Paideia," in Albrecht, Dillon, George, Lurje and Du Toit (eds.), pp. 221–53.

Lutz, C. E. (ed.) 1939. *Iohannis Scotti Annotationes in Marcianum*. Cambridge, MA: Mediaeval Academy of America.

(ed.) 1962–1965. *Remigii Autissiodorensis Commentum in Martianum Capellam*. 2 vols. Leiden: Brill.

Luzzatto, M. T. 1996. "Dialettica o retorica? La *polytropia* di Odisseo da Antistene a Porfirio," *Elenchos* 17.2: 275–357.

Maaz, W. 1998. "Metempsychotica mediaevalia. Pictagoras redivivus," in Holzhausen (ed.), pp. 385–416.

MacIntosh Turfa, J. 2006. "Appendix A: The Etruscan Brontoscopic Calendar," in Grummond and Simon (eds.), pp. 173–90.

Macris, C. 2001. *Πορφυρίου Πυθαγόρου βίος*. Athens: Katarti [in modern Greek].

    2002. "Jamblique et la littérature pseudo-pythagoricienne," in Mimouni, S. C. (ed.). *Apocryphité*. Turnhout: Brepols, pp. 77–129.

    2003. "Pythagore, un maître de sagesse charismatique de la fin de l'époque archaïque," in Filoramo, G. (ed.). *Carisma profetico: fattore di innovazione religiosa*. Brescia: Morcelliana, pp. 243–89.

    2004. "Le Pythagore des Néoplatoniciens. Recherches et commentaires sur 'Le Mode de vie pythagoricien' de Jamblique." 3 vols. Diss. Paris, École pratique des hautes études.

    2006a. "Autorità carismatica, direzione spirituale e genere di vita nella tradizione pitagorica," in Filoramo, G. (ed.). *Storia della direzione spirituale*. Vol. 1: *L'età antica*. Brescia: Morcelliana, pp. 75–102 = "Charismatic Authority, Spiritual Guidance and Way of Life in the Pythagorean Tradition," in Chase, M., Clark, St. R. L. and McGhee, M. (eds.). 2013. *Philosophy as a Way of Life: Ancients and Moderns, Essays in Honor of Pierre Hadot*, Malden/Oxford: Wiley-Blackwell, pp. 57–83.

    2006b. "Becoming Divine by Imitating Pythagoras," *Metis* n.s. 4: 297–329.

    2009a. "Pythagoras," in Oppy, G. and Trakakis, N. (eds.). *The History of Western Philosophy of Religion*. Vol. 1: *Ancient Philosophy of Religion*. London: Acumen, pp. 23–39.

    2009b. "Le pythagorisme érigé en *hairesis*, ou comment (re)construire une identité philosophique. Remarques sur un aspect méconnu du projet pythagoricien de Jamblique," in Belayche, N. and Mimouni, S. C. (eds.). *Entre lignes de partage et territoires de passage. Les identités religieuses dans les mondes grec et romain*. Paris: Peeters, pp. 139–68.

    2010. "Σημαίνοντες θάνατοι φιλοσόφων στον Διογένη Λαέρτιο: μια επανεκτίμηση," *Υπόμνημα στη φιλοσοφία* 9 [special issue *Θάνατοι φιλοσόφων στην Αρχαιότητα*]: 11–52 [in modern Greek].

    2012. "Ptolémaïs de Cyrène," in Goulet (ed.) Vol. 5b, 1717–18.

Macris, C. and Goulet, R. 2012. "Porphyre de Tyr – *Vie de Pythagore*," in Goulet (ed.) Vol. 5b, 1333–5.

Macris, C. and Skarsouli, P. 2012. "La sagesse et les pouvoirs du mystérieux τις du fragment 129 d'Empédocle," *Revue de métaphysique et de morale* 74.3: 357–77.

Magee, J. 2010. "Boethius," in Gerson (ed.), pp. 788–812.

Makarov, I. A. 1999. "Orphism and the Greek Society in VI–IV centuries B.C.," *Vestnik drevnej istorii* 228.1: 8–19 [in Russian with an English summary].

Maniatis, Y. N. 2009. "Pythagorean Philolaus' Pyrocentric Universe," *ΣΧΟΛΗ: Ancient Philosophy and the Classical Tradition* 3: 401–15.

Mansfeld, J. 1971. *The Pseudo-Hippocratic Tract ΠΕΡΙ ʹΕΒΔΟΜΑΔΩΝ Ch. 1–11 and Greek Philosophy*. Assen: Van Gorcum.

1986. "Diogenes Laertius on Stoic Philosophy," *Elenchos* 7: 295–382.

1988. "Compatible Alternatives: Middle Platonist Theology and the Xenophanes Reception," in van der Broek, B. and Mansfeld, J. (eds.). *Knowledge of God in the Graeco-Roman World*. Leiden: Brill, pp. 92–117.

1989a. "Fiddling the Books (Heraclitus B 129)," in Boudouris (ed.), pp. 229–34.

1989b. Review of Kühn, J.-H., and Fleischer, U., *Index Hippocraticus*, Fasc. I–II, *Mnemosyne* 42: 182–6.

1990. "Doxography and Dialectic. The *Sitz im Leben* of the 'Placita'," *ANRW* 36.4: 3056–229.

1992. *Heresiography in Context. Hippolytus' Elenchos as a Source for Greek Philosophy*. Leiden: Brill.

1994. *Prolegomena. Questions to Be Settled before the Study of an Author or Text*. Leiden: Brill.

1998. *Prolegomena mathematica. From Apollonius of Perga to Late Neoplatonism*. Leiden: Brill.

Mansfeld, J. and Primavesi, O. 2011. *Die Vorsokratiker Griechisch-Deutsch*. Stuttgart: Reclam.

Mansfeld, J. and Runia, D. 1997–2010. *Aëtiana: The Method and Intellectual Context of a Doxographer*. 3 vols. Leiden: Brill.

Marcaccini, C. 1998. "Hdt. 4.93–96: Zalmoxis Dioniso del nord," *Sileno* 24: 135–58.

Marincola, J. 2001. *Greek Historians*. Oxford University Press.

Martinelli, M. C., Pelosi, F. and Pernigotti, C. (eds.) 2009. *La musa dimenticata. Aspetti dell'esperienza musicale greca in età ellenistica*. Pisa: Edizioni della Normale.

Masi, M. (ed.) 1981. *Boethius and the Liberal Arts: A Collection of Essays*. Bern: Lang.

Mason, S. 1996. "*Philosophiai*: Graeco-Roman, Judean and Christian," in Kloppenborg, J. S. and Wilson, S. G. (eds.). *Voluntary Associations in the Graeco-Roman World*. London: Routledge, pp. 31–58.

Masson, O. 1995. "La patrie de Diogène Laërce est-elle inconnue?," *Museum Helveticum* 52: 225–30.

Mathieu, B. 1987. "Archytas de Tarente, pythagoricien et ami de Platon," *Bulletin de l'Association Guillaume Budé*: 239–55.

McCoy, J. (ed.) 2013. *Early Greek Philosophy: The Presocratics and the Emergence of Reason*. Washington, DC: The Catholic University of America Press.

McKinnon, J. 1978. "Iubal vel Pythagoras, quis sit inventor musicae?," *Musical Quarterly* 64: 1–28.

Meibom, M. (ed.) 1977. *Antiquae musicae auctores septem*. 2 vols. New York: Broude Brothers [repr. of 1652 edn.].

Meier, C. 1970. *Die Entstehung des Begriffs Demokratie*. Frankfurt: Suhrkamp.

Meinwald, C. C. 1998. "Prometheus's Bounds: *peras* and *apeiron* in Plato's *Philebus*," in Gentzler, J. (ed.). *Method in Ancient Philosophy*. Oxford: Clarendon, pp. 165–80.

2002. "Plato's Pythagoreanism," *Ancient Philosophy* 22.1: 87–101.

Meister, K. 1967. "Die sizilische Geschichte bei Diodor von den Anfängen bis zum Tod des Agathokles. Quellenuntersuchungen zu Buch IV–XXI." Diss. Munich.

1990. *Die griechische Geschichtsschreibung. Von den Anfängen bis zum Ende des Hellenismus.* Stuttgart/Berlin/Cologne: Kohlhammer.

Mejer, J. 1978. *Diogenes Laertius and His Hellenistic Background.* Wiesbaden: Steiner.

Mele, A. 1984. "Crotone e la sua storia," in Mele, A., *Crotone: Atti del ventitreesimo Convegno di studi sulla Magna Grecia.* Taranto: Istituto per la storia e l'archeologia della Magna Grecia, pp. 9–97.

Menn, S. 2001. "Longinus on Plotinus," *Dionysius* 29: 113–23.

Meredith, A. 1976. "Asceticism – Christian and Greek," *Journal of Theological Studies* 27: 313–32.

Merkelbach, R. 1962. "Antonius Diogenes," in Merkelbach, R., *Roman und Mysterium in der Antike.* Munich/Berlin: Beck, pp. 225–33.

1967. "Die Heroen als Geber des Guten und Bösen," *Zeitschrift für Papyrologie und Epigraphik* 1: 97–9.

1968. "Ein ägyptischer Priestereid," *Zeitschrift für Papyrologie und Epigraphik* 2: 7–30.

Merlan, P. 1960. *From Platonism to Neoplatonism.* 2nd edn. The Hague: Martinus Nijhoff.

Meuli, K. 1935. "Scythica," *Hermes* 70: 121–76.

Mewaldt, J. 1904. "De Aristoxeni Pythagoricis Sententiis et Vita Pythagorica." Diss. Berlin.

Meyer, C. 2000. *Jean de Murs. Écrits sur la musique.* Paris: CNRS.

(tr.) 2004. *Boèce: Traité de la musique.* Turnhout: Brepols.

Michel, P.-H. 1950. *De Pythagore à Euclide: contribution à l'histoire des mathématiques préeuclidiennes.* Paris: Les Belles Lettres.

1958. *Les Nombres figurés dans l'arithmétique pythagoricienne.* Paris: Les Conférences du Palais de la Découverte.

Minar, E. L. 1942. *Early Pythagorean Politics in Practice and Theory.* Baltimore, MD: Waverly.

Minio-Paluello, L. (ed.) 1950. *Phaedo interprete Henrico Aristippo.* London: The Warburg Institute.

Mirhady, D. C. 2001. "Dicaearchus of Messana: The Sources, Text and Translation," in Fortenbaugh and Schütrumpf (eds.), pp. 1–142.

Moehring, H. R. 1995. "Arithmology as an Exegetical Tool in the Writings of Philo of Alexandria," in Kenney, J. P. (ed.). *The School of Moses: Studies in Philo and Hellenistic Religion.* Atlanta, GA: Scholars' Press, pp. 141–76.

Momigliano, A. 1987. "Ancient Biography and the Study of Religion in the Roman Empire," in Momigliano, A. (ed.). *On Pagans, Jews and Christians.* Middletown, CT: Wesleyan University Press, pp. 159–77.

1993. *The Development of Greek Biography.* Cambridge, MA: Harvard University Press.

Mora, F. 1986. *Religione e religioni nelle storie di Erodoto*. Milan: Jaca Book.

Morani, M. (ed.) 1987. *Nemesii Emeseni de natura hominis*. Leipzig: Teubner.

Moraux, P. 1950. "Cléarque de Soles disciple d'Aristote," *Les Études classiques* 18: 22–6.

1965. *Aristote: Du Ciel*. Paris: Les Belles Lettres.

1984. *Der Aristotelismus bei den Griechen 2. Der Aristotelismus im I. und II. Jahrhundert n. Chr*. Berlin/New York: De Gruyter.

Morrison, J. S. 1956. "Pythagoras of Samos," *Classical Quarterly* n.s. 6: 135–56.

1958. "The Origins of Plato's Philosopher-Statesman," *Classical Quarterly* n.s. 8: 198–218.

1961. Review of Dodds 1959. *Phoenix* 15: 234–9.

Mourelatos, A. P. D. (ed.) 1993. *The Pre-Socratics: A Collection of Critical Essays*. 2nd edn. Princeton University Press.

Muccioli, F. 2002. "Pitagora e i Pitagorici nella tradizione antica," in Vattuone (ed.), pp. 341–409.

Mueller, I. 1981. *Philosophy of Mathematics and Deductive Structure in Euclid's Elements*. Cambridge, MA: MIT Press.

Münxelhaus, B. 1976. *Pythagoras musicus. Zur Rezeption der pythagoreischen Musiktheorie als quadrivialer Wissenschaft im lateinischen Mittelalter*. Bonn: Verlag für systematische Musikwissenschaft.

Murray, O. 1972. "Herodotus and Hellenistic Culture," *Classical Quarterly* n.s. 22: 200–13.

Musial, D. 2001. "'Sodalicium Nigidiani': les pythagoriciens à Rome à la fin de la République," *Revue de l'histoire des religions* 218: 339–67.

Musti, D. 1989. "Pitagorismo, storiografia e politica tra Magna Grecia e Sicilia," *AION (filol.) [Annali dell' Istituto Universitario Orientale di Napoli]* 11: 13–56.

1990. "Le rivolte antipitagoriche e la concezione pitagorica del tempo," *Quaderni Urbinati di Cultura Classica* 36: 35–65.

Naiden, F. S. 2006. *Ancient Supplication*. Oxford University Press.

Nauck, A. 1884. *Iamblichi de vita pythagorica liber*. St. Petersburg: Eggers [repr. 1965. Amsterdam: Hakkert].

Navia, L. E. 1990. *Pythagoras: An Annotated Bibliography*. New York: Garland.

Netz, R. 1997. "Classical Mathematics in the Classical Mediterranean," *Mediterranean Historical Review* 12: 1–24.

1999. *The Shaping of Deduction in Greek Mathematics: A Study in Cognitive History*. Cambridge University Press.

2002. "Counter Culture: Towards a History of Greek Numeracy," *History of Science* 40: 321–52.

2004. *The Transformation of Mathematics in the Early Mediterranean*. Cambridge University Press.

2005. "The Pythagoreans," in Koetsier, T. and Bergmans, L. (eds.). *Mathematics and the Divine*. Amsterdam: Elsevier, pp. 77–97.

2009. *Ludic Proof: Greek Mathematics and the Alexandrian Aesthetic*. Cambridge University Press.

2010. "What Did Greek Mathematicians Find Beautiful?," *Classical Philology* 105: 426–44.

Netz, R., Acerbi, F. and Wilson, N. 2004. "Towards a Reconstruction of Archimedes' Stomachion," *SCIAMVS* 5: 67–100.

Netz, R., Noel, W., Tchernetska, N. and Wilson, N. 2011. *The Archimedes Palimpsest*. Vol. 1: *Catalogue and Commentary*. Cambridge University Press.

Nock, A. D. 1933. *Conversion. The Old and the New in Religion from Alexander the Great to Augustine of Hippo*. Oxford: Clarendon.

1944. "The Cult of Heroes," *Harvard Theological Review* 37: 141–73.

North, J. A. 2012. "Sappho Underground," in Dignas and Smith (eds.), pp. 37–67.

North, J. A. and Price, S. R. F. (eds.) 2011. *The Religious History of the Roman Empire. Pagans, Jews, and Christians*. Oxford University Press.

Novokhatko, A. A. 2009. *The Invectives of Sallust and Cicero*. Berlin/New York: De Gruyter.

Nussbaum, M. C. 1979. "Eleatic Conventionalism and Philolaus on the Conditions of Thought," *Harvard Studies in Classical Philology* 83: 63–108.

O'Connell, R. J. 1968. *St. Augustine's Early Theory of Man, A.D. 386–391*. Cambridge, MA: Harvard University Press.

Ogden, D. 2007. *In Search of the Sorcerer's Apprentice. The Traditional Tales of Lucian's Lover of Lies*. Swansea: Classical Press of Wales.

Oldfather, W. A. 1938. "Pythagoras on Individual Differences and the Authoritarian Principle," *Classical Journal* 33: 537–9.

O'Meara, D. J. 1989. *Pythagoras Revived: Mathematics and Philosophy in Late Antiquity*. Oxford: Clarendon.

2003. *Platonopolis: Platonic Political Philosophy in Late Antiquity*. Oxford: Clarendon.

2005a. "The Music of Philosophy in Late Antiquity," in Sharples (ed.), pp. 131–47.

2005b. "Plotin 'historien' de la philosophie (*Enn*. IV 8 et V 1)," in Brancacci, A. (ed.). *Philosophy and Doxography in the Imperial Age*. Florence: Olschki, pp. 103–12.

2007. "Hearing the Harmony of the Spheres in Late Antiquity," in Bonazzi, Lévy and Steel (eds.), pp. 147–61.

2010. "L'éloge des sciences mathématiques dans la philosophie de l'Antiquité tardive," in Lernould, A. (ed.). *Études sur le commentaire de Proclus au premier livre des Éléments d'Euclide*. Villeneuve d'Ascq: Presses Universitaires du Septentrion, pp. 57–66.

2013. "Pythagoreanism in Late Antique Philosophy, after Proclus," in Cornelli, McKirahan and Macris (eds.), pp. 405–20.

O'Meara, D. and Dillon, J. 2008. *Syrianus: On Aristotle Metaphysics 3–4*. London: Duckworth.

Oosthout, H. and Schilling, I. (eds.) 1999. *Anicii Manlii Severini Boethii De institutione arithmetica*. Turnhout: Brepols.

Parker, R. 1983. *Miasma: Pollution and Purification in Early Greek Religion.* Oxford: Clarendon.

2005. *Polytheism and Society at Athens.* Oxford University Press.

Patillon, M. and Brisson, L. 2001. *Longin: Fragments-Art rhétorique.* Paris: Les Belles Lettres.

Patterson, R., Karasmanis, V. and Hermann, A. (eds.) 2012. *Presocratics and Plato: Festschrift at Delphi in Honor of Charles Kahn.* Las Vegas, NV: Parmenides.

Pearson, L. 1987. *The Greek Historians of the West. Timaeus and His Predecessors.* Atlanta, GA: Scholars' Press.

Pelosi, F. 2010. *Plato on Music, Soul and Body.* Cambridge University Press.

Penella, R. J. 1979. *The Letters of Apollonius of Tyana.* Leiden: Brill.

Pépin, J. 1974. "*Merikôteron – epoptikôteron* (Proclus, *In Tim.* I, 204, 24–7): deux attitudes exégétiques dans le néoplatonisme," in *Mélanges d'histoire des religions offerts à Henri-Charles Puech.* Paris: Presses universitaires de France, pp. 323–30.

1992. "*Philólogos/philósophos* (*VP* 14, 18–20)," in Brisson, L., Goulet-Cazé, M.-O., Goulet, R. and O'Brien, D. (eds.) 1992. *Porphyre. La Vie de Plotin,* Vol. 2: *Études d'introduction, texte grec et traduction française, commentaire, notes complémentaires, bibliographie.* Paris: Vrin, pp. 477–501.

Pernot, L. 1993. *La Rhétorique de l'éloge dans le monde gréco-romain.* Paris: Institut d'études augustiniennes.

Petit, A. 1997. "Le silence pythagoricien," in Lévy, C. and Pernot, L. (eds.). *Dire l'évidence: philosophie et rhétorique antiques.* Paris: L'Harmattan, pp. 287–96.

Petsalis-Diomidis, A. 2010. *Truly beyond Wonders. Aelius Aristides and the Cult of Asklepios.* Oxford University Press.

Petzke, G. 1970. *Die Traditionen über Apollonius von Tyana und das Neue Testament.* Leiden: Brill.

Philip, J. A. 1959. "The Biographical Tradition – Pythagoras," *Transactions of the American Philological Association* 90: 185–94.

1966. *Pythagoras and Early Pythagoreanism.* University of Toronto Press.

Piccione, R. 2002. "Encyclopédisme et *enkyklios paideia*? À propos de Jean Stobée et de l'*Anthologion*," *Philosophie antique* 2: 169–97.

Piras, G. 1998. *Varrone e i poetica verba. Studio sul settimo libro del De lingua Latina.* Bologna: Pàtron.

Powell, J. E. 1938. *A Lexicon to Herodotus.* Cambridge University Press.

Prelog, J. 1990. "'De Pictagora Phylosopho.' Die Biographie des Pythagoras in dem Walter Burley zugeschriebenen 'Liber de vita et moribus philosophorum'," *Medioevo* 16: 191–251.

Preus, A. (ed.) 2001. *Essays in Ancient Greek Philosophy VI: Before Plato.* Albany: State University of New York Press.

Primavesi, O. 2009. "Zur Genealogie der Poesie (Kap. 4)," in Höffe, O. (ed.). *Aristoteles Poetik.* Berlin: Akademie, pp. 47–67.

2012a. "Aristotle, *Metaphysics A.* A New Critical Edition with Introduction," in Steel (ed.), pp. 385–516.

2012b. "Second Thoughts on Some Presocratics (*Metaphysics A* 989ᵃ18–990ᵃ32)," in Steel (ed.), pp. 225–63.

Provenza, A. 2012. "Aristoxenus and Music Therapy: Fr. 26 Wehrli within the Tradition on Music and Catharsis," in Huffman (ed.) 2012c, pp. 91–128.

Purvis, A. L. (tr.) 2007. *The Landmark Herodotus. The Histories*. New York: Pantheon.

Quack, J. F. 1997. "Ein ägyptisches Handbuch des Tempels und seine griechische Übersetzung," *Zeitschrift für Papyrologie und Epigraphik* 119: 297–300.

Quandt, W. (ed.) 1955. *Orphei hymni*. Berlin: Weidmann.

Radicke, J. 1999. *Felix Jacoby. Die Fragmente der griechischen Historiker Continued. IV A: Biography. Fascicle 7: Imperial and Undated Authors*. Leiden: Brill.

Raffa, M. 2002. *La scienza armonica di Claudio Tolemeo*. Messina: A. Sfameni.

Ramelli, I. 2003. "Diogene Laerzio e Clemente Alessandrino nel contesto di un dibattito culturale comune," *Espacio, Tiempo y Forma* ser. II. 15: 207–24.

Rangos, S. 2004. "Images of Socrates in Neoplatonism," in Karasmanis, V. (ed.). *Socrates: 2400 Years since His Death*. Athens/Delphi: European Cultural Centre of Delphi/Hellenic Ministry of Culture, pp. 463–80.

Rankin, S. 2005. "*Naturalis concordia vocum cum planetis*: Conceptualizing the Harmony of the Spheres in the Early Middle Ages," in Clark and Leach (eds.), pp. 3–19.

Rathmann, W. 1933. "Quaestiones pythagoreae orphicae empedocleae." Diss. Halle.

Raven, J. E. 1951. "Polyclitus and Pythagoreanism," *Classical Quarterly* 3–4: 147–52.

Rawson, E. 1985. *Intellectual Life in the Late Roman Republic*. London: Duckworth.

Redfield, J. M. 2003. *The Locrian Maidens. Love and Death in Greek Italy*. Princeton University Press.

Reiffersheid, A. (ed.) 1860. *C. Suetoni Tranquilli praeter Caesarum libros reliquiae*. Leipzig: Teubner.

Reitzenstein, R. 1914. *Des Athanasius Werk über das Leben des Antonius: Ein philologischer Beitrag zur Geschichte des Mönchtums*. Sitzungsberichte der Heidelberger Akademie der Wissenschaften, Philosophisch-historische Klasse 5. Heidelberg: Winter.

Reydams-Schils, G. (ed.) 2003. *Plato's Timaeus as Cultural Icon*. Notre Dame, IN: University of Notre Dame Press.

2006. "Calcidius on the Human and the World Soul and Middle-Platonist Psychology," *Apeiron* 39: 178–92.

Reyhl, K. 1969. "Antonios Diogenes. Untersuchungen zu den Roman-Fragmenten der Wunder jenseits von Thule und zu den Wahren Geschichten des Lukian." Diss. Tübingen.

Rico, G. 2005a. "'Auctoritas cereum habet nasum': Boethius, Aristotle, and the Music of the Spheres in the Thirteenth and Early Fourteenth Centuries," in Clark and Leach (eds.), pp. 20–8.

2005b. "Music in the Arts Faculty of Paris in the Thirteenth and Early Fourteenth Centuries." Diss. Oxford.

Riedweg, C. 2002. *Pythagoras. Leben – Lehre – Nachwirkung.* Munich: Beck.

2004. "Zum Ursprung des Wortes 'Philosophie,' oder Pythagoras von Samos als Wortschöpfer," in Bierl, A., Schmitt, A. and Willi, A. (eds.). *Antike Literatur in neuer Deutung.* Munich/Leipzig: K. G. Saur, pp. 147–81.

2005. *Pythagoras: His Life, Teaching and Influence.* S. Rendall (tr.). Ithaca, NY/London: Cornell University Press.

2007. *Pythagoras. Leben, Lehre, Nachwirkung. Eine Einführung.* Munich: Beck. 2nd edn.

2008. *Pythagoras: His Life, Teaching and Influence*, 2nd edn. S. Rendall (tr.), Ithaca, NY/London: Cornell University Press.

Rispoli, G. M. 2009. "La musica e le forme," in Martinelli, Pelosi and Pernigotti (eds.), pp. 101–39.

Rivaud, A. 1932. "Platon et la 'politique pythagoricienne'," in *Mélanges Gustave Glotz.* Vol. 2. Paris: Presses universitaires de France, pp. 779–92.

Rives, J. B. 2010. "*Magus* and Its Cognates in Classical Latin," in Gordon and Marco Simón (eds.), pp. 53–77.

Robert, L. 1980. *À travers l'Asie Mineure. Poètes et prosateurs, monnaies grecques, voyageurs et géographie.* Paris: École française d'Athènes.

Robiano, P. 2003. "Lucien, un témoignage-clé sur Apollonios de Tyana," *Revue de philologie, de littérature et d'histoire anciennes* 77: 259–73.

Robson, E. and Stedall, J. (eds.) 2009. *The Oxford Handbook of the History of Mathematics.* Oxford University Press.

Rocca-Serra, G. 1971. "La *lettre à Marcella* de Porphyre et les *Sentences* des Pythagoriciens," in Schuhl, P. M. and Hadot, P. (eds.). *Le Néoplatonisme.* Paris: CNRS, pp. 193–9 and 200–2.

Rohde, E. 1901. "Die Quellen des Iamblichus in seiner Biographie des Pythagoras," in *Kleine Schriften II.* Tübingen: Mohr, pp. 102–72 = *Rheinisches Museum* 26 (1871): 554–76 and 27 (1872): 23–61.

1925. *Psyche. Seelencult und Unsterblichkeitsglaube der Griechen.* 2 vols. Tübingen: Mohr = *Psyche: The Cult of Souls and Belief in Immortality among the Greeks.* Hillis, W. B. (tr.). 2 vols. London: Routledge & Kegan Paul.

Rohloff, E. (ed.) 1943. *Der Musiktraktat des Johannes de Grocheo.* Leipzig: Kommissionsverlag Gebrüder Reinecke.

Romano, F. 2006. *Giamblico, Summa pitagorica: Vita di Pitagora, Esortazione alla filosofia, Scienza matematica commune, Introduzione all'aritmetica di Nicomaco, Teologia dell'aritmetica.* Milan: Bompiani.

Rose, V. 1863. *Aristoteles Pseudepigraphus.* Leipzig: Teubner [repr. 1971. Hildesheim: Olms].

1886. *Aristotelis fragmenta.* 3rd edn. Leipzig: Teubner.

Rosén, H. B. 1987. *Herodoti Historiae.* Vol. 1: Libros I–IV continens. Leipzig: Teubner.

Rosenthal, F. 1937. "Arabische Nachrichten über Zenon den Eleaten," *Orientalia* n.s. 6: 21–67 [repr. in Rosenthal, F. 1990. *Greek Philosophy in the Arab World. A Collection of Essays.* Aldershot: Variorum, pp. 21–67].

Ross, W. D. 1908. *Metaphysica* (= *The Works of Aristotle Translated into English under the Editorship of J. A. Smith / W. D. Ross.* Vol. 8). Oxford: Clarendon.

1924. *Aristotle's Metaphysics. A Revised Text with Introduction and Commentary.* Vol. 1. Oxford: Clarendon.

1928. *Metaphysica. Second Edition* (= *The Works of Aristotle Translated into English under the Editorship of W. D. Ross.* Vol. 8). Oxford: Clarendon.

1955. *Aristotelis fragmenta selecta.* Oxford: Clarendon.

Rostagni, A. 1924. *Il verbo di Pitagora.* Turin: Bocca [repr. 2005: Forlì: Victrix].

Rowe, C. and Schofield, M. (eds.) 2000. *The Cambridge History of Greek and Roman Political Thought.* Cambridge University Press.

Rubenson, S. 2006. "Antony and Pythagoras: A Reappraisal of the Appropriation of Classical Biography in Athanasius' *Vita Antonii,*" in Brakke, D., Jacobsen, A-.C. and Ulrich, J. (eds.). *Beyond Reception: Mutual Influences between Antique Religion, Judaism, and Early Christianity.* Frankfurt: Peter Lang, pp. 191–208.

Runia, D. T. 2001. *On the Creation of the Cosmos according to Moses. Introduction, Translation and Commentary.* Leiden: Brill.

2008. "The Sources for Presocratic Philosophy," in Curd and Graham (eds.), pp. 27–54.

Rusjaeva, A. S. 1978. "Orfism i kult Dionisa v Olvii," *Vestnik Drevnej Istorii* 143: 87–104.

Ruska, J. 1931. *Turba philosophorum: ein Beitrag zur Geschichte der Alchemie.* Berlin: Springer.

Russell, B. 1945. *History of Western Philosophy.* New York: Simon and Schuster.

Rutgers, L. V. 1994. "Roman Policy toward the Jews: Expulsions from the City of Rome during the First Century C.E.," *Classical Antiquity* 13: 56–74.

Sachs, E. 1917. *Die fünf Platonischen Körper.* Berlin: Weidmann.

Sachs, K.-J. 1991. "Boethius and the Judgement of the Ears: A Hidden Challenge in Medieval and Renaissance Music Theory," in Burnett, Fend and Gouk (eds.), pp. 169–98.

Saffrey, H. D. 1992. "Pourquoi Porphyre a-t-il édité Plotin?," in Brisson *et al.* (eds.), pp. 31–57.

Saffrey, H. D. and Westerink, L. G. 1968–2003. *Proclus: Théologie platonicienne.* Paris: Les Belles Lettres.

Saito, K. 1998. "Mathematical Reconstructions Out, Textual Studies In: 30 Years in the Historiography of Greek Mathematics," *Revue d'histoire des mathématiques* 4: 131–42.

Sallmann, K. 2002. "Varro [2]," *DNP* 12: 1130–44.

Sansone, D. 1997. "Hermippus, Fragment 22 Wehrli," *Illinois Classical Studies* 22: 51–64.

Santangelo, F. 2011. "Whose Sacrilege? A Note on *Sal.* 5.14," *Classical World* 104: 333–8.

Sassi, M. M. (ed.) 2006. *La costruzione del discorso filosofico nell'età dei Presocratici/ The Construction of Philosophical Discourse in the Age of the Presocratics.* Pisa: Edizioni della Normale.

Sauron, G. 1994. *Quis deum? L'Expression plastique des idéologies politiques et religieuses à Rome.* Rome: École française de Rome.

Schepens, G. and Delcroix, K. 1996. "Ancient Paradoxography: Origin, Evolution, Production and Reception," in Pecere, O. and Stramaglia, A. (eds.). *La letteratura di consumo nel mondo greco-latino.* Cassino: Università degli studi di Cassino, pp. 373–460.

Schibli, H. S. 1990. *Pherekydes of Syros.* Oxford: Clarendon.

  1997. "On 'The One' in Philolaus, Fragment 7," *Classical Quarterly* n.s. 46.1: 114–30.

Schirren, T. 2005. *"Philosophos Bios." Die antike Philosophenbiographie als symbolische Form. Studien zur "Vita Apollonii" des Philostrat.* Heidelberg: Winter.

Schmeling, G. 1969. "A Pythagorean Element of the Subterranean Basilica at the Porta Maggiore," *Latomus* 28: 1071–3.

Schmidt, P. L. 2000. "Nigidius Figulus, P.," *DNP* 8: 890–1.

Schofield, M. 1997. "APXH," *Hyperboreus* 3: 218–36.

  2012. "Pythagoreanism: Emerging from the Presocratic Fog. *Metaphysics* A 5," in Steel (ed.), pp. 141–66.

  (ed.) 2013. *Aristotle, Plato and Pythagoreanism in the First Century BC.* Cambridge University Press.

Schorn, S. 2004. *Satyros aus Kallatis: Sammlung der Fragmente mit Kommentar.* Basel: Schwabe.

  2007. "'Periegetische Biographie', 'Historische Biographie': Neanthes von Kyzikos (FgrHist 84) als Biograph," in Erler and Schorn (eds.), pp. 115–56.

  2009. "On Eating Meat and Human Sacrifice. Anthropology in Asclepiades of Cyprus and Theophrastus of Eresus," in van Nuffelen, P. (ed.). *Faces of Hellenism.* Leuven: Peeters, pp. 11–47.

  2012. "Aristoxenus' Biographical Method," in Huffman 2012c, pp. 177–221.

  2013. "Bio-Doxographie in hellenistischer Zeit," in Zecchini, G. (ed.). *L'Ellenismo come categoria storica e come categoria ideale.* Milan: Vita e Pensiero, pp. 27–67.

  forthcoming. "Die Pythagoreer im zehnten Buch der Bibliothek Diodors. Zitate, Traditionen – und Manipulationen," in Berti, M. and Costa, V. (eds.). *Ritorno ad Alessandria. Storiografia greca e cultura bibliotecaria. Tracce di una relazione perduta.* Tivoli: Tored.

Schröter, R. 1963. "Die varronische Etymologie," in *Varron. Entretiens sur l'antiquité classique IX.* Geneva: Fondation Hardt, pp. 79–116.

Schütrumpf, E., Stork, P., van Ophuijsen, J. and Prince, S. (eds.) 2008. *Heraclides of Pontus: Texts and Translation.* New Brunswick, NJ/London: Transaction.

Schwartz, E. 1894. "Alexandros (88)," in *RE* 1.2: 1449–52.

  1903a. "Diodoros 38," *RE* 5.1: 663–704.

  1903b. "Diogenes Laertios," *RE* 5.1: 738–63.

Seaford, R. 2004. *Money and the Early Greek Mind.* Cambridge University Press.

Sedley, D. 1976. "Epicurus and the Mathematicians of Cyzicus," *Cronache Ercolanesi* 6: 23–54.

    1995. "The Dramatis Personae of Plato's *Phaedo*," in Smiley (ed.), pp. 3–26.

    2003. *Plato's Cratylus.* Cambridge University Press.

    2007. *Creationism and Its Critics in Antiquity.* Berkeley: University of California Press.

    (ed.) 2012. *The Philosophy of Antiochus.* Cambridge University Press.

Segal, C. 1969. "Myth and Philosophy in the *Metamorphoses*: Ovid's Augustianism and the Augustan Conclusion of Book XV," *American Journal of Philology* 90: 257–92.

Segonds, A.-P. 1982. "Les fragments de l'*Histoire de la philosophie*," in Des Places (ed.), pp. 163–97.

Seltman, C. 1933. *Greek Coins.* London: Methuen.

    1949. "The Problem of the First Italiote Coins," *Numismatic Chronicle* 6: 1–21.

    1956. "Pythagoras: Artist, Statesman, Philosopher: I. Pythagoras in Samos. II. Pythagoras in Italy," *History Today* 6: 522–7 and 592–7.

Sepúlveda, J. G. 1527. *Alexandri Aphrodisiei commentaria in duodecim Aristotelis libros de prima philosophia.* Rome: Silber.

Sfameni Gasparro, G. 1987–1989. "Critica del sacrificio cruento e antropologia in Grecia: da Pitagora a Porfirio. I. La tradizione pitagorica, Empedocle e l'orfismo. II. Il *De abstinentia* porfiriano," in Vattioni, F. (ed.). *Sangue e antropologia – riti e culto.* Vol. I, pp. 107–55 and *Sangue e antropologia nella teologia.* Vol. I, pp. 461–505. Rome: Edizione Pia Unione Preziosissimo Sangue.

Shackleton Bailey, D. R. (tr.) 2000. *Valerius Maximus: Memorable Doings and Sayings.* 2 vols. Loeb Classical Library. Cambridge, MA: Harvard University Press.

Sharples, R. W. (ed.) 2005. *Philosophy and the Sciences in Antiquity.* Aldershot: Ashgate.

Sharples, R. W. and Sorabji, R. (eds.) 2007. *Greek and Roman Philosophy 100 BC–200 AD.* 2 vols. London: Institute of Classical Studies.

Shirokogoroff, S. 1935. *The Psychomental Complex of the Tungus.* London: Kegan Paul.

Shrimpton, G. S. 1991. *Theopompus the Historian.* Montreal: McGill-Queen's University Press.

Skutch, O. 1985. *The Annals of Q. Ennius.* Oxford: Clarendon.

Slaveva-Griffin, S. 2008. "Unity of Thought and Writing: *Enn.* 6. 6. and Porphyry's Arrangement of the *Enneads*," *Classical Quarterly* 58.1: 277–85.

    2009. *Plotinus on Number.* Oxford University Press.

Smiley, T. J. (ed.) 1995. *Philosophical Dialogues: Plato, Hume, Wittgenstein.* Oxford University Press.

Smith, A. 1984. "Did Porphyry Reject the Transmigration of Human Souls into Animals?," *Rheinisches Museum* 127: 276–84 [repr. in Smith, A. 2011. *Plotinus, Porphyry and Iamblichus: Philosophy and Religion in Neoplatonism.* Burlington, VT: Ashgate – Variorum].

(ed.) 1993. *Porphyrii philosophi fragmenta. Fragmenta arabica David Wasserstein interpretante.* Stuttgart/Leipzig: Teubner.

Smith, M. 1988. "A Hidden Use of Porphyry's *History of Philosophy* in Eusebius' *Preparatio Evangelica*," *Journal of Theological Studies* 39: 494–504.

Sodano, A. R. 1991. "Porfirio 'gnomologo': Contributo alla tradizione e alla critica testuale delle sillogi gnomiche," *Sileno* 17: 5–41.

1997. *Porfirio. Storia della filosofia: frammenti.* Milan: Rusconi.

Sodano, A. R. and Girgenti, G. 1998. *Porfirio. Vita di Pitagora.* Milan: Rusconi.

Sokolowski, F. 1955. *Lois sacrées de l'Asie Mineure (LSAM).* Paris: De Boccard.

1969. *Lois sacrées des cités grecques (LSCG).* Paris: De Boccard.

Solmsen, F. 1957. "The Vital Heat, the Inborn Pneuma, and the Aether," *Journal of Hellenic Studies* 77: 119–23.

Solomon, J. 2000. *Ptolemy. Harmonics: Translation and Commentary.* Leiden: Brill.

Sommerstein, A. H. (tr.) 2008. *Aeschylus: Fragments.* Loeb Classical Library. Cambridge, MA: Harvard University Press.

Sorabji, R. (ed.) 1990. *Aristotle Transformed: The Ancient Commentators and Their Influence.* Ithaca, NY: Cornell University Press.

Speyer, W. 1974. "Zum Bild des Apollonios von Tyana bei Heiden und Christen," *Jahrbuch für Antike und Christentum* 17: 47–63.

Staab, G. 2002. *Pythagoras in der Spätantike. Studien zu "De Vita Pythagorica" des Iamblichos von Chalkis.* Munich: K. G. Saur.

2003. "Iamblich von Chalkis: Antiquar-Kompilator-Pädagoge. Strategie und Technik der Quellentransformation in *De vita Pythagorica*," in Piccione, R. and Perkams, M. (eds.). *Selecta colligere, I. Akten des Kolloquiums "Sammeln, Neuordnen, Neues Schaffen. Methoden der Überlieferung von Texten in der Spätantike und in Byzanz."* Alessandria: Edizioni dell'Orso, pp. 145–68.

2007. "Der Gewährsmann 'Apollonios' in den neuplatonischen Pythagorasviten – Wundermann oder hellenistischer Literat?," in Erler and Schorn (eds.), pp. 195–217.

Städele, A. 1980. *Die Briefe des Pythagoras und der Pythagoreer.* Meisenheim: Hain.

Staehle, K. 1931. *Die Zahlenmystik bei Philon von Alexandria.* Leipzig/Berlin: Teubner.

Stählin, O. (ed.) 1905–1936. *Clemens Alexandrinus.* 4 vols. Leipzig: Hinrichs.

Stangl, T. (ed.) 1912. *Ciceronis orationum scholasticae.* Vienna: Tempsky.

Steel, C. 2002. "A Neoplatonic Speusippus?," in Barbanti, Giardina and Manganaro (eds.), pp. 469–76.

2007. "Proclus on Divine Figures. An Essay on Pythagorean–Platonic Theology," in Bonazzi, Lévy and Steel (eds.), pp. 215–42.

(ed.) 2012. *Aristotle's Metaphysics Alpha (Symposium Aristotelicum).* Oxford University Press.

Stephens, S. 1996. "Fragments of Lost Novels," in Schmeling, G. (ed.). *The Novel in the Ancient World.* Leiden: Brill, pp. 655–84.

Stephens, S. and Winkler, J. J. (eds.) 1995. *Ancient Greek Novels: The Fragments.* Princeton University Press.

Stern-Gillet, S. and Corrigan, K. (eds.) 2007. *Reading Ancient Texts.* Vol. 1: *Presocratics and Plato.* Leiden: Brill.

Swoboda, A. 1889. *P. Nigidi Figuli operum reliquiae.* Vienna: Tempsky.

Swogger, J. H. 1975. "Antonio degli Agli's *Explanatio symbolorum Pythagorae*: An Edition and Study of Its Place in the Circle of Marsilio Ficino." Diss. University of London.

Szlezák, T. A. 1972. *Pseudo-Archytas über die Kategorien.* Berlin: De Gruyter.

Tannery, P. 1893. *Diophanti Alexandrini opera omnia.* Vol. 2. Leipzig: Teubner.

Taormina, D. 1999. *Jamblique critique de Plotin et de Porphyre.* Paris: Vrin.

　　2012. "Platonismo e pitagorismo," in Chiaradonna, R. (ed.). *Filosofia tardoantica.* Rome: Carocci, pp. 103–27.

Tarán, L. 1981. *Speusippus of Athens.* Leiden: Brill.

　　1987. "Syrianus and Pseudo-Alexander's Commentary on Metaphysics E-N," in Wiesner, J. (ed.). *Aristoteles: Werk und Wirkung: Kommentierung, Überlieferung, Nachleben.* Berlin: De Gruyter, pp. 215–32.

Tarrant, H. 1993. *Thrasyllan Platonism.* Ithaca, NY/London: Cornell University Press.

Taufer, M. 2008. "Zalmoxis nella tradizione greca. Rassegna e rilettura delle fonti," *Quaderni di Storia* 68: 131–64.

Teeuwen, M. 2007. "L'armonia delle sfere nel nono secolo: Nuove prospettive su fonti antiche," in Cristiani, Panti and Perillo (eds.), pp. 95–113.

Theiler, W. 1965. "Philo von Alexandria und der Beginn des kaiserzeitlichen Platonismus," in Flasch, K. (ed.). *Parusia. Studien zur Philosophie Platons und zur Problemgeschichte des Platonismus.* Frankfurt am Main: Minerva, pp. 199–218.

Thesleff, H. 1961. *An Introduction to the Pythagorean Writings of the Hellenistic Period.* Åbo: Åbo Akademi.

　　1965a. *The Pythagorean Texts of the Hellenistic Period.* Åbo: Åbo Akademi.

　　1965b. Review of Adriana Della Casa, *Nigidio Figulo,* Rome 1962. *Gnomon* 37: 44–8.

　　1972. "On the Problem of the Doric Pseudopythagorica," in von Fritz (ed.), pp. 57–87.

Thom, J. C. 1994. "'Don't Walk on the Highways': The Pythagorean Akousmata and Early Christian Literature," *Journal of Biblical Literature* 113: 93–112.

　　1995. *The Pythagorean Golden Verses. With Introduction and Commentary.* Leiden: Brill.

　　2008. "The Passions in Neopythagorean Writings," in Fitzgerald, J. T. (ed.). *Passions and Moral Progress in Greco-Roman Thought.* London: Routledge, pp. 67–78.

　　2013. "The Pythagorean Akousmata and Early Pythagoreanism," in Cornelli, McKirahan and Macris (eds.), pp. 77–102.

Thomson, G. 1938. *The Oresteia of Aeschylus.* Cambridge University Press.

　　1941. *Aeschylus and Athens.* London: Lawrence and Wishart.

Thomson, W. 1930. *The Commentary of Pappus on Book X of Euclid's Elements.* Cambridge, MA: Harvard University Press.

Thurn, H. (ed.) 2000. *Ioannis Malalae Chronographia*. Berlin/New York: De Gruyter.

Tomlinson, G. 1993. *Music in Renaissance Magic: Towards a Historiography of Others*. Chicago/London: University of Chicago Press.

Tortorelli Ghidini, M. 2000. "Da Orfeo agli orfici," in Tortorelli Ghidini, M., Storchi Marino, A. and Visconti, A. (eds.), pp. 11–41.

Tortorelli Ghidini, M., Storchi Marino, A. and Visconti, A. (eds.) 2000. *Tra Orfeo e Pitagora. Origini e incontri di culture nell'antichità*. Naples: Bibliopolis.

Trapp, M. 2007. "Neopythagoreans," in Sharples and Sorabji, Vol. 2, pp. 347–63.

Trinkaus, C. 1970. *In Our Image and Likeness: Humanity and Divinity in Italian Humanist Thought*. 2 vols. London: Constable.

van der Waerden, B. L. 1965. "Pythagoras – Die Schriften und die Fragmente des Pythagoras," in *RE* Suppl. 10: 843–64.

1979. *Die Pythagoreer*. Zurich: Artemis.

van Uytfanghe, M. 2009. "La *Vie d'Apollonius de Tyane* et le discours hagiographique," in Demoen and Praet (eds.), pp. 335–74.

van Winden, J. C. M. 1965. *Calcidius on Matter: His Doctrine and Sources. A Chapter in the History of Platonism*. Leiden: Brill.

Vattuone, R. 1991. *Sapienza d'occidente. Il pensiero storico di Timeo di Tauromenio*. Bologna: Pàtron.

(ed.) 2002a. *Storici greci d'occidente*. Bologna: Società editrice il Mulino.

2002b. "Timeo di Tauromenio," in R. Vattuone (ed.), pp. 177–323.

Vernant, J. P. 1983. *Myth and Thought among the Greeks*. London: Routledge.

Vitebsky, P. 1993. *Dialogues with the Dead: The Discussion of Mortality among the Sora of Eastern India*. Cambridge University Press.

Viveiros de Castro, E. 2009. *Métaphysiques cannibales*. Paris: Presses universitaires de France.

Vlastos, G. 1952. "Theology and Philosophy in Early Greek Thought," *Philosophical Quarterly* 2: 97–123.

1996. "Raven's *Pythagoreans and Eleatics*," in Graham, D. (ed.). *Studies in Greek Philosophy*. Princeton University Press, pp. 180–8.

Voss, A. 2000. "Marsilio Ficino, the Second Orpheus," in Horden, P. (ed.). *Music as Medicine: The History of Music Therapy since Antiquity*. Aldershot: Ashgate, pp. 154–72.

2002. "Orpheus redivivus: The Musical Magic of Marsilio Ficino," in Allen and Rees (eds.), pp. 227–41.

Wachsmuth, C. and Hense, O. (eds.) 1884–1912. *Stobaeus: Anthologium*. 5 vols. Berlin: Weidmann.

Walker, D. P. 1958. *Spiritual and Demonic Magic: From Ficino to Campanella*. London: Warburg Institute.

Walker, D. P. and Gouk, P. 1985. *Music, Spirit and Language in the Renaissance*. London: Variorum.

Walsh, P. G. (tr.) 1998. *Cicero: The Nature of the Gods*. Oxford: Clarendon.

Warden, J. 1982. "Orpheus and Ficino," in Warden, J. (ed.). *Orpheus: The Metamorphoses of a Myth*. University of Toronto Press, pp. 85–110.

Waszink, J. H. 1966. "Porphyrios und Numenios," in Dörrie, H. (ed.). *Porphyre*. Entretiens sur l'Antiquité classique 12. Vandœuvres-Genève: Fondation Hardt, pp. 33–78.

1975. *Timaeus a Calcidio translatus commentarioque instructus*. 2nd edn. London: Warburg Institute.

Waterfield, R. (tr.) 1988. *The Theology of Arithmetic*. Grand Rapids, MI: Phanes.

Waterhouse, W. C. 1972. "The Discovery of the Regular Solids," *Archive for History of Exact Sciences* 9: 212–21.

Weber, L. 1933. "Zu Herodot II 81," *Philologische Wochenschrift* 53: 1180–3.

Weber, M. 1948. *From Max Weber: Essays in Sociology*. Gerth, H. H. and Mills, C. W. (tr. and ed.). London: Kegan Paul.

Webster, T. B. L. 1970. *Studies in Later Greek Comedy*. 2nd edn. Manchester University Press.

Węcowski, M. 2012. "Pseudo-Democritus, or Bolos of Mendes (263)," in I. Worthington (ed.). *Brill's New Jacoby*. Online at http://referenceworks. brillonline.com/entries/brill-s-new-jacoby/pseudo-democritus-or-bolos-of-mendes-263-a263.

Wehrli, F. 1967–1978. *Die Schule des Aristoteles: Texte und Kommentar*. Vol. 1. *Dikaiarchos*, ²1967; Vol. 2. *Aristoxenos*, ²1967; Vol. 3. *Klearchos*, ²1969; Vol. 4. *Demetrios von Phaleron*, ²1968; Vol. 5. *Straton von Lampsakos*, ²1969; Vol. 6. *Lykon und Ariston von Keos*, ²1968; Vol. 7. *Herakleides Pontikos*, ²1969; Vol. 8. *Eudemos von Rhodos*, ²1969; Vol. 9. *Phanias von Eresos, Chamaileon, Praxiphanes*, ²1969; Vol. 10. *Hieronymos von Rhodos, Kritolaos und seine Schüler. Rückblick: Der Peripatos in vorchristlicher Zeit. Register*, ²1969; Suppl. 1. *Hermippos der Kallimacheer*, 1974; Suppl. 2. *Sotion*, 1978. Basel: Schwabe.

Wellmann, M. 1919. "Eine Pythagoreische Urkunde des IV. Jahrhunderts v. Chr.," *Hermes* 54: 225–48.

West, M. L. 1971a. "The Cosmology of 'Hippocrates,' *De Hebdomadibus*," *Classical Quarterly* n.s. 21, 365–88.

1971b. "Stesichorus," *Classical Quarterly* 21: 302–14.

1982. "The Orphics of Olbia," *Zeitschrift für Papyrologie und Epigraphik* 45: 17–29.

1983. *The Orphic Poems*. Oxford: Clarendon.

1992. *Ancient Greek Music*. Oxford: Clarendon.

Westra, J. J. (ed.) 1986. *The Commentary on Martianus Capella's "De nuptiis Philologiae et Mercurii" Attributed to Bernardus Silvestris*. Toronto: Pontifical Institute of Mediaeval Studies.

White, S. 2001. "*Principes Sapientiae*: Dicaearchus' Biography of Philosophy," in Fortenbaugh and Schütrumpf (eds.), pp. 195–236.

2004. "Hieronymus of Rhodes: The Sources, Text and Translation," in Fortenbaugh and White (eds.), pp. 79–276.

Whittaker, John 1969. "Neopythagoreanism and Negative Theology," *Symbolae Osloenses* 44: 109–25.

Wiersma, W. 1942. "Das Referat des Alexandros Polyhistor über die Pythagoreische Philosophie," *Mnemosyne* 10: 97–112.

Wilamowitz-Moellendorff, U. von 1931–1932. *Der Glaube der Hellenen.* 2 vols. Berlin: Weidmann.

Willis, J. (ed.) 1970. *Ambrosii Theodosii Macrobii Commentarii in Somnium Scipionis.* Leipzig: Teubner.

Wilpert, P. 1940. "Reste verlorener Aristotelesschriften bei Alexander von Aphrodisias," *Hermes* 75: 369–96.

Wind, E. 1968. *Pagan Mysteries in the Renaissance.* Rev. edn. New York: Norton.

Wöhrle, G. 1995. "Wer entdeckte die Quelle des Mondlichts?," *Hermes* 123: 244–7.

Zambon, M. 2002. *Porphyre et le moyen-platonisme.* Paris: Vrin.

2004. "Porfirio biografo di filosofi," in Monaci Castagno, A. (ed.). *La biografia di Origene fra storia e agiografia.* Villa Verucchio (Rimini): P. G. Pazzini, pp. 117–42.

2012. "Porphyre de Tyr – *Histoire philosophique,*" in Goulet (ed.), Vol. 5b, pp. 1326–33.

Zeller, E. 1919. *Die Philosophie der Griechen in ihrer geschichtlichen Entwicklung.* 6th edn. W. Nestle. Leipzig: Reisland [repr. 1963 Darmstadt: Wissenschaftliche Buchgesellschaft].

Zhmud, L. 1989. "'All Is Number?,'" *Phronesis* 34: 270–92.

1992a. "*Mathematici* and *Acusmatici* in the Pythagorean School," in Boudouris (ed.), pp. 240–9.

1992b. "Orphism and Graffiti from Olbia," *Hermes* 120: 159–68.

1997. *Wissenschaft, Philosophie und Religion im frühen Pythagoreismus.* Berlin: Akademie.

1998a. "Plato as 'Architect of Science,'" *Phronesis* 43: 211–44.

1998b. "Some Notes on Philolaus and the Pythagoreans," *Hyperboreus* 4: 243–70.

2002. "Eudemus' History of Mathematics," in Bodnár and Fortenbaugh (eds.), pp. 263–306.

2006. *The Origin of the History of Science in Classical Antiquity.* Berlin/New York: De Gruyter.

2010/2011. "Pythagorean Communities: From Individuals to a Collective Portrait," *Hyperboreus* 16/17: 311–27.

2012a. "Aristoxenus and the Pythagoreans," in Huffman (ed.) 2012c, pp. 223–49.

2012b. *Pythagoras and the Early Pythagoreans.* Oxford University Press.

Zoepffel, R. 2001. "Sokrates und die Pythagoreer," in Kessler, H. (ed.). *Sokrates: Nachfolge und Eigenwege.* Zug: Die Graue Edition, pp. 167–200.

Zuntz, G. N. 1971. *Persephone: Three Essays on Religion and Thought in Magna Graecia.* Oxford: Clarendon.

General index

Please also consult the Index locorum, the Table of contents, and the subheadings within chapters.

abacus, 10, 177–9
Abaris, 258
absolute and relative, Academic categories, 263, 323
Academy, New, and Pythagoreanism, 260, 271
Academy, Old, 261
  and Pythagoreanism, 13–14, 250–60
acme calculations, 170
acoustics, 186–8, 200
active and passive principles, 327
acusmata, 8, 13, 18, 92, 133–6, 137, 138, 141–2, 143–4, 145, 146, 154, 159, 219, 368–70, 376
  and Egyptian traditions, 140
  and Hesiod, 29
  and pseudo-Pythagorean writings, 333
  and *Pythagorean Precepts*, 294
  emphasis on purity in, 214
  explanations of, 377
  in Aristotle, 40, 248
  in the Renaissance, 22
  not attested for historical Pythagoreans, 111
  nucleus of the Pythagorean life, 133
  on naming, 347
  physics in, 48, 135, 163
  Plato's attitude to, 32, 44
  ritual material in, 288
  see also symbola
acusmatici and *mathematici*, 7, 26, 92–4, 111, 136, 286, 287–8, 367
admonitions, 290
adultery, 145
aether, 252, 374
Aëtius, 275
age groupings, 7, 114, 122, 239
Aglaophamus, 149, 150
air, in the Orphic cosmogony, 165
aither, *see* aether
Alcmaeon, 7, 34, 97–102, 106, 212
Alexander of Abonouteichos, 342, 358–9

Alexander of Aphrodisias, summary of Aristotle's monograph on the Pythagoreans, 236–46
Alexander Polyhistor, 18, 260, 264, 269, 349, 371–7
Alexandria, 16
alien wisdom, 396
allegorical interpretation, 160, 163, 445
alphabet, as an example of science, 55
Ambrose, St., 435
Ameinias, 146
amphidromia, 163
Amyclas, 109
analogy, in theology, 418
anarchy, 206, 294
Anaxagoras, 58, 66, 100, 107, 277, 281
Anaxilaus of Larissa, 350
Anaximander of Miletus, author of book on *acusmata*, 133, 249, 274, 302, 369, 377
Androcydes, 133, 271, 369, 414
Andron of Ephesus, 303
Andronicus of Rhodes, 79, 325
anger, 70, 209, 290
animals, 61
anthropocentrism, in the Renaissance, 443
Antonius Diogenes, 387, 389, 398
Apollo, 7, 113, 115–16, 166, 402
  Hyperborean, 10, 13, 132, 166, 248, 288
Apollonius of Tyana, 17, 138, 307, 341, 342, 353–8
  Life of Pythagoras, 94, 357, 412, 413
  On Sacrifices, 356–7
application, mathematical, 181
archēgos, 410–11
Archimedes, 167, 169–70, 184
Archippus, 130
Archytas, 3, 4, 5–6, 26, 44, 69–87
  and Aristotle, 78–82
  and Plato, 12, 72–3, 218
  and sophists, 85
  as an inventor, 86

494

Index locorum

Greek index

Select index of Greek words and phrases discussed in the text. (The reader should supplement this list with transliterated forms and other entries in the general index.)